Law of Success

The 21st-Century Edition

LAW OF SUCCESS

The 21st-Century Edition

Revised and Updated

NAPOLEON HILL

Edited by

Ann Hartley
Bill Hartley

HIGHROADS MEDIA, INC.

ISBN: I-932429-24-7

First edition

10 9 8 7 6 5 4 3 2

Contributing editors, volumes I and II:

Arthur Morey

Matthew Sartwell

Cover design by Lisa-Theresa Lenthall

DEDICATED TO

ANDREW CARNEGIE

who suggested the writing of the course, and to

HENRY FORD

whose astounding achievements form the foundation
for practically all of the lessons of the course, and to

EDWIN C. BARNES

a business associate of Thomas A. Edison,
whose close personal friendship over a period
of more than fifteen years served to help me carry on
in the face of a great variety of adversities
and much temporary defeat met with in organizing the course.

A publicity photo of the author, Napoleon Hill, 1955. Photograph courtesy of the Napoleon Hill Foundation.

TRIBUTES TO "LAW OF SUCCESS"
From Great American Leaders

The publishers feel that you will realize more keenly the enormous value of these lessons if you first read a few tributes from great leaders in finance, science, invention, and political life.

Supreme Court of the United States
Washington, D.C.

MY DEAR MR. HILL: I have now had an opportunity to finish reading your Law of Success textbooks, and I wish to express my appreciation of the splendid work you have done in this philosophy. It would be helpful if every politician in the country would assimilate and apply the 15 principles upon which the Law of Success is based. It contains some very fine material which every leader in every walk of life should understand.

WILLIAM H. TAFT
(Former President of the United States and Chief Justice)

Laboratory of
Thomas A. Edison

MY DEAR MR. HILL: Allow me to express my appreciation of the compliment you have paid me in sending me the original manuscript of Law of Success. I can see you have spent a great deal of time and thought in its preparation. Your philosophy is sound and you are to be congratulated for sticking to your work over so long a period of years. Your students . . . will be amply rewarded for their labor.

THOMAS A. EDISON

PUBLIC LEDGER
Philadelphia

DEAR MR. HILL: Thank you for your Law of Success. It is great stuff; I shall finish reading it. I would like to reprint that story "What I Would Do if I Had a Million Dollars" in the Business Section of the *Public Ledger.*

CYRUS H. K. CURTIS

(Publisher of *Saturday Evening Post, Ladies Home Journal*)

King of the 5 and 10 Cent Stores

By applying many of the 15 fundamentals of the Law of Success philosophy we have built a great chain of successful stores. I presume it would be no exaggeration of fact if I said that the Woolworth Building might properly be called a monument to the soundness of these principles.

F. W. WOOLWORTH

Historic American Labor Leader

Mastery of the Law of Success philosophy is the equivalent of an insurance policy against failure.

SAMUEL GOMPERS

A Former President

May I congratulate you on your persistence. Any man who devotes that much time . . . must of necessity make discoveries of great value to others. I am deeply impressed by your interpretation of the "Master Mind" principles which you have so clearly described.

WOODROW WILSON

A Department Store Founder

I know that your 15 fundamentals of success are sound because I have been applying them in my business for more than 30 years.

JOHN WANAMAKER

From the Founder of Kodak

I know that you are doing a world of good with your Law of Success. I would not care to set a monetary value on this training because it brings to the student qualities which cannot be measured by money alone.

GEORGE EASTMAN

A Food and Candy Chief

Whatever success I may have attained I owe, entirely, to the application of your 15 fundamental principles of the Law of Success. I believe I have the honor of being your first student.

WILLIAM WRIGLEY, JR.

At the time these Tributes were written, the Law of Success had been based on fifteen principles.

CONTENTS

THE SEVENTEEN LESSONS COMPRISING
LAW OF SUCCESS:

Volume I

EDITORS' NOTE

LAW OF SUCCESS IS COMPRISED OF THE KEY PRINCIPLES THAT FORM the foundation of Napoleon Hill's philosophy of personal achievement.

The genesis of the principles explored in *Law of Success* date from the day in 1908 when Napoleon Hill was assigned to write a magazine profile on steel baron and philanthropist Andrew Carnegie. During their interview Carnegie became so impressed with the young writer that what was to have been a brief interview stretched into a three-day marathon. It concluded with Carnegie offering to introduce Napoleon Hill to the most powerful men of the day in order that Hill could learn from each of them the secrets of their success. It was Carnegie's vision that, in so doing, Hill would be able to formulate a philosophy that could be used by anyone to help themselves create their own success and realize their dreams.

As Napoleon Hill pursued his mission, he wrote thousands of articles and profiles, launched his own magazines, developed home-study courses, started training centers, and opened a business college —all inspired by his evolving philosophy. He also created a lecture series that brought him wide recognition as an inspiring public speaker on the subject of success and personal achievement. Through it all, Napoleon Hill was constantly testing and modifying his theories until they became refined into a set of specific principles that together formed the cohesive philosophy Andrew Carnegie had envisioned.

In 1927 Napoleon Hill finally assembled what would become the first edition of *Law of Success*. Then, in what proved to be a brilliant marketing concept, his publisher chose to release it not as a single book but as a set of eight volumes. The entire collection was an immediate and astounding success.

In its first edition *Law of Success* presented fifteen principles. In later editions the number was expanded to sixteen as Hill came to believe that The Master Mind, which had been part of the introduction to the first edition, was in fact a separate principle unto itself. Later still, he concluded that there was another key principle that in effect unified the others. This newly recognized principle he termed Cosmic Habitforce, which, when he began working with W. Clement Stone, was also referred to as the Universal Law. Over the years there have been at least five authorized editions that revised or added material, and in its various forms the book has been reprinted more than fifty times. This newly revised and updated twenty-first-century edition is the first to include all seventeen principles.

In preparing this edition of *Law of Success*, the editors have attempted to allow Hill to be as modern an author as if he were still among us, and we have treated the text as we would the text of a living author. When we encountered what modern grammarians would consider run-on sentences, outdated punctuation, or other matters of form, we opted for contemporary usage. If something was obscure or misleading because the author's language was idiosyncratic or archaic, or when it might be construed as out of step with modern thinking, minor alterations were made.

A more challenging issue was the question of how to update the actual content of the book. In carefully reviewing the original text, it became clear that the answer was not to simply replace the examples cited by Hill with similar stories about contemporary people. The anecdotes and examples used by Napoleon Hill were so integral to the point being made or the principle being discussed that to replace them just for the sake of having a more contemporary name would do nothing to make it better. The editors concluded that the best course was to instead augment with additional stories that would serve as confirmation that the Law of Success is a living philosophy. The additional examples have been judiciously inserted as reminders that the principles upon which *Law of Success* is based were relevant when the first book was published in 1928, they were still applicable seventy-five years later in 2003, and they will no doubt continue to be relevant and applicable for at least the *next* seventy-five years.

In addition to contemporary examples, where the editors felt it would be of interest to the reader, we have also included marginal notes that provide background information, historical context, and, where applicable, we have suggested books that complement various aspects of Napoleon Hill's philosophy. All marginal commentary in these volumes is set off in a different font and style. You will also notice that sometimes Law of Success is italicized in the text and at other times it is not. The italicized usage is in reference to the book; unitalicized, it is a general reference to the concept and its principles.

As you read this edition of *Law of Success* you will find that certain key commentaries and references that appear early in the book are also repeated in later chapters. That is intentional. When this updated edition was first published in 2003 as four separate leather-bound collector's volumes, the key commentaries were included where relevant in each book for the benefit of readers who may not have been reading all four volumes consecutively. And because of their relevance to the lessons in which each appears, when this edition combining all seventeen lessons into one volume was being assembled, the decision was made to maintain the commentaries as they were.

Throughout the preparation of the revised editions, the editors have enjoyed the cooperation of the Napoleon Hill Foundation and the Napoleon Hill World Learning Center. With their assistance we have drawn upon the previous editions of the work, as well as on other books and materials written by Napoleon Hill, in order to incorporate the final evolution of his philosophy and thereby present the most comprehensive edition of *Law of Success.*

—Ann Hartley
Bill Hartley

THE AUTHOR'S ACKNOWLEDGMENT
OF HELP RENDERED HIM
IN THE WRITING OF THIS COURSE

―――――――――

THIS COURSE IS THE RESULT OF CAREFUL ANALYSIS OF THE lifework of over one hundred men and women who have achieved unusual success in their respective callings.

I have spent more than twenty years in gathering, classifying, testing, and organizing the lessons upon which the course is based. In this labor I have received valuable assistance either in person or by studying the lifework of the following:

Henry Ford	Henry L. Doherty
Thomas A. Edison	George S. Parker
Harvey S. Firestone	Dr. C. O. Henry
John D. Rockefeller	General Rufus A. Ayers
Charles M. Schwab	Judge Elbert H. Gary
Woodrow Wilson	William Howard Taft
Darwin P. Kingsley	Dr. Elmer Gates
William Wrigley, Jr.	John W. Davis
A. D. Lasker	Captain George M. Alexander
E. A. Filene	(to whom I was formerly
James J. Hill	an assistant)
Edward Bok	Hugh Chalmers
Cyrus H. K. Curtis	Dr. E. W. Strickler
George W. Perkins	Edwin C. Barnes

Robert L. Taylor
    (Fiddling Bob)
George Eastman
E. M. Statler
Andrew Carnegie
John Wanamaker
Marshall Field
Samuel Gompers
F. W. Woolworth
Judge Daniel T. Wright
    (one of my law
    instructors)

Elbert Hubbard
Luther Burbank
O. H. Harriman
John Burroughs
E. H. Harriman
Charles P. Steinmetz
Frank Vanderlip
Theodore Roosevelt
William H. French
Dr. Alexander Graham Bell
    (to whom I owe credit
    for most of Lesson One)

Of the people named, perhaps Henry Ford and Andrew Carnegie should be acknowledged as having contributed most toward the building of this course, for the reason that it was Andrew Carnegie who first suggested the writing of the course and Henry Ford whose lifework supplied much of the material out of which the course was developed.

I have studied the majority of these people at close range, in person. With many of them I enjoy, or did enjoy before their death, the privilege of close personal friendship which enabled me to gather from their philosophy facts that would not have been available under other conditions.

I am grateful for having enjoyed the privilege of enlisting the services of the most powerful human beings on earth, in the building of the Law of Success course. That privilege has been remuneration enough for the work done, if nothing more were ever received for it. They have been the backbone and the foundation and the skeleton of American business, finance, industry, and statesmanship.

The Law of Success course epitomizes the philosophy and the rules of procedure which made each of these men a great power in his chosen field of endeavor. It has been my intention to present the course in the plainest and most simple terms available, so it could also be mastered by very young men and young women of high school age.

With the exception of the psychological law referred to in Lesson One as the Master Mind, I don't claim to have created anything basically new in this course. What I have done, however, has been to organize old truths and known laws into practical, usable form.

Commenting on the Law of Success, Judge Elbert H. Gary said: "Two outstanding features connected with the philosophy impress me most. One is the simplicity with which it has been presented, and the other is the fact that its soundness is so obvious to all that it will be immediately accepted."

The student of this course is warned against passing judgment upon it before having read *all* of the lessons. The reader who takes up this course with an open mind, and sees to it that his or her mind remains open until the last lesson is finished, will be richly rewarded with a broader and more accurate view of life as a whole.

A PERSONAL STATEMENT
BY NAPOLEON HILL

from the 1928 edition

SOME THIRTY YEARS AGO A YOUNG CLERGYMAN BY THE NAME of Gunsaulus announced in the newspapers of Chicago that he would preach a sermon the following Sunday morning entitled "What I Would Do if I Had a Million Dollars!"

The announcement caught the eye of Philip D. Armour, the wealthy packing-house king, who decided to hear the sermon.

In his sermon Dr. Gunsaulus pictured a great school of technology where young men and young women could be taught how to succeed in life by developing the ability to think in practical rather than in theoretical terms; where they would be taught to "learn by doing." "If I had a million dollars," said the young preacher, "I would start such a school."

After the sermon was over, Mr. Armour walked down the aisle to the pulpit, introduced himself, and said, "Young man, I believe you could do all you said you could, and if you will come down to my office tomorrow morning I will give you the million dollars you need." There is always plenty of capital for those who can create practical plans for using it.

That was the beginning of the Armour Institute of Technology, one of the very practical schools of the country. The school was born in the imagination of a young man who never would have been heard of outside the community in which he preached had it not been for the imagination, plus the capital, of Philip D. Armour.

COMMENTARY

The Armour Institute of Technology opened in 1893, offering courses in engineering, chemistry, architecture, and library science, and in 1940 it became the Illinois Institute of Technology when the Armour Institute merged with the Lewis Institute, a Chicago college that had opened in 1895 and offered liberal arts as well as science and engineering courses. In 1949 the Institute of Design, founded in 1937, also merged with IIT, followed in 1969 by the Chicago-Kent College of Law and the Stuart School of Business, and in 1986 by the Midwest College of Engineering. Today there are several campuses in downtown Chicago. IIT has been called the alma mater of accomplishments.

Every great railroad and every outstanding financial institution and every mammoth business enterprise and every great invention began in the imagination of some one person.

F. W. Woolworth created the 5 and 10 Cent Stores plan in his imagination before it became a reality and made him a multimillionaire.

Thomas A. Edison created sound recorders, moving pictures, the electric light bulb, and scores of other useful inventions, in his own imagination before they became a reality.

After the Chicago fire, scores of merchants whose stores went up in smoke stood near the smoldering embers of their former places of business, grieving over their loss. Many of them decided to go away into other cities and start over again. In the group was Marshall Field, who saw, in his own imagination, the world's greatest retail store, standing on the same spot where his former store had stood, which was then but a ruined mass of smoking timbers. That store became a reality.

Fortunate is the young man or young woman who learns, early in life, to use imagination—and doubly so in this age of greater opportunity.

Imagination is a faculty of the mind that can be cultivated, developed, extended, and broadened by use. If this were not true, this course on the laws of success never would have been created, because it was first conceived in my imagination, from the mere seed of an idea which was sown by a chance remark of the late Andrew Carnegie.

Wherever you are, whoever you are, whatever you may be following as an occupation, there is room for you to make yourself more useful, and in that manner more productive, by developing and using your imagination.

Success in this world is always a matter of individual effort, yet you will only be deceiving yourself if you believe that you can succeed without the cooperation of other people. Success is a matter of individual effort only to the extent that each person must decide, in his or her own mind, what is wanted. This involves the use of imagination. From this point on, achieving success is a matter of skillfully and tactfully inducing others to cooperate.

Before you can secure cooperation from others, before you have the right to ask for or expect cooperation from other people, you must first show a willingness to cooperate with them. For this reason the ninth lesson of this course, the Habit of Doing More Than Paid For, is one that should have your serious and thoughtful attention. The law upon which this lesson is based would, of itself, practically ensure success to all who practice it in all they do.

Following, you will find a Personal Analysis Chart in which nine well-known people have been analyzed for your study and comparison. Observe this chart carefully and note the danger points that mean failure to those who do not observe these signals. Of the nine people analyzed seven are known to be successful, while two may be considered failures. Study, carefully, the reasons why these two men failed.

Then, study yourself. In the two columns which have been left blank for that purpose, at the beginning of this course give yourself a rating on each of the laws of success; at the end of the course rate yourself again and observe the improvements you have made.

The purpose of the Law of Success course is to enable you to find out how you may become more capable in your chosen field of work. To this end you will be analyzed and all of your qualities classified so that you may organize them and make the best possible use of them.

You may not like the work in which you are now engaged. There are two ways of getting out of that work. One way is to take little interest in it and do just enough to get by. Very soon you will find a way out, because the demand for your services will cease.

The other and better way is by making yourself so useful and efficient in what you are now doing that you will attract the favorable attention of those who have the power to promote you into more responsible work that is more to your liking.

It is your privilege to take your choice as to which way you will proceed.

Thousands of people walked over the great Calumet Copper Mine without discovering it. Just one lone man used his imagination, dug down into the ground a few feet, investigated, and discovered the richest copper deposit on earth.

You and every other person walk, at one time or another, over your "Calumet mine." Discovery is a matter of investigation and use of imagination. This course on the laws of success may lead the way to your "Calumet," and you may be surprised when you discover that you were standing right over this rich mine, in the work in which you are now engaged. In his lecture "Acres of Diamonds," Russell Conwell tells us that we need not seek opportunity in the distance; that we may find it right where we stand.

This is a truth well worth remembering!

ALL YOU ARE

OR EVER SHALL BECOME

IS THE RESULT OF

THE USE TO WHICH

YOU PUT YOUR MIND.

—Napoleon Hill

AN EXERCISE IN COMPARISON

The Seventeen Laws of Success	Henry Ford	Benjamin Franklin	George Washington	Abraham Lincoln	
1. The Master Mind**	100	100	100	100	
2. A Definite Chief Aim	100	100	100	100	
3. Self-Confidence	100	90	80	75	
4. The Habit of Saving	100	100	75	20	
5. Initiative & Leadership	100	60	100	60	
6. Imagination	90	90	80	70	
7. Enthusiasm	75	80	90	60	
8. Self-Control	100	90	50	95	
9. The Habit of Doing More Than Paid For	100	100	100	100	
10. A Pleasing Personality	50	90	80	80	
11. Accurate Thinking	90	80	75	90	
12. Concentration	100	100	100	100	
13. Cooperation	75	100	100	90	
14. Profiting by Failure	100	90	75	80	
15. Tolerance	90	100	80	100	
16. Practicing the Golden Rule	100	100	100	100	
17. Universal Law**	70	100	100	100	
Average	91	92	86	84	

The nine people who have been analyzed above are all well known. Seven of them are commonly considered to be successful. Two are generally regarded as failures, but of very different sorts. Napoleon had success within his grasp but squandered it. Jesse James gained notoriety and some cash but little else except a very short life. Observe where they each attained a zero and you will see why they failed. A grade of zero in any one of the laws of success is sufficient to cause failure, no matter how high any other grade may be.

Notice that all the successful figures grade 100 percent on A Definite Chief Aim. This is a prerequisite to success, in all cases, without exception. If you wish to conduct an interesting

Study this chart carefully and compare the ratings of these nine people before grading yourself, at the start and end of this course, in the two columns to the right.

	Napoleon Bonaparte	Helen Keller*	Eleanor Roosevelt*	Bill Gates*	Jesse James	Yourself Before	Yourself After
	100	100	80	100	100		
	100	100	100	100	0		
	100	90	80	80	75		
	40	75	80	100	0		
	100	90	90	90	90		
	90	70	80	80	60		
	80	70	70	60	80		
	40	85	90	100	50		
	100	100	100	100	0		
	100	95	80	70	50		
	90	75	80	100	20		
	100	100	80	100	75		
	50	100	90	100	50		
	40	100	90	90	0		
	10	100	100	90	0		
	0	100	100	75	0		
	0	100	100	75	0		
	67	91	88	89	38		

experiment, replace the above names with the names of nine people whom you know, half of whom are successful and half of whom are failures, and grade each of them. When you are through, grade yourself, taking care to see that you really know what are your weaknesses.

* Helen Keller, Eleanor Roosevelt, and Bill Gates replace Theodore Roosevelt, William Howard Taft, Woodrow Wilson, and Calvin Coolidge in Hill's original chart.

** These more recently defined laws were added to the original chart and scored by the editors.

Volume I

THE PRINCIPLES OF
SELF-MASTERY

Introduction to the Master Mind

A Definite Chief Aim

Self-Confidence

The Habit of Saving

Lesson One

Introduction to
the Master Mind

TIME IS A MASTER WORKER

THAT HEALS THE WOUNDS

OF TEMPORARY DEFEAT

AND EQUALIZES THE

INEQUALITIES AND

RIGHTS THE WRONGS

OF THE WORLD.

THERE IS NOTHING

IMPOSSIBLE WITH TIME!

Lesson One

INTRODUCTION TO THE MASTER MIND

"You Can Do It if You Believe You Can!"

T HIS IS A COURSE ON THE FUNDAMENTALS of success. Success is largely a matter of adjusting one's self to the ever-varying and changing environments of life, in a spirit of harmony and poise. Harmony is based on an understanding of the forces constituting one's environment. Therefore, this course is in reality a blueprint that may be followed straight to success, because it helps you interpret, understand, and make the most of these environmental forces of life.

Before you begin reading the Law of Success lessons you should know something of the history of the course. You should know exactly what the course promises to those who follow it until they have assimilated the laws and principles upon which it is based. You should know its limitations as well as its possibilities as an aid in your fight for a place in the world.

From the viewpoint of entertainment, the Law of Success course would be a poor second to most any of the monthly periodicals that may be found on the newsstands.

COMMENTARY

It has been said that Napoleon Hill and his philosophy of success have made more millionaires than any other person in history. It might equally well be said that Napoleon Hill inspired more motivational experts than any other man in history. Napoleon Hill was, and more than thirty years after his death continues to be, America's most influential motivational author. That is due partly to the fact that he came to prominence at the beginning of the age of mass communications, but it is due in even larger part to the diligence he applied to the research upon which he based his seventeen principles that comprise the Law of Success.

It is practically impossible to find a motivational speaker who does not draw upon Hill's work. His influence can be seen in the writings of his early peers, Dale Carnegie and Norman Vincent Peele. Later, many successful authors and speakers such as W. Clement Stone, Og Mandino, Earl Nightingale, and Chicken Soup for the Soul *author Mark Victor Hansen worked directly with either Napoleon Hill or the Napoleon Hill Foundation. Echoes of Hill's principles can be seen in books by people as diverse as Jose Silva, Mary Kay Ash, Dr. Maxwell Maltz, Shakti Gawain, Wally "Famous" Amos, and Dr. Bernie Siegel. Anthony Robbins, arguably the most successful motivational speaker in recent times, has often cited Napoleon Hill as his inspiration, and bestselling author Stephen R. Covey's* 7 Habits of Highly Effective People *can be found in the seventeen principles Hill wrote about more than seventy years earlier.*

AN OVERVIEW

This course has been created for the serious-minded person who devotes at least a portion of his or her time to the business of succeeding in life. I have not intended to compete with those who write purely for the purpose of entertaining.

My aim, in preparing this course, has been two-fold: first, to help you discover your weaknesses, and second, to help you create a *definite plan* for bridging those weaknesses.

The most successful men and women on earth have had to correct certain weak spots in their personalities before they began to succeed. The most notable of these weaknesses that stand between men and women and success are *intolerance, greed, jealousy, suspicion, revenge, egotism, conceit, the tendency to reap where they have not sown, and the habit of spending more than they earn.*

All of these common enemies of mankind, and many more not here mentioned, are covered by the Law of Success course in such a manner that any person of reasonable intelligence may master them with but little effort or inconvenience.

You should know, at the very outset, that this course has long since passed through the experimental state; that it already has to its credit a record of achievement that is worthy of serious thought and analysis. You should know also that the Law of Success course has been examined and endorsed by some of the most practical minds of modern times.

The Law of Success Lectures

This course was first used as a lecture, which I delivered in practically every city and in many of the smaller localities throughout the United States, over a period of more than seven years. During these lectures I had assistants located in the audiences to interpret the reaction of those who heard the lecture, and in this manner we learned exactly what effect it had upon people. As a result of this study and analysis, many changes were made.

The first big victory of the Law of Success philosophy was gained when it was used as the basis of a course that trained three thousand men and women as a sales army. Few of these people had previous experience of any sort in the field of selling. Through this training they were enabled to earn more than $1 million for themselves and paid me $30,000 for my services, over a period of approximately six months.

The individuals and small groups of salespeople who have found success through the aid of this course are too numerous to be mentioned here, but the number is large and the benefits they derived from the course were definite.

The Law of Success philosophy was brought to the attention of the late Don R. Mellett, former publisher of the *Canton* (Ohio) *Daily News,* who formed a partnership with me and was preparing to resign as publisher of the *Canton Daily News* and take up the business management of my affairs, when he was assassinated on July 16, 1926.

Prior to his death Mr. Mellett had made arrangements with Judge Elbert H. Gary, who was then Chairman of the Board of the United States Steel Corporation, to present the Law of Success course to every employee of the steel corporation, at a total cost of something like $150,000. This plan was halted because of Judge Gary's death, but it proves that the Law of Success is an educational plan of an enduring nature. Judge Gary was eminently prepared to judge the value of such a course, and the fact that he analyzed the Law of Success philosophy and was preparing to invest the huge sum of $150,000 in it is proof of the soundness of all that is said on behalf of the course.

Terminology

You will observe, in this introductory lesson, a few technical terms that may not be clear to you. Don't let this bother you. Make no attempt at first reading to understand these terms. They will become clear to you after you read the remainder of the course. This entire introductory lesson is intended only as a background for the other sixteen lessons of the course, and you should read it as such. You should read this lesson several times, as you will get from it at each reading a thought or an idea that you did not get on previous readings.

In this introduction you will find a description of a newly discovered law of psychology that is the very foundation stone of all outstanding personal achievements. I refer to this as the Master Mind, meaning a mind that is developed through the harmonious Cooperation of two or more people who ally themselves for the purpose of accomplishing any given task.

If you are engaged in the business of selling, you may profitably experiment with this law of the Master Mind in your daily work. It has been found that a group of six or seven salespeople may use the law so effectively that their sales may be increased to unbelievable proportions.

Life insurance is supposed to be the hardest thing on earth to sell. This ought not to be true, with an established necessity such as life insurance, but it is. Nevertheless, a small group of men working for the Prudential Life Insurance Company, whose sales are mostly small policies, formed a little friendly group for the purpose of experimenting with the law of the Master Mind, with the result that every man in the group wrote more insurance during the first three months of the experiment than he had ever written in an entire year before.

What may be accomplished through the aid of this principle by any small group of intelligent salespeople who have learned how to apply the law of the Master Mind will stagger the imagination of the most highly optimistic and imaginative person.

Bear this in mind as you read this first lesson of *Law of Success*, and it is not unreasonable to expect that this lesson alone may give you sufficient understanding of the law to change the entire course of your life.

COMMENTARY

As you read this book you will occasionally encounter a term such as Master Mind *that has, in the years since Napoleon Hill coined the term, taken on a connotation that he never intended. Hill first published this work in 1928, a time when Freud and Jung were still developing the study of human psychology, and the terminology had not yet found its way into common usage. The now commonly accepted psychological term that comes closest to capturing what Napoleon Hill meant by the Master Mind is what Jung called the collective unconscious. But what Hill was describing goes beyond Jung's theory to include other concepts including Edward de Bono's techniques of lateral thinking and brainstorming, and many of the ideas behind modern management buzzwords such as* Quality Circle, synergy, *and* thinking outside the box.

Hill's term Master Mind *may seem quaint to the modern reader, but for all the psychobabble that is now part of everyday speech, there is no other term that encompasses all that Hill had in mind.*

Personalities

It is the personalities behind a business that determine the measure of success the business will enjoy.

Modify those personalities so they are more pleasing and more attractive to the patrons of the business, and the business will thrive. In any of the great cities of the United States merchandise of similar nature and price can be found in scores of stores, yet you will find there is always one outstanding store that does more business than any of the others. The reason for this is that behind that store is someone who is paying close attention to the personalities of those who come in contact with the public. People buy personalities as much as merchandise, and it is a question if they are not influenced more by the personalities with which they come in contact than they are by the merchandise.

COMMENTARY

Hill is prophetic in these paragraphs. His description of the importance of personality and service in business anticipates the growth of the service industries that, by the end of the twentieth century, dominated the economy.

Service

Life insurance has been reduced to such a scientific basis that the cost of insurance does not vary to any great extent, regardless of the company from which one purchases it, yet out of the hundreds of life insurance companies doing business, less than a dozen companies do the bulk of the business of the United States.

Why? Personalities! Ninety-nine people out of every hundred who purchase life insurance policies do not know what is in their policies and, what seems more startling, do not seem to care. What they really purchase is the Pleasing Personality of some man or woman who knows the value of cultivating such a personality.

Your business in life, or at least the most important part of it, is to achieve success. Success, within the meaning of that term as covered by this course on the laws of success, is "the attainment of your Definite Chief Aim without violating the rights of other people." Regardless of what your major aim in life may be, you will attain it with much less difficulty after you learn how to cultivate a Pleasing Personality and after you have learned the delicate art of allying yourself with others in a given undertaking without friction or envy.

One of the greatest problems of life, if not in fact the greatest, is that of learning the art of harmonious negotiation with others. This course was created for the purpose of teaching people how to negotiate their way through life with harmony and poise, free from the destructive effects of disagreement and friction which bring millions of people to misery, want, and failure every year.

NO MAN HAS

A CHANCE TO ENJOY

PERMANENT SUCCESS

UNTIL HE BEGINS

TO LOOK IN A MIRROR

FOR THE REAL CAUSE

OF ALL HIS MISTAKES.

With this statement of the purpose of the course, you should be able to approach the lessons with the feeling that a complete transformation is about to take place in your personality.

You cannot enjoy outstanding success in life without power, and you can never enjoy power without sufficient personality to influence other people to cooperate with you *in a spirit of harmony.* This course shows you step by step how to develop such a personality.

Lesson by lesson, the following is a statement of what you may expect from the seventeen laws of success:

The Master Mind will outline the physical and psychological laws that underly these lessons.

A Definite Chief Aim will teach you how to save the wasted effort the majority of people expend in trying to find their life's work. This lesson will show you how to do away forever with aimlessness and fix your heart and hand on a definite, well-conceived purpose as a life's work.

Self-Confidence will help you master the six basic fears with which every person is cursed—the fear of poverty, the fear of ill health, the fear of old age, the fear of criticism, the fear of loss of love of someone, and the fear of death. It will teach you the difference between egotism and real Self-Confidence that is based on definite, usable knowledge.

The Habit of Saving will teach you how to distribute your income systematically so that a definite percentage of it will steadily accumulate, thus forming one of the greatest known sources of personal power. No one may succeed in life without saving money. There is no exception to this rule, and no one may escape it.

Initiative and Leadership will show you how to become a leader instead of a follower in your chosen field of endeavor. It will develop in you the instinct for Leadership that will cause you gradually to gravitate to the top in all of your undertakings.

Imagination will stimulate your mind so that you will conceive new ideas and develop new plans that will help you in attaining the object of your Definite Chief Aim. This lesson will teach you how to "build new houses out of old stones," so to speak. It will show you how to create new ideas out of old, well-known concepts, and how to put old ideas to new uses.

Enthusiasm will enable you to saturate all with whom you come in contact with interest in you and in your ideas. Enthusiasm is the foundation of a Pleasing Personality, and you must have such a personality in order to influence others to cooperate with you.

Self-Control is the balance wheel with which you control your Enthusiasm and direct it where you wish it to carry you. This lesson will teach you, in a most practical manner, to become "the master of your fate, the captain of your soul."

The Habit of Doing More Than Paid For is one of the most important lessons of this Law of Success course. It will teach you how to take advantage of the law of increasing returns, which will eventually ensure you a return in money far out of proportion to the service you render. No one may become a real leader in any walk of life without practicing the habit of doing more work and better work than that for which they are paid.

A Pleasing Personality is the fulcrum on which you must place the crowbar of your efforts, and when so placed, with intelligence, it will enable you to remove mountains of obstacles. This one lesson alone has made scores of master salespeople. It has developed leaders overnight. It will teach you how to transform your personality so that you may adapt yourself to any environment, or to any other personality, in such a manner that you may easily dominate.

Accurate Thinking is one of the important foundation stones of all enduring success. This lesson teaches you how to separate facts from mere information. It teaches you how to organize known facts into two classes: the important and the unimportant. It teaches you how to determine what is an important fact. It teaches you how to build definite working plans, in the pursuit of any calling, based on facts.

Concentration teaches you how to focus your attention on one subject at a time until you have worked out practical plans for mastering that subject. It will teach you how to ally yourself with others in such a manner that you may have the use of their entire knowledge to back you up in your own plans and purposes. It will give you a practical working knowledge of the forces around you and show you how to harness and use these forces in furthering your own interests.

Cooperation will teach you the value of teamwork in all you do. In this lesson you will be taught how to apply the law of the Master Mind described in this introduction and in Lesson Two. This lesson will show you how to coordinate your own efforts with those of others, in such a manner that friction, jealousy, strife, envy, and greed will be eliminated. You will learn how to make use of all that other people have learned about the work in which you are engaged.

Profiting by Failure will teach you how to make steppingstones out of all of your past and future mistakes and failures. It will teach you the difference between failure and temporary defeat, a difference which is very great and very important. It will teach you how to profit by your own failures and by the failures of other people.

Tolerance will teach you how to avoid the disastrous effects of racial and religious prejudices, which mean defeat for millions of people who permit themselves to become entangled in foolish argument over these subjects, thereby poisoning their own minds and closing the door to reason and investigation. This lesson is a companion to the one on accurate thought, because no one could become an accurate thinker without practicing Tolerance. Intolerance closes the book of knowledge and writes on the cover, "Finis! I have learned it all!" Intolerance makes enemies of those who should be friends. It destroys opportunity and fills the mind with doubt, mistrust, and prejudice.

Practicing the Golden Rule will teach you to make use of this great universal law of human conduct in such a way that you may easily get harmonious Cooperation from any individual or group of individuals. Lack of understanding of the law upon which the Golden Rule philosophy is based is one of the major causes of failure for millions of people who remain in misery, poverty, and want all their lives. This lesson has nothing whatsoever to do with religion in any form, nor with sectarianism, and nor do any of the other lessons of this course.

The Universal Law of Cosmic Habitforce, the last lesson, will show you how to apply the principles in the first sixteen lessons to transform not only your thoughts but also your habits. Through this change in the ways you behave and respond, you will put yourself in total harmony with your environment. Success is a result of achieving such harmony.

When you have mastered these seventeen laws and made them your own, as you could do within a period of fifteen to thirty weeks, you will be ready to develop sufficient personal power to ensure the attainment of your Definite Chief Aim.

The purpose of these seventeen laws is to develop or help you to organize all the knowledge you have, and all you acquire in the future, so you may turn this knowledge into power.

You should read this book with a notebook by your side, for you will observe that ideas will begin to flash into your mind as you read, as to ways and means of using these laws in advancing your own interests.

You should also begin teaching these laws to others about whom you care, as it is a well-known fact that the more one tries to teach a subject the more one learns about that subject. A parent, for example, may so indelibly fix these seventeen laws of success in the minds of their children that this teaching will change the entire course of their lives. If you are married, you should also interest your spouse in studying this course, for reasons that will be clear before you have finished reading this lesson.

Power is one of the three basic objects of human endeavor.

Power is of two types—that developed through coordination of natural physical laws, and that developed by organizing and classifying knowledge.

Power growing out of organized knowledge is the more important because it places in your possession a tool with which you may transform, redirect, and to some extent harness and use the other form of power.

The object of this course is to mark the route by which you may safely travel in gathering the facts that you wish to weave into your fabric of knowledge.

There are two major methods of gathering knowledge: by studying, classifying, and assimilating facts which have been organized by other people, and through one's own process of gathering, organizing, and classifying facts, generally called personal experience.

This lesson deals mainly with the ways and means of studying the facts and data gathered and classified by other people.

THE MASTER MIND AND THE STRUCTURE OF THE UNIVERSE

In the past few centuries, scientists have discovered and catalogued the physical elements of which all material forms in the universe consist.

IF YOU MUST SLANDER SOMEONE,

DON'T SPEAK IT—BUT WRITE IT—

WRITE IT IN THE SAND,

NEAR THE WATER'S EDGE!

COMMENTARY

In the following pages, Hill explains basic laws of physics as they were understood in his time. There are errors in his understanding that will be recognized by even nonscientists. Hill, for example, says that electrons may be either positive or negative. An electron, we now know, always carries a negative charge. And a whole branch of physics studies particles much smaller than the electron, a world of which Hill hadn't an inkling.

Where Hill digresses to discuss specifics, small sections have been deleted. Hill would have deleted them himself had he known more. But it is important to read the outlines of his description of physical matter as a metaphor or parallel for the laws that govern human behavior. That is the way he intended this section to be read. Here Hill is trying to find a physical basis to explain the extremely mysterious but altogether indisputable power of the Master Mind.

By study and analysis and accurate measurements, humans have discovered the "bigness" of the material side of the universe as represented by planets, suns, and stars, some of which are known to be over ten million times as large as the little earth on which we live.

On the other hand, man has discovered the "littleness" of the physical forms that constitute the universe by reducing the physical elements to molecules, atoms, and, finally, to the smallest particle, the electron. An electron cannot be seen; it is but a center of force consisting of a positive or a negative. The electron is the beginning of everything of a physical nature.

Molecules, Atoms, and Electrons

To understand both the detail and the perspective of the process through which knowledge is gathered, organized, and classified, it seems essential to begin with the smallest and simplest particles of physical matter, because these are the ABCs with which Nature has constructed the entire framework of the physical portion of the universe.

The molecule consists of atoms, which are little invisible particles of matter revolving continuously with the speed of lightning on exactly the same principle that the earth revolves around the sun. These little particles of matter known as atoms, which revolve in one continuous circuit in the molecule, are made up of electrons, the smallest particles of physical matter.

As already stated, the electron is nothing but two forms of force. The electron is uniform, of but one class, size, and nature; thus, in a grain of sand or a drop of water the entire principle upon which the whole universe operates is duplicated.

How marvelous! How stupendous! You may gather some slight idea of the magnitude of it all the next time you eat a meal, by remembering that every piece of food you eat, the plate on which you eat it, the tableware, and the table itself are, in final analysis, but a collection of *electrons*.

In the world of physical matter, whether one is looking at the largest star that floats through the heavens or the smallest grain of sand to be found on earth, the object under observation is but an organized collection of molecules, atoms, and electrons revolving around one another at inconceivable speed.

Nothing is ever still, although nearly all physical matter may appear, to the physical eye, to be motionless. There is no solid physical matter. The hardest piece of steel is but an organized mass of revolving particles. Moreover, the electrons in a piece of steel are of the same nature and move at the same rate of speed as the electrons in gold, silver, brass, or pewter.

The forms of physical matter appear to be different from one another, and they *are* different, because they are made up of different combinations of atoms (although the electrons in these atoms are always the same, except that some electrons are positive and some are negative, meaning that some carry a positive charge of electrification while others carry a negative charge).

Through the science of chemistry, matter may be broken up into atoms, which are, within themselves, unchangeable. The elements are created through, and by reason of, the combining and changing of the positions of the atoms. Thus it may be seen that the physical elements of the universe differ from one another only in the number of electrons composing their atoms, and in the number and arrangement of those atoms in the molecules of each element.

As an illustration, an atom of mercury contains eighty positive charges (electrons) in its nucleus and eighty negative outlying charges (electrons). If only the chemist were to expel two of its positive electrons it would instantly become the metal known as platinum. If only the chemist could then go a step further and transform the platinum into *gold!*

The formula through which this electronic change might be produced has been the object of diligent search by the alchemists all down the ages, and by the modern chemists of today.

It is a fact known to every chemist that literally tens of thousands of synthetic substances may be composed out of only four kinds of atoms—hydrogen, oxygen, nitrogen, and carbon.

It may be stated as a literal truth that the atom is the universal particle with which Nature builds all material forms, from a grain of sand to the largest star that floats through space. The atom is Nature's building block out of which she erects an oak tree or a pine, a rock of sandstone or granite, a mouse or an elephant.

COMMENTARY

Hill is indicating here that the universe is filled with invisible untapped energy. It is the kind of energy that would later be demonstrated in the explosion of the first atomic bomb.

But the essential message of this example is this: Around a clump of matter there is a swirl of energy. That energy determines whether something attracts other objects or whether it repels them. The nature of this energy can allow two hydrogen atoms to bond with an oxygen atom to form a molecule of water, or a sodium and a chloride atom to join to create a molecule of salt. The nucleuses of the atoms are never changed, but the atoms themselves are joined into something new because of the nature of their energy.

In a Master Mind group, the energy of their individual minds surrounds the people who comprise the group. Their energies interact, and what results is something new and different.

These facts concerning the smallest analyzable particles of matter have been briefly referred to as a starting point from which we shall undertake to ascertain how to develop and apply the law of *power.*

Vibrating Matter

It has been noticed that all matter is in a constant state of vibration or motion; that the molecule is made up of rapidly moving particles called atoms, which, in turn, are made up of rapidly moving particles called electrons.

In every particle of matter is an invisible force which causes the atoms to circle around one another at an inconceivable rate of speed.

One rate of vibration causes what is known as sound. The human ear can detect only the sound that is produced through from 20 to about 20,000 cycles per second.

As the rate of cycles per second increases above that which we call sound, they begin to manifest themselves in the form of heat. *[Today this phenomenon is used in microwave ovens.]*

Still higher up the scale, vibrations or cycles begin to register in the form of light. Ultraviolet rays are normally invisible, and energy with a wavelength of higher order than ultraviolet is also invisible but can have a tremendous effect on physical objects. Science is still probing these upper limits and perhaps future discoveries will explain what today remains a mystery.

Yet still higher up the scale—just how high no one is able to say at this point—the vibrations or cycles create the power, I believe, with which humans *think*. It is my belief that all vibrations which produce energy are simply varying forms of the same thing; the difference is in the rate of vibration. The difference between light and sound is only the rate of vibration. Thoughts, too, are energy. Therefore, the only difference between thought, sound, heat, or light is the number of vibrations per second.

Just as there is only one form of physical matter of which the earth and all the other planets, suns, and stars are composed, so is there but one form of energy, which causes all matter to remain in a constant state of rapid motion.

Dr. Alexander Graham Bell, inventor of the long distance telephone and one of the accepted authorities on the subject of vibration, is here introduced in support of my theories of vibration:

> Suppose you have the power to make an iron rod vibrate with any desired frequency in a dark room. At first, when vibrating slowly, its movement will be indicated by only one sense, that of touch. As soon as the vibrations increase, a low sound will emanate from it and it will appeal to two senses.
>
> At about 32,000 vibrations to the second the sound will be loud and shrill, but at 40,000 vibrations it will be silent and the movements of the rod will not be perceived by touch. Its movements will be perceived by no ordinary human sense.
>
> From this point up to about 1,500,000 vibrations per second, we have no sense that can appreciate any effect of the intervening vibrations. After that stage is reached, movement is indicated first by the sense of temperature and then, when the rod becomes red hot, by the sense of sight.

DON'T BE AFRAID

OF A LITTLE OPPOSITION.

REMEMBER THAT

THE KITE OF SUCCESS

GENERALLY RISES AGAINST

THE WIND OF ADVERSITY—

NOT WITH IT!

At 3,000,000 it sheds violet light. Above that it sheds ultra-violet rays and other invisible radiations, some of which can be perceived by instruments and employed by us.

Now, it has occurred to me that there must be a great deal to be learned about the effect of those vibrations in the great gap where the ordinary human senses are unable to hear, see, or feel the movement. The power to send wireless messages by ether vibrations lies in that gap, but the gap is so great that it seems there must be much more. You must make machines to practically supply new senses, as the wireless instruments do.

Can it be said, when you think of that great gap, that there are not many forms of vibrations that may give us results as wonderful as, or even more wonderful than, the wireless waves? It seems to me that in this gap lie the vibrations that we have assumed to be given off by our brains and nerve cells when we think. But then, again, they may be higher up, in the scale beyond the vibrations that produce the ultraviolet rays.

[NOTE: The last sentence suggests my theory.]

Do we need a wire to carry these vibrations? Will they not pass through the ether without a wire, just as the wireless waves do? How will they be perceived by the recipient? Will he hear a series of signals or will he find that another man's thoughts have entered into his brain?

We may indulge in some speculations based on what we know of the wireless waves, which, as I have said, are all we can recognize of a vast series of vibrations that theoretically must exist. If the thought waves are similar to the wireless waves, they must pass from the brain and flow endlessly around the world and the universe. The body and the skull and other solid obstacles would form no obstruction to their

---

RENDER MORE SERVICE

THAN THAT FOR WHICH

YOU ARE PAID AND

YOU WILL SOON BE PAID

FOR MORE THAN YOU RENDER.

THE LAW OF INCREASING RETURNS

TAKES CARE OF THIS.

---

passage, as they pass through the ether that surrounds the molecules of every substance, no matter how solid and dense.

You ask if there would not be constant interference and confusion if other people's thoughts were flowing through our brains and setting up thoughts in them that did not originate with ourselves?

How do you know that the thoughts of others are not interfering with yours now? I have noticed many phenomena of mind disturbances that I have never been able to explain. For instance, there is the inspiration or the discouragement that a speaker feels in addressing an audience. I have experienced this many times in my life and have never been able to define exactly the physical causes of it.

Many recent scientific discoveries, in my opinion, point to a day not too far distant perhaps, when we will read one another's thoughts, when thoughts will be conveyed directly from brain to brain without intervention of speech, writing, or any of the present known methods of communication.

It is not unreasonable to look forward to a time when we shall see without eyes, hear without ears, and talk without tongues. Briefly, the hypothesis that mind can communicate directly with mind rests on the theory that thought or vital force is a form of electrical disturbance, that it can be taken up by induction and transmitted to a distance either through a wire or simply through the all-pervading ether, as in the case of wireless telegraph waves.

There are many analogies suggesting that thought is of the nature of an electrical disturbance. A nerve, which is of the same substance as the brain, is an excellent conductor of the electric current. When we first passed an electrical current through the nerves of a dead man we were shocked and amazed to see him sit up and move. The electrified nerves produced contraction of the muscles very much as in life.

The nerves appear to act upon the muscles very much as the electric current acts upon an electromagnet. The current magnetizes a bar of iron placed at right angles to it, and the nerves produce, through the intangible current of vital force that flows through them, contraction of the muscular fibers that are arranged at right angles to them.

It would be possible to cite many reasons why thought and vital force may be regarded as of the same nature as electricity. The electric current is held to be a wave motion of the ether, the hypothetical substance that fills all space and pervades all substances. We believe there must be ether because without it the electric current could not pass through a vacuum, or sunlight through space. It is reasonable to believe that only a wave motion of a similar character can produce the phenomena of thought and vital force. We may assume that the brain cells act as a battery and that the current produced flows along the nerves.

But does it end there? Does it not pass out of the body in waves that flow around the world unperceived by our senses, just as the wireless waves passed unperceived before Hertz and others discovered their existence?

Every Mind Both a Broadcasting and a Receiving Station

More times than I can enumerate, I have proven to my own satisfaction at least, that every human brain is both a broadcasting and a receiving station for vibrations of thought frequency.

If this theory should turn out to be a fact, and methods of reasonable control should be established, imagine the part it would play in the gathering, classifying, and organizing of knowledge. The possibility, much less the probability, of such a reality is staggering!

Thomas Paine was one of the great minds of the American revolutionary period. To him more, perhaps, than to any other one person, we

owe both the beginning and the happy ending of the Revolution, for it
was his keen mind that both helped in drawing up the Declaration of
Independence and in persuading the signers of that document to translate it into terms of reality.

In speaking of the source of his great storehouse of knowledge,
Paine thus described it:

> Any person, who has made observations on the state of progress
> of the human mind by observing his own, cannot but have
> observed that there are two distinct classes of what are called
> thoughts: those that we produce in ourselves by reflection
> and the act of thinking, and those that bolt into the mind of
> their own accord. I have always made it a rule to treat these
> voluntary visitors with civility, taking care to examine, as well
> as I was able, if they were worth entertaining; and it is from
> them I have acquired almost all the knowledge that I have. As
> to the learning that any person gains from school education,
> it serves only like a small capital, to put him in the way of
> beginning learning for himself afterwards. Every person of
> learning is finally his own teacher, the reason for which is, that
> principles cannot be impressed upon the memory; their place of
> mental residence is the understanding, and they are never so
> lasting as when they begin by conception.

In the foregoing words Paine described an experience that at one
time or another is the experience of every person. Who is there so
unfortunate as not to have received positive evidence that thoughts
and even complete ideas will pop into the mind from outside sources?

I believe that every thought vibration released by every brain is
picked up by the ether and kept in motion in circuitous wavelengths
corresponding in length to the intensity of the energy used in their
release; that these vibrations remain in motion forever; that they are

EVERY FAILURE IS A

BLESSING IN DISGUISE,

PROVIDING IT TEACHES

SOME NEEDED LESSON

ONE COULD NOT HAVE

LEARNED WITHOUT IT.

MOST SO-CALLED

FAILURES ARE ONLY

TEMPORARY DEFEATS.

one of the two sources from which thoughts that pop into one's mind emanate, the other source being direct and immediate contact through the ether with the brain releasing the thought vibration.

Thus it will be seen that if this theory is a fact, the boundless space of the whole universe is now and will continue to become literally a mental library wherein may be found all the thoughts released by human beings.

COMMENTARY

Imagine what a part this principle plays in every walk of life. You have probably experienced it with those you love, or with someone you work alongside. There you are, both of you considering the solution to some problem, and you hit on the same idea at the same moment.

You have probably also noticed that the intensity of thoughts can increase their power to affect other minds. When you listen to a passionate speaker, don't you sometimes know what will be said next, even the words that will be used? This may sometimes be due to simple logical interpretation, yet it is just as likely to happen when you are hearing someone speak on something you know little about. In such a case, you have little basis for anticipating anything. Yet the power of the other person's thoughts conveys to you the ideas that are being expounded.

Imagine, then, applying this effect to your pursuit of success through harmonious and purposeful alliance of two or more minds. Two words are key here: harmonious *and* purposeful.

Organized Knowledge

Here I am laying the foundation for one of the most important hypotheses enumerated in Lesson Three.

This is a lesson on organized knowledge. Most of the useful knowledge to which the human race has become heir has been preserved and accurately recorded in Nature's bible. By turning back the pages of this unalterable bible, we have read the story of the terrific struggle through and out of which the present civilization has grown. The pages of this bible are made up of the physical elements of which this earth and the other planets consist, and of the ether that fills all space.

By turning back the pages written on stone and covered near the surface of this earth on which we live, we have uncovered the bones, skeletons, footprints, and other unmistakable evidence of the history of animal life on this earth, planted there for our enlightenment and guidance by the hand of Mother Nature throughout unbelievable periods of time. The evidence is plain and unmistakable. The great stone pages of Nature's bible found on this earth, and the endless pages of that bible represented by the ether wherein all past human thought has been recorded, constitute an authentic source of communication between the Creator and his creation. This bible was begun before humankind had reached the thinking stage; indeed before life had reached the ameba (one-cell animal) stage of development.

This bible is above and beyond our power to alter. Moreover, it tells its story not in the ancient dead languages or hieroglyphics but in universal language which all who have eyes may read. Nature's bible, from which we have derived all the knowledge that is worth knowing, is one that no one may alter or in any manner tamper with.

The most marvelous discovery yet made is that of the recently discovered radio principle. Imagine picking up the ordinary vibration of sound and transforming that vibration from audio frequency into radio frequency, sending it to a properly attuned receiving station and there transforming it back into its original form of audio frequency, all in the flash of a second. It should surprise no one that such a force could gather up the vibration of thought and keep that vibration in motion forever.

The instantaneous transmission of sound, by means of the modern radio apparatus, makes not only possible but also probable my theory— that thought vibration can connect mind to mind.

COMMENTARY

Napoleon Hill wrote these words in 1927, a time of great optimism in America. The economy was booming, and advances in science and industry were happening so swiftly that it seemed to many people that nothing was impossible.

Needless to say, mind-to-mind communication did not happen in Hill's lifetime. However, if you take the extraordinary work being done at the beginning of the twenty-first century in communications technology and artificial intelligence, and combine it with the knowledge being gained about DNA and the human genome, it seems possible, perhaps even probable, that in some form Hill's theory of mind-to-mind communication will be realized.

THE MASTER MIND

We come now to the next step in the description of the ways and means by which one may gather, classify, and organize useful knowledge, through the harmonious alliance of two or more minds, out of which grows a Master Mind.

I have searched in vain through all the textbooks and essays available on the subject of the human mind, but nowhere did I find even the slightest reference to the principle here described as the Master Mind. The term first came to my attention through an interview with Andrew Carnegie, as described in Lesson Two.

Mind Chemistry

It is my belief that the mind is made up of the same universal energy as that which fills the universe. It is a fact as well known to the layman as to the scientist, that some minds clash the moment they come in contact with each other, while other minds show a natural affinity for each other. Between the two extremes of natural antagonism and natural affinity growing out of the meeting or contacting of minds, there is a wide range of possibility for varying reactions of mind upon mind.

Some minds are so naturally adapted to each other that love at first sight is the inevitable outcome of the contact. Who has not known of such an experience? In other cases minds are so antagonistic that violent mutual dislike shows itself at first meeting. These results occur without a word being spoken, and without the slightest signs of any of the usual causes for love and hate acting as a stimulus.

It is quite probable that the mind is made up of energy, and when two minds come close enough to form a contact, the mixing of the units of this mind stuff sets up a chemical reaction and starts vibrations that affect the two individuals pleasantly or unpleasantly.

The effect of the meeting of two minds is obvious to even the most casual observer. Every effect must have a cause! What could be more reasonable than to suspect the cause of the change in attitude between two minds that have just come in close contact is none other than the disturbance of the electrons or units of each mind in the process of rearranging themselves in the new field created by the contact?

For the purpose of establishing this lesson on a sound foundation, we have gone a long way toward success by admitting that the meeting or coming in close contact of two minds sets up in each of those minds a certain noticeable effect or state of mind quite different from the one existing immediately prior to the contact. While it is desirable, it is not essential to know the cause of this reaction of mind upon mind. That the reaction takes place, in every instance, gives us a starting point from which we may show what is meant by the term *Master Mind.*

A Master Mind may be created through the bringing together or blending, in a spirit of perfect harmony, of two or more minds. Out of this harmonious blending, the chemistry of the mind creates a third mind which may be appropriated and used by one or all of the individual minds. This Master Mind will remain available as long as the friendly, harmonious alliance between the individual minds exists. It will disintegrate and all evidence of its former existence will disappear the moment the friendly alliance is broken.

COMMENTARY

There is a strong parallel between what Hill is saying here about the interrelation of minds and the theories of the revolutionary philosopher/scientist/designer Buckminster Fuller. In the introduction to Synergetics, *Fuller writes, "[H]umanity has been deprived of comprehensive understanding. Specialization has bred feelings of isolation, futility, and confusion in individuals." Hill believed that the Master Mind draws its members out of their fields of specialization into a group the power of which is greater than its component parts.*

Macrocosmically, Fuller says that we must understand all elements and operations of the universe as interconnected. In Synergetics 303.00 *he defines* Universe *as, "The comprehensive, historically synchronous, integral-aggregate system embracing all the separate integral-aggregate systems of all men's consciously apprehended and communicated (to self or others) nonsimultaneous, nonidentical, but always complementary and only partially overlapping, macro-micro, always-and-everywhere, omnitransforming, physical and metaphysical, weighable and unweighable event sequences. Universe is a dynamically synchronous scenario…"*

The Meeting of Minds

This principle of mind chemistry is the basis and cause for practically all the soul-mate and eternal-triangle cases, so many of which unfortunately find their way into the divorce courts and meet with popular ridicule from ignorant and uneducated people who manufacture vulgarity and scandal out of one of the greatest of Nature's laws.

The entire civilized world knows that the first two or three years of association after marriage are often marked by much disagreement, of a more or less petty nature. These are the years of adjustment. If the marriage survives them, it is more than apt to become a permanent alliance. These facts no experienced married person will deny. Again we see the effect without understanding the cause.

TO BELIEVE

IN THE HEROIC

MAKES HEROES.

—Disraeli

While there are yet other contributing causes, lack of harmony during these early years of marriage is often due to the slowness of the chemistry of the minds in blending harmoniously. Stated differently, the electrons or units of the energy called the mind are often neither extremely friendly nor antagonistic upon first contact, but through constant association they gradually adapt themselves in harmony, except in rare cases where association has the opposite effect of leading, eventually, to open hostility between these units.

It is a well-known fact that after a man and a woman have lived together for ten to fifteen years they become practically indispensable to each other, even though there may not be the slightest evidence of the state of mind called love. Moreover, this association and relationship not only develops a natural affinity between the two minds sexually, but it actually causes the two people to take on a similar facial expression and to resemble each other closely in many other marked ways.

So marked is the effect of the chemistry of the human mind that any experienced public speaker may quickly interpret the manner in which his or her statements are accepted by the audience. Antagonism in the mind of but one person in an audience of one thousand may be readily detected by the speaker who has learned how to feel and register the effects of antagonism. Moreover, the public speaker can make these interpretations without observing or in any manner being influenced by the expression on the faces of those in the audience. Because of this, an audience may cause a speaker to rise to great heights of oratory, or heckle him or her into failure, without making a sound or denoting a single expression of satisfaction or dissatisfaction through the features of the face.

All master salespeople know the moment the "psychological time for closing" has arrived, not by what the prospective buyer says but from the effect of the chemistry of his or her mind as interpreted or felt by that salesperson. Words often belie the intentions of those speaking them, but a correct interpretation of the chemistry of the mind leaves no loophole for such a possibility. Every able salesperson knows that the majority of buyers have the habit of affecting a negative attitude almost to the very climax of a sale.

Every able lawyer has developed a sixth sense whereby he or she is enabled to feel their way through the most artfully selected words of the clever witness who is lying, and correctly interpret what is in the witness's mind, through the chemistry of the mind. Many lawyers have developed this ability without knowing the real source of it; they possess the technique without the scientific understanding upon which it is based. Many salespeople have done the same thing.

One who is gifted in the art of correctly interpreting the chemistry of the minds of others may, figuratively speaking, walk in at the front door of the mansion of a given mind and leisurely explore the entire building, noting all its details, walking out again with a complete picture of the interior of the building, without the owner of the building so much as knowing that he or she has entertained a visitor. You will observe in Lesson Eleven, on accurate thought, that this principle may be put to a very practical use (having reference to the principle of the chemistry of the mind).

Enough has already been said to introduce the principle of mind chemistry, and to prove, with the aid of your own everyday experiences and casual observations, that the moment two minds come within close range of each other a noticeable mental change takes place in both—sometimes registering in the nature of antagonism and at other times registering in the nature of friendliness. Every mind has what might be termed an electric field. The nature of this field varies, depending upon the mood of the individual mind and upon the nature of the chemistry of the mind creating the field.

It is my belief that the normal or natural condition of the chemistry of any individual mind is the result of physical heredity plus the nature of thoughts which have dominated the mind. Every mind is continuously changing to the extent that the individual's philosophy and general habits of thought change the chemistry of the mind. This is my theory. That any individual may voluntarily change the chemistry of his or her mind so that it will attract or repel all with whom it comes in contact is a *known fact!* Stated in another way, any person may assume a mental attitude that will attract and please others or repel and antagonize them, and this without the aid of words or facial expression or other form of bodily movement or demeanor.

Go back now to the definition of a Master Mind, a mind which grows out of the blending and coordination of two or more minds *in a spirit of perfect harmony*, and you will catch the full significance of the word *harmony.* Two minds will not blend, nor can they be coordinated, unless the element of perfect harmony is present. That is the secret of success or failure of practically all business and social partnerships.

Every sales manager and every military commander and every leader in any walk of life understands the necessity of an *esprit de corps*—a spirit of common understanding and Cooperation—in the attainment of success. This mass spirit of harmony of purpose is obtained through discipline, voluntary or forced, of such a nature that the individual minds become blended into a Master Mind. That is, the chemistry of the individual minds is modified in such a manner that these minds blend and function as one.

The methods through which this blending process takes place are as numerous as the individuals engaged in all the various forms of Leadership. Every leader has a method of coordinating the minds of his or her followers. One will use force; another persuasion. One will play upon the fear of penalties while another plays upon rewards. The aim will be to reduce the individual minds of a given group of people to the point that they may be blended into a mass mind. You will not have to search deeply into the history of statesmanship, politics, business, or finance to discover the techniques employed by the leaders in these fields in the process of blending the minds of individuals into a mass mind.

IF YOU DO NOT BELIEVE

IN COOPERATION,

LOOK WHAT HAPPENS

TO A WAGON THAT

LOSES A WHEEL.

The really great leaders of the world, however, have been provided by Nature with mind chemistry favorable as a nucleus of attraction for other minds. Napoleon was a notable example of a man with a magnetic type of mind that had a very decided tendency to attract all minds with which it came in contact. Soldiers followed Napoleon to certain death without flinching, because of the impelling or attracting nature of his personality, and that personality was nothing more nor less than the chemistry of his mind.

COMMENTARY

Hill is here creating his own definition and explanation of "charisma," which originally meant a kind of religious power or leadership that made certain individuals unusually magnetic. The subject fascinated religious and political historians, psychologists, and other social scientists for many years. For a century after his death, because of the power he apparently was able to exert on those around him, Bonaparte was a prime example of a charismatic leader. When Hill first wrote Law of Success, *Napoleon Bonaparte held the same kind of interest for many people that Hitler holds today.*

The Making of the Master Mind

No group of minds can be blended into a Master Mind if one of the individuals of that group possesses an extremely negative mind. The negative and positive minds will not blend in the sense here described as a Master Mind. Lack of knowledge of this fact has brought many an otherwise able leader to defeat.

Any able leader who understands this principle of mind chemistry may temporarily blend the minds of individuals into a mass mind, but the composition will disintegrate almost the very moment the leader's presence is removed from the group. The most successful life insurance sales organizations and other sales forces meet once a week, or more often, for the purpose of . . . *what?*

For the purpose of merging the individual minds into a Master Mind which will, for a few days, serve as a stimulus to the individual minds!

It may be, and generally is, true that the leaders of these groups do not understand what actually takes place in those meetings. The routine of such meetings is usually given over to talks by the leader and other members of the group, and occasionally from someone outside of the group. Meanwhile the minds of the individuals are contacting and recharging one another.

The brain of a human being may be compared to an electric battery in that it will become exhausted or run down, causing the owner of that brain to feel despondent, discouraged, and lacking in energy. Who is so fortunate as never to have had such a feeling? The human brain, when in this depleted condition, must be recharged, and the manner in which this is done is through contact with a more vital mind or minds.

COMMENTARY

A great deal of New Age thinking and the study of the practices of Asian philosophy and religion have created a number of ways unknown to Hill of "recharging the mind." Yoga, meditation, various forms of prayer, spinning, and other techniques all have their devotees. The latter part of the twentieth century also saw tremendous interest in what is often referred to as the personal-growth or human-potential movement. It has fostered countless bestselling books, audiotape courses, and video programs, and every week thousands of people pay to attend seminars, lectures, and retreats to hear motivational speakers or spiritual leaders inspire them to be better in some aspect of their lives.

Some pundits have belittled the lasting effects of such techniques, referring to those who attend as seminar junkies who need a new guru every week to get themselves pumped up. Hill would not have agreed with such a cynical view. He saw diminishing motivation as a perfectly logical aspect of human nature.

Sexuality and the Master Mind

The great leaders understand the necessity of this recharging process and, moreover, they understand how to accomplish this result. *This knowledge is the main feature that distinguishes a leader from a follower!* Fortunate is the person who understands this principle sufficiently well to keep his or her brain vitalized or recharged by periodically connecting it with a more vital mind.

Sexual contact is one of the most effective of the stimuli through which a mind may be recharged, providing the contact is intelligently made, between a man and woman who have genuine affection for each other. (Any other sort of sexual relationship is a devitalizer of the mind.) Any competent practitioner of psychotherapy can recharge a brain within a few minutes.

Before moving on from this brief reference to sexual contact as a means of revitalizing a depleted mind, it seems appropriate to point out that all of the great leaders, in whatever walks of life they have arisen, have been and are people of highly sexed natures.

COMMENTARY

> Hill's position on the relationship between sexuality and creativity is complex and it changes several times throughout his life. While here recommending the bond between a man and a woman he seems not to feel impelled to recommend that leaders draw women into their Master Mind groups. In later works, notably Think and Grow Rich, *he alters his position to recommend sublimation of sexual energy.*
>
> A factor in this may be that Hill seems to have perceived his audience to be entirely masculine. (Practically speaking, the business climate of the 1920s and 1930s did not encourage independent achievement by women.) In the original version of Law of Success, *virtually all examples are of men, and references to human potentiality are always written with masculine examples. (He talks, for example, about what a man may or must do.)*

There is a growing tendency on the part of the best-informed physicians and other health practitioners to accept the theory that all diseases begin when the brain of the individual is in a depleted or devitalized state. Stated in another way, a person who has a perfectly vitalized brain is practically, if not entirely, immune from disease.

Health practitioners know that Nature, or the mind, cures disease in every instance where a cure is effected. Medicines, faith, laying on of hands, chiropractic, osteopathy, and all other forms of outside stimulant are nothing more than aids to Nature, or, to state it correctly, mere methods of setting the chemistry of the mind into motion to the end that it readjusts the cells and tissues of the body, revitalizes the brain, and otherwise causes the human machine to function normally.

The most conventional practitioner will admit the truth of this statement.

What, then, may be the possibilities of the future developments in the field of mind chemistry?

Through the principle of harmonious blending of minds, perfect health may be enjoyed. Through the aid of this same principle, sufficient power may be developed to solve the problem of economic pressure which constantly presses upon every individual.

We may judge the future possibilities of mind chemistry by taking inventory of its past achievements, keeping in mind that these achievements have been largely the result of accidental discovery and of chance groupings of minds.

COMMENTARY

In his references to health and the power of the mind, Napoleon Hill once again demonstrates not only insight but also what can now be seen as foresight. Beginning in the 1960s, what is now commonly called the body-mind connection moved from the fringes of the New Age into the mainstream of American life.

Virtually every newspaper, television news program, and popular magazine regularly features stories on the crucial role the mind plays in helping the immune system to heal the body. Techniques to utilize the healing powers of the mind are now taught in most medical schools and are the basis of bestselling books by Dr. O. Carl Simonton, Louise Hay, Dr. Bernie Siegel, Ken Dychtwald, Dr. Deepak Chopra, and Dr. Andrew Weil, to mention but a few of the more high-profile authors.

Mind Chemistry and Economic Power

Mind chemistry may be appropriately applied to the workaday affairs of the economic and commercial world.

Through the blending of two or more minds in a spirit of perfect harmony, the principle of mind chemistry may be made to develop sufficient power to enable the individuals whose minds have been thus blended to perform seemingly superhuman feats. Power is the force with which humans achieve success in any undertaking. Power, in unlimited quantities, may be enjoyed by any group of people who possess the wisdom with which to submerge their own personalities and their own immediate individual interests, through the blending of their minds in a spirit of perfect harmony.

Observe, profitably, the frequency with which the word *harmony* appears throughout this chapter. There can be no development of a Master Mind where this element of perfect harmony does not exist. The units of one mind will not blend with the units of another mind until the two minds have been aroused and warmed, as it were, with a spirit of perfect harmony of purpose. The moment two minds begin to take divergent roads of interest, the individual units of each mind separate, and the third element—the Master Mind that grew out of the friendly or harmonious alliance—will disintegrate.

COMMENTARY

Before you read the following comments on Ford, Edison, and Firestone, it is once again worth noting that Hill wrote this work before many of the great fortunes of America were made and before many of the industries and businesses that play a role in contemporary life were even conceived. Hill was writing at a time when the possibility of an airline industry was barely born, and the entertainment industries including the great Hollywood studios, the music business, and the television networks were still awaiting the inventions that would make them possible. IBM and the aerospace industry didn't exist, and the computer revolution and the Internet were hardly imaginable.

As this revised edition is being readied for publication in 2004, it seems somewhat anachronistic to imagine three such powerful business leaders getting together to share ideas. Today, instead of Ford, Firestone, and Edison, it would be a group such as Bill Gates, Jeff Bezos, and Michael Dell. As interesting as such a meeting would probably be, it's hard to imagine them meeting in perfect harmony, and if they did they might well be violating a half-dozen antitrust laws.

Antitrust violations notwithstanding, there are more than enough modern examples of the Master Mind at work. What else would you term the coming together of Spielberg, Katzenberg, and Geffen to create DreamWorks? And who hasn't heard the classic example of Wozniak and Jobs huddled in a garage putting together the first Apple computer that launched the computer revolution?

Examples of Mind Chemistry in Action

We come now to the study of some well-known men who have accumulated great power (and also great fortunes) through the application of mind chemistry.

Let us begin our study with three men who are known to be men of great achievement in their respective fields of economic, business, and professional endeavor. Their names are Henry Ford, Thomas A. Edison, and Harvey S. Firestone.

Of the three, Henry Ford is by far the most powerful, if measured in economic and financial power. Mr. Ford is the most powerful man now living on earth. Many who have studied Mr. Ford believe him to be the most powerful man who ever lived.

As far as is known, Ford is the only person now living, or who ever lived, with sufficient power to outwit the money trust of the United States. Ford gathers millions of dollars with as great ease as a child fills a bucket with sand when playing on the beach. It has been said, by those who were in position to know, that Ford, if he needed it, could send out the call for money, gather in a billion dollars, and have it available for use within one week. No one who knows Ford's achievements doubts this. Those who know him well know that he could do it with no more effort than the average person expends in raising the money to pay a month's house rent. And he could get this money, if he needed it, through the intelligent application of the principles on which this course is based.

While Mr. Ford's new automobile was in the process of perfection in 1927, it is said that he received advance orders, with cash payments, for more than 375,000 cars. At an estimated price of $600 per car, this would amount to $225,000,000 that he received before a single car was delivered. Such is the power of confidence in Ford's ability.

Thomas Edison, as everyone knows, is a philosopher, scientist, and inventor. He is, perhaps, the keenest bible student on earth; a student of Nature's bible, however, and not of the myriad manmade Bibles. Mr. Edison has such a keen insight that he has harnessed and combined, for the good of mankind, more of Nature's laws than any other person now living or who ever lived. It was he who brought together the point of a needle and a piece of revolving wax in such a way that the vibration of the human voice could be recorded and reproduced through the early phonograph.

Edison first harnessed lightning and made it serve as a light for man's use, through the aid of the incandescent bulb.

COURAGE IS

THE STANDING ARMY

OF THE SOUL

WHICH KEEPS IT

FROM CONQUEST, PILLAGE,

AND SLAVERY.

—Henry van Dyke

Edison gave the world the modern moving picture.

These are but a few of his outstanding achievements. The miracles that he performed (not by trickery, under the pretense of superhuman power, but in the very midst of the bright light of science) transcend all of the so-called miracles described in books of fiction.

Harvey Firestone is the moving spirit behind the great Firestone Tire industry in Akron, Ohio.

All three of these men began their business careers without capital and with little formal education. All three men are now well-educated. All three are wealthy. All three are powerful.

Now let us consider the source of their wealth and power. Thus far we have been dealing only with effect; the true philosopher wishes to understand the cause of a given effect.

It is a matter of general knowledge that Ford, Edison, and Firestone are close personal friends and have been so for many years, and that in former years they were in the habit of going away to the woods once a year for a period of rest, meditation, and recuperation.

But it is not generally known—it may be doubted that these men know it themselves—that there exists between the three a bond of harmony that has caused their minds to become blended into a Master Mind, which is the real source of the power of each. This mass mind, developing from the coordination of the individual minds of Ford, Edison, and Firestone, has enabled these men to tune in on forces (and sources of knowledge) with which most people are unfamiliar.

More than half this theory is known fact. For example, it is known that these men have great power and that they are wealthy. It is also known that they began without capital and with little schooling. And it is known that they form periodic mind contacts. It is known that they are harmonious and friendly. It is known that their achievements are too outstanding to be easily compared with those of others in their respective fields of activity.

These men work with natural laws well known to all economists and natural scientists. As yet, chemistry of the mind is not sufficiently developed to be classed, by scientific men, in their catalogue of known laws.

A Master Mind may be created by any group of people who will coordinate their minds, in a spirit of perfect harmony. The group may consist of any number from two upward. Best results appear to come from the blending of six or seven minds.

It has been suggested that Jesus Christ discovered how to make use of the principle of mind chemistry, and that His seemingly miraculous performances grew out of the power He developed through the blending of the minds of the twelve disciples. It has been pointed out that when one of the disciples (Judas Iscariot) broke faith, the Master Mind immediately disintegrated and Jesus met with supreme catastrophe.

COMMENTARY

An opposite example is Adolf Hitler, whose ability to hold the minds of his people in thrall allowed him to dominate Europe, terrify the world, and commit countless crimes against humanity. His immoral use of the Master Mind was defeated only by a greater Master Mind in which leaders like Franklin Roosevelt and Winston Churchill united their people in a valiant effort. It is interesting to note that in the United States many people had opposed going to war against Hitler and his allies. President Roosevelt, however, applied many of the principles of the laws of success to persuade the public of the necessity and rightness of his course. Truly great leaders have the ability to create harmony where it does not already exist. Roosevelt's Master Mind, like that of Christ's, survived his death. Hitler's perished with him.

Not every Master Mind changes the course of history, but they can still offer important and valuable contributions. In a time when it was unusual for women to start up businesses, Mary Kay Ash invested her life savings in developing and marketing a line of cosmetics. To make her venture a success, she created a Master Mind with the women who sold her products. Because so many doors to success *were closed to women in that time, she found that when she gave her sales reps an opportunity no one else offered, they responded by working hard for themselves and for her. She used a series of distinctive, highly visible rewards as incentives, most notably the famous pink Mary Kay Cadillacs. Today, more than 200,000 women worldwide sell Mary Kay cosmetics, part of a powerfully successful Master Mind.*

When two or more people harmonize their minds and produce the effect known as a Master Mind, each person in the group becomes vested with the power to contact and gather knowledge through the subconscious minds of all the other members of the group. This power becomes immediately noticeable, having the effect of stimulating the mind to a higher rate of vibration and otherwise evidencing itself in the form of a more vivid Imagination and the consciousness of what appears to be a sixth sense. It is through this sixth sense that new ideas will flash into the mind. These ideas take on the nature and form of the subject dominating the mind of the individual. If the entire group has met for the purpose of discussing a given subject, ideas concerning that subject will come pouring into the minds of all present, as if an outside influence were dictating them. The minds of those participating in the Master Mind become like magnets, attracting ideas and thoughts of the most highly organized and practical nature, from no one knows where!

The process of mind-blending here described as a Master Mind may be likened to the act of one who connects many electric batteries to a single transmission wire, thereby stepping up the power flowing over that line. Each battery added increases the power passing over the line by the amount of energy the battery carries. It is the same with blending individual minds into a Master Mind. Each mind, through the principle of mind chemistry, stimulates all the other minds in the group, until the mind energy becomes so great that it penetrates to and connects with the universal energy known as ether, which, in turn, touches every atom of the entire universe.

The modern radio apparatus substantiates, to a considerable extent, this same theory. Powerful sending or broadcasting stations must be erected through which the vibration of sound is stepped up before it can be picked up by the much higher vibrating energy of the ether and carried in all directions. A Master Mind made up of many individual minds, so blended that they produce a strong vibrating energy, constitutes almost an exact counterpart of the radio broadcasting station.

Every public speaker has felt the influence of mind chemistry, for it is a well-known fact that as soon as the individual minds of an audience become en rapport with the speaker (attuned to the rate of vibration of the mind of the speaker), there is a noticeable increase of Enthusiasm in the speaker's mind, and he or she often rises to heights of oratory which surprise all, including themself.

The first five to ten minutes of the average speech are devoted to what is known as warming up. This is the process through which the minds of the speaker and the audience are becoming blended in a spirit of *perfect harmony.*

Every speaker knows what happens when this state of perfect harmony fails to materialize on part of their audience.

The seemingly supernatural phenomena occurring in spiritualistic meetings are the result of the reaction, upon one another, of the minds in the group. These phenomena seldom begin to manifest themselves in less than ten to twenty minutes after the group is formed, for the reason that this is about the time required for the minds in the group to become harmonized or blended.

Vibrations

The "messages" received by members of a spiritualistic group probably come from one of two sources, or from both:

- From the vast storehouse of the subconscious mind of some member of the group; or

• From the universal storehouse, in which I believe all thought vibration is preserved.

Neither any known natural law nor human reason supports the theory of communication with a person who has died.

Any individual may explore the store of knowledge in another's mind through this principle of mind chemistry, and it seems reasonable to suppose that this power may be extended to include contact with whatever vibrations are available in the ether, if there are any.

Matter and energy (the two known elements of the universe) may be transformed, but neither created nor destroyed. The theory that all the higher and more refined vibrations, such as those of thought, are preserved grows out of that fact. It is reasonable to suppose that all vibrations that have been stepped up sufficiently will go on forever. The lower vibrations probably live a natural life and die out.

All the so-called geniuses probably gained their reputations because by mere chance or otherwise, they formed alliances with other minds which enabled them to step up their own mind vibrations and enabled them to contact the vast Temple of Knowledge recorded and filed in the ether of the universe.

Inquiring further into the source of economic power as manifested by achievements in the field of business, let us study the Chicago group known as the Big Six, consisting of William Wrigley Jr., who owns the chewing gum business bearing his name, and whose individual income is said to be more than $15 million a year; John R. Thompson, who operates the chain of lunch rooms bearing his name; Mr. Lasker, who owns the Lord & Thomas Advertising Agency; Mr. McCullough, who owns the Parmalee Express Company, the largest transfer business in America; and Mr. Ritchie and Mr. Hertz, who own the Yellow Taxicab business. A reliable financial reporting company has estimated the yearly income of these six men at upward of $25 million, or an average of more than $4 million a year per man.

MEN CEASE TO INTEREST US

WHEN WE FIND THEIR LIMITATIONS.

THE ONLY SIN IS LIMITATION.

AS SOON AS YOU ONCE

COME UP TO A MAN'S LIMITATIONS,

IT IS ALL OVER WITH HIM.

—Emerson

Analysis of this entire group of six men indicates that not one of them had any special educational advantages; that all began without capital or extensive credit; that their financial achievement has been due to their own individual plans, and not to any fortunate turn of the wheel of chance.

Many years ago these six men formed a friendly alliance, meeting at stated periods for the purpose of assisting one another with ideas and suggestions in their various lines of business.

With the exception of Hertz and Ritchie, none of the six men was in any manner associated in a legal partnership. These meetings were strictly for the purpose of cooperating on a give-and-take basis, assisting one another with ideas and suggestions, and occasionally endorsing notes and other securities to assist some member of the group who had met with an emergency.

It is said that each of the individuals belonging to this Big Six group is a millionaire many times over. As a rule there is nothing worthy of special comment about a man who does nothing more than accumulate a few million dollars. However, there is something connected with the financial success of this particular group of men that is well worth comment, study, analysis, and even emulation, and that something is the fact that they have learned how to coordinate their individual minds by blending them in a spirit of perfect harmony, thereby creating a Master Mind that unlocks, to each member of the group, doors which are closed to most of the human race.

The United States Steel Corporation is one of the strongest and most powerful industrial organizations in the world. The idea out of which this great industrial giant grew was born in the mind of Elbert H. Gary, a more or less commonplace small-town lawyer who was born and reared near Chicago.

Mr. Gary surrounded himself with a group of men whose minds he successfully blended in a spirit of perfect harmony, thereby creating the Master Mind that is the moving spirit of the United States Steel Corporation.

Search where you will, wherever you find an outstanding success in business, finance, industry, or in any of the professions, you may be sure that behind the success is some individual who has applied the principle of mind chemistry, out of which a Master Mind has been created. These outstanding successes often appear to be the handiwork of just one person, but search closely and the other individuals whose minds have been coordinated with the creator's mind may be found.

Remember that two or more persons may operate the principle of mind chemistry so as to create a Master Mind.

COMMENTARY

> One of the notable success stories of the computer age is the Intel corporation, and as this edition is being readied for publication it is one of the leaders in the computer-chip industry. The most famous figure at Intel is Andrew Grove, the company's CEO, once an immigrant who supported himself waiting tables. Grove's keen skills as a manager, however, are only a part of the reason for Intel's success, for Grove is part of a Master Mind that includes Robert Noyce and Gordon Moore, the men whose technical knowledge and innovation helped drive the company forward. Each of these men is brilliant in his own right, but together they have made Intel into one of the dominating companies in its field—and one of the most consistently profitable businesses in the volatile high-tech industry.

When Knowledge Is Power

Power is organized knowledge, expressed through intelligent efforts. No effort can be said to be *organized* unless the individuals engaged in that effort coordinate their knowledge and energy in a spirit of perfect harmony. Lack of such harmonious coordination of effort is the main cause of practically every business failure.

I conducted an interesting experiment in collaboration with the students of a well-known college. Each student was requested to write an essay—"How and Why Henry Ford Became Wealthy." Each was required to describe, as a part of his or her essay, what was believed to be the nature of Ford's real assets and of what these assets consisted in detail.

The majority of the students gathered financial statements and inventories of the Ford assets and used these as the basis of their estimates of Ford's wealth.

The sources of Ford's wealth included cash in banks; raw and finished materials in stock; real estate (land and buildings); and goodwill, estimated at from 10 to 25 percent of the value of the material assets.

One student out of the entire group of several hundred answered as follows:

Henry Ford's assets consist, in the main, of two items, i.e., (1) Working capital and raw and finished materials; (2) The knowledge, gained from experience, of Henry Ford himself, and the cooperation of a well-trained organization which understands how to apply this knowledge to best advantage from the Ford viewpoint. It is impossible to estimate, with anything approximating correctness, the actual dollars and cents value of either of these two groups of assets, but it is my opinion that their relative values are:

The organized knowledge of the Ford
Organization   75 percent

The value of cash and physical assets of every
nature, including raw and finished materials   25 percent

Unquestionably the biggest asset that Henry Ford has is his own brain. Next would come the brains of his immediate circle of associates, for it has been through coordination of these that the physical assets he controls were accumulated.

YOU CANNOT BECOME

A POWER IN YOUR COMMUNITY

NOR ACHIEVE ENDURING SUCCESS

IN ANY WORTHY UNDERTAKING

UNTIL YOU BECOME BIG ENOUGH

TO BLAME YOURSELF

FOR YOUR OWN MISTAKES

AND REVERSES.

Destroy every plant the Ford Motor Company owns, every piece of machinery, every atom of raw or finished material, every finished automobile, and every dollar on deposit in any bank, and Ford would still be the most powerful man, economically, on earth. The brains that have built the Ford business could duplicate it again in short order. Capital is always available, in unlimited quantities, to such brains as Ford's.

Ford is the most powerful man (economically) because he has the keenest and most practical conception of the principle of *organized knowledge* of any man on earth.

Despite Ford's great power and financial success, it may be that he has blundered often in the application of the principles through which he accumulated this power. There is little doubt that Ford's methods of mind coordination have often been crude; they were bound to be so in the earlier days of his experience, before he gained the wisdom of application that would naturally go with maturity of years.

There can't be much doubt that Ford's application of the principle of mind chemistry was, at least at the start, the result of a chance alliance with other minds, particularly the mind of Edison. It is more than probable that Mr. Ford's remarkable insight into the laws of Nature was first begun as the result of his friendly alliance with his own wife, long before he ever met either Mr. Edison or Mr. Firestone. Many a man who never knows the real source of his success is made by his wife, through application of the Master Mind principle. Mrs. Ford is a most remarkably intelligent woman, and I believe that it was her mind, blended with Mr. Ford's, that gave him his first real start toward power.

It may be mentioned, without in any way depriving Mr. Ford of any honor or glory, that in his earlier days he had to combat the powerful enemies of illiteracy and ignorance to a greater extent than did either Edison or Firestone, both of whom were gifted by natural heredity with a most fortunate aptitude for acquiring and applying knowledge. Ford had to hew this talent out of the rough, raw timbers of his hereditary estate.

Within an inconceivably short period of time, Ford has mastered three of the most stubborn enemies of mankind and transformed them into assets constituting the very foundation of his success.

These enemies are ignorance, illiteracy, and poverty!

Anyone who can stay the hand of these three savage forces, much less harness and use them to good account, is well worth close study by the less fortunate individuals.

This is an age of *industrial power* in which we are living, and the source of all this *power is organized effort.* Not only has the management of industrial enterprises efficiently organized individual workers, but in many instances mergers of industry have been effected in such a way and to the end that these combinations (as in the case of the United States Steel Corporation, for example) have accumulated practically unlimited power.

One may hardly glance at the day's news without seeing a report of some business, industrial, or financial merger, bringing under one management enormous resources and thus creating great power.

One day it is a group of banks; another day a chain of railroads; the next day it is a combination of steel plants, all merging for the purpose of developing power through highly organized and coordinated effort.

Knowledge, general in nature and unorganized, is not *power;* it is only potential power—the raw material out of which real power may be developed. Any modern library contains an unorganized record of all the knowledge of value to which the present stage of civilization is heir, but this knowledge is not power because it is not organized.

Every form of energy and every species of animal or plant life, to survive, must be organized. The oversized animals whose remains have filled Nature's boneyard through extinction have left mute but certain evidence that nonorganization means annihilation.

From the smallest particle of matter to the largest star in the universe, these and every material thing in between these two extremes offer proof positive that one of Nature's first laws is that of *organization.* Fortunate is the individual who recognizes the importance of this law and makes it his or her business to familiarize themself with the various ways in which the law may be applied to advantage.

The astute businessperson has not only recognized the importance of the law of *organized effort,* but they have made this law the warp and the woof of their *power.*

Without any knowledge whatsoever of the principle of mind chemistry, or even that such a principle exists, many influential persons have accumulated great power by merely organizing the knowledge that they possessed. The majority of those who have discovered the principle of mind chemistry, and developed that principle into a Master Mind, have stumbled upon this knowledge by the merest of accident, often failing to recognize the real nature of their discovery or to understand the source of their power.

I am of the opinion that all living persons who at the present time are consciously making use of the principle of mind chemistry in developing power through the blending of minds may be counted on the fingers of two hands, with perhaps several fingers left to spare.

If this estimate is even approximately true, there is little danger that the field of mind chemistry will become overcrowded.

It is a known fact that one of the most difficult tasks anyone in business must perform is inducing associates to coordinate their efforts in a spirit of harmony. To induce continuous Cooperation between a group of workers in any undertaking is next to impossible. Only the most efficient leaders can accomplish this highly desired objective. But once in a great while such a leader will rise above the horizon in the field of industry, business, or finance, and then the world hears of a Henry Ford, Thomas A. Edison, John D. Rockefeller Sr., E. H. Harriman, or James J. Hill.

Power and success are practically synonymous terms!

One grows out of the other. Therefore, any person who has the knowledge and the ability to develop power through the principle of harmonious coordination of effort between individual minds, or in any other manner, may be successful in any reasonable undertaking that is possible of successful termination.

Harmony

It must not be assumed that a Master Mind will immediately spring, mushroom-fashion, out of every group of minds that makes pretense of coordination in a spirit of *harmony!*

Harmony, in the real sense of the meaning of the word, is as rare among groups of people as is genuine Christianity among those who proclaim themselves Christians.

Harmony is the nucleus around which the state of mind known as a Master Mind must be developed. Without this element there can be no Master Mind—a truth that cannot be repeated too often.

In his proposal for establishing the League of Nations, Woodrow Wilson had in mind the development of a Master Mind to be composed of groups of minds representing the civilized nations of the world. Wilson's conception was the most far-reaching humanitarian idea ever created in the mind of man, because it dealt with a principle that embraces sufficient power to establish a real brotherhood of man on earth. The League of Nations, or some similar blending of international minds in a spirit of harmony, is sure to become a reality.

COMMENTARY

The League of Nations that Hill refers to was established in 1920, after the First World War, for the purpose of promoting world peace and cooperation. And though it was first proposed by President Woodrow Wilson, the United States never joined the organization, which seriously impeded its effectiveness.

After the Second World War, The League of Nations was superceded by the creation of the United Nations, of which America was one of the founding nations. Unfortunately, the UN has not often lived up to Hill's conception of a Master Mind, which requires that the participants come together in perfect harmony.

The time when such unity of minds will take place will be measured largely by the time required for the great universities and nonsectarian institutions of learning to supplant ignorance and superstition with understanding and wisdom. This time is rapidly approaching.

COMMENTARY

Failure to develop a Master Mind can create enormous, embarrassing fiascoes. The Metropolitan Transit Authority of New York owned a valuable piece of property on Columbus Circle, one of the city's busiest intersections. The old Coliseum there had been made obsolete by a new Convention Center, so the Transit Authority decided to sell the land to a developer for a new building. Several companies bid, and a winner was selected. When the design for the building was unveiled, however, there was enormous public outcry, for the building was so large that its shadow would lie over vast stretches of Central Park.

So the developers paid for a new building design, but it, too, was greeted with public dismay, for it made only a token effort to address the many objections. Citizen groups circulated petitions and threatened lawsuits. Wealthy individuals who lived in the neighborhood protested just as loudly as did people on the street, because all felt that the park was threatened. The Transit Authority, the developer, even the city government tried to make the building happen, but at every turn they were stymied by people who were outraged.

Finally, the developer gave up. Hundreds of millions of dollars had been spent on the project, the Transit Authority lost its sale, construction jobs were lost, and the Coliseum sat empty and unused for a decade. All this because the leaders of the project failed to create harmony among the people of the city.

NEVER, IN THE HISTORY

OF THE WORLD, HAS THERE BEEN

SUCH ABUNDANT OPPORTUNITY

AS THERE IS NOW FOR THE PERSON

WHO IS WILLING TO SERVE

BEFORE TRYING TO COLLECT.

The old religious orgy known as the revival meeting offers a favorable opportunity to study the principle of mind chemistry created within a Master Mind.

It will be observed that music plays no small part in bringing about the harmony essential to the blending of a group of minds in such a meeting. Without music the revival meeting would be a tame affair.

During revival services the leader of the meeting has no difficulty in creating harmony in the minds of his devotees, but it is well known that this state of harmony lasts no longer than the presence of the leader, after which the Master Mind that leader has temporarily created disintegrates.

By arousing the emotional nature of his followers, the revivalist has no difficulty, with the proper stagesetting music, in creating a Master Mind which becomes noticeable to all who come in contact with it. The very air becomes charged with a positive, pleasing influence that changes the entire chemistry of all minds present.

The revivalist calls this energy "the Spirit of the Lord."

Through experiments conducted with a group of scientific investigators and laymen (all of whom were unaware of the nature of the experiment), I have created the same state of mind and the same positive atmosphere without calling it the Spirit of the Lord.

On several occasions I have witnessed the creation of this same positive atmosphere among a group of men and women engaged in the business of salesmanship, without calling it the Spirit of the Lord.

I once helped conduct a school of salesmanship for Harrison Parker, founder of the Cooperative Society, of Chicago, and, by the use of the principle of mind chemistry that revivalists call the Spirit of the Lord, so transformed the nature of a group of three thousand men and women (all of whom were without former sales experience) that they sold more than $10 million worth of securities in less than nine months and earned more than $1 million for themselves.

It was found that the average person who joined this school would reach the zenith of his or her selling power within one week, after which it was necessary to revitalize the individual's brain through a group sales meeting. These sales meetings were conducted on very much the same order as are the modern revival meetings, with much the same stage equipment, including music and high-powered speakers who could exhort the salespeople.

COMMENTARY

Not to belabor the obvious, but the style of presentation that Hill refers to in commenting on the similarity between revival meetings and his sales meetings can also be seen at almost any self-help or personal-growth seminar.

Call it religion, psychology, mind chemistry, or anything you please (they are all based on the same principle), but there is nothing more certain than that wherever a group of minds are brought into contact, in a spirit of *perfect harmony*, each mind becomes immediately supplemented and reinforced by the noticeable energy called a Master Mind.

For all I profess to know, this uncharted energy may be the Spirit of the Lord, but it operates just as favorably when called by any other name. The human brain and nervous system constitute a piece of intricate machinery which but few, if any, understand. When controlled and properly directed, this piece of machinery can be made to perform wonders of achievement; and if not controlled it will perform wonders fantastic and phantomlike in nature, as may be seen by observing the patients of any psychiatric hospital.

The human brain has direct connection with a continuous influx of energy from which we derive our power to think. The brain receives this energy, mixes it with the energy created by the food taken into the body, and distributes it to every portion of the body through the aid of the blood and the nervous system. It thus becomes what we call life.

Every normal human body has a first-class chemical laboratory and a stock of chemicals sufficient to carry on the business of breaking up, assimilating, and properly mixing and compounding the food we take into the body, preparatory to distributing it to wherever it is needed as a body builder.

Tests have been made, both with humans and animals, to prove that the energy known as the mind plays an important part in this chemical operation of compounding and transforming food into the required substances to build and keep the body in repair. It is known that worry, excitement, or fear will interfere with the digestive process, and in extreme cases stop this process altogether, resulting in illness or death. It is obvious, then, that the mind enters into the chemistry of food digestion and distribution.

It is believed by many eminent authorities, although it may never have been scientifically proved, that the energy known as mind or thought may become contaminated with negative or "unsociable" elements, causing the entire nervous system to be thrown out of working order—digestion is interfered with and various diseases will manifest themselves. Financial difficulties and unrequited love affairs head the list of causes of such emotional disturbances.

A negative environment, such as that existing where some member of the family is constantly nagging, will interfere with the chemistry of the mind to the point that the individual loses ambition and gradually sinks into oblivion. It is because of this fact that the old saying that a man's wife may either make or break him is literally true. In a subsequent lesson a section on this subject is addressed to spouses.

Anyone knows that certain food combinations will, if taken into the stomach, result in indigestion, violent pain, and even death. Good health depends, at least in part, on a food combination that harmonizes. But harmony of food combinations is not sufficient to ensure good health; there must also be harmony between the elements of energy known as the mind.

A MAN IS HALF WHIPPED

THE MINUTE HE BEGINS

TO FEEL SORRY FOR HIMSELF,

OR TO SPIN AN ALIBI

WITH WHICH HE WOULD

EXPLAIN AWAY HIS DEFECTS.

Harmony seems to be one of Nature's laws without which there can be no such thing as organized energy, or life in any form whatsoever.

The health of the body as well as the mind is literally built out of, around, and on the principle of harmony! The energy known as life begins to disintegrate and death approaches when the organs of the body stop working in harmony.

The moment harmony ceases at the source of any form of organized energy (power), the units of that energy are thrown into a chaotic state of disorder and the power is rendered neutral or passive.

Harmony is also the nucleus around which the principle of mind chemistry known as a Master Mind develops power. Destroy this harmony and you destroy the power that can grow out of the coordinated effort of a group of individual minds.

This truth has been stated, restated, and presented in every manner that I could conceive, with unending repetition. But unless you grasp this principle and learn to apply it, this lesson is useless.

Success in life, no matter what one may call success, is very largely a matter of adaptation to environment in such a manner that there is harmony between the individual and their environment. The palace of a king becomes as a hovel of a peasant if harmony does not abound within its walls. Conversely, the hut of a peasant may be made to yield more happiness than the mansion of the rich man, if harmony exists in the former and not in the latter.

Without perfect harmony the science of astronomy would be as useless as the bones of a saint because the stars and planets would clash with one another, and all would be in a state of chaos and disorder.

Without the law of harmony an acorn might grow into a heterogeneous tree consisting of the wood of the oak, poplar, maple, and whatnot.

Without the law of harmony there cannot be proper organization of knowledge, for what, may one ask, is organized knowledge except the harmony of facts and truths and natural laws?

The moment discord begins to creep in at the front door, harmony edges out at the back door, so to speak, whether this application is made to a business partnership or the orderly movement of the planets of the heavens.

If you get the impression that I am laying undue stress on the importance of *harmony*, remember that lack of harmony is the first, and often the last and only, cause of failure!

There can be no poetry nor music nor oratory worthy of notice without the presence of harmony.

Good architecture is largely a matter of harmony. Without harmony a house is nothing but a mass of building material, more or less a monstrosity.

Sound business management plants the very sinews of its existence in harmony.

Every well-dressed man or woman is a living picture and a moving example of harmony.

With all these workaday illustrations of the important part that harmony plays in the affairs of the world—no, in the operation of the entire universe—how could any intelligent person leave harmony out of their Definite Chief Aim in life? Could *any* definite aim in life omit harmony as the chief stone of its foundation?

KNOWLEDGE AND POWER

The human body is a complex organization of organs, glands, blood vessels, nerves, brain cells, muscles, etc. The mind that stimulates to action and coordinates the efforts of the component parts of the body is also a plurality of ever-varying and changing energies. From birth until death there is continuous struggle, often assuming the nature of open combat, between the forces of the mind. For example, the lifelong struggle between the motivating forces and desires of the mind, which takes place between the impulses of right and wrong, is well known to everyone.

Every human being possesses at least two distinct personalities, and as many as six distinct personalities have been discovered in one person. One of man's most delicate tasks is that of harmonizing these mind forces so that they may be organized and directed toward the orderly attainment of a given objective. Without this element of harmony, no individual can become an accurate thinker.

It is no wonder that leaders in business and industrial enterprises, as well as those in politics and other fields of endeavor, can find it so difficult to organize groups of people so that they will function in the attainment of a given objective, without friction. Each individual human being possesses inner forces that are difficult to harmonize, even when placed in the environment most favorable to harmony. If the chemistry of the individual's mind is such that the units of the mind cannot be easily harmonized, think how much more difficult it must be to harmonize a group of minds so they will function as one, in an orderly manner, through a Master Mind.

The leader who successfully develops and directs the energies of a Master Mind must possess tact, patience, persistence, Self-Confidence, intimate knowledge of mind chemistry, and the ability to adapt (in a state of perfect poise and harmony) to quickly changing circumstances, without showing the least sign of annoyance.

How many are there who can measure up to this requirement?

The successful leader must have the ability to change the color of the mind, chameleonlike, to fit every circumstance that arises in connection with the object of Leadership. Moreover, he or she must have the ability to change from one mood to another without showing the slightest signs of anger or lack of Self-Control. The successful leader must understand the seventeen laws of success and be able to put into practice any combination of these seventeen laws whenever the occasion demands.

Without this ability no leader can be powerful, and without power no leader can long endure.

The Meaning of Education

There has long been a general misconception of the meaning of the word *educate*. The dictionaries have not aided in the elimination of this misunderstanding, because they have defined the word *educate* as an act of imparting knowledge. The word *educate* has its roots in the Latin word *educo*, which means to develop *from within;* to educe; to draw out; to grow through the law of *use.*

Nature hates idleness in all its forms. She gives continuous life only to those elements that are in use. Tie up an arm, or any other portion of the body, taking it out of use, and the idle part will soon atrophy and become lifeless. Reverse the order, give an arm more than normal use, such as that engaged in by the blacksmith who wields a heavy hammer all day long, and that arm (developed from within) grows strong.

Organized Knowledge in Action

Power grows out of *organized knowledge.* But, mind you, it grows out of it only through application and use.

A person may become a walking encyclopedia of knowledge without possessing any power of value. This knowledge becomes power only to the extent that it is organized, classified, and put into action. Some of the best-educated people the world has known possessed much less general knowledge than some who have been known as fools, the difference between the two being that the former put into use what knowledge they possessed while the latter made no such application.

An educated person is one who knows how to acquire everything needed in the attainment of their main purpose in life—without violating the rights of others. By that definition, many knowledgeable individuals come nowhere near qualifying as "educated." Similarly, it might also be a great surprise to many who believe they suffer from lack of learning to know that they are *well* educated.

COMMENTARY

Henry Ford, as cited often, is one example. Another is Albert Einstein, who could barely eke out a living as a patent clerk until he began organizing his knowledge of physics. And U.S. President Harry S. Truman had nothing more than a high school education. He laughed once that he was such a poor speller that when he wrote the word dictionary, *"I had to look on the back to see how to spell the book itself." But all of these men commanded power in different ways.*

The Uses of Learning

The successful lawyer is not necessarily the one who memorizes the greatest number of the principles of law. On the contrary, the successful lawyer is the one who knows where to find a principle of law, plus a variety of opinions supporting that principle, which fit the immediate needs of a given case.

In other words, the successful lawyer is the one who knows where to find the law he or she wants when needed.

This principle applies, with equal force, to the affairs of industry and business.

Henry Ford had but little elementary schooling, yet he is one of the best-educated men in the world because he has acquired the ability to combine natural and economic laws, to say nothing of the minds of other men, that he has the power to get anything of a material nature he wants.

During the world war, Mr. Ford brought suit against the *Chicago Tribune*, charging the newspaper with libelous publication of statements about him, one of which was that Ford was an "ignoramus," an ignorant pacifist, and so forth.

When the suit came up for trial, the attorneys for the *Tribune* undertook to prove, through Ford himself, that their statement was true, that he was indeed ignorant, and with this object in view they catechized and cross-examined him on all manner of subjects.

SEEK THE COUNSEL OF THOSE

WHO WILL TELL YOU

THE TRUTH ABOUT YOURSELF,

EVEN IF IT HURTS YOU TO HEAR IT.

MERE COMMENDATION

WILL NOT BRING

THE IMPROVEMENT YOU NEED.

One question they asked was:

"How many soldiers did the British send over to subdue the rebellion in the Colonies in 1776?"

With a dry grin on his face, Ford nonchalantly replied:

"I do not know just how many, but I have heard that it was a lot more than ever went back."

Loud laughter erupted from court, jury, courtroom spectators, and even from the frustrated lawyer who had asked the question.

This line of interrogation continued for an hour or more, with Ford keeping perfectly calm in the meantime. Finally, however, he was tired of the smart-alec lawyers, and in reply to a question that was particularly obnoxious and insulting, Ford straightened himself up, pointed his finger at the questioning lawyer, and replied: "If I should really wish to answer the foolish question you have just asked, or any of the others you have been asking, let me remind you that I have a row of electric push buttons hanging over my desk and by placing my finger on the right button I could call in men who could give me the correct answer to all the questions you have asked and to many that you have not the intelligence either to ask or answer. Now, will you kindly tell me why I should bother about filling my mind with a lot of useless details in order to answer every fool question that anyone may ask, when I have able men all about me who can supply me with all the facts I want when I call for them?"

This answer is quoted from memory but it substantially relates Ford's answer.

There was silence in the courtroom. The questioning attorney's jaw dropped down and his eyes opened wide. The judge leaned forward from the bench and stared at Ford. Many of the jury awoke and looked around as if they had heard an explosion (which they actually had).

A prominent clergyman who was present in the courtroom at the time said later that the scene reminded him of what must have existed when Jesus Christ was on trial before Pontius Pilate, just after He had given His famous reply to Pilate's question, "Are you a king?"

In the vernacular of the day, Ford's reply knocked the questioner cold.

Up until that reply, the lawyer had been enjoying considerable fun at what he had believed to be Ford's expense, by adroitly displaying his general knowledge and comparing it with what he inferred to be Ford's ignorance as to many events and subjects.

That answer spoiled the lawyer's fun!

It also proved once more (to all who had the intelligence to accept the proof) that true education means mind development, not merely the gathering and classifying of knowledge.

Ford could not, in all probability, have named the capitals of all the states of the United States, but he could have, and in fact had, gathered the "capital" with which to turn many wheels within every state in the Union.

Education, let us not forget this, consists of the power with which to get everything one needs, when one needs it, without violating the rights of others. Ford comes well within that definition, as the foregoing incident shows.

COMMENTARY

As the example of Henry Ford demonstrates, power is organized knowledge expressed through intelligent efforts. Let us consider how a Master Mind facilitates the exercise of power. The current era has been called the Information Age, due in large part to the ease with which information is transferred through computers at speeds and in such volume that were unthinkable even a generation ago.

But information is not organized knowledge. In fact, one of the chief complaints of many people is that they have far more information at their disposal than they know what to do with. A few minutes surfing the Internet in search of the answer to a particular question can produce a deluge of conflicting, ambiguous information that does nothing to increase one's knowledge. *Thousands of facts may have been gathered, but an* understanding *of those facts, including which are significant and which are not, is necessary before they can be considered knowledge. Still, as Napoleon Hill says, even such knowledge is not power; it is only potential power—the material out of which real power may be developed. Application of this potential power requires properly organized effort.*

Suppose you had collected the name and address of every CEO of a Fortune 500 company. Having this information represents a potential power—the ability to contact these men and women. Such power might or might not be useful to you. If you were attempting to sell a small starter home in need of much repair, you would be targeting a very unlikely group of buyers. If, on the other hand, you were selling a luxurious estate with state-of-the-art security and communications capability, this group of people would likely be more interested. Clearly, the knowledge you acquire must be suited to your task.

If you were indeed selling such an estate and you never attempted to contact these CEOs, you would not be exercising the potential power of your knowledge —simply because you would have made no effort. And if you sent each of them a box of chocolates and some balloons with a handwritten note about your property, you would be making an effort but it would not be appropriate.

However, if you printed a handsome brochure featuring photographs of the estate and outlining all its unique aspects, you would be applying your knowledge much more usefully—giving you the power to attract the attention of your potential buyers.

So far, the selling of this estate has involved at least three separate tasks. First, the collection of the names of potential buyers; second, the creation of an appropriate selling tool; and third, its distribution to your potential buyers. Supposing you interested some of these people, you would also need someone to show the property and eventually to negotiate the terms of the deal. This means at least five different tasks, all requiring different kinds of knowledge. You could work to educate yourself for each of these jobs, or you could create a Master Mind alliance.

You could begin by enlisting a direct-mail specialist to collect the list of names; that person could also contribute ideas for the brochure, which would be designed by a graphics artist familiar with all the necessary steps for production. You would handle showing the estate and selling it to your prospective buyers, and the fine points of the deal could be hammered out by an attorney. You would all be united behind a common purpose, dedicating your special skills to the task of making the sale. But who would have truly been responsible for making the sale happen? You, since you were the one who assembled the team that got the job done.

There are many learned people who could easily entangle Ford, theoretically, with a maze of questions, none of which he, personally, could answer. But Ford could turn right around and wage a battle in industry or finance that would exterminate those same people, with all of their knowledge and all of their wisdom.

Ford could not go into his chemical laboratory and separate water into its component atoms of hydrogen and oxygen and then recombine these atoms in their former order, but he knows how to surround himself with chemists who can do this for him if he wants it done.

The person who can intelligently use the knowledge possessed by another is as much, or more, a person of education as the one who merely has the knowledge but does not know what to do with it.

The president of a well-known college inherited a large tract of very poor land. This land had no timber of commercial value, no minerals or other valuable appurtenances, therefore it was nothing but a source of expense to him, for he had to pay taxes on it. The state built a highway through the land. An "uneducated" man who was driving his automobile over this road observed that this poor land was on top of a mountain that commanded a wonderful view for many miles in all directions. He (the ignorant one) also observed that the land was covered with a growth of small pines and other saplings.

This man bought fifty acres of the land for $10 an acre. Near the public highway he built a unique log house to which he attached a large dining room. Near the house he put in a gasoline filling station. Next he built a dozen single-room log houses along the road; these houses he rented out to tourists at $3 a night each. The dining room, the gasoline station, and the log houses brought him a net income of $15,000 the first year. The next year he extended his plan by adding fifty more log houses, with three rooms each, which he now rents out as summer country homes to people in a nearby city, at a rental of $150 each for the season.

The building material cost him nothing, for it grew on his land in abundance (that same land which the college president believed to be worthless).

Moreover, the unique and unusual appearance of the log bungalows served as an advertisement for the plan, whereas many would have considered it a real calamity had they been compelled to build out of such crude materials.

Less than five miles from the location of these log houses, this same man purchased an old worked-out farm of 150 acres, for $25 an acre, a price the seller believed to be extremely high.

By building a dam, one hundred feet in length, the purchaser of this old farm turned a stream of water into a lake that covered fifteen acres of the land, stocked the lake with fish, then sold the farm off in building lots to people who wanted summer places around the lake. The total profit realized from this simple transaction was more than $25,000, and the time required was one summer.

Yet this man of vision and Imagination was not educated, in the orthodox meaning of the term.

Let us keep in mind that it is through these simple illustrations of the use of organized knowledge that one may become educated and powerful.

In speaking of that transaction, the college president who sold the fifty acres of "worthless" land for $500 said:

"Just think of it! That man, whom most of us might call ignorant, mixed his ignorance with fifty acres of worthless land and made the combination yield more yearly than I earn from five years of application of so-called education."

————————

There is an opportunity, if not scores of them, in every state in America to make use of the idea here described. From now on, make it your business to study the lay of all land you see that is similar to the land that this man saw, and you may find a suitable place for developing a similar money-making enterprise.

The automobile has caused a great system of public highways to be built throughout the United States. On practically every one of these highways there is a suitable spot for a "cabin city" for tourists which can be turned into a regular money-making mint by the person with the Imagination and Self-Confidence to do it.

COMMENTARY

If you think that Hill's example of starting what we now know as a motel is out of date and no longer applicable, you are not seeing the ideas for the words.

As this edition is being edited, Hill's advice is more than seventy-five years old, yet one of the most exciting new business ventures of this era might well have been inspired by that "out of date" story. Jeff Bezos did exactly what Hill suggested. He looked for a highway on which to set up a business. When he found the right place he opened a bookstore. The highway that Bezos found was the information highway and the bookstore was Amazon.com.

Sometimes the innovation requires specialized education or technical expertise, but just as often the business itself is not especially new. The innovation is in finding the right highway.

Lora Brody is another example of someone whose inspiration made her greater than the so-called experts. The author of several cookbooks, she noticed that many people were buying and enjoying the bread machines that had become so popular. But when she noticed that they were not fully satisfied with the bread they were making, her first right move was to write a new cookbook for bread machines. It was an instant success. Then she took her good idea even further.

Huge corporations were manufacturing these machines, and other huge corporations were making mixes to use in them. But Brody alone realized that these appliances were different enough from traditional techniques that the old methods weren't enough. What bread machine bakers needed were additives, simple natural ingredients that professional bakeries used all the time. So she created a line of dough enhancers that could be added to any bread machine recipe, creating a better, more tasty loaf.

Soon her "Bread Machine Magic" was in grocery stores and cooks' catalogs around the country, making home bakers happier and Lora Brody a wealthy and popular entrepreneur. The experts who had been involved in creating these machines, and the flour companies that thought to profit from their popularity, had looked right past a tremendous opportunity that one woman who organized her knowledge profited from.

In the mid-1970s, computers were used by big businesses. They were giant, complicated machines too expensive for anyone else to afford, or such was the conventional wisdom at companies like IBM. Steve Jobs and Steven Wozniak thought differently. In a garage in California they built a small computer that could fit on a desktop. The company they founded was called Apple. The Apple computer created a revolution in the computer industry—and made multimillionaires of Jobs and Wozniak, because they organized their knowledge in a way that no one had before.

Ray Kroc saw that people wanted fast food, and he created McDonald's. Frederick W. Smith saw that people wanted safe reliable delivery, and he created Federal Express. Bill Bowerman saw people jogging, and he created Nike to make special shoes for the new fad.

There are similar opportunities everywhere, in every walk of life, in every area of human endeavor, to achieve success. This course can reveal new opportunities and strategies for personal success, but what it cannot do is give you the benefit of real education, of creating an understanding based on your own efforts. You must resolve to take the ideas that you absorb here and apply them in all your efforts.

As this course proceeds, you will learn more about the Master Mind, as well as all the other significant principles you must apply. You will begin to see how they all fit together into a harmonious whole, a manner of acting and thinking that takes best advantage of the way the world operates. But only through applying each of these principles will you truly understand how to integrate them.

Remember: your own actions will educate you in the laws of success.

There are opportunities all around you to make money. This course was designed to help you see these opportunities and to inform you how to make the most of them after you discover them.

WHO CAN PROFIT MOST BY THE
LAW OF SUCCESS PHILOSOPHY?

Transportation Officials who want a better spirit of Cooperation between their employees and the public they serve.

Salaried People who wish to increase their earning power and market their services to better advantage.

Salespeople who wish to become masters in their chosen field. The Law of Success philosophy covers every known law of selling and includes many features not included in any other course.

Industrial Plant Managers who understand the value of greater harmony among their employees.

Employees who wish to establish records of efficiency that will lead to more responsible positions, with greater pay.

Merchants who wish to extend their business by adding new customers. The Law of Success philosophy will help any merchant increase business by teaching how to make a walking advertisement of every customer who comes into the store.

Sales Agents or Managers who wish to increase the selling power of their sales force. A large part of the Law of Success course was developed from the lifework and experience of the greatest automobile salesman, and it is therefore of unusual help to the sales manager who is directing the efforts of a sales force.

Life Insurance Agents who wish to add new policyholders and increase the insurance on present policyholders. One life insurance salesman in Ohio sold a $50,000 policy to one of the officials of the Central Steel Company, as the result of just one reading of the lesson on Profiting by Failure. This same salesman has become one of the star men of the New York Life Insurance Company's staff, as the result of his training in the seventeen laws of success.

School Teachers who wish to advance to the top in their present occupation or who are looking for an opportunity to enter the field of business as a life's work.

Students, both college and high school, who are undecided as to the field of endeavor they wish to enter. The Law of Success course includes a personal analysis chart that will help the student of the philosophy to determine the work for which he or she is best suited.

Bankers who wish to extend their business through better service and more courteous methods of serving their clients.

Mid-level Managers who are ambitious to prepare themselves for executive positions in some commercial or industrial field.

Physicians and Dentists who wish to extend their practice without violating the ethics of their profession by direct advertising. A prominent physician has said that the Law of Success course is worth $1,000 to any professional man or woman whose professional ethics prevent direct advertising.

WHO SAID IT COULD NOT BE DONE?

AND WHAT GREAT VICTORIES

HAS HE TO HIS CREDIT

WHICH QUALIFY HIM

TO JUDGE OTHERS ACCURATELY?

Entrepreneurs and Promoters who wish to develop new and previously unworked combinations in business or industry.

Real Estate Agents who wish to create new methods for promoting sales. This lesson contains a description of an entirely new real estate promotion plan which is sure to make fortunes for many who will put it to use. This plan may be put into operation in practically every state. Moreover, it may be used by agents who never promoted an enterprise. (In fact the principle described in this introductory lesson is said to have made a small fortune for a man who used it as the basis of a real estate promotion.)

Farmers who wish to discover new methods of marketing their products so as to give them greater net returns, and those who own lands suitable for subdivision promotion under the plan referred to at the end of this lesson. Many farmers have "gold mines" in the land they own that is not suitable for cultivation, but could be used for recreation and resort purposes on a highly profitable basis.

Entry-level Service Workers who are looking for a practical plan to promote themselves into higher and better-paying positions. The Law of Success course is said to be the best course ever written on the subject of marketing personal services.

Printers who want a larger volume of business as well as more efficient production through better Cooperation among their own employees.

Laborers who have the ambition to advance into more responsible positions, in work that has greater responsibilities and consequently offers more pay.

Lawyers who wish to extend their clientele through dignified, ethical methods that will bring them to the attention, in a favorable way, of a greater number of people who need legal services.

Business Executives who wish to expand their present business, or who wish to handle their present volume with less expense, as the result of greater Cooperation among their employees.

Service Industry Owners who wish to extend their business by teaching their drivers how to serve more courteously and efficiently.

Life Insurance General Agents who wish bigger and more efficient sales organizations.

Chain Store Managers who want a greater volume of business as the result of more efficient individual sales efforts.

Married People who are unhappy, and therefore unsuccessful, because of lack of harmony and Cooperation in the home.

To all described in the foregoing classification, the Law of Success philosophy offers both *definite* and *speedy* aid.

SUMMARY, THE MASTER MIND

The main purpose of this lesson is to introduce some of the principles upon which the course is founded. These principles are more accurately described, and the student is taught in a very definite manner how to apply them, in the individual lessons which follow.

All new ideas, and especially those of an abstract nature, will settle comfortably into the human mind only after much repetition, a well-known truth that accounts for the restatement, in this summary, of the principle known as the Master Mind.

A Master Mind may be developed by a friendly alliance, in a spirit of harmony of purpose, between two or more minds.

This is an appropriate place at which to explain that out of every alliance of minds, whether in a spirit of harmony or not, there is developed another mind which affects all participating in the alliance. No two or more minds ever met without creating, out of that contact, another mind, but this creation is not always a Master Mind.

There may be, and altogether too often there is, developed out of the meeting of two or more minds a negative power which is just the opposite of a Master Mind.

There are certain minds which, as has been stated throughout this lesson, cannot be made to blend in a spirit of harmony. This principle has its analogy in chemistry.

For example, the chemical formula H_2O (meaning the combining of two atoms of hydrogen with one atom of oxygen) changes these two elements into water. But one atom of hydrogen and one atom of oxygen will not produce water; moreover, they cannot be made to associate themselves in harmony!

There are many known elements which, when combined, are immediately transformed from harmless into deadly poisonous substances. Stated differently, many well-known poisonous elements are neutralized and rendered harmless when combined with certain other elements.

Just as the combining of certain elements changes their entire nature, the combining of certain minds changes the nature of those minds, producing either a certain degree of what has been called a Master Mind, or its opposite which is highly destructive.

Some minds will not be harmonized and cannot be blended into a Master Mind—a fact that all leaders will do well to remember. It is the leader's responsibility to group his or her subordinates so that those who have been placed at the most strategic points in the organization are those whose minds can and will be blended in a spirit of friendliness and harmony.

Ability to bring people together is the chief outstanding quality of Leadership. In Lesson Two of this course you will discover that this ability was the main source of both the power and fortune accumulated by the late Andrew Carnegie.

AN AIM IN LIFE

IS THE ONLY FORTUNE

WORTH FINDING;

AND IT IS NOT TO BE FOUND

IN FOREIGN LANDS,

BUT IN THE HEART ITSELF.

—Robert Louis Stevenson

Knowing nothing whatsoever about the technical end of the steel business, Carnegie so combined and grouped the people of which his Master Mind was composed that he built the most successful steel industry known to the world during his lifetime.

Henry Ford's gigantic success may be traced to the successful application of this selfsame principle. With all the self-reliance that a man could have, Ford, nevertheless, did not depend on himself for the knowledge necessary in the successful development of his industries.

Like Carnegie, he surrounded himself with people who supplied the knowledge that he, himself, did not and could not possess.

Moreover, Ford picked men who could and did harmonize in group effort.

The most effective alliances, which have resulted in the creation of the principle known as the Master Mind, have been those developed out of the blending of the minds of men and women. The reason for this is that the minds of male and female will more readily blend in harmony than will the minds of only one gender. As well, the added stimulus of potential sexual contact often enters into the development of a Master Mind between a man and a woman.

The road to success may be, and generally is, obstructed by many influences that must be removed before the goal can be reached. One of the most detrimental of these obstacles is that of unfortunate alliance with minds that do not harmonize. In such cases the alliance must be broken or the end is sure to be defeat and failure.

Those who master the six basic fears, one of which is the fear of criticism, will have no hesitancy in taking what may seem to the more convention-bound type of mind to be drastic action when they find themselves circumscribed and bound down by antagonistic alliances, no matter of what nature or with whom they may be.

It is a million times better to meet and face criticism than to be dragged down to failure and oblivion as a result of alliances that are not harmonious, whether the alliances be of a business or social nature.

While it is true that some minds will not blend in a spirit of harmony, and cannot be forced or induced to do so because of the chemical nature of the individuals' brains, do not be too ready to charge the other party to your alliance with all the responsibility for lack of harmony—remember, the trouble may be *with your own brain!*

Remember, also, that a mind that cannot and will not harmonize with one person or persons may harmonize perfectly with other types of minds. Discovery of this has resulted in radical changes in methods of hiring. It is no longer customary to dismiss an employee who does not fit the position for which he or she was originally hired. The discriminating leader endeavors to place such a person in some other position, where, it has been proved more than once, such individuals may become valuable.

You should be sure that the principle described as the Master Mind is thoroughly understood before proceeding with the remaining lessons of the course. The reason for this is that practically the entire course is closely associated with this law of mind operation.

If you are not sure you understand this law, analyze the record of anyone who has accumulated a great fortune, and you will find that they have, either consciously or unconsciously, employed the Master Mind principle.

No amount of time spent in serious thought and contemplation in connection with the law of the Master Mind is too much, for when you have mastered this law, and learned how to apply it, new worlds of opportunity will open to you.

Any sales organization may make effective use of the law of the Master Mind by grouping the sales force into groups of two or more people who will ally themselves in a spirit of friendly Cooperation and apply this law as suggested in this lesson.

An agent for a well-known make of automobile, who employs a sales force of twelve, has grouped the organization into six groups of two each, with the object of applying the law of the Master Mind. As a result, all the salespeople have established new high-sales records.

This same organization has created what it calls the "One-A-Week Club," meaning that every member of the club has averaged the sale of one car a week since the club was organized.

The results of this effort have been surprising to all! Each member of the club was provided with a list of one hundred prospective purchasers of automobiles. Each salesperson sends one postcard a week to each of those one hundred prospective purchasers, and makes personal calls on at least ten of these each day.

Each postcard is confined to the description of just one advantage of the automobile and asks for a personal interview.

Interviews have increased rapidly, as have sales!

The agent who employs this sales force has offered an extra cash bonus to anyone who earns the right to membership in the One-A-Week Club by averaging the sale of one car a week.

This plan has injected new vitality into the entire organization, and the results are showing in the weekly sales record. A similar plan could also be adopted very effectively by life insurance agencies. Any enterprising general agent might easily double or even triple the volume of business through the use of this plan.

Practically no changes whatsoever would need to be made in the method of use of the plan. The club might be called the Policy-A-Week Club, meaning that each member pledges to sell at least one policy, of an agreed minimum amount, each week.

The student of this course who has mastered the second lesson, A Definite Chief Aim, and understands how to apply the fundamentals of that lesson, will be able to make much more effective use of the plan here described.

It is not suggested or intended that anyone undertake to apply the principles of this lesson until they have mastered at least the next five lessons of the Law of Success course.

The automobile sales organization to which I have here referred holds a lunchtime meeting once a week. An hour and a half is devoted

IF YOU CANNOT

DO GREAT THINGS YOURSELF,

REMEMBER THAT YOU MAY

DO SMALL THINGS

IN A GREAT WAY.

to the meeting and to the discussion of ways and means of applying the principles of this course. This gives each individual member an opportunity to profit by the ideas of all the other members.

Two tables are set for the lunch. At one table, all who have earned the right to membership in the One-A-Week Club are seated. At the other table, which is serviced with tinware instead of china, are those who did not earn the right to membership in the club. These, needless to say, become the object of considerable good-natured chiding from the more fortunate members seated at the other table.

It is possible to make an almost endless variety of adaptations of this plan.

The justification for its use is that *it pays!*

It pays not only the leader or the manager of the organization, but every member of the sales force as well.

I have briefly described this plan here for the purpose of showing you one of many ways to make practical application of the principles outlined in this course.

The final acid test of any theory or rule or principle is that it will actually work. The law of the Master Mind has been proved sound because it *works!*

If you understand this law, you are now ready to proceed with Lesson Two, A Definite Chief Aim, in which you will be further and much more deeply initiated in the application of the principles described in this introductory lesson.

Lesson Two

A Definite Chief Aim

THE BEST ROSE BUSH,

AFTER ALL, IS NOT

THAT WHICH HAS

THE FEWEST THORNS,

BUT THAT WHICH BEARS

THE FINEST ROSES.

—Henry van Dyke

Lesson Two

A DEFINITE CHIEF AIM

"You Can Do It if You Believe You Can!"

You ARE AT THE BEGINNING OF A COURSE of philosophy which, for the first time in the history of the world, has been organized from the known factors that have been used and must always be used by successful people.

Literary style has been completely subordinated so that I may state the principles and laws included in this course in such a manner that they can be quickly and easily assimilated by people in every walk of life.

Some of the principles described in this course are familiar to all who will read it. Others are presented here for the first time. It should be kept in mind, from the first lesson to the last, that the value of the philosophy lies entirely in the thought stimuli it will produce in the mind of the reader, and not merely in the lessons themselves.

Stated another way, this course is intended as a mind stimulant that will cause you to organize and direct to a *definite* end the forces of your mind, thus harnessing the stupendous power which most people waste in purposeless thought.

Singleness of purpose is essential for success, no matter what may be one's idea of the definition of success. Yet singleness of purpose is also a quality which may, and generally does, call for thought on many allied subjects.

I traveled a long distance to watch Jack Dempsey train for an upcoming fight. It was observed that he did not rely entirely on one form of exercise but resorted to many forms. The punching bag helped him develop one set of muscles and also trained his eye to be quick. The dumbbells trained yet another set of muscles. Running developed the muscles of his legs and hips. A well-balanced diet supplied the materials needed for building muscle without fat. Proper sleep, relaxation, and rest habits provided still other qualities that he needed in order to win.

You should be engaged in the business of training for success in the battle of life. To win there are many factors that must have attention. A well-organized, alert, and energetic mind is produced by various and sundry stimuli, all of which are plainly described in these lessons.

It should be remembered, however, that just as the physical body, to be properly developed, calls for many forms of systematic exercise, the mind also requires, for its development, a variety of exercise.

Horses are trained to certain gaits by trainers who jump them over hurdles to help them develop the desired steps, through habit and repetition. The human mind must be trained in a similar manner, by a variety of thought-inspiring stimuli.

You will observe, before you have gone very far into this philosophy, that reading these lessons will induce a flow of thoughts covering a wide range of subjects. For this reason you should read this course with a notebook and pencil at hand, and follow the practice of recording these thoughts or ideas as they come to your mind.

By following this suggestion you will have a collection of ideas, by the time the course has been read two or three times, sufficient to transform your entire life plan.

By following this practice it will be noticed, very soon, that the mind has become like a magnet in that it will attract useful ideas right out of thin air, to use the words of a noted scientist who has experimented with this principle for a great number of years.

COMMENTARY

In the time since Hill wrote these words, considerable research has been done on creativity, intuition, and various thinking styles and techniques. In almost all cases, books written on these subjects tend to support Hill's theory that the act of writing down what you think or dream prompts the human mind to make leaps of insight and spontaneously create original ideas. This in turn has prompted a whole subset of books about what is now termed journaling.

If you wish to explore the possibilities further, you will find the following books of interest: The Intuitive Edge by Philip Goldberg, The Right-Brain Experience by Marilee Zdenek, Creative Dreaming by Patricia Garfield, and Writing the Natural Way by Gabriele Rico. Books on methods of thinking include numerous works by Tony Buzan, and an extensive collection of influential bestsellers written by Edward de Bono. Books on journaling include Writing Down the Bones by Natalie Goldberg, At a Journal Workshop by Ira Progoff, and The Artist's Way by Julia Cameron.

You will be doing yourself a great injustice if you undertake this course with even a remote feeling that you do not stand in need of more knowledge than you now possess. In truth, no one knows enough about any worthwhile subject to entitle them to feel that they have the last word on that subject.

In the long, hard task of trying to wipe out some of my own ignorance and make way for some of the useful truths of life, I have often seen, in my imagination, the Great Marker who stands at the gateway entrance of life and writes "Poor Fool" on the brow of those who believe they are wise, and "Poor Sinner" on the brow of those who believe they are saints.

Translated into workaday language, this means that none of us knows very much, and by the very nature of our being can never know as much as we need to know in order to live sanely and enjoy life while we live.

Humility is a forerunner of success!

Until we become humble in our own hearts, we are not apt to profit greatly by the experiences and thoughts of others.

Sounds like a preachment on morality? Well, what if it does?

Even sermons, as dry and lacking in interest as they generally are, may be beneficial if they serve to reflect the shadow of our real selves so we may get an approximate idea of our smallness and superficiality.

Success in life is largely predicated upon who we know!

The best place to study the human animal is in your own mind, by taking as accurate an inventory as possible of *yourself*. When you know yourself thoroughly (if you ever do) you will also know much about others.

To know others, not as they seem to be but as they really are, study them through:

- the posture of the body and the way they walk
- the tone of the voice, its quality, pitch, volume
- the eyes, whether shifty or direct
- the use of words, their trend, nature, and quality

Through these open windows you may literally "walk right into a person's soul" and take a look at the *real* human being!

Going a step further, if you would know people, study them:

- when angry
- when in love
- when money is involved

- when eating (alone, and unobserved, as they believe)

- when writing

- when in trouble

- when joyful and triumphant

- when downcast and defeated

- when facing catastrophe of a hazardous nature

- when trying to make a good impression on others

- when informed of another's misfortune

- when informed of another's good fortune

- when losing in any sort of a game of sport

- when winning at sport

- when alone, in a meditative mood

Before you can know people as they really are, you must observe them in all the foregoing moods, and perhaps more, which is practically the equivalent of saying that you have no right to judge others at sight.

Appearances count, there can be no doubt of that, but appearances are often deceiving.

This course has been so designed that the student who masters it may take inventory of themselves and of others by something more than "snap-judgment" methods. When you master this philosophy you will be able to look through the outer crust of personal adornment, clothes, so-called culture, and the like, and down deep into the heart.

This is a very broad promise!

It would not have been made if I had not known, from years of experimentation and analysis, that the promise can be met.

Some who have examined the manuscripts of this course have asked why it was not called a course in master salesmanship. The answer is that the word *salesmanship* is commonly associated with the marketing of goods or services, and it would, therefore, narrow down and circumscribe

NO PERSON IS EDUCATED

WHO HAS NOT AT LEAST

A SPEAKING ACQUAINTANCE

WITH THE LAW OF COMPENSATION,

AS IT IS DESCRIBED BY EMERSON.

the real nature of the course. It is true that this is a course in master salesmanship, providing one takes a deeper-than-the-average view of the meaning of salesmanship.

This philosophy is intended to enable those who master it to sell their way through life successfully, with a minimum of resistance and friction. Such a course, therefore, must help the student organize and make use of much truth that is overlooked by the majority of people who go through life as mediocrities.

Not all people are so constituted that they wish to know the truth about all matters vitally affecting life. One of the great surprises I met with, in connection with my research, is that so few people are willing to hear the truth when it shows up their own weaknesses.

We prefer illusions to realities!

New truths, if accepted at all, are taken with the proverbial grain of salt. Some of us demand more than a mere pinch of salt; we demand enough to pickle new ideas so they become useless.

For these reasons, the first lesson of this course, and this lesson as well, cover subjects intended to pave the way for new ideas so those ideas will not be too severe a shock to the mind of the reader.

The thought I want to get across has been quite plainly stated by the editor of *The American Magazine* in an editorial that appeared in a recent issue, in the following words:

> On a recent rainy night, Carl Lomen, the reindeer king of Alaska, told me a true story. It has stuck in my crop ever since. And now I am going to pass it along.
>
> "A certain Greenland Eskimo," said Lomen, "was taken on one of the American North Polar expeditions a number of years ago. Later, as a reward for faithful service, he was brought to New York City for a short visit. At all the miracles of sight and sound he was filled with a most amazed wonder. When he returned to

his native village he told stories of buildings that rose into the very face of the sky; of street cars, which he described as houses that moved along the trail, with people living in them as they moved; of mammoth bridges, artificial lights, and all the other dazzling concomitants of the metropolis.

"His people looked at him coldly and walked away. And forthwith throughout the whole village he was dubbed 'Sagdluk,' meaning 'the Liar,' and this name he carried in shame to his grave. Long before his death his original name was entirely forgotten.

"When Knud Rasmussen made his trip from Greenland to Alaska he was accompanied by a Greenland Eskimo named Mitek (Eider Duck). Mitek visited Copenhagen and New York, where he saw many things for the first time and was greatly impressed. Later, upon his return to Greenland, he recalled the tragedy of Sagdluk, and decided that it would not be wise to tell the truth. Instead, he would narrate stories that his people could grasp and thus save his reputation.

"So he told them how he and Doctor Rasmussen maintained a kayak on the banks of a great river, the Hudson, and how, each morning, they paddled out for their hunting. Ducks, geese, and seals were to be had aplenty, and they enjoyed the visit immensely.

"Mitek, in the eyes of his countrymen, is a very honest man. His neighbors treat him with rare respect."

The road of the truth-teller has always been rocky. Socrates sipping the hemlock, Christ crucified, Stephen stoned, Bruno burned at the stake, Galileo terrified into retraction of his starry truths—forever could one follow that bloody trail through the pages of history.

Something in human nature makes us resent the impact of new ideas.

We all hate to be disturbed in the beliefs and prejudices that have been handed down with the family furniture. At maturity too many of us go into hibernation and live off the fat of ancient fetishes. If a new idea invades our den we rise up snarling from our winter sleep.

The Eskimos in *The American Magazine* editor's story at least had some excuse. They were unable to visualize the startling pictures drawn by Sagdluk. Their simple lives had been too long circumscribed by the brooding arctic night.

OPEN YOUR MIND

There is no adequate reason why the average person should ever close their mind to fresh slants on life. But they do, just the same. Nothing is more tragic—or more common—than mental inertia. For every ten people who are physically lazy there are ten thousand others with stagnant minds. And stagnant minds are the breeding places of fear.

An old farmer in Vermont always used to end his prayers with this plea: "Oh, God, give me an open mind!" If more people followed his example they might escape being hamstrung by prejudices. And what a pleasant place to live the world would be.

———————

Every person should make it his or her business to gather new ideas from sources other than the environment in which he or she daily lives and works.

The human mind becomes withered, stagnant, narrow, and closed unless it searches for new ideas. The farmer should come to the city quite often, and walk among the strange faces and the tall buildings. He will go back to his farm, his mind refreshed, with more courage and greater Enthusiasm.

And city people should take a trip to the country every so often to freshen their minds with sights new and different from those associated with their daily routines.

Everyone needs a change of mental environment at regular periods, the same as a change and variety of food are essential. The mind becomes more alert, more elastic, and more ready to work with speed and accuracy after it has been bathed in new ideas, outside of one's own field of daily labor.

As a student of this course you will temporarily lay aside the set of ideas with which you perform your daily labors and enter a field of entirely new (and in some instances, heretofore unheard-of) ideas.

Splendid! You will come out, at the other end of this course, with a new stock of ideas that will make you more efficient, more enthusiastic, and more courageous, *no matter in what sort of work you may be engaged.*

Do not be afraid of new ideas. They may mean to you the difference between success and failure. Some of the ideas introduced in this course will require no further explanation or proof of their soundness because they are familiar to practically everyone. Some of the other ideas introduced here are new, and for that very reason many students of this philosophy may hesitate to accept them as sound.

I have thoroughly tested every principle described in this course, and the majority of the principles covered have been tested by scores of scientists and others who were quite capable of distinguishing between the merely theoretic and the practical.

For these reasons all principles here covered are known to be workable in the exact manner claimed. However, no reader of this book is asked to accept any statement made in these lessons without having first satisfied himself or herself, by tests, experiments, and analysis, that the statement is sound.

The major evil you are requested to avoid is that of forming opinions without definite *facts* as the basis, which brings to mind Herbert Spencer's famous admonition: "There is a principle which is a bar against all information; which is proof against all argument; and which cannot fail to keep a man in everlasting ignorance. This principle is contempt prior to examination."

It may be well to bear this principle in mind as you study the law of the Master Mind described in these lessons. This law embodies an entirely new principle of mind operation, and, for this reason alone, it will be difficult for you to accept it as sound until after you have experimented with it.

When the fact is considered, however, that the law of the Master Mind is believed to be the real basis of most of the achievements of those who are considered geniuses, this law takes on an aspect which calls for more than snap-judgment opinions.

It is believed by many scientists, whose opinions on the subject have been passed on to me, that the law of the Master Mind is the basis of practically all of the more important achievements resulting from group or cooperative effort.

The late Dr. Alexander Graham Bell said he believed that the law of the Master Mind, as it has been described in this philosophy, was not only sound, but that all the higher institutions of learning would soon be teaching that law as a part of their courses in psychology.

Charles P. Steinmetz said that he had experimented with the law and had arrived at the same conclusion as that stated in these lessons, long before he talked to me about the subject.

Luther Burbank and John Burroughs made similar statements.

Edison was never questioned on the subject, but other statements of his indicate that he would endorse the law as being a possibility, if not in fact a reality.

Dr. Elmer Gates also endorsed the law, when I spoke with him some years ago. Dr. Gates is a scientist of the highest order, ranking along with Steinmetz, Edison, and Bell.

I have spoken with scores of intelligent businessmen who, while they were not scientists, admitted they believed in the soundness of the law of the Master Mind. It is hardly excusable, therefore, for those of less ability to judge such matters, to form opinions as to this law, without serious, systematic investigation.

BY AND LARGE,

THERE IS NO SUCH THING

AS SOMETHING FOR NOTHING.

IN THE LONG RUN

YOU GET EXACTLY

THAT FOR WHICH YOU PAY,

WHETHER YOU ARE BUYING

AN AUTOMOBILE

OR A LOAF OF BREAD.

COMMENTARY

To recap, the Master Mind is a mental state that is developed through the harmonious cooperation of two or more people who ally themselves for the purpose of accomplishing any given task. The Master Mind harnesses the dedicated effort of a group of people, pools their resources, both tangible and intangible, and creates a new whole that is greater than the sum of its parts.

A Master Mind operates (or should operate) among the members of the board of directors for huge international corporations. It operates among a team of engineers designing a new car. It operates in the production of a movie, the conduct of a political campaign, or the launch of a new advertising strategy. A Master Mind occurs when a church begins a fundraising program for a new building, when a group of neighbors organizes to increase the safety of their community, and when a couple commits to a lifetime of marriage.

A Master Mind is not simply teamwork. People can work together on a team simply because they like the leader, or because they are paid to. But in a Master Mind alliance each member must be passionately committed to the same goals.

Let me lay before you a brief outline of what this lesson is and what it is intended to do for you.

Having prepared myself for the practice of law, I will offer this introduction as a statement of my case. And the evidence with which to back up my case will be presented in the seventeen lessons of which the course is comprised.

The facts out of which this course has been prepared have been gathered through more than twenty-five years of business and professional experience, and my only explanation of the rather free use of the personal pronoun throughout the course is that I am writing from *first-hand experience.*

Before this course on the Law of Success was published, the manuscripts were submitted to two prominent universities with the request they be read by competent professors—with the object of eliminating or correcting any statements that appeared to be unsound, from an economic viewpoint.

This request was complied with and the manuscripts were carefully examined, with the result that not a single change was made, with the exception of one or two slight changes in wording.

One of the professors who examined the manuscripts expressed himself, in part, as follows: "It is a tragedy that every boy and girl who enters high school is not efficiently drilled on the seventeen major parts of your course in the Law of Success. It is regrettable that the great university with which I am connected, and every other university, does not include your course as a part of its curriculum."

Inasmuch as this course is intended as a map or blueprint that will guide you in the attainment of that coveted goal called success, may it not be well here to define success?

Success is the development of the power with which to get whatever one wants in life without interfering with the rights of others.

I lay particular stress on the word *power* because it is inseparably related to success. We are living in a world and during an age of intense competition, and the law of the survival of the fittest is everywhere in evidence. Because of this, all who would enjoy enduring success must go about its attainment through the use of power.

And what is power?

Power is *organized* energy or effort. This course is appropriately called the Law of Success because it teaches how one may organize *facts* and *knowledge*, and the faculties of one's mind, into a unit of power.

The course brings you a definite promise: Through its mastery and application you can get whatever you want, with but two qualifying words—"within reason."

This qualification takes into consideration your education, your wisdom or your lack of it, your physical endurance, your temperament, and all of the other qualities mentioned in the seventeen lessons of this course as being the factors most essential in the attainment of success.

Without a single exception, those who have attained unusual success have done so, either consciously or unconsciously, through the aid of all or a portion of the seventeen major factors of which this course is compiled. If you doubt this statement, then master these seventeen lessons so you can go about the analysis with reasonable accuracy and analyze such men as Carnegie, Rockefeller, Hill, Harriman, Ford, and others of this type who have accumulated great fortunes of material wealth, and you will see that they understood and applied the principle of *organized effort.*

COMMENTARY

Anyone who has ever participated in a "Quality Circle" at work knows how business employs the Master Mind. The assembly teams that have replaced assembly lines at the most modern and efficient factories reflect the same use of the Master Mind.

Stephen Covey, author of The 7 Habits of Highly Effective People *(Fireside),* speaks of the Master Mind when he writes of the "interdependent person." "As an interdependent person . . ." he says, "I have access to the vast resources and potential of other human beings."

Dennis Connor, the two-time winner of sailing's America's Cup, has a philosophy of teamwork that is a perfect expression of the Master Mind, emphasizing the power of commitment and dedication to a task. Read his book The Art of Winning *(St. Martin's Press)* for a vivid explanation of how Connor used the Master Mind to create a winning team.

From restaurant kitchens to football teams, from factories to scientific laboratories, the Master Mind harnesses the potential power of a group of minds focused on a goal. Can you afford to ignore this valuable resource in your quest for success?

WHAT DO YOU MEAN BY SUCCESS?

Nearly twenty years ago I interviewed Mr. Carnegie for the purpose of writing a story about him. During the interview I asked him to what he attributed his success. With a merry little twinkle in his eyes he said:

"Young man, before I answer your question will you please define your term 'success'?"

After waiting until he saw that I was somewhat embarrassed by this request, he continued: "By success you make reference to my money, do you not?" I assured him that money was the term by which most people measured success, and he then said: "Oh, well, if you wish to know how I got my money—if *that* is what you call success —I will answer your question by saying that we have a Master Mind here in our business, and that mind is made up of more than a score of men who constitute my personal staff of superintendents and managers and accountants and chemists and other necessary types. No one person in this group is the Master Mind of which I speak, but the sum total of all the minds in the group, coordinated, organized, and directed to a *definite* end in a spirit of harmonious Cooperation, is the power that got my money for me. No two minds in the group are exactly alike, but each man in the group does the thing that he is supposed to do and he does it better than any other person in the world could do it."

Then and there, the seed out of which this course has since been developed was sown in my mind. But that seed did not take root or germinate until later. This interview marked the beginning of years of research which led, finally, to the discovery of the principle of psychology described in the introductory lesson as the Master Mind.

I heard all that Mr. Carnegie had said, but it took the knowledge gained from many years of subsequent contact with the business world to enable me to assimilate what he said and to clearly grasp and understand the principle behind it—which was nothing more nor less than the principle of *organized effort* upon which this course on the Law of Success is founded.

Carnegie's group of men constituted a Master Mind and that mind was so well-organized, so well-coordinated, so powerful, that it could have accumulated millions of dollars for Mr. Carnegie in practically any sort of endeavor of a commercial or industrial nature. The steel business in which that mind was engaged was but an incident in connection with the accumulation of the Carnegie wealth. The same wealth could have been accumulated had the Master Mind been directed in the coal business or the banking business or the grocery business, because behind that mind was *power*—the sort of power that *you* may attain when you have organized the faculties of your own mind and allied yourself with other well-organized minds for the attainment of a Definite Chief Aim in life.

A careful checkup with several of Mr. Carnegie's former business associates, which was made after this course was begun, proves conclusively not only that there *is* such a law as that which has been called the Master Mind, but that this law was the chief source of Mr. Carnegie's success.

Perhaps there was never anyone associated with Mr. Carnegie who knew him better than did Mr. C. M. Schwab, who, in the following words, has very accurately described that "subtle something" in Mr. Carnegie's personality which enabled him to rise to such stupendous heights:

> I never knew a man with so much imagination, lively intelligence, and instinctive comprehension. You sensed that he probed your thoughts and took stock of everything that you had ever done or might do. He seemed to catch at your next word before it was spoken. The play of his mind was dazzling and his habit of close observation gave him a store of knowledge about innumerable matters.
>
> But his outstanding quality, from so rich an endowment, was the power to inspire other men. Confidence radiated from him. You might be doubtful about something and discuss the matter with Mr. Carnegie. In a flash he would make you see that it was right and then you would absolutely believe it; or he might settle your doubts by pointing out its weakness. This quality of attracting others, then spurring them on, arose from his own strength.

IF YOU CAN RUN

A LOSING RACE WITHOUT

BLAMING YOUR LOSS

ON SOMEONE ELSE,

YOU HAVE BRIGHT

PROSPECTS OF SUCCESS

FURTHER DOWN

THE ROAD IN LIFE.

The results of his leadership were remarkable. Never before in history of industry, I imagine, was there a man who, without understanding his business in its working details, making no pretense of technical knowledge concerning steel or engineering, was yet able to build up such an enterprise.

Mr. Carnegie's ability to inspire others rested on something deeper than any faculty of judgment.

In his last sentence, Mr. Schwab had conveyed a thought which corroborates the theory of the Master Mind to which I attributed the chief source of Mr. Carnegie's power.

Mr. Schwab has also confirmed the statement that Mr. Carnegie could have succeeded as well in any other business as he did in the steel business. It is obvious that his success was due to his understanding of his own mind and the minds of other men, and not to mere knowledge of the steel business itself.

This thought is most consoling to those who have not yet attained outstanding success, for it shows that success is solely a matter of correctly applying laws and principles which are available to all; and these laws, let us not forget, are fully described in the seventeen lessons of this course.

Mr. Carnegie learned how to apply the law of the Master Mind. This enabled him to organize the faculties of his own mind and the faculties of other men's minds, and to coordinate the whole behind a Definite Chief Aim.

Every strategist, whether in business or war or industry or other callings, understands the value of *organized*, coordinated effort. Every military strategist understands the value of sowing seeds of dissension in the ranks of the opposing forces, because this breaks up the power of coordination behind the opposition. During the world war, much was heard about the effects of propaganda, and it seems not an exaggeration to say that the disorganizing forces of propaganda were much more destructive than were all the guns and explosives.

One of the most important turning points of the world war came when the allied armies were placed under the direction of the French marshall, Ferdinand Foch. There are some well-informed military historians who claim that this was the move that spelled doom for the opposing armies.

Any modern railroad bridge is an excellent example of the value of *organized effort*, because it demonstrates quite simply and clearly how thousands of tons of weight may be borne by a comparatively small group of steel bars and beams which are arranged so that the weight is spread over the entire group.

There is a story about a man who had seven sons who were always quarreling among themselves. One day he called them all together and informed them that he wished to demonstrate just what their lack of cooperative effort meant. He had prepared a bundle of seven sticks which he had carefully tied together. One by one he asked his sons to take the bundle and break it. Each son tried, but in vain. Then he cut the strings and handed one of the sticks to each of his sons and asked each to break it over his knee. After those sticks had all been broken with ease, he said: "When you boys work together in a spirit of harmony you resemble the bundle of sticks, and no one can defeat you; but when you quarrel among yourselves, anyone can defeat you one at a time."

There is a worthwhile lesson in this story of the man and his seven quarrelsome sons, and it may be applied to the people of a community, the employees and employers in a given place of business, or to the state and nation in which we live.

Organized effort may be made a power, but it may also be a dangerous power unless guided with intelligence, which is the chief reason why the sixteenth lesson of this course is devoted largely to describing how to direct the power of *organized effort* so that it will lead to success; the sort of success that is founded on truth and justice and fairness which leads to ultimate *happiness*.

One of the greatest tragedies of this age of struggle and money madness is that so few people are engaged in the effort that they like best. One of the objects of this course is to help each reader to find his or her particular niche in the world's work, where both material prosperity and *happiness* in abundance may be found. To accomplish this purpose, the various lessons of this course are skillfully designed to help you take inventory and find out what latent ability and hidden forces lie sleeping within.

This entire course is intended as a stimulus with which to enable you to see yourself and your hidden forces as they are, and to awaken in you the ambition and the vision and the determination to cause you to go forth and claim what is rightfully yours.

Less than thirty years ago a man was working in the same shop with Henry Ford, doing practically the same sort of work that he was doing. It has been said that this man was really a more competent worker, in that particular sort of work, than Ford. Today this man is still engaged in the same sort of work, at wages of less than a hundred dollars a week, while Mr. Ford is the world's richest man.

What outstanding difference is there between these two men that has so widely separated them in terms of material wealth? Just this— Ford understood and applied the principle of *organized effort* while the other man did not.

In the little city of Shelby, Ohio, this principle of *organized effort* was applied for the purpose of creating a closer alliance between the churches and the businesses of a community.

The clergymen and businessmen formed an alliance, with the result that practically every church in the city was squarely behind every businessman, and every businessman was squarely behind every church. The effect was the strengthening of the churches and the businesses to such an extent that it has been said it would be practically impossible for any individual member of either to fail in their calling; the others who belong to the alliance will permit no such failures.

Here is an example of what may happen when groups form an alliance for the purpose of placing the combined power of the group behind each individual. The alliance has brought both material and moral advantages to the city of Shelby such as are enjoyed by few other cities of its size in America. The plan has worked so effectively and so satisfactorily that a movement is now under way to extend it into other cities throughout America.

COMMENTARY

> *E. Colin Lindsey was a shoe salesman for the Belk Brothers store in Charlotte, North Carolina. There were many other clerks in that store, but Lindsey had the idea of proposing a new store in cooperation with the Belk family. Forty years later, he headed the thirty-five-store chain of Belk Lindsey department stores in the South, while the other salespeople he worked with still wondered what had happened. All that happened was that Lindsey applied organized effort and the others did not.*
>
> *Jean Nidetch was one of millions of overweight people in America during the 1960s, and she knew many other people who were in a similar position. She realized how powerful it would be to bring those people together to inspire each other, to share experiences in losing weight. So Jean Nidetch founded Weight Watchers. From a first meeting with just fifty people, Weight Watchers grew into an organization of more than a million members—because Nidetch understood the importance of organized effort in helping others.*

Alliances

In order that you may gain a still more concrete vision of just how this principle of *organized effort* can be made powerful, stop for a moment and try to imagine what would likely be the result if every church and every newspaper and every Rotary Club and every Kiwanis Club and every advertising club and every women's club and every other civic organization of a similar nature, in your city or in any other city in the

United States, should get together and form an alliance for the purpose of pooling their power and using it for the benefit of all members of these organizations.

The results that might easily be attained by such an alliance stagger the imagination!

There are three outstanding powers in the world of *organized effort:* the churches, the schools, and the newspapers. Think what might easily happen if these three great powers and molders of public opinion were to ally themselves for the purpose of bringing about any needed change in human conduct. They could, in a single generation, so modify the present standard of business ethics, for example, that it would practically be business suicide for any company or individual to attempt to transact business under any standard except that of the Golden Rule. Such an alliance could be made to produce sufficient influence to change, in a single generation, the business, social, and moral tendencies of the entire civilized world. Such an alliance would have sufficient power to force on the minds of the upcoming generations any ideals desired.

Power is *organized effort,* as has already been stated. And success is based upon power!

That you may have a clear concept of what is meant by the term *organized effort,* I have made use of the foregoing illustrations. For the sake of further emphasis, I am going to repeat the statement that the accumulation of great wealth and the attainment of any high station in life, such as those that constitute what we ordinarily call success, are based on the vision to comprehend and the ability to assimilate and apply the major principles of the seventeen lessons of this course.

This course is in complete harmony with the principles of economics and the principles of applied psychology. You will observe that when a lesson depends, for its practical application, on the student having knowledge of psychology, that lesson has been supplemented with sufficient explanation of the psychological principles involved to render it easily understood.

A GOOD ENCYCLOPEDIA

CONTAINS MOST

OF THE KNOWN FACTS

OF THE WORLD,

BUT THEY ARE AS USELESS

AS SAND DUNES UNTIL

ORGANIZED AND EXPRESSED

IN TERMS OF ACTION.

Before the manuscripts for this course went to the publisher they were submitted to some of the foremost bankers and businessmen of America so that they might be examined, analyzed, and criticized by the most practical of minds. One of the best-known bankers in New York City returned the manuscripts with the following comment:

> I hold a master's degree from Yale, but I would willingly exchange all that this degree has brought me in return for what your course on the Law of Success would have brought me had I been afforded the privilege of making it a part of my training while I was studying at Yale.
>
> My wife and daughter have also read the manuscripts, and my wife has named your course "the master keyboard of life" because she believes that all who understand how to apply it may play a perfect symphony in their respective callings, just as a pianist may play any tune once the keyboard of the piano and the fundamentals of music have been mastered.

No two people on earth are exactly alike, and for this reason no two people would be expected to gain from this course the same viewpoint. You should read the course, understand it, and then appropriate from it whatever you need to develop a well-rounded personality.

ANALYZE YOURSELF

This book has been compiled for the purpose of helping you find out what are your natural talents, and for the purpose of helping organize, coordinate, and put into use the knowledge gained from experience. For more than twenty years I have been gathering, classifying, and organizing this material. During the past fourteen years I have analyzed more than 16,000 men and women, and all of the vital facts gathered from these analyses have been carefully organized and woven into this course. These analyses brought out many interesting facts that have helped to make this course practical and usable. For example, it was discovered that

95 percent of all who were analyzed were failures and only 5 percent were successes. (Here the term failure means they had failed to find happiness and the ordinary necessities of life without almost unbearable struggle.) Perhaps this is about the proportion of successes and failures that might be found if all the people of the world were accurately analyzed. The struggle for a mere existence is tremendous among people who have not learned how to organize and direct their natural talents, while the attainment of those necessities, as well as the acquiring of many of the luxuries, is comparatively simple among those who have mastered the principle of *organized effort*.

One of the most startling facts brought to light by those 16,000 analyses was the discovery that the 95 percent who were classed as failures were in that class because they had *no Definite Chief Aim in life,* while the 5 percent of successful ones not only had purposes that were *definite* but they also had *definite plans* for the attainment of their purposes.

Another important fact disclosed by these analyses was that the 95 percent constituting the failures were engaged in work they did not like, while the 5 percent constituting the successful ones were doing what they liked best. It is doubtful whether a person could be a failure while engaged in work he or she liked best. Another vital fact learned from the analyses was that all of the 5 percent who were succeeding had formed the habit of systematically saving money, while the 95 percent who were failures saved little. This is worthy of serious thought.

One of the chief objects of this course is to aid you in performing your chosen work in such a way that it will yield the greatest returns in both money and happiness.

Take your measure; make a self-analysis. If you will answer each of these questions truthfully, you will know more about yourself than the majority of people. Study the questions carefully, come back to them once each week for several months, and you will be astounded at the amount of additional knowledge of great value to yourself you will have gained by answering truthfully. If you are not certain as to the answers to some of the questions, seek the counsel of those who know you well, especially those who have no motive in flattering you, and see yourself through their eyes.

COMMENTARY

The following is Hill's self-analysis test, which is taken from his book Think and Grow Rich:

Do you often complain of "feeling bad"? If so, why?

Do you find fault with other people easily?

Do you often make mistakes in your work?

Are you sarcastic and obnoxious?

Do you deliberately avoid anyone? Why?

Does life seem futile and hopeless to you?

Do you often feel self-pity? If so, why?

Do you envy people who are more successful?

Do you devote more time to thinking about success or failure?

Are you gaining or losing self-confidence as you grow older?

Do you learn from your mistakes?

Are you permitting a relative or friend to worry you?

Are you sometimes elated and sometimes depressed?

Who is the most inspiring person you know?

Do you put up with negative influences?

Are you careless about your personal appearance?

Do you avoid your troubles by being busy?

Do you let other people do your thinking for you?

Are you annoyed by petty disturbances?

Do you resort to liquor, drugs, or cigarettes to calm you down?

Does anyone nag you?

Do you have an aim in life and a plan for achieving it?

Do you suffer from any of the six basic fears?

Do you have a way to shield yourself from the negative effects of others?

Do you actively attempt to keep your mind positive?

What do you value more: your physical possessions or your ability to control your own thoughts?

Are you easily influenced by others?

Have you learned anything of value today?

Do you accept responsibility for problems?

Do you analyze mistakes and try to learn from them?

Can you name your three most damaging weaknesses and explain what you are doing to combat them?

Do you encourage others to bring their troubles to you for sympathy?

Does your presence have a negative influence on others?

What habits in others annoy you the most?

Do you form your own opinions or do you let yourself be influenced by others?

Does your job inspire you?

Do you have spiritual forces powerful enough to keep you free from fear?

If you believe that "birds of a feather flock together," what do you know about your friends?

Do you see any connection between your friends and some unhappiness in your life?

Is it possible that some close friend or associate has a negative influence on your mind?

What criteria do you use to determine who is helpful to you and who is harmful?

Are your intimate associates mentally superior or inferior to you?

How much time out of every day to you devote to:

- *your occupation?*
- *sleep?*
- *play and relaxation?*
- *acquiring useful knowledge?*
- *plain waste?*

Who among your friends and family:

- *encourages you the most?*
- *cautions you the most?*
- *discourages you the most?*

What is your greatest worry? Why do you tolerate it?

When others offer you unsolicited advice, do you accept it without question or do you analyze their motive for giving it?

What, above all else, do you desire? Do you intend to get it? Are you willing to subordinate all other goals for this one? How much time do you devote to it daily?

Do you change your mind often?

Do you usually finish what you start?

Are you easily impressed by other people's business titles, college degrees, or wealth?

Are you often concerned about what other people might think or say of you?

Do you try to make friends with people because of their social status or wealth?

Whom do you believe to be the greatest person living? How is this person superior to you?

How much time have you devoted to studying and answering these questions?

At least one full day is needed to contemplate your answers, in order to truthfully answer these questions.

A DEFINITE CHIEF AIM

The keynote of this entire lesson may be found in the word *definite.*

It is most appalling to know that 95 percent of the people of the world are drifting aimlessly through life, without the slightest concept of the work for which they are best fitted, and with no concept whatsoever of even the need for such a thing as a *definite* objective toward which to strive.

There is a psychological, as well as an economic, reason for the selection of a Definite Chief Aim in life. Let us devote our attention to the psychological side of the question first. It is a well-established principle of psychology that a person's acts are always in harmony with the dominating thoughts of his or her mind.

NO POSITION IN LIFE

CAN BE SECURE,

AND NO ACHIEVEMENT

CAN BE PERMANENT

UNLESS BUILT UPON

TRUTH AND JUSTICE.

Any Definite Chief Aim that is deliberately fixed in the mind and held there, with the firm determination to realize it, finally saturates the entire subconscious mind until it automatically influences the physical action of the body toward the attainment of that purpose.

Your Definite Chief Aim in life should be selected with deliberate care, and after it has been selected it should be written out and placed where you will see it at least once a day. The psychological effect of this is to impress this purpose upon your subconscious mind so strongly that it accepts the purpose as a pattern or blueprint that will eventually dominate your activities in life and lead you, step by step, toward the attainment of the object behind that purpose.

The principle of psychology through which you can impress your Definite Chief Aim on your subconscious mind is *autosuggestion,* or suggestion that you repeatedly make to yourself. It is a degree of self-hypnotism, but do not be afraid of it, for it was through the aid of this same principle that Napoleon lifted himself from the lowly station of poverty-stricken Corsican to the dictatorship of France.

It is through the aid of this same principle that Thomas Edison has risen from his lowly beginning to become accepted as the leading inventor of the world. It was also through the aid of this principle that Lincoln bridged the mighty chasm between his lowly birth, in a log cabin in the mountains of Kentucky, and the presidency of the greatest nation on earth. And it was through the aid of this principle that Theodore Roosevelt became one of the most aggressive leaders that ever reached the presidency of the United States.

Autosuggestion

You need have no fear of the principle of autosuggestion as long as you are sure that the objective for which you are striving is one that will bring you happiness of an enduring nature. Be sure that your *definite purpose* is constructive; that its attainment will bring hardship and misery to no one; that it will bring you peace and prosperity. Then apply, to the limit of your understanding, the principle of self-suggestion for the speedy attainment of this purpose.

On the street corner, just opposite the room in which I am writing, I see a man who stands there all day long and sells peanuts. He is busy every minute. When not actually engaged in making a sale, he is roasting peanuts and packing them in little bags. He is one of that great army constituting the 95 percent who have no *definite purpose* in life. He is selling peanuts not because he likes the work better than anything else he might do, but because he never sat down and thought out a *definite purpose* that would bring him greater returns for his labor. He is selling peanuts because he is a drifter on the sea of life, and one of the tragedies of his work is that the same amount of effort he puts into it, if directed along other lines, would bring him much greater returns.

Another of the tragedies of this man's work is that he is unconsciously making use of the principle of self-suggestion, but he is doing it to his own disadvantage. No doubt, if a picture could be made of his thoughts, there would be nothing in that picture except a peanut roaster, some little paper bags, and a crowd of people buying peanuts. This man could get out of the peanut business if he had both the vision and the ambition, first to imagine himself in a more profitable calling and then the perseverance to hold that picture before his mind until it influenced him to take the necessary steps to enter a more profitable calling. He puts sufficient labor into his work to bring him a substantial return if that labor were directed toward the attainment of a *definite purpose* that offered bigger returns.

One of my closest personal friends is also one of the best-known writers and public speakers in this country. About ten years ago he saw the possibilities of this principle of self-suggestion and began immediately to harness it and put it to work. He worked out a plan for its application that proved to be very effective. At the time he was neither a writer nor a speaker.

Each night, just before going to sleep, he would shut his eyes and see, *in his Imagination,* a long council table at which he placed, also in his Imagination, certain well-known men whose characteristics he wished to absorb into his own personality. At the end of this table he placed Lincoln, and on either side of the table he placed Napoleon, Washington, Emerson, and Elbert Hubbard. He then proceeded to talk to these imaginary figures that he had seated at his imaginary council table, in something like this manner:

Mr. Lincoln: I desire to build in my own character those qualities of patience and fairness toward all mankind, and a keen sense of humor, which were your outstanding characteristics. I need these qualities and I shall not be content until I have developed them.

Mr. Washington: I desire to build in my own character those qualities of patriotism and self-sacrifice and Leadership which were your outstanding characteristics.

Mr. Emerson: I desire to build in my own character those qualities of vision and the ability to interpret the laws of Nature as written in the rocks of prison walls and growing trees and flowing brooks and growing flowers and the faces of little children, which were your outstanding characteristics.

Napoleon: I desire to build in my own character those qualities of self-reliance and the strategic ability to master obstacles and profit by mistakes and develop strength out of defeat, which were your outstanding characteristics.

Mr. Hubbard: I desire to develop the ability to equal and even to excel the ability which you possessed to express yourself in clear, concise, and forceful language.

Night after night for many months this man saw these men seated around that imaginary council table until finally he had imprinted their outstanding characteristics upon his own subconscious mind so clearly that he began to develop a personality which was a composite of their personalities.

COMMENTARY

Napoleon Hill was by no means the first to encourage the use of autosuggestion. Perhaps the best-known advocate was French psychiatrist, Emil Coué. A contemporary of Freud in the late 1800s, Coué advocated the use of autosuggestion by the repetition of statements that he termed positive affirmations. *He developed what he considered to be a perfect positive statement that was nonspecific and could be used to improve any aspect of anyone's life. Coué instructed his patients to repeat the following phrase several times a day: "Every day in every way I am getting better and better." Word of his success with the method quickly spread, and the use of the phrase practically became a movement in Europe.*

When Coué traveled to America on a lecture tour, the press of the day found his idea to be too simplistic and parodied his affirmation with their own version, "Hells bells, I'm well." It made Coué a laughingstock, and just as had happened when stage magicians cast doubt on the efficacy of hypnosis, Coué's method of positive affirmation fell into disrepute.

Serious scientists and therapists continued to work with these methods, but as with Hill's theories about the power of the mind to heal the body, it took the openness of the latter part of the twentieth century before the techniques of self-hypnosis, autosuggestion, and positive affirmations began to gain general acceptance once again.

If you wish to increase your knowledge of these techniques, the following books will provide you with a diversity of information: Creative Visualization *by Shakti Gawain,* Psycho-Cybernetics *by Dr. Maxwell Maltz,* Visualization: Directing the Movies of Your Mind *by Adelaide Bry,* Getting Well Again *by Dr. O. Carl Simonton,* Self-Hypnosis *by Leslie M. LeCron.*

The subconscious mind may be likened to a magnet; when it has been vitalized and thoroughly saturated with any definite purpose, it has a decided tendency to attract all that is necessary for the fulfillment of that purpose.

Like attracts like, and you may see evidence of this law in every blade of grass and every growing tree. The acorn attracts from the soil and the air the necessary materials out of which to grow an oak tree. It never grows a tree that is part oak and part poplar.

Every grain of wheat that is planted in the soil attracts the materials out of which to grow a stalk of wheat. It never makes a mistake and grows both oats and wheat on the same stalk.

People, too, are subject to this same law of attraction. Go into any cheap boardinghouse district in any city and there you will find people of the same general trend of mind associated together. Or go into any prosperous community and there you will also find people of the same general tendencies associated together. Those who are successful always seek the company of others who are successful; those who are on the ragged side of life always seek the company of those who are in similar circumstances. "Misery loves company."

Water seeks its level with no finer certainty than we all seek the company of those who occupy our own general status financially and mentally. A Yale University professor and an illiterate hobo have nothing in common. They would be miserable if thrown together for any length of time. Oil and water will mix about as readily as will people who have nothing in common.

All of which leads up to this: You will attract to you people who harmonize with your own philosophy of life, whether you wish it or not. This being true, can you not see now the importance of vitalizing your mind with a Definite Chief Aim that will attract to you people who will be of help to you and not a hindrance? Suppose your Definite Chief Aim is far above your present station in life. What of it? It is your privilege—in fact it is your *duty*—to aim high in life. You owe it to yourself, and to the community in which you live, to set a high standard for yourself.

There is much evidence to justify the belief that nothing, *within reason*, is beyond the possibility of attainment by the person whose Definite Chief Aim has been well developed. Some years ago, Louis Victor Eytinge was given a life sentence in the Arizona penitentiary.

DO NOT "TELL" THE WORLD

WHAT YOU CAN DO—"SHOW" IT!

At the time of his imprisonment he was an all-around "bad man," by his own admissions. In addition to this it was believed that he would die of tuberculosis within a year.

Eytinge had reason to feel discouraged, if anyone ever had. Public feeling against him was intense and he did not have a single friend in the world who came forth and offered him encouragement or help.

Then something happened in his own mind that gave him back his health, put the dreaded disease to rout, and finally unlocked the prison gates and gave him his freedom. What was that "something"?

It was that he had made up his mind to whip the white plague and regain his health. It was a very Definite Chief Aim. In less than a year from the time his decision was made he had won. Then he extended that Definite Chief Aim by making up his mind to gain his freedom. Soon the prison walls melted from around him.

COMMENTARY

The details of this case are interesting. In prison, Louis Eytinge decided to become a writer. He took magazines, catalogs, and anything else that contained marketing copy, and he began to rewrite it. As his confidence in what he was doing grew, he sent the revised copy to the companies that had produced it. Some were not flattered, but others recognized that he had skill. Soon he was earning a good sum of money. But more important, his dedication impressed a group of his clients and they decided to help him. They petitioned the governor of Arizona for clemency. It took some time, but Eytinge was eventually freed and walked out of the prison and into a job with a public relations firm.

No undesirable environment is strong enough to hold the man or woman who understands how to apply the principle of autosuggestion in the creation of a Definite Chief Aim. Such a person can throw off the shackles of poverty; destroy the most deadly disease germs; rise from a lowly station in life to power and plenty.

All great leaders base their Leadership on a Definite Chief Aim. Followers are willing followers when they know their leader is a person with a Definite Chief Aim who has the courage to back up that purpose with action. Even a balky horse knows when a driver with a Definite Chief Aim takes hold of the reins, and it yields to that driver. When a person with a Definite Chief Aim starts through a crowd, everybody stands aside and makes way for them. But let that person hesitate and show by their actions that they are not sure which way they want to go, and the crowd will step all over their toes and refuse to budge an inch out of the way.

Nowhere is the lack of a Definite Chief Aim more noticeable or more detrimental than it is in the relationship between parent and child. Children sense very quickly the wavering attitude of their parents and they will take advantage of that attitude quite freely. It is the same all through life—those with a Definite Chief Aim command respect and attention at all times.

COMMENTARY

In 1990 Douglas Grant was paralyzed in an accident that left him in a wheelchair. But instead of deciding that his life was over, Grant embarked on the pursuit of a Definite Chief Aim. His father had told him he would never walk again unless he had a vision in life. Grant's vision was not just to walk, but to win a gold medal as a weightlifter. "I decided I would make it happen," he says. He created his own strategy for rehabilitation and it started to restore his mobility. By 1993 he was not only walking but he had also won the World Championships of Powerlifting —getting that gold medal he had dreamed of.

Grant's battle to restore his strength had also excited his interest in nutrition. He created a Master Mind with a leading authority on enzymes, and developed an enzyme-activated nutritional system called Infinity2. The program is now used by such professional teams as the New York Yankees and the Houston Rockets, and Grant's company is doing millions of dollars of business each year.

The Definite Purpose and Finance

So much for the psychological viewpoint of a *definite purpose.* Let us now look at its economic side.

If a ship lost its rudder in mid-ocean and began circling around, it would soon exhaust its fuel supply without reaching shore, despite that it would use up enough energy to carry it to shore and back several times.

The person who labors without a *definite purpose* backed by a definite plan for its attainment resembles the ship that has lost its rudder. Hard labor and good intentions are not sufficient to carry anyone through to success, for how may any of us be sure that we have attained success unless a definite desired objective had been established in our minds?

Every well-built house started in the form of a *definite purpose* plus a definite plan in the nature of a set of blueprints. Imagine what would happen if one tried to build a house by the haphazard method, without plans. Workmen would be in each other's way, building materials would be piled all over the lot before the foundation was even completed, and everybody on the job would have a different notion as to how the house ought to be built. Result: chaos and misunderstandings, and costs that would be prohibitive.

Yet have you ever stopped to think that most people finish school, take up employment or enter a trade or profession, without the slightest concept of anything that even remotely resembles a *definite purpose* or a definite plan? In view of the fact that science has provided reasonably accurate ways and means of analyzing character and determining the work for which people are best fitted, does it not seem a modern tragedy that 95 percent of the adult population of the world is made up of men and women who are failures because they have not found their proper niches in the world's work?

If *success* depends upon power, and if power is *organized effort,* and if the first step in the direction of organization is a *definite purpose,* then one may easily see why such a purpose is essential.

Until you select a *definite purpose* in life you dissipate your energies and spread your thoughts over so many subjects and in so many different directions that they lead not to power but to indecision and weakness.

With the aid of a magnifying glass you can teach yourself a great lesson on the value of *organized effort*. Through the use of such a glass you can focus the sun's rays on a *definite* spot so strongly that they will burn a hole through a plank. Remove the glass (which represents the *definite purpose*) and the same rays of sun may shine on that same plank for a million years without burning it.

One thousand electric dry batteries, when properly organized and connected together with wires, will produce enough power to run a good-sized piece of machinery for several hours. But take those same battery cells singly, disconnected, and not one of them would exert enough energy to turn the machinery over once. The faculties of your mind might properly be likened to those dry cells. When you organize your faculties, according to the plan laid down in the seventeen lessons of this course on the laws of success, and then direct them toward the attainment of a *definite purpose* in life, you will be taking advantage of the cooperative or accumulative principle out of which *power* is developed, which is called *organized effort*.

Andrew Carnegie's advice was: "Place all your eggs in one basket and then watch the basket to see that no one kicks it over." By that he meant, of course, that we should not dissipate any of our energies by engaging in sidelines. Carnegie was a sound economist and he knew that most people would do well if they harnessed and directed their energies so that some one thing would be done well.

When the plan behind this course was initially developed, I had taken the first manuscript to a professor at the University of Texas. In a spirit of Enthusiasm I suggested to him that I had discovered a principle that would be of aid to me in every public speech I delivered in future, because I would be better prepared to organize and marshal my thoughts.

He looked at the outline of the points for a few minutes, then turned to me and said:

"Yes, your discovery is going to help you make better speeches, but that is not all it will do. It will help you become a more effective writer, for I have noticed in your previous writings a tendency to scatter your thoughts. For instance, if you started to describe a beautiful mountain yonder in the distance, you would be apt to sidetrack your description by calling attention to a beautiful bed of wild flowers, or a running brook, or a singing bird, detouring here and there, zigzag fashion, before finally arriving at the proper point from which to view the mountain. In the future you are going to find it much less difficult to describe an object, whether you are speaking or writing, because your seventeen points represent the *very foundation* of organization."

A man who had no legs once met a man who was blind. He proposed to the blind man that they form an alliance that would be of great benefit to both. "You let me climb upon your back," said he to the blind man, "then I will use your legs and you may use my eyes. Between the two of us we will get along more rapidly."

COMMENTARY

Marty and Helen Shih are a brother-and-sister team that has proven the value of a Master Mind in turning organized effort into success. In 1979 they opened a flower stall on a street corner in Los Angeles. Their first day they took in just $1.99.

Together they worked hard. One of their smartest decisions was to record as many details as possible about each of their customers. This allowed them to call and remind people of approaching birthdays, anniversaries, and special events— saving many a forgetful customer from embarrassment and earning the Shihs enormous goodwill. From this simple start, the Shihs began compiling a valuable database. This value was increased by the fact that the Shihs were targeting the Asian-American community, one that many businesses had overlooked.

> *From there the Shihs developed a full-service referral company for new Asian immigrants, who can call and talk to operators who speak Mandarin, Cantonese, Korean, or Japanese. Internet Web pages are available in the same languages. Their Asian-American Association then allied with such major companies as DHL, New York Life, and Sprint, marketing services to a community that is often hard to reach. Annual sales are more than $200 million.*
>
> *The Shihs' simple venture into flower-selling showed them an opportunity. Their dedicated, organized effort gave them the means to fill it. Now Fortune 500 companies are their allies in growing their business.*

Out of allied effort comes greater power. This is a point worthy of much repetition. The great fortunes of the world have been accumulated through the use of this principle of allied effort. What one individual can accomplish single-handedly, during an entire lifetime, is but meager at best, no matter how well-organized that individual may be. But what one person may accomplish through the principle of alliance with others is practically without limitation.

That Master Mind to which Andrew Carnegie referred during my interview with him was made up of more than a score of minds. In that group were men of practically every temperament and inclination. Each was there to play a certain part and he did nothing else. There was perfect understanding and teamwork among them. It was Carnegie's business to keep harmony among them.

And he did it wonderfully well.

If you are familiar with team sports you know, of course, that the winning team is the one that best coordinates the efforts of its players. Teamwork wins. It is the same in the great game of life.

In your struggle for *success* you should constantly keep in mind the necessity of knowing what it is that you want—of knowing precisely what your *definite purpose* is. At the same time, keep in mind the value of the principle of *organized effort* in the attainment of whatever it is that constitutes your *definite purpose*.

In a vague sort of way nearly everyone has a definite purpose—the desire for *money*. But this is not a *definite purpose* within the meaning of the term as it is used in this lesson. Before your purpose could be considered *definite*, even though that purpose were the accumulation of money, you would have to reach a decision as to the precise method through which you intend to accumulate that money. It would be insufficient for you to say that you would make money by going into some sort of business. You would have to decide just what line of business. You would also have to decide just where you would locate. And you would also have to decide the business policies under which you would conduct your business.

In answering the question "What is your *definite purpose* in life?" which appears in the questionnaire that I have used for the analysis of more than 16,000 people, many answered in somewhat this way:

"My definite purpose in life is to be of as much service to the world as possible and to earn a good living."

That answer is about as *definite* as a frog's concept of the size of the universe is accurate!

The object of this lesson is not to inform you as to what your life's work should be, for indeed this could be done with accuracy only after you have been completely analyzed. What this lesson *is* intended to do is to impress upon your mind a clear concept of the value of a *definite purpose* of some nature, and, as has also been stated, to be sure that you understand the value of *organized effort* as a means of attaining the necessary power with which to achieve that *definite purpose*.

Careful observation of the business philosophy of more than one hundred men and women who have attained outstanding success in their respective callings disclosed the fact that each was a person of prompt and definite decision.

The habit of working with a Definite Chief Aim will create in you the habit of prompt decision, and this habit will come to your aid in all that you do.

THE BEST COMPENSATION

FOR DOING THINGS

IS THE ABILITY TO DO MORE.

Moreover, the habit of working with a Definite Chief Aim will help you to concentrate all your attention on any given task until you have mastered it.

Concentration of effort and the habit of working with a Definite Chief Aim are two of the essential factors in success which are always found together. One leads to the other.

The best-known, most successful business leaders were all people of prompt decision who always worked with one main, outstanding purpose as a chief aim.

The following are some notable examples:

F. W. Woolworth chose as his Definite Chief Aim the belting of America with a chain of stores, and concentrated his mind on this one task until "he made it and it made him."

William Wrigley concentrated on the production and sale of a five-cent package of chewing gum and turned this one idea into millions of dollars.

Thomas Edison concentrated his efforts on the understanding of physical laws and he created more useful inventions than any other man who ever lived.

R. H. Ingersoll concentrated on a one-dollar watch and girdled the earth with them.

E. M. Statler concentrated on "homelike hotel service" and made himself wealthy and useful to millions of people.

Woodrow Wilson concentrated on the White House for twenty-five years and became its chief tenant, because he knew the value of sticking to a Definite Chief Aim.

Abraham Lincoln concentrated his mind on freeing the slaves and became our greatest American president while doing it.

John D. Rockefeller concentrated on oil and he became the richest man of his generation.

Henry Ford concentrated on inexpensive transportation for ordinary people and made himself the richest and most powerful man alive.

Andrew Carnegie concentrated on steel, made a great fortune, and plastered his name on public libraries throughout America.

King Gillette concentrated on a safety razor, gave the entire world a "close shave," and made himself a multimillionaire.

George Eastman concentrated on the Kodak camera and made the idea yield him a fortune while bringing much pleasure to millions of people.

William Randolph Hearst concentrated on publishing sensational newspapers and made the idea worth millions of dollars.

Helen Keller concentrated on learning to speak, and, though she was deaf, dumb, and blind, she realized her Definite Chief Aim.

Marshall Field concentrated on the world's greatest retail store and it rose before him, a reality.

Philip Armour concentrated on the butchering business and established a great industry as well as a big fortune.

The Wright brothers concentrated on the airplane and mastered the air.

George Pullman concentrated on the sleeping car and the idea made him rich and millions of people comfortable in travel.

Millions of people are concentrating daily on *poverty* and *failure,* and getting both in overabundance.

COMMENTARY

There are many more examples:

Marie Curie concentrated on scientific investigation and was the first woman to win a Nobel Prize. And the first person to ever win it twice.

Coco Chanel concentrated on elegant fashion and defined the way women dressed for a generation.

Henry Kaiser concentrated on building ships and built the American Navy during the Second World War.

Ray Kroc concentrated on hamburgers and made McDonald's the world's most successful restaurant.

Martin Luther King Jr. concentrated on civil rights and led Americans of all colors forward.

Sam Walton concentrated on low prices and spread his stores across the country like a carpet.

George Lucas concentrated on Star Wars *and made it into the most successful movie franchise of all time.*

Stephen King concentrated on supernatural suspense novels and became the bestselling writer of his day.

Ted Turner concentrated on cable television and built an enormous media conglomerate.

Harry Helmsley concentrated on real estate and amassed more than $1 billion in land in New York City.

Oprah Winfrey concentrated on succeeding as a television broadcaster, got her own talk show, created her own studio, and became the most successful and wealthiest woman in the media.

Bill Gates concentrated on software and became America's richest person. Whom would you add?

Finding Your Life's Work

Thus it will be seen that all who succeed work with some definite, outstanding aim as the object of their labors.

There is some one thing that you can do better than anyone else in the world could do it. Search until you find out what this particular line of endeavor is, make it the object of your Definite Chief Aim, and then organize all of your forces and attack it with the belief that you are going to win. In your search for the work for which you are best suited, it will be well if you bear in mind that you will most likely attain the greatest success by finding out what work you like best. It is a well-known fact that a person generally best succeeds in the particular line of endeavor into which they can throw their whole heart and soul.

ANYONE CAN START

BUT ONLY THE THOROUGHBRED

WILL FINISH!

COMMENTARY

As with so much of what Hill wrote, his advice to focus on that for which you are best suited as your life's work has also been expanded upon by many other authors. It is the genesis of numerous bestsellers including Feel the Fear and Do It Anyway *by Susan Jeffers and* Wishcraft *by Barbara Sher with Annie Gottlieb.*

Let us go back, for the sake of clarity and emphasis, to the psychological principles upon which this lesson is founded, because it will mean a loss you can ill afford if you fail to grasp the real reason for establishing a Definite Chief Aim in your mind. These principles are:

First, every voluntary movement of the human body is caused, controlled, and directed by *thought*, through the operation of the mind.

Second, the presence of any thought or idea in your consciousness tends to produce an associated feeling and urge you to transform that feeling into appropriate muscular action that is in perfect harmony with the nature of the thought.

For example, if you think of winking your eyelid and there are no counterinfluences or thoughts in your mind at the time to stop that action, the motor nerve will carry your thought from the seat of government, in your brain, and the appropriate or corresponding muscular action takes place immediately.

Stating this principle from another angle: You choose, for example, a *definite purpose* as your life's work and make up your mind that you will carry out that purpose. *From the very moment that you make this choice, this purpose becomes the dominating thought in your consciousness, and you are constantly on the alert for facts, information, and knowledge with which to achieve that purpose.* From the time that you plant a *definite purpose* in your mind, your mind begins, both consciously and unconsciously, to gather and store away the material with which you are to accomplish that purpose.

Desire is the factor that determines what your *definite purpose* in life shall be. No one can select your dominating *desire* for you, but once you select it yourself it becomes your Definite Chief Aim and occupies the spotlight of your mind until it is transformed into reality, unless you permit it to be pushed aside by conflicting desires.

To emphasize the principle I am trying to make clear, I believe it not unreasonable to suggest that to be sure of successful achievement, one's Definite Chief Aim in life should be backed with a burning desire for its achievement. I have noticed that boys and girls who enter college and pay their way through by working seem to get more out of their schooling than do those whose expenses are paid for them. The secret of this may be found in the fact that those who are willing to work their way through are blessed with a burning desire for education. And such a desire, if the object of the desire is within reason, is practically sure of realization.

Science has established, beyond the slightest room for doubt, that through the principle of autosuggestion any deeply rooted desire saturates the entire body and mind with the nature of the desire and literally transforms the mind into a powerful magnet that will attract the object of the desire, if it is within reason. For those who might not properly interpret the meaning of this statement, I will explain this principle in another way. For example, merely desiring an automobile will not cause that automobile to come rolling in. But if there is a *burning desire* for an automobile, that desire will lead to the appropriate action through which an automobile may be paid for.

Similarly, merely desiring freedom would never release a prisoner if that desire were not sufficiently strong to cause him to do something to entitle himself to freedom.

Beyond Your Burning Desire

These are the steps leading from desire to fulfillment: first the burning desire, then the crystallization of that desire into a *definite purpose*, then sufficient appropriate *action* to achieve that purpose. *Remember that these three steps are always necessary to ensure success.*

I knew a very poor girl from a troubled family who had a *burning desire* for friends. She finally got many of them, and a husband too, but not without having transformed that desire into the development of a very attractive personality which, in turn, attracted other people.

I once had a *burning desire* to be able to analyze character accurately. That desire was so persistent and so deeply seated that it practically drove me into ten years of research and study of men and women.

George S. Parker makes one of the best fountain pens in the world, and despite the fact that his business is conducted from the little city of Janesville, Wisconsin, he has spread his product all around the globe and has his pen on sale in every civilized country. More than twenty years ago Mr. Parker's *definite purpose* was established in his mind, and that purpose was to produce the best fountain pen that money could buy. He backed that purpose with a *burning desire* for its realization, and if you carry a fountain pen the chances are that you have evidence in your own possession that it has brought him abundant success.

You are a contractor and builder, and, like those who build houses of wood and brick and steel, you must draw up a set of plans from which to construct your building. You are living in a wonderful age, when the materials that go into success are plentiful and cheap. You have at your disposal, in the archives of the public libraries, the carefully compiled results of two thousand years of research, covering practically every possible line of endeavor in which one would wish to engage.

If you wish to become a member of the clergy you have at hand the entire history of what has been learned by men and women who have preceded you in this field. If you want to become a mechanic you have at hand the entire history of the inventions of machines and the discovery and use of metals. If you wish to become a lawyer you have at your disposal the entire history of law procedure. Through the Department of Agriculture in Washington, D.C., you have at your disposal all that has been learned about farming and agriculture, should you wish to find your life's work in this field.

COMMENTARY

Here, as in many other places, Hill seems very far ahead of his time. In the preceding passage, he anticipates the age of the Internet, recognizing that information may be the most valuable commodity any man or woman can possess.

The world was never so resplendent with *opportunity* as it is today. Everywhere there is an ever-increasing demand for the services of the man or the woman who makes a better mousetrap or performs a better service or preaches a better sermon or digs a better ditch or runs a more accommodating bank.

This lesson will not be completed until you have made your choice as to what your Definite Chief Aim in life is to be and then recorded a description of that definite purpose in writing and placed it where you will see it every morning when you arise and every night before you retire.

Procrastination is . . . but why preach about it? You know that *you* are the hewer of your own wood and the drawer of your own water and the shaper of your own Definite Chief Aim in life. Therefore, why dwell on what you already know?

A *definite purpose* is something that you must create for yourself. No one else will create it for you and it will not create itself. What are you going to do about it? and when? and how?

Desire

Start now to analyze your desires and find out what it is that you wish, then make up your mind to get it. Lesson Three will point out to you the next step and show you how to proceed. Nothing is left to chance in this course. Every step is clearly marked. Your part is to follow the directions until you arrive at your destination, as represented by your Definite Chief Aim. Make that aim clear and back it up with a persistence that does not recognize the word *impossible.*

When you come to select your Definite Chief Aim, just keep in mind that you cannot aim too high.

Also keep in mind the never-varying truth that you'll get nowhere if you start nowhere. If your aim in life is vague, your achievements will also be vague, and, it might well be added, very meager. *Know what you want, when you want it, why you want it, and how you intend to get it.* This is known to teachers and students of psychology as the WWWH formula—"what, when, why, and how."

Read this lesson four times, at intervals of one week apart.

You will see much in the lesson the fourth time you read it that you did not see the first time.

Your success in mastering this course and in making it bring you success will depend very largely, if not entirely, on how well you follow *all* the instructions it contains.

Do not set up your own rules of study. Follow those laid down in the course; they are the result of years of thought and experimentation. If you wish to experiment, wait until you have mastered this course in the manner suggested. You will then be in a position to experiment more safely. For the present, content yourself by being the student. You will, let us hope, become the teacher as well as the student, after you have followed the course until you have mastered it.

If you follow the instructions laid down in this course, you can no more fail than water can run uphill above the level of its source.

APPLYING THE PRINCIPLES OF THIS LESSON

Through the introductory lesson you became familiar with the Master Mind principle of psychology.

You are now ready to begin using this principle as a means of transforming your Definite Chief Aim into reality. It must have occurred to you that one might as well have no Definite Chief Aim unless one also has a very definite and practical plan for turning that aim into a

EVERY LINE A MAN WRITES,

AND EVERY ACT

IN WHICH HE INDULGES,

AND EVERY WORD HE UTTERS,

SERVES AS INESCAPABLE EVIDENCE

OF THE NATURE OF THAT

WHICH IS DEEPLY EMBEDDED

IN HIS OWN HEART,

A CONFESSION

THAT HE CANNOT DISAVOW.

reality. Your first step is to decide what your major aim in life shall be. Your next step is to write out a clear, concise statement of this aim. This should be followed by a statement, in writing, of the plan or plans through which you intend to attain the object of your aim.

COMMENTARY

Almost ten years later, when Hill wrote Think and Grow Rich, *he placed even greater emphasis on the need to write down your chief aim. And, as was mentioned earlier in this revised edition of* Law of Success, *most of the self-improvement and motivational books written since agree that it is not enough for you to just know intellectually what you want; you must commit it to paper. If Hill believed the actual act was important, and if hundreds of other motivational experts agree, then you would be foolish not to follow this simple advice. Just do it.*

Your next and final step will be the forming of an alliance with some person or persons who will cooperate with you in carrying out these plans and transforming your Definite Chief Aim into reality.

The purpose of this friendly alliance is to employ the law of the Master Mind in support of your plans. The alliance should be made between yourself and those who have your highest and best interests at heart. If you are married, your spouse should be one of the members of this alliance, providing there exists between you a normal state of confidence and sympathy. Other members of this alliance may be your mother, father, brothers or sisters, or some close friend or friends.

If you are a single person your sweetheart, if you have one, should become a member of your alliance. This is no joke. You are now studying one of the most powerful laws of the human mind, and you will serve your own best interests by seriously and earnestly following the rules laid down in this lesson, even though you may not be sure where they will lead you.

Those who join with you in the formation of a friendly alliance for the purpose of aiding you in the creation of a Master Mind should sign, with you, your statement of the object of your Definite Chief Aim. Every member of your alliance must be fully acquainted with the nature of your objective in forming the alliance. Moreover, every member must be in hearty accord with this objective and in full sympathy with you. Each member of your alliance must be supplied with a written copy of your statement of your Definite Chief Aim. With this exception, however, you are explicitly instructed to keep the object of your chief aim to yourself. The world is full of "doubting Thomases" and it will do you no good to have these rattle-brained people scoffing at you and your ambitions. Remember, what you need is friendly encouragement and help, not derision and doubt.

If you believe in prayer you are instructed to make your Definite Chief Aim the object of your prayer at least once every twenty-four hours, and more often if convenient. If you believe there is a God who can and will aid those who are earnestly striving to be of constructive service in the world, surely you feel that you have a right to petition Him for aid in the attainment of what should be the most important thing in life to you.

If those who have been invited to join your friendly alliance believe in prayer, ask them to also include the object of this alliance as a part of their daily prayer.

We come now one of the most essential rules that you *must follow.* Arrange with one or all of the members of your friendly alliance to tell you, in the most positive and definite terms at their command, that they know you can and will realize the object of your Definite Chief Aim. This affirmation or statement should be made to you at least once a day; more often if possible.

These steps must be followed persistently, with full faith that they will lead you where you wish to go! It will not suffice to carry out these plans for a few days or a few weeks and then discontinue them. *You must follow the described procedure until you attain the object of your Definite Chief Aim, regardless of the time required.*

From time to time it may become necessary to change the plans that you have adopted for the achievement of your Definite Chief Aim. Make these changes without hesitation. No one has sufficient foresight to build plans that need no alteration or change.

If any member of your friendly alliance loses faith in the law known as the Master Mind, immediately remove that member and replace him or her with some other person.

Andrew Carnegie said to me that he, too, had found it necessary to replace some of the members of his Master Mind. In fact, he said that practically every member of whom his alliance was originally comprised had, in time, been removed and replaced with some other person who could adapt himself more loyally and enthusiastically to the spirit and objective of the alliance.

You cannot succeed when surrounded by disloyal and unfriendly associates, no matter what the object of your Definite Chief Aim may be. Success is built upon loyalty, faith, sincerity, Cooperation, and the other positive forces essential to your environment.

Many of you will want to form friendly alliances with those with whom you are associated professionally or in business, with the object of achieving success in your business or profession. In such cases the same rules of procedure which have been here described should be followed. The object of your Definite Chief Aim may be one that will benefit you individually, or it may be one that will benefit the business or profession with which you are connected. The law of the Master Mind will work the same in either case. If you fail, either temporarily or permanently, in the application of this law, it will be because some member of your alliance did not enter into the spirit of the alliance with faith, loyalty, and sincerity of purpose.

The last sentence is worthy of a second reading!

The object of your Definite Chief Aim should become your hobby.

"YES, HE SUCCEEDED . . .

BUT HE ALMOST FAILED!"

SO DID ROBERT FULTON

AND ABRAHAM LINCOLN

AND NEARLY ALL THE OTHERS

WHOM WE CALL SUCCESSFUL.

NO MAN EVER ACHIEVED

WORTHWHILE SUCCESS WHO DID NOT,

AT ONE TIME OR OTHER,

FIND HIMSELF WITH AT LEAST

ONE FOOT HANGING WELL OVER

THE BRINK OF FAILURE.

You should ride this hobby continuously; you should sleep with it, eat with it, play with it, work with it, live with it, and *think* with it.

Whatever you want you may get—if you want it with sufficient intensity, and keep on wanting it, providing the object wanted is one within reason, and you *actually believe you will get it!* There is a difference, however, between merely wishing for something and *actually believing* you will get it. A lack of understanding of this difference has meant failure to millions of people. The doers are the believers in all walks of life. Those who *believe* that they can achieve the object of their Definite Chief Aim do not recognize the word *impossible*. Neither do they acknowledge a temporary defeat. They *know* they are going to succeed, and if one plan fails they quickly replace it with another plan.

Every noteworthy achievement met with some sort of temporary setback before success came. Edison conducted more than ten thousand experiments before he succeeded in making the first talking machine *[audio recorder and playback]* record the words "Mary had a little lamb."

If there is one word that should stand out in your mind in connection with this lesson, it is the word *persistence!*

You now have within your possession the key to achievement. You have but to unlock the door to the Temple of Knowledge and walk in. But you must go to the temple; it will not come to you. If these laws are new to you, the going will not be easy at first. You will stumble many times. But keep moving! Very soon you will come to the brow of the mountain you have been climbing, and you will behold, in the valleys below, the rich estate of *knowledge* which shall be your reward for your faith and efforts.

Everything has a price. There is no such possibility as "something for nothing." In your experiments with the law of the Master Mind you are jockeying with Nature in her highest and noblest form. Nature cannot be tricked or cheated. She will give up to you the object of your struggles only after you have paid her price, which is *continuous, unyielding, persistent effort!*

What more could be said on this subject?

You have been shown *what to do, when to do it, how to do it,* and *why you should do it.* If you will master the next lesson, on Self-Confidence, you will then have the faith in yourself to enable you to carry out the instructions laid down for your guidance in this lesson.

Master of human destinies am I!
Fame, love, and fortune on my footsteps wait.
Cities and fields I walk; I penetrate
Deserts and seas remote, and passing by
Hovel and mart and palace—soon or late
I knock, unbidden, once at every gate!
If sleeping, wake—if feasting, rise before
I turn away. It is the hour of fate,
And they who follow me reach every state
Mortals desire, and conquer every foe
Save death; but those who doubt or hesitate,
Condemned to failure, penury, and woe,
Seek me in vain and uselessly implore.
I answer not, and I return no more!

—JOHN J. INGALLS

NEGLECTING TO BROADEN THEIR VIEW

HAS KEPT SOME PEOPLE

DOING ONE THING ALL THEIR LIVES.

Lesson Three

Self-Confidence

———————————

AMIDST ALL THE MYSTERIES

BY WHICH WE ARE SURROUNDED,

NOTHING IS MORE CERTAIN THAN

THAT WE ARE IN THE PRESENCE

OF AN INFINITE AND ETERNAL ENERGY

FROM WHICH ALL THINGS PROCEED.

—Herbert Spencer

———————————

Lesson Three

SELF-CONFIDENCE

"You Can Do It if You Believe You Can!"

BEFORE APPROACHING THE FUNDAMENTAL principles upon which this lesson is founded it will be of benefit to you to keep in mind that it is practical—that it brings you the discoveries of more than twenty-five years of research —and that it has the approval of the leading scientific men and women of the world who have tested every principle involved.

Skepticism is the deadly enemy of progress and self-development. You might as well lay this book aside and stop right here as to approach this lesson with the feeling that it was written by some theorist who had never tested the principles upon which the lesson is based.

Surely this is no age for the skeptic, because it is an age in which we have seen more of Nature's laws uncovered and harnessed than had been discovered in all past history of the human race. Within three decades we have witnessed the mastery of the air; we have explored the ocean; we have all but annihilated distances on the earth; we have harnessed the lightning and made it turn the wheels of industry; we have made seven blades of grass grow where but one grew before; we have instantaneous communication between the nations of the world. Truly, this is an age of illumination and unfoldment, but we have as yet barely scratched the surface of knowledge. However, when we shall have unlocked the gate that leads to the secret power that is stored up within us, it will bring us knowledge that will make all past discoveries pale into oblivion by comparison.

Thought is the most highly organized form of energy known, and this is an age of experimentation and research that is sure to bring us into greater understanding of that mysterious force called thought. We have already found out enough about the human mind to know that one may throw off the accumulated effects of a thousand generations of *fear*, through the aid of the principle of *autosuggestion*. We have already discovered the fact that *fear* is the chief reason for poverty and failure and misery that takes on a thousand different forms. We have already discovered the fact that the person who masters *fear* may continue on to successful achievement in practically any undertaking, despite all efforts to defeat them.

The development of Self-Confidence starts with the elimination of this demon called *fear*, which sits on a person's shoulder and whispers into their ear: "You can't do it—you are afraid to try—you are afraid of public opinion—you are afraid that you will fail—you are afraid you do not have the ability."

This *fear* demon is getting into close quarters. Science has found a deadly weapon with which to put it to flight, and this lesson on Self-Confidence has brought you this weapon for use in your battle with that enemy of progress: *fear*.

THE SIX BASIC FEARS OF MANKIND

Every person falls heir to the influence of six basic fears. Under these six fears may be listed the lesser fears. The six basic or major fears are identified here and the sources from which they are believed to have developed are described. The six basic fears are:

- The fear of poverty
- The fear of old age
- The fear of criticism
- The fear of loss of love of someone
- The fear of ill health
- The fear of death

Study the list, then take inventory of your own fears and ascertain under which of the six headings you can classify them.

Every human being who has reached the age of understanding is bound down, to some extent, by one or more of these six basic fears. As the first step in the elimination of these six evils, let us examine the sources from which we inherited them.

Physical and Social Heredity

All that man is, both physically and mentally, he came by through two forms of heredity. One is known as physical heredity and the other is called social heredity.

Through the law of physical heredity, man has slowly evolved from the ameba (a single-cell animal form), through the stages of development corresponding to all known animal forms now on this earth, including those known to have existed but which are now extinct.

Every generation through which man has passed has added to his nature something of the traits, habits, and physical appearance of that generation. Our physical inheritance, therefore, is a heterogeneous collection of many habits and physical forms.

There seems little if any doubt that while the six basic human fears could not have been inherited through physical heredity (these six fears being mental states of mind and therefore not capable of transmission through physical heredity), it is obvious that through physical heredity a most favorable lodging place for these six fears has been provided.

By far the most important part of a person's makeup comes through the law of social heredity. This term refers to the methods by which one generation imposes upon the minds of the generation under its immediate control the superstitions, beliefs, legends, and ideas that it, in turn, inherited from the generation preceding.

The term *social heredity* should be understood to mean any and all sources through which a person acquires knowledge, such as schooling of religious and all other natures, reading, word-of-mouth conversation, storytelling, and all manner of thought inspiration coming from his or her personal experiences.

Through the operation of the law of social heredity, anyone having control of the mind of a child may, through intense teaching, plant in that child's mind any idea, whether false or true, in such a manner that the child accepts it as true and it becomes as much a part of the child's personality as any cell or organ of its physical body (and just as hard to change in its nature).

It is through the law of social heredity that the religionist plants in a child's mind dogmas, creeds, and religious ceremonies too numerous to describe, holding those ideas before that mind until the mind accepts them and forever seals them as a part of its irrevocable belief.

The mind of a child which has not come into the age of general understanding, during an average period covering, let us say, the first two years of its life, is plastic, open, clean, and free. Any idea planted in such a mind by one in whom the child has confidence takes root and develops in such a manner that it never can be eradicated or wiped out, no matter how opposed to logic or reason that idea may be.

Many religionists claim that they can so deeply implant the tenets of their religion in the mind of a child that there can never be room in that mind for any other religion, either in whole or in part. The claims are not greatly overstated.

With this explanation of the manner in which the law of social heredity operates, you will be ready to examine the sources from which humans inherit the six basic fears. Moreover, any reader (except those who refuse to examine truth that steps on their own beliefs) may check the soundness of the principle of social heredity as it is here applied to the six basic fears, without going outside of his or her own personal experiences.

Fortunately, practically the entire mass of evidence submitted in this lesson is of such a nature that all who sincerely seek the truth may ascertain, for themselves, whether the evidence is sound or not.

For the moment at least, lay aside your prejudices and preconceived ideas (you may always go back and pick them up again, you know) while we study the origin and nature of man's worst enemies, the six basic fears.

COMMENTARY

Hill continued to reexamine the six fears throughout his life. His discussion of them appears in several variations. It appears first in the original version of Law of Success, *published in pamphlet form. There, in the Lesson One Appendix, he lists the fears in a different order. Fear of ill health comes third and fear of criticism fifth; here their positions are reversed.

In Think and Grow Rich, *he lists poverty, criticism, and ill health as the primary fears, saying that they are at the core of one's worries. Here one sees the reason for his fascination with the subject. "Indecision is the seedling of fear," he says. "Indecision crystallizes into doubt and the two become fear." Fear, then, becomes a symptom of the thought and action Hill shows us how to reform.

His commentaries differ also. The most significant departures are noted following.

———————

REMEMBER THAT WHEN YOU

MAKE AN APPOINTMENT

WITH ANOTHER PERSON

YOU ASSUME THE RESPONSIBILITY

OF PUNCTUALITY, AND

THAT YOU HAVE NOT THE RIGHT

TO BE A SINGLE MINUTE LATE.

———————

The Fear of Poverty

It requires courage to tell the truth about the origins of this fear, and still greater courage, perhaps, to accept the truth after it has been told. The fear of poverty grew out of man's inherited tendency to prey upon his fellow man economically. Nearly all lower forms of animals have instinct but appear not to have the power to reason and think; therefore, they prey upon one another physically. We, with our superior sense of intuition, thought, and reason, do not eat our fellow human beings bodily; we get more satisfaction out of eating others *financially!*

Of all the ages of the world of which we know anything, the age in which we live seems to be the age of money worship. A person is considered less than the dust of the earth unless they can display a fat bank account. Nothing brings us so much suffering and humiliation as does poverty. No wonder we *fear* poverty. Through a long line of inherited experiences with others like us, we have learned for certain that this animal cannot always be trusted where matters of money and other evidences of earthly possessions are concerned.

Many marriages have their beginning (and oftentimes their ending) solely on the basis of the wealth possessed by one or both of the parties. It is no wonder that the divorce courts are busy!

"Society" could quite properly be spelled "$ociety," because it is inseparably associated with the dollar sign. So eager are we to possess wealth that we will acquire it in whatever manner we can; through legal methods if possible, through other methods if necessary.

The fear of poverty is a terrible thing!

A man may commit murder, engage in robbery, rape, and all other manner of violation of the rights of others and still regain a high station in the minds of people of his society, providing always that he does not lose his wealth. Poverty, therefore, is a crime—an unforgivable sin, as it were.

No wonder we fear it!

Every statute book in the world bears evidence that the fear of poverty is one of the six basic fears of mankind, for in every such book of laws may be found various and sundry laws intended to protect the weak from the strong. To spend time trying to prove either that the fear of poverty is one of man's inherited fears, or that this fear has its origin in man's nature to cheat his fellow man, would be similar to trying to prove that three times two are six.

COMMENTARY

> *From the Appendix to Lesson One: "Humans are such great offenders in this respect that nearly every state and nation has been obliged to pass laws, scores of laws, to protect the weak from the strong. Every code of laws ever written provides indisputable evidence of humanity's nature to prey upon its weaker members economically."*
>
> *In* Think and Grow Rich, *Hill lists six symptoms of the fear of poverty: indifference (lack of ambition, laziness, and so forth); indecision; doubt (expressed through alibis and excuses); worrying (expressed through fault-finding;) overcaution (shown in general negativity); and procrastination.*

Obviously no one would ever fear poverty if we had any grounds for trusting our fellow men, for there is food and shelter and raiment and luxury of every nature sufficient for the needs of every person on earth, and all these blessings would be enjoyed by every person except for the swinish habit that humans have of trying to push all the other swine out of the trough, even after everyone has all and more than needed.

The Fear of Old Age

This fear grows mainly out of two sources. First, the thought that old age may bring with it *poverty*. Second, human beings have learned to fear old age because it meant the approach of another, and a possibly much more horrible, world than this one which is known to be bad enough.

In the basic fear of old age, humans have two very sound reasons for their apprehension: the one growing out of distrust of those who may seize whatever worldly goods we possess, and the other arising from the terrible pictures of the world to come which were deeply planted in our minds, through the law of social heredity, long before any of us came into possession of that mind.

Is it any wonder that so many fear the approach of old age?

The Fear of Criticism

Just how humans acquired this basic fear it would be difficult, if not impossible, to definitely determine. But one thing is certain, we all have it in well-developed form.

I am inclined to attribute the basic fear of criticism to that part of our inherited nature that prompts many of us not only to take away our fellow human's goods and wares but also to justify our actions by *criticism* of the character of others.

The fear of criticism takes on many different forms, the majority of which are petty and trivial in nature, even to the extent of being childish in the extreme.

The makers of all manner of clothing have not been slow to capitalize on this basic fear of criticism with which all humankind is cursed. Every season, it will be observed, the styles in many articles of apparel change. Who establishes the styles? Certainly not the purchasers, but the manufacturers of clothes. Why do they change the styles so often? Obviously so that they can sell more clothes.

For the same reason the manufacturers of automobiles (with a few rare and very sensible exceptions) change styles every season.

The manufacturers of clothing know how the human animal fears to wear a garment that is one season out of step with what "they" are all wearing now.

Is this not true? Does your own experience not back it up?

Powerful and mighty is the fear of criticism.

IN EVERY SOUL

THERE HAS BEEN DEPOSITED

THE SEED OF A GREAT FUTURE,

BUT THAT SEED

WILL NEVER GERMINATE,

MUCH LESS GROW TO MATURITY,

EXCEPT THROUGH THE RENDERING

OF USEFUL SERVICE.

COMMENTARY

From Think and Grow Rich: *"The fear of criticism robs man of his initiative, destroys his power of imagination, limits his individuality, takes away his self-reliance, and does him damage in a hundred other ways. Parents often do their children irreparable injury by criticizing them. . . . It should be recognized as a crime (in reality it is a crime of the worst nature), for any parent to build an inferiority complex in the mind of a child, through unnecessary criticism. Employers who understand human nature get the best there is in employees, not by criticism but by constructive suggestion."*

The Fear of Loss of Love of Someone

The source from which this fear originated needs but little description, for it is obvious that it grew out of man's nature to steal his fellow man's mate, or at least to take liberties with her.

There can be little doubt that jealousy and all other similar forms of more or less mild dementia praecox (insanity) grew out of the fear we all inherited of the loss of love of someone.

Of all the sane fools I have studied, the jealous lover is the oddest and strangest. Fortunately, I have had personal experience of this form of insanity, and from that experience I learned that the fear of the loss of love of someone is one of the most painful, if not in fact the most painful, of all the six basic fears. It seems reasonable to add that this fear plays more havoc with the human mind than do any of the other six basic fears of mankind, often leading to the more violent forms of permanent insanity.

COMMENTARY

From the Appendix to Lesson One: *"This fear fills the asylums with the insanely jealous, for jealousy is nothing but a form of insanity. It also fills the divorce courts and causes murders and other forms of cruel punishment. It is a holdover, handed down through social heredity, from the Stone Age when man preyed upon his fellow man by stealing his mate by physical force. The method, but not the practice, has now changed to some extent. Instead of physical force man now steals his fellow man's mate with pretty colorful ribbons and fast motor cars and bootleg whisky and sparkling rocks and stately mansions."*

The Fear of Ill Health

This fear has its origin, to considerable extent also, in the same sources from which the fears of poverty and old age are derived.

The fear of ill health is closely associated with both poverty and old age because it also leads toward the borderline of terrible worlds of which people know little, but about which there are many discomforting stories.

I strongly suspect that those engaged in the business of selling good health methods have had considerable to do with keeping the fear of ill health alive in the human mind.

For longer than the record of the human race can be relied upon, the world has known of various and sundry forms of therapy and health purveyors. If a person gains a living from keeping others in good health, it seems natural that he or she would use every possible means to persuade them of the need for caregiving services. Thus, in time, it might be that people would inherit a fear of ill health.

COMMENTARY

From the Appendix to Lesson One: "This fear is born of both physical and social heredity. From birth until death there is eternal warfare within every physical body; warfare between groups of cells, one group being known as the friendly builders of the body, and the other as the destroyers, or "disease germs." The seed of fear is born in the physical body to begin with, as the result of nature's cruel plan of permitting the stronger forms of cell life to prey upon the weaker. Social heredity has played its part though lack of cleanliness and knowledge of sanitation. Also, through the law of suggestion cleverly manipulated by those who profited by ill health."

> *In* Think and Grow Rich *Hill suggests that ill health comes from fear: "Thought impulses immediately begin to translate themselves into their physical equivalent, whether those thoughts are voluntary or involuntary.... All thought has a tendency to clothe itself in its physical equivalent."*

The Fear of Death

To many this is the worst of all the six basic fears, and the reason why it is regarded as such becomes obvious to even the casual student of psychology.

The terrible pangs of fear associated with death may be charged directly to religious fanaticism—the source that is more responsible for it than are all other sources combined.

So-called heathens are not as much afraid of *death* as are the civilized, especially that portion of the civilized population that has come under the influence of theology.

For hundreds of millions of years we have all been asking the still unanswered (and, it may be, the unanswerable) questions, *whence?* and *whither? Where did I come from and where am I going after death?*

The more cunning and crafty, as well as the honest but credulous, of the race have not been slow to offer the answer to these questions. In fact the answering of these questions has become one of the so-called learned professions, despite little learning being required to enter this profession.

Witness now the major source of origin of the fear of *death.*

"Come into my tent, embrace my faith, accept my dogmas (and pay my salary) and I will give you a ticket that will admit you straightway into heaven when you die," says the leader of one form of sectarianism. "Remain out of my tent," says this same leader, "and you will go direct to hell, where you will burn throughout eternity."

While, in fact, the self-appointed leader may not be able to provide safe-conduct into heaven nor, by lack of such provision, allow the unfortunate seeker after truth to descend into hell, the possibility of the latter seems so terrible that it takes hold of the mind and creates that fear of fears—the fear of *death*.

In truth no one knows, and no one has ever known, what heaven or hell is like, or if such places exist, and this very lack of definite knowledge opens the door of the human mind to the charlatan to enter and control that mind with his stock of various brands of trickery, deceit, and fraud.

The truth is this—nothing less and nothing more—*no person knows nor has any person ever known where we come from at birth or where we go at death.* Anyone claiming otherwise is either deceiving themself or is a conscious impostor who makes it a business to live without rendering service of value, while preying upon the credulity of humanity.

Be it said in their behalf, however, the majority of those engaged in selling tickets into heaven actually believe not only that they know where heaven exists, but that their creeds and formulas will give safe passage to all who embrace them.

This belief may be summed up in one word—*credulity!*

Religious leaders, generally, make the broad, sweeping claim that the present civilization owes its existence to the work done by the churches. I am willing to grant their claims to be correct if, at the same time, I am permitted to add that even if this claim were true, the theologians haven't a great deal to brag about.

But it is not—cannot be—true that civilization has grown out of the efforts of the organized churches and creeds, if the term *civilization* means the uncovering of the natural laws and the many inventions to which the world is the present heir.

If the theologians wish to claim the part of civilization that has to do with man's conduct toward his fellow man, then they are perfectly welcome to it, as far as I am concerned. On the other hand, if they presumed to gobble up the credit for all the scientific discovery of mankind, I would protest vigorously.

COMMENTARY

From the Appendix: "You can make and put into action a plan of attack on fear. Ask yourself which of the six basic fears is doing you the greatest damage.

"We are slowly discovering more about these six basic fears. The most effective tool with which to fight them is organized knowledge. Ignorance and fear are twins. They are generally found together. But for ignorance, the six basic fears would disappear from human thought. In every public library you can find the remedy for these six enemies.

"Begin with Ralph Waldo Emerson's essay on Compensation. Then select some of the other books on self-suggestion and inform yourself about the principle through which your beliefs of today become the realities of tomorrow.

"Through the principle of social heredity, the ignorance and superstition of the past have been passed on to you. But you are living in a modern age. On every hand you may see evidence that every effect has a natural cause. Begin now to study effects by their causes, and soon you will emancipate your mind from the burden of the six basic fears.

"Begin by selecting two people whom you know close at hand; one should represent your idea of failure and the other should correspond to your idea of success. Find out what made one a failure and the other a success. Get the real facts. In the process of gathering these facts you will have taught yourself a great lesson on cause and effect.

"Nothing ever just happens. In a single month of properly directed self-suggestion you may place your foot upon the neck of every one of your six basic fears. In twelve months of persistent effort you may drive the entire herd into the corner where it will never again do you any serious injury.

"You will resemble tomorrow the dominating thoughts that you keep alive in your mind today. Plant in your mind the seed of determination to whip your six basic fears, and the battle will have been half won then and there. Keep this intention in your mind and it will slowly push your six worst enemies out of sight, as they exist nowhere except in your own mind.

"A person who is powerful fears nothing; not even God. The powerful person loves God, but fears Him never! Enduring power never grows out of fear. Any power that is built upon fear is bound to crumble and disintegrate. Understand this great truth and you will never be so unfortunate as to try to raise yourself to power through the fears of other people who may owe you temporary allegiance."

HOW LESSONS ARE LEARNED

It is hardly sufficient to say that social heredity is the method through which humans gather all knowledge that reaches us through the five senses. It is more to the point to say *how* social heredity works, in as many different applications as will give you a comprehensive understanding of that law.

COMMENTARY

Appropriately enough, Hill here turns to animal stories as a way of discussing the development of human character. Hill's frequent references to Nature's bible demonstrate that he believed human beings are a part of Nature. But he also values the importance of the human social environment. In weighing in on the relative influences of Nature and nurture, Hill uses the term physical heredity *for what we today might call* genetic predisposition. *By* social heredity *he means what we might simply call* conditioning *or* social conditioning *or* socialization.

The Law of Social Heredity

Let us begin with some of the lower forms of animal life and examine the manner in which they are affected by the law of social heredity.

COMMENTARY

Many authors and lecturers of Napoleon Hill's day prided themselves on being storytellers, and they often drew upon the natural world for examples around which to spin a yarn that would entertain while conveying the points they were trying to make. However, the America in which most of us live today is not nearly as bucolic as the one in which Hill grew up. There's a lot less catching of frogs in the creek or watching of grouse in the fields, and kids think chickens come as a half-dozen thighs or breasts shrink-wrapped in a package from the supermarket.

For that reason, as this edition was being prepared, there was considerable discussion among the editors about the inclusion of Hill's animal analogies. It was concluded that the points made are as valid today as they were when Hill wrote them, and though they might be considered quaint by the modern reader, the stories themselves provide interesting insights into the life and times of Napoleon Hill.

Shortly after I began, some thirty-odd years ago, to examine the major sources from which we gather the knowledge that makes us what we are, I discovered the nest of a ruffed grouse. The nest was so located that the mother bird could be seen from a considerable distance when she was on the nest. With the aid of a pair of field glasses, I watched the bird closely until the young birds were hatched. It happened that my regular daily observation was made but a few hours after the young birds came out of the shell. Desiring to know what would happen, I approached the nest. The mother bird remained nearby until I was within ten or twelve feet of her, then she disarranged her feathers, stretched one wing over her leg, and went hobbling away, making a pretense of being crippled. Being somewhat familiar with the tricks of mother birds, I did not follow but instead went to the nest to take a look at the little ones. Without the slightest signs of fear they turned their eyes toward me, moving their heads first one way and then another. I reached down and picked one of them up. With no signs of fear it stood in the palm of my hand. I laid the bird back in the nest and went away to a safe distance to give the mother bird a chance to return.

The wait was short. Very soon she began cautiously to edge her way back toward the nest until she was within a few feet of it, when she spread her wings and ran as fast as she could, uttering, meanwhile, a

YOU ARE FORTUNATE

IF YOU HAVE LEARNED

THE DIFFERENCE BETWEEN

TEMPORARY DEFEAT AND FAILURE;

MORE FORTUNATE STILL,

IF YOU HAVE LEARNED

THE TRUTH THAT THE VERY

SEED OF SUCCESS IS DORMANT

IN EVERY DEFEAT

THAT YOU EXPERIENCE.

series of sounds similar to those of a hen when she has found some morsel of food and wishes to call her brood to partake of it.

She gathered the little birds around and continued to quiver in a highly excited manner, shaking her wings and ruffling her feathers. One could almost hear her words as she gave the little birds their first lesson in self-defense, through the law of social heredity.

"You silly little creatures! Do you not know that humans are your enemies? Shame on you for allowing that man to pick you up in his hands. It's a wonder he didn't carry you off and eat you alive! The next time you see a man approaching, make yourselves scarce. Lie down on the ground, run under leaves, go anywhere to get out of sight, and remain out of sight until the enemy is well on his way."

The little birds stood around and listened to the lecture with intense interest. After the mother bird had quieted down, I again started to approach the nest. When within twenty feet or so of the guarded household, the mother bird again started to lead me in the other direction by crumpling up her wing and hobbling along as if she were crippled. I looked at the nest but the glance was in vain. The little birds were nowhere to be found! They had learned rapidly to avoid their natural enemy, thanks to their natural instinct.

Again I retreated, waited until the mother bird had reassembled her household, then came out to visit them, but with similar results. When I approached the spot where I last saw the mother bird, not the slightest signs of the little fellows were to be found.

————————

When I was a small boy I captured a young crow and made a pet of it. The bird became quite satisfied with its domestic surroundings and learned to perform many tricks requiring considerable intelligence. After the bird was big enough to fly, it was permitted to go wherever it pleased. Sometimes it would be gone for many hours, but it always returned home before dark.

One day some wild crows became involved in a fight with an owl in a field near the house where the pet crow lived. As soon as the pet heard the "caw, caw, caw" of its wild relatives it flew up on top of the house, and with signs of great agitation walked from one end of the house to the other. Finally it took wing and flew in the direction of the battle. I followed to see what would happen. In a few minutes I found the pet sitting on the lower branches of a tree. Two wild crows were on a limb just above, chattering and walking back and forth, acting very much in the same manner that angry parents behave toward their offspring when chastising them.

As I approached, the two wild crows flew away, one of them circling around the tree a few times while letting out a terrible flow of the most abusive language, which, I expect, was directed at its foolish relative who hadn't enough sense to fly while the flying was good.

The pet was called but it paid no attention. That evening it returned home but would not come near the house. It sat on a high limb of an apple tree and talked in crow language for about ten minutes, saying, no doubt, that it had decided to go back to the wild. It then flew away and did not return until two days later, when it came back and did some more talking in crow language, while keeping at a safe distance. It then went away and never returned.

Social heredity had robbed me of a fine pet! The only consolation I got from the loss of my crow was the thought that it had shown fine sportsmanship by coming back and giving notice of its intention to depart. Many farm hands have left the farm without going to the trouble of this formality.

It is a well-known fact that a fox will prey upon all manner of fowl and small animals, with the exception of the skunk. No reason need be stated as to why Mr. Skunk enjoys immunity. A fox may tackle a skunk once, but never twice! For this reason a skunk hide, when nailed to a chicken roost, will keep all but the very young and inexperienced foxes at a safe distance.

The odor of a skunk, once experienced, is never to be forgotten. No other smell even remotely resembles it. It is nowhere recorded that any mother fox ever taught her young how to detect and keep away from the familiar smell of a skunk, but all who are informed on fox lore know that foxes and skunks never seek lodging in the same cave.

Just one lesson is sufficient to teach the fox all it cares to know about skunks. Through the law of social heredity, operating via the sense of smell, one lesson serves for an entire lifetime.

———————————

A bullfrog can be caught on a fishhook by attaching a small piece of red cloth or any other small red object to the hook and dangling it in front of the frog's nose. That is, Mr. Frog may be caught in this manner provided he is hooked the first time he snaps at the bait. But if he is poorly hooked and makes a getaway, or if he feels the point of the hook when he bites at the bait but is not caught, he will never make the same mistake again. I spent many hours in stealthy attempt to hook a particularly desirable specimen which had snapped and missed, before learning that just one lesson in social heredity is enough to teach even a humble croaker that bits of red flannel are things to be left alone.

———————————

Once I owned a very fine male Airedale dog that caused no end of annoyance by his habit of coming home with a young chicken in his mouth. Each time the chicken was taken away from the dog and he was soundly switched, but to no avail; he continued in his liking for fowl.

For the purpose of saving the dog, if possible, and as an experiment with social heredity, this dog was taken to the farm of a neighbor who had a hen and some newly hatched chickens. The hen was placed in the barn and the dog was put in with her. As soon as everyone was out of

IS IT NOT STRANGE

THAT WE FEAR MOST

THAT WHICH NEVER HAPPENS?

WE DESTROY OUR INITIATIVE

BY THE FEAR OF DEFEAT,

WHEN, IN REALITY, DEFEAT IS

A MOST USEFUL TONIC AND

SHOULD BE ACCEPTED AS SUCH.

sight, the dog slowly edged up toward the hen, sniffed the air in her direction a time or two (to make sure she was the kind of meat for which he was looking), then made a dive toward her. Meanwhile, Mrs. Hen had been doing some surveying of her own, for she met Mr. Dog more than halfway; moreover, she met him with a surprise of wings and claws such as he had never before experienced. The first round was clearly the hen's. But a nice fat bird, reckoned the dog, was not to slip between his paws so easily; therefore he backed away a short distance, then charged again. This time Mrs. Hen lit upon his back, drove her claws into his skin, and made effective use of her sharp bill! Mr. Dog retreated to his corner, looking for all the world as if he were listening for someone to ring the bell and call the fight off until he got his bearings. But Mrs. Hen craved no time for deliberation; she had her adversary on the run and showed that she knew the value of the offensive by keeping him on the run.

One could almost understand her words as she flogged the poor Airedale from one corner to another, keeping up a series of rapid-fire sounds that for all the world resembled the remonstrations of an angry mother who had been called upon to defend her offspring from an attack by older boys.

The Airedale was a poor soldier. After running around the barn from corner to corner for about two minutes, he spread himself on the ground as flat as he could and did his best to protect his eyes with his paws. Mrs. Hen seemed to be making a special attempt to peck out his eyes.

The owner of the hen then stepped in and retrieved her—or, more accurately stating it, he retrieved the dog—which in no way appeared to meet with the dog's disapproval.

The next day a chicken was placed in the cellar where the dog slept. As soon as he saw the bird he tucked his tail between his legs and ran for a corner. He never again attempted to catch a chicken. One lesson in social heredity, via the sense of touch, was sufficient to teach him that while chicken-chasing may offer some enjoyment, it is also fraught with many hazards.

All these illustrations, with the exception of the first, describe the process of gathering knowledge through direct experience. Observe the marked difference between knowledge gathered by direct experience and that which is gathered through the training of the young by the old, as in the case of the ruffed grouse and her young.

The most impressive lessons are those learned by the young from the old, through highly colored or emotionalized methods of teaching. When the mother grouse spread her wings, stood her feathers on end, shook herself like a man suffering with the palsy, and chattered to her young in a highly excited manner, she planted the fear of humans in their hearts in a manner which they were never to forget.

The term *social heredity*, as used in this lesson, refers to all methods through which a child is taught any idea, dogma, creed, religion, or system of ethical conduct, by its parents or by those who may have authority over it, before reaching the age at which it may reason and reflect upon such teaching in its own way. I would estimate the age of such reasoning power at between seven and twelve years.

Fear in Middle Age

There are myriad forms of *fear*, but none more deadly than the fear of poverty and old age. We drive our bodies as if they were slaves because we are so afraid of poverty that we wish to hoard money. For what? *Old age!* This common form of *fear* drives us so hard that we overwork our bodies and bring on the very thing we are struggling to avoid.

What a tragedy to watch men and women drive themselves when they begin to arrive at about the forty-year milepost of life—the age at which they are just beginning to mature mentally. At forty, we are just entering the age in which we are able to see and understand and assimilate the handwriting of Nature, as it appears in the forests and flowing brooks and faces of other adults and little children. Yet this devil *fear* drives us to the point that we become blinded and lost in the entanglement of a maze of conflicting *desires.* The principle of *organized effort* is lost sight of, and instead of taking hold of Nature's forces that are in evidence all around us, and permitting those forces to carry us to the heights of great achievement, we defy them and they become forces of destruction.

THE POWER OF SELF-CONFIDENCE

Perhaps none of these great forces of Nature are more available for our personal growth and self-improvement than is the principle of auto-suggestion. But ignorance of this force is leading the majority of people to apply it so that it acts as a hindrance and not as a help.

Following are four examples, arbitrarily two men and two women, that show how this misapplication of a great force of Nature takes place.

Here is a man who meets with some disappointment—a friend proves false, or a neighbor seems indifferent. So he decides (through self-suggestion) all people are untrustworthy and all neighbors unappreciative. These thoughts so deeply embed themselves in this man's subconscious mind that they color his whole attitude toward others. Go back to what was said in Lesson Two about the way the dominating thoughts of our minds attract others whose thoughts are similar.

Apply the law of attraction and you will soon see and understand why the unbeliever attracts other unbelievers.

Reverse the principle:

Here is a woman who sees nothing but the best in all whom she meets. If her neighbors seem indifferent she takes no notice of it, for she makes it *her business* to fill her mind with dominating thoughts of optimism and good cheer and faith in others. If people speak to her harshly she speaks back in tones of softness. Through the operation of this same eternal law of attraction, she draws to herself the attention of people whose attitude toward life and whose dominating thoughts harmonize with her own. Tracing the principle a step further:

Here is a man who has been well schooled and has the ability to render the world some needed service. Somewhere, sometime, he has heard it said that modesty is a great virtue and that to push himself to the front of the stage in the game of life shows egotism. He quietly slips in through the back door and takes a seat at the rear while other players in the game of life boldly step to the front. He remains in the back row because he *fears* "what *they* will say." Public opinion, or what he believes to be public opinion, has him pushed to the rear and the world hears little of him. His schooling counts for naught because he is *afraid* to let the world know that he has had it. He is constantly *suggesting to himself* (thus using the great force of autosuggestion to his own detriment) that he should remain in the background lest he be criticized, as if criticism would do him any damage or defeat his purpose.

Here is a woman who was born of poor parents. Since the first day that she can remember, she has seen evidence of poverty. She has heard talk of poverty. She has felt the icy hand of poverty on her shoulders and it has so impressed her that she fixes it in her mind as a curse to which *she must submit.* Quite unconsciously she permits herself to fall victim to the belief "once poor always poor" until that belief becomes the dominating thought of her mind. She resembles a horse that has been harnessed and broken until it forgets that it has the potential power with which to throw off that harness. Autosuggestion is rapidly relegating her to the back of the stage of life. Finally she becomes a *quitter.* Ambition is gone. Opportunity no longer comes her way, or if it does she hasn't the vision to see it. *She has accepted her fate!* It is a well-established fact that the faculties of the mind, like the limbs of the body, atrophy and wither away if not used. Self-Confidence is no exception. It develops when used but disappears if not used.

One of the chief disadvantages of inherited wealth is that it too often leads to inaction and loss of Self-Confidence. Some years ago a baby boy was born to Mrs. E. B. McLean in the city of Washington. His inheritance was said to be around $100 million. When this baby was taken for an airing in his carriage it was surrounded by nurses and assistant nurses and detectives and other servants whose duty was to see that no harm befell it. As the years passed by, this same vigilance was kept up. This child did not have to dress himself; he had servants who did that. Servants watched over him while he slept and while he was at play. He was not permitted to do anything that a servant could do for him. He had grown to the age of ten years. One day he was playing in the yard and noticed that the back gate had been left open. In all his life this boy had never been outside of that gate alone, and naturally that was just the thing he wished to do. During a moment when the servants were not looking, he dashed out the gate and was run down and killed by an automobile before he reached the middle of the street.

He had used his servants' eyes until his own no longer served him as they might have done had he learned to rely on them.

Twenty years ago the man to whom I served as secretary had sent his two sons away to school. One went to the University of Virginia and the other to a college in New York. Each month it was a part of my task to make out a check for $100 to each of these boys. *[The 2004 value would be at least $1,800.]* This was their pin money, to be spent as they wished. How profitably I remember the way I envied those boys as I made out those checks each month. I often wondered why the hand of fate bore me into the world in poverty. I could look ahead and see how these boys would rise to the high stations in life while I remained a humble clerk.

In due time the two boys returned home with their sheepskins. Their father was a wealthy man who owned banks and railroads and coal mines and other property of great value. Good positions were waiting for the boys in their father's employ.

But twenty years of time can play cruel tricks on those who have never had to struggle. Perhaps a better way to state this would be that time gives those who have never had to struggle a chance to play cruel tricks on themselves! At any rate, these two boys brought home from school other things besides their sheepskins. They came back with well-

YOUR WORK AND MINE

ARE PECULIARLY AKIN; I AM

HELPING THE LAWS OF NATURE

CREATE MORE PERFECT SPECIMENS

OF VEGETATION, WHILE YOU

ARE USING THOSE SAME LAWS,

THROUGH THE LAW OF

SUCCESS PHILOSOPHY, TO CREATE

MORE PERFECT SPECIMENS

OF THINKERS.

—Luther Burbank

developed capacities for strong *drink—capacities they developed because the $100 that each of them received each month made it unnecessary for them to struggle.*

Theirs is a long and sad story, the details of which will not interest you, but you will be interested in the outcome. As this lesson is being written I have on my desk a copy of the newspaper published in the town where these boys lived. Their father has been bankrupted and his costly mansion, where the boys were born, has been placed on the block for sale. One of the boys died of alcohol-related causes and the other one has been confined to a mental-health facility.

The lives of not all rich men's sons turn out so unfortunately, but the fact remains, nevertheless, that inaction leads to atrophy and this, in turn, leads to the loss of ambition and Self-Confidence, and without these essential qualities an individual will be carried through life on the wings of uncertainty, just as a dry leaf may be carried here and there in the stray winds.

Far from being a disadvantage, struggle is a decided advantage, because it develops those qualities that would forever lie dormant without it. Many have found their place in the world due to having been forced to struggle for existence early in life. Lack of knowledge of the advantages accruing from struggle has prompted many a parent to say, "I had to work hard when I was young, but I shall see to it that my children have an easy time!" Poor foolish creatures. An "easy" time usually turns out to be a greater handicap than the average young man or young woman can survive. There are worse things in this world than being forced to work in early life. Forced idleness is far worse than forced labor. Being forced to work, and forced to do your best, will breed in you temperance and Self-Control and strength of will and content and a hundred other virtues which the idle will never know.

Not only does lack of the necessity for struggle lead to weakness of ambition and willpower, but, what is more dangerous still, it sets up in a person's mind a state of lethargy that leads to the loss of Self-Confidence. The person who has quit struggling because effort is no longer necessary is literally applying the principle of autosuggestion, undermining his or her own power of Self-Confidence. Such a person will finally drift into a frame of mind in which he or she will actually look with contempt upon the person who is forced to carry on.

The human mind, if you will pardon the repetition, may be likened to an electric battery. It may be positive or negative. Self-Confidence is the quality with which the mind is recharged and made positive.

Let us apply this line of reasoning to salesmanship and see what part Self-Confidence plays in this great field of endeavor. One of the greatest salesmen this country has ever seen was once a clerk in a newspaper office.

It will be worth your while to analyze the method through which he gained his title as "the world's leading salesman."

He was a timid young man with a more or less retiring sort of nature. He was one of those who believe it best to slip in by the back door and take a seat at the rear of the stage of life. One evening he heard a lecture on the subject of this lesson, Self-Confidence, and that lecture so impressed him that he left the lecture hall with a firm determination to pull himself out of the rut into which he had drifted.

He went to the business manager of the newspaper, asked for a position as an advertising salesman, and was put to work on a commission basis. Everyone in the office expected to see him fail, as this sort of salesmanship calls for the most positive type of sales ability. He went to his room and made out a list of certain merchants on whom he intended to call. One would think that he would naturally have made up his list of the names of those whom he believed he could sell with the least effort, *but he did nothing of the sort*. He listed only the names of the merchants on whom other advertising salespeople had called without making a sale. His list consisted of only twelve names. Before he made a single call he went to the city park, took out his list of twelve names, and read it over a hundred times, saying to himself as he did so, "You will purchase advertising space from me before the end of the month."

Then he began to make his calls. The first day he closed sales with three of the twelve "impossibilities." During the remainder of the week he made sales to two others. By the end of the month he had opened advertising accounts with all but one of the merchants on his list. For the ensuing month he made no sales because he made no calls, except on this one obstinate merchant. Every morning when the store opened he was there to speak with this merchant and every morning the merchant said no. The merchant knew he was not going to buy advertising space, but this young man didn't know it. When the merchant said no, the young man did not hear it; he kept right on coming. On the last day of the month, after having told this persistent young man no for thirty consecutive times, the merchant said: "Look here, young man, you have wasted a whole month trying to sell to me. What I would like to know is this—why have you wasted your time?"

"Wasted my time nothing," he retorted, "I have been going to school and you have been my teacher. Now I know all the arguments that a merchant can bring up for not buying, and besides that I have been drilling myself in self-confidence."

Then the merchant said: "I will make a little confession of my own. I, too, have been going to school, and you have been my teacher. You have taught me a lesson in persistence that is worth money to me, and to show you my appreciation I am going to pay my tuition fee by giving you an order for advertising space."

And that was the way in which the *Philadelphia North American's* best advertising account was brought in. That one sale also marked the beginning of a reputation that has since made that same young man a millionaire. He succeeded because he deliberately charged his own mind with sufficient Self-Confidence to make that mind an irresistible force. When he sat down to make up that list of twelve names he did something that ninety-nine people out of a hundred would not have done—he selected the names of those whom he believed it would be hard to sell, because he understood that out of the resistance he would meet with in trying to sell them would also come strength and Self-Confidence. He was one of the very few who understand that all rivers and some people are crooked because of following the line of least resistance.

––––––––––

I am going to digress and break the line of thought for a moment to offer a word of advice to spouses and companions.

From having analyzed more than 16,000 people, the majority of whom were married, I have learned something that may be of value.

You have it within your power to send your mate away to his or her work, business, or profession each day with a feeling of Self-Confidence that will carry them successfully over the rough spots of a day and bring them home again at night, smiling and happy. A man I know well married a woman who had a set of false teeth. One day his wife dropped her teeth and broke the plate. The husband picked up the pieces and began examining them. He showed such interest in them that his wife said:

"You could make a set of teeth like those if you made up your mind to do it."

This man was a farmer whose ambitions had never carried him beyond the bounds of his little farm until his wife made that remark. She walked over, laid her hand on his shoulder, and encouraged him to try his hand at dentistry. She finally coaxed him to make the start, and today he is one of the most prominent and successful dentists in the state of Virginia. I know him well, for he is my father!

No one can foretell the possibilities of achievement available to the man or woman whose partner supports and encourages bigger and better endeavor. It is your right and your duty to encourage your mate in worthy undertakings until he or she finds an appropriate place in the world. You can induce your mate to put forth greater effort than can any other person in the world. Make him or her believe that nothing within reason is beyond reach, and you will have rendered a service that will go a long way toward winning the battle of life.

One of the most successful men in his line in America gives entire credit for his success to his wife. When they were first married she wrote a creed which he signed and placed over his desk. This is what it said:

> I believe in myself. I believe in those who work with me. I believe in my employer. I believe in my friends. I believe in my family. I believe that God will lend me everything I need with which to succeed if I do my best to earn it through faithful and honest service. I believe in prayer and I will never close my eyes in sleep without praying for divine guidance to the end that I will be patient with other people and tolerant with those who do not believe as I do. I believe that success is the result of intelligent effort and does not depend upon luck or sharp practices or double-crossing friends, fellow men, or my employer. I believe I will get out of life exactly what I put into it, therefore I will be careful to conduct myself toward others as I would want them to act toward me. I will not slander those whom I do not like. I will not slight my work no matter what I may see others doing. I will render the best service of which I am capable because I have pledged myself to succeed in life and I know that success is always the result of conscientious and efficient effort. Finally, I will forgive those who offend me because I realize that I shall sometimes offend others and I will need their forgiveness.
>
> Signed . . . .

The woman who wrote this creed was a practical psychologist of the first order. With the influence and guidance of such a marriage partner as a helpmate any man or woman could achieve noteworthy success.

Analyze this creed and you will observe how freely the personal pronoun is used. It starts off with the affirmation of Self-Confidence,

---

NO MAN CAN BECOME

A GREAT LEADER OF MEN

UNLESS HE HAS THE MILK

OF HUMAN KINDNESS

IN HIS OWN HEART,

AND LEADS BY SUGGESTION

AND KINDNESS,

RATHER THAN BY FORCE.

---

which is perfectly appropriate. You could not make this creed your own without developing the positive attitude that would attract people who would aid you in your struggle for success.

This would be a splendid creed for every salesperson to adopt. It might not hurt your chances for success if *you* adopted it. Mere adoption, however, is not enough. You must *practice* it! Read it over and over until you know it by heart. Then repeat it at least once a day until you have literally transformed it into your mental makeup. Keep a copy of it in front of you as a daily reminder of your pledge to practice it. By doing so you will be making efficient use of the principle of autosuggestion as a means of developing Self-Confidence. Never mind what anyone may say about your procedure. Just remember that it is your business to succeed, and this creed, if mastered and applied, will go a long way toward helping you.

You learned in Lesson Two that any idea you firmly fix in your subconscious mind, by repeated affirmation, automatically becomes a plan or blueprint that an unseen power uses in directing your efforts toward the attainment of the objective named in the plan.

You have also learned that the principle through which you may fix in your mind any idea you choose is called autosuggestion, which simply means a suggestion that you give to your own mind. It was this principle of autosuggestion that Emerson had in mind when he wrote:

"Nothing can bring you peace but yourself!"

Similarly, you might well remember that nothing can bring you *success* but yourself. Of course, you will need the Cooperation of others if your aim is success of a far-reaching nature, but you will never get that Cooperation without the positive attitude of Self-Confidence.

Perhaps you have wondered why a few will advance to highly paid positions while others all around them, who have as much training and who seemingly perform as much work, do not get ahead. Select any two people of these two types, and study them, and the reason why one advances and the other stands still will be quite obvious to you. You will find that the one who advances *believes in themself,* and that he or she backs their belief with such dynamic, aggressive action that others can recognize it in them. You will also notice that this Self-Confidence is contagious; it is impelling; it is persuasive; it attracts others.

You will also find that the one who does *not* advance shows clearly, by the look on their face, by the posture of their body, by the lack of briskness in their step, by the uncertainty with which they speak, that he or she lacks Self-Confidence. No one is going to pay much attention to the person who has no confidence in themself.

They do not attract others because their mind is a negative force that repels rather than attracts.

In no other field of endeavor does Self-Confidence, or the lack of it, play such an important part as in the field of sales, and one does not need to be a character analyst to determine, on first meeting, whether a salesperson possesses this quality. If you have it, the signs of its influence are written all over you. The moment you speak you inspire customers with confidence in you and in the goods you are selling.

We come now to the point at which you are ready to take hold of the principle of autosuggestion and make direct use of it in developing yourself into a positive, dynamic, self-reliant person. You are instructed to copy the following formula, sign it, and commit it to memory:

SELF-CONFIDENCE FORMULA

1. I know that I have the ability to achieve the object of my definite purpose, therefore I demand of myself persistent, aggressive, and continuous action toward its attainment.

2. I realize that the dominating thoughts of my mind will eventually reproduce themselves in outward, bodily action and then gradually transform themselves into physical reality. Therefore, I will concentrate my mind for thirty minutes daily on the task of thinking of

the person I intend to be, by creating a mental picture of this person and then transforming that picture into reality through my actions.

3. I know that through the principle of autosuggestion, any desire I persistently hold in my mind will eventually seek expression through some practical means of realizing it. Therefore I shall devote ten minutes daily to demanding of myself the development of the factors named in the seventeen lessons of the Law of Success course.

4. I have clearly mapped out, and written down, a description of my Definite Purpose in life, for the next five years. I have set a price on my services for each of these five years, a price that I intend to *earn* and *receive* through strict application of the principle of efficient, satisfactory service, which I will render in advance.

5. I fully realize that no wealth or position can long endure unless it is built upon truth and justice. Therefore, *I will engage in no transaction that does not benefit all whom it affects.* I will succeed by attracting to me the forces I wish to use and the Cooperation of other people. I will induce others to serve me because I will first serve them. I will eliminate hatred, envy, jealousy, selfishness, and cynicism by developing love for all humanity, because I know that a negative attitude toward others can never bring me success. I will cause others to believe in me because I will believe in them and in myself.

I will sign my name to this formula, commit it to memory, and repeat it aloud once a day with full faith that it will gradually influence my entire life so that I will become a successful and happy worker in my chosen field of endeavor.

Signed . . . .

Before you sign your name to this formula, make sure that you intend to carry out its instructions. Behind this formula is a law that is

IF YOU WANT A THING DONE WELL,

CALL ON SOME BUSY PERSON TO DO IT.

BUSY PEOPLE ARE GENERALLY

THE MOST PAINSTAKING

AND THOROUGH IN ALL THEY DO.

difficult to explain. Psychologists refer to this law as autosuggestion and let it go at that, but you should bear in mind one point about which there is no uncertainty, and that is the fact that whatever this law is, it *actually works!*

Another point to be kept in mind is that just as electricity will turn the wheels of industry and serve mankind in a million other ways, or snuff out life if wrongly applied, so will this principle of autosuggestion lead you up the mountainside of peace and prosperity, or down into the valley of misery and poverty, according to the application you make of it. If you fill your mind with doubt and unbelief in your ability to achieve, then the principle of autosuggestion takes this spirit of unbelief and sets it up in your subconscious mind as your dominating thought and slowly but surely it draws you into the whirlpool of *failure.* But if you fill your mind with radiant Self-Confidence, the principle of auto-suggestion takes this belief and sets it up as your dominating thought and helps you master the obstacles that fall in your way until you reach the mountaintop of *success.*

THE POWER OF HABIT

Having, myself, experienced all the difficulties that stand in the road of those who lack the understanding to make practical application of this great principle of autosuggestion, let me tell you a little about the principle of habit, through the aid of which you may easily apply the principle of autosuggestion in any way and for any purpose whatsoever.

Habit grows out of environment, out of doing the same thing or thinking the same thoughts or repeating the same words over and over again. Habit may be likened to the groove in a record, while the human mind may be likened to the needle that fits into that groove. When any habit has been well formed, through repetition of thought or action, the mind has a tendency to attach itself to and follow the course of that habit as closely as a phonograph needle follows the groove in a record.

Habit is created by *repeatedly* directing one or more of the five senses of seeing, hearing, smelling, tasting, and feeling, in a given direction. After habit has been well established, it will automatically control and direct our bodily activity, wherein may be found a thought that can be transformed into a powerful factor in the development of Self-Confidence: *Voluntarily, and by force if necessary, direct your efforts and your thoughts along a desired line until you have formed the habit that will take hold and continue, voluntarily, to direct your efforts along the same line.*

The object in writing out and repeating the Self-Confidence formula is to form the habit of making *belief in yourself* the dominating thought of your mind until that thought has been thoroughly embedded in your subconscious mind, through the principle of habit.

You learned to write by repeatedly directing the muscles of your arm and hand over certain letter outlines, until finally you formed the habit of tracing these outlines. Now you write quickly and easily, without tracing each letter slowly. Writing has become a *habit* with you.

The principle of habit will take hold of the faculties of your mind just the same as it will influence the physical muscles of your body, as you can easily prove by mastering and applying this lesson on Self-Confidence. Any statement that you repeatedly make to yourself, or any *desire* that you deeply plant in your mind through repeated statement, will eventually seek expression through your physical, outward bodily efforts. The principle of habit is the very foundation upon which this lesson on Self-Confidence is built, and if you will understand and follow the directions laid down in this lesson, you will soon know more about the law of habit, from firsthand knowledge, than could be taught to you by a thousand such lessons as this.

You have little concept of the possibilities that lie sleeping within you, just awaiting the wakening hand of vision to arouse you, and you will never have a better concept of those possibilities unless you develop sufficient Self-Confidence to lift you above the commonplace influences of your present environment.

The human mind is a marvelous, mysterious piece of machinery, which I was reminded of a few months ago when I picked up *Emerson's Essays* and reread his essay on spiritual laws. A strange thing happened. I saw in that essay, which I had read scores of times previously, much that I had never noticed before. I saw more in this essay than I had seen during previous readings, because the unfoldment of my mind since the last reading had prepared me to interpret more.

The human mind is constantly unfolding, like the petals of a flower, until it reaches the maximum of development. What this maximum is, where it ends, and whether or not it ends at all, are unanswerable questions, but the degree of unfoldment seems to vary according to the nature of the individual and the degree to which they keep their mind at work. A mind that is forced or coaxed into analytical thought every day seems to keep on unfolding and developing greater powers of interpretation.

Down in Louisville, Kentucky, lives Mr. Lee Cook, a man who has practically no legs and has to wheel himself around on a cart. Despite Mr. Cook having been without legs since birth, he is the owner of a great industry and is a millionaire through his own efforts. He has proved that people can get along very well without legs if they have a well-developed Self-Confidence.

In the city of New York one may see a young man, without legs but otherwise able-bodied and able-headed, rolling himself down Fifth Avenue every afternoon with cap in hand, begging for a living. His head is perhaps as sound and as able to think as the average. This young man could duplicate anything that Mr. Cook of Louisville has done, *if he thought of himself as Mr. Cook thinks of himself.*

Henry Ford has more money than he will ever need or use. Not so many years ago, he was working as a laborer in a machine shop, with but little schooling and without capital. Scores of other men, some of them with better-organized brains than his, worked near him. Ford threw off the poverty consciousness, developed confidence in himself,

YOU CAN ALWAYS

BECOME THE PERSON

YOU WOULD HAVE LIKED TO BE.

thought of success, and attained it. Those who worked around him could have done as well had they *thought* as he did.

Milo C. Jones of Wisconsin was stricken with paralysis a few years ago. So bad was the stroke that he could not turn himself in bed or move a muscle of his body. His physical body was useless, but there was nothing wrong with his brain, so it began to function in earnest, probably for the first time in its existence. Lying flat on his back in bed, Mr. Jones made that brain create a *definite purpose.* That purpose was prosaic and humble enough in nature, but it was *definite* and it was a *purpose*, something that he had never known before.

His *definite purpose* was to make pork sausage. Calling his family around him, he told of his plans and began directing them in carrying the plans into action. With nothing to aid him except a sound mind and plenty of Self-Confidence, Milo C. Jones spread the name and reputation of "Little Pig Sausage" all over the United States, and at the same time accumulated a fortune.

All this was accomplished after paralysis had made it impossible for him to work with his hands.

COMMENTARY

Many more modern examples can also be cited. There is a powerful disease called amyotrophic lateral sclerosis, which is also known as Lou Gehrig's disease. It affects the nerves that control the muscles, causing them to waste away, bringing paralysis and usually death in just a few short years. This condition afflicts the famous physicist, Dr. Stephen Hawking, and has for more than two decades. Dr. Hawking's body is severely limited, but his mind is not. He has taken his mind down incredible roads where he explores the secrets of the universe, studying black holes, quantum physics, even the very nature of time. Dr. Hawking's mind has unfolded to a previously unimagined degree because he made it his habit to develop it.

Peter Leonard seemed to have been dealt a tough hand in life. He had learning disabilities that made reading and writing very difficult. By the time he reached *middle age, he was divorced and unemployed. But he conceived an idea that came to dominate his mind. He wanted to serve in the New Hampshire legislature. He lost his first campaign, and his second. Others would have given up, but Leonard looked at himself and realized that his best chances lay in his own efforts, despite the fact that he had no experience and less money. So for his next campaign he began going door to door in his district. He met everyone he could, he walked in parades, and attended community meetings. He spent just $12 on some posters and $36 on filing fees, and that was the extent of his spending. And Peter Leonard was elected! His path was unusual, but he found it by making a habit of working toward being elected.*

Where *thought* prevails, power may be found! Henry Ford has made millions of dollars, and is still making millions of dollars each year, because *he believed in Henry Ford* and transformed that belief into a *definite purpose* backed with a definite plan. The other machinists who worked along with Ford during the early days of his career envisioned nothing but a weekly pay envelope and that was all they ever got; they demanded nothing out of the ordinary of themselves. If you want to *get* more, be sure to *demand* more of yourself. Notice that this demand is to be made on *yourself.*

This brings to mind a familiar poem which expresses a great psychological truth:

> *If you think you are beaten, you are;*
> *If you think you dare not, you don't;*
> *If you like to win, but you think you can't,*
> *It is almost certain you won't.*

> *If you think you'll lose, you've lost,*
> *For out of the world we find*
> *Success begins with a fellow's will—*
> *It's all in the state of mind.*

If you think you are outclassed, you are—
You've got to think high to rise.
You've got to be sure of yourself before
You can ever win a prize.

Life's battles don't always go
To the stronger or faster man;
But soon or late the man who wins
Is the man who thinks he can.

It can do no harm if you commit this poem to memory and use it as a part of your working equipment in the development of your Self-Confidence.

Somewhere in your makeup there is a "subtle something" which, if it were aroused by the proper outside influence, would carry you to heights of achievement such as you have never before anticipated. Just as a master player can take hold of a violin and make it pour forth the most beautiful and entrancing strains of music, so is there some outside influence that can take hold of your mind and cause you to go forth into the field of your chosen endeavor and play a glorious symphony of success. No one knows what hidden forces lie dormant within *you.* You, yourself, do not know your capacity for achievement, and you never will know until you come in contact with the particular stimulus that arouses you to greater action and extends your vision, develops your Self-Confidence, and moves you with a deeper *desire* to achieve.

It is not unreasonable to expect that some statement, some idea, or some stimulating word of this course on the Law of Success will serve as the needed stimulus that will reshape your destiny and redirect your thoughts and energies along a pathway that will lead you, finally, to your coveted goal in life. It is strange but true that the most important turning points of life often come at the most unexpected times and in the most unexpected ways.

I have in mind a typical example of this, and of what a person can accomplish when he or she awakens to a full understanding of the value of Self-Confidence. The incident to which I refer happened in the city of Chicago, while I was engaged in the work of character analysis.

One day a homeless man presented himself at my office and asked for an interview. As I looked up from my work and greeted him, he said, "I have come to see the man who wrote this little book," and he removed from his pocket a copy of a book entitled *Self-Confidence*, which I had written many years previously. "It must have been the hand of fate," he continued, "that slipped this book into my pocket yesterday afternoon, because I was about ready to go out there and punch a hole in Lake Michigan. I had about come to the conclusion that everything and everybody, including God, had it in for me, until I read this book and it gave me a new viewpoint and brought me the courage and the hope that sustained me through the night. I made up my mind that if I could see the man who wrote this book he could help me get on my feet again. Now I am here and I would like to know what you can do for a man like me."

While he was speaking I had been studying him from head to foot and I am frank to admit that down deep in my heart I did not believe there was anything I could do for him, but I did not wish to tell him so. The glassy stare in his eyes, the lines of discouragement in his face, the posture of his body, the ten days' growth of beard on his face, the nervous manner about this man all conveyed to me the impression that he was hopeless, but I did not have the heart to tell him.

So I asked him to sit down and tell me his whole story. I asked him to be perfectly frank and tell me, as nearly as possible, just what had brought him down to the ragged edge of life. I promised him that after I heard his entire story I would then tell him whether or not I could be of service to him. He related his story, in lengthy detail, the sum and substance of which was this: He had invested his entire fortune in a small manufacturing business. When the world war began in 1914, it was impossible for him to get the raw materials necessary for the operation of his factory, and he therefore failed. The loss of his money broke his heart and so disturbed his mind that he left his wife and children and went to live on the streets. He had actually brooded over his loss until he reached the point at which he was contemplating suicide.

After he had finished his story, I said to him: "I have listened to you with a great deal of interest, and I wish that there was something I could do to help you. *But there is absolutely nothing.*"

He became as pale as he will be when he is laid away in a coffin. He settled back in his chair and dropped his chin on his chest as much as to say, "That settles it." I waited for a few seconds, then said:

"While there is nothing that *I* can do for you, there is a man in this building to whom I will introduce you, if you wish, who can help you regain your lost fortune and put you back on your feet again." These words had barely fallen from my lips when he jumped up, grabbed me by the hands, and said, "For God's sake lead me to this man."

It was encouraging to note that he had asked this "for God's sake." This indicated that there was still a spark of hope within him, so I took him by the arm and led him out into the laboratory where my psychological tests in character analysis were conducted, and stood with him in front of what looked to be a curtain over a door. I pulled the curtain aside and uncovered a tall mirror in which he saw himself from head to foot. Pointing my finger at the glass, I said:

"There stands the man to whom I promised to introduce you. He is the only man in this world who can put you back on your feet again. And unless you sit down and become acquainted with that man, as you never became acquainted with him before, you might just as well go on over and 'punch a hole' in Lake Michigan, because you will be of no value to yourself or to the world until you know this man better."

He stepped over to the glass, rubbed his hands over his bearded face, studied himself from head to foot for a few moments, then stepped back, dropped his head, and began to weep. I knew that the lesson had

———

THE ONLY MAN WHO MAKES NO

MISTAKES IS THE MAN WHO NEVER

DOES ANYTHING. DO NOT BE AFRAID

OF MISTAKES, PROVIDING YOU DO NOT

MAKE THE SAME ONE TWICE.

—Theodore Roosevelt

———

been driven home, so I led him back to the elevator and sent him on his way. I never expected to see him again, and I doubted that the lesson would be sufficient to help him regain his place in the world, because he seemed too far gone for redemption. He seemed to be not only *down*, but almost *out*.

A few days later I met this man on the street. His transformation had been so complete that I hardly recognized him. He was walking briskly, with his head tilted back. That old, shifting, nervous posture of his body was gone. He was dressed in new clothes from head to foot. He looked prosperous and he felt prosperous. He stopped me and related what had happened to bring about his rapid transformation from a state of abject failure to one of hope and promise.

"I was just on my way to your office," he explained, "to bring you the good news. I went out the very day that I was in your office, a down-and-out tramp, and despite my appearance I sold myself at a salary of $3,000 a year. *Think of it, man, $3,000 a year!* And my employer advanced me money enough to buy some new clothes, as you can see for yourself. He also advanced me some money to send home to my family, and I am once more on the road to success. It seems like a dream when I think that only a few days ago I had lost hope and faith and courage, and was actually contemplating suicide.

"I was coming to tell you that one of these days, when you are least expecting me, I will pay you another visit, and when I do I will be a successful man. I will bring with me a blank check, signed and made payable to you, and you may fill in the amount because you have saved me from myself by introducing me to myself—that self I never knew until you stood me in front of that mirror and pointed out the real me."

As he turned and departed into the crowded streets of Chicago, I saw, for the first time in my life, what strength and power and possibility lie hidden in the mind of the person who has never discovered the value of *self-reliance*. Then and there I made up my mind that I, too, would stand in front of that same mirror and point an accusing finger at myself for not having discovered the lesson that I had helped another to learn. I did stand before that same mirror. And as I did so, I then and there fixed in my mind, as my *definite purpose* in life, the determination to help men and women discover the forces that lie sleeping within them. The book you hold in your hands is evidence that my definite purpose is being carried out.

The man whose story I have related here is now the president of one of the largest and most successful concerns of its kind in America, with a business that extends from coast to coast and from Canada to Mexico.

A short while after the incident just related, a woman came to my office for personal analysis. She was then a teacher in the Chicago public schools. I gave her an analysis chart and asked her to fill it out. She had been at work on the chart but a few minutes when she came to my desk, handed back the chart, and said, "I do not believe I will fill this out." I asked her why she had decided not to fill out the chart, and she replied: "To be perfectly frank with you, one of the questions in this chart started me thinking and I now know what is wrong with me. Therefore I feel it unnecessary to pay you a fee to analyze me." With that the woman went away and I did not hear from her for two years. She went to New York City, became a writer of advertising copy for one of the largest agencies in the country, and her income at the time she wrote me was $10,000 a year. *[In today's terms, and depending on the nature of the work or the company, this would be in the range of $175,000 to $200,000.]*

This woman later sent me a check to cover the cost of my analysis fee because she felt that the fee had been earned, even though I did not render her the service that I usually render my clients. It is impossible for anyone to foretell what seemingly insignificant incident may lead to an important turning point in one's career, but there is no denying that these "turning points" may be more readily recognized by those who have well-developed confidence in themselves.

One of the irreparable losses is the lack of knowledge that there is a definite method through which Self-Confidence can be developed in any person of average intelligence. What an immeasurable loss it is to civilization that young men and women are not taught this known method of developing Self-Confidence before they complete their schooling, for no one who lacks faith in themself is really educated in the proper sense of the term.

Oh, what glory and satisfaction would be the happy heritage of the man or woman who could pull aside the curtain of *fear* that hangs over humanity and shuts out the sunlight of understanding that Self-Confidence brings, wherever it is in evidence.

Where *fear* controls, noteworthy achievement becomes an impossibility. This brings to mind the definition of *fear* as stated by a great philosopher:

"Fear is the dungeon of the mind into which it runs and hides and seeks seclusion. Fear brings on superstition, and superstition is the dagger with which hypocrisy assassinates the soul."

In front of the typewriter on which I am writing the manuscripts for this course hangs a sign with the following wording, in big letters:

"Day by day in every way I am becoming more *successful*."

A skeptic who read that sign asked if I really believed "that stuff" and I replied, "Of course not. All it ever did for me was to help me get out of the coal mines, where I started as a laborer, and find a place in the world in which I am serving upwards of 100,000 people, in whose minds I am planting the same positive thought that this sign brings out. Therefore, why should I believe in it?"

As this man started to leave, he remarked, "Well, perhaps there *is* something to this sort of philosophy, after all, for I have always been afraid that I would be a failure, and so far my fears have been thoroughly realized."

You are condemning yourself to poverty, misery, and failure, or you are driving yourself on toward the heights of great achievement,

LOVE, BEAUTY, JOY, AND WORSHIP

ARE FOREVER BUILDING,

TEARING DOWN, AND REBUILDING

THE FOUNDATION

OF EACH MAN'S SOUL.

solely by the thoughts you think. If you *demand* success of yourself, and also back up this demand with intelligent action, you are sure to win. Bear in mind, though, that there is a difference between *demanding* success and just merely wishing for it. You should find out what this difference is and take advantage of it.

Do you remember what the Bible says about those who have faith as a grain of mustard seed? (Look it up in the book of Matthew, chapter 13.) Go at the task of developing Self-Confidence with at least that much faith if not more. Never mind "what *they* will say" because you might as well know that *"they"* will be of little aid to you in your climb up the mountainside of life toward the object of your *definite purpose.* You have within you all the power necessary to get whatever you want or need in this world, and about the best way to avail yourself of this power is to *believe in yourself.*

"Know thyself, man; know thyself."

This has been the advice of the philosophers all down the ages. When you *really* know yourself, you will know that there is nothing foolish about hanging a sign in front of you that reads "Day by day in every way I am becoming more successful," with due apologies to Emile Coué, who made this motto popular. I am not afraid to place this sort of suggestion in front of my desk, and, what is more to the point, I am not afraid to believe that it will influence me so that I will become a more positive and aggressive human being.

More than twenty-five years ago I learned my first lesson in Self-Confidence building. One night I was sitting before an open fireplace, listening to a conversation between some older men on the subject of capital and labor. Without invitation I joined the conversation and said something about employers and employees settling their differences on the Golden Rule basis. My remarks attracted the attention of one of the men, who turned to me with a look of surprise on his face, and said:

"Why, you are a bright boy, and if you would go out and get a schooling you would make your mark in the world."

His remark fell on fertile ears. It was the first time that anyone outside my family had ever told me that I was bright, or that I might accomplish anything worthwhile in life. It started me thinking, and the more I allowed my mind to dwell on those thoughts, the more certain I became that the remark had behind it a possibility.

It might be truthfully stated that whatever service I am rendering the world and whatever good I accomplish should be credited to that offhand remark.

Suggestions such as this are often powerful, and none the less so when they are both deliberate and self-expressed. Go back now to the Self-Confidence formula and master it, for it will lead you into the "powerhouse" of your own mind, where you will tap a force that can be made to carry you to the very top of the ladder of success.

Others will believe in you only when you believe in yourself. They will "tune in" on your thoughts and feel toward you just as you feel toward yourself. The law of mental telepathy takes care of this. You are continuously broadcasting what you think of yourself, and if you have no faith in yourself, others will pick up the vibrations of your thoughts and mistake them for their own. Once you understand the law of mental telepathy, you will know why Self-Confidence is the third of the seventeen laws of success.

You should be cautioned, however, to learn the difference between Self-Confidence, which is based on sound knowledge of what you know and what you can do, and egotism, which is based only on what you *wish* you knew or could do. Learn the difference between these two terms or you will make yourself boring, ridiculous, and annoying to people of culture and understanding. Self-Confidence is something that should never be proclaimed or announced except through intelligent performance of constructive deeds.

If you have Self-Confidence, those around you will discover this fact. Let them make the discovery. They will feel proud of their alertness in having made the discovery, and you will be free from the suspicion of egotism. Opportunity never stalks the person with a highly developed state of egotism, but brickbats and ugly remarks do. Opportunity forms affinities much more easily and quickly with Self-Confidence than it does with egotism. Self-praise is never a proper measure of self-reliance. Bear this in mind and let your Self-Confidence speak only through the tongue of constructive service rendered without fuss or flurry.

Self-Confidence is the product of knowledge. Know yourself, know how much you know (and how little), why you know it, and how you are going to use it. Four-flushers come to grief; therefore, do not pretend to know more than you actually do know. There's no use of pretense, because any educated person will measure you quite accurately after hearing you speak for three minutes. What you really are will speak so loudly that what you claim you are will not be heard.

If you heed this warning, the last few pages of this one lesson may mark one of the most important turning points of your life.

Believe in yourself but do not *tell* the world what you can do. *Show it!*

DISCONTENTMENT—
AN AFTER-THE-LESSON VISIT WITH THE AUTHOR

The marker stands at the entrance gate of life and writes "Poor Fool"
on the brow of the wise man and "Poor Sinner" on the brow of the saint.

The supreme mystery of the universe is life! We come here without our consent, from whence we know not. We go away without our consent, whither we know not.

We are eternally trying to solve this great riddle of *life*, and for what purpose and to what end?

That we are placed on this earth for a definite reason there can be no doubt by any thinker. May it not be possible that the power which placed us here will know what to do with us when we pass on beyond the Great Divide?

Would it not be a good plan to give the Creator who placed us here on earth credit for having enough intelligence to know what to do with us after we pass on? Or should we assume the intelligence and the ability to control the future life in our own way? May it not be possible that we can cooperate with the Creator very intelligently by assuming to control our conduct on this earth to the end that we may be decent to one another and do all the good we can in all the ways we can during this life, leaving the hereafter to one who probably knows, better than we, what is best for us?

From birth until death, the mind is always reaching out for what it does not possess.

The little child, playing with its toys on the floor, sees another child with a different toy and immediately tries to lay hands on that toy.

Adults continue to pursue what they perceive as bigger, better, and more toys; the more the better.

F. W. Woolworth, the 5 and 10 Cent Stores king, stood on Fifth Avenue in New York City and gazed upward at the tall Metropolitan Building and said, "How wonderful! I will build one much taller." The crowning achievement of his life was measured by the Woolworth Building. That building stands as a temporary symbol of man's nature to excel the handiwork of other men. *A monument to the vanity of man, with but little else to justify its existence!*

———————

The little ragged newsboy on the street stands, with wide-open mouth, and envies the businessman as he alights from his automobile at the curb and starts into his office. "How happy I would be," the newsboy says to himself, "if I owned a car like that." And the businessman, as he sits at his desk in his office, thinks how happy he would be if he could add another million dollars to his already overswollen bankroll.

The grass is always sweeter on the other side of the fence says the jackass, as he stretches his neck in the attempt to get to it.

Let a crowd of boys into an apple orchard and they will pass by the nice mellow apples on the ground. The red, juicy ones hanging dangerously high at the top of the tree look much more tempting, and up the tree they will go.

The married man takes a sheepish glance at the ladies on the street and thinks how fortunate he would be if his wife were as pretty as they. Perhaps she is much prettier, but he misses that beauty because —well, because "the grass is always sweeter on the other side of the fence."

Happiness is always just around the bend; always in sight but just out of reach. Life is never complete, no matter what we have or how much of it we possess. One thing calls for something else to go with it.

You long for a home—just a plain little house sitting off in the edge of the woods. You build it, but it is not complete; now you must have shrubbery and flowers and landscaping to go with it. Still it is not complete; you must have a beautiful fence around it, with a graveled driveway.

This calls for a second car and a garage.

All these little touches have been added, but to no avail. The place is now too small. You must have a house with more rooms. The Ford must be replaced by a Cadillac.

On and on the story goes, ad infinitum!

You receive a salary sufficient to keep yourself and your family fairly comfortable. Then comes a promotion, with an advance in salary of $1,000 a year. Do you put the extra $1,000 away in a savings account and continue living as before? You do nothing of the sort. Immediately you must trade the old car in for a new one. A porch must be added to the house. Someone needs a new wardrobe. The table must be set with better food. . . . At the end of the year are you better off with such an increase? Not at all! The more you get the more you want, and the rule applies to the millionaire as much as it does to someone with only a few thousand dollars.

A young man selects the girl of his choice, believing he cannot live without her. After he gets her he is not sure that he can live with her. If a man remains a bachelor he wonders why he is so stupid as to deprive himself of the joys of married life. If he marries he wonders how she happened to catch him off guard long enough to "harpoon" him.

And the god of destiny cries out "O fool, O fool! You are damned if you do and you are damned if you don't."

At every crossroad of life the imps of discontentment stand in the shadows of the background, with a grin of mockery on their faces, crying, "Take the road of your own choice! We will get you in the end!"

At last many become disillusioned and begin to learn that happiness and contentment are not of this world. Then begins the search for the password that will open the door to some world of which we know nothing. Surely there must be happiness on the other side of the Great Divide. In desperation the tired, careworn heart turns to religion for hope and encouragement.

But one's troubles are not over; they are just starting!

In the midst of sectarian claims and counterclaims, we become undecided. Not knowing whether to turn this way or that, we wonder which brand of religion offers the safest passageway, until hope vanishes. As expressed in the Rubayat of Omar Khayyam (in the Fitzgerald translation):

Myself when young did eagerly frequent
Doctor and Saint and heard great argument
About it and about; but evermore
Came out by the same door where in I went.

Always seeking but never finding—this might describe the human struggle for happiness and contentment. We try one religion after another, finally joining the "Big Church" that the world has named the "damned." Our minds become eternal question marks, searching hither and yon for an answer to the questions "Whence and Whither?"

The worldly hope men set their Hearts upon
Turns Ashes—or it prospers; and anon,
Like Snow upon the Desert's Dusty Face
Lighting a little Hour or two—is gone.

Life is an everlasting question mark.

That which we want most is always in the embryonic distance of the future. Our power to acquire is always a decade or so behind our power to *desire*.

And if we catch up with the thing we want, we no longer want it!

Our favorite author is a hero and a genius until we meet him or her and learn the sad truth that this author is only human. As Emerson wrote, "How often must we learn this lesson? People cease to interest us when we find their limitations. The only sin is limitation. As soon as you once come up with a man's limitations, it is all over with him."

How beautiful the mountain yonder in the distance. But the moment we draw near it we find it to be nothing but a wretched collection of rocks and dirt and trees.

Out of this truth grew the oft-repeated adage "Familiarity breeds contempt."

Beauty and happiness and contentment are states of mind. They can never be enjoyed except through vision of the afar. The most beautiful painting by Rembrandt becomes a mere smudge of daubed paint if we come too near it.

Destroy the hope of unfinished dreams in a person's heart and he or she is finished.

The moment we cease to cherish the vision of future achievement we are through. Nature has built us so that our greatest and only lasting happiness is that which we feel in the pursuit of some yet unattained object. Anticipation is sweeter than realization. That which is at hand does not satisfy. The only enduring satisfaction is that which comes to the person who keeps alive in their heart the hope of future achievement. When that hope dies, write *finis* across the human heart.

Life's greatest inconsistency is that most of what we believe is not true. Russell Conwell wrote an extremely popular lecture called "Acres of Diamonds." The central idea of the lecture was that one need not seek opportunity in the distance; that opportunity may be found in the vicinity of one's birth. Perhaps, but how many believe it?

Opportunity may be found wherever one really looks for it, and nowhere else! To most of us the picking looks better on the other side of the fence. How futile it is to urge one to try their luck in their little hometown, when it is human nature to look for opportunity in some other locality.

Do not worry because the grass looks sweeter on the other side of the fence. Nature intended it so. Thus does she allure us and groom us for the lifelong task of *growth through struggle*.

SOME MODERN "MIRACLES"

Some people doubt the authenticity of the Bible because they believe that if miracles could have been performed over two thousand years ago, before the dawn of science, while the world was still steeped in illiteracy and superstition, it should be just as easy to perform them today.

I have read the Bible very carefully, some parts of it many times, and I am convinced that it contains no account of any alleged miracle that has not been more than matched in our times, in the open light of science. Moreover, these modern day miracles are subject to analysis and proof. Any child of average intelligence, above the age of twelve years, may understand the miracles of today.

The Greatest of All Miracles Is Faith

This is a wonderful age. It is an age of provable miracles. These are the modern miracles that have impressed me most:

The miracle which Edison performed when, after thousands of temporary failures, he wrested from Nature the secret by which the sound of the human voice may be recorded on a wax record and re-produced perfectly. That miracle was wrought through Edison's *faith*. He had no precedent to guide him. No other person had ever performed such a miracle.

One of the strange things about this miracle is that Edison began at the very outset to experiment with the rudimentary principle and the mechanical apparatus through which the talking machine *[audio recorder and playback]* was later revealed. The principle was vibration and the apparatus was a tube made of wax which revolved on a cylinder that contacted the point of a needle. Nothing but faith could have enabled Edison to have begun so near the source of the secret that he sought, and nothing but faith could have given him the persistence to stick to his experiments through more than ten thousand failures.

It was faith that enabled Edison to concentrate his mind on the task which led him through many thousand failures before he created the incandescent lamp with which he harnessed the energy known as electricity and made it serve to light the world.

It was faith that prompted Edison to continue his experiments with the moving-picture machine *[camera and projector]* until he made it actually perform the miracle that he must have seen through his own Imagination before he even began.

It was faith that sustained the Wright brothers through the years of hazardous experiments before they conquered the air and created a machine that excels, in both speed and endurance, the swiftest bird.

It was faith that prompted Christopher Columbus to set sail on an uncharted sea, in search of a land that, as far as he was concerned, existed nowhere except in his own Imagination. Considering the frailties of the little sailing vessels in which he embarked on that momentous voyage, his faith must have been of the kind that enables a person to see the object of their labor already attained, even before they begin.

It was faith that inspired Copernicus to see that portion of a universe which human eyes had never beheld. It was at a time in the history of the world when such revelations as those he wrought through his faith and his crude mechanical equipment might mean his destruction at the hands of his contemporaries who *believed* there were no stars except those within range of the human eyes.

It was faith that enabled "Golden Rule" Nash to transform a failing business into a shining example of success, by dealing with his customers on the basis of a rule that Christ recommended nearly two thousand years earlier. Arthur Nash turned to faith after every other business principle failed him. By following the Golden Rule through the remainder of his life, Nash accumulated a vast fortune in money, to say nothing of leaving the world richer in spirit because of his example.

It was his faith in a cause that enabled Mahatma Gandhi of India to blend into a single mass the minds of more than two hundred million of his countrymen, every one of whom would do Gandhi's bidding, even though it meant immediate death. No other influence except faith could have performed this miracle. Because his mind is capable of sustained faith, Gandhi wields this power passively. Gandhi has proved that faith can accomplish that which trained soldiers and money and implements of warfare cannot achieve.

It was faith that cut the shackles of limitation from the mind of Professor Einstein and revealed to him mathematical principles that the world had not even suspected to exist. No fear-bound mind could have uncovered such a miracle.

It was faith that sustained our own beloved Washington and drove him on to victory in opposition to vastly superior physical forces—a form of faith born of his love for freedom for mankind.

The profound principle known as faith is as available to you as it ever was to any human being who has passed this way.

If your world is one of limitation, misery, and want, it is because you have not yet realized that you have in your own mind a laboratory that is equipped to engender the power of faith.

If we may judge the possibilities of the future by the achievements of the past, the miracles remaining to be uncovered are vastly greater in number and nature than those that have been revealed in the past. It is not yet revealed what our destiny may be.

This is an age of revelation!

Those who believe that the power of revelation passed away with the superstition and ignorance which prevailed a few hundred years ago have but little comprehension of our modern history.

Men like Edison, the Wright brothers, Columbus, Copernicus, Arthur Nash, Gandhi, Einstein, and Washington are all miracle men. They have removed the horizons of men's minds and discovered unto us new worlds. Ours is a day of miracles; and this is an age of faith.

The world is passing through an experience that will call for many forms of readjustment of human relationships. The real Leadership will be found among those who have great capacity for faith. There will be no place in the immediate future for the weaklings and those who still believe that miracles belong only in the age of the dead past, or that they are wrapped up in unfathomable mystery.

The miracles of the future will be revealed by science.

Lesson Four

The Habit of Saving

THE ONLY LASTING FAVOR

WHICH THE PARENT

MAY CONFER UPON THE CHILD

IS THAT OF HELPING THE CHILD

TO HELP ITSELF.

Lesson Four

The Habit of Saving

"You Can Do It if You Believe You Can!"

To advise one to save money, without describing *how* to save, would be somewhat like drawing a picture of a horse and writing under it, "This is a horse." It is obvious to all that the saving of money is one of the essentials for success, but the big question uppermost in the minds of the majority of those who do not save is: "How can I do it?"

The saving of money is solely a matter of *habit*. For that reason, this lesson begins with a brief analysis of the law of habit.

It is literally true that an individual, through the law of habit, shapes their own personality. Through repetition, any act indulged in a few times becomes a habit, and the mind appears to be nothing more than a mass of motivating forces growing out of our daily habits.

When once fixed in the mind, a habit voluntarily impels one to action. For example, follow a given route to your daily work, or to some other place that you frequently visit, and very soon the habit has been formed and your mind will lead you over that route without thought on your part. Moreover, if you start out with the intention of traveling in another direction, without keeping the thought of the change in routes constantly in mind, you will find yourself following the old route.

Public speakers have found that the telling over and over again of a story, which may be based on pure fiction, brings into play the law of habit, and very soon they forget whether the story is true or not.

LIMITATION BUILT THROUGH HABIT

Millions of people go through life in poverty and want because they have made destructive use of the law of habit. Not understanding either the law of habit or the law of attraction through which "like attracts like," those who remain in poverty seldom realize that they are where they are as the result of their own acts.

Fix in your mind the thought that your ability is limited to a given earning capacity and you will never earn more than that—the law of habit will set up a definite limitation of the amount you can earn. Your subconscious will accept this limitation, and very soon you will feel yourself "slipping" until finally you will become so hedged in by a fear of poverty (one of the six basic fears) that opportunity will no longer knock at your door; your doom will be sealed; your fate fixed.

The formation of the Habit of Saving does not mean that you shall limit your earning capacity; it means just the opposite—that you shall apply this law so that it not only conserves what you do earn, in a systematic manner, but it also places you in the way of greater opportunity and gives you the vision, the Self-Confidence, the Imagination, the Enthusiasm, the Initiative and Leadership to actually increase your earning capacity.

Stating this great law in another way, when you thoroughly understand the law of habit you may ensure yourself success in the great game of moneymaking by "playing both ends of that game against the middle."

You proceed in this manner:

First, through your Definite Chief Aim, you set up in your mind an accurate, definite description of what you want, including the amount of money you intend to earn. Then your subconscious mind takes over this picture you have created and uses it as a blueprint, chart, or map by which to mold your thoughts and actions into practical plans for attaining the object of your chief aim, or purpose. Through the law of habit you keep the object of your Definite Chief Aim fixed in your mind (in the manner described in Lesson Two) until it becomes firmly and permanently implanted there. This practice will destroy the poverty consciousness and set up in its place a prosperity consciousness. You will actually begin to *demand* prosperity, you will begin to expect it, you will begin to prepare yourself to receive it and to use it wisely, thus paving the way or setting the stage for the development of the Habit of Saving.

Second, having in this manner increased your earning power, you will then make further use of the law of habit by provision—in your written statement of your Definite Chief Aim—for saving a definite proportion of all the money you earn.

Therefore, as your earnings increase, your savings will, likewise, increase in proportion.

By ever urging yourself on and demanding of yourself increased earning power, on the one hand, and by systematically laying aside a definite amount of all your earnings, on the other hand, you will soon reach the point at which you have removed all imaginary limitations from your own mind and you will then be well started on the road toward financial independence.

Nothing could be more practical—or more easily accomplished—than this.

Reverse the operation of the law of habit, by setting up in your mind the fear of poverty, and very soon this fear will reduce your earning capacity until you will be barely able to earn sufficient money to take care of your actual necessities.

The publishers of newspapers could create a panic in a week's time by filling their columns with news items concerning the actual business failures of the country, despite the fact that few businesses, compared with the total number in existence, actually fail. The so-called "crime waves" are very largely the products of sensational journalism. A single murder case, when exploited by the newspapers of the country through scare headlines, is sufficient to start a regular wave of similar crimes in various localities.

We are the victims of our habits, no matter who we are or what may be our life-calling. Any idea that is deliberately fixed in the mind, or any idea that is permitted to set itself up in the mind as the result of suggestion, environment, the influence of associates, is sure to cause us to indulge in acts that conform to the nature of the idea.

Form the habit of thinking and talking of prosperity and abundance, and very soon material evidence of these will begin to manifest itself in the nature of wider opportunity, and new and unexpected opportunity.

Like attracts like! If you are in business and have formed the habit of talking and thinking about business being bad, business will be bad. One pessimist, providing that person is permitted to continue his or her destructive influence long enough, can destroy the work of half a dozen competent people, and the pessimist will do it by setting adrift in the minds of his or her associates the thought of poverty and failure.

Don't be this type of man or woman.

One of the most successful bankers in the state of Illinois has this sign hanging in his private office:

"We talk and think only of abundance here. If you have a tale of woe please keep it, as we do not want it."

No business firm wants the services of a pessimist, and those who understand the law of attraction and the law of habit will no more tolerate the pessimist than they would permit a burglar to roam around their place of business, because just one such person will destroy the usefulness of those around them.

In tens of thousands of homes, the general topic of conversation is poverty and want, and that is just what they are getting. They think of poverty, they talk of poverty, they accept poverty as their lot in life. They reason that because their ancestors had all been poor, they too must remain poor.

The poverty consciousness is the result of the habit of thinking of and fearing poverty. "The thing I had feared has come upon me!"

THE SLAVERY OF DEBT

Debt is a merciless master, a fatal enemy of the savings habit. Poverty alone is sufficient to kill off ambition, destroy Self-Confidence, and destroy hope, but add to it the burden of debt and all who are victims of these two cruel taskmasters are practically doomed to failure.

No one can do their best work, no one can find self-expression in terms that command respect, no one can either create or carry out a *definite purpose* in life, with heavy debt hanging over his or her head. Someone bound in the slavery of debt is just as helpless as the slave who is bound by ignorance, or by actual chains.

I have a very close friend whose income is $1,000 a month. His wife loves "society" and she tries to make a $20,000 showing on a $12,000 income, with the result that this poor fellow is usually about $8,000 in debt. From the mother, every member of his family has also acquired the spending habit. The children, two girls and one boy, are now of the age when they are thinking of going to college, but this is impossible because of the father's debts. The result is dissension between the father and his children, which makes the entire family unhappy and miserable.

———

YOU ARE A HUMAN MAGNET

AND YOU ARE CONSTANTLY

ATTRACTING TO YOU PEOPLE

WHOSE CHARACTERS

HARMONIZE WITH YOUR OWN.

———

It is terrible to even think of going through life like a prisoner in chains, bound down and owned by somebody else on account of debts. The accumulation of debts is a habit. It starts in a small way and grows to enormous proportions slowly, step by step, until finally those debts take charge of one's very soul.

Thousands of young people start their married lives with unnecessary debts hanging over their heads and never manage to get out from under the load. After the novelty of marriage begins to wear off, the couple begins to feel the embarrassment of want, and this feeling grows until it leads, oftentimes, to open dissatisfaction with one another and eventually to the divorce court.

Those bound by the slavery of debt have no time or inclination to set up or work out ideals, with the result that they drift downward with time until they eventually begin to set up limitations in their own minds, and by these they hedge themselves behind prison walls of fear and doubt from which they never escape.

No sacrifice is too great to avoid the misery of debt!

"Think of what you owe yourself and those who are dependent upon you, and resolve to be no man's debtor" is the advice of one very successful man whose early chances were destroyed by debt. This man, however, had been able to throw off the habit of buying what he did not need and eventually he worked his way out of slavery.

Most of those who develop the habit of debt will not be so fortunate as to come to their senses in time to save themselves, because debt is something like quicksand—it has a tendency to draw its victim deeper and deeper into the mire.

The fear of poverty is one of the most destructive of the six basic fears described in Lesson Three. The person who becomes hopelessly in debt is seized with this fear, their ambition and Self-Confidence become paralyzed, and they sink gradually into oblivion.

There are two types of debts, and these are so different in nature that I will describe them here:

- Debts incurred for luxuries that become a dead loss
- Debts incurred in the course of professional or business trading which represent service or merchandise that can be converted back into assets

The first type of debt is the one to be avoided. The second type may be indulged in, providing the one incurring the debts uses judgment and does not go beyond the bounds of reasonable limitation. The moment a person buys beyond his or her limitations, that person enters the realm of speculation, and speculation swallows more of its victims than it enriches.

Practically all people who live beyond their means are tempted to speculate with the hope that they may recoup, at a single turn of the wheel of fortune, so to speak, their entire indebtedness. The wheel generally stops at the wrong place and, far from finding themselves out of debt, those who indulge in speculation are bound more closely as slaves of debt.

The fear of poverty breaks down the willpower of its victims and they then find themselves unable to restore their lost fortunes. What is still more sad, they lose all ambition to extricate themselves from the slavery of debt.

In wartime, millions face combat without flinching, knowing that death might overtake them at any moment. But those same people, when facing the fear of poverty, often cringe and out of sheer desperation, which paralyzes their reason, sometimes commit suicide.

The person who is free from debt may whip poverty and achieve outstanding financial success, but, if bound by debt, such achievement is only a remote possibility, and never a probability.

Fear of poverty is a negative, destructive state of mind. Moreover, one negative state of mind has a tendency to attract other similar states of mind. For example, the fear of poverty may attract the fear of ill health, and these two may attract the fear of old age, so that the victim finds themself poverty-stricken, in ill health, and actually growing old long before the time they should begin to show signs of old age.

Millions of untimely, nameless graves have been filled by this cruel state of mind known as the fear of poverty.

About ten years ago a young man held a responsible position with the City National Bank of New York City. Through living beyond his income he incurred a large amount of debt, which caused him to worry until this destructive habit began to show up in his work and he was dismissed from the bank's service.

He secured another position, but at less money, and his creditors embarrassed him to such a degree that he decided to resign and move to another city, where he hoped to escape them until he had accumulated sufficient money to pay off his indebtedness. Creditors have a way of tracing debtors, and very soon they were again close on the heels of this young man, whose employer found out about his indebtedness and dismissed him from his position.

He then searched in vain for employment for two months. One cold night he went to the top of one of the tall buildings on Broadway and jumped off. Debt had claimed another victim.

COMMENTARY

As you read Napoleon Hill's comments about debt and poverty, the stories may seem melodramatic and you may feel that they don't bear much relationship to conditions in your world. People's sense of responsibility and personal obligation has changed, and financial debt no longer has the taint about it that it had in Hill's day. After all, the America Hill was writing about was before the crash of 1929 and the Great Depression that followed. It was before the modern stock market, the antitrust laws, the FTC, and the Federal Reserve; well before credit cards, and light years before e-commerce and dot-com billionaires.

The times have indeed changed, but the changing social mores have not altered the basic principles of success. The tales that Hill tells may be from another era, but as was stated earlier, the philosophy they convey has made more millionaires than any other philosophy. Those stories inspired people to succeed during the Great Depression, and through the Second World War, and they were the touchstone for many who made America boom during the '50s and the '60s. It was those same stories and the philosophy behind them that made some of the most successful entrepreneurs of the baby boom generation, and for those who look past the words and learn the lessons, it will be the making of the new-millennium millionaires.

MASTER THE FEAR OF POVERTY

To whip the fear of poverty one must take two very definite steps if one is in debt. First, quit the habit of buying on credit, and follow this by gradually paying off the debts that you have already incurred.

Being free from the worry of indebtedness, you are ready to revamp the habits of your mind and redirect your course toward prosperity. Adopt, as a part of your Definite Chief Aim, the habit of saving a regular portion of your income, even if it is no more than a penny a day. Very soon this habit will begin to take hold of your mind and you will actually get joy out of saving.

Any habit may be discontinued by building in its place some other and more desirable habit. The spending habit must be replaced by the saving habit by all who wish to attain financial independence.

Merely to discontinue an undesirable habit is not enough, as such habits have a tendency to reappear unless the place they had occupied in the mind is filled by some other habit of a different nature.

The discontinuance of a habit leaves a hole in the mind, and this hole must be filled with some other form of habit or the old one will return and claim its place.

Throughout this course many psychological formulas, which you are requested to memorize and practice, have been described. You will find such a formula in Lesson Three, the object of which is to develop Self-Confidence.

These formulas may be assimilated so that they become a part of your mental machinery, through the law of habit, if you will follow the instructions for their use which accompany each of them.

It is assumed that you are striving to attain financial independence. The accumulation of money is not difficult—once you have mastered the fear of poverty and developed in its place the Habit of Saving.

I would be greatly disappointed to know that any student of the course got the impression from anything in this or any of the other lessons that success is measured by dollars alone.

However, money does represent an important factor in success, and it must be given its proper value in any philosophy intended to help people in becoming useful, happy, and prosperous.

The cold, cruel, relentless truth is that in this age of materialism a person is no more than so many grains of sand, which may be blown helter-skelter by every stray wind of circumstance, unless entrenched behind the power of money!

Genius may offer many rewards to those who possess it, but the fact still remains that genius without money with which to give it expression is but an empty honor.

The person without money is at the mercy of the person who has it—regardless of the amount of ability one may possess, the training they have had, or their native genius or natural gifts.

There is no escape from the fact that people will weigh you very largely in the light of bank balances, no matter who you are or what you can do. The first question that arises in the minds of most people when they meet a stranger is how much money does he or she have? If they have money they are welcomed into homes, and business opportunities are thrown their way. All sorts of attention is lavished on them. They are entitled to the best of the land.

But if, for example, a man's shoes are run down at the heels, his clothes are not pressed, his collar is dirty, and he shows plainly the

WHO TOLD YOU

IT COULDN'T BE DONE?

AND WHAT GREAT ACHIEVEMENT

HAS HE TO HIS CREDIT

THAT ENTITLES HIM TO USE

THE WORD "IMPOSSIBLE"

SO FREELY?

signs of impoverished finances, woe be his lot, for the passing crowd will step on his toes and blow the smoke of disrespect in his face.

These are not pretty statements but they have one virtue: *they are true*. This tendency to judge people by the money they have, or their power to control money, is not confined to any one class of people. We all have a touch of it, whether we recognize it or not.

Thomas A. Edison is one of the best-known and most respected inventors in the world because he is also a good businessman. It is no misstatement of facts to say that he may have remained a practically unknown person had he not followed the habit of saving his money, which allowed him to turn his inventions into a business.

Henry Ford never would have got to first base with his "horseless carriage" had he not developed, quite early in life, the Habit of Saving. Moreover, had Ford not conserved his resources and hedged himself behind their power, he would have been swallowed up by his competitors or those who covetously desired to take his business away from him, long, long years ago.

Many of us have gone a very long way toward success, only to stumble and fall, never again to rise, because of lack of money in times of emergency. The mortality rate in business each year, due to lack of reserve capital for emergencies, is stupendous. To this one cause are due more of the business failures than to all other causes combined.

Reserve funds are essential in the successful operation of business!

Likewise, savings accounts are essential to success on the part of individuals. Without a savings fund the individual suffers in two ways: first, by their inability to seize opportunities that come only to the person with some ready cash, and, second, by embarrassment due to some unexpected emergency calling for cash.

It might also be said that the individual suffers in still a third respect by not developing the saving habit, and that is through the lack of certain other qualities essential for success which grow out of the practice of the Habit of Saving.

The nickels, dimes, and pennies that the average person allows to slip through their fingers would, if systematically saved and properly put to work, eventually bring financial independence.

Through the courtesy of a building and loan association, the table on the following page has been compiled showing what a monthly saving of $5, $10, $25, or $50 will amount to at the end of ten years. These figures are startling when one considers that the average person spends from $5 to $50 a month for useless merchandise or so-called "entertainment."

The making and saving of money is a science, yet the rules by which money is accumulated are so simple that anyone may follow them. The main prerequisite is a willingness to subordinate the present to the future, by eliminating unnecessary expenditures for luxuries.

A young man, who was earning only $20 a week as chauffeur for a prominent New York banker, was induced by his employer to keep an accurate account of every cent he spent for one week. The following is an itemized list of his expenses:

Cigarettes	$0.75
Chewing gum	$0.30
Soda fountain	$1.80
Cigars for associates	$1.50
Moving-picture show	$1.00
Shaves, including tips	$1.60
Newspaper, daily and Sunday	$0.22
Shoeshines	$0.30
	$7.47
Board and room	$12.00
Money on hand	$0.53
	$20.00

THE AMAZING WAY YOUR MONEY GROWS

Save $5 a Month (Only 17 cents a day)

	Amount Saved	Profit [at about 7% interest]	Savings Plus Profits	Withdrawal Value
1st year	$60.00	$4.30	$64.30	$61.30
2nd year	$120.00	$16.55	$136.00	$125.00
3rd year	$180.00	$36.30	$216.30	$191.55
4th year	$240.00	$64.00	$304.00	$216.20
5th year	$300.00	$101.00	$401.00	$338.13
6th year	$360.00	$140.00	$500.00	$414.75
7th year	$420.00	$197.10	$617.00	$495.43
8th year	$480.00	$157.05	$737.50	$578.32
9th year	$540.00	$324.95	$864.95	$687.15
10th year	$600.00	$400.00	$1000.00	$1000.00

Save $10 a Month (Only 33 cents a day)

	Amount Saved	Profit [at about 7% interest]	Savings Plus Profits	Withdrawal Value
1st year	$120.00	$8.60	$128.60	$122.60
2nd year	$240.00	$33.11	$273.11	$250.00
3rd year	$360.00	$72.60	$432.60	$383.10
4th year	$480.00	$128.00	$608.00	$520.40
5th year	$600.00	$202.00	$802.00	$676.25
6th year	$720.00	$280.00	$1000.00	$829.50
7th year	$840.00	$394.20	$1234.20	$990.85
8th year	$960.00	$514.10	$1474.10	$1156.64
9th year	$1080.00	$649.90	$1729.90	$1374.30
10th year	$1200.00	$800.00	$2000.00	$2000.00

Save $25 a Month (Only 83 cents a day)

	Amount Saved	Profit [at about 7% interest]	Savings Plus Profits	Withdrawal Value
1st year	$300.00	$21.50	$321.50	$306.50
2nd year	$600.00	$82.75	$682.75	$625.00
3rd year	$900.00	$181.50	$1081.50	$957.75
4th year	$1200.00	$320.00	$1520.00	$1301.00
5th year	$1500.00	$505.00	$2005.00	$1690.63
6th year	$1800.00	$700.00	$2500.00	$2073.75
7th year	$2100.00	$985.50	$3085.50	$2477.13
8th year	$2400.00	$1285.25	$3685.25	$2891.60
9th year	$2700.00	$1624.75	$4324.75	$3435.75
10th year	$3000.00	$2000.00	$5000.00	$5000.00

Save $50 a Month (Only $1.66 a day)

	Amount Saved	Profit [at about 7% interest]	Savings Plus Profits	Withdrawal Value
1st year	$600.00	$43.00	$643.00	$613.00
2nd year	$1200.00	$165.00	$1365.00	$1250.00
3rd year	$1800.00	$363.00	$2163.00	$1915.50
4th year	$2400.00	$640.00	$3040.00	$2602.00
5th year	$3000.00	$1010.00	$4010.00	$3381.25
6th year	$3600.00	$1400.00	$5000.00	$4147.50
7th year	$4200.00	$1971.00	$6171.00	$4954.25
8th year	$4800.00	$2570.50	$7370.00	$5783.20
9th year	$5400.00	$3249.50	$8649.50	$6871.50
10th year	$6000.00	$4000.00	$10,000.00	$10,000.00

EVERY FAILURE,

EVERY ADVERSITY,

EVERY HEARTACHE

MAY BE A BLESSING IN DISGUISE

PROVIDING IT SOFTENS

THE ANIMAL PORTION

OF OUR NATURE.

These figures tell a tragic story that might as well apply to thousands of other people as to the young man who kept this account. His actual saving out of $20 was only 53 cents. He spent $7.47 for items, every one of which could have been greatly reduced, and most of which could have been eliminated entirely. And if he also shaved himself and shined his own shoes, he could have saved every cent of the $7.47.

COMMENTARY

Wayne Wagner and Al Winnikoff, authors of Millionaire, *make a similar point in modern terms. They argue for investment in index funds, which are relatively secure and typically increase in value at a rate of more than 10 percent per year. They work backwards from the goal of saving a million dollars.*

If you begin investing at this age	Years to a million dollars at age 65	Monthly investment required	Daily investment required
25	40	$179	$5.97
30	35	$292	$9.73
35	30	$481	$16.03
40	25	$805	$28.63
45	20	$1382	$46.07
50	15	$2491	$83.03

Now turn back to the table compiled by the building and loan association and observe what the saving of $7.47 a week would amount to. Suppose the amount this young man actually saved had been only $25 a month; the saving would have increased to the sum of $5,000 by the end of the first ten years.

The young man in question was twenty-one years old at the time he kept this expense account. By the time he reached the age of thirty-one he could have had a substantial amount in the bank had he saved $25 a month, and this saving would have brought him many opportunities that would have led directly to financial independence.

Some who are shortsighted pseudophilosophers are fond of pointing to the fact that no one can become rich merely by saving a few dollars a week.

This may be true enough, as far as the reasoning goes (which is not very far), but the other side of the story is that the saving of even a small sum of money places one in a position where, oftentimes, even this small sum may enable one to take advantage of business opportunities that lead directly and quite rapidly to financial independence.

The table *[page 269]* showing what a saving of $5 a month will amount to at the end of ten years, should be copied and pasted on your mirror, where it will stare you in the face every morning when you get up and every night as you retire, providing you have not already acquired the habit of systematically saving money. This table should be reproduced, in letters and figures an inch tall, and placed on the walls of every public school throughout the land, where it might serve as a constant reminder to all children of the value of the savings habit.

COMMENTARY

A modern example might look something like this. Terry, a twenty-six-year-old professional, is earning $36,000 a year. Terry's monthly financial picture is as follows:

Income:	*$3,000*
Outgo:	
Taxes	*$900*
Food	*$200*
Rent and bills	*$750*
Car payment	*$200*
Car insurance	*$100*

Gas	$100
New clothes	$150
Credit card bills	$150
Student loan	$200
"Spending money"	$250
Total outgo:	$3,000

Terry is saving nothing. It seems impossible, with a car and an apartment and a professional wardrobe to keep up, let alone a college loan and a big credit card debt, which is how Terry pays for such things as birthday gifts, vacations, car repairs, and so forth. That $250 spending money vanishes on lunches, dinners out, toiletries, and other small things. How could Terry ever get ahead?

Terry has made some poor choices. The down payment on a new-car lease emptied the savings account, and car insurance is steep. A professional appearance can be important to success, but Terry has long since established a good basic wardrobe, making additional purchases unnecessary. With a credit card balance of over $4,000, Terry is paying more than $600 a year in interest, more than $50 a month. A cheaper apartment alone would provide enough money to pay off half the credit card debt in a year, saving another $300. The car lease is, unfortunately, an obligation Terry is locked into for two years, at the end of which time a new lease will have to be signed or the outright purchase would be several thousand dollars.

Terry decides to bite the bullet and moves to a cheaper apartment, freeing up $200 monthly. Half of that goes to credit card bills and the remainder is used to pay cash for purchases that otherwise would have been charged. Additionally, Terry decides to set aside $20 each week—not a large amount, but for Terry an important beginning.

At the end of a year, Terry will be only $1,200 in debt to credit card companies and able to retire that debt completely in six months more. At the end of that same year, Terry will have more than $1,000 in the bank. After the liberating moment when the last credit card bill is paid, there will be an extra $250 each month. But instead of spending that newly available cash, Terry will be in the grip of the saving habit and will devote all of it to savings, socking away $4,040 over the next twelve months.

Assuming the continuation of that annual savings of $4,040, there will be more than $10,500 in the bank by Terry's thirtieth birthday. And assuming just 3 percent growth and the annual savings contribution, Terry will reach the age of forty with more than $55,000. Having a healthy nest egg to fall back on is a great antidote to the fear of poverty, making it much easier to develop the self-confidence you need to pursue your Definite Chief Aim. How much easier would it be for you to take a risk if you knew that you had $55,000 backing you up?

Some years ago, before giving serious thought to the value of the savings habit, I made a personal account of the money that had slipped through my fingers. The amount was so alarming that it resulted in the writing of this lesson and adding The Habit of Saving as one of the seventeen laws of success.

Following is an itemized statement of that account:

Inherited; invested in automobile supply business with a friend who lost the entire amount in one year	$4,000
Extra money earned from sundry writing for magazines and newspapers, all spent uselessly	$3,600
Earned from training 3,000 salesmen, with the aid of the Law of Success philosophy, and invested in a magazine that was not a success because there was no reserve capital behind it	$30,000
Extra money earned from public addresses, lectures, etc., all of which was spent as it came in	$3,400
Estimated amount that could have been saved during a period of ten years out of regular earnings, at the rate of only $50 a month	$6,000
	$47,000

This amount, had it been saved and invested as received, in building and loan associations or in some other manner that would have earned compound interest, would have grown to the sum of $94,000 at the time this lesson is being written.

I have never been a victim of any of the usual habits, such as gambling, drinking, or excessive entertaining. It is almost unbelievable that someone whose habits of living are reasonably moderate could spend $47,000 within a little over ten years without having anything to show for the money. But it can be done!

I recall one occasion when the president of a large corporation sent me a check for $500 for an address I delivered at a banquet given for the employees, and I distinctly recall what went through my mind when I opened the letter and saw the check. I had wanted a new automobile and this check was exactly the amount required for the first payment. I had it spent before it had been in my hands thirty seconds.

Perhaps this is the experience of the majority of people. They think much more about how they will *spend* whatever they have than they do about *saving*. The idea of saving, and the Self-Control and self-sacrifice that would be needed to do so, is always accompanied by thoughts of an unpleasant nature. But oh, how it thrills one to think of spending.

There is a reason for this, and it is that most of us have developed the habit of spending while neglecting the Habit of Saving, and any idea that seldomly frequents the mind is not as welcome as the idea that frequents it often. In truth, the Habit of Saving can be made as fascinating as the habit of spending might seem, but not until it has become a regular, well-grounded, systematic habit. We like to do things that are often repeated, which is but another way of saying what the scientists have discovered: that we are victims of our habits.

The Habit of Saving requires more force of character than most people have developed, because saving means self-denial and sacrifice of amusements and pleasures in scores of different ways. For this very reason, one who develops the savings habit acquires, at the same time, many of the other needed habits that lead to success, especially Self-Control, Self-Confidence, courage, poise, and freedom from fear.

COMMENTARY

Though some people spend a great deal of money, it does not mean they are rich. In The Millionaire Next Door, *Thomas J. Stanley and William Danko reveal that spending is something most wealthy people avoid. Their research shows that:*

- *More than 80 percent of America's millionaires accumulated their own wealth—they did not inherit it.*

- *Most millionaires do not live in fancy neighborhoods but in the houses they owned when they began to accumulate their fortunes.*

- *Most millionaires drive mid-size American cars, not fancy imports, and one out of three of them always buys used cars.*

- *The average millionaire has an income of just over $130,000—their real wealth comes from their habit of saving 20 percent of their income.*

In short, most millionaires are not actors or Fortune 500 CEOs or athletes pulling down millions of dollars a season. They are people earning good but not fantastic incomes, who have made a habit of saving.

HOW MUCH SHOULD YOU SAVE?

The question of how much a person should save cannot be answered in a few words, for the amount each should save depends upon many conditions, some of which may be within one's control and some of which may not be.

Generally speaking, a salaried worker should apportion his or her income about as follows:

Savings Account	20 percent
Living: Clothes, Food, and Shelter	50 percent
Education	10 percent
Recreation	10 percent

Life Insurance	10 percent
	100 percent

The following, however, indicates the approximate distribution that the average person actually makes of their income:

Savings Account	*NOTHING*
Living: Clothes, Food, and Shelter	60 percent
Education	0 percent
Recreation	35 percent
Life Insurance	5 percent
	100 percent

An experienced analyst has said that he could tell very accurately, by examining anyone's personal monthly budget, what sort of a life that person is living. Moreover, the analyst will get most of the information from looking at the figure for the "recreation" item. This, then, is a figure to be watched as carefully as the greenhouse keeper watches the thermometer that controls the life and death of their plants.

Nothing in this lesson is intended as a sermon on morality, or on any other subject. We are dealing here with cold facts which, to a large extent, constitute the materials out of which success may be created.

Regardless, this is an appropriate place to state some facts which have such a direct bearing on the subject of achieving success that they cannot be omitted without weakening this entire course in general and this lesson in particular.

I am speaking not as a reformer! Nor am I preaching morals, as this field of useful endeavor is quite well covered by others who are able workers. What is here stated, therefore, is intended as a necessary part of a course of philosophy whose purpose is to mark a safe road over which one may travel to honorable achievement.

CAREFUL ANALYSIS OF 178 MEN

WHO ARE KNOWN TO BE SUCCESSFUL

DISCLOSED THE FACT

THAT ALL HAD FAILED

MANY TIMES BEFORE ARRIVING.

COMMENTARY

In the following section Napoleon Hill goes on at length citing examples of people spending their money on bootleg alcohol instead of saving. The editors have chosen to include these examples in this new edition as a short lesson in human nature. As you read the following section, in your mind replace the word liquor *with the words* drugs, video games, lottery tickets, *or any other current trend, and no doubt you will experience Hill's stories from 1927 suddenly becoming as contemporary as today's headlines.*

During 1926 I was in partnership with the late Don R. Mellett, who was, at that time, the publisher of the *Canton* (Ohio) *Daily News.* Mr. Mellett became interested in the Law of Success philosophy because it offered, as he believed, sound counsel to young men and young women who really wish to get ahead in life. Through the pages of the *Daily News* Mr. Mellett was conducting a fierce battle against the underworld forces of Canton. With the aid of detectives and investigators, some of whom were supplied by the governor of Ohio, Mr. Mellett and I gathered accurate data as to the way most of the people in Canton were living.

In July 1926, Mr. Mellett was assassinated. During the investigation into crime conditions in Canton all reports came to my office, and the data described following are, therefore, absolutely accurate.

A bank teller, whose salary was $150 a month, was spending an average of $75 a month for liquor, and in addition to this unpardonable waste of money, out of a salary that was none too great at most, he was traveling at a pace and with a crowd that meant ruin for him later on.

The superintendent of a large manufacturing plant, whose salary was $5,000 a year and who should have been saving at least $125 a month, was saving nothing. His bootlegger's bill averaged $150 a month.

A policeman whose income was $160 a month was spending over $400 a month on dinner parties at a nearby roadhouse. Where he got the difference between his legitimate income and his actual expenditures is a question that reflects no particular credit on the policeman.

A young man who was attending high school was spending large sums for liquor. The actual amount was not obtainable for the reason that he paid cash as he got the liquor, and the bootlegger's records did not, therefore, disclose the actual amount. Later this boy's parents had him locked up "to save him from himself." It was found that he was stealing money from a savings fund kept by his mother, somewhere in the house. He had stolen and spent more than $300 of this money when discovered.

A few years ago I set up a lecture bureau in forty-one high schools, where I lectured once each month throughout the school season. The principals of these high schools stated that less than 2 percent of the students showed any tendency toward saving money, and an examination through the aid of a questionnaire prepared specifically for that purpose disclosed that only 5 percent of the students, out of a total of 11,000 of high school age, believed that the savings habit was one of the essentials for success.

COMMENTARY

According to the 1999 EBRI Youth and Money Survey, 64 percent of students say they do not know as much about money as they should. Even among students who say they do a very good job of managing their money, 49 percent think they should know more.

It is no wonder that the rich are becoming richer and the poor are becoming poorer!

We are all victims of *habit*.

Unfortunately for most of us, we are reared by parents who have no concept whatsoever of the psychology of habit, and without being aware of their fault, most parents aid and abet their offspring in the development of the spending habit by overindulgence with spending money, and by lack of training in the Habit of Saving.

The habits of early childhood cling to us all through life.

Fortunate indeed is the child whose parents have the foresight, as well as the understanding of the value of the savings habit as a builder of character, to instill this habit in the minds of their children.

It is a training that yields rich rewards.

Give the average person a $100 windfall and what will become of it? Why, the lucky person will begin to ponder how to spend the money. Dozens of things that are needed, or are perceived as being needed, will flash into that person's mind, but it is a rather safe bet that it will never occur to the recipient (unless he or she has acquired the savings habit) to make this $100 the beginning of a savings account. Before night comes, the $100 will be spent, or at least a decision will have been made as to how to spend it, thus adding more fuel to the already too bright flame of the habit of spending.

We are ruled by our habits!

It requires force of character, determination, and the power of firm decision to open a savings account and then add to it a regular, even if small, portion of all subsequent income.

There is one rule by which anyone may determine, well in advance, whether or not financial freedom and independence, which is so universally desired, is attainable. And this rule has absolutely nothing to do with the amount of one's income.

The rule is that if you follow a systematic habit of saving a definite proportion of all money you earn or receive in other ways, you are practically sure to place yourself in a position of financial independence. If you save nothing, you are *absolutely sure never to be financially independent,* no matter how much your income may be.

The one and only exception to this rule is that someone who does not save might possibly inherit such a large sum of money that he or she could not spend it, or might inherit it under a trust which would protect it, but these eventualities are rather remote. So much so, in fact, that you cannot rely upon such a miracle happening to you.

ALL SALES PEOPLE

WILL DO WELL TO REMEMBER

THAT NO ONE WANTS ANYTHING

THAT SOMEONE ELSE

IS TRYING TO GET RID OF.

I enjoy a rather close acquaintance with many hundreds of people throughout the United States and in some foreign countries. For nearly twenty-five years I have been watching many of these acquaintances, and I know therefore, from actual experience, how they live, why some of them have failed while others have succeeded, and the *reasons* for both failure and success.

This list of acquaintances includes men who control hundreds of millions of dollars, and who actually own many millions that they have acquired. I also know men who have *had* millions of dollars, all of which passed through their fingers and they are now penniless.

For the purpose of showing the student of this philosophy just how the law of habit becomes a sort of pivotal point on which success or failure turns, and exactly why no one can become financially independent without developing the habit of *systematic saving*, the living habits of some of these many acquaintances will be described.

We will begin with a complete history, in his own words, of a man who made a million dollars in the field of advertising but who was left with nothing to show for his efforts. The story is true, in every respect, and it has been included as a part of this lesson because the author of the story, Mr. W. C. Freeman, is willing to have his mistakes made public with the hope that others may avoid them.

This story first appeared in *The American Magazine,* and it is here reprinted through the courtesy of the publishers of that publication. (Copyright, The Crowell Publishing Company, 1927.)

A SAD BUT TRUE STORY

I HAVE MADE A MILLION DOLLARS
BUT I HAVEN'T GOT A CENT

While it is embarrassing, yes, humiliating, publicly to confess to an outstanding fault that has made a good deal of a mess of my life today, nevertheless I have decided to make this confession for the good it may do.

I am going to make a clean breast of how I let slip through my fingers all the money I have earned thus far in my lifetime, which approximates one million dollars. This amount I made through my work in the field of advertising, except a few thousand dollars I earned up to twenty-five years of age by teaching in country schools and by writing news letters to some country weeklies and daily newspapers.

Maybe one lone million does not seem a lot of money in these days of many millions and even billions; but it is a big sum of money, just the same. If there are any who think to the contrary, let them count a million. I tried to figure out the other night how long it would take to do so. I found I could count an average of one hundred a minute. On this basis it would take me twenty days of eight hours each, plus six hours and forty minutes on the twenty-first day to do the stunt. I doubt very much if you or I were given an assignment to count one million one-dollar bills, on the promise that all of them would be ours at the end of that time, that we could complete it. It would probably drive us mad —and a lot of use the money would be to us then, wouldn't it?

Let me say at the outset of my story that I do not regret, not for one minute, that I spent 90 percent of the money I made. To wish any of this 90 percent back at this time would make me feel that I would have denied much happiness to my family and to many others.

My only regret is that I spent all of my money, and more besides. If I had today the 10 percent I could have saved easily, I would have one hundred thousand dollars safely invested, and no debts. If I had this money I would feel really and truly that I was rich; and I mean just this, for I have never had a desire to accumulate money for money's sake.

Those schoolteaching and newspaper-correspondence days of mine brought some cares and responsibilities, but they were met optimistically.

I married at the age of twenty-one with the full approval of parents on both sides, who believed thoroughly in the doctrine preached by Henry Ward Beecher, that "early marriages are virtuous marriages."

Just one month and one day after I was married my father met a tragic death. He was suffocated by coal gas. Having been an educator all his life—and one of the best—he had not accumulated any money.

When he passed out of our family circle it was up to all of us to pull together and get along somehow, which we did.

Apart from the void left in our home by my father's death (my wife and I and my mother and only sister lived together), we had a joyful life, despite the fact that it was a tight squeeze to make ends meet.

My mother, who was exceptionally talented and resourceful (she had taught school with my father until I was born), decided to open our home to a married couple, old friends of the family. They came to live with us and their board helped to pay expenses. My mother was known far and wide for the wonderful meals she served. Later on, two well-to-do women friends of the family were taken into our home, thus increasing our revenue.

My sister helped very substantially by teaching a kindergarten class, which met in the big living room of our home; my wife contributed her share to the household by taking charge of the sewing and mending.

Those were very happy days. Nobody in the household was extravagant or had any extravagant tendencies except perhaps myself, for I was always inclined to be free with money. I liked to make gifts to the family and to entertain friends.

THINK WELL BEFORE YOU SPEAK

BECAUSE YOUR WORDS

MAY PLANT THE SEED OF

EITHER SUCCESS OR FAILURE

IN THE MIND OF

SOME OTHER PERSON.

When the first baby came into our home—a boy—we all thought heaven had opened its doors to us. My wife's parents, who took the keenest and deepest interest in our affairs, and who were always ready to lend a helping hand, were equally happy over the coming of their first grandchild. My brother-in-law, much older than my wife, and a bachelor, could not understand at first the joy we all felt; but even he began to strut around like a proud peacock after a while. What a difference a baby makes in a home!

I am injecting these details into my story merely to emphasize how the early days of my life were lived. I had no opportunity to spend much money, and yet I had as much happiness in those days as I have ever had since.

The strange thing about it all is that the experience of those days did not teach me the value of money. If anybody ever had a practical lesson to guide him in his future, I certainly had it.

But let me tell you how this early experience affected me. The birth of my son inspired me to do something that would make more money than I was getting at teaching school and in writing for newspapers. I did not want my wife, mother, and sister to feel that they would have to continue indefinitely to do their part in sustaining the household. Why should a fellow, big and strong and healthy as I have always been, and with a reasonable amount of ability, be content to remain a spoke in the wheel? Why shouldn't I be the whole wheel, as far as providing for the family was concerned?

Following my desire to make more money, I took on the selling of books in addition to teaching and writing for newspapers. This earned for me quite a little extra money. Finally, I gave up teaching and concentrated on selling books, and writing for newspapers.

My bookselling took me to Bridgeton, New Jersey. It was here that I got my first real start in making money. I had to be away from home a great deal to do this work, but the sacrifice was worthwhile. I earned enough money in a few weeks to send more money home than I had contributed to the household in any year from my school teaching and newspaper correspondence. After combing the territory in the Bridgeton zone, I became interested in a newspaper in that city, the *Morning Star.* It seemed to me that the editor and publisher of this paper needed a helper. I called on him and told him so. He said, "Heavens, young man, how can I hire you? I am not earning enough money to pay for my own living!"

"That's just it," said I. "I believe together we can make the *Star* a success. I'll tell you what I'll do:

"I'll work for you for one week for one dollar a day. At the end of the week, if I have made good, I'll expect you to pay me three dollars a day for the second week; and then, if I continue to do well, I'll expect you to pay me six dollars a day for the third week, and will continue from then on until the paper makes enough money to pay me fifty dollars a week."

The owner agreed to my proposition. At the end of two months, I was being paid fifty dollars a week, which in those days was considered a big salary. I began to feel that I was well on my way toward making money—but all I wanted it for was to make my family more comfortable. Fifty dollars a week was just four times as much as I had made teaching school.

My job on the *Star* embraced editorial writing (not very brilliant), reporting (just ordinary), the writing and selling of advertisements (fairly successful), proofreading, bill collecting, and so forth. It kept me humping six days a week; but I could stand it, for I was strong and healthy, and, besides, the work was very interesting. I also contributed correspondence to the

New York Sun, *Philadelphia Record*, and the *Trenton* (N.J.) *Times*, which brought me in an average of one hundred and fifty dollars a month, for this was a good news territory.

I learned a lesson on the *Star* that eventually shaped the course of my life. I found out that there is a great deal more money to be earned by selling advertising for newspapers than in writing for them. Advertising brings grist to the mill.

I put over one advertising stunt on the *Star*—a write-up of the south Jersey oyster industry, paid for by the oyster men—that brought in three thousand dollars cash, which the publisher divided with me fifty-fifty. I had never seen so much money at one time in all my life. Think of it! Fifteen hundred dollars —25 percent more than I had made in two years of school teaching and odd tasks.

Did I save this money or any part of it? I did not. What was the use? I could do so much with it to make my wife, boy, mother, and sister happy that I let it go far easier than I had made it. But would it not have been a fine thing if I had put this money away for a rainy day?

My work in Bridgeton attracted the attention of Sam Hudson, New Jersey correspondent of the *Philadelphia Record*, who was a shining example of that type of newspapermen whose greatest pleasure in life is doing things for others.

Sam told me that it was time for me to get located in a big city. He thought I had it in me to make good. He said he would get me a job in Philadelphia. He did, and I moved with my wife and baby to Germantown. I was given charge of the advertising department of the *Germantown* (Philadelphia) *Gazette*, a weekly newspaper.

At the start I did not make as much money as I had earned in Bridgeton, because I had to give up my newspaper correspondence. The news for this section was covered by other correspondents. But very soon I was making 25 percent more money. The *Gazette* increased its size three times to accommodate its advertising, and each time I received a very substantial increase in salary.

In addition to this, I was given a job to gather social news for the Sunday edition of the *Philadelphia Press*. Bradford Merrill, managing editor of that newspaper, now a very important New York newspaper executive, assigned me a big territory to cover. This kept me busy every night in the week except Saturdays. I was paid five dollars a column; but I averaged seven columns every Sunday, which made me thirty-five dollars a week extra.

It was more money for me to spend, and I spent it. I did not know anything about budgeting my expenses. I just let it go as it came. I did not have time, or thought I hadn't, to watch my step in spending.

A year later I was invited to join the advertising staff of the *Philadelphia Press*, a big opportunity for a young man, for I got wonderful training under the management of William L. McLean, now the owner of the *Philadelphia Evening Bulletin*. I still retained my job as gatherer of social news—so my income was just about the same as I had been making in Germantown.

But before long my work attracted the attention of James Elverson Sr., publisher of the old *Saturday Night* and *Golden Days*, who had just purchased the *Philadelphia Inquirer*. I was offered and accepted the advertising management of this newspaper.

This meant a big increase in my income. And soon afterward there came a happy increase in my family, the birth of a daughter. Then I was able to do what I had longed to do since the birth of my son. I got the family together again under one roof—my wife and two babies, my mother and sister. At last I was able to relieve my mother of any cares or responsibilities, and never again did she have either as long as she lived. She died in her eighty-first year, twenty-five years after my father's death. I shall never forget her last words to me: "Will, you have never caused me a moment's worry since you were born, and I could not have had more than you have given me had I been the Queen of England."

I was making at this time four times more money than my father had made as superintendent of public schools in my hometown of Phillipsburg, New Jersey.

All the money, however, passed out of my pockets as easily as water flows through a sieve. Expenses increased with every increase in my income, which is the habit, I suppose, with most people. There was no sane reason, though, for letting my expenses go beyond my income, which I did. I found myself piling up debts, and from this time on I was never out of debt. I did not worry about my debts, though, for I thought I could pay them off at any time. It never occurred to me—not until fully twenty-five years later—that debt eventually would bring upon me not only great anxiety and unhappiness, but that I would lose friends and credit as well.

But I must pat myself on the back for one thing: I was giving full rein to my big fault—spending money as fast as I made it, often faster; but I never shirked my work. I was always trying to find more things to do, and I always found them. I spent very little time with my family. I would go home to dinner every night and romp with the babies until their bedtime, then I would return to the office and often work.

So the years went by. Another daughter arrived. Presently I wanted my daughters to have a pony and cart, and I wanted my son to have a riding horse. Then I thought I needed a team to take me around with the family. I got them all. Instead of one horse and a carry-all, or perhaps a team, which would have been sufficient for our needs and something we could have

———————

I AM THANKFUL FOR THE ADVERSITIES

THAT HAVE CROSSED MY PATHWAY,

FOR THEY HAVE TAUGHT ME

TOLERANCE, SYMPATHY,

SELF-CONTROL, PERSEVERANCE

AND SOME OTHER VIRTUES

I MIGHT NEVER HAVE KNOWN.

———————

afforded, I had to have a stable, with all that goes with it. This outfit cost me nearly one-fourth of my annual income.

Then I took up golf. This was in my forty-first year. I went at my play the same way I went at my work—put my whole heart into it. I learned to play pretty well. My son and elder daughter played with me, and they learned to play well, too.

It was necessary that my younger daughter should spend the winter in the South and summers in the Adirondacks; but instead of her mother going with her alone, I felt it would be fine if the son and other daughter went along with them. This arrangement was carried out. They went to Pinehurst, North Carolina, every winter and to expensive resorts in the Adirondacks or in New Hampshire in the summer.

All of this took a great deal of money. My son and elder daughter were keen about golf and spent a lot of money on it. I also disbursed quite a little on golf courses around New York. Between the three of us we won eighty prizes, most of which are now in storage. I sat down one day and calculated what these prizes had cost me. I discovered that each trophy had cost me $250 or a total of $45,000 over a period of fifteen years, an average of $3,000 a year. Ridiculous, wasn't it?

I entertained lavishly at my home. Montclair folks thought I was a millionaire. I frequently invited groups of businessmen to have a day of golf at the club, and then to have dinner with me in the evening. They would have been satisfied with a plain home dinner, but, no, I must serve them an elaborate affair staged by a famous caterer. These dinners never cost less than ten dollars a plate, which did not include the money spent for music while they were dining. I had a quartet come to the house. Our dining room comfortably seated twenty people, and it was filled to capacity many times.

It was all very lovely and I was glad to be their host. In fact, I was very happy over it. I never stopped to think how rapidly I was piling up debts. The day came when they began to bother me a lot. I had entertained so many guests at the golf club one month, paying for luncheons, cigars, and greens fees, that my bill was four hundred and fifty dollars. This attracted the attention of the directors of the club, who were all good friends of mine and very much interested in my welfare. They made it their business to tell me that I was spending entirely too much money, and they wished for my sake that I could check my expenses.

This gave me a bit of a jolt. It made me think seriously long enough to get rid of my horses and traps—at a big sacrifice, of course. I gave up our home and moved back to the city; but I did not leave any unpaid bills in Montclair. I borrowed the money to pay them. It was always easy for me to get all the money I wanted, despite my well-known financial shortcomings.

Here are two sidelights on my experience during my "flaring forties."

Besides spending money foolishly and perhaps recklessly, I loaned it with equal abandon. In cleaning out my desk at home before moving to the city I looked over a package of due bills, the total of which was over forty thousand dollars. That was money handed out to just anybody who came along. I tore them all up; but I realized that if I had that money in hand I wouldn't owe a dollar.

One of the prosperous businessmen I had entertained many times and who in turn had entertained me, said to me: "Billy, I've got to stop going on outings with you. You spend entirely too much money for me. I can't keep up with you."

Think of that coming from a man who was making more money than I was! It should have struck home, but it didn't. I went on spending just the same, and foolishly thinking that I was having a good time, and with no thought of the future. This man is now one of the vice presidents of one of New York's greatest financial institutions, and is reported to be worth many millions of dollars.

I should have taken his advice.

In the fall of 1908, after my disastrous experience of six months in another line of business following my resignation from the Hearst organization, I resumed newspaper work as advertising manager of the *New York Evening Mail.* I had known Henry L. Stoddard, editor and owner, back in the Philadelphia days, when he was political correspondent for the *Press.*

Despite the fact that I was bothered by debts, I did the best work of my life on the *Evening Mail,* and made more money during the five years I was associated with it than I had ever made before. Moreover, Mr. Stoddard gave me the privilege of syndicating advertising talks, which ran in his paper for one thousand consecutive publication days, and earned for me more than fifty-five thousand dollars.

Mr. Stoddard was very generous in many other ways, and frequently paid me special sums of money for doing what he considered unusual things in the way of developing business. During this period, I was so deeply in debt that, in order to keep things moving as smoothly as possible, but without retrenching in the slightest way in my expenses, I borrowed money from Peter to pay Paul and from Paul to pay Peter. That item of fifty-five thousand dollars earned from syndicating advertising talks would have more than paid all my debts and left a nice nest egg besides. But all of it was spent as easily as though I hadn't a care in the world.

In 1915 I went on my own in the advertising business. From that time until the spring of 1922 my fees ran into very big figures. I was still making more money than I ever did, and was spending it just as fast as I made it, until finally my friends got tired of making me loans.

If I had shown the slightest inclination to curb my expenses to the extent of only 10 percent, these wonderful men would have been willing to divide fifty-fifty with me, letting me pay them 5 percent of it and saving 5 percent. They did not care so much about the return of the money they had loaned me, as that they wanted to see me pull myself together.

The crash in my affairs came five years ago. Two friends who had stood by me loyally became impatient, and told me frankly that I needed a drastic lesson. And they gave it to me all right. I was forced into bankruptcy, which nearly broke my heart. I felt that every person I knew was pointing the finger of scorn at me. This was very foolish. While there was comment, it was not at all unfriendly. It was expressive of keen regret that a man who had attained so much prestige in his profession, and had earned so much money, should have allowed himself to get into financial difficulties.

Proud and sensitive to the core, I felt the disgrace of bankruptcy so keenly that I decided to go to Florida, where I had once done a special piece of work for a client. It seemed to me to be the coming El Dorado. I figured that maybe I could make sufficient money in a few years so that I could return to New York, not only with a competency but with enough to pay all my debts in full. For a time it looked as though I would realize this ambition; but I was caught in the big real estate collapse. So here I am back in the old town where I once had big earning power and hundreds of friends and well-wishers.

It has been a strange experience.

One thing is certain: I have learned my lesson at last. I feel sure that opportunities will come my way to redeem myself, and that my earning power will be restored to me. And when that time comes, I know that I shall be able to live as well as I ever did, on 40 percent of my income. Then I shall divide the remaining 60 percent into two parts, setting aside 30 percent to pay my creditors and 30 percent for insurance and savings.

If I allowed myself to feel depressed over my past, or filled my mind with worries, I would not be capable of carrying on the fight to redeem myself.

Besides, I would be ungrateful to my Maker for having endowed me with wonderful health all my life. Is there any greater blessing?

I would be ungrateful to the memory of my parents, whose splendid training has kept me anchored pretty safely to moral standards. Slipping from moral moorings is infinitely more serious, in the end, than slipping from the thrift standard.

I would lack appreciation for the encouragement and support I have had in generous measure from hundreds of businessmen and to many good friends who helped me build a fine reputation in my profession.

These memories are the sunshine of my life. And I shall use them to pave the way to my future achievement.

With abundance of health, unfaltering faith, unflagging energy, unceasing optimism, and unbounded confidence that a man can win his fight, even though he commences late in life to realize the kind of fight he must make—is there anything but death to stop him?

Mr. Freeman's story is the same as that which might be told by thousands of others who save nothing, with the exception that the amounts of their incomes would vary. The manner of living, the way the money was spent, and why, as told in Mr. Freeman's narrative, show the way the spender's mind works.

FORTUNATE IS THE PERSON

WHO HAS LEARNED THAT

THE MOST CERTAIN WAY TO GET

IS TO FIRST GIVE,

THROUGH SOME SORT

OF USEFUL SERVICE.

The installment plan of buying has become so common, and it is so easy to purchase practically anything one desires, that the tendency to spend out of proportion to one's income is rapidly increasing. This tendency must be curbed by the person who has made up his or her mind to gain financial independence.

It can be done by anyone who is willing to try.

There is no virtue in keeping up with the neighbors when this means sacrifice of the habit of saving a regular part of one's income. It is far better, in the long run, to be considered a bit behind the times than it is to go through youth, into the days of maturity, and finally into old age, without having formed the habit of systematic saving.

It is a common practice today for families to purchase automobiles on monthly payments which involve too great an expenditure compared with their income. If you have a Ford income you have no business purchasing a more expensive car. You should curb your desires and content yourself with a Ford. Many people spend their entire incomes, and often go into debt besides, because they maintain automobiles out of keeping with their incomes. This common practice is fatal to success, as far as financial independence may be considered a part of success.

It is better to sacrifice during the age of youthfulness, than it is to be compelled to do so during the age of maturity, as all who have not developed the Habit of Saving generally have to do.

There is nothing quite so humiliating, that carries such great agony and suffering, as poverty in old age when personal services are no longer marketable, and one must turn to relatives or to charitable institutions for existence.

A budget system should be maintained by every person, both the married and the single, but no budget will work if the person trying to keep it lacks the courage to cut expenses on such items as entertainment and recreation. If you have so little willpower that you think it necessary to "keep up with the Joneses" with whom you associate socially, and whose income is greater than yours, or who spend all of their income foolishly, then no budget system can be of service to you.

I AM THANKFUL THAT

I WAS BORN POOR—

THAT I DID NOT

COME INTO THIS WORLD

BURDENED BY THE WHIMS

OF WEALTHY PARENTS,

WITH A BAG OF GOLD

AROUND MY NECK.

Forming the savings habit means that, to some extent at least, you must seclude yourself from all except a well-selected group of friends who enjoy you without elaborate entertaining on your part.

To admit you lack the courage to trim down your expenditures so that you can save money, even if only a small amount, is the equivalent of admitting at the same time a lack of the sort of character that leads to success.

It has been proved, times too numerous to mention, that people who have formed the Habit of Saving are always given preference in positions of responsibility. Therefore, the saving of money not only adds advantages in the nature of preferred employment and a larger bank account, but it also increases the actual earning capacity. Any business will prefer to employ a person who saves money regularly, not only because that person saves money, but more because of the characteristics possessed by such a person which make him or her more efficient.

It should be a common practice for all businesses to require all employees to save money. This would be a blessing to the many who would not otherwise have the willpower to form the savings habit.

Henry Ford has gone a very long way, perhaps as far as is expedient, to induce his employees not only to save their money but also to spend what they do spend wisely, and to live sanely and economically. The manager who induces their employees to form the Habit of Saving is a practical philanthropist.

COMMENTARY

The smart course is to resolve to save a certain percentage of every check that comes to you. This is called "paying yourself first." While 20 percent may seem daunting, it will become easier to manage as you experience the excitement of watching your savings grow. If your current situation absolutely will not allow you to set aside 20 percent, select another amount, even just 5 percent. Out of every

$1,000 this is just $50, but repeat that 5 percent savings ten times and you will have $500.

You will find that as you watch your savings grow, you will gain self-confidence. You will realize that you are capable of saving. "What would happen," you'll ask, "if I were saving 10 percent, or even 15 percent?" Soon 20 percent will seem far more attainable.

You should strive to reach a point where you have at least three months' take-home pay in your savings account. This will provide you with an important cushion in the event of some unexpected difficulty. Even better, a year's worth of living expenses set aside will bring you a great sense of freedom.

If you have nothing more in the bank than what it will take to get you through next week, this will seem an enormous goal. Even by setting aside 20 percent of your income, you will still need almost five years to reach this level of savings. But if you do nothing, in five years you will still be as strapped for cash as you are today.

Perhaps your friends will wonder why you are driving the same car, or why you haven't made other significant purchases. The fear of criticism may concern you, but if these people are measuring you solely by how extravagantly you spend your money, maybe they aren't the best friends to have.

Avoid the temptation to boast about your savings. Unless you are embarking on a business relationship, this is no one else's concern. It's too easy to find yourself the butt of jokes about being a skinflint or the target of a so-called friend who comes, hat in hand, for a loan that you will never see repaid.

Learn more about what you can do with your savings. There are many good guides to money management.

Of course, accumulating savings will also be very useful to you in pursuing your Definite Chief Aim. When the time comes for that pursuit, be sure to hold back a part of your savings. Few people leap to success immediately. There will be surprises and probably some setbacks along the way. Keeping a cushion ready gives you the resiliency to bounce back from disappointment and take advantage of the lessons it has taught you.

Your commitment to the habit of saving will prepare you to embrace and use all the lessons of the Law of Success.

OPPORTUNITIES THAT COME TO THOSE
WHO HAVE SAVED MONEY

A few years ago a young man came to Philadelphia from the farming district of Pennsylvania and went to work in a printing plant. One of his fellow workers owned some shares in a building and loan company and had formed the habit of saving $5 a week. This young man was influenced by his associate to also open an account with the building and loan company, and at the end of three years he had saved $900. Then the printing plant got into financial difficulty and was about to fail. He came to the rescue with his $900, which he had saved in small amounts, and in return was given a half interest in the business.

By inaugurating a system of close economy he helped the business to pay off its indebtedness, and today he is drawing out of it, as his half of the profits, a little better than $25,000 a year.

This opportunity never would have come, or if it had he would not have been prepared to take it, had he not formed the Habit of Saving.

When the Ford automobile was perfected, during the early days of its existence, Henry Ford needed capital to promote the manufacture and sale of his product. He turned to a few friends who had saved up a few thousand dollars, one of whom was Senator Couzens. These friends came to his rescue, put in a few thousand dollars with him, and later drew out millions of dollars in profits.

When Woolworth first started his 5 and 10 Cent Stores plan he had no capital, but he turned to a few friends who had saved, by the closest sort of economy and great sacrifice, a few thousand dollars. These friends staked him and later they were paid back hundreds of thousands of dollars in profits.

Van Heusen, the famed shirt manufacturer, conceived the idea of producing a semi-soft collar for men. His idea was sound but he had not a cent to promote it. He turned to a few friends who had only a few hundred dollars. They gave him a start, and the collar made each of them wealthy.

The men who started the El Producto Cigar business had but little capital, and what they did have was money they had saved from their small earnings as cigar makers. They had a good idea and knew how to make a good cigar, but the idea would have died before it could be carried out had they not saved a little money. With their meager savings they launched the cigar, and a few years later they sold out their business to the American Tobacco Company for $8,000,000.

Behind practically every great fortune one may find, as its beginning, a well-developed habit of saving money.

John D. Rockefeller was an ordinary bookkeeper when he conceived the idea of developing the oil business, which was then not even considered a business. He needed capital, and because he had developed the Habit of Saving, and had thereby proved that he could conserve the funds of other people, he had no difficulty in borrowing the money he needed. It may be truthfully stated that the real basis of the Rockefeller fortune is the habit of saving money that Mr. Rockefeller developed while working as a bookkeeper at a salary of $40 a month.

James J. Hill was a poor young man, working as a telegrapher at a salary of $30 a month. He conceived the idea of the Great Northern Railway System, but his idea was out of proportion to his ability to finance. However, he had formed the habit of saving money, and on the meager salary of $30 a month had saved enough to enable him to pay his expenses on a trip to Chicago, where he interested capitalists in financing his plan. The fact that he, himself, had saved money on a small salary was considered good evidence that he would be a safe man to trust with other people's money.

Most people in business will not trust another person with their money unless that person has demonstrated an ability to take care of their own and use it wisely. The test, while it is often embarrassing to those who have not formed the Habit of Saving, is a very practical one.

A young man who worked in a printing plant in the city of Chicago wanted to open a small print shop and go into business for himself. He went to a printing supply-house manager and made his wants known, saying he needed credit for a printing press and some type and other small equipment.

The first question asked by the manager was: "Have you saved any money of your own?"

And he had! Out of his salary of $30 a week, he had saved $15 a week regularly for nearly four years. He got the credit he wanted. Later on he got more credit, until today he has built up one of the most successful printing plants in the city of Chicago. His name is George B. Williams.

Many years after this incident, I became acquainted with George Williams, and at the end of the war, in 1918, I went to Mr. Williams and asked for credit amounting to many thousands of dollars, for the purpose of publishing the Golden Rule Magazine. The first question he asked was:

"Have you formed the habit of saving money?" Despite that all the money I had saved was lost in the war, the fact that I had actually formed the savings habit was the real basis on which I got credit for upward of $30,000.

There are opportunities on every corner, but they exist only for those who have ready money, or who can command money because they have formed the Habit of Saving. Those who have developed the savings habit generally also have the other character attributes that go with its formation.

The late J. P. Morgan once said he would rather loan $1,000,000 to a person of sound character, who had formed the habit of saving money, than he would $1,000 to a person without character, who was a spendthrift.

Generally speaking, this is the attitude that the world takes toward all those who save money.

It often happens that a small savings account of no more than two or three hundred dollars is sufficient to start one on the highway to

———————————

LOVE AND JUSTICE

ARE THE REAL ARBITERS

OF ALL DISPUTES.

GIVE THEM A CHANCE

AND YOU WILL NO LONGER

WANT TO DEFEAT

A BROTHER SOJOURNER

BY THE WAYSIDE OF LIFE.

———————————

financial independence. A few years ago a young inventor invented a household article which was unique and practical. But he was at a disadvantage, as inventors so often are, because he did not have the money to market his invention. Moreover, not having formed the Habit of Saving, he found it impossible to borrow money through banking sources.

His roommate was a young machinist who had saved $200. He came to the inventor's aid with this small sum of money, and that allowed them to have enough of these articles manufactured to give them a start. They went out and sold the first supply from house to house, then came back and had another supply made up, and so on, until they had accumulated (thanks to the thrift and savings ability of the roommate) a capital of $1,000. With this, plus some credit they secured, they bought the tools for manufacturing their own product.

The young machinist sold his half interest in the business six years later, for $250,000. He never would have handled this much money during his entire life had he not formed the Habit of Saving, which enabled him to come to the rescue of his inventor friend.

This case might be multiplied a thousand times, with only slight variation in details, as it is fairly descriptive of the beginning of many great fortunes that have been made, and are now in the making, in the United States.

COMMENTARY

There may be times when you find that, even having saved money, it is difficult to persuade others to back you, simply because your vision is greater than theirs. Women entrepreneurs, unfortunately, have often had this experience. But a small savings account of no more than a few thousand dollars can often be enough to get you started. Mary Kay Ash started her cosmetics company with $5,000 of her own money. Lillian Vernon began with $2,000 she had saved. They created their opportunities with their habit of saving.

It may seem a cruel fact, but it is a *fact* nonetheless, that if you have no money, and have not developed the Habit of Saving, you are out of luck as far as availing yourself of the opportunity to make money is concerned.

It can do no harm to repeat—in fact it should be repeated over and over again—that the real start of nearly all fortunes, whether great or small, is the formation of the habit of saving money.

Get this basic principle firmly founded in your mind and you will be well on the road toward financial independence!

It is a sad sight to see someone who is well along in years and self-sentenced to the wearisome treadmill of hard labor because he or she neglected to form the habit of saving money when they were younger. Yet there are millions of such men and women, of all ages and types, living in the United States alone.

The greatest thing in life is *freedom!*

But there can be no real freedom without a reasonable degree of financial independence. It is a terrible thing to be compelled to be at a certain place, at a certain task (perhaps a task that one does not like) for a certain number of hours every working day of the week, for a whole lifetime. In some ways this is the same as being in prison, since one's choice of action is always limited. It is really no better than being in prison with the privilege of a "trustee," and in some ways it is even worse because the person who is imprisoned has escaped the responsibility of providing themself a place to sleep, something to eat, and clothes to wear.

The only hope of escape from this lifelong toil which curtails freedom is to form the habit of saving money, and then live up to that habit, no matter how much sacrifice it may require. There is no other way out for millions of people, and unless you are one of the rare exceptions, this lesson and all these statements of fact are meant *for* you and apply *to* you!

Neither a borrower, nor a lender be;
For loan oft loses both itself and friend,
And borrowing dulls the edge of husbandry.
This above all: to thine own self be true,
And it must follow, as the night the day,
Thou canst not then be false to any man.

—SHAKESPEARE

Volume II

THE PRINCIPLES OF
PERSONAL POWER

Initiative and Leadership

Imagination

Enthusiasm

Self-Control

Lesson Five

Initiative and Leadership

EVERYTHING PASSES AT PAR,

TEMPORARILY;

TRUTH ALONE REMAINS

PERMANENTLY.

INITIATIVE AND LEADERSHIP

"You Can Do It if You Believe You Can!"

BEFORE YOU PROCEED TO THE MASTERY OF this lesson, let me again remind you that there is perfect coordination of thought running throughout this course on the laws of success. The entire seventeen lessons harmonize and blend with each other so that they constitute a perfect chain that has been built, link by link, out of the factors that enter into the development of power through *organized effort*.

You will find also that the same fundamental principles of applied psychology form the foundation of each of these seventeen lessons, although different application is made of these principles in each of the lessons.

This lesson on Initiative and Leadership comes after the lesson on Self-Confidence for the reason that no one could become an efficient leader or take the Initiative in any great undertaking without belief in himself or herself.

THE POWER OF INITIATIVE

The reason why *Initiative* and *Leadership* are associated terms in this lesson is that Leadership is essential for the attainment of success, and Initiative is the very foundation upon which this necessary quality of Leadership is built. Initiative is as essential to success as a hub is essential to a wheel.

Initiative is that exceedingly rare quality which impels a person to do what ought to be done *without being told to do it*. Elbert Hubbard expressed himself on the subject of Initiative in these words:

> The world bestows its big prizes, both in money and honors, for one thing, and that is *initiative*.
>
> What is initiative? I'll tell you: It is doing the right thing without being told.
>
> But next to doing the right thing without being told is to do it when you are told once. That is to say, "Carry the message to Garcia." Those who can carry a message get high honors, but their pay is not always in proportion.
>
> Next, there are those who do the right thing only when necessity kicks them from behind, and these get indifference instead of honors, and a pittance for pay.
>
> This kind spends most of the time polishing a bench with a hard-luck story.
>
> Then, still lower down in the scale than this, we have the person who will not do the right thing even when someone goes along to demonstrate and stays to see that the work is done right. This person is always out of a job, and receives deserved

contempt, unless there is a rich relative in the background, in which case destiny patiently waits around the corner with a club.

To which class do *you* belong?

Inasmuch as you will be expected to take inventory of yourself and determine which of the factors of this course you need most, after you have completed the last lesson, it may be well if you begin to get ready for this analysis by answering the question that Elbert Hubbard has asked: *To which class do you belong?*

One of the peculiarities of Leadership is the fact that it is never found in those who have not acquired the *habit* of taking the Initiative. Leadership is something that you must invite yourself into; it will never thrust itself upon you. If you will carefully analyze all leaders whom you know, you will see that they not only exercised Initiative but they also went about their work with a *definite purpose* in mind. You will also see that they possessed the quality described in the third lesson of this course: Self-Confidence.

These facts are mentioned in this lesson because it will profit you to observe that successful people make use of *all* the factors covered by the seventeen lessons of the course. They are also mentioned for the more important reason that it will profit you to understand thoroughly the principle of *organized effort,* which this course is intended to establish in your mind.

This seems an appropriate place to point out that this course is not intended as a *shortcut* to success, nor is it intended as a mechanical formula that you may use in noteworthy achievement without effort on your part. The *real* value of the course lies in the *use* that you will make of it, and not in the course itself. Its chief purpose is to help you develop in yourself the qualities covered by the seventeen lessons, and one of the most important of these qualities is Initiative, the subject of this lesson.

We will now proceed to apply the principle on which this lesson is founded by describing, in detail, just how it served successfully to complete a business transaction that most people would call difficult.

In 1916 I needed $25,000 with which to create an educational institution, but I had neither the money nor sufficient collateral with which to borrow it through the usual banking sources. Did I bemoan my fate or think of what I might accomplish if some rich relative or Good Samaritan would come to my rescue by loaning me the necessary capital?

I did nothing of the sort!

I did just what you will be advised, throughout this course, to do. First of all, I made the securing of this capital my Definite Chief Aim. Second, I laid out a complete plan through which to transform this aim into reality. Backed by sufficient Self-Confidence and spurred on by Initiative, I proceeded to put my plan into action. But before the "action" stage of the plan had been reached, more than six weeks of constant, persistent study and effort and thought were put into it. If a plan is to be sound it must be built of carefully chosen material.

You will next observe the application of the principle of *organized effort*, through which it is possible for one to ally or associate several interests in such a way that *each of these interests* is greatly strengthened and each supports all the others, just as one link in a chain supports all the other links.

I wanted this $25,000 in capital for the purpose of creating a school of advertising and salesmanship. Two things were necessary for the organization of such a school. One was the $25,000, which I did not have, and the other was the proper course of instruction, which I *did* have. My problem was to *ally myself* with some group who needed what I had, and who would supply the $25,000.

This alliance had to be made through a plan that would benefit all concerned.

After my plan had been completed, and I was satisfied that it was equitable and sound, I presented it to the owner of a well-known and reputable business college which just then was finding competition quite keen and was badly in need of a plan for meeting this competition.

My plan was presented in about these words:

Whereas, you have one of the most reputable business colleges in the city; and,

Whereas, you need some plan with which to meet the stiff competition in your field; and,

Whereas, your good reputation has provided you with all the credit you need; and,

Whereas, I have the plan that will help you meet this competition successfully, be it resolved that we ally ourselves through a plan that will give you what you need and at the same time supply me with something that I need.

Then I proceeded to unfold my plan further, in these words:

I have written a very practical course on advertising and salesmanship. Having built this course out of my actual experience in training and directing salesmen, and my experience in planning and directing many successful advertising campaigns, I have behind it plenty of evidence of its soundness.

If you will use your credit in helping market this course, I will place it in your business college as one of the regular departments of your curriculum and take entire charge of this newly created department. No other business college in the city will be able to meet your competition, because no other college has a course such as this. The advertising that you do in marketing this course will also serve to create the demand for your regular business course. You may charge to my department the entire amount that you spend for this advertising, and the advertising bill will be paid out of that department, leaving for you the accumulative advantage that will accrue to your other departments without cost to you.

Now, I suppose you will want to know where I will profit by this transaction, and I will tell you. I want you to enter into a contract with me in which it will be agreed that when the cash receipts from my department equal the amount you have paid out or contracted to pay

THERE IS NO SECURITY

ON THIS EARTH,

THERE IS ONLY OPPORTUNITY.

—General Douglas MacArthur

out for advertising, my department and my course in advertising and salesmanship become my own and I may have the privilege of separating this department from your school and running it under my own name.

The plan was agreeable and the contract was closed.

(Please keep in mind that my *definite purpose* was to secure the use of $25,000 for which I had no security to offer.)

COMMENTARY

> A powerful example of initiative can be found in one the greatest modern success stories: the founding of Microsoft by Bill Gates and Paul Allen.
>
> Gates and Allen became friends in high school. They were early examples of the now-familiar computer nerd, people so obsessed with programming that they seemed to think of little else.
>
> In 1974, Gates was attending Harvard while Allen was working for Honeywell and also living in Cambridge, Massachusetts. It was there that they began to exhibit the initiative that would guide their careers. An issue of Popular Electronics magazine had a cover article on a new computer, the Altair 8800, a $400 device that was the first computer meant for the general public.
>
> Today the Altair would seem very primitive. It had no keyboard and was designed to be connected to a teletype. But Gates and Allen knew that it would be tremendously appealing if someone wrote a simple version of the programming language BASIC to give the Altair instructions.
>
> For two months they worked on writing BASIC language for the Altair—though they didn't even own one of the machines—and then contacted Ed Roberts, the engineer who had designed the Altair.
>
> Their version of BASIC worked, and Roberts was so impressed that he offered Gates and Allen a contract. By the summer, Gates and Allen had formed a company they called Microsoft, which earned royalties on every Altair sold with their language. Soon they were adapting other programming languages for the Altair.
>
> Sometimes it seems that when anyone wants to make a point about any aspect of success they cite Bill Gates and the founding of Microsoft. So what is the point of the story in the context of initiative?

It is quite possible to be successful without demonstrating any particular initiative. Some people simply follow the tried-and-true path and become successes. And Bill Gates and Paul Allen were smart enough about computers early on that they surely would have been successful.

On the other hand, some people have terrific ideas but their ideas don't make them successful because they never get beyond using those ideas to amuse themselves and their friends. That, too, could have been the story of Gates and Allen.

But it wasn't. And that's where initiative played a huge part in the story. Bill Gates and Paul Allen weren't content just to go along to get along. And they weren't content to wait until someone else told them what a good idea they had. Without initiative they could have had enough success to satisfy most people, but because they did have initiative, they stepped up to the plate, thought outside the box, pushed the envelope, and had not just success but the biggest success ever in the history of the world.

In a little less than a year the business college had paid out slightly more than $25,000 for advertising and marketing my course and for the other expenses incidental to the operation of this newly organized department. Meanwhile the department had collected and turned back to the college, in tuition fees, a sum equaling the amount the college had spent, and I took the department over as a going and self-sustaining business, according to the terms of my contract.

As a matter of fact, this newly created department not only served to attract students for the other departments of the college, but at the same time the tuition fees collected through this new department were sufficient to place it on a self-sustaining basis before the end of the first year.

So you can see that while the college did not loan me one penny of actual capital, it nevertheless supplied me with credit, which served exactly the same purpose.

I said that my plan was founded on equity; that it contemplated a benefit to all parties concerned. The benefit accruing to me was the use of the $25,000, which resulted in an established and self-sustaining business by the end of the first year. The benefit accruing to the college was the new students secured for its regular commercial and business course as a result of the money spent in advertising my department, all advertising having been done under the name of the college.

Today that business college is one of the most successful schools of its kind, and it stands as a monument of sound evidence with which to demonstrate the value of *allied effort*.

COMMENTARY

> While not perfectly parallel, the stories of Hill's course and the story of the rise of Microsoft share the basic principles of this law of success. In both cases the entrepreneurs didn't have the money to launch their projects themselves. In both cases they took the initiative to find someone who did, and then made the case for why it was in that party's interests to finance the project. As Hill has pointed out, once his course had paid back the seed capital he then owned the business, and the partner college went on to become the most successful college of its kind.
>
> To continue the example of Microsoft, in 1980 IBM wanted someone to write the software for a personal computer line they were about to launch that was far more sophisticated than the Altair. They wanted results in just three months. Microsoft agreed to do it.
>
> Allen and Gates bought an operating system from another company and began adapting it for IBM. They called it MS-DOS—for Microsoft Disk Operating System. Gates, Allen, and their staff met IBM's deadline, and the IBM PC caused a sensation.
>
> It also inspired an immediate wave of clones, less expensive versions of the IBM PC. Microsoft's deal with IBM allowed them to license their software to whomever they pleased. And that's what they did, riding the huge surge in popularity of home computers. But Microsoft didn't stop there. They created a worldwide sales force to license their software in other countries and they continually worked to improve MS-DOS. In four years their sales quadrupled.

Today Microsoft dominates the software market worldwide. Is it luck? Were Paul Allen and Bill Gates just in the right place at the right time? Certainly not. From the moment they saw the Altair on the cover of Popular Electronics *they pursued a definite aim, one that continued to grow as time passed. They were determined to make themselves indispensable to the manufacturers and owners of personal computers.*

Once they had their initial success, they continued to drive themselves and their employees forward to offer further improvement to what they had already done.

Microsoft is the leader in the software industry precisely because it has always been willing to take the initiative, and with it the risks, of pursuing its founders' aims.

This story and the previous not only show the value of initiative and leadership, but they also lead up to the subject covered by the next lesson of this course on the laws of success—which is imagination.

There are generally many plans through which a desired object may be achieved, and it is often true that the obvious and usual methods are not the best. The usual method of procedure would have been to borrow from a bank. But you can see that in this case this method was impractical because no collateral was available.

A great philosopher once said: *"Initiative is the passkey that opens the door to opportunity."* I do not recall who this philosopher was, but I know that he was *great* because of the soundness of his statement.

I will next outline the exact procedure that you must follow if you are to become a person of Initiative and Leadership.

ELIMINATE PROCRASTINATION

First you must master the habit of procrastination and eliminate it from your makeup. This habit of putting off until tomorrow what you should have done last week or last year or a score of years ago is gnawing at your very being, and you can accomplish nothing until you throw it off.

The method through which you eliminate procrastination is based on a well-known and scientifically tested principle of psychology that has been referred to in the two preceding lessons of this course as *auto-suggestion.*

Copy the following formula and put it in a conspicuous place in your room where you will see it as you retire at night and as you arise in the morning.

> Having chosen a Definite Chief Aim as my life's work, I now understand it to be my duty to transform this aim into reality. Therefore I will form the habit of taking some definite action each day that will carry me one step nearer the attainment of my Definite Chief Aim.
>
> I know that procrastination is a deadly enemy of all who would become leaders in any undertaking, and I will eliminate this habit from my makeup by:
>
> 1. Doing some one definite thing each day, something that ought to be done, without anyone telling me to do it.
>
> 2. Looking around until I find at least one thing that I can do each day that I have not been in the habit of doing, and that will be of value to others, without expectation of pay.
>
> 3. Telling at least one other person, each day, of the value of practicing this habit of doing something that ought to be done without being told to do it.
>
> I can see that the muscles of the body become strong in proportion to the extent to which they are used. Therefore I understand that the *habit* of Initiative also becomes fixed in proportion to the extent that it is practiced.
>
> I realize the place to begin developing the *habit* of Initiative is in the small, commonplace things connected with my daily work. Therefore I will go at my work each day as if I were doing it solely for the purpose of developing this necessary *habit* of Initiative.

I understand that by practicing this *habit* of taking the Initiative in connection with my daily work I will be not only developing that habit, but I will also be attracting the attention of those who will place greater value on my services as a result of this practice.

Signed . . . .

Regardless of what you are now doing, every day brings you a chance to render some service, outside of the course of your regular duties, that will be of value to others. In rendering this additional service of your own accord, you of course understand that you are not doing so with the objective of receiving monetary pay. You are rendering this service because it provides you with ways and means of exercising, developing, and making stronger the aggressive spirit of Initiative, a quality which you must possess before you can ever become an outstanding figure in your chosen field.

Those who work for money alone, and who receive as their pay nothing but money, are always underpaid, no matter how much they receive. Money is of course necessary, but the big prizes of life cannot be measured in dollars and cents.

No amount of money could possibly be made to take the place of the happiness and joy and pride that belong to the person who digs a better ditch, or builds a better chicken coop, or sweeps a cleaner floor, or cooks a better meal. Every normal person loves to create something that is better than the average. The joy of *creating* a work of art is a joy that cannot be replaced by money or any other form of material possession.

I employ a woman who opens, sorts, and answers much of my personal mail. She began in my employ more than three years ago. At that time her duties were to take dictation. Her salary was about the same as what others receive for similar service. One day I dictated the following motto which I asked her to type for me:

Remember that your only limitation is the one you set up in your own mind.

As she handed the typewritten page back to me, she said, "Your motto has given me an idea that is going to be of value to both you and me."

I told her I was glad to have been of service to her. The incident made no particular impression on my mind, but from that day on I could see that it had made a *tremendous* impression on her mind. She began to come back to the office after supper and perform service that she was neither paid for nor expected to do. Without anyone telling her to do it, she would bring to my desk letters that she had answered for for me. She had studied my style and these letters were written as well as I could have done it; in some instances even better. She kept up this habit until my personal secretary resigned. When I began to look for someone to take his place, what was more natural than to turn to this young woman to fill the place. Before I had time to give her the position, *she took it on her Initiative.* My personal mail began to come to my desk with a new secretary's name attached, and she was that secretary. On her own time, after hours, and without additional pay, she had prepared herself for the best position on my staff.

But that is not all. She soon became so noticeably efficient that she began to attract the attention of others who offered her attractive positions. I have increased her salary many times and she now receives four times what she earned when she first went to work for me as a stenographer. And, to tell you the truth, I am helpless in the matter, because she has made herself so valuable to me that I cannot get along without her.

That is Initiative transformed into practical, understandable terms. I would be remiss if I failed to also point out an advantage, other than a greatly increased salary, that this young lady's Initiative has brought her. It has developed in her a spirit of cheerfulness that brings her happiness that most stenographers never know. Her work is not work—it is a great interesting game at which she is playing. Even though she arrives at the office ahead of any of the other stenographers and remains there long

———————

"WHAT HELPED YOU OVER

THE GREAT OBSTACLES OF LIFE?"

WAS ASKED OF A

HIGHLY SUCCESSFUL MAN.

"THE OTHER OBSTACLES," HE REPLIED.

———————

after they have watched the clock tick off five o'clock and quitting time, her hours are shorter by far than are those of the other workers. Hours of labor do not drag on the hands of those who are happy at their work.

This brings us to the next step in the description of the exact procedure you must follow in developing Initiative and Leadership.

INSPIRE OTHERS

The only way to get *happiness* is by giving it away, to others. The same applies to the development of Initiative. It is a well-known fact that one learns best that which they endeavor to teach others. If a person embraces a certain faith, the first thing that person does is to go out and try to "sell" it to others. And in exact proportion to the extent to which one impresses others does he or she impress *themself*.

In the field of salesmanship it is a well-known fact that no salesperson is successful in selling others until they have first done a good job of selling *themself*. Stated conversely, no salesperson can do their best to sell others without sooner or later selling themself that which they are trying to sell to others.

Any statement that a person repeats over and over again for the purpose of inducing others to believe it, that person will also come to believe. And this holds good whether the statement is false or true.

You can now see the advantage of making it your business to *talk* Initiative, *think* Initiative, *eat* Initiative, *sleep* Initiative, and *practice* Initiative. By so doing you *become* a person of Initiative and Leadership, for it is a well-known fact that people will readily, willingly, and voluntarily follow someone who shows by their actions that he or she is a person of Initiative.

In the place where you work or the community in which you live you come in contact with other people. Make it your business now to interest every one of them who will listen to you, in the development of Initiative. It will not be necessary for you to give your reasons for doing this, nor will it be necessary for you to announce the fact that you are doing it. Just go ahead and do it. In your own mind you will understand, of course, that you are doing it because this practice will help you and will at least do those whom you influence in the same practice no harm.

If you wish to try an experiment that will prove both interesting and profitable to you, pick out any acquaintance whom you know to be a person who never does anything that he or she is not expected to do, and begin selling them your idea of Initiative. Do not stop by merely discussing the subject once; keep it up every time you have a convenient opportunity. Approach the subject from a different angle each time. If you go about this in a tactful and forceful manner, you will soon observe a change in the person on whom you are trying the experiment. And you will observe something else of more importance still: you will observe a change in yourself! Do not fail to try this experiment. You cannot talk Initiative to others without developing a desire to practice it yourself.

Through the operation of the principle of autosuggestion, every statement that you make to others leaves its imprint on your own subconscious mind, and this is also the case whether your statements are false or true. You have often heard the saying "He who lives by the sword will die by the sword." Properly interpreted, this simply means that we are constantly attracting to ourselves and weaving into our own characters and personalities those qualities that our influence is helping to create in others. If we help others develop the habit of Initiative, we, in turn, develop this same habit. If we sow the seeds of hatred and envy and discouragement in others, we, in turn, develop these qualities in ourselves.

We come now to another step in the procedure you must follow in developing Initiative and Leadership.

LEADERSHIP AND TEAMWORK

Before we go further, let it be understood what is meant by the term *leadership* as it is used in connection with this course. There are two brands of Leadership, and one of them is as deadly and destructive as the other is helpful and constructive. The deadly brand, which leads not to *success* but to *absolute failure,* is the brand adopted by pseudoleaders who *force* their leadership on unwilling followers.

Napoleon Bonaparte was a *leader,* there can be no doubt about this, but he led his followers and himself to destruction. It is not Napoleon's brand of leadership that is recommended in this course, although I will admit that Napoleon possessed all the necessary fundamentals for great leadership, excepting one—he lacked the spirit of helpfulness to others as an objective. His desire for leadership was based solely upon self-aggrandizement. It was built upon personal ambition, and not upon a desire to lift the French people to a higher and nobler station in the affairs of nations.

COMMENTARY

> As was noted in Lesson One, Napoleon Hill often cited Napoleon Bonaparte because when Hill was composing this work in 1927 his namesake was thought to be the personification of charismatic but misguided leadership. At that time the world had yet to experience Hitler or Stalin, not to mention the many other dictators, strong-men, cult leaders, terrorists, and fanatics who ruthlessly abused their positions of power throughout the later years of the twentieth century and the beginning of the new millennium.

The brand of Leadership that is recommended throughout this course is the brand that leads to self-determination and freedom and self-development and enlightenment and justice. This is the brand that endures. For example, and as a contrast with the brand of leadership through which Napoleon raised himself into prominence, consider our

———

THEY ALWAYS SAY THAT

TIME CHANGES THINGS,

BUT YOU ACTUALLY HAVE TO

CHANGE THEM YOURSELF.

—Andy Warhol

———

own American commoner, Lincoln. The object of Lincoln's Leadership was to bring truth and justice and understanding to the people of the United States, and even though he died a martyr to his belief in this brand of Leadership, his name has been engraved upon the heart of the world in terms of loving kindliness that brings good to the world.

Both Lincoln and Napoleon led armies in warfare, but the objects of their Leadership were as different as night is from day. Your own ability to look around and analyze people who take the leading parts in all lines of endeavor is sufficient to enable you to pick out the Lincoln as well as the Napoleon types. Your own judgment will help you decide which type you prefer to emulate.

There can be no doubt in your mind as to the brand of Leadership that I recommend, and there should be no question in your mind as to which of the two brands described you will adopt as your brand. I make no recommendations on this subject. However, because this course has been prepared as a means of providing for its students the fundamental principles upon which power is developed, and not as a preachment on ethical conduct, I present both the constructive and the destructive possibilities of the principles outlined in this course, that you may become familiar with both. But I leave entirely to your own discretion the choice and application of these principles, believing that your own intelligence will guide you to make a wise selection.

THE PRICE OF LEADERSHIP

(WITH COMPLIMENTS OF THE CADILLAC MOTOR CAR CO.)

In every field of human endeavor, he that is first must perpetually live in the white light of publicity. Whether the leadership be vested in a man or in a manufactured product, emulation and envy are ever at work.

In art, in literature, in music, in industry, the reward and the punishment are always the same. The reward is widespread recognition; the punishment, fierce denial and detraction.

When a man's work becomes a standard for the whole world, it also becomes a target for the shafts of the envious few. If his work be merely mediocre, he will be left severely alone—if he achieves a masterpiece, it will set a million tongues a-wagging.

Jealousy does not protrude its forked tongue at the artist who produces a commonplace painting.

Whatsoever you write, or paint, or play, or sing, or build, no one will strive to surpass or slander you, unless your work be stamped with the seal of a genius.

Long, long after a great work or a good work has been done, those who are disappointed or envious continue to cry out that it cannot be done.

The leader is assailed *because* he or she is a leader, and the effort to equal them is merely added proof of their Leadership.

Failing to equal or to excel, the follower seeks to depreciate and to destroy—but only confirms the superiority of what it is that the follower strives to supplant. There is nothing new in this. It is as old as the world and as old as the human passions—envy, fear, greed, ambition, and the desire to surpass.

And it all avails nothing.

Spiteful little voices in the domain of art were raised against the painter Whistler long after the big world acclaimed him its greatest artistic genius.

Multitudes worship at the musical shrine of the composer Wagner, while the little group of those whom he had dethroned and displaced argued angrily that he was no musician at all.

The little world continued to protest that the inventor Fulton could never build a steamboat, while the big world flocked to the riverbanks to see his boat steam by.

Small, narrow voices cried out that Henry Ford would not last another year, but above and beyond the din of their childish prattle,

Ford went silently about his business and made himself the richest and most powerful man on earth.

Mean voices were raised against me personally before the ink was dry on the first copies of the Law of Success. Poisoned pens were released against both my ideas and me, the moment the first edition of this course was printed.

But the leader who truly leads remains the leader!

Master poet, master painter, master workman, each in their turn is assailed, and each holds their laurels through the ages.

That which is good or great makes itself known, no matter how loud the clamor of denial.

A real leader cannot be slandered or damaged by lies of the envious, because all such attempts serve only to turn the spotlight on the leader's ability, and real ability always finds a generous following.

Attempts to destroy real Leadership is love's labor lost, because that which deserves to live, lives!

COOPERATION

We return now to the discussion of the third step of the procedure you must follow in developing Initiative and Leadership. This step takes us back for a review of the principle of *organized effort*, as described in Lesson One and Lesson Two.

You have already learned that no one can accomplish enduring results of a far-reaching nature without the aid and Cooperation of others. And you have learned that when two or more persons ally themselves in any undertaking, in a spirit of harmony and understanding, each person in the alliance thereby multiplies his or her own powers of achievement. Nowhere is this principle more in evidence than it is in an industry or business in which there is perfect teamwork between the employer and the employees. Wherever you find this teamwork you find prosperity and goodwill on both sides. Without it, prosperity suffers.

THE WORLD IS DIVIDED INTO

PEOPLE WHO DO THINGS

AND PEOPLE WHO GET THE CREDIT.

TRY, IF YOU CAN, TO BELONG TO

THE FIRST CLASS.

THERE'S FAR LESS COMPETITION.

—Dwight Morrow

Cooperation is said to be the most important word in the English language. It plays an important part in the affairs of the home, in the relationship of men and women, parents and children. It plays an important part in the affairs of state. So important is this principle of Cooperation that no leader can become powerful or last long who does not understand and apply it in their Leadership.

Lack of Cooperation has destroyed more business enterprises than have all other causes combined. In my twenty-five years of active business experience and observation, I have witnessed the destruction of all manner of business enterprises because of dissension and lack of application of this principle of Cooperation. In the practice of law I have observed the destruction of homes, and divorce cases without end, as a result of the lack of Cooperation between man and wife. In the study of the histories of nations it becomes alarmingly obvious that lack of cooperative effort has been a curse to the human race throughout the ages.

Turn back the pages of these histories and study them and you will learn a lesson in Cooperation that will impress itself indelibly on your mind for ages and ages to come.

You are paying, and your children and your children's children will continue to pay for the cost of waging wars, because nations have not yet learned that a part of the world cannot suffer without damage and suffering to the whole world.

This same rule applies, with telling effect, in the conduct of modern business and industry. When any industry becomes disorganized and torn asunder by strikes and other forms of disagreement, both the employers and employees suffer irreparable loss. But the damage does not stop here; this loss becomes a burden to the public and takes on the form of higher prices and scarcity of the necessities of life. In the final analysis it becomes obvious that the evils of government and of industry have grown out of lack of Cooperation.

COMMENTARY

There was a time in this country when businesses flourished and great fortunes were made by their owners, while the common laborers who toiled in factories made a pittance. It was hardly surprising that labor unions sprang up to represent those at the bottom. The United States went through many decades of unrest as labor and capital struggled with each other to achieve a balance between the interests of both parties. Ultimately the hard-won cooperation between the two sides benefited everyone as demand for products increased and so did worker output. America became the world's greatest industrial power, enjoying a standard of living that was the envy of the world.

The so-called captains of industry would have been reduced to failures if they had not cooperated with those they led. You, too, must learn to inspire co-operation among everyone you work with. Otherwise it will be forced upon you or you will be forced out of your position of leadership.

If you would be a real leader, you must realize that everyone in the world will not share your ambitions. Some people will oppose you directly. Others will agree with you in small ways, and still others will say, "Yes, that is a worthwhile goal, but I would go about it another way."

The key is to find those points on which your interests intersect with those around you, and to use those points as a means of moving forward. You may eventually part ways with some or most of your followers, but if you have been an effective leader, they will all go their own way feeling that they benefited from their association with you.

Nor can it be truthfully said that all the evils of the world are confined to the affairs of state and industry. Look at the churches and you will observe the damaging effects of lack of Cooperation. No particular church is cited, but analyze any church or group of churches where lack of coordination of effort prevails and you will see evidence of disintegration that limits the service those churches could render.

My complaint is not against the work the churches have done, but the work that they *could have done* through Leadership that was based on the principle of coordinated, cooperative effort that would have carried civilization at least a thousand years ahead of where it is today. These possibilities are not mentioned in a spirit of criticism, but only as a means of illustrating the power of Cooperation, and to emphasize my belief in the potential power of all the churches of the world. Had it not been for the influence of the churches, none of us would be safe in walking down the street. People would be at each other's throats like wolves, and civilization would still be in the pre-historic age. Through harmonized effort and through Cooperation, the churches of the world could wield sufficient influence to render war an impossibility. It is not yet too late for such Leadership.

COMMENTARY

> Since the first publication of Law of Success *in the early part of the twentieth century, there have been profound changes in practically every aspect of our way of life. Yet none of those changes have made Hill's basic concepts less relevant or his advice less applicable. In fact, as has been said before, many of the changes came about because of the influence of Napoleon Hill's philosophy on those who have become the leaders in every aspect of American life.*
>
> *The last quarter of the twentieth century saw the emergence of a subset within the publishing industry that specializes in books and audiobooks on personal growth, motivation, leadership, and management style, all of which are testament to the enduring quality of the principles enunciated in* Law of Success. *Many of these recent books became the biggest bestsellers of their day, and in them you will find Napoleon Hill's ideas, elaborated upon, personalized, and told from different perspectives that will further illuminate the principles you are learning in these pages.*
>
> *The editors suggest that when you have finished reading* Law of Success *you should then read or listen to the audiobook of Hill's classic,* Think and Grow Rich, *followed by reading or listening to the work of others who have explored the same ground. The following list is a sampling of books that are also available on*

audio. The editors feel confident you will find these similarly enlightening: You Can Negotiate Anything *by Herb Cohen;* The 7 Habits of Highly Effective People *by Stephen Covey;* Feel the Fear and Do It Anyway *by Susan Jeffers;* In Search of Excellence *by Tom Peters;* Awaken the Giant Within *by Anthony Robbins, and the complete Anthony Robbins library of* PowerTalk! *audiobooks;* Wishcraft *by Barbara Sher;* Do What You Love, The Money Will Follow *by Marsha Sinetar;* Sell Your Way to the Top *by Zig Zigler.*

THE CHARACTER OF
A GREAT LEADER

During the world war, I was fortunate enough to listen to a great soldier's analysis of how to be a *leader*. This analysis was given to the student officers of the Second Training Camp at Fort Sheridan, by Major C. A. Bach, a quiet, unassuming army officer acting as an instructor. I have preserved a copy of this address because I believe it to be one of the finest lessons on Leadership ever recorded.

The wisdom of Major Bach's address is so vital to the businessperson aspiring to Leadership, or to the section boss, or to the clerk, or to the foreman of the shop, or to the president of the company, that I have preserved it as a part of this course. It is my earnest hope that this remarkable dissertation on Leadership will find its way into the hands of every employer and every worker and every ambitious person who aspires to Leadership in any walk of life. The principles upon which the address is based are as applicable to Leadership in business and industry and finance as they are in the successful conduct of warfare. Major Bach spoke as follows:

> In a short time each of you men will control the lives of a certain number of other men. You will have in your charge loyal but untrained citizens, who look to you for instruction and guidance. Your word will be their law. Your most casual remark will be remembered. Your mannerisms will be aped.

Your clothing, your carriage, your vocabulary, your manner of command will be imitated.

When you join your organization you will find there a willing body of men who ask from you nothing more than the qualities that will command their respect, their loyalty, and their obedience.

They are perfectly ready and eager to follow you so long as you can convince them that you have these qualities. When the time comes that they are satisfied you do not possess them, you might as well kiss yourself good-bye. Your usefulness in that organization is at an end.

How remarkably true this is in all manner of leadership.

From the standpoint of society, the world may be divided into leaders and followers. The professions have their leaders, the financial world has its leaders. In all this leadership it is difficult, if not impossible, to separate from the element of pure leadership that selfish element of personal gain or advantage to the individual, without which any leadership would lose its value.

It is in military service only, where men freely sacrifice their lives for a faith, where men are willing to suffer and die for the right or the prevention of a wrong, that we can hope to realize leadership in its most exalted and disinterested sense. Therefore, when I say *leadership*, I mean *military leadership*.

In a few days the great mass of you men will receive commissions as officers. These commissions will not make you leaders; they will merely make you officers. They will place you in a position where you *can* become leaders if you possess the proper attributes. But you must make good, not so much with the men over you as with the men under you.

Men must and will follow into battle officers who are not leaders, but the driving power behind these men is not enthusiasm but discipline. They go with doubt and trembling that prompts the unspoken question: "What will he do next?"

BEGIN NOW—NOT TOMORROW,

NOT NEXT WEEK, BUT TODAY—

TO SEIZE THE MOMENT

AND MAKE THIS DAY COUNT.

REMEMBER, YESTERDAY IS GONE

AND TOMORROW MAY NEVER COME.

—Ellen Kreidman

Such men obey the letter of their orders but no more. Of devotion to their commander, of exalted enthusiasm that scorns personal risk, of *self-sacrifice* to ensure his personal safety, they know nothing. Their legs carry them forward because their brain and their training tell them they *must* go. Their spirit does not go with them.

Great results are not achieved by cold, passive, unresponsive soldiers. They don't go very far and they stop as soon as they can. Leadership not only demands but receives the willing, unhesitating, unfaltering obedience and loyalty of other men; and a devotion that will cause them, when the time comes, to follow their uncrowned king to hell and back again, if necessary.

You will ask yourselves: "Of just what, then, does leadership consist? What must I do to become a leader? What are the attributes of leadership, and how can I cultivate them?"

Leadership is a composite of a number of qualities. [Just as success is a composite of the factors out of which this course on the laws of success was built.] Among the most important I would list self-confidence, moral ascendancy, self-sacrifice, paternalism, fairness, initiative, decision, dignity, courage.

Self-confidence results, first, from exact knowledge; second, the ability to impart that knowledge; and third, the feeling of superiority over others that naturally follows. All these give the officer poise. To lead, you must *know*. You may bluff all of your men some of the time, but you can't do it all the time. Men will not have confidence in an officer unless he knows his business, and he must know it from the ground up.

The officer should know more about paperwork than his first sergeant and company clerk put together; he should know more about messing than his mess sergeant; more about diseases of the horse than his troop farrier. He should be at least as good a shot as any man in his company.

If the officer does not know, and demonstrates the fact that he does not know, it is entirely human for the soldier to say to himself, "To hell with him. He doesn't know as much about this as I do," and calmly disregard the instructions received.

There is no substitute for accurate knowledge!

Become so well-informed that men will hunt you up to ask questions; that your brother officers will say to one another, "Ask Smith—he knows."

And not only should each officer know thoroughly the duties of his own grade, but he should study those of the two grades next above him. A twofold benefit attaches to this. He prepares himself for duties that may fall to his lot anytime during battle, and he further gains a broader viewpoint which enables him to appreciate the necessity for the issuance of orders and join more intelligently in their execution.

Not only must the officer know, but he must be able to put what he knows into grammatical, interesting, forceful English. He must learn to stand on his feet and speak without embarrassment.

I am told that in British training camps student officers are required to deliver ten-minute talks on any subject they choose. That is excellent practice. For to speak clearly one must think clearly, and clear, logical thinking expresses itself in definite, positive orders.

While self-confidence is the result of knowing more than your men, moral ascendancy over them is based upon your belief that you are the better man. To gain and maintain this ascendancy you must have self-control, physical vitality, and endurance and moral force. You must have yourself so well in hand that, even though in battle you be scared stiff, you will never show fear. For if by so much as a hurried movement or a trembling of the hands, or a change of expression or a hasty order hastily revoked you indicate your mental condition, it will be reflected in your men in a far greater degree.

In garrison or camp, many instances will arise to try your temper and wreck the sweetness of your disposition. If at such times you "fly off the handle," you have no business to be in charge of men. For men in anger say and do things that they almost invariably regret afterward.

An officer should never apologize to his men; also, an officer should never be guilty of an act for which his sense of justice tells him he should apologize.

Another element in gaining moral ascendancy lies in the possession of enough physical vitality and endurance to withstand the hardships to which you and your men are subjected, and a dauntless spirit that enables you not only to accept them cheerfully but to minimize their magnitude.

Make light of your troubles, belittle your trials, and you will help vitally to build up within your organization an esprit whose value in time of stress cannot be measured.

Moral force is the third element in gaining moral ascendancy. To exert moral force you must live clean; you must have sufficient brainpower to see the right and the will to do right.

Be an example to your men!

An officer can be a power for good or a power for evil. Don't preach to them—that will be worse than useless. Live the kind of life you would have them lead, and you will be surprised to see the number that will imitate you.

A loud-mouthed, profane captain who is careless of his personal appearance will have a loud-mouthed, profane, dirty company. *Remember what I tell you. Your company will be the reflection of yourself!* If you have a rotten company it will be because you are a rotten captain.

Self-sacrifice is essential to leadership. You will give, give, all the time. You will give of yourself physically, for the longest hours, the hardest work, and the greatest responsibility are the lot of the captain. He is the first man up in the morning and the last man in at night. He works while others sleep.

You will give of yourself mentally, in sympathy and appreciation for the troubles of the men in your charge. This one's mother has died, and that one has lost all his savings in a bank failure. They may desire help, but more than anything else they desire *sympathy*. Don't make the mistake of turning such men down with the statement that you have troubles of your own, for every time you do that *you knock a stone out of the foundation of your house*. Your men are your foundation, and your house of leadership will tumble about your ears unless it rests securely upon them.

Finally, you will give of your own slender financial resources. You will frequently spend your own money to conserve the health and well-being of your men or to assist them when in trouble. Generally you get your money back. Very frequently you must charge it off to profit and loss.

Even so, it is worth the cost.

When I say that paternalism is essential to leadership, I use the term in its better sense. I do not now refer to that form of paternalism that robs men of initiative, self-reliance, and self-respect. I refer to the paternalism that manifests itself in watchful care for the comfort and welfare of those in your charge.

Soldiers are much like children. You must see that they have shelter, food, and clothing, the best that your utmost efforts can provide. You must see that they have food to eat before you think of your own; that they have each as good a bed as can be provided before you consider where you will sleep.

You must be far more solicitous of their comfort than of your own. You must look after their health. You must conserve their strength by not demanding needless exertion or useless labor.

By doing all these things you are breathing life into what would be otherwise a mere machine. You are creating a soul in your organization that will make the mass respond to you as though it were one man. And that is esprit.

And when your organization has this esprit you will wake up some morning and discover that the tables have been turned; that instead of your constantly looking out for them, they have, without even a hint from you, taken up the task of looking out for *you.* You will find that a detail is always there to see that your tent, if you have one, is promptly pitched; that the most and the cleanest bedding is brought to your tent; that from some mysterious source two eggs have been added to your supper when no one else has any; that an extra man is helping your men give your horse a super grooming; that your wishes are anticipated; that every man is "Johnny-on-the-spot." And then you have *arrived!*

You cannot treat all men alike! A punishment that would be dismissed by one man with a shrug of the shoulders is mental anguish for another. A company commander who, for a given offense, has a standard punishment that applies to all is either too indolent or too stupid to study the personalities of his men. In his case justice is certainly blind.

Study your men as carefully as a surgeon studies a difficult case. And when you are sure of your diagnosis, apply the remedy. Remember that you apply the remedy to effect a cure, not merely to see the victim squirm. It may be necessary to cut deep, but when you are satisfied as to your diagnosis, don't be diverted from your purpose by any false sympathy for the patient.

Hand in hand with fairness in awarding punishment walks fairness in giving credit. Everybody hates a human hog. When one of your men has accomplished an especially creditable piece of work, see that he gets the proper reward. *Turn heaven and earth upside down to get it for him.* Don't try to take it away from him and hog it for yourself. You may do this and get

NO ACCURATE THINKER

WILL JUDGE ANOTHER PERSON

BY THAT WHICH

THE OTHER PERSON'S ENEMIES

SAY ABOUT HIM.

away with it, but you have lost the respect and loyalty of your men. Sooner or later your brother officers will hear of it and shun you like a leper. In war there is glory enough for all. Give the man under you his due. The man who always takes and never gives is not a leader. He is a parasite.

There is another kind of fairness—that which will prevent an officer from abusing the privileges of his rank. When you exact respect from soldiers, be sure you treat them with equal respect. Build up their manhood and self-respect. Don't try to pull it down. For an officer to be overbearing and insulting in the treatment of enlisted men is the act of a coward. He ties the man to a tree with the ropes of discipline and then strikes him in the face knowing full well that the man cannot strike back.

Consideration, courtesy, and respect from officers toward enlisted men are not incompatible with discipline. They are parts of our discipline. Without initiative and decision, no man can expect to lead.

In maneuvers you will frequently see, when an emergency arises, certain men calmly give instant orders which later, on analysis, prove to be, if not exactly the right thing, very nearly the right thing to have done. You will see other men in emergency become badly rattled; their brains refuse to work, or they give a hasty order, revoke it; give another, revoke that; in short, show every indication of being in a blue funk.

Regarding the first man you may say: "That man is a genius. He hasn't had time to reason this thing out. He acts intuitively." Forget it! Genius is merely the capacity for taking infinite pains. The man who was ready is the man who has prepared himself. He has studied beforehand the possible situations that might arise; he has made tentative plans covering such situations. When he is confronted by the emergency he is ready to meet it. He must have sufficient mental alertness to appreciate the problem that confronts him and the power of quick reasoning to determine what changes are necessary in his already formulated plan. He must have the decision to order the execution and stick to his orders.

Any reasonable order in an emergency is better than no order. The situation is there. Meet it. It is better to do something and do the wrong thing than to hesitate, hunt around for the right thing to do, and wind up by doing nothing at all. And, having decided on a line of action, stick to it. Don't vacillate. Men have no confidence in an officer who doesn't know his own mind.

Occasionally you will be called upon to meet a situation that no reasonable human being could anticipate. If you have prepared yourself to meet other emergencies that you could anticipate, the mental training you have thereby gained will enable you to act promptly and with calmness.

You must frequently act without orders from higher authority. Time will not permit you to wait for them. Here again enters the importance of studying the work of officers above you. If you have a comprehensive grasp of the entire situation and can form an idea of the general plan of your superiors, that and your previous emergency training will enable you to determine that the responsibility is yours and to issue the necessary orders without delay.

The element of personal dignity is important in military leadership. Be the friend of your men, but do not become their intimate. Your men should stand in awe of you—not in fear! If your men presume to become familiar it is your fault, not theirs. Your actions have encouraged them. And, above all things, don't cheapen yourself by courting their friendship or currying their favor. They will despise you for it. If you are worthy of their loyalty, respect, and devotion, they will surely give all these without asking. If you are not, nothing that you can do will win them.

It is exceedingly difficult for an officer to be dignified while wearing a dirty, spotted uniform and three-days' stubble of whiskers on his face. Such a man lacks self-respect, and self-respect is an essential of dignity.

There may be occasions when your work entails dirty clothes and an unshaved face. Your men all look that way. At such times there is ample reason for your appearance. In fact, it would be a mistake to look too clean—they would think you were not doing your share. But as soon as this unusual occasion has passed, set an example for personal neatness.

And then I would mention courage. Moral courage you need as well as mental courage—that kind of moral courage which enables you to adhere without faltering to a determined course of action which your judgment has indicated is the one best suited to secure the desired results.

You will find many times, especially in action, that after having issued your orders to do a certain thing, you will be beset by misgivings and doubts; you will see, or think you see, other and better means for accomplishing the object sought. You will be strongly tempted to change your orders. Don't do it until it is clearly manifested that your first orders were radically wrong. For, if you do, you will be again worried by doubts as to the efficacy of your second orders.

Every time you change your orders without obvious reason you weaken your authority and impair the confidence of your men. Have the moral courage to stand by your order and see it through.

Moral courage further demands that you assume responsibility for your own acts. If your subordinates have loyally carried out your orders and the movement you directed is a failure, the failure is *yours*, not theirs. Yours would have been the honor had it been successful. Take the blame if it results in disaster. Don't try to shift it to a subordinate and make him the goat. That is a cowardly act.

Furthermore, you will need moral courage to determine the fate of those under you. You will frequently be called upon for recommendations for promotion or demotion of officers and noncommissioned officers in your immediate command.

THERE IS SOMETHING WRONG

ABOUT THE MAN WHOSE

WIFE AND CHILDREN DO NOT

GREET HIM AFFECTIONATELY

ON HIS HOMECOMING.

Keep clearly in mind your personal integrity and the duty you owe your country. Do not let yourself be deflected from a strict sense of justice by feelings of personal friendship. If your own brother is your second lieutenant and you find him unfit to hold his commission, eliminate him. If you don't, your lack of moral courage may result in the loss of valuable lives. If, on the other hand, you are called upon for a recommendation concerning a man whom, for personal reasons, you thoroughly dislike, do not fail to do him full justice. Remember that your aim is the general good, not the satisfaction of an individual grudge.

I am taking it for granted that you have physical courage. I need not tell you how necessary that is. Courage is more than bravery. Bravery is fearlessness—the absence of fear. The merest dolt may be brave, because he lacks the mentality to appreciate his danger; he doesn't know enough to be afraid.

Courage, however, is that firmness of spirit, that moral backbone which, while fully appreciating the danger involved, nevertheless goes on with the undertaking. Bravery is physical; courage is mental and moral. You may be cold all over; your hands may tremble; your legs may quake; your knees be ready to give way—that is fear. If, nevertheless, you go forward; if, in spite of this physical defection you continue to lead your men against the enemy, you have courage. The physical manifestations of fear will pass away. You may never experience them but once. They are the "buck fever" of the hunter who tries to shoot his first deer. You must not give way to them.

A number of years ago, while taking a course in demolitions, the class of which I was a member was handling dynamite. The instructor said, regarding its manipulation: "I must caution you gentlemen to be careful in the use of these explosives. One man has but one accident." And so I would caution you. If you give way to fear that will doubtless beset you in your first action, if you show the white feather, if you let your men go forward while you hunt a shell crater, you will never again have the opportunity of leading those men.

Use judgment in calling on your men for displays of physical courage or bravery. *Don't ask any man to go where you would not go yourself.* If your common sense tells you that the place is too dangerous for you to venture into, then it is too dangerous for him. You know his life is as valuable to him as yours is to you.

Occasionally some of your men must be exposed to danger that you cannot share. A message must be taken across a fire-swept zone. You call for volunteers. If your men know you and know that you are "right" you will never lack volunteers, for they will know your heart is in your work, that you are giving your country the best you have, that you would willingly carry the message yourself if you could. Your example and enthusiasm will have inspired them.

And, lastly, if you aspire to leadership, I would urge you to study men. Get under their skins and find out what is inside. Some men are quite different from what they appear to be on the surface. Determine the workings of their minds.

Much of General Robert E. Lee's success as a leader may be ascribed to his ability as a *psychologist.* He knew most of his opponents from West Point days, knew the workings of their minds, and he believed that they would do certain things under certain circumstances. In nearly every case he was able to anticipate their movements and block the execution.

You cannot know your opponent in this war in the same way. But you can know your own men. You can study each to determine wherein lies his strength and his weakness, which man can be relied upon to the last gasp and which cannot.

Know your men, know your business, know yourself!

In all literature you will not find a better description of Leadership than this. Apply it to yourself, to your business, or to your place of employment and you will observe how well it serves as your guide.

Major Bach's address is one that might well be delivered to every boy and girl who graduates from high school. It might well be delivered to every college graduate. It might well become the book of rules for every person who is placed in a position of Leadership over others, no matter in what calling, business, or profession.

MAKE BOLD DECISIONS QUICKLY

In Lesson Two you learned the value of a Definite Chief Aim. Here, I want to emphasize that your definite aim will never be anything else but a mere wish unless you become a person of Initiative and aggressively and persistently pursue that aim until it has been fulfilled. Your aim must be active and not passive.

You can get nowhere without persistence, a fact that cannot be too often repeated.

The difference between persistence and lack of it is the same as the difference between wishing for a thing and positively determining to get it.

To become a person of Initiative, you must form the habit of *aggressively* and *persistently* following the object of your Definite Chief Aim until you acquire it, whether this requires one year or twenty years. You might as well have no Definite Chief Aim as to have such an aim without *continuous* effort to achieve it.

You are not making the most of this Law of Success course if you do not take some step each day that brings you nearer the realization of your Definite Chief Aim. Do not fool yourself, or permit yourself to be misled to believe that the object of your Definite Chief Aim will materialize if you just wait. The materialization will come only through your own determination, backed by your own carefully laid plans and your own Initiative in putting those plans into action, or it will not come at all.

One of the major requisites for Leadership is the power of quick and firm *decision!*

Analysis of more than 16,000 people disclosed the fact that leaders always make ready decisions, even in matters of small importance, while followers *never* make quick decisions.

This is worth remembering!

The follower, in whatever walk of life that person is found, is one who seldom knows what he or she wants. The follower vacillates, procrastinates, and actually refuses to reach a decision, even in matters of the smallest importance, unless a leader induces him or her to do so.

To know that the majority of people cannot and will not reach decisions quickly, if at all, is of great help to the leader who knows what he or she wants and has a plan for getting it.

Here it will be observed how closely allied are the two laws covered by Lesson Two and by this lesson. The leader not only works with a Definite Chief Aim, but also has a very *definite plan* for attaining the object of that aim. It will be seen, as well, that Self-Confidence becomes an important part of the working equipment of the leader.

The chief reason why the follower does not reach decisions is that he or she lacks the Self-Confidence to do so. Every leader makes use of the law of a Definite Chief Aim, the law of Self-Confidence, and the law of Initiative and Leadership. And an outstanding, successful leader also makes use of the laws of Imagination, Enthusiasm, Self-Control, Pleasing Personality, Accurate Thinking, Concentration, and Tolerance. Without the combined use of all these laws, no one may become a really great leader. Omission of a single one of these laws lessens the power of the leader proportionately.

A salesman for the LaSalle Extension University called on a real estate dealer, in a small western town, for the purpose of trying to sell the realtor a course in salesmanship and business management.

When the salesman arrived at the prospective student's office, he found the gentleman pecking out a letter by the two-finger method, on an antiquated typewriter. The salesman introduced himself, stated his business, and then described the course he had come to sell.

The realtor listened with apparent interest. After his sales talk had been completed the salesman hesitated, waiting for some signs of yes or no from his prospective client. Thinking that perhaps he had not made his talk quite strong enough, he briefly went over the merits of the course he was selling, a second time. Still there was no response from the prospective student.

The salesman then asked the direct question, "You want this course, do you not?"

In a slow, drawling tone of voice, the realtor then replied: "Well, I hardly know whether I do or not."

And no doubt he was telling the truth, because he was one of the millions who find it hard to reach decisions.

Being an able judge of human nature, the salesman then arose, put on his hat, placed his literature back in his briefcase, and made ready to leave. Then he resorted to tactics that were somewhat drastic, and took the realtor by surprise with this startling statement:

"I am going to take it upon myself to say something to you that you will not like, but it may be of help to you.

"Take a look at this office in which you work! The floor is dirty, the walls are dusty, the typewriter you are using looks as if it might be the one Mr. Noah used in the Ark during the big flood. Your pants are bagged at the knees, your collar is dirty, your face is unshaved, and you have a look in your eyes that tells me you are defeated.

"Please go ahead and get mad—that's just what I want you to do, because it may shock you into doing some thinking that will be helpful to you and to those who are dependent upon you.

"I can see, in my imagination, the home in which you live. Several little children, none too well-dressed, and perhaps none too well-fed; a mother whose dress is three seasons out of style, whose eyes carry the same look of defeat that yours do. This woman whom you married has stuck by you but you have not made good in life as she had hoped, when you were first married, that you would.

IF YOU HAVE A TALENT,

USE IT IN EVERY WAY POSSIBLE.

DON'T HOARD IT.

DON'T DOLE IT OUT LIKE A MISER.

SPEND IT LAVISHLY LIKE A

MILLIONAIRE INTENT ON GOING BROKE.

—Brendan Francis

"Please remember that I am not now talking to a prospective student, because I would not sell you the course—at this particular moment—if you offered to pay cash in advance, because if I did, you would not have the initiative to complete it, and we want no failures on our student list.

"The talk I am now giving you will make it impossible, perhaps, for me ever to sell you anything, but it is going to do something for you that has never been done before, providing it makes you think.

"I will tell you, in a very few words, exactly why you are defeated; why you are pecking out letters on an old typewriter, in an old dirty office, in a little town: *It is because you do not have the power to reach a decision!*

"All of your life you have been forming the habit of dodging the responsibility of reaching decisions, until you have come now to where it is well-nigh impossible for you to do so.

"If you had told me that you wanted the course, or that you did not want it, I could have sympathized with you, because I would have known that lack of funds was what caused you to hesitate. But what did you say? Why, you admitted that you did not know whether you wanted it or not.

"If you will think over what I have said, I am sure that you will acknowledge that it has become a habit with you to dodge the responsibility of reaching clear-cut decisions on practically all matters that affect you."

The realtor sat glued in his chair, with his underjaw dropped and his eyes bulged in astonishment, but he made no attempt to answer the biting indictment.

The salesman said good-bye and started for the door.

After he had closed the door behind him, he again opened it and walked back in. With a smile on his face, he took his seat in front of the astonished realtor and explained his conduct in this way:

"I do not blame you at all if you feel hurt by my remarks. In fact, I sort of hope that you have been offended. But now let me say this, face to face, that I think you have intelligence and I am sure you have ability, but you have fallen into a habit that has whipped you. Nobody is ever down and out until he is under the sod. You may be temporarily down, but you can get up again, and I am just sportsman enough to give you my hand and offer you a lift, if you will accept my apologies for what I have said.

"You do not belong in this town. You would starve to death in the real estate business in this place, even if you were a leader in your field. Get yourself a new suit of clothes, even if you have to borrow the money with which to do it, then go over to St. Louis with me and I will introduce you to a real estate agent who will give you a chance to earn some money and at the same time teach you some of the important things about this line of work that you can later capitalize on.

"If you do not have enough credit to get the clothes you need, I will stand good for you at a store in St. Louis where I have a charge account. I am in earnest and my offer to help you is based upon the highest motive that can actuate a human being. I am successful in my own field, but I have not always been so. I went through just what you are now going through, but the important thing is that I went through it, and got it over with, just as you are going to do if you will follow my advice.

"Will you come with me?"

The realtor started to rise, but his legs wobbled and he sank back into his chair. Despite the fact that he was a great big fellow, a "he-man" type, his emotions got the better of him and he actually wept.

He made a second attempt and got on his feet, shook hands with the salesman, thanked him for his kindness, and said he was going to follow the advice but he would do so in his own way.

Asking for an application blank, he signed for the course on salesmanship and business management, made the first payment in nickels and dimes, and told the salesman he would hear from him again.

Three years later this realtor had an organization of sixty salesmen and one of the most successful real estate businesses in the city of St. Louis. I have been in this realtor's office many times and have observed him over a period of more than fifteen years. He is an entirely different human being from the person interviewed by the LaSalle salesman over fifteen years ago. And the thing that made him different is the same that will make *you* different: It is the power of *decision* that is so essential to Leadership.

This realtor is now a leader in the real estate field. He is directing the efforts of other salesmen and helping them to become more efficient. This one change in his philosophy has turned temporary defeat into success. Every new salesperson who goes to work for him is called into his private office, before going to work, and told the story of his own transformation, word for word, just as it occurred when the LaSalle salesman first met him in his shabby little real estate office.

Some eighteen years ago I made my first trip to the little town of Lumberport, West Virginia. At that time the only means of transportation leading from Clarksburg, the largest nearby center, to Lumberport was both the Baltimore & Ohio Railroad and an interurban electric line which ran within three miles of the town. One could walk the three miles if they chose.

Upon my arrival at Clarksburg I found that the only train going to Lumberport in the forenoon had already gone, and not wishing to wait for the later afternoon train I made the trip by trolley, with the intention of walking the three miles. On the way down, the rain began to pour, and those three miles had to be navigated on foot, through deep yellow mud. When I arrived at Lumberport my shoes and pants were muddy, and my disposition was none the better for the experience.

MASTERY OF THE

SEVENTEEN LAWS OF SUCCESS

IS THE EQUIVALENT OF

AN INSURANCE POLICY

AGAINST FAILURE.

—Samuel Gompers

The first person I met was V. L. Hornor, who was then cashier of the Lumberport Bank. In a rather loud tone of voice I asked of him, "Why do you not get that trolley line extended from the junction over to Lumberport so your friends can get in and out of town without drowning in mud?"

"Did you see a river with high banks, at the edge of town, as you came in?" he asked. I replied that I had seen it. "Well," he continued, "that's the reason we have no streetcars running into town. The cost of a bridge would be about $100,000 and that is more than the company owning the trolley line is willing to invest. We have been trying for ten years to get them to build a line into town."

"Trying!" I exploded. "How hard have you tried?"

"We have offered them every inducement we could afford, such as free right of way from the junction into the town, and free use of the streets, but that bridge is the stumbling block. They simply will not stand the expense. Claim they cannot afford such an expense for the small amount of revenue they would receive from the three-mile extension."

Then the Law of Success philosophy began to come to my rescue!

I asked Mr. Hornor if he would take a walk over to the river with me, that we might look at the spot that was causing so much inconvenience. He said he would be glad to do so.

When we got to the river I began to take inventory of everything in sight. I observed that the Baltimore & Ohio Railroad tracks ran up and down the river banks, on both sides of the river, and that the county road crossed the river on a rickety wooden bridge, both approaches to which were over several strands of railroad track, as the railroad company had its switching yards at that point.

While we were standing there, a freight train blocked the crossing and several teams of horses stopped on both sides of the train, waiting for an opportunity to get through. The train kept the road blocked for about twenty-five minutes.

With this combination of circumstances in mind, it required little Imagination to see that *three different parties* were or could be interested in the building of the bridge such as would be needed to carry the weight of a streetcar.

It was obvious that the Baltimore & Ohio Railroad Company would be interested in such a bridge, because that would remove the county road from their switching tracks. It would also save them a possible accident on the crossing, to say nothing of much loss of time and expense in cutting trains to allow the wagon teams to pass.

It was also obvious that the County Commissioners would be interested in the bridge, because it would raise the county road to a better level and make it more serviceable to the public. And of course the street railway company was interested in the bridge, *but it did not wish to pay the entire cost.*

All of this passed through my mind as I stood there watching the freight train being cut for the traffic to pass through.

A Definite Chief Aim took place in my mind. Also a *definite plan* for its attainment. The next day I got together a committee of townspeople, consisting of the mayor, councilmen, and some of the leading citizens, and called on the Division Superintendent of the Baltimore & Ohio Railroad Company at Grafton. We convinced him that it was worth one-third of the cost of the bridge to get the county road off his company's tracks. Next we went to the County Commissioners and found them to be quite enthusiastic over the possibility of getting a new bridge by paying for only one-third of it. They promised to pay their one-third, providing we could make arrangements for the other two-thirds.

We then went to the president of the Traction Company which owned the trolley line at Fairmont, and laid before him an offer to donate all the rights of way and pay for two-thirds of the cost of the bridge, providing he would begin building the line into town promptly. We found him receptive also.

Three weeks later a contract had been signed between the Baltimore & Ohio Railroad Company, the Monongahela Valley Traction Company, and the County Commissioners of Harrison County, providing for the construction of the bridge, one-third of its cost to be paid by each.

Just two months later, the right of way was being graded and the bridge was under way. And three months after that, the streetcars were running into Lumberport on regular schedule.

This incident meant much to the town of Lumberport, because it provided transportation that enabled people to get in and out of the town without undue effort.

It also meant a great deal to me, because it served to introduce me as one who "got things done." Two very definite advantages resulted from this transaction. The Chief Counsel for the Traction Company gave me a position as his assistant, and later on it was the means of an introduction that led to my appointment as the advertising manager of the LaSalle Extension University.

Lumberport, West Virginia, was then and still is a small town, and Chicago was a large city and located a considerable distance away, but news of Initiative and Leadership has a way of taking on wings and traveling.

Four of the seventeen laws of success were combined in the transaction I have described here: a Definite Chief Aim, Self-Confidence, Imagination, and Initiative and Leadership. The law of Doing More Than Paid For also entered, somewhat, into the transaction, because I was not offered anything and, in fact, did not expect pay for what I did.

To be perfectly frank, I appointed myself to that job of getting the bridge built more as a sort of challenge to those who had said it could not be done than I did with the expectation of getting paid for it. By my attitude I rather intimated to Mr. Hornor that I could get it done, and he was not slow to snap me up and put me to the test.

TIME IS THE MIGHTY HAND

THAT ROCKS THE ETERNAL CRADLE

OF PROGRESS AND

NURSES STRUGGLING HUMANITY

THROUGH THAT PERIOD

WHEN MAN NEEDS PROTECTION

AGAINST HIS OWN IGNORANCE.

It would be helpful here to point out the part that Imagination played in this transaction. For ten years the townspeople of Lumberport had been trying to get a streetcar line built into town. It must not be concluded that the town was without any citizens of ability, because that would be inaccurate. In fact there were many able people in the town, but they had been making the mistake, which is so commonly made by us all, of trying to solve their problem through one single source, whereas there were actually *three sources* of solution available to them.

One hundred thousand dollars was too much for one company to assume for the construction of a bridge, but when that cost was distributed among three interested parties, the amount to be borne by each was more reasonable.

The question might be asked, why did some of the local townspeople not think of this three-way solution?

In the first place, they were so close to their problem that they failed to take a perspective bird's-eye view of it, which would have suggested the solution. This is a common mistake, and one that is always avoided by great leaders. In the second place, these townspeople had never before coordinated their efforts or worked as an organized group with the sole purpose in mind of finding a way to get a streetcar line built into town. This is another common error made by people in all walks of life—that of failure to work in unison, in a thorough spirit of Cooperation.

I, being an outsider, had less difficulty in getting cooperative action than one of their own group might have had. Too often there is a spirit of selfishness in small communities which prompts each individual to think that their ideas are the ones that should prevail. It is an important part of the leader's responsibility to induce people to subordinate their own ideas and interests for the good of the whole, and this applies to matters of a civic, business, social, political, financial, or industrial nature.

Success, no matter what may be one's concept of that term, is nearly always a question of one's ability to get others to subordinate their own individual interests and follow a leader. The leader who has the Personality and the Imagination to induce followers to accept his or her plans and carry them out faithfully is always an able leader.

The next lesson, Imagination, will take you further into the art of tactful Leadership. Leadership and Imagination are so closely allied and so essential for success that one cannot be gainfully applied without the other. Initiative is the moving force that pushes the leader ahead, but Imagination is the guiding spirit that tells him or her which way to go.

Imagination is what enabled me to analyze the Lumberport bridge problem, break it up into its three component parts, and assemble those parts into a practical working plan. Nearly every problem may be broken up into parts which are more easily managed, as parts, than they are when assembled as a whole. Perhaps one of the most important advantages of Imagination is that it enables one to separate all problems into their component parts and to reassemble them in more favorable combinations.

It has been said that all battles in warfare are won or lost not on the firing line but behind the lines, through the sound strategy, or the lack of it, used by the generals who plan the battles.

What is true of warfare is equally true in business, and in most other problems that confront us throughout life. We win or lose according to the nature of the plans we build and carry out, a fact which serves to emphasize the value of the laws of Initiative and Leadership, Imagination, Self-Confidence, and a Definite Chief Aim.

With the intelligent use of these four laws, one may build plans, for any purpose whatsoever, which cannot be defeated by any person or group of persons who do not employ or understand these laws.

There is no escape from this truth. *Organized effort* is effort that is directed according to a plan that was conceived with the aid of Imagination, guided by a Definite Chief Aim, and given momentum with Initiative and Self-Confidence. These four laws blend into one and become a power in the hands of a leader. Without their aid, effective Leadership is impossible.

INTOLERANCE—
AN AFTER-THE-LESSON VISIT WITH THE AUTHOR

If you must give expression to prejudice and hatred and intolerance,
do not speak it, but write it; write it in the sands, near the water's edge.

When the dawn of intelligence shall spread over the eastern horizon of human progress, and ignorance and superstition shall have left their last footprints on the sands of time, it will be recorded in the last chapter of the book of humanity's crimes that our most grievous sin was that of intolerance.

The bitterest intolerance grows out of religious, racial, and economic prejudices and differences of opinion. How long until we will understand the folly of trying to destroy one another because we are of different religious beliefs and racial tendencies?

Our allotted time on this earth is but a fleeting moment. Like a candle, we are lighted, shine for a moment, and flicker out. Why can we not learn to so live during this brief earthly visit that when the great caravan called Death draws up and announces this visit completed, we will be ready to fold our tents and silently follow out into the great unknown without fear and trembling?

I am hoping that I will find no Jews or Gentiles, Catholics or Protestants, Germans, English, or French when I shall have crossed the bar to the other side. I am hoping that I will find there only human souls, brothers and sisters all, unmarked by race, creed, or color, for I shall want to be done with intolerance so I may rest in peace throughout eternity.

DESTINY IS NOT

A MATTER OF CHANCE;

IT IS A MATTER OF CHOICE.

IT IS NOT A THING TO BE WAITED FOR;

IT IS A THING TO BE ACHIEVED.

—William Jennings Bryan

There is a famous picture that, to my mind, perfectly describes the futility of combat.

Two male deer have engaged in a fight to the finish, each believing that he will be the winner. Off at the side, a doe awaits the victor, little dreaming that tomorrow the bones of both combatants will be bleaching in the sun.

Twenty years ago a great educational institution was doing a thriving business and rendering a worthy service to thousands of students. The two owners of the school married two beautiful and talented young women who were especially accomplished in the art of piano playing. The two wives became involved in an argument as to which one was the more accomplished in this art. The disagreement was taken up by each of the husbands. They became bitter enemies. Now the bones of that once prosperous school "lie bleaching in the sun."

In one of the great industrial plants, two young managers "locked horns" because one received a promotion that the other should have had. For more than five years the silent undertow of hatred and intolerance showed itself. Those who worked under each of them became inoculated with the spirit of dislike that they saw cropping out in their superiors. Slowly the spirit of retaliation began to spread over the entire plant. The employees became divided into little cliques. Production began to fall off. Then came financial difficulty and finally bankruptcy for the company. Now the bones of a once prosperous business "lie bleaching in the sun," and the two managers and several thousand others were compelled to start all over again, in another field.

In a fashionable suburb of Philadelphia, certain people of wealth have built their homes. The word *intolerance* might just as well be inscribed on each door. One owner builds a high steel fence in front of their house. The neighbor, not to be outdone, builds a fence twice as high. Another buys a new car, and the next-door neighbor goes one better by purchasing two new cars. Another remodels, adding a Colonial-style porch. Then another adds a new porch and a Spanish-style garage for good measure. The big mansion on top of the hill gives a reception which brings a long line of cars filled with people who have nothing in particular in common with the host. Then follows a series of "receptions" all down the "gold-coast" line, each trying to outshine all the others.

Andrew Carnegie and Henry C. Frick did more than any other two men to establish the steel industry. Both made millions of dollars for themselves. Then came the day when economic intolerance sprang up between them. To show his contempt for Frick, Carnegie built a tall skyscraper and named it the Carnegie Building. Frick retaliated by erecting a much taller building, right alongside of the Carnegie Building, naming it the Frick Building.

These two gentlemen had "locked horns" in a fight to the finish. Carnegie lost his mind and perhaps more, for all we know. What Frick lost is known only to Frick himself and the keeper of the Great Records. In memory, their bones "lie bleaching in the sun" of posterity.

Poverty has some advantages—it never drives those who are poverty-stricken to lock horns in the attempt to out-poverty their neighbors.

Wherever you see people with their "horns locked" in conflict, you may trace the cause of the combat to one of the three causes of intolerance—religious difference of opinion, economic competition, or sexual competition.

The next time you observe two people engaged in hostility toward each other, just close your eyes and think for a moment and you will be surprised how much they begin to resemble two deer with their horns locked over a doe, a religious emblem, or a pile of gold.

Seventeen factors enter into the attainment of success. One of these is Tolerance. The other sixteen are mentioned many times in this series of lessons.

Intolerance binds our legs with the shackles of ignorance and covers our eyes with the scales of fear and superstition. Intolerance closes the book of knowledge and writes on the cover: "Open not this book again. The last word has been herein written."

It is not your *duty* to be tolerant; it is your *privilege!*

Remember, as you read this, that sowing the seed of intolerance is the sole and exclusive business of *some.* All wars and all other forms of human suffering bring profit to *some.* If this were not true, there would be no wars or other similar forms of hostility.

―――――――――

When you feel yourself preparing to lock horns with someone, remember that it will be more profitable if you *lock hands* instead! A handshake leaves no bones bleaching in the sun.

> *Love* is the only bow on life's dark cloud. It is the Morning and the Evening Star. It shines upon the cradle of the babe, and sheds its radiance upon the quiet tomb. It is the mother of Art, inspirer of poet, patriot and philosopher. It is the air and light of every heart, builder of every home, kindler of every fire on every hearth. It was the first to dream of immortality. It fills the world with melody, for Music is the voice of Love. Love is the magician, the enchanter that changes worthless things to Joy, and makes right royal kings and queens of common clay. It is the perfume of the wondrous flower—the heart—and without that sacred passion, that divine swoon, we are less than beasts; but with it, earth is heaven and we are gods.
>
> —INGERSOLL

Cultivate *love* for your fellow human being and you will no longer want to lock horns with them in futile combat. Love makes each of us our brother's keeper.

> *Love, indeed, is light from heaven;*
> *A spark of that immortal fire*
> *With angels shared, by Allah given,*
> *To lift from earth our low desire.*
> *Devotion wafts the mind above,*
> *But heaven itself descends in love;*
> *A feeling from the Godhead caught,*
> *To wean from self each sordid thought;*
> *A ray of Him who form'd the whole;*
> *A glory circling round the soul.*
>
> —BYRON

There are twenty qualities a leader must possess. Rubber-spined people will have no part in the Leadership of the future. They will have been supplanted because they lacked the qualities essential for Leadership at a time when the whole country was literally bleeding to death because of poor Leadership. Leaders of the future must possess these qualities:

1. Complete mastery over the six basic fears.

2. Willingness to subordinate personal interests for the good of their followers. Complete mastery over avarice and greed.

3. Singleness of purpose, represented by a definite program of Leadership which harmonizes with the needs of the times.

4. Understanding and application of the Master Mind principle, by which power may be achieved through coordination of effort in a spirit of harmony.

5. Self-Confidence in its highest form.

6. Ability to reach decisions quickly and stand by them firmly.

7. Imagination sufficient to enable them to anticipate the needs of the times and to create plans for supplying those needs.

8. Initiative in its keenest form.

9. Enthusiasm and the ability to transmit it to their followers.

10. Self-Control in its highest form.

11. A willingness to render more service than that for which direct compensation is received.

12. A pleasing, magnetic personality.

13. The ability to think accurately.

14. The ability to cooperate with others in a spirit of harmony.

15. The persistence to concentrate thoughts and efforts upon a given task until it has been completed.

16. The ability and "hindsight" to profit by mistakes and failures.

17. Tolerance in its highest form.

18. Temperance in all of its forms.

19. Intentional honesty of both purpose and deed.

20. Last, but by no means least, strict adherence to the Golden Rule as the basis of all relationships with others.

This may appear to be a formidable list of qualities with which the leader of the future must be equipped, but time will prove that those leaders who endure will possess and make use of every one of these qualities. The leaders of the future will be compelled to avoid the mistakes of the leaders of the past, the chief of which has been *exploitation of their followers.* Great fortunes accumulated at the expense of the masses will not be among the possessions of the leaders of the future.

Wise beyond room for comparison will be the aspirant to future Leadership who realizes that no business or profession of the future may be successfully conducted without recognition of the fact that the followers and patrons of that business or profession are *partners in it,* and as such are entitled to share in the benefits to be derived from it.

COMMENTARY

If you think that sounds like pie-in-the-sky optimism, let us offer you an example: Sam Walton. At his death in 1992, Sam Walton was the richest person in America, worth $28 billion. He made that fortune through his Wal-Mart stores, providing everyday necessities to everyday people.

Walton's customers benefited from his business because it provided them the things they needed at lower prices than any other store. They also benefited from shopping in a place where the clerks were friendly and eager to help. That spirit was a direct result of Walton's dedication to working hard alongside his employees. He would show up on loading docks late at night with bags of donuts for his crews, jump up on tables at store openings and lead the staff in a cheer, and once paid up—by doing the hula down Wall Street—on a dare to them to bring in improved profits.

Walton also shared the company's wealth very generously, paying yearly bonuses in the company's valuable stock. People who were committed to Wal-Mart were repaid with retirement accounts that, even for salesclerks, could be worth hundreds of thousands of dollars. It may have cost Walton a little more up front, but it earned him an unbelievable return in terms of the enthusiasm of his employees.

Sam Walton's dynamic leadership style encompassed all twenty of the qualities Napoleon Hill proposes in this lesson—and more.

Before beginning the next lesson it may be helpful if you take inventory of yourself and determine your rating on the twenty qualities of Leadership. Self-analysis is always beneficial, provided the analysis is accurate. Every essential for Leadership can be cultivated by anyone who makes a reasonable effort to apply the Law of Success philosophy.

If you wish to be certain that your self-analysis is accurate, give yourself a rating on each of the twenty qualities of Leadership and then have it checked by two or three people who know you well enough to judge you accurately.

Here is a simple method of rating yourself: Copy the twenty qualities of Leadership on a sheet of paper. After each of the qualities write the word "perfect, fair, or poor" according to what you believe your rating to be. Perfect will entitle you to a rating of 5 percent, fair will entitle you to a rating of 2.5 percent, and poor should be rated as zero. Enter your rating for each quality on your analysis sheet. If your total gives you an average of less than 75 percent, you will know that you are not yet passable as a leader in your chosen occupation. The chart will disclose where you are weak. Mastery of this philosophy will provide all you need with which to eliminate or bridge your weakness.

This self-analysis should be made before you continue on to the next lesson, because it will help you get more from that lesson and from all the lessons that follow. Remember, as you make this analysis, that its purpose is to let you see yourself as you are, through eyes that are dependable and friendly.

You are now ready for the lesson on Imagination. Read that lesson with the thought in mind of all that has been stated here and it will take on a deeper meaning.

Lesson Six

Imagination

I CALL THAT MAN IDLE

WHO MIGHT BE BETTER EMPLOYED.

—Socrates

Lesson Six

──────────

IMAGINATION

──────────

"You Can Do It if You Believe You Can!"

I MAGINATION IS THE WORKSHOP OF THE HUMAN mind, wherein old ideas and established facts may be reassembled into new combinations and put to new uses. Webster's Third International Dictionary defines *imagination* as follows:

> 1. an act or process of forming a conscious idea or mental image of something never before wholly perceived in reality by the imaginer (as through a synthesis of remembered elements of previous sensory experiences or ideas . . .) 2. creative ability . . . resourcefulness. . . .

Imagination has been called the creative power of the soul, but this is somewhat abstract and goes more deeply into the meaning than is necessary from the viewpoint of a student of this course who wishes to use the course only as a means of attaining material or monetary advantages in life.

IMAGINATION CAN BE DEVELOPED

If you have mastered and thoroughly understood the preceding lessons you know that the materials out of which you built your Definite Chief Aim were assembled and combined in your Imagination. You also know that Self-Confidence, and Initiative and Leadership, must be created in your Imagination before they can become a reality, for it is in the workshop of your Imagination that you will put the principle of autosuggestion into operation in creating these necessary qualities.

This lesson on Imagination might be called the "hub" of this course, because every other lesson of the course leads to this lesson and makes use of the principle upon which it is based, just as all the telephone wires lead to the exchange office for their source of power. You will never have a *definite purpose* in life, you will never have Self-Confidence, you will never have Initiative and Leadership unless you first create these qualities in your Imagination and see yourself in possession of them.

Just as the oak tree develops from the germ that lies in the acorn, and the bird develops from the germ that lies asleep in the egg, so will your material achievements grow out of the *organized* plans that you create in your Imagination. First comes the thought; then organization of that thought into ideas and plans; then transformation of those plans into reality. The beginning, as you will observe, is in your Imagination.

The Imagination is both interpretative and creative in nature. It can examine facts, concepts, and ideas, and it can create new combinations and plans out of these.

COMMENTARY

Imagination is too often regarded as nothing more than fanciful dreams, but it is a tremendously practical, exciting tool. Forget the pejorative terms you may have heard, such as "having your head in the clouds" or "contemplating your navel." This lesson will help you regard your imagination as a useful, vigorous ally in your pursuit of success.

If further proof were needed, consider that much of the vast Walt Disney empire was born out of the fanciful thinking of a group that Walt dubbed his Imagineers, that the space program and many advances in medicine have been achieved by imagining what might be and then applying science and technology to making those "pipe dreams" real, and that even our military leaders openly drew upon Hollywood screenwriters to create imagined scenarios so that those in charge of the War on Terrorism could prepare countermeasures to the kind of attacks that weren't covered in conventional military strategy.

Through its interpretative capacity, the Imagination has one power not generally attributed to it: the power to register vibrations and thought waves that are put into motion from outside sources, just as the radio-receiving apparatus picks up the vibrations of sound. The principle through which this interpretative capacity of the Imagination functions is called telepathy—the communication of thought from one mind to another, at long or short distances, without the aid of physical or mechanical appliances, in the manner explained in Lesson One, Introduction to the Master Mind.

COMMENTARY

At the time Napoleon Hill was writing the original edition of this book, research was being conducted which strongly implied that telepathy would soon be a proven fact. However, by the beginning of the twenty-first century, the evidence in its favor is still largely anecdotal.

It is the opinion of the editors of this updated edition that Napoleon Hill would not have been deterred by the lack of scientific evidence. Hill's interest in telepathy was purely practical, not in proving the existence of some parapsychic phenomenon. The editors advise the reader to suspend any skepticism you might have because the term telepathy *has, in the intervening years, fallen out of favor. Instead, pay attention to the perfectly logical and practical application Hill had in mind when he used the term.*

Telepathy can be an important factor to a student who is preparing to make effective use of Imagination, because this telepathic capacity of the Imagination is constantly picking up thought waves and vibrations of every description. So-called "snap judgment" and "hunches," which prompt one to form an opinion or decide upon a course of action that is not in harmony with logic and reason, are usually the result of stray thought waves that have registered in the Imagination.

That you may understand how closely interwoven are the seventeen factors upon which this course is based, consider, for example, what happens when a salesperson who lacks confidence in themself, and in their goods, walks in to see a prospective buyer. Whether or not the prospective buyer is conscious of it, his or her Imagination immediately "senses" that lack of confidence in the salesperson's mind. The salesperson's own *thoughts* are actually undermining their own efforts. This will explain, from another angle, why Self-Confidence is one of the most important factors entering into the great struggle for success.

The principle of telepathy and the law of attraction, through which like attracts like, explain many a failure. If the mind has a tendency to attract those thought vibrations which harmonize with the dominating thoughts of a given mind, you can easily understand why a negative mind that dwells on failure and lacks Self-Confidence would not attract a positive mind that is dominated by thoughts of success.

Perhaps these explanations are somewhat abstract, but it seems necessary to inject them here as a means of enabling the student to understand and make practical use of the subject of this lesson. The Imagination is too often regarded merely as an indefinite, untraceable, indescribable something that does nothing but create fiction. It is this popular disregard of the powers of the Imagination that has made necessary these more or less abstract references to the subject. Not only is the subject of Imagination an important factor in this course, but it is also one of the most interesting subjects, as you will observe when you begin to see how it affects all that you do toward the achievement of your Definite Chief Aim.

You will see the importance of the subject of Imagination when you stop to realize that it is the only thing in the world over which you have absolute control. Others may deprive you of your material wealth and cheat you in a thousand ways, but no one can deprive you of the control and use of your Imagination. Others may deal with you unfairly, as they often do; they may deprive you of your liberty, but they *cannot* take from you the privilege of using your Imagination as you wish.

The most inspiring poem in all literature was written by Leigh Hunt while he was a poverty-stricken inmate in an English prison, where he had been unjustly confined because of his advanced views on politics. This poem is entitled "Abou Ben Adhem," and it is here reprinted as a reminder that one of the great things each of us may do, in our own Imaginations, is to forgive those who have dealt unjustly with us:

> *Abou Ben Adhem (may his tribe increase)*
> *Awoke one night from a deep dream of peace*
> *And saw within the moonlight of his room,*
> *Making it rich and like a lily in bloom,*
> *An angel writing in a book of gold,*
> *Exceeding peace had made Ben Adhem bold,*
> *And to the presence in the room he said:*
> *"What writest thou?"—the vision raised its head,*

THE MAN WHO SLANDERS

HIS FELLOWMAN UNWITTINGLY

UNCOVERS THE REAL NATURE

OF HIS INNER SELF.

And, with a look made of all sweet accord,
Answered, "The names of those who love the Lord."
"And is mine one?" said Abou. "Nay, not so,"
Replied the angel. Abou spoke more low,
But cheerily still; and said, "I pray thee, then,
Write me as one that loves his fellow men."
The angel wrote, and vanished. The next night
It came again, with a great wakening light,
And showed the names whom love of God had blessed.
And, lo! Ben Adhem's name led all the rest!

Civilization itself owes its existence to such poets as Leigh Hunt, in whose fertile Imaginations have been pictured the higher and nobler standards of human relationship. "Abou Ben Adhem" is a poem that will never die, thanks to this poet who pictured in his Imagination the hope of an ideal that is constructive.

THE POWER OF IMAGINATION

The major trouble with this world today lies in our lack of understanding of the power of Imagination, for if we understood this great power we could use it as a weapon with which to wipe out poverty and misery and injustice and persecution, and this could be done in a single generation. This is a rather broad statement, and no one understands better than I how useless such a statement would be if the principle on which it is founded were not explained in the most practical of terms. Therefore, let me describe what is meant.

I will devote no time to proving that telepathy is a reality. To make this description understandable we must simply accept the principle of telepathy, in the sense that every thought we release is registering itself in the minds of other people.

You have often heard of "mob psychology," which is nothing more nor less than some strong, dominating idea that has been created in the mind of one or more persons and registers itself in the minds of other persons through the principle of telepathy. So strong is the power of mob psychology that two men fighting in the street will often start a "free-for-all" fight in which bystanders will engage each other in battle without even knowing what they are fighting about, or with whom they are fighting.

On Armistice Day 1918, we had extraordinary anecdotal evidence of the principle of telepathy, on a scale such as the world had never before witnessed. I remember, distinctly, the impression made on my mind on that eventful day. So strong was this impression that it had awakened me at about three o'clock in the morning, just as effectively as if someone had aroused me by physical force. As I sat up in bed I knew that something out of the ordinary had happened, and so strange and impelling was the effect of this experience that I got up, dressed, and went out in the streets of Chicago where I was met by thousands of others who had felt the touch of the same influence. Everyone was asking: *What has happened?*

What had happened was this:

Millions of men had received instructions to cease fighting, and it was their combined joy that set into motion a thought wave which swept the entire world. Perhaps never in the history of the world had so many millions of people *thought of the same thing, in the same manner, at the same time.* For once in the history of the world, *everybody* felt something in common, and the effect of this harmonized thought was the worldwide "mob psychology" that we witnessed on Armistice Day. It will help you to better understand this statement if you recall what was said in the introductory lesson of this course about the method of creating a Master Mind—through the harmony of thought of two or more persons.

We will bring the application of this principle a little nearer home by showing how it may either make or break the harmonious working relationship of a business or industry. You may doubt that it was the harmony of thought of millions of soldiers that registered in the minds of the people of the world and caused the "mob" psychological condition on Armistice Day, but you will need no proof that a disgruntled person always disturbs everyone with whom he or she comes in contact. It is a well-established fact that one such person in a place of employment will disrupt the entire organization.

Apply the principle in another way:

Place among a group of workers one person whose personality is positive and optimistic, and who makes it his or her business to sow the seeds of harmony around the place where they work, and their influence will reflect itself in every person who works with them.

If every business is the "extended shadow of one man," as Emerson wrote, then it behooves that one man to reflect a shadow of confidence and good cheer and optimism and harmony, that these qualities may, in turn, reflect themselves in all who are connected with the business.

PUT IMAGINATION TO WORK

In continuing on to the next step in our application of the power of Imagination in the attainment of success, I will cite some of the most recent and modern examples of its use in the accumulation of material wealth and in the perfection of some of the leading inventions of the world.

In approaching this next step, bear in mind that "there is nothing new under the sun." Life on this earth may be likened to a great kaleidoscope before which the scenes and facts and material substances are ever shifting and changing, and all anyone can do is to take these facts and substances and rearrange them in new combinations.

The process through which this is done is called Imagination.

I have said that the Imagination is both interpretative and creative in its nature. It can receive impressions or ideas and out of these it can form new combinations.

TOWERING GENIUS

DISDAINS A BEATEN PATH.

IT SEEKS REGIONS

HITHERTO UNEXPLORED.

—Abraham Lincoln

As our first illustration of the power of Imagination in modern business achievement, take the case of Clarence Saunders who organized the Piggly-Wiggly system of self-help grocery stores.

Saunders was a grocery clerk in a small southern retail store. One day he was standing in a line, with a tin tray in his hands, waiting his turn to get food in a cafeteria. He had never earned more than twenty dollars a week before that time, and no one had ever noticed anything about him that indicated unusual ability, but something took place in his mind, as he stood in the line of waiting people, that put his Imagination to work. With the aid of his Imagination he lifted that "self-help" idea out of the cafeteria (not creating anything new, but merely shifting an old idea into a new use) and he set it down in a grocery store. In an instant the Piggly-Wiggly chain-store grocery plan had been created, and Clarence Saunders, the twenty-dollar-a-week grocery clerk, rapidly became the million-dollar chain-store groceryman of America.

Where in that transaction do you see the slightest indication of a performance that you could not duplicate?

Analyze the transaction and measure it by the previous lessons of this course and you will see that Clarence Saunders had created a very *definite purpose.* He supported this purpose with a sufficient degree of Self-Confidence to cause him to take the Initiative to transform it into reality. His Imagination was the workshop in which these three factors —a Definite Chief Aim, Self-Confidence, and Initiative—were brought together and they supplied him with the momentum for the first step in the organization of the Piggly-Wiggly plan.

Thus are great ideas changed into realities.

COMMENTARY

A few years later, Sylvan Goldman, who owned several Piggly-Wiggly stores in Oklahoma, noticed his customers struggling to carry everything in small baskets. One night, while trying to figure out how to enable them to purchase more at one time, he found himself staring at a basket sitting on the seat of a wooden folding chair. Goldman had an idea. He called his mechanic, who added wheels to the chair legs, added another basket below the seat, and the first shopping cart was born.

Thomas Stemberg was the manager of another supermarket, and he began to wonder if there wasn't some other kind of retail operation that could be run the same way. He decided to apply the supermarket concept to office supplies and he, with Leo Kahn, gave their first new store the name Staples.

When Thomas A. Edison invented the incandescent electric light bulb he merely brought together two old, well-known principles and associated them in a new combination. He, and practically all others who were informed on the subject of electricity, knew that a light could be produced by heating a small wire with electricity, but the problem was to do this without burning the wire in two. In his experimental research Mr. Edison tried out every conceivable sort of wire, hoping to find some substance that would withstand the tremendous heat to which it had to be subjected before a light could be produced.

Edison's Imagination finally delivered for him when he compared his problem with the making of charcoal. Charcoal is created by burning wood under a mound of dirt. This cuts off most of the available oxygen that is necessary for combustion. Edison needed to make the wire burn like charcoal. His solution was to enclose the wire in a glass bulb and then pump out almost all the oxygen. Combustion still occurred, but at such a slow rate that the wire lasted long enough for the light bulb to be useful.

Even then, Edison's idea still required many refinements in terms of the right kind of wire and the proper thickness and type of glass. Those refinements continue today, but nothing obscures the fact that it was Mr. Edison who made the essential connection, and he did it by repeated attempts to apply his Imagination.

When the sun goes down tonight, you step to the wall and press a button to bring it back again, a performance that would have mystified the people of a few generations ago. Thanks to the use of Edison's

Imagination, you have simply brought together two principles, both of which were in existence since the beginning of time.

No one who knew him intimately ever accredited Andrew Carnegie with unusual ability, or with the power of genius, except in one respect, and that was his ability to select men who could and would cooperate, in a spirit of harmony, in carrying out his wishes. But what additional ability did he need in the accumulation of his millions of dollars?

COMMENTARY

> Throughout this course, your imagination should prompt you to make connections between principles and apply them in ways that are unique to your situation.
>
> Begin with your definite chief aim. Look at the written statement you have made of it. Is there some way that you might now modify that statement to make it clearer, more accurate, or closer to what you truly want?
>
> Sometimes you will discover that you have misplaced the emphasis in what you have set out to do. This is not uncommon, and hardly cause for despair or frustration. Some of the greatest successes have come when people have looked at their goals and seen that they were not right for their situation.

Anyone who understands the principle of *organized effort* as Carnegie understood it, and knows enough about human nature to be able to select just those types that are needed in the performance of a given task, could duplicate all that Carnegie accomplished.

Carnegie was a leader of Imagination. He first created a *definite purpose* and then surrounded himself with people who had the training and the vision and the capacity necessary for the transformation of that purpose into reality. He did not always create his own plans for the attainment of his *definite purpose*. Carnegie made it his business to know what he wanted, then found others who could create plans through which to procure it. And that was not only Imagination, it was genius of the highest order.

But it should be made clear that individuals of Mr. Carnegie's type are not the only ones who can make profitable use of Imagination. This great power is as available to the beginner in business as it is to the person who has "arrived."

One morning Charles M. Schwab's private car was backed onto the side track at his Bethlehem Steel plant. As he alighted from the car he was met by a young male stenographer who announced that he had come to make sure that any letters or telegrams Mr. Schwab might wish to write would be taken care of promptly. No one told this young man to be on hand, but he had enough Imagination to see that his being there would not hurt his chances of advancement. From that day on, this young man was "marked" for promotion. Mr. Schwab singled him out for promotion because he had done what any of the dozen or so other stenographers in the employ of the Bethlehem Steel Company might have done, but didn't. Today this same man is the president of one of the largest drug concerns in the world and has all of this world's goods and wares that he wants and much more than he needs.

COMMENTARY

> The Sony Corporation once tried to make a very small stereo tape recorder that would work with standard-size cassettes. They could make a small playback machine, but at the time the electronics needed to also make it a recording machine just couldn't be made small enough. They concluded that the design was a failure.
>
> Then one day Sony's honorary chairman, Masaru Ibuka, walked into the laboratory and saw that a few of the engineers were using the prototypes of the failed tape recorder to listen to music tapes. They didn't seem to care that it couldn't record, they just liked to be able to walk around listening to their favorite music.
>
> Then Ibuka remembered that another division was working on lightweight headphones, and his imagination made the connection that the rest of the engineers' had not. In Ibuka's view they hadn't made a failed "recorder," they'd created a successful "private stereo listener." They added the headphones, named it the Walkman, and it revolutionized both the music business and the electronics industry.

A few years ago I received a letter from a young man who had just finished business college, and who wanted to secure employment in my office. With his letter he sent a crisp ten-dollar bill that had never been folded. The letter read as follows:

> I have just finished a commercial course in a first-class business college and I want a position in your office because I realize how much it would be worth to a young man, just starting out on his business career, to have the privilege of working under the direction of a man like you.
>
> If the enclosed ten-dollar bill is sufficient to pay for the time you would spend in giving me my first week's instructions I want you to accept it. I will work the first month without pay and you may set my wages after that at whatever I prove to be worth.
>
> I want this job more than I ever wanted anything in my life and I am willing to make any reasonable sacrifice to get it.
>
> Very cordially . . .

This young man got his chance in my office. His Imagination gained for him the opportunity that he wanted, and before his first month had expired, the president of a life insurance company who heard of this incident offered the young man a private secretaryship at a substantial salary. He is today an official of one of the largest life insurance companies in the world.

Some years ago a young man wrote to Thomas A. Edison for a position, but for some reason Mr. Edison did not reply. By no means discouraged on this account, the young man made up his mind that not only would he get a reply from Mr. Edison, but what was more important still, he would actually secure the position he sought. He lived a long distance from West Orange, New Jersey, where the Edison industries are located, and he did not have the money with which to pay his railroad fare. *But he did have Imagination.* He went to West Orange in a freight car, got his interview, told his story in person, and got the job he sought.

Today this same man has retired from active business, having made all the money he needs. His name, in case you wish to confirm what I have said, is Edwin C. Barnes.

COMMENTARY

Edwin C. Barnes not only got a job with Edison, but he ultimately became a business associate of the famed inventor. It was largely through Barnes' belief in the Edison dictating machine, and his unflagging salesmanship, that the device became a staple in business offices throughout the country.

By using his Imagination, Edwin Barnes saw the advantage of close association with a man like Thomas A. Edison. He saw that such an association would give him the opportunity to study Mr. Edison and at the same time it would bring him into contact with Mr. Edison's friends, who are among the most influential people in the world.

These are but a few cases in which I have personally observed how people have climbed to high places in the world and accumulated wealth in abundance by making practical use of their Imagination.

COMMENTARY

When the first Xerox copies were introduced, the machines were very expensive. So Xerox didn't sell the machines, they leased them and charged customers for each copy that was made. It was a whole new way of doing business, it was imaginative, and it changed the way modern offices worked.

Ruth Handler's daughter Barbara liked playing dress-up and she liked playing with dolls. When Ruth went looking for a doll that could be dressed up, she found that there weren't any on the market. Every doll had just one dress. Why doesn't somebody combine these two favorite pastimes, Handler wondered. So she did it herself and named the doll for her daughter, calling it Barbie.

George de Mestrel went hunting one day with his dog. When they got home, he realized that they were both covered with burrs. The burrs were a real nuisance to remove and, curious, de Mestrel put them under a magnifying glass to see why. They were covered with tiny hooks that attached themselves to fur and fabric. De Mestrel began to wonder what else could be attached with tiny hooks, and the result of his wondering was Velcro.

In each of these examples an existing concept was given a new application.

Theodore Roosevelt engraved his name on the tablets of time by one single act during his tenure of office as President of the United States; after all else that he did while in that office will have been forgotten, this one transaction will record him in history as a person of Imagination:

He started the steam shovels to work on the Panama Canal.

Every president, from Washington on up to Roosevelt, could have started the canal and it would have been completed, but it seemed such a colossal undertaking that it required not only Imagination but daring courage as well. Theodore Roosevelt had both, and the people of the United States have the canal.

COMMENTARY

Many years later, when Franklin Delano Roosevelt was president of the United States through one of the most difficult times in its history, he used his imagination to strengthen his self-confidence. FDR had been a vigorous and active man until polio cost him the use of his legs. For a leader who guided the country through the Great Depression and World War II, paralysis was a terrible specter and it would have been disastrous if he had let the limitations of his legs affect his spirit.

Often, when he was troubled and unable to sleep, Roosevelt would imagine himself on a hillside near his boyhood home, standing in the snow with his sled. He would push off on his sled and imagine himself skimming across the snow, negotiating sharp turns, avoiding obstacles, until he reached the bottom and stood up, ready to race back up the hill and do it again. As his biographer, Doris Kearns Goodwin, writes, it was "an imaginative act of will."

THE FUTURE BELONGS TO THOSE

WHO BELIEVE IN THE BEAUTY

OF THEIR DREAMS.

—Eleanor Roosevelt

At the age of forty—the age at which the average man or woman begins to think they are too old to start anything new—James J. Hill was still working as a telegraph operator, at a salary of thirty dollars per month. He had no capital, and he had no influential friends with capital. But he did have something that is more powerful than either —he had Imagination.

In his mind's eye he saw a great railway system that would penetrate the undeveloped northwest and unite the Atlantic and Pacific oceans. So vivid was his Imagination that he was also able to make others see the advantages of such a railway system. I would emphasize the part of the story that most people never mention—that Hill's Great Northern Railway system became a reality in his own Imagination first. This railroad was built with steel rails and wooden cross-ties, just as most other railroads are built, and these things were paid for with capital that was secured in very much the same manner that capital for all railroads is secured. But if you want the real story of James J. Hill's success, you must go back to that little country railway station where he worked at thirty dollars a month and there pick up the little threads that he wove into a mighty railroad, with materials no more visible than the thoughts that he organized in his Imagination.

What a mighty power is Imagination, the workshop of the soul, in which *thoughts* are woven into railroads and skyscrapers and mills and factories and all manner of material wealth.

> *I hold it true that thoughts are things;*
> *They're endowed with bodies and breath and wings;*
> *And that we send them forth to fill*
> *The world with good results or ill.*
> *That which we call our secret thought*
> *Speeds forth to earth's remotest spot,*
> *Leaving its blessings or its woes,*
> *Like tracks behind it as it goes.*

We build our future, thought by thought,
For good or ill, yet know it not,
Yet so the universe was wrought.
Thought is another name for fate;
Choose, then, thy destiny and wait,
For love brings love and hate brings hate.

—ELLA WHEELER WILCOX

If your Imagination is the mirror of your soul, then you have a perfect right to stand before that mirror and see yourself as you wish to be. You have the right to see, reflected in that magic mirror, the mansion you intend to own, the factory you intend to manage, the bank of which you intend to be president, the station in life you intend to occupy. Your Imagination belongs to you. Use it! The more you use it the more efficiently it will serve you.

COMMENTARY

You have already learned that the power of self-suggestion makes you become the thoughts that you permit to occupy your mind. If you imagine that you have no imagination, this valuable faculty will devote itself to nothing more than creating images of yourself being unable to respond to opportunities and new situations. What you must do instead is imagine yourself being imaginative.

Acquire a small notebook that you can keep accessible as much of the day as possible. Get one for work and one for home, if you need to. In this book, as often as you can, write down ideas that come to you for anything that it seems to you could be done differently. You don't have to know how these things could be done differently, just that a better way might be possible or useful. They can be big, enormous things, or small, everyday things. Don't worry about feeling silly, or that you're just making things up to put something on the page. Even making things up requires that you use your imagination.

IMAGINATION DOES THE IMPOSSIBLE

At the east end of the great Brooklyn Bridge in New York City, an old man operates a cobbler shop. When the engineers began driving stakes and marking the foundation place for that great steel structure, this man shook his head and said, *"It can't be done!"*

Now he looks out from his dingy little shoe-repair shop, shakes his head, and asks himself, *"How did they do it?"*

He saw the bridge grow before his very eyes and still he lacks the Imagination to analyze what he saw. The engineer who planned the bridge saw it as a reality long before a single shovel of dirt had been removed for the foundation stones. The bridge became a reality in his Imagination because he had trained that Imagination to weave new combinations out of old ideas.

In one of the cities on the coast of California, all the land that was suitable for building lots had been developed and put into use. On one side of the city there were some steep hills that could not be used for building purposes, and on the other side the land was unsuitable for buildings because it was so low that the backwater covered it once a day.

And then an imaginative newcomer arrived in town. People of Imagination usually have keen minds, and this man was no exception. The first day of his arrival he saw the possibilities for making money from real estate. He secured an option on those hills that were unsuitable for use because of their steepness. He also secured an option on the ground that was unsuitable for use because of the backwater that covered it daily. He secured these options at a very low price because the land was supposed to be without substantial value.

With a few tons of explosives he turned those steep hills into loose dirt. With the aid of a few tractors and some road scrapers he leveled the ground and turned it into beautiful building lots. With the aid of a few mules and carts he dumped the surplus dirt on the low ground, raised it above the water level, and turned that into building lots too.

He made a substantial fortune, *for what?*

For removing some dirt from where it was not needed to where it was needed! *For mixing some useless dirt with Imagination!*

The people of that little city gave this man credit for being a genius, and he was—the same sort of genius that any one of them could have been had they used their Imagination as this man used his.

COMMENTARY

You will often find yourself in situations where you face a problem that offers no obvious solutions. The following four techniques for focusing your imagination are designed to help you get around problems in your quest for success.

Imagination helps you look at a situation in a novel way and make connections that you've not seen before. These exercises may not present you with million-dollar solutions, but they do have the power to stimulate your mind to consider new approaches.

Call a Council of Advisers: *In Lesson Two there's a story about a man who imagined himself at a table surrounded by great figures whom he wanted to emulate. The purpose for this imaginary group of great leaders is to ask each of them how they would tackle a particular problem.*

Seek Random Inspiration: *Select a book of inspiring words, perhaps the Bible or a book of quotations, or the autobiography of someone you admire. Open it anywhere and read the first sentence your eyes fall upon.*

Turn the World Upside Down: *Make a list of the four or five major components of your problem. Underneath each, write down what the opposite situation would be.*

Go Away: *Strange as it may seem, sometimes focusing your imagination on a problem can be a trap. You need a way to break free of the mental boundaries you have created. The key is to reduce pressure on yourself and allow your mind a freedom that you have not been giving it.*

In the field of chemistry it is possible to mix two or more chemical ingredients in such proportions that the mere act of mixing gives each ingredient a tremendous amount of energy that it did not possess. It is also possible to mix certain chemical ingredients in such proportions that *all the ingredients of the combination take on an entirely different nature*, as in the case of H_2O, which is a mixture of two parts hydrogen and one part oxygen, creating water.

Chemistry is not the only field in which a combination of physical materials can be so assembled that each takes on a greater value, or the result is a product entirely foreign in nature to that of its component parts. The man who blew up those useless hills of dirt and stone and moved the surplus from where it was not needed, to the low land where it was needed, gave that dirt and stone a value that it did not have before.

A ton of iron is worth little. Add to it carbon, silicon, manganese, sulfur, and phosphorus, in the right proportions, and you have transformed it into steel, which is of much greater value. Add still other substances, in the right proportion, including some skilled labor, and that same ton of steel is transformed into watch springs worth a small fortune. But in all these transformation processes the one ingredient that is worth most is the one that has no material form—Imagination!

Here lie great piles of loose brick, lumber, nails, and glass. In its present form it is worse than useless for it is a nuisance and an eyesore. But mix it with the architect's Imagination and add some skilled labor and it becomes a beautiful mansion worth a king's ransom.

On one of the great highways between New York and Philadelphia stood an old ramshackle, timeworn barn worth less than fifty dollars. With the aid of a little lumber and some cement, plus Imagination, this old barn has been turned into a beautiful automobile supply station that earns a small fortune for the man who provided the Imagination.

Across the street from my office is a little print shop that earns coffee and rolls for its owner and his helper, but no more. Less than a dozen blocks away stands one of the most modern printing plants in the world, whose owner spends most of his time traveling and has far more wealth than he will ever use. Twenty-two years ago those two printers were in business together.

I KNOW I AM HERE.

I KNOW I HAD NOTHING TO DO

WITH MY COMING, AND I SHALL

HAVE BUT LITTLE, IF ANYTHING,

TO DO WITH MY GOING.

THEREFORE I WILL NOT WORRY

BECAUSE WORRIES ARE OF NO AVAIL.

The one who owns the big print shop had the good judgment to ally himself with a man who mixed Imagination with printing. This man of Imagination is an advertising writer who brings in more business than the shop can handle, by analyzing its clients' business, creating attractive advertising features, and supplying the necessary printed material with which to make these features of service. This plant receives top-notch prices for its printing because the Imagination mixed with that printing produces a product that most printers cannot supply.

In the city of Chicago the level of a certain boulevard was raised, which spoiled a row of beautiful residences because the sidewalk was raised to the level of the second-story windows. While these owners were bemoaning their ill fortune, a man of Imagination came along. He purchased the property for a "song," converted the second stories into business property, and now enjoys a handsome income from his rentals.

As you read these lines please keep in mind all that was said at the beginning of this lesson, especially that the greatest and most profitable thing you can do with your Imagination is to rearrange old ideas into new combinations.

If you properly use your Imagination, it will help you to convert your failures and mistakes into assets of priceless value. It will lead you to discovery of a truth known only to those who use their Imagination: that the greatest reverses and misfortunes of life often open the door to golden opportunities.

One of the finest and most highly paid engravers in the United States was formerly a mail carrier. One day he was fortunate enough to be on a streetcar that met with an accident and he had one of his legs cut off. The street railway company paid him $5,000 for his leg. With this money he paid his way through school and became an engraver. The product of his hands, plus his Imagination, is worth much more than he could earn with his legs as a mail carrier. He discovered that he had Imagination when it became necessary to redirect his efforts, as a result of the streetcar accident.

You will never know what *your* capacity is for achievement until you learn how to mix your efforts with Imagination. The products of your hands, minus Imagination, will yield you but a small return. But those selfsame hands, when properly guided by Imagination, can be made to earn you all the material wealth you can use.

There are two ways in which you can profit by Imagination. You can develop this faculty in your own mind, or you can ally yourself with those who have already developed it. Andrew Carnegie did both. He not only made use of his own fertile Imagination, but he gathered around him a group of others who also possessed this essential quality, for his *definite purpose* in life called for specialists whose Imaginations ran in numerous directions. In the group that constituted Mr. Carnegie's Master Mind were men whose Imaginations were confined to the field of chemistry. He had others in the group whose Imaginations were confined to finances. He had still others whose Imaginations were confined to salesmanship, one of whom was Charles M. Schwab, who is said to have been the most able salesman on Mr. Carnegie's staff.

If you feel that your own Imagination is inadequate, you should form an alliance with someone whose Imagination is sufficiently developed to supply your deficiency. There are various forms of alliance, including the alliance of marriage, the alliance of a business partnership, the alliance of friendship, and the alliance of employer and employee. Not all workers have the capacity to serve their own best interests as employers, and those who haven't this capacity may profit by allying themselves with people of Imagination who do have such capacity.

It is said that Mr. Carnegie made more millionaires of his employees than any other employer in the steel business. Among these was Charles M. Schwab, who displayed evidence of the soundest sort of Imagination by his good judgment in allying himself with Mr. Carnegie. It is no disgrace to serve in the capacity of employee. To the contrary, it often proves to be the most profitable side of an alliance since not all of us are fitted to assume the responsibility of directing others.

COMMENTARY

Figures like Michelangelo or Georgia O'Keeffe are renowned for their imaginations, but the essence of what they did is simple: They looked at the world in a way that no one else had before, and they translated their visions into work.

Imagination is always reshaping the world as people connect seemingly disparate things. And once the connection is made, it may seem obvious, but making these supposedly obvious connections has brought success to many people.

John D. Rockefeller was a partner in an oil refining business in Cleveland, Ohio. In the early days of petroleum production, the business was extremely volatile. The price of a barrel of oil fluctuated enormously. Determined to make his company succeed, Rockefeller realized that if he couldn't control oil prices, he might help himself by controlling his costs. So he set up a barrel-making operation that cut barrel costs by more than 60 percent. That move was so profitable, Rockefeller began investigating what other parts of the business his company could control. Soon he owned pipelines and oil wells, along with his refineries. He had created the first vertical corporation—one that supplied all its own needs, and one that became the huge Standard Oil.

You must learn to focus your imagination, and then to act on the right ideas that you develop. This is not an overnight process; a multimillion-dollar idea will not spring from your brain tomorrow simply because you will it. In most people, imagination is handicapped by two things. First, it is not usefully focused. It flits from object to object, driven by circumstance. Today your imagination may be stimulated by a movie you saw, tomorrow by a newspaper headline, and the next day by a bit of conversation you overhear. Its powers are scattered. Or, second, it may be in thrall to the six basic fears, creating visions of some rare and dreaded disease, a disaster at work, or romantic betrayal. In such situations its powers are at work, but only to your detriment.

If you do begin to focus your imagination, it will not take long at all for you to have many small ideas of surprising usefulness. As you begin to apply these ideas, your confidence in your imagination and in yourself will grow.

> *There are numerous books and audiobooks specifically designed to help stimulate the imagination and create solutions to problems. Here are just a few that will help readers tap into their creativity and imagination:* Super Creativity *by Tony Buzan;* The Artist's Way *by Julia Cameron;* Lateral Thinking, Six Thinking Hats, *and* Super Thinking *by Edward De Bono;* Drawing on the Right Side of the Brain *by Betty Edwards;* The Zen of Seeing *by Frederick Franck;* Writing Down the Bones *by Natalie Goldberg;* Peak Learning *by Ronald Gross;* Thinkertoys *by Michael Michalko;* Superlearning *by Sheilah Ostrander and Lynn Schroeder;* Writing the Natural Way by *Gabriele Rico;* A Kick in the Seat of the Pants *by R. von Oech. There are also numerous computer programs designed to stimulate new ideas and creativity.*

Perhaps there is no field of endeavor in which Imagination plays such an important part as it does in salesmanship. The master salesperson see the merits of the goods he or she sells or the service they are rendering, in their own Imagination, and if they fail to do so they will not make the sale.

A few years ago a sale was made which is said to have been the most far-reaching and important sale of its kind. The object of the sale was not merchandise but the freedom of a man who was confined in the Ohio penitentiary, and the development of a prison reform system which promises a sweeping change in the method of dealing with the unfortunate men and women who have become entangled in the meshes of the law.

IMAGINATION AND PERSUASION

That you may observe just how Imagination plays the leading part in salesmanship, I will analyze this sale for you, with due apologies for the personal references which cannot be avoided without destroying much of the value of the illustration.

A few years ago I was invited to speak before the inmates of the Ohio penitentiary. When I stepped upon the platform I saw in the audience a man whom I had known as a successful businessman more than ten years previously. That man was B——, whose pardon I later secured, and the story of whose release has been spread across the front page of practically every newspaper in the United States. Perhaps you will recall it.

After I had completed my address I interviewed Mr. B—— and found out that he had been sentenced for forgery, for a period of twenty years. After he told me his story I said, "I will have you out of here in less than sixty days!"

With a forced smile he replied: "I admire your spirit but question your judgment. Why, do you know that at least twenty influential men have tried every means at their command to get me released, without success? *It can't be done!*"

I suppose it was that last remark—*It can't be done*—that challenged me to show him that it could be done. I then returned to New York City and requested that my wife pack her trunks and get ready for an indefinite stay in the city of Columbus, where the Ohio penitentiary is located.

I had a *definite purpose* in mind! That purpose was to get B—— out of the Ohio penitentiary. Not only did I have in mind securing his release, but I intended to do it in such a way that his release would erase from his breast the scarlet letter of "convict" and at the same time reflect credit upon all who helped to bring about his release.

Not once did I doubt that I would achieve it, for no salesman can make a sale if he doubts that he can do it. My wife and I returned to Columbus and took up permanent headquarters.

The next day I called on the governor of Ohio and stated the object of my visit in about these words:

"Governor, I have come to ask you to release B—— from the Ohio penitentiary. I have sound reason for asking his release, and I hope you will give him his freedom at once, but I have come prepared to stay until he is released, no matter how long that may be.

THE REAL VOYAGE OF DISCOVERY

CONSISTS NOT IN SEEKING

NEW LANDSCAPES

BUT IN HAVING NEW EYES.

—Marcel Proust

"During his imprisonment, B—— has inaugurated a system of correspondence instruction in the Ohio penitentiary, as you of course know. He has influenced 1,729 of the 2,518 prisoners of the Ohio penitentiary to take up courses of instruction. He has managed to beg sufficient textbooks and lesson materials with which to keep these men at work on their lessons, and has done this without a penny of expense to the state of Ohio. The warden and the chaplain of the penitentiary tell me that he has carefully observed the prison rules. Surely a man who can influence 1,729 prisoners to turn their efforts toward self-betterment cannot be a very bad sort of fellow.

"I have come to ask you to release B—— because I wish to place him at the head of a prison school that will give the 160,000 inmates of the other penitentiaries of the United States a chance to profit by his influence. I am prepared to assume full responsibility for his conduct after his release.

"That is my case, but before you give me your answer, I want you to know that I am not unmindful of the fact that your enemies will probably criticize you if you release him. In fact if you release him it may cost you many votes if you run for office again."

With his fist clinched and his broad jaw set firmly, Governor Vic Donahey of Ohio said: "If that is what you want with B—— I will release him if it costs me five thousand votes. However, before I sign the pardon I want you to see the Clemency Board and secure its favorable recommendation. I want you also to secure the favorable recommendation of the warden and the chaplain of the Ohio penitentiary. You know that a governor is amenable to the court of public opinion, and these gentlemen are the representatives of that court."

The sale had been made! And the whole transaction had required less than five minutes.

The next day I returned to the governor's office, accompanied by the chaplain of the Ohio penitentiary, and notified the governor that the Clemency Board, the warden, and the chaplain all joined in recommending the release. Three days later the pardon was signed and B—— walked through the big iron gates, a free man.

I have cited the details to show you that there was nothing difficult about the transaction. The groundwork for the release had all been prepared before I came on the scene. B—— had done that, by his good conduct and the service he had rendered those 1,729 prisoners. When he created the world's first prison correspondence-school system he created the key that unlocked the prison doors for himself.

Why, then, had the others who asked for his release failed to secure it? They failed because they used no Imagination!

Perhaps they asked the governor for B——'s release on the ground that his parents were prominent people, or on the ground that he was a college graduate and not a bad sort of fellow. *But they failed to supply the governor of Ohio with a sufficient motive to justify him in granting a pardon,* for had this not been so, he would undoubtedly have released B—— long before I came on the scene and asked for his release.

Before I went to see the governor I went over all the facts, and in my own Imagination I saw myself in the governor's place and made up my mind what sort of a presentation would appeal most strongly to me if I were in reality in his place.

When I asked for B——'s release I did so in the name of the 160,000 unfortunate men and women inmates of the prisons of the United States who would enjoy the benefits of the correspondence-school system that he had created. I said nothing about his prominent parents. I said nothing about my friendship with him during former years. I said nothing about his being a deserving fellow. All these matters might have been used as sound reasons for his release, but they seemed insignificant when compared with the bigger and sounder reason that his release would be of help to 160,000 other people who would feel the influence of his correspondence-school system after his release.

When the governor of Ohio came to a decision I do not doubt that B—— was of secondary importance as far as his decision was

concerned. The governor no doubt saw a possible benefit not to B——
alone, but to 160,000 other men and women who needed the influence
that B—— could supply, if released.

And that was Imagination!

It was also salesmanship. In speaking of the incident after it was
over, one of those who had worked diligently for more than a year in
trying to secure B——'s freedom, asked:

"How did you do it?"

And I replied: "It was the easiest task I ever performed, because
most of the work had been done before I became involved. In fact I
didn't do it. B—— did it himself."

This man looked at me in bewilderment. He did not see what I
am here trying to make clear: that practically all difficult tasks are easily
performed if one approaches them from the right angle. There were two
important factors entering into B——'s release. The first was that he
had supplied the material for a good case before I took it in charge, and
the second was that before I called on the governor I had so completely
convinced myself that I had a right to ask for B——'s release that I
had no difficulty presenting my case effectively.

Go back to what was said at the beginning of this lesson, on the
subject of telepathy, and apply it to this case. The governor could tell,
long before I had stated my mission, that *I knew I had a good case.* If
my brain did not telegraph this thought to his brain, then the look of
Self-Confidence in my eyes and the positive tone of my voice made
obvious my belief in the merits of my case.

Again I apologize for these personal references, with the explanation
that I have used them only because the whole of America was familiar
with the B—— case that I have described. I disclaim all credit for
the small part I played in the case, for I did nothing except use my
Imagination as an assembly room in which to piece together the factors
out of which the sale was made. I did nothing except that which any
salesperson of Imagination could have done.

ONLY PASSIONS,

GREAT PASSIONS,

CAN ELEVATE THE SOUL

TO GREAT THINGS.

—Denis Diderot

I cannot recall an incident in my entire life in which the soundness of the seventeen factors that enter into this course was more clearly manifested than it was in securing the release of B———.

It is but another link in a long chain of evidence that proves to my entire satisfaction the power of Imagination as a factor in salesmanship. There are endless millions of approaches to every problem, but there is *only one* best approach. Find this one best approach and your problem is easily solved. No matter how much merit your goods may have, there are millions of *wrong* ways in which to offer them. Your Imagination will assist you in finding the *right* way.

In your search for the right way to offer your merchandise or your services, remember this peculiar trait of mankind:

People will grant favors that you request for the benefit of a third person when they would not grant them if requested for your benefit.

Compare this statement with the fact that I had asked the governor to release B——— not as a favor to me, and not as a favor to B———, but for the benefit of the 160,000 unfortunate inmates of the prisons of America.

Salespeople of Imagination always offer their wares in such terminology that the advantages of those wares to the prospective purchaser are obvious. It is seldom that anyone makes a purchase of merchandise or renders another a favor just to accommodate the salesperson. It is a prominent trait of human nature that prompts us all to do that which advances our own interests. This is a cold, indisputable fact, claims of the idealist to the contrary notwithstanding.

To be perfectly plain, *people are selfish!*

To understand the truth is to understand how to present your case, whether you are asking for the release of someone from prison or offering for sale some commodity. In your own Imagination, plan the presentation of your case so that the strongest and most impelling advantages to the buyer are made clear.

This is Imagination!

A farmer moved to the city, taking with him his well-trained shepherd dog. But he soon found that the dog was out of place in the city, so he decided to "get rid of him." Taking the dog with him, he went out into the country and knocked on the door of a farmhouse. A man came hobbling to the door, on crutches. The man with the dog greeted the man in the house in these words:

"You wouldn't care to buy a fine shepherd dog that I wish to get rid of, would you?"

The man on crutches replied *No!* and closed the door.

The man with the dog called at half a dozen other farmhouses, asking the same question, and received the same answer. He made up his mind that no one wanted the dog and returned to the city. That evening he was telling of his misfortune, to someone with Imagination. The man heard how the owner of the dog had tried in vain to "get rid of him."

"Let me dispose of the dog for you," said the man of Imagination. The owner was willing. The next morning the man of Imagination took the dog out into the country and stopped at the first farmhouse at which the owner of the dog had called the day before. The same old man hobbled out on crutches and answered the knock at the door.

The man of Imagination greeted him in this fashion:

"I see you are all crippled with rheumatism. What you need is a fine dog to run errands for you. I have a dog here that has been trained to bring home the cows, drive away wild animals, herd the sheep, and perform other useful services. You may have this dog for a hundred dollars."

"All right," said the crippled man, "I'll take him."

That, too, was Imagination!

Most anyone would like to own a dog that would herd sheep and bring home the cows and perform other useful services. The dog was the same one that the crippled buyer had refused the day before, but the man who sold the dog was not the man who had tried to "get rid of him." If you use your Imagination, you will know that no one wants anything that someone else is trying to "get rid of."

Remember what was said about the law of attraction through the operation of which "like attracts like." If you look and act the part of a failure, you will attract nothing but failures.

Whatever your life's work, it calls for the use of Imagination.

Niagara Falls was nothing but a great mass of roaring water until a man of Imagination harnessed it and converted the wasted energy into electric current that now turns the wheels of industry. Before this man of Imagination came along, millions of people had seen and heard those roaring falls but lacked the Imagination to harness them.

The first Rotary Club of the world was born in the fertile Imagination of Paul Harris of Chicago, who saw in this child of his brain an effective means of cultivating prospective clients and the extension of his law practice, since the ethics of the legal profession forbid commercial advertising. Paul Harris's Imagination found a way to extend his law practice without advertising in the usual way.

If the winds of fortune happen to be temporarily blowing against you, remember that you can harness them and make them carry you toward your *definite purpose* through the use of your Imagination. A kite rises against the wind—not with it!

Dr. Frank Crane was a struggling "third-rate" preacher until the starvation wages of the clergy forced him to use his Imagination. Now he earns upward of a hundred thousand dollars a year for an hour's work a day, writing essays.

Woolworth was a poorly paid clerk in a retail store—poorly paid, perhaps, because he had not yet found out that he had Imagination. Before he died he built the tallest office building in the world and girdled the United States with 5 and 10 Cent Stores, through the use of his Imagination.

You will observe, by analyzing these illustrations, that a close study of human nature played an important part in each of the achievements mentioned. To make profitable use of your Imagination you must make it give you a keen insight into the motives that cause people to do or refrain from doing a given act. If your Imagination leads you to understand how quickly people grant your requests when those requests appeal to their self-interest, you can have practically anything you go after.

COMMENTARY

The story of David Lloyd provides not only an example of imaginative use of appealing to someone's self-interest but it also speaks to the value of going the extra mile.

David Lloyd grew up in a small Alabama town, an African American in a place where Black people owned few businesses. He had only a high school education. On a trip to San Diego, California, for the first time, he saw the ocean—and a marina full of boats.

Lloyd was fascinated. He got a job working for a company that repaired yachts. His excitement about his work, and his dedication to doing it well, quickly won him attention, and soon he was overwhelmed with offers of freelance work on some of San Diego's finest yachts.

Lloyd saw an opportunity. One handsome yacht in the marina was in particular need of work. Lloyd approached the owner and offered to make all repairs for the cost of the materials if the owner would allow him to take before-and-after photographs to show to prospective clients.

Lloyd probably could have got himself hired to fix the yacht anyway, but he went the extra mile and appealed to the owner's self-interest by offering to do the work for free. Naturally the owner accepted, and Lloyd got his photos, but even more important, he had so impressed the yacht owner that the man began referring more work to Lloyd—eventually more than fifty clients.

Even with his business so brisk that he could barely keep up, Lloyd continued to teach himself the skills he needed. He read books on everything from accounting fundamentals to varnishing. He received certification that allowed him to bid on the biggest and most lucrative contracts for aircraft carriers and cruise ships.

From there, Lloyd built his business into one of the largest and most successful shipbuilding and repair companies in the nation, working with clients like General Dynamics, Exxon, and the U.S. Navy. He was always willing to work harder, using his imagination to demonstrate his initiative and leadership.

I saw my wife make a very clever sale to our baby not long ago. The baby was pounding the top of our mahogany library table with a spoon. When my wife reached for the spoon, the baby refused to give it up. Being a woman of Imagination, she then offered him a nice stick of red candy. He dropped the spoon immediately and centered his attention on the more desirable object.

That was Imagination! It was also salesmanship. She won her point without using force.

There is one form of Imagination against which I would caution you. It is the brand that prompts some people to *imagine* that they can get something for nothing, or that they can force themselves ahead in the world without observing the rights of others. There are more than 160,000 prisoners now in the penal institutions of the United States, practically every one of whom is in prison because they imagined they could get something for nothing.

There is a man in the Ohio penitentiary who has served more than thirty-five years for forgery, and the largest amount he ever got from his misapplication of Imagination was twelve dollars.

There are a few people who direct their Imaginations in the vain attempt to show what happens when "an immovable body comes in contact with an irresistible force," but these types belong in a psychiatric hospital.

There is also another form of misapplied Imagination: that of the young boy or girl who knows more about life than their dad, but this form is subject to modification with time. My own boys have taught me much that my dad tried, in vain, to teach me when I was their age.

Time and Imagination (which is often the product of time) teach us many things, but nothing of more importance than this: *All of us are much alike in many ways.*

If you are a salesperson and would like to know what your customer is thinking, study yourself and imagine what you would be thinking if you were in your customer's place.

NOTHING IN LIFE IS MORE

EXCITING AND REWARDING THAN

THE SUDDEN FLASH OF

INSIGHT THAT LEAVES YOU

A CHANGED PERSON—

NOT ONLY CHANGED,

BUT FOR THE BETTER.

—Arthur Gordon

Study yourself, find out what the motives are that inspire you to perform certain deeds and that cause you to refrain from performing other deeds, and you will have gone far toward perfecting yourself in the accurate use of Imagination.

The detective's biggest asset is Imagination. The first question he asks when called in to solve a crime is: *What was the motive?* If he can find out the motive he can usually find the perpetrator of the crime.

A man who had lost a horse posted a reward of five dollars for its return. Several days later a boy who was supposed to have been "weak-minded" came leading the horse home and claimed the reward. The owner was curious to know how the boy found the horse. "How did you ever think where to look for the horse?" he asked, and the boy replied, "Well, I just thought where I would have gone if I had been a horse, and went there, and he had." Not so bad for a "weak-minded" fellow. Some who are not accused of being weak-minded go all through life without displaying as much evidence of Imagination as did this boy.

If you want to know what the other person will do, use your Imagination. Put yourself in the place of the other and find out what you would have done. That's Imagination.

Every person should be somewhat of a dreamer. Every business needs the dreamer. Every industry and every profession needs them. But the dreamer must also be a doer, or else they must form an alliance with someone who can and does translate dreams into reality.

IMAGINATION AND ACTION

The greatest nation on the face of this earth was conceived, born, and nurtured, through the early days of its childhood, by Imagination in the minds of people who combined dreams with *action!*

Your mind is capable of creating many new and useful combinations of old ideas, but the most important thing it can create is a Definite Chief Aim that will give you what you most desire.

Your Definite Chief Aim can be speedily translated into reality after you have first created it in your Imagination. If you have faithfully followed the instructions set down for your guidance in Lesson Two, you are now well on the road toward success, because it would mean that you know what it is that you want—and you have a plan for getting what you want.

The battle for the achievement of success is half won when one knows definitely what they want. The battle is all over except for the "shouting," when one knows what is wanted and has made up his or her mind to get it, whatever the price may be.

Your selection of a Definite Chief Aim calls for the use of both Imagination and *decision!* The power of decision grows with its use. A prompt decision in forcing your Imagination to create a Definite Chief Aim renders more powerful the capacity to reach decisions in other matters.

Adversities and temporary defeat are generally blessings in disguise, because they force one to use both Imagination and decision. This is why all of us usually make a better fight when our backs are to the wall and we know there is no retreat. We then reach the decision to fight instead of running.

COMMENTARY

Ben Nighthorse Campbell got used to people saying no, and he found imaginative ways around those negative answers. Campbell had a tough childhood, in and out of foster homes. He dropped out of high school, wound up in the Air Force, worked his way through college, and then moved to Japan to study judo. He won a gold medal in judo in the 1963 Pan Am Games and was captain of the U.S. Olympic team a year later in Tokyo. He returned to the United States that year.

In Japan he had learned a jewelry-making technique that could be applied to traditional Native American arts. Though Campbell's father had been reluctant to acknowledge his roots, he had passed along the craft of jewelry-making to his son. Ben began executing his own designs in the new technique, and displaying them at shows.

When his jewelry won popular success, Campbell began to further explore his Native American roots. His commitment to his heritage led him into politics. He was drafted in 1982 as a candidate for the Colorado state house of representatives, and four years later was the only Native American elected to the U.S. House of Representatives. In 1994 he became only the second Native American to be elected to the U.S. Senate.

Campbell still designs his jewelry, and is one of the most popular artists in the country. Though the circumstances of his life presented him with a series of situations in which Campbell was told to ignore or forget his aspirations, his imagination allowed him to see possibility where others saw only limitation.

John H. Johnson is another who became a success because he wouldn't take no for an answer. In 1939 Johnson was editor of "The Guardian," the in-house publication of Supreme Liberty, the largest life insurance firm in America targeted to African Americans. In the publication, positive news items about Blacks were reprinted for the edification of company employees.

Johnson came to see that what "The Guardian" did for the company's employees was something that ought to be done for African Americans everywhere. But the respected editor of The Crisis, *the NAACP's magazine, told him, "Save your money, young man. Save your energy. Save yourself a lot of disappointment." A banker he approached for start-up capital told him, "Boy, we don't make loans to colored people."*

But Johnson's determination convinced executives at Supreme Liberty to give him their mailing list of 20,000 names. By November 1942, the first issue of Negro Digest *was on newsstands, featuring reprints of articles by the likes of Carl Sandburg and the director of the NAACP.*

Within a year, Negro Digest *was carrying original articles by prominent people of all colors, including First Lady Eleanor Roosevelt. The success of* Negro Digest *gave Johnson the money to pursue even bigger projects, including the launch in 1945 of* Ebony.

He knew that getting one major advertiser would help keep his company afloat. He targeted the Zenith corporation, also based in Chicago, and went after it with consummate imagination.

Zenith's chairman, Eugene McDonald, was famous for having gone to the North Pole. Johnson decided to appeal to McDonald's interests by running a feature on Matthew Henson, a Black man who had made it to the North Pole ahead of the famed Robert Peary. When Johnson arrived at McDonald's office, he saw on the wall a pair of snowshoes that Henson had given to the executive. McDonald was easily persuaded that Ebony *was a good place to advertise.*

For the next twenty years, Johnson continued his campaign to interest big companies in the Black consumer. His publishing operations were successful and by the mid-1960s Johnson was a member of the board of companies like Zenith and Twentieth Century-Fox. In 1982 he was the first Black person to appear on the Forbes 400 list of wealthiest Americans.

The late Dr. Harper, who was formerly president of the University of Chicago, was one of the most efficient college presidents of his time. He had a penchant for raising funds in large amounts. It was he who induced John D. Rockefeller to contribute millions of dollars to the support of the University of Chicago.

It may be helpful to the student of this course to study Dr. Harper's technique, because he was a leader of the highest order. Moreover, I have his own word for it that his Leadership was never a matter of chance or accident, but always the result of carefully planned procedure.

The following incident will serve to show just how Dr. Harper made use of Imagination in raising money in large sums.

Dr. Harper needed an extra million dollars for the construction of a new building. Taking inventory of the wealthy men of Chicago to whom he might turn for this large sum, he decided upon two, each of whom was a millionaire, and both were bitter enemies.

One of these was, at that time, the head of the Chicago street railway system. Choosing the noon hour, when the office force and this man's secretary, in particular, would be apt to be out at lunch, Dr. Harper nonchalantly strolled into the office. Finding no one on guard at the outer door, he walked into the office of his intended "victim," whom he surprised by his appearance unannounced.

"My name is Harper," said the doctor, "and I am president of the University of Chicago. Pardon my intrusion, but I found no one in the outer office [which was no mere accident] so I took the liberty of walking on in.

"I have thought of you and your street railway system many, many times. You have built up a wonderful system, and I understand that you have made lots of money for your efforts. I never think of you, however, without it occurring to me that one of these days you will be passing out into the Great Unknown, and after you are gone there will be nothing left as a monument to your name, because others will take over your money, and money has a way of losing its identity very quickly, as soon as it changes hands.

"I have often thought of offering you the opportunity to perpetuate your name by permitting you to build a new Hall out on the University grounds, and naming it after you. I would have offered you this opportunity long ago had it not been for the fact that one of the members of our Board wishes the honor to go to Mr.——— [the streetcar head's enemy]. Personally, however, I have always favored you, and I still favor you, and if I have your permission to do so I am going to try to swing the opposition over to you.

"I have not come to ask for any decision today, however, as I was just passing and thought it a good time to drop in and meet you. Think the matter over and if you wish to talk to me about it again, phone me at your leisure.

"Good day, sir. I am happy to have had this opportunity of meeting you."

With this he bowed himself out without giving the head of the streetcar company a chance to say either yes or no. In fact the streetcar

A MAN'S MIND,

ONCE STRETCHED BY A NEW IDEA,

NEVER REGAINS ITS

ORIGINAL DIMENSIONS.

—Oliver Wendell Holmes

man had very little chance to do any talking; Dr. Harper did all of the talking, which was as he had planned it. He went into the office merely to plant the seed, believing that it would germinate and spring into life in due time.

His belief was not without foundation. He had hardly returned to his office at the University when the telephone rang. It was the streetcar man, asking for an appointment with Dr. Harper. The two met in Dr. Harper's office the next morning, and a check for a million dollars was in Dr. Harper's hands an hour later.

Despite the fact that Dr. Harper was a small, rather insignificant-looking man, it was said of him that "he had a way about him that enabled him to get everything he went after."

As to this "way" that he was reputed to have had—what was it?

It was nothing more nor less than his understanding of the power of Imagination. Suppose he had gone to the office of the streetcar head and asked for an appointment. Sufficient time would have elapsed between the time he called and the time when he would have actually seen this man, to have enabled the latter to anticipate the reason for his call and also to formulate a good, logical excuse for saying no.

Suppose, again, he had opened his interview with the streetcar man something like this: "The University is badly in need of funds and I have come to ask your help. You have made lots of money and you owe something to the community in which you have made it. [Which perhaps was true.] If you will give us a million dollars, we will place your name on a new Hall that we wish to build."

What might have been the result?

In the first place, there would have been no motive suggested that was sufficiently appealing to sway the mind of the streetcar man. While it may have been true that he owed something to the community from which he had made his fortune, he probably would not have admitted it. In the second place, he would have enjoyed the position of being on the offensive instead of the defensive side of the proposal.

But Dr. Harper, shrewd in the use of Imagination as he was, provided for just such contingencies by the way he stated his case. First, he placed the streetcar man on the defensive by informing him that it was not certain that he (Dr. Harper) could get the permission of his Board to accept the money and name the Hall after him. In the second place, he intensified the desire of the streetcar man to have his name on that building because of the thought that his enemy and competitor might get the honor if it got away from him. Moreover (and this was no accident either), Dr. Harper had made a powerful appeal to one of the most common of all human weaknesses—by showing this streetcar man how to perpetuate his own name.

All of this required that he make practical application of the law of Imagination.

Dr. Harper was a master salesman. When he asked for money, he always paved the way for success by planting in the mind of the person of whom he asked it a good sound reason why the money should be given—a reason which emphasized some advantage accruing to the person as the result of the gift.

Often this would take the form of a business advantage. Again it would be an appeal to that part of man's nature which prompts him to wish to perpetuate his name so it will live after him. But, always, the request for money was carried out according to a plan that had been carefully thought out, embellished, and smoothed down with the use of Imagination.

COMMENTARY

When the editors of this revised and updated edition set about the task of reviewing the material in the original edition, it was concluded that there were certain instances where the text would benefit from the inclusion of contemporary stories. However, once the task was actually begun, it became clear that very often Napoleon Hill's stories illustrated certain concepts so well that replacing those would have resulted in little more than mentioning names that are more familiar to the modern reader while adding little of consequence to the point being made.

It was with that in mind that the editors decided to include the following section from the original text in which Hill offers his readers ideas that he suggests the imaginative person could take and develop into products or businesses. As you might guess, every one of the concepts he offered was taken up by someone and turned into a reality.

While the Law of Success philosophy was in the embryonic stage, long before it had been organized into a systematic course of instruction and reduced to textbooks, I was lecturing on this philosophy in a small town in Illinois.

One of the members of the audience was a young life insurance salesman. After hearing what was said on the subject of Imagination, he began to apply what he had heard to his own problem of selling life insurance. Something was said during the lecture about the value of allied effort, through which people may enjoy greater success by cooperative effort through a working arrangement under which each "boosts" the interests of the other.

Taking this suggestion, the young man in question immediately formulated a plan whereby he gained the Cooperation of a group of businessmen who were in no way connected with the insurance business.

Going to the leading grocer in his town he made arrangements with that grocer to give a thousand-dollar insurance policy to every customer purchasing no less than fifty dollars' worth of groceries each month. He then made it a part of his business to inform people of this arrangement and brought in many new customers. The grocer had a large, neatly lettered card placed in his store, informing his customers of this offer of free insurance, thus helping himself by offering all his customers an inducement to do all their trading in the grocery line with him.

This young insurance man then went to the leading gas station and made arrangements with the owner to insure all customers who purchased all their gasoline, oil, and other motor supplies from him.

TO KNOW IS NOTHING AT ALL;

TO IMAGINE IS EVERYTHING.

—Anatole France

Next he went to the leading restaurant in the town and made a similar arrangement with the owner. Incidentally, this alliance proved to be quite profitable to the restaurateur, who promptly began an advertising campaign in which it was stated that the food was so pure, wholesome, and good that all who ate there regularly would be apt to live much longer. Therefore he would insure the life of each regular customer for one thousand dollars.

The life insurance salesman then made arrangements with a local builder and real estate man to insure the life of each person buying property from him, for an amount sufficient to pay off the balance due on the property in case the purchaser died before payments were completed.

The young man in question is now the General Agent for one of the largest life insurance companies in the United States, with headquarters in one of the largest cities in Ohio.

The turning point in his life came when he discovered how he might make practical use of the law of Imagination.

There is no patent on his plan. It may be duplicated over and over again by other life insurance sellers who know the value of Imagination. Just now, if I were engaged in selling life insurance, I think I would make use of this plan by allying myself with a group of automobile distributors in each of several cities, thus enabling them to sell more automobiles and at the same time providing for the sale of a large amount of life insurance, through their efforts.

Financial success is not difficult to achieve after one learns how to make practical use of creative Imagination. Someone with sufficient Initiative and Leadership, and the necessary Imagination, will duplicate the fortunes being made each year by the owners of five-and-ten-cent stores, by developing a system of marketing the same sort of goods now sold in these stores, with the aid of vending machines. This will save a fortune in clerk hire, ensure against theft, and cut down the overhead of store operation in many other ways. Such a system can be conducted just as successfully as food can be dispensed with the aid of automatic vending machines.

The seed of the idea has been here sown. It is yours for the taking!

Someone with an inventive mind is going to make a fortune, and at the same time save thousands of lives each year, by perfecting an automatic railroad-crossing "control" that will reduce the number of automobile accidents on crossings.

Imagination, plus some mechanical skill, will give the motorist this much needed safeguard, and make the person who perfects the system all the money they need and much more besides.

Some inventor who understands the value of Imagination and has a working knowledge of the radio principle, may make a fortune by perfecting a burglar alarm system that will signal police headquarters and at the same time switch on lights and ring a gong in the place about to be burglarized, with the aid of apparatus similar to that now used for broadcasting.

Any farmer with enough Imagination to create a plan, plus the use of a list of all automobile licenses issued in his state, may easily create a clientele of motorists who will come to his farm and purchase all the vegetables he can produce and all the chickens he can raise, thus saving him the expense of hauling his products to the city. By contracting with each motorist for the season, the farmer may accurately estimate the amount of produce that he should provide. The advantage to the motorists is that they will be sure of direct-from-the-farm produce, at less cost than they could purchase it from local dealers.

The roadside gasoline-station owner can make effective use of Imagination by placing a lunch stand near their filling station, and then doing some attractive advertising along the road in each direction, calling attention to "barbecue," "home-made sandwiches," or whatever else the owner may wish to specialize in. The lunch stand will cause the motorists to stop, and many of them will purchase gasoline before starting on their way again.

These are simple suggestions, involving no particular difficulty in connection with their use, yet it is just such uses of Imagination that bring financial success.

The Piggly-Wiggly self-help store plan, which made millions of dollars for its originator, was a very simple idea that anyone could have adopted, yet considerable Imagination was required to put the idea to work in a practical sort of way.

The more simple and easily adapted to a need an idea is, the greater is its value, as no one is looking for ideas that are involved with great detail or are in any way complicated.

COMMENTARY

The billions of McDonald's hamburgers sold, the invention of Wite-Out by a secretary, and the success of Mrs. Field's Cookies are stories that have been cited so often as modern examples of a simple idea transformed by imagination that they may have begun to lose some of their power to inspire. If that is so, the story of Josie Natori's simple idea should once again ignite your imagination.

Raised in the Philippines, Josie Natori came to the United States to study economics and had a successful career as an investment banker. But, she recalls, "I was bored. It all came too easy." She and her husband were mulling over starting their own business, considering items they could import from the Philippines, when a friend sent her some children's clothes with elaborate embroidery.

Natori took one look at the clothes and was inspired. The look might not work for kids, but she knew it would be dynamite on women's lingerie. She began creating her own designs and soon had orders from major department stores like Saks and Bloomingdale's.

"From the beginning," Natori told an interviewer, "I wasn't consciously trying to challenge the established ideas of lingerie. I simply followed my instincts. I had no preconceived ideas and asked questions that forced buyers to reconsider what [a garment] should look like. I naturally asked questions like, 'Why can't a nightgown look like an evening gown?' or 'Who says you can't wear these slippers with that dress?'"

Today Josie Natori's company does $40 million worth of business annually and sells lingerie across America and in Canada, Italy, Japan, and France. Natori's imagination continues to be the fuel that drives her business forward. "Even when I'm shopping in a flea market, I am searching for inspiration."

IMAGINATION AND SALESMANSHIP

Imagination is the most important factor entering into the art of selling. The master salesperson is always the one who makes systematic use of Imagination. The outstanding merchant relies upon Imagination for the ideas that make their business excel.

COMMENTARY

During the first quarter of the twentieth century, when Napoleon Hill was developing the Law of Success, business in America was booming. But, in many ways, how people conducted their day-to-day business affairs was still quite traditional. Most merchants had yet to embrace what was to become one of the defining hallmarks of American business—the concept of business as a service industry.

In the following, Napoleon Hill addresses the issue of imaginative salesmanship and customer service, and to make his point he uses everyday examples drawn from his personal experience. Today Hill's suggestions may seem somewhat quaint compared with our drive-through shopping center/infomercial/e-commerce way of life, but as with the previous section in which Hill gave away ideas, much of what is common business practice today is so because of what Napoleon Hill wrote in the original edition of this book.

Imagination may be used effectively in the sale of even the smallest articles of merchandise, such as shirts or ties.

I walked into one of the best-known haberdasheries in the city of Philadelphia to purchase some shirts and ties.

I picked up two or three ties from the counter and examined them briefly, then laid down all but one light blue that somewhat appealed to me. Finally I laid this one down also, and began to look through the remainder of the assortment.

The young man behind the counter then had a happy idea. Picking up a gaudy-looking yellow tie, he wound it around his fingers to show how it would look when tied, and asked:

"Isn't this a beauty?"

Now, I hate yellow ties, and the salesman made no particular hit with me by suggesting that a gaudy yellow tie is pretty. If I had been in that salesman's place I would have picked up the blue tie, for which I had shown a decided preference, and I would have wound it around my fingers so as to bring out its appearance after being tied. I would have known what my customer wanted by watching the kinds of ties that he picked up and examined. If given the opportunity, any customer will give the alert salesperson a clue as to the particular merchandise that should be stressed in an effort to make a sale.

I then moved over to the shirt counter. Here I was met by an elderly gentleman who asked:

"Is there something I can do for you today?"

Well, I thought to myself, if he ever did anything for me it would have to be today, as I might never come back to that particular store again. I told him I wanted to look at shirts, and described the style and color of shirt that I wanted.

The old gentleman replied: "I am sorry, sir, but they are not wearing that style this season, so we are not showing it."

I said that I knew "they" were not wearing the style for which I had asked, and for that very reason, among others, I was going to wear it, providing I could find it in stock.

If I were selling goods, I might think what I pleased about a customer's taste, but I surely would not be so lacking in diplomacy as to tell a customer that I thought he didn't know his own business. Rather, I would tactfully show him what I believed to be more appropriate merchandise, if what he wanted was not in stock.

A SENSE OF CURIOSITY

IS NATURE'S ORIGINAL SCHOOL

OF EDUCATION.

—Smiley Blanton

The old gentleman finally pulled down some shirt boxes and began laying out shirts that were not even similar to the shirt for which I had asked. I told him that none of these suited, and as I started to walk out he asked if I would like to look at some nice suspenders.

It is proper for a salesperson to try to interest a customer in wares for which they make no inquiry, but judgment should be used and care taken to offer something which the salesperson has reason to believe the customer may want

I walked out of the store without having bought either shirts or ties, and feeling somewhat resentful that I had been so grossly misjudged as to my tastes for colors and styles.

A little further down the street I went into a small, one-man shop which had shirts and ties on display in the window.

Here I was handled differently!

The salesperson asked no unnecessary or stereotypical questions. He took one glance at me as I entered the store, sized me up quite accurately, and greeted me with a very pleasant "Good morning, sir!"

He then inquired, "Which shall I show you first, shirts or ties?" I said I would look first at shirts. He glanced at the style of shirt I was wearing, asked my size, and began laying out shirts of the very type and color for which I was searching, without my saying another word. He laid out six different styles and watched to see which I would pick up first. I looked at each shirt and laid them all back on the counter, but the salesman observed that I examined one of the shirts a little more closely than the others and held it a little longer. No sooner had I laid this shirt down than the salesman picked it up and began to explain how it was made. He then went to the tie counter and came back with three very beautiful blue ties, tied each, and held it in front of the shirt, pointing out the perfect harmony between the colors of the ties and the shirt.

Before I had been in the store five minutes I had purchased three shirts and three ties, and was on my way with the package under my arm, feeling that here was a store to which I would return.

DREAM. DREAM *BIG* DREAMS!

OTHERS MAY DEPRIVE YOU OF YOUR

MATERIAL WEALTH AND CHEAT YOU

IN A THOUSAND WAYS, BUT NO MAN

CAN DEPRIVE YOU OF THE CONTROL

AND USE OF YOUR IMAGINATION.

MEN MAY DEAL WITH YOU UNFAIRLY,

AS MEN OFTEN DO; THEY MAY DEPRIVE

YOU OF YOUR LIBERTY; BUT THEY

CANNOT TAKE FROM YOU THE PRIVILEGE

OF USING YOUR IMAGINATION.

IN YOUR IMAGINATION *YOU ALWAYS WIN!*

—Jesse Jackson

I learned afterwards that the merchant who owns the little shop where I made these purchases pays a monthly rental of $500 for the small store and makes a handsome income from the sale of nothing but shirts, ties, and collars. He would have gone out of business, with a fixed $500 a month for rent, if it were not for his knowledge of human nature which enables him to make a very high percentage of sales to all who come into his store.

I was once walking down Michigan Avenue in Chicago, when my eye was attracted to a beautiful gray suit in the window of a men's store. I had no notion of buying the suit, but was curious to know the price, so I opened the door and, without entering, merely pushed my head inside and asked the first person I saw how much the suit in the window was.

Then followed one of the cleverest bits of sales maneuvering I have ever observed. The salesman knew he could not sell me the suit unless I came into the store, so he said, "Will you not step inside, sir, while I find out the price of the suit?"

Of course he knew the price all the time, but that was his way of disarming me of the thought that he intended trying to sell me the suit. In less than two minutes I found myself standing in front of a case, with my coat off, getting ready to try on a coat like the one I had observed in the window.

After I was in the coat, which happened to fit almost perfectly (and this was no accident, thanks to the accurate eyes of an observing salesman) my attention was called to the nice, smooth touch of the material. I rubbed my hand up and down the arm of the coat, as I had seen the salesman do while describing the fabric, and, sure enough, it was a very fine piece of material. By this time I had again asked the price, and when I was told that the suit was only fifty dollars I was agreeably surprised, as I had come to believe that it might have been priced much higher. However, when I first saw this suit in the window, my guess had been that it would have been been priced at about thirty-five dollars, and I doubt that I would have paid that much for it had I not fallen into the hands of a salesman who knew how to show the suit to best advantage.

If the first coat tried on me had been about two sizes too large, or a size too small, I doubt that any sale would have been made. I bought that suit "on the impulse of the moment." A single slip on the part of the salesman would have lost him the sale of that suit. If he had said "fifty dollars" when I first asked the price, I would have said thank you and gone on my way without looking at the suit.

Later in the season I purchased two more suits from this same salesman, and if I now lived in Chicago the chances are that I would buy still other suits from him, because he always showed me suits that were in keeping with my personality.

The Marshall Field's store in Chicago gets more for merchandise than any other store of its kind in the country. Moreover, people knowingly pay more at this store, and feel better satisfied than if they bought the merchandise at another store for less money.

Why is this?

Well, there are many reasons, among them the fact that anything purchased at the Field's store, if it is not entirely satisfactory, may be returned and the purchase price will be refunded. A guarantee goes with every article sold in the Field's store.

Another reason why people will pay more at the Field's store is that the merchandise is displayed and shown to better advantage than it is at most other stores. The Field's window displays are truly works of art. The same is true of the goods displayed in the store. There is harmony and proper grouping of merchandise throughout the Field's establishment, and this creates an "atmosphere" that is more—much more—than merely an imaginary one.

Still another reason why the Field's store can get more for their merchandise than can most other stores is due to the careful selection and supervision of the salespeople. One would seldom find a person employed in the Field's store whom one would not be willing to accept as a neighbor.

Merchandise purchased at the Field's store is packed or wrapped more artistically than is common in other stores, which is yet another reason why people will go out of their way and pay higher prices to shop there.

While we are on the subject of the artistic wrapping of merchandise, I wish to relate the experience of a friend of mine which shows how Imagination may be used even in wrapping merchandise.

This friend had a very fine silver cigarette case that he had carried for years, and of which he was very proud because it was a gift from his wife.

Constant usage had banged the case up rather badly, so he decided to take it to Caldwell, a jewelry store in Philadelphia, to be repaired. He left the case and asked them to send it to his office when it was ready.

About two weeks later a splendid-looking new livery wagon with the Caldwell name on it drew up in front of his office, and a nice-looking young man in a neat uniform stepped out with a package. It was artistically wrapped and tied with a ribbon.

His secretary and other workers in his office gathered around his desk to watch him open up his "present." He cut the ribbon and then removed the outer covering. Under this was a covering of tissue paper, fastened with beautiful gold seals bearing the Caldwell initials and their trademark. This paper was removed, and a most beautiful plush-lined box met his eyes. The box was opened, and, after removing the tissue-paper packing, there was the cigarette case he had left to be repaired.

GREAT ACHIEVEMENT IS

USUALLY BORN OF GREAT SACRIFICE,

AND IS NEVER THE RESULT

OF SELFISHNESS.

But it did not look like the same case, thanks to the Imagination of the Caldwell manager. Every dent had been carefully straightened out. The hinges had been trued and the case had been polished and cleaned so it shone as it did when it was first purchased.

And the bill? Oh, it was plenty, and yet the price charged for the repair did not seem too high. As a matter of fact everything that entered into the transaction, from the packing of the case with the fine tissue paper and gold seals to the delivery of the package, was based upon carefully calculated psychology which laid the foundation for a high price for the repair.

To me there was a great lesson in this cigarette-case incident. The goods you are selling may actually be worth all you are asking for them, but if you do not carefully study the subjects of display and packaging, you may be accused of overcharging your customers.

On Broad Street, in the city of Philadelphia, there is a fruit shop where those who patronize the store are met at the door by a man in uniform who opens the door for them. He does nothing else but merely open the door, but he does it with a smile.

This fruit merchant specializes in baskets of fruit decorated with fancy wrapping and ribbons. Just outside the store is a large blackboard on which are listed the sailing dates of the various ocean liners leaving from New York City. This merchant caters to people who wish baskets of fruit delivered on board departing boats on which friends are sailing.

This merchant's store is a small affair, no larger than the average small store, but he pays a rent of at least $15,000 a year for the place and makes more money than half a hundred ordinary fruit stands combined, merely because he knows how to display and deliver his wares so they appeal to the vanity of the buyers. He gets from $10 to

$25 for a basket of fruit which one could purchase just around the corner for from $3 to $7.50, with the exception that the latter would not be embellished with the seventy-five cents' worth of frills which the former contains.

This is but further proof of the value of Imagination.

The American people—and this means all of them, not merely the so-called rich—are the most extravagant spenders on earth, but they insist on "class" when it comes to appearances such as wrapping and delivery and other embellishments which add no real value to the merchandise they buy. The merchant who understands this, and has learned how to mix Imagination with his merchandise, may reap a rich harvest in return for his knowledge.

And a great many are doing it, too.

The salesperson who understands the psychology of proper display, wrapping, and delivery of merchandise, and who knows how to show their wares to fit the whims and the characteristics of their customers, can make ordinary merchandise bring fancy prices. And what is more important still, they can do so and still retain the patronage of their customers more readily than if they sold the same merchandise without the "studied" appeal and the artistic wrapping and delivery service.

In a "cheap" restaurant, where coffee is served in heavy, thick cups and the silverware is tarnished or dirty, a ham sandwich is only a ham sandwich, and if the restaurant gets fifteen cents for it they are doing well. But just across the street, where the coffee is served in dainty thin cups, on neatly covered tables, a much smaller ham sandwich will bring a quarter, to say nothing of the cost of the tip for service. The only difference in the sandwiches is merely in appearances. The difference in price is considerable, but the difference in the merchandise is not a difference of either quality or quantity so much as it is of "atmosphere" or appearances.

People love to buy appearance or atmosphere, which is simply a more refined way of saying what P. T. Barnum said about "one being born every minute."

It is no overstatement to say that a master of sales psychology could go into the average merchant's store, where the stock of goods was worth, let us say, $50,000, and at very slight additional expense make the stock bring $60,000 to $75,000. That person would have to do nothing except coach the salespeople on the proper showing of the merchandise, after having purchased a small amount of more suitable fixtures, perhaps, and repackaging the merchandise in more suitable coverings and boxes.

A shirt or blouse, packed one to a box, in the right sort of box, with a piece of ribbon and a sheet of tissue paper added for embellishment, can be made to bring a dollar or a dollar and a half more than the same shirt would bring without more artistic packing. I know this is true, and I have proved it more times than I can recall, to convince some skeptical merchant who had not studied the effect of "proper displays."

Conversely stated, I have proved, many times, that the finest shirt made cannot be sold for half its value if it is removed from its box and placed on a bargain counter with inferior-looking shirts.

COMMENTARY

As was noted at the beginning of this section, merchandising has changed radically in the years since Napoleon Hill wrote those words, but the basic principles he described are still at work in contemporary life. The editors are confident that if you stop to think about the last time you went into Starbucks or Wal-Mart, bought a cell phone, a computer, a car, or just a pair of jeans at the Gap, you will recognize that you were being influenced by those same principles of imaginative salesmanship that Hill was writing about in 1927. The editors are equally confident that you, too, can take those "old-fashioned" concepts and use them in your own "new-fashioned" way.

Lesson Seven

Enthusiasm

THE LUCKY OR

SUCCESSFUL PERSON

HAS LEARNED A SIMPLE SECRET.

CALL UP, CAPTURE,

EVOKE THE FEELING OF SUCCESS.

WHEN YOU FEEL SUCCESSFUL

AND SELF-CONFIDENT,

YOU WILL ACT SUCCESSFULLY.

—Maxwell Maltz

Lesson Seven

ENTHUSIASM

"You Can Do It if You Believe You Can!"

ENTHUSIASM IS A STATE OF MIND THAT inspires and arouses one to put *action* into the task at hand. And it does more than this—it is contagious, and vitally affects not only the enthusiast, but all with whom they come in contact as well.

Enthusiasm bears the same relationship to a human being that steam does to the locomotive—it is the vital moving force that impels action. The greatest leaders are the ones who know how to inspire Enthusiasm in their followers. Enthusiasm is the most important factor entering into salesmanship, and, by far, the most vital factor that enters into public speaking.

HOW ENTHUSIASM WILL AFFECT YOU

Mix Enthusiasm with your work and it will not seem difficult or monotonous. Enthusiasm will so energize your entire body that you can get along with less than half the usual amount of sleep and at the same time it will enable you to perform two to three times as much work as you usually perform in a given period, without fatigue.

For many years I have done most of my writing at night. One night, while I was enthusiastically working at my typewriter, I looked out the window of my study, just across the square from the Metropolitan tower in New York City, and saw what seemed to be the most peculiar reflection of the moon on the tower. It was a silvery gray shade, such as I had never seen before. Upon closer inspection I found that the reflection was that of the early morning sun and not that of the moon. It was daylight! I had been at work all night, but I was so engrossed in my work that the night had passed as though it were but an hour. I worked at my task all that day and all the following night without stopping, except for a small amount of light food.

Two nights and one day without sleep, and with little food, without the slightest evidence of fatigue, would not have been possible had I not kept my body energized with Enthusiasm over the work at hand.

Enthusiasm is not merely a figure of speech; it is a vital force that you can harness and use. Without Enthusiasm you would resemble an electric battery without electricity.

Enthusiasm is the vital force with which you recharge your body and develop a dynamic personality. Some people are blessed with natural Enthusiasm, while others must acquire it. The procedure through which it may be developed is simple. It begins by doing work you like. If you cannot engage in the work that you like best, for the time being, then you can continue in another line very effectively by adopting a Definite Chief Aim that contemplates your engaging in your chosen work at some future time.

Lack of money and other circumstances over which you have no control may force you to engage in work that you do not like, but no one can stop you from determining in your own mind what your Definite Chief Aim in life shall be. Nor can anyone stop you from planning ways and means for translating this aim into reality, and nor can anyone stop you from mixing Enthusiasm with your plans.

Happiness, the final object of all human effort, is a state of mind that can be maintained only through the hope of future achievement. The happy person is the one who dreams of heights of achievement that are yet unattained. The home you intend to own, the money you intend to earn and place in the bank, the trip you intend to take when you can afford it, the position in life you intend to fill when you have prepared yourself, and the preparation itself—these are the things that produce happiness. Likewise, these are the materials out of which your Definite Chief Aim is formed, and these are the things over which you may become *enthusiastic,* no matter what your present station in life may be.

More than twenty years ago I became *enthusiastic* over an idea. When the idea first took form in my mind, I was unprepared to take even the first step toward its transformation into reality. But I nursed it in my mind and I became enthusiastic as I looked ahead, in my Imagination, and saw the time when I would be prepared to make it a reality.

The idea was this: I wanted to become the editor of a magazine, based on the Golden Rule, through which I could inspire people to keep up courage and deal with one another squarely.

Finally my chance came, and on Armistice Day 1918, I wrote the first editorial for what was to become the material realization of a hope that had lain dormant in my mind for nearly twenty years.

With Enthusiasm I poured into that editorial the emotions which I had been developing in my heart. My dream had come true—my editorship of a national magazine had become a reality.

As I have said, this editorial was written with Enthusiasm. I took it to a man of my acquaintance, and with Enthusiasm I read it to him. The editorial ended in these words: "At last my twenty-year-old dream is about to come true. It takes money, and a lot of it, to publish a national magazine, and I haven't the slightest idea where I am going to get this essential factor, but this is worrying me not at all because *I know I am going to get it somewhere!*" As I wrote those lines, I mixed Enthusiasm and faith with them.

I had hardly finished reading this editorial when the man to whom I read it—the first and only person to whom I had shown it—said:

"I can tell you where you are going to get the money, for I am going to supply it." And he did!

Enthusiasm is a vital force; so vital, that until you have it highly developed you cannot even begin to imagine its potential power in the achievement of success.

Before moving to the next step in this lesson, I wish to repeat and to emphasize the fact that you may develop Enthusiasm over your Definite Chief Aim in life whether you are in position to achieve that purpose at this time or not. You may be a long way from realization of your Definite Chief Aim, but if you will kindle the fire of Enthusiasm in your heart, and keep it burning, before very long the obstacles that now stand in the way of your attainment of that purpose will melt away as if by magic, and you will find yourself in possession of power that you did not know you possessed.

HOW YOUR ENTHUSIASM WILL AFFECT OTHERS

We come now to the discussion of one of the most important subjects of this course—*suggestion.* Suggestion is the principle through which your words and your acts and *even your state of mind* influence others.

COMMENTARY

In Lesson Two, Napoleon Hill discusses at length the subject of autosuggestion, or self-suggestion, and in Lesson Three he introduces a related concept which he called the law of mental telepathy. As noted earlier, in the time since Hill's writing most experiments in telepathy have done little to convince the skeptical. What Hill meant by the term, however, had little to do with hocus-pocus and much to do with common sense. Here he briefly recaps his thoughts on telepathy as it relates to suggestion.

If you accept the principle of telepathy (the communication of thought from one mind to another without the aid of signs, symbols, or sounds) as a reality, you of course understand why Enthusiasm is contagious and why it influences all within its radius.

When your own mind is vibrating at a high rate because it has been stimulated with Enthusiasm, that vibration registers in the minds of all within its radius, and especially in the minds of those with whom you come in close contact. When a public speaker "senses" their audience is "en rapport" (in harmony) with him or her, they are merely recognizing that their own Enthusiasm has influenced the minds of the listeners until the listeners' minds are vibrating in harmony with the speaker's own.

When the salesperson senses that the "psychological" moment for closing a sale has arrived, he or she merely feels the effect of their own Enthusiasm as it influences the mind of the prospective buyer and places that mind "en rapport" with the salesperson's own.

The subject of *suggestion* constitutes so important a part of this lesson, and of this entire course, that I will describe the three mediums through which it usually operates, which are: what you say, what you do, and what you *think!*

When you are enthusiastic over the goods you are selling or the services you are offering, or the speech you are delivering, your state of mind becomes obvious to all who hear you, *by the tone of your voice.* Whether you have ever thought of it in this way or not, it is the tone in which you make a statement, more than it is the statement itself, that carries conviction or fails to convince. No mere combination of words can ever take the place of a deep belief in a statement that is expressed with burning Enthusiasm. Words are but devitalized sounds unless colored with feeling that comes from Enthusiasm.

ONE FEELS THE NOBLEST,

AND ACTS THE BEST,

WHEN THE INSPIRATION OF

ENTHUSIASM DRIVES

HIM ONWARD TOWARD

THE ATTAINMENT OF

SOME PREESTABLISHED GOAL.

Here the printed word fails me, for I can never express with mere type and paper the difference between words that fall from unemotional lips, without the fire of Enthusiasm behind them, and those that seem to pour forth from a heart that is bursting with eagerness for expression. The difference is there, however.

Thus, *what* you say, and the *way* in which you say it, conveys a meaning that may be just the opposite of what is intended. This accounts for many a failure by the salesperson who presents their arguments in words that seem logical enough, but lack the coloring that can come only from Enthusiasm that is born of sincerity and belief in the goods they are trying to sell. Their words said one thing, but their tone of voice *suggested* something entirely different. Therefore, no sale was made.

What you *say* is of course an important factor in the operation of the principle of suggestion, but not nearly so important as what you *do*. *Your acts will count for more than your words,* and woe unto you if the two fail to harmonize.

If you preach the Golden Rule as a sound rule of conduct, your words will fall upon deaf ears if you do not practice what you preach. The most effective sermon a person can preach on the soundness of the Golden Rule is the one that is preached by *suggestion,* when that person applies this rule in their relationships with others.

If a salesman of Ford automobiles drives up to his prospective purchaser in a Buick, all the arguments he can present in behalf of the Ford will be without effect.

Your *thoughts* constitute the most important of the three ways in which you apply the principle of suggestion, because they control the tone of your words and, to some extent at least, your actions. If your thoughts and your actions and your words harmonize, you are bound to influence others.

We will now analyze the subject of *suggestion,* and I will show you exactly how to apply the principle upon which it operates. As we have already seen, suggestion differs from autosuggestion in only one way—

we use suggestion, consciously or unconsciously, when we influence others, while we use *autosuggestion* as a means of influencing ourselves.

Before you can influence another person through suggestion, that person's mind must be in a state of neutrality; that is, it must be open and receptive to your method of suggestion. Right here is where most salespeople fail—they try to make a sale before the mind of the prospective buyer has been rendered receptive or neutralized. This is such a vital point in this lesson that I feel impelled to dwell on it until there can be no doubt that you understand the principle that I am describing.

When I say that the salesperson must neutralize the mind of the prospective purchaser before a sale can be made I mean that the prospective purchaser's mind must be credulous. A state of confidence must have been established and it is obvious that there can be no set rule for either establishing confidence or neutralizing the mind to a state of openness. Here the ingenuity of the salesperson must supply that which cannot be set down as a hard-and-fast rule.

I know a life insurance salesman who sells nothing but large policies. Before this man even approaches the subject of insurance with a prospective client he familiarizes himself with that person's complete history, including their education, financial status, eccentricities if they have any, religious preferences, and other data too numerous to be listed. Armed with this information, he manages to secure an introduction under conditions that permit him to know the prospective client in a social as well as a business way. Nothing is said about the sale of life insurance during his first visit, nor his second, and sometimes he does not approach the subject of insurance until he has become very well acquainted with the prospective client.

All this time, however, he is not dissipating his efforts. He is taking advantage of these friendly visits for the purpose of neutralizing his prospective client's mind. That is, he is building up a relationship of confidence so that when the time comes for him to talk life insurance, what he says will fall upon ears that *willingly* listen.

Some years ago I wrote a book entitled *How to Sell Your Services.* Just before the manuscript went to the publisher, it occurred to me to ask some celebrities to write letters of endorsement to be published in the book. The printer was waiting for the manuscript, therefore I hurriedly wrote a letter to some eight or ten people, in which I briefly outlined exactly what I wanted. But the letter brought back no replies, for I had failed to observe two important prerequisites for success—I had written the letter so hurriedly that I had failed to inject the spirit of Enthusiasm into it, and I had neglected to word the letter so that it had the effect of neutralizing the minds of those to whom it was sent. I had not paved the way for the application of the principle of suggestion.

After I realized my mistake, I then wrote a letter that was based on strict application of the principle of suggestion. This letter not only brought back replies from all to whom it was sent, but many of the replies were masterpieces and served, far beyond my fondest hopes, as valuable supplements to the book. For the purpose of comparison, to show you how the principle of suggestion may be used in writing a letter and what an important part Enthusiasm plays in giving the written word "flesh," the two letters are here reproduced. It will not be necessary to indicate which letter failed, as that will be quite obvious.

My dear Mr. Ford:

I am just completing a manuscript for a new book entitled How to Sell Your Services. I anticipate the sale of several hundred thousand of these books and I believe those who purchase the book would welcome the opportunity of receiving a message from you as to the best method of marketing personal services.

Would you, therefore, be good enough to give me a few minutes of your time by writing a brief message to be published in my book? This will be a big favor to me personally, and I know it would be appreciated by the readers of the book.

A CAREFUL INVENTORY

OF ALL YOUR PAST EXPERIENCES

MAY DISCLOSE THE

STARTLING FACT

THAT EVERYTHING

HAS HAPPENED FOR THE BEST.

Thanking you in advance for any consideration you may care to show me, I am,

Yours very truly . . .

Hon. Thomas R. Marshall,
Vice President of the United States,
Washington, D. C.

My dear Mr. Marshall:

Would you care for the opportunity to send a message of encouragement, and possibly a word of advice, to a few hundred thousand of your fellow men who have failed to make their mark in the world as successfully as you have done?

I have about completed a manuscript for a book to be entitled How to Sell Your Services. The main point made in the book is that service rendered is *cause* and the pay envelope is *effect*, and that the latter varies in proportion to the efficiency of the former.

The book would be incomplete without a few words of advice from a few men who, like yourself, have come up from the bottom to enviable positions in the world. Therefore, if you will write me of your views as to the most essential points to be borne in mind by those who are offering personal services for sale, I will pass your message on through my book, which will ensure its getting into hands where it will do a world of good for a class of earnest people who are struggling to find their places in the world's work.

I know you are a busy man, Mr. Marshall, but please bear in mind that by simply calling in your secretary and dictating a brief letter you will be sending forth an important message to possibly half a million people. In money this will not be worth to you the two-cent stamp that you will place on the letter, but, if estimated from the viewpoint of the good it may do others who are less fortunate than yourself, it may be worth the difference between success and failure to many a worthy person who will read your message, believe in it, and be guided by it.

Very cordially yours . . .

Now, let us analyze the two letters and find out why one failed in its mission while the other succeeded. This analysis should start with one of the most important fundamentals of salesmanship: *motive.* In the first letter it is obvious that the motive is entirely one of self-interest. The letter states exactly what is wanted, but the wording of it leaves a doubt as to *why* the request is made or whom it is intended to benefit. Study the sentence in the second paragraph, "This will be a big favor to me personally," et cetera. Now, it may seem to be a peculiar trait, but the truth is that most people will not grant favors just to please others. If I ask you to render a service that will benefit me, without bringing you some corresponding advantage, you will not show much Enthusiasm in granting that favor; you may refuse altogether if you have a plausible excuse for refusing. But if I ask you to render a service that will ben-efit a third person, even though the service must be rendered through me, and if that service is of such a nature that it is likely to reflect credit on you, the chances are that you will render the service willingly.

We see this psychology demonstrated by the person who gives only small change to the beggar on the street, but willingly hands over hun-dreds of thousands of dollars to the charity worker who is soliciting in the name of others.

But the most damaging suggestion of all is contained in the last and most important paragraph of the letter: "Thanking you in advance for *any consideration you may care to show me.*" This sentence strongly suggests that the writer of the letter anticipates a refusal of their request. It clearly indicates lack of Enthusiasm. It paves the way for a refusal of the request. There is not one single word in the entire letter that places in the mind of anyone to whom it is sent a satisfactory reason for complying with the request. On the other hand, the reader can clearly see that the object of the letter is to secure a letter of endorsement that will help sell the book. The most important selling argument—in fact, the only selling argument in connection with this request—has been lost because it was not brought out and established as the real motive for making the request. This argument was but faintly mentioned in the sentence, "I believe those who purchase the book would welcome the opportunity of receiving a message from you as to the best method of marketing personal services."

The opening paragraph of the letter violates an important fundamental of salesmanship, because it clearly suggests that the object of the letter is to gain some advantage for its writer and does not even hint at any advantage to the person to whom it is sent. Instead of neutralizing the mind of the recipient of the letter, as it should do, it has just the opposite effect; it makes it easy for him to say no.

It reminds me of a salesman—or, perhaps I should say someone who wanted to be a salesman—who once approached me in an effort to sell me a subscription to the *Saturday Evening Post.* As he held a copy of the magazine in front of me he suggested the answer I should give, by this question:

"You wouldn't subscribe for the *Post* to help me out, would you?"

He had made it too easy for me to say no. There was no Enthusiasm behind his words, and he suggested nothing that appealed to my self-interest motive, therefore he lost a sale.

A few weeks later another subscription agent approached me. She was selling a combination of six magazines, one of which was the *Saturday Evening Post,* but how different her approach was. She glanced at my library table, on which she saw several magazines, then at my bookshelves, and exclaimed with Enthusiasm:

"Oh! I see you are a lover of books and magazines."

PEAK PERFORMERS ARE PEOPLE

WHO APPROACH ANY SET OF

CIRCUMSTANCES WITH THE ATTITUDE

THAT THEY CAN GET IT

TO TURN OUT THE WAY

THEY WANT IT TO.

NOT ONCE IN A WHILE.

REGULARLY. THEY CAN

COUNT ON THEMSELVES.

—Charles Garfield

I proudly pleaded guilty to the charge. Observe the word *proudly*, for it has an important bearing on this incident. I laid down the manuscript that I was reading when this saleswoman came in, for I could see that she was a woman of intelligence. Just how I came to see this you will see too, from this story. The important point is that I laid down the manuscript and actually felt myself wanting to hear what she had to say.

With the aid of eleven words, plus a pleasant smile, plus a tone of genuine Enthusiasm, she had neutralized my mind sufficiently to make me want to hear her. She had performed her most difficult task with those few words, because I had made up my mind when she was announced that I would keep my manuscript in my hands and thereby convey to her mind, as politely as I could, that I was busy.

Being a student of salesmanship and of suggestion, I carefully watched to see what her next move would be. She had a bundle of magazines under her arm and I expected she would unroll it and begin to urge me to purchase, but she didn't. You will recall that I said she was *selling* a combination of six magazines; not merely *trying* to sell them.

She walked over to my bookshelves, pulled out a copy of *Emerson's Essays*, and for the next ten minutes she talked about Emerson's essay on Compensation so interestingly that I lost sight of the roll of magazines that she carried. (She was neutralizing my mind some more.)

Incidentally, she gave me a sufficient number of new ideas about Emerson's works to provide material for an excellent editorial.

Then she asked me which magazines I received regularly, and after I told her, she smiled as she unrolled her bundle of magazines and laid them on the table in front of me. She analyzed her magazines one by one, and explained just why I should have each of them. *The Saturday Evening Post* would bring me the cleanest fiction; *Literary Digest* would bring me the news of the world in condensed form, such as a busy man like myself would demand; the *American Magazine* would bring me the latest biographies of those who were leading in business and industry, and so on, until she had covered the entire list.

But I was not responding to her argument as freely as she thought I should have, so she slipped me this gentle *suggestion:*

"A man of your position is bound to be well-informed, and if he isn't it will show up in his own work!"

She spoke the truth! Her remark was both a compliment and a gentle reprimand. She made me feel somewhat sheepish because she had taken inventory of my reading matter—and six of the leading magazines were not on my list. (The six that she was selling.)

Then I began to "slip" by asking her how much the six magazines would cost. She put on the finishing touches of a well-presented sales talk by this tactful reply: "The cost? Why, the cost of the entire number is less than you receive for a single page of the typewritten manuscript that you had in your hands when I came in."

Again she spoke the truth. And how did she happen to guess so well what I was getting for my manuscript? The answer is, she didn't guess— *she knew!* She made it a part of her business to draw me out tactfully as to the nature of my work (which in no way made me angry). She became so deeply interested in the manuscript, which I had laid down when she came in, that she actually induced me to talk about it. (I am not saying, of course, that this required any great amount of skill or coaxing; after all, it was *my* manuscript.)

For all I know, it was a part of her plan to observe carefully all that she saw and heard, with the object of finding out just what my weaknesses were and in what I was most interested. Some salespeople take the time to do this; some do not. She was one of those who did.

Yes, she went away with my order for the six magazines, but that was not all the benefit she derived from tactful suggestion plus Enthusiasm. She also got my consent to canvass my office, and before she left she had five other orders from my employees.

At no time during her stay did she leave the impression that I was favoring her by purchasing her magazines. Just to the contrary, she distinctly impressed me with the feeling that she was rendering me a favor. This was tactful suggestion.

Before we get away from this incident, I wish to make an admission. When she drew me into conversation, she did it in such a way that I talked with Enthusiasm, and I am sure I caught the spirit of Enthusiasm from this clever saleswoman when she made that opening remark as she came into my study. I am just as sure that her Enthusiasm was not a matter of accident. She had trained herself to look for something in her prospective purchaser's office, or their work, or their conversation, over which she could express Enthusiasm.

Remember, suggestion and Enthusiasm go hand in hand!

I can remember, as though it were yesterday, the feeling that came over me when that other would-be salesman pushed that *Saturday Evening Post* in front of me, as he remarked, "You wouldn't subscribe for the *Post* to help me out, would you?"

His words were chilled, they were lifeless; they lacked Enthusiasm. They registered an impression in my mind, but that impression was one of coldness. I wanted to see the man go out the door at which he had come in. Mind you, I am not naturally unsympathetic, but the tone of his voice, the look on his face, his general bearing *suggested* that he was there to ask a favor and not to offer one.

Suggestion is one of the most subtle and powerful principles of psychology. You are making use of it in all that you do and say and think. But, unless you understand the difference between negative suggestion and positive suggestion, you may be using it in such a way that it is bringing you defeat instead of success.

Science has established the fact that through the negative use of suggestion, life may be extinguished. In the little town where I was raised, there lived an old lady who constantly complained that she feared death from cancer. During her childhood she had seen a woman who had cancer and the sight had so impressed itself upon her mind that she began to look for symptoms in her own body. She was sure that every little ache and pain was the beginning of her long-looked-for symptom of cancer. I have seen her place her hand on her breast and have heard her exclaim, "Oh, I am sure I have a cancer growing here. I can feel it," when complaining of this left breast, where she believed the cancer was attacking her.

A few weeks ago she died—*with cancer on her left breast!* If suggestion will actually transform healthy body cells into parasites out of which cancer will develop, can you not imagine what it will do in destroying disease germs—if properly directed? Suggestion is the law through which mental healers work what appear to be miracles. I have personally witnessed the removal of parasitical growths known as warts, through the aid of suggestion, within forty-eight hours.

COMMENTARY

By the 1980s the medical aspects of the principle Napoleon Hill wrote about in the preceding paragraph were embraced by a growing segment of the population commonly referred to as the New Age. Among the adherents were numerous medical professionals who incorporated the concept under the term "the body-mind connection," and by the turn of the twenty-first century the belief that the mind can manifest physical changes in the body had become a part of mainstream medical practice.

Following is a listing of the seminal books and audiobooks that explain in greater detail the medical applications of the power of suggestion: Visualization *by Adelaide Bry;* Ageless Body, Timeless Mind *by Deepak Chopra, M.D.;* Creative Visualization *by Shakti Gawain;* Focusing *by Eugene Gendlin, Ph.D.;* You Can Heal Your Life *by Louise Hay;* Healing With Body Energy *by W. Brugh Joy, M.D.;* Psycho-Cybernetics *by Maxwell Maltz, M.D.;* Superimmunity *by Paul Pearsall, Ph.D.;* Healing Back Pain *by John E. Sarno, M.D.;* Love, Medicine, and Miracles *by Bernie S. Siegel, M.D.;* Getting Well *by O. Carl Simonton, M.D.;* Eight Weeks to Optimum Health and Spontaneous Healing *by Andrew Weil, M.D.*

A few months ago I received one of the most effective pieces of advertising I ever saw. It was a little book in which a clever automobile insurance salesman had reprinted press dispatches that he had gathered from all over the country, showing that sixty-five automobiles had been stolen in a single day. On the back page of the book was this highly suggestive statement:

"Your car may be the next one to go. Is it insured?"

At the bottom of the page was the salesman's name, address, and telephone number. Before I had finished reading the first two pages of the book I called the salesman on the telephone and made inquiry about rates. He came right over to see me, and you know the rest of the story.

Go back now to the two letters *[pages 457 and 459]* and let us analyze the second one, which brought the desired replies from all to whom it was sent. Study, carefully, the first paragraph and you will observe that it asks a question that can be answered in only one way. Compare this opening paragraph with that of the first letter, by asking yourself which of the two would have impressed you most favorably. This paragraph is worded as it is for a twofold purpose. First, it is intended to serve the purpose of neutralizing the mind of the reader so he will read the remainder of the letter with an open-minded attitude. And second, it asks a question that can be answered in only one way, for the purpose of committing the reader to a viewpoint that harmonizes with the nature of the service which in subsequent paragraphs of the letter he is to be requested to render.

In the second lesson of this course, you observed that Andrew Carnegie refused to answer my question, when I asked him to what he attributed his success, until he had asked me to define the word *success*. He did this to avoid misunderstanding. The first paragraph of the letter we are analyzing is so worded that it states the object of the letter and at the same time practically forces the reader to accept that object as being sound and reasonable.

HALF THE WRECKS THAT

STREW LIFE'S OCEAN,

IF SOME STAR

HAD BEEN THEIR GUIDE,

MIGHT IN SAFETY NOW BE RIDING,

BUT THEY DRIFTED WITH THE TIDE.

Any person who would answer the question in the negative would convict themself on the charge of selfishness, and no one wants to live with a guilty conscience on such a charge. Just as the farmer first plows his ground, then fertilizes it in order that he may be sure of a crop, so does this paragraph fertilize the mind of the reader and prepare it for the seed that is to be placed there through the subtle suggestion the paragraph contains.

Now carefully study the second paragraph of the letter and you will observe that it carries a statement of fact that the reader can *neither question nor deny!* It provides him no reason for argument because it is obviously based on a sound fundamental. It takes him the second step of the psychological journey that leads straight toward compliance with the request that is carefully clothed in the third paragraph of the letter, but you will also notice that the paragraph begins by indirectly paying the reader a nice little compliment: "Therefore, if you will write me of your views as to the most essential points to be borne in mind by those who are offering personal services for sale," et cetera. Study the wording of this sentence, together with the setting in which it has been placed, and you will observe that it hardly appears to be a request at all, and certainly there is nothing about it to suggest that the writer of the letter is requesting a favor *for his personal benefit.* At most, it can be construed merely as a request for a favor for others.

Next study the closing paragraph and notice how tactfully concealed is the suggestion that if the reader should refuse the request he is placing himself in the awkward position of one who does not care enough about those who are less fortunate than himself to spend a stamp and a few minutes of time for their benefit.

The whole construction of the letter is such that if the reader lays it aside without complying with the request that it makes, *he will have to reckon with his own conscience!* This effect is intensified by the last sentence of the last paragraph and especially by the last thirteen words of that sentence: *"who will read your message, believe in it, and be guided by it."*

CONCEIT IS A FOG THAT

ENVELOPS A MAN'S

REAL CHARACTER BEYOND

HIS OWN RECOGNITION.

IT WEAKENS HIS

NATIVE ABILITY AND

STRENGTHENS ALL

HIS INCONSISTENCIES.

This letter brings the reader up with a bang and turns his own conscience into an ally of the writer; it corners him, just as a hunter might corner a rabbit by driving it into a carefully prepared net.

The best evidence I can offer that this analysis is correct is that the letter brought replies from every person to whom it was sent, despite the fact that every one of the recipients was of the type that is generally supposed to be too busy to answer a letter of this nature. Not only did the letter bring the desired replies, but those to whom it was sent also replied in person, with the exception of the late Theodore Roosevelt, who replied under the signature of a secretary.

John Wanamaker and Frank A. Vanderlip wrote two of the finest letters I have ever read—each a masterpiece which might well have adorned the pages of a more dignified volume than the one for which the letters were requested. Andrew Carnegie also wrote a letter that was well worth consideration by all who have personal services for sale. William Jennings Bryan wrote a fine letter, as did, also, the late Lord Northcliffe.

None of these wrote merely to please me, for I was unknown to all of them, with the exception of four. They did not write to please me—they wrote to please themselves and to render a worthy service. Perhaps the wording of the letter had something to do with this, but, as to that, I make no point other than to state that all of those whom I have mentioned, and most others of their type, are generally the most willing to render service for others when they are properly approached.

I wish to take advantage of this appropriate opportunity to state that all of the really big public figures whom I have had the pleasure of knowing have been the most willing and courteous men of my acquaintance when it came to rendering service that was of benefit to others. Perhaps that was one reason why they were really major figures.

The human mind is a marvelous piece of machinery! One of its outstanding characteristics is that all impressions which reach it, either through outside suggestion or autosuggestion, are recorded together in groups which harmonize in nature. The negative impressions are all stored away in one portion of the brain, while the positive impressions are stored in another portion. When one of these impressions (or past experiences) is called into the conscious mind through the principle of memory there is a tendency to recall with it all others of a similar nature, just as the raising of one link of a chain brings up other links with it.

For example, anything that causes a feeling of doubt to arise in a person's mind is sufficient to call forth all of their experiences that caused them to become doubtful. If a person is asked by a stranger to cash a check, he or she may immediately remember having cashed checks that were not good, or of having heard of others who did so. Through the law of association, all similar emotions, experiences, and sense impressions that reach the mind are filed away together, so that the recalling of one tends to bring back to memory all the others.

To arouse a feeling of distrust in a person's mind has a tendency to bring back every doubt-building experience that person ever had. For this reason, successful salespeople endeavor to keep away from the discussion of subjects that may arouse the buyer's "chain of doubt impressions" from previous experiences. The successful salesperson quickly learns that "knocking" a competitor may result in bringing to the buyer's mind certain negative emotions that might make it impossible for the salesperson to "neutralize" the buyer's mind.

This principle applies to, and controls, every sense impression that is lodged in the human mind. Take the feeling of fear, for example; the moment we permit a single emotion that is related to fear to reach the conscious mind, it calls with it all of its unsavory relations. A feeling of courage cannot claim the attention of the conscious mind while a feeling of fear is there. One or the other must dominate. They make poor roommates because they do not harmonize in nature. Like attracts like. Every thought held in the conscious mind has a tendency to draw to it other thoughts of a similar nature. These feelings, thoughts, and emotions growing out of past experiences, which claim the attention of the conscious mind, are backed by a regular army of supporting soldiers of a similar nature that stand ready to aid them in their work.

COMMENTARY

As noted earlier, many people built on the basic principles about which Napoleon Hill wrote and lectured. Some took inspiration from Hill's principles of success and turned their inspiration into businesses, a number of which went on to become not just businesses but industries unto themselves. Others built on the ideas by elaborating on certain concepts and they themselves became bestselling authors and famous motivational speakers.

To experience firsthand just how influential Napoleon Hill has been in this regard, the editors urge you to attend seminars and workshops by today's popular speakers. You will hear new buzzwords, and the speakers will illustrate their concepts with contemporary stories, but behind each modern catch phrase or story you will also hear the echo of one of Hill's original seventeen principles of success. Two of the most prominent and powerful motivational speakers of the latter part of the twentieth century and beginning of the twenty-first century are Anthony Robbins and Stephen Covey, both of whom readily acknowledge Napoleon Hill as a major inspiration in their work.

ENTHUSIASM AND SUGGESTION

Deliberately place in your own mind, through the principle of auto-suggestion, the ambition to succeed through the aid of a Definite Chief Aim, and notice how quickly all of your latent or undeveloped ability in the nature of past experiences will become stimulated and aroused to action on your behalf. Plant in a child's mind, through the principle of suggestion, the ambition to become a successful lawyer or doctor or engineer or businessperson or financier, and if you plant that suggestion deeply enough, and keep it there, by repetition, it will begin to move the child toward the achievement of the object of that ambition.

If you would plant a suggestion "deeply," mix it generously with Enthusiasm, for Enthusiasm is the fertilizer that will ensure its rapid growth as well as its permanency. When that kind-hearted old gentleman planted in my mind the suggestion that I was a "bright boy" and that I could make my mark in the world if I would educate myself, it was not so much *what* he said, as it was the *way* in which he said it that made such a deep and lasting impression on my mind. It was the way in which he gripped my shoulders, and the look of confidence in his eyes, that drove his suggestion so deeply into my subconscious mind that it never gave me any peace until I commenced taking the steps that led to the fulfillment of the suggestion.

This is a point I would stress with all the power at my command. *It is not so much what you say as it is the TONE and MANNER in which you say it that makes a lasting impression.*

It naturally follows, therefore, that sincerity of purpose, honesty, and earnestness must be placed behind all that one says if one would make a lasting and favorable impression.

Whatever you successfully sell to others you must first sell to *yourself!*

Not long ago I was approached by an agent of the government of a certain country. The agent sought my services as a writer of propaganda for the administration in charge at that time. His approach was about as follows:

"Whereas, you have a reputation as an exponent of the Golden Rule philosophy; and whereas, you are known throughout the United States as an independent who is not allied with any political faction, would you be gracious enough to come to our country, study the economic and political affairs, then return to the United States and write a series of articles to appear in the newspapers, recommending to the people of America the immediate recognition of the government by the United States," et cetera.

For this service, I was offered more money than I shall, perhaps, ever possess during my entire life. But I refused the commission, and for a reason that will fail to impress anyone except those who understand the principle that makes it necessary for all who would influence others to remain on good terms with their own conscience.

I could not write convincingly of that country's cause because I did not believe in that cause. Therefore, I could not have mixed sufficient Enthusiasm with my writing to have made it effective, even if I had been willing to prostitute my talent and dip my pen into ink that I believed to be muddy.

I will not endeavor further to explain my philosophy on this incident, as those who are far enough advanced in the study of autosuggestion will not need further explanation, while those who are not far enough advanced would not and could not understand.

No one can afford to express, through words or acts, anything that is not in harmony with their own belief, and if they do, they must pay by the loss of their ability to influence others.

Please read aloud the foregoing paragraph! It is worth emphasizing by repetition, for it is by lack of observation of the principle on which it is based that many a person's Definite Chief Aim has been dashed.

I do not believe that I can afford to try to deceive anyone, about anything, but I *know* that I cannot afford to try to deceive *myself.* To do so would destroy the power of my pen and render my words ineffective.

It is only when I write with the fire of Enthusiasm burning in my heart that my writing impresses others favorably; and it is only when I speak from a heart that is bursting with belief in my message, that I can move my audience to accept that message.

I urge you to also read aloud the foregoing paragraph. Commit it to memory. Write it out and place it where it may serve as a daily reminder of a principle, as immutable as the law of gravity, *without which you can never become a power in your chosen life's work.*

There have been times, and many of them, when it appeared that if I stood by this principle it would mean starvation!

There have been times when even my closest friends and business advisers have strongly urged me to shade my philosophy for the sake of gaining a needed advantage here and there, but somehow I have managed to cling to it, mainly, I suppose, because I have preferred peace and harmony in my own heart to the material gain that I might have had by compromising my integrity.

Strange as it may seem, my refusal to strangle my own conscience has seldom been based on what is commonly called "honesty." My refusal to write or speak anything that I did not believe has been solely a question of honor between my conscience and myself. I have tried to express what my heart dictated because I have aimed to give my words "flesh." It might be said that my motive was based more on self-interest than on a desire to be fair with others, though I have never desired to be unfair with others, so far as I am able to analyze myself.

No one can become a master salesperson if they compromise falsehood. Even if no one ever catches them red-handed in expressing what they do not believe, their words will fail in the accomplishment of their purpose because a person cannot give their words "flesh" if they do not come from the heart, and if they are not mixed with genuine, unadulterated Enthusiasm.

I would also ask you to read, aloud, the foregoing paragraph, for it embraces a great law that you must *understand* and *apply* before you can become a person of influence in any undertaking.

I should point out that I am quite serious when I ask you to read aloud or memorize certain phrases. It is not that I don't give you full credit for being an adult, a thinker, an intelligent person, but I know how likely you are to skip over these vital laws without being sufficiently impressed by them to make them a part of your everyday philosophy. I know *your* weakness because I know *my own*. It has required the better part of twenty-five years of ups and downs—mostly downs—to impress these basic truths on my own mind so that they influenced me. I have tried both them and their opposites; therefore, I can speak not as one who merely *believes* in their soundness, but as one who *knows*.

And what do I mean by "these truths"?

So that you cannot possibly misunderstand my meaning, and so that these words of warning cannot possibly convey an abstract meaning, I will state that by "these truths" I mean this:

You cannot afford to suggest to another person, by word of mouth or by an act of yours, anything that you do not believe.

Surely, that is plain enough.

And the reason you cannot afford to do so, is this:

If you compromise with your own conscience, it will not be long before you will have no conscience; for your conscience will fail to guide you, just as an alarm clock will fail to awaken you if you do not heed it.

Surely, that is plain enough also.

And how do I happen to be an authority on this vital subject? I am an authority because I have experimented with the principle until I know how it works!

"But," you may ask, "how do I know that you are telling the truth?"

The answer is *you will know only by experimenting for yourself, and by observing others who faithfully apply this principle and those who do not apply it.*

If my evidence needs backing, then consult anyone whom you know to be a person who has "tried to get by" without observing this principle, and if they will not or cannot give you the truth, you can get it nevertheless by analyzing the character of the person.

There is but one thing in the world that gives us real and enduring power, and that is *character*. Reputation, bear in mind, is not character. Reputation is that which people are believed to be; character is that which people *are!* If you would be a person of great influence, then be a person of real *character*.

Character is the philosopher's lodestone through which all who have it may turn the base metals of their life into pure gold. Without character you have nothing, you are nothing, and you can be nothing. Character is something that you cannot beg or steal or buy. You can get it only by building it; and you can build it by your own thoughts and deeds, and in no other way. Through the aid of autosuggestion, any person can build a sound character, no matter what his or her past has been. I wish to emphasize the fact that all who have character also have Enthusiasm and Personality sufficient to attract others who have character.

Following are three simple but valuable instructions as to how to develop Enthusiasm.

First: Complete the remaining lessons of this course, because other important instructions that are to be coordinated with this one will be found in subsequent lessons.

Second: If you have not already done so, write out your Definite Chief Aim in clear, simple language, and follow this by writing out the plan through which you intend to transform your aim into reality.

Third: Read over the description of your Definite Chief Aim each night just before retiring, and as you read, see yourself (in your Imagination) in full possession of the object of your aim. Do this with full faith in your ability to transform your Definite Chief Aim into reality. Read aloud, with all the Enthusiasm at your command, emphasizing every word. Repeat this reading until the small still voice within you tells you that your purpose will be realized. Sometimes you will feel the effects of this voice from within the first time you read your Definite Chief Aim, while at other times you may have to read it a dozen or fifty times before the assurance comes. But do not stop until you feel it.

One of the greatest powers for good, on the face of this earth, is *faith*. To this marvelous power may be traced miracles of the most astounding nature. It offers peace on earth to all who embrace it.

Faith involves a principle so far-reaching in its effect that no one can say what its limitations are, or if it has limitations. *Write into the description of your Definite Chief Aim a statement of the qualities that you intend to develop in yourself, and the station in life that you intend to attain, and have faith, as you read this description each night, that you can transform this purpose into reality.* Surely, you cannot miss the suggestion contained in this lesson.

To become successful you must be a person of *action.* Merely to "know" is not sufficient. It is necessary both to know and to do.

Enthusiasm is the mainspring of the mind that urges one to put knowledge into action.

Billy Sunday is the most successful evangelist this country has ever known. For the purpose of studying his technique and checking up on his psychological methods, I went through three campaigns with Reverend Sunday.

His success is based very largely on one word—ENTHUSIASM!

By making effective use of the law of suggestion, Billy Sunday conveys his own spirit of Enthusiasm to the minds of his followers and they become influenced by it. He sells his sermons by exactly the same sort of strategy employed by many master salespeople.

Enthusiasm is as essential to a salesperson as water is to a duck!

All successful sales managers understand the psychology of Enthusiasm and make use of it, in various ways, as a practical means of helping their group produce more sales.

Practically all sales organizations have get-together meetings for the purpose of revitalizing the minds of all members of the sales force and injecting the spirit of Enthusiasm, which can be best done en masse through group psychology.

Sales meetings might properly be called "revival" meetings, because their purpose is to revive interest and arouse Enthusiasm that will enable the salespeople to take up the fight with renewed ambition and energy.

During his administration as sales manager of the National Cash Register Company, Hugh Chalmers (who later became famous in the

IF YOU THINK YOUR LOT

IN LIFE HAS BEEN HARD,

READ *UP FROM SLAVERY*

BY BOOKER T. WASHINGTON,

AND YOU MAY SEE HOW

FORTUNATE YOU HAVE BEEN.

motor car industry) faced a most embarrassing situation which threatened to wipe out his position as well as that of thousands of salesmen under his direction.

The company was in financial difficulty. This fact had become known to the salesmen in the field, and as a result they began to lose their Enthusiasm. Sales began to dwindle until finally the conditions became so alarming that a general meeting of the sales organization was called, to be held at the company's plant in Dayton, Ohio. The salesmen were called in from all over the country.

Mr. Chalmers presided over the meeting. He began by calling on several of his best salesmen to tell what was wrong out in the field that orders had fallen off. One by one they got up, as called, and each had a most terrible tale of grief to tell. Business conditions were bad, money was scarce, people were holding off buying until after the presidential election, and so forth. As the fifth man began to enumerate the difficulties that had kept him from making his usual quota of sales, Mr. Chalmers jumped up on top of a table, held up his hands for silence, and said, "Stop! I order this convention to come to a close for ten minutes while I get my shoes shined."

Then turning to a small boy who sat nearby, he ordered the boy to bring his shoeshine outfit and shine his shoes, right where he stood, on top of the table.

The salesmen in the audience were astounded! They began to whisper among themselves. Meanwhile, the boy shined first one and then the other shoe, taking plenty of time and doing a first-class job.

After the job was finished, Mr. Chalmers handed the boy a dime, then went ahead with his speech:

"I want each of you," he said, "to take a good look at this boy. He has the concession for shoe-shining throughout our plant and offices. His predecessor was considerably older than himself, and despite the fact that the company subsidized him with a salary, he could not make a living in this plant, where thousands of people are employed.

"This boy not only makes a good living, without any subsidy from the company, but he is actually saving money out of his earnings each week, working under the same conditions, in the same plant, for the same people.

"Now I wish to ask you a question. Whose fault was it that the older boy did not get more business? Was it his fault, or the fault of his buyers?"

In a mighty roar from the crowd the answer came back:

"It was the boy's fault, of course!"

"Just so," replied Chalmers, "and now I want to tell you this, that you are selling cash registers in the same territory, to the same people, with exactly the same business conditions that existed a year ago, yet you are not producing the business that you were then. Now whose fault is that? Is it yours, or the buyers'?"

And again the answer came back with a roar:

"It is our fault, of course!"

"I am glad that you are frank to acknowledge your faults," Chalmers continued, "and I now wish to tell you what your trouble is: You have heard rumors about this company being in financial trouble and that has killed off your enthusiasm so that you are not making the effort that you formerly made. If you will go back into your territories with a definite promise to send in five orders each during the next thirty days, this company will no longer be in financial difficulty, for that additional business will see us clear. Will you do it?"

They said they would, and they did!

That incident has gone down in the history of the National Cash Register Company under the name Hugh Chalmers' Million-Dollar Shoe Shine, for it is said that this turned the tide in the company's affairs and was worth millions of dollars.

Enthusiasm knows no defeat! The sales manager who knows how to send out an army of enthusiastic salespeople may set his or her own price on their services. What is more important even than this, they can increase the earning capacity of every person under their direction. Thus, the sales manager's Enthusiasm benefits not only themself, but perhaps hundreds of others as well.

Enthusiasm is never a matter of chance. There are certain stimuli that produce Enthusiasm, the most important being as follows:

1. Occupation in the work that one loves best.

2. Environment where one comes in contact with others who are enthusiastic and optimistic.

3. Financial success.

4. Complete mastery and application, in one's daily work, of the seventeen laws of success.

5. Good health.

6. Knowledge that one has served others in some helpful manner.

7. Good clothes, appropriate to the needs of one's occupation.

These sources of stimuli are self-explanatory, with the exception of the last. The psychology of clothes is understood by very few people and will therefore be explained here in detail. Clothes are the most important part of the embellishment that every person must have in order to feel self-reliant, hopeful, and enthusiastic.

THE PSYCHOLOGY OF GOOD CLOTHES

COMMENTARY

Needless to say, clothing and what is acceptable to wear in business today is a far cry from what was considered appropriate in the early part of the twentieth century. As you begin to read the following you may wonder what Napoleon Hill, who wore celluloid collars and spats, could have to say to a world where Casual Friday is common and billion-dollar deals are signed by people dressed in blue jeans or sweats.

> *The editors assure you that if you read on, it will become abundantly clear that the philosophy behind the words supercedes the fashion of any particular era, and that in fact Hill's Psychology of Good Clothes has a much more significant point than "Can I wear checks with stripes?"*

When the good news came from the theatre of war on November the eleventh, 1918, my worldly possessions amounted to little more than they did the day I came into the world.

The war had destroyed my business and made it necessary for me to make a new start.

My wardrobe consisted of three well-worn business suits and two uniforms which I no longer needed.

Knowing all too well that the world forms its first and most lasting impressions of a person by the clothes he or she wears, I lost no time in visiting my tailor.

My tailor had known me for many years, and therefore he did not judge me entirely by the clothes I wore. If he had, I would have been "sunk."

With less than a dollar in change in my pocket, I picked out the cloth for three of the most expensive suits I ever owned, and ordered that they be made up for me at once. The three suits came to $375!

I shall never forget the remark made by the tailor as he took my measure. Glancing first at the three bolts of expensive cloth that I had selected, and then at me, he inquired:

"Dollar-a-year man, eh?"

COMMENTARY

> *The term "dollar-a-year man" was used to refer to those individuals who were wealthy enough to leave their businesses and contribute their time and skills to helping the government manage essential industries during the First World War. In exchange for helping with the war effort, they were paid one dollar a year.*

"No," said I, "if I had been fortunate enough to get on the dollar-a-year payroll I might now have enough money to pay for these suits."

The tailor looked at me with surprise. I don't think he got the joke.

One of the suits was a beautiful dark gray; one was a dark blue; the other was a light blue with a pin stripe.

Fortunately I was in good standing with my tailor, therefore he did not ask when I was going to pay for those expensive suits. I knew that I could and would pay for them in due time, but could I have convinced him of that? This was the thought that was running through my mind, with hope against hope that the question would not be brought up.

I then visited my haberdasher, from whom I purchased three less expensive suits and a complete supply of the best shirts, collars, ties, hosiery, and underwear that he carried.

With an air of prosperity I nonchalantly signed the charge ticket. A feeling of renewed self-reliance and success began to come over me, even before I had attired myself in my newly purchased clothing.

I was out of the war and $675 in debt, all in less than twenty-four hours.

The following day the first of the three suits I ordered from the haberdasher was delivered. I put it on at once, stuffed a new silk handkerchief in the outside pocket of my coat, shoved the fifty dollars I had borrowed on my ring down into my pants pocket, and walked down Michigan Avenue in Chicago, feeling as rich as Rockefeller.

Every morning I dressed in an entirely new outfit, and walked down that same street at precisely the same hour. That hour "happened" to be the time when a certain wealthy publisher usually walked down the same street on his way to lunch.

I made it my business to speak to him each day, and occasionally we would stop for a minute's chat.

After this daily meeting had been going on for about a week, one day when I saw this publisher I decided to see if he would let me get by him without our speaking to each other.

PUT VIM, FORCE, VITALITY INTO

EVERY MOVEMENT OF YOUR BODY.

LET YOUR VERY ATMOSPHERE BE THAT

OF [ONE] WHO IS . . .

DETERMINED TO

STAND FOR SOMETHING,

AND TO BE SOMEBODY. . . .

DARE TO STEP OUT OF THE CROWD

AND BLAZE YOUR OWN PATH.

—Orison Swett Marden

Watching him from under my eyelashes I looked straight ahead and started to pass him, when he stopped and motioned me over to the edge of the sidewalk, placed his hand on my shoulder, looked me over from head to foot, and said: "You look damned prosperous for a man who has just laid aside a uniform. Who makes your clothes?"

"Well," I said, "Wilkie & Sellery made this particular suit."

He then wanted to know what sort of business I was engaged in. I said, "Oh, I am preparing the copy for a new magazine that I am going to publish."

"A new magazine, eh?" he queried. "And what are you going to call it?"

"It is to be named Hill's Golden Rule."

"Don't forget," said my publisher friend, "that I am in the business of printing and distributing magazines. Perhaps I can serve you also."

That was the moment for which I had been waiting. And I can assure you, that conversation never would have taken place had this publisher observed me walking down that street from day to day with a "whipped-dog" look on my face, an unpressed suit on my back, and a look of poverty in my eyes.

An appearance of prosperity attracts attention always, with no exceptions whatsoever. Moreover, a look of prosperity attracts favorable attention, because the one dominating desire in every human heart is to be prosperous.

My publisher friend invited me to his club for lunch. Before the coffee and cigars had been served he had "talked me out of" the contract for printing and distributing my magazine. I had even "consented" to permit him to supply the capital, without any interest charge.

For the benefit of those who are not familiar with the publishing business, let me point out that considerable capital is required for launching a new nationally distributed magazine.

The capital necessary for launching *Hill's Golden Rule Magazine* was well above $30,000, and every cent of it was raised because of the way I was dressed, and perhaps more important, the way it made me feel.

To some it may seem an unpardonable extravagance for one who was "broke" to have gone into debt for $675 worth of clothes, but the psychology behind that investment more than justified it.

The appearance of prosperity not only made a favorable impression on those to whom I had to look for favors, but of more importance still was the effect that proper attire had on me.

I not only knew that correct clothes would impress others favorably, but I knew also that good clothes would give me an air of self-reliance, without which I could not hope to regain my lost fortunes.

I got my first training in the psychology of good clothes from my friend Edwin C. Barnes, whom I mentioned earlier had ridden into West Orange, New Jersey, on a freight train (not being able to raise sufficient money for passenger fare). What I had not elaborated on then is that when Mr. Barnes arrived, he had announced at the Edison offices that he had come to enter into a partnership with Mr. Edison.

Nearly everybody around the Edison plant had laughed at Barnes, except Edison himself. He saw something in the square jaw and determined face of young Barnes that most of the others did not see, despite the fact that the young man looked more like a tramp than he did a future partner of the greatest inventor on earth.

Barnes got his start, sweeping floors in the Edison offices! That was all he sought—just a chance to get a toehold in the Edison organization. From there on he made history.

He is now a multimillionaire, prosperous and happy, and a close associate of Thomas A. Edison's. He has retired from active business, even though he is still a comparatively young man, and spends most of his time at his two beautiful homes in Bradentown, Florida, and Damariscotta, Maine.

I first became acquainted with Barnes during the early days of his association with Edison, before he had "arrived."

In those days he had the largest and most expensive collection of clothes I had ever seen or heard of one man owning. His wardrobe consisted of thirty-one suits; one for each day of the month. He never wore the same suit two days in succession.

One day, in a spirit of fun, I asked him to save some of his old suits that he did not need, for me.

He informed me that he hadn't a single suit that he did not need!

He then gave me a lesson on the psychology of clothes that is well worth remembering: "I do not wear thirty-one suits of clothes entirely for the impression they make on other people; I do it mostly for the impression they have on me."

Barnes then told me of the day when he presented himself at the Edison plant for a position. He said he had to walk around the plant a dozen times before he worked up enough courage to announce himself, because he knew he looked more like a tramp than he did a desirable employee.

Barnes is said to be the most able salesman ever connected with the great inventor of West Orange. His entire fortune was made through his ability as a salesman, but he has often said that he never could have accomplished the results that have made him both wealthy and famous had it not been for his understanding of the psychology of clothes.

I have met many salespeople in my time. During the past ten years I have personally trained and directed the efforts of more than three thousand, both men and women, and I have observed that, without a single exception, the star producers were all people who understood and made good use of the psychology of clothes. I have yet to see the first poorly dressed salesperson who became a star producer.

I have studied the psychology of clothes for so long, and I have watched its effect on people in so many different walks of life, that I am fully convinced there is a close connection between clothes and success.

WE ACT AS THOUGH COMFORT

AND LUXURY WERE THE

CHIEF REQUIREMENTS OF LIFE,

WHEN ALL WE NEED

TO MAKE US HAPPY

IS SOMETHING

TO BE ENTHUSIASTIC ABOUT.

—Charles Kingsley

Personally I feel no need of thirty-one suits of clothes, but if my personality demanded a wardrobe of this size I would manage to get it, no matter how much it might cost.

It may be true, as a well-known poet has said, that "clothes do not make the man," but no one can deny that good clothes go a very long way toward giving a person a favorable start.

A bank will generally loan you all the money you want when you do not need it—when you are prosperous—but never go to your bank for a loan with shabby-looking clothes on your back and a look of poverty in your eyes, for if you do you'll get the gate. Success attracts success! There is no escape from this fact. Therefore, if you wish to attract success, make sure that you look the part of success, whether your calling is that of day laborer or merchant prince.

For the benefit of the more "dignified" students of this philosophy who may object to resorting to "trick clothing" as a means of achieving success, let me say that the real lesson here is that practically every successful person has discovered some form of stimulus through which they can and do drive themself on to greater effort.

Times too numerous to mention I have gone into conference with colleagues who had the appearance of worry written all over them, only to see those same colleagues straighten up their shoulders, tilt their chins at a higher angle, soften their faces with smiles of confidence, and get down to business with the sort of Enthusiasm that knows no defeat.

The change took place at the moment harmony of purpose was established.

If a person goes about the affairs of life devoid of Enthusiasm, they are doomed to failure. Nothing can save them until they change their attitude and learn how to stimulate their mind and body to unusual heights of Enthusiasm *at will!*

Your business in life, you are reminded once again, is to achieve success!

LET US GO SINGING

AS FAR AS WE GO;

THE ROAD WILL BE LESS TEDIOUS.

—Virgil

With the motivation you will derive from studying this philosophy, you should be able to create a *definite plan* that will lift you to great heights of achievement. However, there is no plan that can produce this desirable result without the aid of some influence that will cause you to lift yourself, in a spirit of Enthusiasm, to where you will exert greater than the ordinary effort that you put into your daily work.

You are now ready for the lesson on Self-Control, which describes the law that serves as the balance wheel of this entire philosophy. You will find that it has a vital bearing on this lesson, just as this lesson has a direct connection with the preceding lessons on a Definite Chief Aim, Self-Confidence, Initiative and Leadership, and Imagination.

THE SEVEN DEADLY HORSEMEN— AN AFTER-THE-LESSON VISIT WITH THE AUTHOR

The "seven horsemen" are labeled
Intolerance, Greed, Revenge, Egotism, Suspicion, Jealousy, and "?"

The worst enemy that anyone has is the one that walks around under his or her own hat. If you could see yourself as others see you, the enemies that you harbor in your own personality might be discovered and thrown out. The seven enemies named in this essay are the commonest that ride millions of men and women to failure without being discovered. Your success will be measured very largely by the way you manage your battle against these swift riders.

If these enemies rode openly, on real horses, they would not be dangerous, because they could be rounded up and put out of commission. But they ride unseen, in our minds. So silently and subtly do they work that most people never recognize their presence.

Take careful inventory of yourself and find out how many of these seven horsemen you are harboring.

In the foreground you will find Intolerance—the most dangerous and commonest of the riders. You will be fortunate if you can discover this enemy and protect yourself against it. This cruel warrior has killed more people, destroyed more friendships, brought more misery and suffering into the world, and caused more wars than all of the other six horsemen.

Until you master Intolerance you will never become an accurate thinker. This enemy of mankind closes the mind and pushes reason and logic and facts into the background. If you find yourself hating those whose viewpoint is different from your own, you may be sure that the most dangerous of the seven deadly horsemen still rides in your brain.

Next come Revenge and Greed. These riders travel side by side. Where one is found the other is always close at hand. Greed warps and twists a person's brain so that he or she wants to build a fence around the earth and keep everyone else on the outside. This is the enemy that drives many to accumulate millions on top of millions of dollars that they do not need and can never use. This is the enemy that causes many to twist the screw until they have wrung the last drop of blood from their fellow human being.

And thanks to Revenge, which rides alongside of Greed, the unfortunate person who gives room to these cruel twins is not satisfied to merely take away a neighbor's earthly belongings; that person wants to destroy the reputation of the other in the bargain.

> *Revenge is a naked sword*
> *It has neither hilt nor guard.*
> *Would'st thou wield this brand of the Lord;*
> *Is thy grasp then firm and hard?*
> *But the closer thy clutch of the blade,*

The deadlier blow thou would'st deal,
Deeper wound in thy hand is made
It is thy blood reddens the steel.
And when thou hast dealt the blow
When the blade from thy hand has flown
Instead of the heart of the foe
Thou may'st find it sheathed in thine own.

If you would know how deadly are Revenge and Greed, study the history of every person who has set out to become ruler of the world!

If you do not wish to undertake such ambitious research, then study the people around you; those who have tried and those who are now trying to "feather their own nests" at the cost of others. Greed and Revenge stand at the crossroads of life, where they turn aside to failure and misery every person who would take the road that leads to success. It is a part of your business not to permit them to interfere with you when you approach one of these crossroads.

Both individuals and nations rapidly decline where Greed and Revenge are in the minds of those who dominate.

Most important of all, take a look at *yourself* and make sure that these two deadly enemies are not riding in your brain!

Turn your attention now to two more twins of destruction—Egotism and Suspicion. Observe that they also ride side by side. There is no hope of success for the person who suffers either from too much self-love or lack of confidence in others.

Someone who likes to manipulate figures has estimated that the largest club in the world is the "It-Can't-Be-Done" club.

If you have no faith in other people, you have not the seed of success in you. Suspicion is a prolific germ. If permitted to get a start, it rapidly multiplies itself until it leaves no room for faith.

Without faith, no one may enjoy enduring success.

Running throughout the Bible is the admonition to have faith. Before civilization lost itself in its mad rush for dollars, people understood the power of faith.

"For verily I say unto you, if ye have faith as a grain of mustard seed, ye shall say unto this mountain, Remove hence to yonder place; and it shall remove; and nothing shall be impossible unto you."

The writer of this passage, which appears in the Bible, understood a great law which but few today understand. Believe in people if you would have them believe in you. Kill off suspicion. If you do not, it will kill you off.

If you would have power, cultivate faith in humankind!

Egotism thrives where suspicion exists. Interest yourself in others and you will be too busy to indulge in self-love. Observe those around you who begin every sentence with the personal pronoun "I," and you will notice that they are suspicious of other people.

The person who can forget themself while engaging in useful service to other people is never cursed with suspicion. Study those who are both suspicious and egotistical and see how many of this type you can name who are successful in their work.

And, while making this study of others, also study yourself!

Be sure that you are not bound down by egotism and suspicion.

———————

Bringing up the rear of this deadly group of riders are two more horsemen. One is Jealousy and the name of the other has been purposely omitted. Each reader may take inventory of himself or herself and give the seventh rider a name that fits whatever they might find in their own mind.

Some will name this rider Dishonesty. Others will name it Procrastination. A few will name it Uncontrolled Sex Desire. As for you, name it whatever you please, but be sure to give it a name.

Perhaps your own imagination will supply an appropriate name as a fellow traveler for Jealousy.

You will be better prepared to give the unnamed rider a name if you know that jealousy is a form of insanity! Facts are sometimes cruel things to face, but it is a fact that jealousy is a form of insanity, known to the medical fraternity as "dementia praecox."

> *O jealousy,*
> *Thou ugliest fiend of hell! thy deadly venom*
> *Preys on my vitals, turns the healthful hue*
> *Of my fresh cheek to haggard sallowness,*
> *And drinks my spirit up!*

You will notice that Jealousy rides just behind Suspicion. Some readers will say that Jealousy and Suspicion should have ridden side by side, as one often leads to the other in the human mind.

Jealousy is the most common form of insanity. It rides in the minds of both men and women, sometimes with a real cause but more often without any cause whatsoever.

This deadly rider is a great friend of the divorce lawyers!

It also keeps the detective agencies busy night and day. It takes its regular toll of murders. It breaks up homes. It makes widows of mothers, and orphans of innocent little children. Peace and happiness can never be yours as long as this rider, Jealousy, remains unharnessed in your brain.

Man and wife may go through life together in poverty and still be very happy, if both are free from this child of insanity known as jealousy. Examine yourself carefully and if you find any evidence of jealousy in your mind, begin at once to master it.

Jealousy rides in many forms. When it first begins to creep into the brain it manifests itself something like this:

"I wonder where she is and what she is doing while I am away?"

EVERY GREAT AND

COMMANDING MOVEMENT

IN THE ANNALS OF THE WORLD

IS A TRIUMPH OF ENTHUSIASM.

—Ralph Waldo Emerson

Or, "I wonder if he does not see another woman when he is away from me?"

Get your foot on Jealousy's neck before it gets its clutches on your throat.

After you have read this essay, lay it aside and think about it. At first you may say, "This does not apply to me. I have no imaginary horsemen in my brain."

Do not fool yourself! The purpose of this essay is to get you to see yourself as you are! If you are suffering failure and poverty and misery in any of their forms, you are sure to discover one or more of these deadly riders in your brain.

Make no mistake about it—those who have all they want, including happiness and good health, have driven the seven horsemen out of their brains.

Come back to this essay a month from now, after you have had time to analyze yourself carefully. Read it again and it may bring you face-to-face with *facts* that will emancipate you from a horde of cruel enemies that now ride within your brain without your knowing it.

Lesson Eight

Self-Control

THE MAN WHO

MASTERS HIMSELF IS

DELIVERED FROM THE FORCE

THAT BINDS ALL CREATURES.

—Johann Wolfgang von Goethe

Lesson Eight

SELF-CONTROL

"You Can Do It if You Believe You Can!"

IN THE PRECEDING LESSON YOU LEARNED OF the value of Enthusiasm. You also learned how to generate Enthusiasm and how to transmit its influence to others, through the principle of *suggestion.*

We come now to the study of Self-Control, through which you may direct your Enthusiasm to constructive ends. Without Self-Control, Enthusiasm resembles the unharnessed lightning of an electrical storm—it may strike *anywhere;* it may destroy life and property.

Enthusiasm is the vital quality that arouses you to action, while Self-Control is the balance wheel that *directs* your action so that it will build up and not tear down.

COMMENTARY

> *Self-control is the ability to direct your thoughts, and thus your actions, in the pursuit of your definite chief aim. In a very large sense, every lesson of* Law of Success *is about self-control, but in this chapter Hill explores the issue with specific regard to your dealings with other people.*

To be a person who is "well-balanced," you must be a person in whom Enthusiasm and Self-Control are equalized. A survey I have just completed of 160,000 adult inmates of penitentiaries in the United States discloses the startling fact that 92 percent of these unfortunate men and women are in prison because they lacked the necessary Self-Control to direct their energies constructively.

Read the foregoing paragraph again; it is authentic, it is startling!

It is a fact that the majority of our personal grief comes about through lack of Self-Control. The holy scriptures are full of admonition in support of Self-Control. They even urge us to love our enemies and to forgive those who injure us.

Study the records of those whom the world calls great, and observe that *every one of them possesses this quality of Self-Control!*

For example, study the characteristics of our own immortal Lincoln. In the midst of his most trying hours he exercised patience, poise, and Self-Control. These were some of the qualities that made him the great man that he was. He found disloyalty in some of the members of his cabinet; but because this disloyalty was toward him, personally, and because those in whom he found it had qualities that made them valuable to his country, Lincoln exercised Self-Control and disregarded the objectionable qualities.

How many people do you know who have Self-Control to equal this?

In language more forceful than polished, Billy Sunday exclaimed from the pulpit: "There is something as rotten as hell about the man who is always trying to show some other fellow up!" I wonder if the "devil" didn't yell "Amen, brother" when Billy made that statement?

Self-Control becomes an important factor in this course on the laws of success because those who do not exercise it suffer the loss of a great power that they need in their struggle for achievement of their Definite Chief Aim.

If you neglect to exercise Self-Control, you are not only likely to injure others but you are sure to injure yourself!

During the early part of my public career I discovered what havoc lack of Self-Control was playing in my life. This discovery taught me one of the most important lessons I have ever learned.

One day, in the building in which I had my office, the janitor and I had a misunderstanding. This led to a most violent form of mutual dislike between us. As a way of showing his contempt for me, this janitor would switch off the lights when he knew I was alone at work in my study. This happened on several occasions until I finally decided to "strike back." My opportunity came one Sunday when I came to my study to prepare an address I had to deliver the following night. I had hardly seated myself at my desk when off went the lights.

I jumped to my feet and ran toward the basement of the building where I knew I would find the janitor.

When I arrived, I found him busily engaged, shoveling coal into the furnace, and whistling as though nothing unusual had happened.

Without ceremony I pitched into him, and for five minutes I hurled adjectives at him which were hotter than the fire that he was feeding. Finally, I ran out of words and had to slow down. Then he straightened himself up, looked back over his shoulder, and in a calm, smooth tone of voice that was full of poise and Self-Control, and with a smile on his face that reached from ear to ear, he said:

"Why, you're just a little bit excited this morning, ain't you?"

That remark cut as though it had been a stiletto! Imagine my feelings as I stood there before a man who could neither read nor write, but who, despite this handicap, had defeated me in a duel that had been fought on ground and with a weapon of my own choice.

THE GROWTH OF WISDOM

MAY BE GAUGED ACCURATELY

BY THE DECLINE OF ILL-TEMPER.

—Friedrich Nietzsche

My conscience pointed an accusing finger at me. I knew that not only had I been defeated but, what was worse, I knew that I was the aggressor and *I was in the wrong,* which only served to intensify my humiliation.

Not only did my conscience point an accusing finger at me, but it placed some very embarrassing thoughts in my mind; it mocked me and it tantalized me. There I stood, a boasted student of advanced psychology, an exponent of the Golden Rule philosophy, having at least a fair acquaintance with the works of Shakespeare, Socrates, Plato, Emerson, and the Bible. And facing me stood a man who knew nothing of literature or of philosophy, but who had, despite this lack of knowledge, whipped me in a battle of words.

I turned and went back to my office as rapidly as I could go. There was nothing else for me to do. As I began to think the matter over, I saw my mistake, but, true to nature, I was reluctant to do what I knew must be done to right the wrong. I knew I would have to apologize to that man before I could place myself at peace in my own heart, much less with him. Finally, I made up my mind to go back down to the basement and suffer this humility which I knew I had to undergo. The decision was not easily reached, nor did I reach it quickly.

I started down, but I walked more slowly than I had when I went down the first trip. I was trying to think how I would make the second approach so as to suffer the least humiliation possible.

When I got to the basement I called to the janitor to come over to the door. In a calm, kindly tone of voice he asked: "What do you wish this time?"

I informed him that I had come back to apologize for the wrong I had done, if he would permit me to do so. Again that smile spread all over his face as he said: "For the love of the Lord, you don't have to apologize. Nobody heard you except these four walls and you and me. I ain't going to tell it and I know you ain't going to tell it, so just forget it."

And that remark hurt more than his first one, for he had not only expressed a willingness to forgive me, but he had actually indicated

LUCK IS NOT CHANCE—

IT'S TOIL—

FORTUNE'S EXPENSIVE SMILE

IS EARNED.

—Emily Dickinson

his willingness to help me cover up the incident so nobody would ever know.

I walked over to him and took him by the hand. But I shook with more than my hand—I shook with my heart—and as I walked back to my office I felt good for having summoned the courage with which to right the wrong I had done.

This is not the end of the story. It is only the beginning! Following this incident, I made a resolution that I would never again place myself in a position where another human being could humiliate me because I had lost my Self-Control.

Following that resolution, a remarkable change began to take place in me. My pen began to take on greater power. My spoken words began to carry greater weight. I began to make more friends and fewer enemies among my acquaintances. The incident marked one of the most important turning points of my life. It taught me that no one can control others unless they first control themself. It gave me a clear concept of the philosophy behind these words: "Whom the gods would destroy, they first make mad." It also gave me a clear concept of the law of nonresistance.

This incident placed in my hands the passkey to a storehouse of knowledge that is illuminating and helpful in all that I do. And later in life, when enemies sought to destroy me, it gave me a powerful weapon of defense that has never failed me.

Lack of Self-Control is the average salesperson's most damaging weakness.

In one of the large department stores of Chicago I witnessed an incident that illustrated the importance of Self-Control. A long line of people was in front of the "complaint" desk, telling their troubles and the store's faults to the young woman in charge. Some were angry and unreasonable and some of them made very ugly remarks. The young woman at the desk received the disgruntled customers without the slightest sign of resentment at their remarks. With a smile on her face she directed them to the proper departments with such charming grace and poise that I marveled at her Self-Control.

Standing just behind her was another young woman who was making notations on slips of paper and passing them in front of her as the customers in the line unburdened their troubles. These slips of paper contained the gist of what the women in the line were saying, minus the "vitriolic coloring" and the anger.

This smiling young woman at the desk who was "hearing" the complaints was deaf! Her assistant supplied her with all the necessary facts, through those slips of paper.

I was so impressed with the plan that I sought the manager of the store and interviewed him. He informed me that he had selected a deaf woman for one of the most trying and important positions in the store because he had not been able to find any other person with sufficient Self-Control to fill the position.

Ever since I witnessed that scene, I have thought of the poise and Self-Control of that young woman at the desk every time I felt myself becoming irritated at remarks I did not like. Often I have thought that everybody should have a set of "mental ear muffs" which they could slip over their ears at times. Life is too short and there is too much constructive work to be done to justify us "striking back" at everyone who says something that we do not wish to hear.

As I stood and watched that line of angry people, I observed what a pleasant effect the smile of the young woman at the desk had on them. Even those who came to her growling like wolves often went away as meek and quiet as sheep. This young woman's Self-Control had made them ashamed of themselves. Those who control themselves usually boss the job, no matter what it may be.

No doubt all people who refuse or neglect to exercise Self-Control are literally turning away opportunity after opportunity without knowing it.

One rainy afternoon an old lady walked into a Pittsburgh department store and wandered around in an aimless sort of way, very much in the manner that people who have no intention of buying often do. Most of the salespeople gave her the "once over" and busied themselves by straightening the stock on their shelves so as to avoid being troubled by her. One of the young men saw her and made it his business to inquire politely if he might serve her. She informed him that she was only waiting for it to stop raining; that she did not wish to make any purchases. The young man assured her that she was welcome, and by engaging her in conversation made her feel that he had meant what he said. When she was ready to go, he accompanied her to the street and raised her umbrella for her. She asked for his card and went on her way.

The incident had been forgotten by the young man, when one day he was called into the office by the head of the firm and shown a letter from a lady who wanted a salesman to go to Scotland and take an order for the furnishings for a mansion.

That lady was Andrew Carnegie's mother; she was also the same woman whom the young man had so courteously escorted to the street many months previously.

In the letter, Mrs. Carnegie specified that this young man was the one whom she desired be sent to take her order. That order amounted to an enormous sum, and the incident brought to the young man an opportunity for advancement that he might never have had except for his courtesy to an old lady who did not look like a "ready sale."

Just as the great fundamental laws of life are wrapped up in the commonest sort of everyday experiences that most of us never notice, so are the *real* opportunities often hidden in the seemingly unimportant transactions of life.

Ask the next ten people whom you meet why it is they have not accomplished more in their respective lines of endeavor, and at least nine of them will tell you that opportunity does not seem to come their way. Go a step further and analyze each of these nine accurately by observing their actions for one single day, and the chances are you

THE MAN WHO ACTUALLY KNOWS

JUST WHAT HE WANTS IN LIFE

HAS ALREADY GONE A LONG WAY

TOWARD ATTAINING IT.

will find that every one of them is turning away the finest sort of opportunities every hour of the day.

One day I went to visit a friend who was associated with a commercial school. When I asked him how he was getting along he replied: "Rotten! I see a large number of people but I am not making enough sales to give me a good living. I am thinking about changing positions as there is no *opportunity* here."

It happened that I was on my vacation and had ten days' time that I could use as I wished, so I challenged his remark that he had no opportunity by telling him that I could turn his position into $250 in a week's time and show him how to make it worth that every week thereafter. He looked at me in amazement and asked me not to joke with him over so serious a matter. When he was finally convinced that I was in earnest, he inquired how I would perform the "miracle."

I informed him that by using *organized effort* he could enroll from five to ten students with the same amount of effort that he had been putting into the enrollment of one or of none. He replied that he was willing to be shown, so I asked him to arrange for me to speak before the employees of one of the local department stores. He made the appointment and I delivered the address. In my talk I outlined a plan by which the employees could not only increase their ability so that they could earn more money in their present positions, but it also offered them an opportunity to prepare themselves for greater responsibilities and better positions. Following my talk, which of course had been designed for that purpose, my friend enrolled eight of those employees for night courses in the commercial school that he represented.

The following night he booked me for a similar address before the employees of a laundry, and following this address he enrolled three more students, two of whom were young women who worked over the washing machines at the hardest sort of labor.

Two days later he booked me for an address before the employees of one of the local banks, and following the address he enrolled four more students, making a total of fifteen new students. The entire time consumed was not more than six hours, including the time required for the delivery of the addresses and the enrollment of the students.

My friend's commission on the transactions was a little over four hundred dollars!

These places of employment were within fifteen minutes' walk of this man's place of business, but he had not thought of looking there for business nor of allying himself with a speaker to assist him in "group" selling. That man now owns a highly successful commercial school of his own.

No "opportunities" come your way? Perhaps they come but you do not see them. Perhaps you will see them in the future as you are preparing yourself, through the laws of success, so that you can recognize an opportunity when you see it. The sixth lesson of this course was on the subject of Imagination, which is the chief factor in this story. Imagination, plus a *definite plan*, plus Self-Confidence, plus *action*, were the main factors that entered into this transaction. You now know how to use all of these, and before you have finished this lesson you will understand how to direct these factors through Self-Control.

Now let us examine the scope of meaning of the term *self-control.* A person with well-developed Self-Control does not indulge in hatred, envy, jealousy, fear, revenge, or any similar destructive emotions. A person with well-developed Self-Control does not go into ecstasies or become ungovernably enthusiastic over anything or anybody.

Greed and selfishness and excessive self-approval indicate lack of Self-Control in one of its most dangerous forms. Self-Confidence is one of the important essentials of success, but when this faculty is developed beyond the point of reason, it becomes very dangerous.

Self-sacrifice is a commendable quality, but when carried to extremes it also becomes one of the dangerous forms of lack of Self-Control.

You owe it to yourself not to permit your emotions to place your happiness in the keeping of another person. Love is essential for happiness, but the person who loves so deeply that his or her happiness is placed entirely in the hands of another is literally out of control.

A person with well-developed Self-Control will not permit himself or herself to be influenced by the cynic or the pessimist; nor will they permit another person to do their thinking for them.

A person with well-developed Self-Control will stimulate their Imagination and their Enthusiasm until they have produced *action,* but will then control that action and not permit it to control them.

A person with well-developed Self-Control will never, under any circumstances, slander another person or seek revenge for any cause whatsoever.

A person with Self-Control will not hate those who do not agree with them; instead, they will endeavor to understand the reason for their disagreement, and profit by it.

We come now to a form of lack of Self-Control that causes more grief than all other forms combined; it is the habit of forming opinions before studying the *facts.* You will find that this subject is covered more fully in Lesson Eleven, on Accurate Thinking, but the subject of Self-Control could not be covered without at least a passing reference to this common evil to which we are all more or less addicted.

No one has any right to form an opinion that is not based either on what they believe to be facts, or on a reasonable hypothesis. Yet, if you will observe yourself carefully, you will catch yourself forming opinions on nothing more substantial than your desire for a thing to be or not to be.

Another grievous form of lack of Self-Control is the habit of spending beyond one's needs.

I am safe in assuming that you are struggling to attain success, for if you were not, you would not be reading this course. Let me remind you, then, that a little savings account will attract many an opportunity that would not come your way without it. The size of the account is not as important as the fact that you have established the Habit of

SPEAK WHEN YOU ARE ANGRY

AND YOU WILL MAKE

THE BEST SPEECH

YOU WILL EVER REGRET.

—Ambrose Bierce

Saving, for this habit marks you as a person who exercises an important form of Self-Control.

The modern tendency of those who work for a salary is to spend it all. If a person who receives $15,000 a year, and manages to get along on it fairly well, receives an increase of $1,000 a year, do they continue to live on $15,000 and put the increased portion of their income into savings or investments? No, not unless he or she is one of the few who have developed the savings *habit*. Then what do they do with this additional $1,000? They trade in the old automobile and buy a new, more expensive one, and at the end of the year they are poorer on a $16,000 income than they were previously on a $15,000 income.

Somewhere between the miser who hoards, in an old sock, every penny they get their hands on, and the person who spends every cent they can earn or borrow, there is a "happy medium." If you wish to enjoy life with reasonable assurance of average freedom and contentment, you must find this halfway point and adopt it as a part of your Self-Control program.

Self-discipline is the most essential factor in the development of personal power. It enables you to control your appetite and your tendency to spend more than you earn, and your habit of "striking back" at those who offend you, as well as the other destructive habits that cause you to dissipate your energies through nonproductive effort which takes on forms too numerous to mention in this lesson.

Very early in my public career I was shocked when I learned how many people there are who devote most of their energies to tearing down what the builders construct. By some queer turn of the wheel of fate, one of these destroyers crossed my path by making it his business to try to destroy my reputation.

At first I was inclined to "strike back" at him, but as I sat at my typewriter late one night, a thought came to me that changed my entire attitude toward this man. Removing the sheet of paper from my typewriter, I inserted another on which I wrote this thought, in these words:

PERSEVERANCE IS

MORE PREVAILING THAN VIOLENCE;

AND MANY THINGS

WHICH CANNOT BE OVERCOME

WHEN THEY ARE TAKEN TOGETHER,

YIELD THEMSELVES UP

WHEN TAKEN LITTLE BY LITTLE.

—Plutarch

"You have a tremendous advantage over the man who does you an injury: You have it within your power to forgive him, while he has no such advantage over you."

As I finished writing those lines, I made up my mind that I had come to the point at which I had to decide on a policy that would serve as a guide concerning my attitude toward those who criticize my work or try to destroy my reputation. I reached this decision by reasoning in somewhat this way:

Two courses of action were open to me. I could waste much of my time and energy in striking back, or I could devote this energy to furthering my life's work and let the result of that work serve as my sole answer to all who would criticize my efforts or question my motives. I decided on the latter as being the better policy and adopted it.

"By their deeds you shall know them!"

If your deeds are constructive and you are at peace with yourself, in your own heart, you will not find it necessary to stop and explain your motives, for they will explain themselves.

The world soon forgets its destroyers. It builds its monuments to and bestows its honors upon none but its builders. Keep this in mind and you will more easily reconcile yourself to the policy of refusing to waste your energies by "striking back" at those who offend you.

Every person who amounts to anything in this world comes to the point, sooner or later, at which they are forced to settle this question of policy toward their enemies. If you want proof that it pays to exercise sufficient Self-Control to refrain from dissipating your vital energies by striking back, then study the records of all who have risen to high stations in life and observe how carefully they curbed this destructive habit.

It is a well-known fact that no one ever reached a high station in life without opposition of a violent nature from jealous and envious enemies. The late President Warren G. Harding and former President Wilson and John H. Patterson of the National Cash Register Company and scores of others whom I could mention, were victims of this cruel

tendency, of a certain type of depraved human being, to destroy reputations. But these people wasted no time explaining or "striking back"
at their enemies. They exercised Self-Control.

It may even be that these attacks, cruel and unjust and untruthful
as they often are, serve a good purpose. In my own case, I know that I
made a discovery that was of great value to me, as a result of a series of
bitter attacks that a journalist launched against me. I paid no attention
to these attacks for four or five years, until finally they became so bold
that I decided to override my policy and strike back at my antagonist.
I sat down at my typewriter and began to write. In all of my experience
as a writer I do not believe I ever assembled such a collection of biting
adjectives as those that I used on this occasion. The more I wrote, the
more angry I became, until I had written all that I could think of on
the subject. As the last line was finished, a strange feeling came over me
—it was not a feeling of bitterness toward the person who had tried to
injure me, it was a feeling of compassion, of sympathy, of forgiveness.

I had unconsciously psychoanalyzed myself by releasing, over the
keys of my typewriter, the repressed emotions of hate and resentment
that I had been unintentionally gathering in my subconscious mind
over a long period of years.

Now if I find myself becoming very angry, I sit down at my typewriter and "write it out of my system," then throw away the manuscript.
Or I file it away so I can refer back in the years to come—after the
evolutionary processes of time have given me greater understanding.

COMMENTARY

*Elsewhere, Hill writes about a negative experience that motivated him: "I was once
engaged by the chamber of commerce in a small town to deliver a series of lectures.
One citizen took it upon himself to announce that I was a charlatan who was riding
into town to fleece the locals of their hard-earned cash. He caused no small amount
of grief to the people who had hired me, and frankly, piqued my anger a little.*

"So, I took my entire fee for the lectures and bought airtime on the local radio station. And I delivered my talks free to a much larger audience than could have fit into the hall where I was supposed to speak.

"I must admit that I caused quite a sensation, creating favorable publicity for myself and for the chamber of commerce. I made no money on that actual transaction, but I did keep myself from becoming engaged in a fruitless battle. I answered the doubting Thomas's charges in a way that completely obliterated them without once sacrificing my dignity, or credibility. I like to think, in fact, that my words carried an extra weight in that town and did far more good than they might otherwise have."

Repressed emotions, especially the emotion of hatred, resemble a bomb that has been constructed of high explosives, and unless they are handled as an expert would handle a bomb, they are as dangerous. A bomb may be rendered harmless by explosion in an open field, or by disintegration in a bath of the proper sort. A feeling of anger or hatred may also be rendered harmless by giving expression to it in a manner that harmonizes with the principle of psychoanalysis.

THOUGHT

Before you can achieve success in the higher and broader sense, you must gain such thorough control over yourself that you will be a person of *poise.*

You are the product of at least a million years of evolutionary change. For countless generations preceding you, Nature has been tempering and refining the materials that have gone into your makeup. Step by step, she has removed from the generations that have preceded you the animal instincts and baser passions until she has produced, in you, the finest specimen of animal that lives. She has endowed you, through this slow evolutionary process, with reason and poise and "balance" sufficient to enable you to control and do with yourself whatever you will.

WHILE OTHERS

MAY SIDETRACK YOUR AMBITIONS

NOT A FEW TIMES,

REMEMBER THAT DISCOURAGEMENT

MOST FREQUENTLY

COMES FROM WITHIN.

No other animal has ever been endowed with such Self-Control as you possess. You have been endowed with the power to use the most highly organized form of energy known—that of *thought*. It is not improbable that thought is the closest connecting link there is between the material, physical things of this world and the world of Divinity.

You have not only the power to *think*, but what is a thousand times more important still, you have the power to *control* your thoughts and *direct* them to do your bidding!

We are coming now to the really important part of this lesson. Read slowly and meditatively!

I approach this part of the lesson almost with fear and trembling, for it brings us face to face with a subject which but few are qualified to discuss with reasonable intelligence.

I repeat, *you have the power to control your thoughts and direct them to do your bidding!*

Your brain may be likened to a dynamo, in that it generates or sets into motion the mysterious energy called *thought*. The stimuli that start your brain into action are of two sorts: one is *autosuggestion* and the other is *suggestion*. You can select the material out of which your thinking is produced, and that is autosuggestion (or self-suggestion). You can permit others to select the material out of which your thinking is produced, and that is suggestion. It is a humiliating fact that most thought is produced by the outside suggestions of others, and it is more humiliating still to have to admit that the majority of us accept this suggestion without examining it or questioning its soundness. We read the daily papers as though every word were based on fact. We are swayed by the gossip and idle chatter of others as though every word were true.

Thought is the only thing over which you have absolute control. Yet you permit other people to enter the sacred mansion of your mind and there deposit, through suggestion, their troubles and woes, adversities and falsehoods, just as though you did not have the power to close the door and keep them out.

You have within your control the power to select the material that constitutes the dominating thoughts of your mind, and just as surely as you are reading these lines, those thoughts which dominate your mind will bring you success or failure, according to their nature.

The fact that thought is the only thing over which you have absolute control is of most profound significance. It strongly suggests that thought is your nearest approach to Divinity on this earthly plane.

Surely, Divine Providence did not make thought the sole power over which you have absolute control, without associating with that power potentialities which, if understood and developed, would stagger the imagination. Thought is your most important tool; the one with which you may shape your worldly destiny according to your own liking.

Self-Control is solely a matter of *thought control!*

Please read the foregoing sentence aloud. Read it thoughtfully and meditate over it before reading further, because it is, without doubt, the most important single sentence of this entire course.

You are studying this course, presumably, because you are earnestly seeking truth and understanding sufficient to enable you to attain some high station in life.

You are searching for the magic key that will unlock the door to the source of power. And yet you have the key in your own hands, and you may make use of it the moment you learn to *control your thoughts.*

Place in your own mind, through the principle of autosuggestion, the positive, constructive thoughts that harmonize with your Definite Chief Aim in life, and that mind will transform those thoughts into physical reality and hand them back to you, as a finished product.

This is thought control!

When you deliberately choose the thoughts that dominate your mind, and firmly refuse admittance to outside suggestion, you are exercising Self-Control in its highest and most efficient form. Human beings are the only animals that can do this.

How many millions of years Nature has required in which to produce this animal, no one knows, but every intelligent student of psychology knows it is the dominating thoughts that determine the actions and the nature of the animal.

The point I wish to clearly establish in this lesson is that *thought*, whether accurate or inaccurate, is the most highly organized functioning power of your mind, and that *you are but the sum total of your dominating or most prominent thoughts.*

If you would be a master salesperson of goods or of personal services, you must exercise sufficient Self-Control to shut out all adverse arguments and suggestions. Most salespeople have so little Self-Control that they hear the prospective purchaser say no, even before it is said. They have so little Self-Control that they actually *suggest* to themselves that their prospective purchaser will say no when asked to purchase their wares.

How different is the person of Self-Control! He or she not only makes the self-suggestion that the prospective purchaser will say yes, but if the desired yes is not forthcoming, he or she stays on the job until the opposition breaks down. If the prospective purchaser says no, the person of Self-Control does not hear it. If the prospective purchaser says no a second, and a third, and a fourth time, he or she does not hear it, for a person of Self-Control permits no suggestions to reach the mind except those which are invited.

The master salesperson, whether engaged in selling merchandise or personal services or sermons or public addresses, understands how to control their own thoughts. Instead of being a person who accepts, with meek submission, the suggestions of others, the master salesperson is one who persuades *others* to accept his or her suggestions. The master salesperson becomes a dominating personality. *This, too, is Self-Control!*

A master salesperson is one who takes the offensive, and never the defensive, side of an argument, if argument arises.

Please read the foregoing sentence again!

———

BOTH TEARS AND SWEAT

ARE SALTY, BUT THEY WILL

RENDER DIFFERENT RESULTS.

TEARS WILL GET YOU SYMPATHY;

SWEAT WILL GET YOU CHANGE.

—Jesse Jackson

———

If you are a master salesperson you know that it is necessary for you to keep your prospective purchaser on the defensive. You also know that it will be fatal to your sale if you permit the buyer to place you on the defensive and keep you there. You may, and of course you will at times, be placed in a position in which you will have to assume the defensive side of the conversation for a time. But it is your business to exercise such perfect poise and Self-Control that you will change places with your prospective purchasers without them noticing that you have done so.

This requires the most consummate skill and Self-Control!

Most salespeople sweep this vital point aside by becoming angry and trying to scare the prospective purchaser into submission, but the master of the craft remains calm and serene, and usually comes out the winner.

When I use the term *salesperson,* I mean all people who try to persuade or convince others by logic or by appeal to self-interest. We are all salespeople, or at least we should be, no matter what form of service we are rendering or what sort of goods we are offering.

The ability to negotiate with other people without friction and argument is the outstanding quality of all successful people. Observe those nearest you and notice how few there are who understand this art of tactful negotiation. Observe, also, how successful are the few who understand this art, despite the fact that they may have less education than those with whom they negotiate.

It is a knack that can be cultivated.

COMMENTARY

An advertising representative for a magazine once received an angry phone call from one of his customers. The magazine's production department had placed incorrect information in a small ad, and the client was furious. For ten minutes he yelled and screamed.

The ad rep was a master salesperson. He listened carefully to everything the client had to say. Then he interrupted with a simple statement: "You feel we hurt your business." Showing that he understood the customer's frustration immediately gave him the offensive.

He continued with, "I know you had big expectations from this ad and that you feel your money has been wasted. I'd like to make it up to you. With your permission, we will correct the ad and run it again, but this time twice as large, at no charge."

The rep's words continued to reinforce the value of his magazine's service, while presenting the customer with a proposition that was difficult to refuse.

More significantly, however, the rep had gotten the customer to agree to a much larger ad. Of course, the first time it ran, the customer paid nothing for it. But the rep knew that once the customer experienced the business that the larger ad would create, he would never go back to a small one.

By exercising self-control in his dealings with an irate customer, the ad rep turned a potential disaster into a positive opportunity.

The art of successful negotiation grows out of patient and painstaking Self-Control. Notice how easily the successful salesperson exercises Self-Control when handling a customer who is impatient. The salesperson may be boiling inside, but you will see no evidence of it in manner or words.

That person has acquired the art of tactful negotiation!

A single frown of disapproval or a single word denoting impatience will often spoil a sale. Successful salespeople exercise Self-Control, and as a reward they set their own salary and choose their own position.

To watch those who have acquired the art of successful negotiation is an education in itself. Watch the public speakers who have acquired this art; notice the firmness of step as they mount the platform; observe the firmness of voice as they begin to speak; study their facial expressions as they sweep the audience with the mastery of their arguments. *These are people who have learned how to negotiate without friction.*

Study those physicians who have acquired this art, as they walk into the sick room and greet their patients with a smile. The bearing, the tone of voice, the look of assurance, clearly identify them as professionals who have acquired the art of successful negotiation. And their patients will tell you it makes them feel better the moment such a doctor enters the sick room.

Watch the managers or supervisors who have acquired this art, and observe how their very presence spurs the employees to greater effort and inspires them with confidence and Enthusiasm.

Watch the lawyer who has acquired this art, and observe how he or she commands the respect and the attention of the court. There is something about the tone of voice, the posture, and expression, that cause opponents to suffer by comparison.

All of this is predicated upon Self-Control. And Self-Control is the result of *thought control!*

Deliberately place in your own mind the sort of thoughts that you wish to have there, and keep out of your mind those thoughts that others place there through suggestion, and you will become a person of Self-Control.

This privilege of stimulating your mind with suggestions and thoughts of your own choosing is your prerogative, and if you will exercise this right there is nothing within the bounds of reason that you cannot attain.

Losing your temper, and with it your case, or your argument, or your sanity, marks you as one who has not yet familiarized yourself with the fundamentals upon which Self-Control is based, and chief of these fundamentals is the privilege of choosing the thoughts that will dominate your mind.

A student in one of my classes once asked how one went about controlling one's thoughts when in a state of intense anger. I replied: "In exactly the same way you would change your manner and the tone of your voice if you were in a heated argument with a member of your family and heard the doorbell ring, warning that company had arrived. You would control yourself because you would desire to do so."

If you have ever been in a similar predicament, where you found it necessary to cover up your real feelings and change the expression on your face quickly, you know how easily it can be done. You also know that it can be done because one *wants* to do it!

Behind all achievement, behind all Self-Control, behind all thought control, is that magic something called *desire.*

It is no misstatement of fact to say that you are limited only by the depth of your desires. When your desires are strong enough, you will appear to possess superhuman powers to achieve. No one has ever explained this strange phenomenon of the mind, and perhaps no one ever will, but if you doubt that it exists, you have but to experiment and be convinced.

If you were in a building that was on fire, and all the doors and windows were locked, chances are that you would develop sufficient strength with which to break down the average door, because of your intense *desire* to free yourself.

If you *desire* to acquire the art of successful negotiation, as you undoubtedly will when you understand its significance in relation to your achievement of your Definite Chief Aim, you will do so, providing your desire is intense enough.

Napoleon *desired* to become emperor of France, and he did rule. Lincoln *desired* to free the slaves, and he accomplished it. The French *desired* that "they shall not pass," at the beginning of the world war, and they didn't pass! Edison *desired* to produce light with electricity, and he produced it—although he was many years in doing so. Roosevelt *desired* to unite the Atlantic and Pacific Oceans, through the Panama Canal, and he did it. Demosthenes *desired* to become a great public speaker, and, despite the handicap of a serious speech impediment, he transformed his desire into reality. Helen Keller *desired* to speak, and, despite the fact that she was deaf, dumb, and blind, she spoke. John H. Patterson *desired* to dominate in the production of cash registers, and he did it. Marshall Field *desired* to be the leading merchant of his time, and he did it. Shakespeare *desired* to become a great playwright, and, despite the fact that he was only a poor itinerant actor, he made his desire come true. Billy Sunday *desired* to quit playing baseball and become a master preacher, and he did. James J. Hill *desired* to become an empire builder, and, despite the fact that he was only a poor telegraph operator, he transformed that desire into reality.

COMMENTARY

Charles Lindbergh flew across the Atlantic, Gandhi led India to independence, Martin Luther King Jr. galvanized the civil rights movement, Mary Kay Ash built a business empire for women, Sam Walton became the richest man in America, Jackie Joyner-Kersee won a string of Olympic gold medals, and no doubt anyone reading this could add the names of other men and women that would go on for pages—and all of them had a definite chief aim that they desired strongly enough to make it a reality.

Don't say it can't be done, or that you are different from these and thousands of others who have achieved noteworthy success in every worthy calling. If you are "different" it is only in this respect: *they desired the object of their achievement with more depth and intensity than you desire yours.*

Plant in your mind the seed of a desire that is constructive, by making the following your creed and the foundation of your code of ethics.

I wish to be of service to others as I journey through life. To do this I have adopted this creed as a guide to be followed in dealing with my fellow beings:

To train myself so that never, under any circumstances, will I find fault with any person, no matter how much I may disagree with them or how inferior their work may be, as long as I know they are sincerely trying to do their best.

To respect my country, my profession, and myself. To be honest and fair with others, as I expect them to be honest

IT IS A PECULIAR TRAIT

OF HUMAN NATURE,

BUT IT IS TRUE,

THAT THE MOST SUCCESSFUL MEN

WILL WORK HARDER

FOR THE SAKE OF RENDERING

USEFUL SERVICE THAN

THEY WILL FOR MONEY ALONE.

and fair with me. To be a loyal citizen of my country. To speak of it with praise, and act always as a worthy custodian of its good name. To be a person whose name carries weight wherever it goes.

To base my expectations of reward on a solid foundation of service rendered. To be willing to pay the price of success in honest effort. To look upon my work as an opportunity to be seized with joy and made the most of, and not as a painful drudgery to be reluctantly endured.

To remember that success lies within myself—in my own brain. To expect difficulties and to force my way through them.

To avoid procrastination in all its forms, and never, under any circumstances, put off until tomorrow any duty that should be performed today.

Finally, to take a good grip on the joys of life, so I may be courteous to others, faithful to friends, true to God—a fragrance in the path I tread.

The energy that most people dissipate through lack of Self-Control would, if organized and used constructively, bring all the necessities and all the luxuries desired.

The time that many people devote to "gossiping" about others would, if controlled and directed constructively, be sufficient to attain the object of their Definite Chief Aim (if they had such an aim).

All successful people grade high on Self-Control. All "failures" grade low, generally zero, on this important law of human conduct.

Study those around you and observe, with profit, that all the successful ones exercise Self-Control, while the "failures" permit their thoughts, words, and deeds to run wild!

One very common and very destructive form of lack of Self-Control is the habit of talking too much. People of wisdom, who know what they want and are determined to achieve it, guard their conversation carefully. There can be no gain from a barrage of uninvited, uncontrolled, loosely spoken words.

It is nearly always more profitable to listen than it is to speak. A good listener may, once in a great while, hear something that will add to their stock of knowledge. It requires Self-Control to become a good listener, but the benefits to be gained are worth the effort.

"Taking the conversation away from another person" is a common form of lack of Self-Control that is not only discourteous but it deprives those who do it of many valuable opportunities to learn from others.

Self-Control was one of the marked characteristics of all successful leaders whom I have analyzed in gathering material for this course. Luther Burbank said that, in his opinion, Self-Control was the most important of these seventeen laws. During all his years of patient study and observation of the evolutionary processes of vegetable life, he had found it necessary to exercise the faculty of Self-Control despite the fact that he was dealing with inanimate life.

John Burroughs, the naturalist, said practically the same thing; that Self-Control stood near the head of the list, in importance, of the seventeen laws of success.

The person who exercises complete Self-Control cannot be permanently defeated, as Emerson has so well stated in his essay on Compensation, because obstacles and opposition have a way of melting away when confronted by the determined mind that is guided to a definite end with complete Self-Control.

Every wealthy person I have analyzed (referring to those who have become wealthy through their own efforts) showed such positive evidence that Self-Control had been one of their strong points that I reached the conclusion no one can hope to accumulate great wealth and keep it without exercising this necessary quality.

The saving of money requires the exercise of Self-Control of the highest order, as I hope has been made quite clear in the fourth lesson of this course.

POVERTY

I am indebted to Edward W. Bok for the following rather colorful description of the extent to which he found it necessary to exercise Self-Control before he achieved success and was crowned with fame as one of the great journalists of America.

WHY I BELIEVE IN POVERTY AS THE
RICHEST EXPERIENCE THAT CAN COME TO A BOY

I make my living trying to edit the *Ladies' Home Journal.* And because the public has been most generous in its acceptance of that periodical, a share of that success has logically come to me. Hence a number of my very good readers cherish an opinion that often I have been tempted to correct, a temptation to which I now yield. My correspondents express the conviction variously, but this extract from a letter is a fair sample:

"It is all very easy for you to preach economy to us when you do not know the necessity for it. To tell us how, as for example in my own case, we must live within my husband's income of eight hundred dollars a year, when you have never known what it is to live on less than thousands. Has it occurred to you, born with the proverbial silver spoon in your mouth, that theoretical writing is pretty cold and futile compared to the actual hand-to-mouth struggle that so many of us live, day by day and year in and year out—an experience that you know not of?"

"An experience that you know not of"!

Now, how far do the facts square with this statement?

Whether or not I was born with the proverbial silver spoon in my mouth, I cannot say. It is true that I was born of well-to-do parents. But when I was six years old my father lost all his means, and faced life at forty-five, in a strange country, without even necessaries. There are men and their wives who know what that means; for a man to try to "come back" at forty-five, and in a strange country! I had the handicap of not knowing one word of the English language. I went to a public school and learned what I could. And sparse morsels they were! The boys were cruel, as boys are. The teachers were impatient, as tired teachers are.

My father could not find his place in the world. My mother, who had always had servants at her beck and call, faced the problems of housekeeping that she had never learned nor been taught. And there was no money.

So, after school hours, my brother and I went home, but not to play. After-school hours meant for us to help a mother who daily grew more frail under the burdens that she could not carry. Not for days, but for years, we two boys got up in the gray cold winter dawn when the beds feel so warm to growing boys, and we sifted the coal ashes of the day before's fire for a stray lump or two of unburned coal, and with what we had or could find we made the fire and warmed up the room. Then we set the table for the scant breakfast, went to school, and directly after school we washed the dishes, swept and scrubbed the floors. Living in a three-family tenement, each third week meant that we scrubbed the entire three flights of stairs from the third story to the first, as well as the doorsteps and the sidewalk outside. The latter work was the hardest; for we did it on Saturdays, with the boys of the neighborhood looking on none too kindly, so we did it to the echo of the crack of the ball and bat on the adjoining lot!

In the evening when the other boys could sit by the lamp or study their lessons, we two boys went out with a basket and picked up wood and coal in the adjoining lots, or went after the dozen or so pieces of coal left from the ton of coal put in that afternoon by one of the neighbors, with the spot hungrily fixed in mind by one of us during the day, hoping that the man who carried in the coal might not be too careful in picking up the stray lumps!

"An experience that you know not of"! Don't I?

At ten years of age I got my first job, washing the windows of a baker's shop at fifty cents a week. In a week or two I was allowed to sell bread and cakes behind the counter after school hours for a dollar a week—handing out freshly baked cakes and warm, delicious-smelling bread, when scarcely a crumb had passed my mouth that day!

Then on Saturday mornings I served a route for a weekly paper, and sold my remaining stock on the street. It meant from sixty to seventy cents for that day's work.

I lived in Brooklyn, New York, and the chief means of transportation to Coney Island at that time was the horse car. Near where we lived the cars would stop to water the horses, the men would jump out and get a drink of water, but the women had no means of quenching their thirst. Seeing this lack I got a pail, filled it with water and a bit of ice, and, with a glass, jumped on each car on Saturday afternoon and all day Sunday, and sold my wares at a cent a glass. And when competition came, as it did very quickly when other boys saw that a Sunday's work meant two or three dollars, I squeezed a lemon or two in my pail, my liquid became "lemonade" and my price two cents a glass, and Sunday meant five dollars to me. Then, in turn, I became a reporter during the evenings, an office boy daytimes, and learned stenography at midnight.

My correspondent says she supports her family of husband and child on eight hundred dollars a year and says I have never known what that means. I supported a family of three on six dollars and twenty-five cents a week—less than one-half of her yearly income. When my brother and I, combined, brought in eight hundred dollars a year we felt rich!

OUR DOUBTS ARE TRAITORS,

AND MAKE US LOSE

THE GOOD WE OFT MIGHT WIN

BY FEARING TO ATTEMPT.

—William Shakespeare

I have for the first time gone into these details in print that you may know, at first hand, that the editor of the *Ladies' Home Journal* is not a theorist when he writes or prints articles that seek to preach economy or that reflect a hand-to-hand struggle on a small or an invisible income. There is not a single step, not an inch, on the road of direct poverty that I do not know of or have not experienced. And, having experienced every thought, every feeling and every hardship that come to those who travel that road I say today that I rejoice with every boy who is going through the same experience.

Nor am I discounting or forgetting one single pang of the keen hardships that such a struggle means. I would not today exchange my years of the keenest hardship that a boy can know or pass through for any single experience that could have come to me. I know what it means to earn—not a dollar, but to earn two cents. I know the value of money as I could have learned it or known it no other way. I could have been trained for my life work in no surer way. I could not have arrived at a truer understanding of what it means to face a day without a penny in hand, not a loaf of bread in the cupboard, not a piece of kindling wood for the fire—with nothing to eat, and then be a boy with the hunger of nine or ten, with a mother frail and discouraged!

"An experience that you know not of "! Don't I?

And yet I rejoice in the experience, and I envy every boy who is in that condition and going through it. But—and here is the pivot of my strong belief in poverty as an undisguised blessing to a boy—I believe in poverty as a condition to experience, to go through, and then to get out of; not as a condition to stay in. "That's all very well," some will say, "easy enough to say, but how can you get out of it!" No one can definitely tell another that. No one told me. No two persons can find the same way out. Each must find his way for himself. That depends on the boy. I was determined to get out of poverty, because my mother was not born in it, could not stand it and did not belong in it. This gave me the first essential: a purpose. Then I backed up the purpose with effort and willingness to work and to work at anything that came my way, no matter what it was, so long as it meant "the way out." I did not pick and choose; I took what came and did it in the best way I knew how; and when I didn't like what I was doing I still did it well while I was doing it, but I saw to it that I didn't do it any longer than I had to do it. I used every rung in the ladder as a rung to the one above. It meant effort, but out of the effort and the work came the experience; the upbuilding, the development; the capacity to understand and sympathize; the greatest heritage that can come to a boy. And nothing in the world can give that to a boy, so that it will burn into him, as will poverty.

That is why I believe so strongly in poverty, the greatest blessing in the way of the deepest and fullest experience that can come to a boy. But, as I repeat: always as a condition to work out of, not to stay in.

THE LAW OF RETALIATION

Before you can develop the habit of perfect Self-Control, you must understand the real need for this quality. Also, you must understand the advantages which Self-Control provides those who have learned how to exercise it.

By developing Self-Control, you also develop other qualities that will add to your personal power. Among other laws that are available to the person who exercises Self-Control is the law of retaliation.

You know what "retaliate" means! But in the sense that we are using here, it means to "return like for like," and not merely to avenge or to seek revenge, as is commonly meant by the use of this word.

If I do you an injury, you retaliate at first opportunity. If I say unjust things about you, you will retaliate in kind, even in greater measure. On the other hand, if I do you a favor you will reciprocate even in greater measure if possible.

Through the proper use of this law, *I can get you to do whatever I wish you to do.* If I wish you to dislike me and lend your influence toward damaging me, I can accomplish this by inflicting upon you the sort of treatment that I want you to inflict upon me through retaliation.

If I wish your respect, your friendship, and your Cooperation, I can get these by extending to you my friendship and Cooperation.

You can compare these statements with your own experience and you will see how beautifully they harmonize.

How often have you heard the remark "What a wonderful personality that person has"? How often have you met people whose personalities you coveted?

People who attract you to them through their Pleasing Personality are merely making use of the law of harmonious attraction, or the law of retaliation, both of which, when analyzed, mean that "like attracts like."

If you will study, understand, and make intelligent use of the law of retaliation, you will be an efficient and successful salesperson. When you have mastered this simple law and learned how to use it, you will have learned all that can be learned about salesmanship.

The first and probably the most important step to be taken in mastering this law is to cultivate complete Self-Control. You must learn to take all sorts of punishment and abuse without retaliating in kind. This Self-Control is a part of the price you must pay for mastery of the law of retaliation.

When an angry person starts in to vilify and abuse you, justly or unjustly, just remember that if you retaliate in a like manner you are being drawn down to that person's mental level. Therefore that person is *dominating you!*

THE HEIGHTS BY GREAT MEN

REACHED AND KEPT

WERE NOT ATTAINED

BY SUDDEN FLIGHT,

BUT THEY,

WHILE THEIR COMPANIONS SLEPT,

WERE TOILING UPWARD

IN THE NIGHT.

—Henry Wadsworth Longfellow

On the other hand, if you refuse to become angry, if you retain your self-composure and remain calm and serene, you take the other person by surprise. You retaliate with a weapon with which he or she is unfamiliar, consequently you easily dominate.

Like attracts like! There's no denying this!

Literally speaking, every person with whom you come in contact is a mental looking-glass in which you may see a perfect reflection of your own mental attitude.

As an example of direct application of the law of retaliation, let me cite an experience that I recently had with my two small boys, Napoleon Junior and James.

We were on our way to the park to feed the birds and squirrels. Napoleon Junior had bought a bag of peanuts and James had bought a box of Cracker Jack. James took a notion to sample the peanuts. Without asking permission he reached over and made a grab for the bag. He missed and Napoleon Junior "retaliated" with his left fist, which landed rather briskly on James' jaw.

I said to James, "Now, see here, son, you didn't go about getting those peanuts in the right manner. Let me show you how to get them." It all happened so quickly that I hadn't the slightest idea when I spoke what I was going to suggest to James.

Then I thought of the experiments we had been doing in connection with the law of retaliation, so I said to James, "Open your box of Cracker Jack, offer your little brother some, and see what happens." After considerable coaxing I persuaded him to do so. Then a remarkable thing happened—out of which I learned my greatest lesson in salesmanship: *Before Napoleon would touch the Cracker Jack, he insisted on pouring some of his peanuts into James' overcoat pocket.* He "retaliated in kind"! Out of this simple experiment with two small boys, I learned more about the art of managing them than I could have learned in any other way.

None of us has advanced far beyond Napoleon Junior and James as far as the operation and influence of this law of retaliation is concerned. We are all just grown-up children and easily influenced through this principle. If a person presents us with a gift, we never feel satisfied until we have "retaliated" with something as good or better than that which we received. If a person speaks well of us, we increase our admiration for that person and we "retaliate" in return!

Through the principle of retaliation we can actually convert our enemies into loyal friends. If you have an enemy whom you wish to convert into a friend you can prove the truth of this statement if you will forget that dangerous millstone hanging around your neck which we call pride, or stubbornness. Make a habit of speaking to this enemy with unusual cordiality. Go out of your way to favor them in every manner possible. They may seem immovable at first, but gradually he or she will give way to your influence and "retaliate in kind"!

One morning in August 1863, a young clergyman was called out of bed in a hotel at Lawrence, Kansas. The man who called him was one of Quantrill's guerrillas, who demanded that he immediately come downstairs. All over the border that morning people were being murdered. A band of raiders had ridden in early to perpetrate the Lawrence massacre.

The guerrilla who called the clergyman was impatient. The latter, when fully awake, was horrified by what he saw going on through his window. As he came downstairs the guerrilla demanded his watch and money, and then wanted to know if he was an abolitionist. The clergyman was trembling. But he decided that if he was to die then and there, it would not be with a lie on his lips. So he said that he was, and followed up the admission with a remark that immediately turned the whole affair in another direction.

He and the guerrilla sat down on the porch, while people were being killed through the town, and had a long talk. It lasted until the raiders were ready to leave. When the clergyman's guerrilla mounted to join his confederates, he was strictly on the defensive. He handed back the New Englander's valuables, apologized for disturbing him, and asked to be thought well of.

That clergyman lived many years after the Lawrence massacre. What did he say to the guerrilla? What was there in his personality that led the latter to sit down and talk? What did they talk about?

"Are you a Yankee abolitionist?" the guerrilla had asked.

"Yes, I am," was the reply, "and you know very well that you ought to be ashamed of what you're doing."

This drew the matter directly to a moral issue. It brought the guerrilla up roundly. The clergyman was only a stripling beside this seasoned border ruffian. But he threw a burden of moral proof onto the raider, and in a moment the latter was trying to demonstrate that he might be a better fellow than circumstances would seem to indicate.

After waking this New Englander to kill him on account of his politics, he spent twenty minutes on the witness stand trying to prove an alibi. He went into his personal history at length. He explained matters from the time when he had been a tough little kid who would not say his prayers, and became quite sentimental in recalling how one thing had led to another, and that led to something worse, until —well, here he was, and "a mighty bad business to be in, pardner." His last request in riding away was: "Now, pardner, don't think too hard of me, will you?"

The New England clergyman made use of the law of retaliation, whether he knew it at that time or not. Imagine what would have happened had he come downstairs with a revolver in his hand and started to meet physical force with physical force!

But he didn't do this. He mastered the guerrilla because he fought him with a force that was unknown to the brigand.

Why is it that when once you begin to make money the whole world seems to beat a pathway to your door?

Take any person that you know who enjoys financial success and they will tell you that they are being constantly sought, and that opportunities to make money are constantly being urged upon them!

"To him that hath shall be given, but to him that hath not shall be taken away even that which he hath."

This quotation from the Bible used to seem ridiculous to me, yet how true it is when reduced to its concrete meaning.

Yes, "to him that hath shall be given." If he "hath" failure, lack of Self-Confidence, hatred, or lack of Self-Control, to him shall these qualities be given in still greater abundance! But if he "hath" success, Self-Confidence, Self-Control, patience, persistence, and determination, to him shall these qualities be increased! Sometimes it may be necessary to meet force with force until we overpower our opponent or adversary, but while they are down is a splendid time to complete the "retaliation" by taking them by the hand and showing them a better way to settle disputes.

It is for you to decide what you want others to do and it is for you to get them to do it through the law of retaliation!

"The Divine Economy is automatic and very simple: we receive only that which we give."

How true it is that "we receive only that which we give." It is not that which we *wish for* that comes back to us, but that which we *give.*

I implore you to make use of this law, not alone for material gain, but, better still, for the attainment of happiness and goodwill.

This, after all, is the only real success for which to strive.

In this lesson we have learned a great principle—probably the most important major principle of psychology! We have learned that our thoughts and actions toward others resemble a magnet which attracts to us the same sort of thought and the same sort of action that we, ourselves, create.

We have learned that "like attracts like," whether in thought or in action. We have learned that the human mind responds, in kind, to whatever thought impressions it receives. We have learned that the human mind resembles mother earth in that it will reproduce action that corresponds, in kind, to the sensory impressions planted in it. We have learned that kindness begets kindness and unkindness and injustice beget unkindness and injustice.

We have learned that our actions toward others, whether of kindness or unkindness, justice or injustice, come back to us, in an even larger measure! We have learned that the human mind responds in kind to all sensory impressions it receives; therefore we know what we must do to influence any desired action on the part of another. We have learned that pride and stubbornness must be brushed away before we can make use of the law of retaliation in a constructive way.

We have *not* learned what the law of retaliation is, but we have learned how it works and what it will do. Therefore, it only remains for us to make intelligent use of this great principle.

THE EVOLUTION OF TRANSPORTATION— AN AFTER-THE-LESSON VISIT WITH THE AUTHOR

Nothing is permanent except change. Time is ever shifting, changing, and rearranging both the stage setting and the players. New friends are constantly replacing the old. Everything is in a state of flux. In every heart is the seed of both rascality and justice. Every human being is both a criminal and a saint, depending on the expediency of the moment as to which will assert itself. Honesty and dishonesty are largely matters of individual viewpoint. The weak and the strong, the rich and the poor, the ignorant and the well-informed are exchanging places continuously.

Know *yourself* and you know the entire human race. There is but one real achievement, and that is the ability to *think accurately*. We move with the procession, or behind it, but we cannot stand still.

Nothing is permanent except change!

The law of evolution is working out improvements in the methods of travel, and all these changes took place first in the human mind.

IF YOU ARE SUCCESSFUL,

REMEMBER THAT SOMEWHERE,

SOMETIME, SOMEONE GAVE YOU

A LIFT OR AN IDEA THAT

STARTED YOU IN THE

RIGHT DIRECTION.

REMEMBER, ALSO,

THAT YOU ARE INDEBTED

TO LIFE UNTIL YOU HELP

SOME LESS FORTUNATE PERSON,

JUST AS YOU WERE HELPED.

Man was not satisfied with the first crude method of transportation. Those two little words, "not satisfied," have been the starting point of all advancement. Think of them as you read this.

As the human brain began to expand, humans discovered how to hitch a bullock to a wagon and thereby escape the toil of pulling the load. That was practical utility. But when the stagecoach was ushered into use, that was both utility and style. Still we were "not satisfied" and this dissatisfaction ultimately created the crude locomotive.

Now these methods of travel have been discarded in almost all parts of the world. The man drawing the cart, the bullock drawing the cart, the stagecoach, and the crude locomotive all belong to ages that have passed.

Think about the transportation methods of the present. Compare them with those of the past and you may have a fair idea of the enormous expansion that has taken place in the human brain and mind. Automobiles that travel at great speed became as common as were the two-wheel carts in ages past. And yet we were still "not satisfied." Travel on the earth was too slow. Turning our eyes upward we watched the birds soaring high in the elements and became *determined* to excel them. And so we mastered the sky. Not only has man made the air carry him at amazing speeds, but he has harnessed the ether and made it carry his words all the way around the earth in a fraction of a second.

Any influence that causes one to think also causes one to grow stronger mentally. Mind stimulants are essential for growth. From the days of the man-drawn cart to the present days of air mastery, the only progress that anyone has made has been the result of some influence that stimulated their mind to greater than normal action.

The two great major influences that cause the human mind to grow are the urge of *necessity* and the urge of *desire to create*. Some minds will develop only after they have undergone failure and defeat and other forms of punishment that arouse them to greater action. Other minds wither away and die under punishment, but grow to unbelievable heights when provided with the opportunity to use their imaginative forces in a creative way.

Understand the evolution of transportation and you will observe one outstanding aspect worth remembering: The whole story has been one of development and advancement that grew out of necessity. Throughout the past, the urge to change was based on necessity.

In the present the urge has been a combination of both necessity and the desire to create. In the future the strong desire to create will be the sole urge that will drive the human mind on and on to heights as yet undreamed of.

It is a long distance from the days of the man-drawn cart to the present, when we have harnessed the lightning of the clouds and made it turn machinery that will perform as much service in a minute as ten thousand workers could perform in a day. But if the distance has been long, the development of man's mind has been correspondingly great, and that development has been sufficient to eventually do the work of the world with machines operated by Nature's forces and not by human muscles.

The evolutionary changes in the methods of transportation have created other problems for our minds to solve. The automobile drove us to build better roads and more of them. The automobile also claims thousands of lives annually. The human mind must now respond to the urge of *necessity* and meet this emergency.

If you have a highly imaginative mind, *you* may be the one who will create the solution and collect the royalties from its sale. The value to you, of this suggestion, lies in the possibility of *thought* that you may devote to it, thereby developing and expanding your own mind. Remember, the purpose of this essay is to give you merely the seed of suggestion; not the finished product of an invention ready to set up and render service.

Study yourself and find out to which of the two great major urges to action your mind responds most naturally—the urge of necessity or the desire to create. If you have children, study them and determine to which of these two motives they respond most naturally. Millions of children have had their imaginations dwarfed and retarded by parents who removed as much as possible of the urge of necessity. By "making it easy" for your child you may be depriving the world of a genius. Bear in mind that most of the progress humans have made came as the result of bitter, biting *necessity!*

———————

The law of evolution is always and everywhere at work—changing, tearing down, and rebuilding every material element on this earth and throughout the universe. Towns, cities, and communities are undergoing constant change. Go back to the place where you lived twenty years ago and you will recognize neither the place nor the people. New faces will have made their appearance. The old faces will have changed. New buildings will have taken the place of the old. Everything will appear different because everything will *be* different.

The human mind is also undergoing constant change. If this were not true we would never grow beyond the child-mind age. Every seven years the mind of a normal person becomes noticeably developed and expanded. It is during these periodical changes of the mind that bad habits may be left off and better habits cultivated.

The mind that is driven by the urge of necessity, or out of the love to create, develops more rapidly than does the mind that is never stimulated to greater action than what is necessary for existence.

The imaginative faculty of the human mind is the greatest piece of machinery ever created. Out of it has come every man-made machine and every man-made object.

Behind every one of the great industries and commercial enterprises is the all-powerful force of Imagination!

Force your mind to *think!* Proceed by combining old ideas into new plans. Every great invention and every outstanding business or industrial achievement that you can name is, in final analysis, but the application of a combination of plans and ideas that have been used before, in some other manner.

> *Back of the beating hammer*
> *By which the steel is wrought,*
> *Back of the workshop's clamor*
> *The seeker may find the Thought;*
> *The thought that is ever Master*
> *Of iron and steam and steel,*
> *That rises above disaster*
> *And tramples it under heel.*

> *The drudge may fret and tinker*
> *Or labor with lusty blows,*
> *But back of him stands the Thinker,*
> *The clear-eyed man who knows;*
> *For into each plow or saber,*
> *Each piece and part and whole,*
> *Must go the brains of labor,*
> *Which gives the work a soul.*

> *Back of the motor's humming,*
> *Back of the bells that ring,*
> *Back of the hammer's drumming,*
> *Back of the cranes that swing,*
> *There is the Eye which scans them,*
> *Watching through stress and strain,*
> *There is the Mind which plans them—*
> *Back of the brawn, the Brain.*

Might of the roaring boiler,
 Force of the engine's thrust,
Strength of the sweating toiler,
 Greatly in these we trust;
But back of them stands the schemer,
 The Thinker who drives things through,
Back of the job the Dreamer
 Who's making the dream come true.

     —BERTON BRALEY

Six months or a year from now, come back and read this essay again and you will observe how much more you will get from it than you did at first reading. *Time* gives the law of evolution a chance to expand your mind so it can see and understand more.

Volume III

THE PRINCIPLES OF
SELF-CREATION

Habit of Doing More Than Paid For

Pleasing Personality

Accurate Thinking

Concentration

—— Lesson Nine ——

The Habit of Doing More Than Paid For

THE PERSON WHO RECEIVES

NO PAY FOR THEIR SERVICES

EXCEPT THAT WHICH COMES

IN THE PAY ENVELOPE

IS UNDERPAID, NO MATTER

HOW MUCH MONEY

THAT ENVELOPE MAY CONTAIN.

—Napoleon Hill

THE HABIT OF DOING MORE THAN PAID FOR

"You Can Do It if You Believe You Can!"

IT MAY SEEM TO BE A DEPARTURE FROM THE subject of this lesson to start with a discussion of love, but after you have completed the lesson you will understand that the subject could not have been omitted without impairing the value of the lesson.

The word *love* is used here in an all-encompassing sense. There are many objects, motives, and people that can inspire love, and one of these inspirations can be work. Great artists, for example, generally love their work.

But it is not uncommon for many people to speak of hating work, and it is easy to envision work that is dull, tiring, and emotionally unsatisfying. Work that you do merely for the sake of earning a living is seldom enjoyable. Time passes slowly, and boredom and weariness are inevitable in such circumstances.

It is possible, however, to be engaged in work that you love, work that gives you personal satisfaction and which you approach in a spirit of anticipation and excitement. When engaged in work that you love, you can labor for unbelievably long periods of time without noticing the clock, because you are focused on the challenge and the satisfaction you are getting.

Your endurance, therefore, depends very largely on the extent to which you like, dislike, or love what you are doing. This is the basis for one of the most important philosophies of this course: *You are most efficient and will more quickly and easily succeed when engaged in work that you love, or work that you perform on behalf of some person whom you love.*

Whenever the element of love enters into any task you perform, the quality of your work becomes immediately improved and the quantity increased, without a corresponding increase in the fatigue caused by that work.

COMMENTARY

Napoleon Hill obviously believed that finding the work you love is of key importance in achieving success, and he wrote extensively about the concept in the previous lessons as well.

The editors of this updated edition of Napoleon Hill's work have, in each of the volumes, added commentary suggesting many books and audiobooks by other authors that have been published in the intervening years and which expand on Hill's basic theses. Two of the most popular bestsellers on this subject are Wishcraft *by Barbara Sher and* Do What You Love, the Money Will Follow *by Marsha Sinetar. Both books offer not only inspiration and motivation but also practical advice on how to get started.*

Some years ago a group of people organized a colony in Louisiana, purchased several hundred acres of farmland, and started to work out an ideal that they believed would give them greater happiness in life and fewer of the worries—through a system which provided each person with work at the sort of labor they preferred.

Their idea was to pay no wages to anyone. Each person did the work they liked best, or that for which they might be best equipped, and the products of their combined labors became the property of all. They had their own dairy, their own brick-making plant, their own cattle, poultry, etc. They had their own schools and a printing plant through which they published a paper.

A Swedish gentleman from Minnesota joined the colony, and at his own request he was placed at work in the printing plant. Very soon he complained that he did not like the work, so he was put to work on the farm, operating a tractor. Two days of this was all he could stand, so he again applied for a transfer, and was assigned to the dairy. But he could not get along with the cows, so he was once more changed, to the laundry, where he lasted only one day.

One by one he tried every job available, but liked none of them. It had begun to look as if he did not fit in with the co-operative idea of living, and he was about to withdraw, when someone happened to think of one job he had not yet tried—in the brick plant. So he was given a wheelbarrow and put to work wheeling bricks from the kilns and stacking them in piles in the brickyard. A week's time went by and no complaint was registered by him. When asked if he liked his job he replied, "This is just the job I like."

Imagine anyone preferring a job wheeling bricks! However, that job suited this man's nature. He worked alone, at a task that called for no thought and placed upon him no responsibility, which was just what he wanted.

He remained at the job until all the bricks had been wheeled out and stacked, then he withdrew from the colony because there was no more brick work to be done. "The nice quiet job is finished, so I think I'll be going back to Minnesota," and back to Minnesota he went.

WORK IS

LOVE MADE VISIBLE.

—Kahlil Gibran

COMMENTARY

It is quite possible that this story became known to Hill when, at the age of fifteen and looking for an alternative to working in the fields or the coal mines, he went to work as a reporter for a weekly newsletter that supplied rural news to the many small newspapers established through the Farmers' Alliance, a forerunner of the farm co-op.

THE MOTIVATING POWER OF
LOVING WHAT YOU DO

When you are engaged in work that you love, it is no hardship to do more work and better work than that for which you are paid. For this reason you owe it to yourself to find the sort of work you like best.

I have a perfect right to offer this advice because I have followed it myself, without reason to regret having done so.

This seems to be an appropriate place to inject a little personal history concerning myself and the Law of Success philosophy, in order to show that labor performed in a spirit of love, for the sake of the labor itself, never has been and never will be lost. This would be empty and useless advice had I not practiced this rule long enough to know how well it works.

For over a quarter of a century I have been engaged in the labor of love out of which this course has been developed, and I am perfectly sincere when I say that I would have been amply paid for my labors, by the pleasure I have had as I went along, even if I had received nothing more.

COMMENTARY

The most successful people have a passion for what they do, which is what motivates them to put greater effort and time into whatever it is that they want to achieve. Few, however, have had the passion and dedication that Napoleon Hill had.

WE MAKE A LIVING

BY WHAT WE GET,

BUT WE MAKE A LIFE

BY WHAT WE GIVE.

—Winston Churchill

In 1908, during a particularly down time in the U.S. economy and with no money and no work, Hill took a job with Bob Taylor's Magazine. *Although it would not provide much in the way of income, it would provide the opportunity to meet and profile the giants of industry and business—the first of whom was the creator of America's steel industry, multimillionaire Andrew Carnegie, who was to become Hill's mentor.*

Carnegie was so impressed by Hill's perceptive mind that following their three-hour interview he invited Hill to spend the weekend at his estate. After two more days of conversation, Carnegie told Hill that he believed any person could achieve greatness if they understood the philosophy of success and the steps required to achieve it, and that this knowledge could be gained by interviewing those who had achieved greatness and then compiling the information and research into a comprehensive set of principles. He believed that it would take at least twenty years, and that the result would be "the world's first philosophy of individual achievement." He offered Hill the challenge—for no more compensation than that Carnegie would make the necessary introductions and cover travel expenses.

It took Hill twenty-nine seconds to accept Carnegie's proposal. Carnegie told him afterward that had it taken him more than sixty seconds to make the decision he would have withdrawn the offer, for "a man who cannot reach a decision promptly, once he has all the necessary facts, cannot be depended upon to carry through any decision he may make."

It was through Hill's unwavering dedication that this book and his others were eventually written. Hill's conversations with Andrew Carnegie during their first meeting would later also become the basis for Think and Grow Rich.

For detailed information on the life of Hill, read or listen to the audiobook of A Lifetime of Riches: The Biography of Napoleon Hill *by Michael J. Ritt Jr. and Kirk Landers. Ritt worked as Hill's assistant for ten years and was the first employee of the Napoleon Hill Foundation, where he served as executive director, secretary, and treasurer. The material in Ritt's book comes from his own personal knowledge of Hill as well as from Hill's unpublished autobiography.*

My labors on this philosophy made it necessary, many years ago, for me to choose between immediate monetary returns, which I might have enjoyed by directing my efforts along purely commercial lines, and the remuneration that can be measured only in terms of the accumulated knowledge that enables one to enjoy the world about them more keenly.

People who engage in work that they love best do not always have the support, in this choice, of the people closest to them. Combating negative comments from friends and relatives has required an alarming proportion of my energies, especially during the early years that I was engaged in the research which has gone into this course.

These personal references are made solely for the purpose of showing the students of this philosophy that seldom, if ever, can one hope to engage in the work one loves best without meeting with obstacles of some nature. Generally, the chief obstacle is that it may not be, as I said, the work that brings the greatest remuneration at the start.

To offset this disadvantage, however, if you engage in the sort of work you love, you are generally rewarded with two very decided benefits. First, you will usually find in such work the greatest of all rewards—happiness—which is priceless. And secondly, your actual reward in money, when averaged over a lifetime of effort, is generally much greater, for labor that is performed in a spirit of love is usually greater in quantity and finer in quality than that which is performed solely for money.

The most trying opposition to my choice of a life's work came from my wife. Her idea was that I should accept a salaried position which would ensure a regular monthly income, because I had shown, by the few salaried positions I had held, that I had marketable ability and could command an income of from $6,000 to $10,000 a year without any very great effort on my part.

COMMENTARY

Through inflation alone, and according to one calculation source, by the early twenty-first century the dollar equivalent of Hill's marketability as a freelance writer would be approximately $120,000 to $200,000 annually. As well, over those years the advertising industry has changed radically and the demand for people with Hill's talents has created salaries that far outstrip inflation. There are, however, many factors and variables in making direct dollar comparisons when it comes to salaries, and the conversion figures also vary among sources.

According to the Bureau of Labor Statistics it took $17.89 in 2002 to buy what $1.00 bought in 1913. If the $17.89 figure were used relative to salaries, that would translate to Hill's annual salary being potentially the equivalent of $107,340 to $178,900.

But that calculation is based on all goods and services purchased by urban households, which is not necessarily reflective of salaries. As we've seen during recessions, the fact that consumers spend less freely doesn't mean salaries are suddenly decreased accordingly, and nor do salaries increase to match the freer spending in a particularly good economic climate.

In a way, I saw my wife's viewpoint, as we had young growing children who needed clothes and education. A regular salary, even though it was not large, seemed to be a necessity.

Despite this logical argument, however, I chose to override my wife's counsel and the criticism of family and friends. I remained adamant. I had made my choice and I was determined to stand by it.

The opposition did not yield to my viewpoint, but it gradually subsided. And the knowledge that my choice had created hardship for my family actually increased the dedication with which I worked for what I believed.

Fortunately, not all of my friends believed my choice unwise. There were a few who not only believed I was following a course that would ultimately bring me out somewhere near the top in the way of useful achievement, but in addition to believing in my plans, they

FIND SOMETHING

YOU LOVE TO DO AND

YOU'LL NEVER HAVE TO

WORK A DAY IN YOUR LIFE.

—Harvey Mackay

actually went out of their way to encourage me not to be whipped by either adversity or the opposition of relatives.

Of this small group of faithful ones who gave me encouragement at a time when it was badly needed, perhaps one man should have the most credit: Edwin C. Barnes, business associate of Thomas A. Edison.

Mr. Barnes became interested in my chosen work at its beginnings, and had it not been for his unwavering faith in the soundness of the philosophy behind the Law of Success, I would have yielded to the persuasion of others and sought the way of least resistance.

This would have saved me much grief and an almost endless amount of criticism, but it would also have wrecked the hopes of a lifetime, and in the end I would in all probability have also lost that finest and most desirable of all things—happiness—for I have been extremely happy in my work, even during the periods when the financial remuneration it brought me could be measured by nothing but a mountain of debts.

Edwin Barnes not only believed in the soundness of the Law of Success philosophy, but his own financial success had also demonstrated, as had his close business relationship with the greatest inventor on earth, that he had the right to speak with authority on the subject of the laws through which success may be achieved.

I began my research with the belief that success could be attained, by anyone with reasonable intelligence and a real desire to succeed, by following certain (at that time unknown to me) rules of procedure. I wanted to know what these rules were and how they could be applied.

Mr. Barnes believed as I did. Moreover, he was in a position to know that the astounding achievements of Mr. Edison had come about entirely through the application of some of the principles that later were tested and included as a part of this philosophy. From his way of thinking it seemed that the accumulation of money, enjoying peace of mind, and finding happiness could be brought about by the application of laws that anyone could master and apply.

That was my belief also. This belief has now been transformed into not merely a provable but a *proved* reality, as I hope every student of this course will have reason to understand when the course has been mastered.

Please keep in mind that during all these years of research I was not only applying this law, by doing more than I was paid for, but I was going much further than this by doing work that I loved and for which I did not, at the time I was doing it, ever hope to receive pay.

DO MORE, RECEIVE MORE

I was invited to deliver an address in Canton, Ohio. It had been well advertised and there was reason to expect that I would have a large audience. But conflicting meetings being held by two large groups of businessmen reduced my audience to the lucky number of thirteen.

It has always been my belief that one should do their very best regardless of how much they receive for their services or the number of people they may be serving. I went at my subject as though the hall were filled. There also arose in me a sort of feeling of resentment at the way the "wheel of fate" had turned against me, and if ever I made a convincing speech I made it that night.

Down deep in my heart, however, I thought I had failed. I did not know until the next day that I was making history that night which was destined to give the Law of Success philosophy its first real impetus.

One of the men who sat in my audience of thirteen was Don R. Mellett, who was then publisher of the *Canton Daily News.*

After I had finished speaking, I slipped out the back door and returned to my hotel, not wanting to face any of my thirteen victims on the way out.

The next day I was invited to Mr. Mellett's office. Inasmuch as it was he who had taken the initiative by inviting me in to see him, I left it to him to do most of the talking. He began something like this:

"Would you mind telling me your entire life story, from the days of your early childhood on up to the present? What I wish you to do," he said, "is to mix the fat with the lean and let me take a look at your very soul, not from its most favorable side, but from all sides."

For three hours I talked while Mellett listened. I omitted nothing. I told him of my struggles, of my mistakes, of my impulses to be dishonest when the tides of fortune swept against me too swiftly, and of my better judgment which prevailed in the end, but only after my conscience and I had engaged in prolonged combat. I told him how I conceived the idea of organizing the Law of Success philosophy, how I had gone about gathering the data which had gone into the philosophy, of the tests I had made that resulted in the elimination of some of the data and of the retention of other parts of it.

After I had finished, Mellett said: "I wish to ask you a very personal question, and I hope you will answer it as frankly as you have told the rest of your story. Have you accumulated any money from your efforts, and if not, do you know why you have not?"

"No," I replied, "I have accumulated nothing but experience and knowledge and a few debts. And the reason, while it may not be sound, is easily explained. The truth is that I have been so busy all these years in trying to eliminate some of my own ignorance so I could intelligently gather and organize the data that has gone into the Law of Success philosophy, that I have had neither the opportunity nor the inclination to turn my efforts to making money."

The serious look on Don Mellett's face, much to my surprise, softened into a smile as he laid his hand on my shoulder and said, "I knew the answer before you stated it, but I had wondered if you knew it. You probably know that you are not the only man who has had to sacrifice immediate monetary remuneration for the sake of gathering knowledge. Your experience has been that of every philosopher from the time of Socrates down to the present."

Those words were like music to my ears!

WHEN YOU GET INTO A TIGHT PLACE

AND EVERYTHING GOES AGAINST YOU,

'TIL IT SEEMS AS THOUGH YOU COULD

NOT HOLD ON A MINUTE LONGER,

NEVER GIVE UP THEN, FOR THAT IS

JUST THE PLACE AND TIME

THAT THE TIDE WILL TURN.

—Harriet Beecher Stowe

I had made one of the most embarrassing admissions of my life; I had laid my soul bare, admitting temporary defeat at almost every crossroad that I had passed in my struggles, and I had capped all this off by admitting that an exponent of the Law of Success was himself a temporary failure.

How incongruous it had seemed! I felt stupid, humiliated, and embarrassed as I sat in front of the most searching pair of eyes and the most inquisitive man I had ever met.

The absurdity of it all came over me in a flash—the philosophy of success, created and broadcasted by a man who was obviously a failure! The thought struck me so forcibly that I expressed it in words.

"What?!" Mellett exclaimed. "A failure? Surely you know the difference between failure and temporary defeat," he continued. "No man is a failure who creates a single idea, much less an entire philosophy that serves to soften the disappointments and minimize the hardships of generations yet unborn."

Before I left Mellett's office we had become business partners, with the understanding that he would resign as publisher of the *Canton Daily News* and take over the management of all my affairs, as soon as this could be arranged.

In the meantime, I began writing a series of Sunday feature-page editorials which were published in the *Canton Daily News*, based on the Law of Success philosophy.

One of these editorials came to the attention of Judge Elbert H. Gary, who was at that time the chairman of the board of the United States Steel Corporation. This resulted in Mellett contacting Judge Gary, and that in turn led to Judge Gary's offer to purchase the Law of Success course for the use of the employees of the Steel Corporation.

The tides had begun to turn in my favor. The seeds of service that I had been sowing over a long period of years, by Doing More Than Paid For, were beginning to germinate at last!

Despite the fact that my partner was assassinated before our plans had barely gotten started, and Judge Gary died before the Law of Success philosophy could be adapted for the Steel Corporation, that fateful night when I spoke to an audience of thirteen in Canton, Ohio, started a chain of events that now move rapidly without thought or effort on my part, and many well-known companies have since purchased the Law of Success course for their employees.

COMMENTARY

Comparing Hill's information here with that in A Lifetime of Riches, *considerable detail has been omitted. His relationship with Mellett in 1926 was an example of a Master Mind alliance, and it was Mellett who was now encouraging Hill to develop his research into a book.*

At this same time it was learned that Prohibition gangsters were selling narcotics and bootleg liquor to schoolchildren in Canton, and members of the local police force were being bribed to do nothing about it. Mellett was outraged and wrote an exposé in the Canton Daily News, *while Hill contacted the governor to implement a state investigation of the corrupt police department. Most others in a position to do anything further about it, however, were all too intimidated by the gangsters to take action.*

A week before the scheduled meeting with Judge Gary, Mellett was ambushed outside his home and assassinated by a gangster and a renegade cop. The same would likely have happened to Hill had he not been delayed by car trouble. But on his return home he received a phone call from that same cop, warning him to get out of town. A few more calls, and Hill spent the next several months in hiding at the home of relatives in the mountains of West Virginia.

During those months Judge Gary took ill and died, as did Hill's hopes of having his success course published at that time.

There are many sound reasons why you should develop the habit of performing more and *better* service than that for which you are paid.

There are two reasons, however, which transcend all others in their importance.

First, by establishing a reputation as being a person who does this, you will benefit by comparison with those around you who do not render such service, and the contrast will be so noticeable that there will be keen competition for your services, no matter what your life's work may be. Whether you are preaching sermons, practicing law, writing books, teaching school, or digging ditches, you will become more valuable and you will be able to command greater pay as you gain recognition for Doing More Than Paid For.

The second, and by far the most important reason, is basic and fundamental in nature. Suppose that you wished to develop a strong right arm, and suppose that you tried to do so by tying your arm to your side to give it a long rest. Would disuse bring strength, or would it bring atrophy and weakness?

You know that if you wanted a strong right arm you would develop it only by exercising and working it harder. Out of resistance comes strength. The strongest tree in the forest is not the one that is protected from the storm and hidden from the sun, but the one that stands in the open, where it is compelled to struggle for its existence against the winds and rains and scorching sun.

The purpose of this lesson is to show you how to harness this law of nature—that struggle and resistance develop strength—and use it to aid you in your struggle for success. By forming the Habit of Doing More Than Paid For, you will eventually develop sufficient strength to enable you to remove yourself from any undesirable station in life, and no one can or will desire to stop you.

If your employer should be so unfortunate as to try to pay you less than you are worth, that won't last long; other employers will discover your unusual quality and offer you employment.

The very fact that most people are rendering as little service as they can possibly get by with serves as an advantage to those who are

NO MAN, WHO CONTINUES TO

ADD SOMETHING TO THE

MATERIAL, INTELLECTUAL, AND

MORAL WELL-BEING OF THE

PLACE IN WHICH HE LIVES,

IS LEFT LONG WITHOUT

PROPER REWARD.

—Booker T. Washington

rendering *more* service. You can "get by" if you render as little service as possible, but that is all you will get; and when work is slack and retrenchment sets in, you will be one of the first to be dismissed.

Personally, I never received a promotion in my life that I could not trace directly to recognition that I had gained by rendering more service and better service than that for which I was paid.

Those who do observe this principle are rewarded with a greater material gain than those who do not. They also gain the happiness and satisfaction that comes only to those who render such service. If you receive no pay except that which comes in your pay envelope, you are underpaid, no matter how much money that envelope contains.

My wife brought me a book from the public library titled *Observation: Every Man His Own University* by Russell H. Conwell. It covers the subject of this lesson as though it had been written for that purpose; covers it in a far more impressive way than I could do it. The following quotation from the chapter Every Man's University will give you an idea of the golden nugget of truth to be found throughout the book:

> The intellect can be made to look far beyond the range of what men and women ordinarily see, but not all the colleges in the world can alone confer this power—this is the reward of *self-culture*; each must acquire it for himself; and perhaps this is why the power of observing deeply and widely is so much oftener found in those men and those women who have never crossed the threshold of any college but the *University of Hard Knocks*.

We will now analyze the law upon which this entire lesson is founded.

THE LAW OF INCREASING RETURNS

Let us begin our analysis by showing how Nature employs this law on behalf of the tillers of the soil. The farmer carefully prepares the

———————————

GIVING PEOPLE A LITTLE MORE

THAN WHAT THEY EXPECT

IS A GOOD WAY TO GET BACK

MORE THAN YOU'D EXPECT.

—Robert Half

———————————

ground, then sows his wheat and waits while the law of increasing returns brings back the seed he has sown—plus a manyfold increase.

Were it not for this law of increasing returns, humankind would perish because we could not make the soil produce sufficient food for our existence. There would be no advantage to be gained by sowing a field of wheat if the harvest yield did not return more than was sown.

With this vital "tip" from Nature, let us proceed to appropriate this law and learn how to apply it to the service we render, so that it may yield returns in excess of the effort put forth.

First let me emphasize that there is no trickery connected with this law, although quite a few seem not to have learned this great truth, judging by the number who spend all of their efforts trying to get something for nothing or something for less than its true value.

A remarkable and noteworthy feature of this law of increasing returns is that it may be used, with as great returns, by those who purchase service as it can be by those who render service. For proof of that, we have but to study the effects of Henry Ford's famous five-dollar-a-day minimum-wage scale.

Those who are familiar with the facts say that Mr. Ford was not playing the part of a philanthropist when he inaugurated this minimum-wage scale. To the contrary, he was merely taking advantage of a sound business principle that probably yielded him greater returns, in both dollars and goodwill, than any other single policy ever inaugurated at the Ford plant.

Through the inauguration of that minimum-wage policy, Ford attracted the best labor on the market and placed a premium on the privilege of working in his plant.

Although I have no hard figures to prove it, I believe that for every five dollars Ford spent under this policy, he received at least seven dollars and fifty cents' worth of service. I also have reason to believe that this policy enabled Ford to reduce the cost of supervision, because employment in his plant became so desirable that no worker would run the risk of losing his position by rendering poor service.

COMMENTARY

As with many of the concepts that Napoleon Hill promoted through his writing, the concept of employee participation soon became common practice in American business. In every decade since, there have been standout examples of companies or industries that have employed the concept to boost sales or improve productivity. One of the most interesting variations on the theme is the so-called new economy and the dot-com companies that exploded on the scene in the late 1990s. Though the Internet industry proved to be a disappointment to many, it has also had some of the most dedicated employees the business world has seen.

In the beginning, in virtually every Internet-related start-up, it was common practice that the employees who signed on early received only modest pay. Yet the stories of kids barely out of school pulling all-nighters to finish writing some computer program, or subsisting on pizza and caffeine in a cramped cubicle in a converted warehouse, became the folklore of the industry. What kept them working late into the night was partly the fact that they were doing what they loved, but just as important was that they had a stake in the success of their company: they got stock options that they could exercise when the companies went public. And when the companies launched their IPOs, many of those employees suddenly found themselves millionaires overnight.

The story of the instant Internet millionaires is of course a very dramatic example of employee participation. Less dramatic but no less significant is the story of how a store that sold household goods, clothing, appliances, and such, used the same principle to become an extraordinary store.

In 1962 Sam Walton opened the first Wal-Mart store in Rogers, Arkansas, selling name-brand products at discounted prices. It soon led to a chain of stores across the country. In 1970, after taking the company public, Walton introduced an employee profit-sharing plan dependent on the profitability of the store. He believed that if an employee's success were dependent on the company's success, they would naturally care more about the company and the result would mean an increase in sales.

In Walton's biography, Made in America: My Story, *he outlines what he believed to be the ten commandments of business management:*

1. *Commit to your goals*
2. *Share your rewards*
3. *Energize your colleagues*
4. *Communicate all you know*
5. *Value your associates*
6. *Celebrate your success*
7. *Listen to everyone*
8. *Deliver more than you promise*
9. *Work smarter than others*
10. *Blaze your own path*

By the 1980s Wal-Mart had over 300 stores across North America, with sales in excess of one billion dollars, and by 1991, with 1,700 stores, Wal-Mart was (and still is in 2004, with more than 4,200 stores worldwide) the world's largest retailer. Walton believed that "individuals don't win, teams do." At the time he died, in 1992, Sam Walton was the world's richest man.

Marshall Field was probably the leading merchant of his time, and the great Field's store in Chicago stands today as a monument to his ability to apply the law of increasing returns.

A customer purchased an expensive garment at the Field's store but did not wear it. Two years later she gave it to her niece as a wedding present. The niece quietly returned the garment to the Field's store and exchanged it for other merchandise—despite the fact that it had been out for more than two years and was then out of style.

Not only did the Field's store take it back, but what is of more importance, it did so *without argument.* Of course there was no obligation, moral or legal, on the part of the store to accept the return at that late date, which makes the transaction all the more significant.

The garment was originally priced at fifty dollars, and of course it had to be thrown on the bargain counter and sold for whatever it would bring, but the keen student of human nature will understand that the Field's store not only did not lose anything on the garment but it actually profited by the transaction to an extent that cannot be measured in mere dollars.

The woman who returned the garment knew that she was not entitled to a refund. Therefore, when the store gave her that to which she was not entitled, the transaction won her as a permanent customer and she then spread the news of the "fair treatment" she had received at the Field's store. The store received more advertising from that transaction than it could have purchased in any other way with ten times the value of the returned garment.

The success of the Field's store was built largely on Marshall Field's understanding of the law of increasing returns, which had prompted him to adopt, as a part of his business policy, the slogan "The customer is always right."

COMMENTARY

Napoleon Hill's example of the Marshall Field's policy once again demonstrates how he was able to anticipate the coming of the service industry that grew to dominate American business by the last half of the twentieth century. In the 1920s, when he predicted the success of the Field's policy, a visit to most retail stores was far from what it is today. They were "business establishments" and were just about as friendly as that austere term implies. Customers were not so much "served" as tolerated.

But by the middle of the twentieth century, "the customer is always right" was practically the watchword of American business. Today there are few department stores, clothing chains, grocery chains, or even direct mail or e-commerce businesses that don't routinely accept returns, no questions asked.

When you do only that for which you are paid, there is nothing out of the ordinary to attract favorable comment about the transaction. But when you willingly do more than that for which you are paid, your action attracts the favorable attention of all who are affected by it, and goes another step toward establishing a reputation that will eventually set the law of increasing returns to work on your behalf, for this reputation will create a demand for your services.

Carol Downes went to work for W. C. Durant, the head of General Motors, in a minor position yet quickly became Mr. Durant's right-hand man and the president of one of his automobile distributing companies. He promoted himself into this profitable position solely through the aid of the law of increasing returns, which he put into operation by rendering more service and better service than that for which he was paid.

In a visit with Mr. Downes I asked him to tell me how he had managed to gain promotion so rapidly. In a few brief sentences he told the whole story.

"When I first went to work for Mr. Durant," he said, "I noticed that he always remained at the office long after all the others had gone home for the day, and I made it my business to stay there also. No one asked me to stay, but I thought someone should be there to give Mr. Durant any assistance he might need. Often he would look around for someone to bring him a file, or render some other trivial service, and always he found me there ready to serve him. He got into the habit of calling on me. That is about all there is to the story."

"He got into the habit of calling on me." Read that sentence again, for it is full of meaning of the richest sort.

And why did Mr. Durant get into the habit of calling on Mr. Downes? Because Mr. Downes made it his business to be on hand where he would be seen. He deliberately placed himself in a position

YOU NEED HAVE NO FEAR OF COMPETITION

FROM THE PERSON WHO SAYS,

"I'M NOT PAID TO DO THIS

AND I'LL NOT DO IT."

HE WILL NEVER BE A DANGEROUS

COMPETITOR FOR YOUR JOB.

BUT WATCH OUT FOR THE FELLOW WHO

REMAINS AT HIS WORK UNTIL IT IS

FINISHED AND PERFORMS A LITTLE

MORE THAN IS EXPECTED OF HIM, FOR

HE MAY CHALLENGE YOU AT THE POST

AND PASS YOU AT THE GRANDSTAND.

—Napoleon Hill

to render service that would make the law of increasing returns work for him.

Was he told to do this? No.

Was he paid to do it? Yes! He was paid by the opportunity it offered for him to bring himself to the attention of the man who had it within his power to promote him.

We are now approaching the most important part of this lesson, because this is an appropriate place to suggest that *you* have the same opportunity to make use of the law of increasing returns that Mr. Downes had, and you can go about the application of the law in exactly the same way that he did—by being on hand and ready to volunteer your services in the performance of work that others may shirk because they are not paid to do it.

Stop. Don't say it—don't even think it—if you have the slightest intention of using the argument "but my employer is different."

Of course yours is different. All people are different in most respects, but the majority are very much alike in being somewhat selfish. In fact they are selfish enough not to want a man such as Carol Downes to go to work for their competitor, and this very selfishness may be made to serve you as an asset, not as a liability—*if* you have the good judgment to make yourself so useful that the person to whom you sell your services cannot get along without you.

One of the most advantageous promotions I ever received came about through an incident that seemed so insignificant at the time that it appeared to be unimportant. One Saturday afternoon, a lawyer whose office was on the same floor as that of my employer came in and asked if I knew where he could get a stenographer to do some work that he was compelled to finish that day.

I told him that all our stenographers had gone to the ball game, and that I would have been gone too had he called five minutes later, but that I would be very glad to stay and do his work as I could go to a ball game any day and his work had to be done then.

I did the work, and when he asked how much he owed me I replied, "Oh, about a thousand dollars, as long as it is you; if it were for anyone else, I wouldn't charge anything." He smiled and thanked me.

Little did I think, when I made that remark, that he would ever pay me a thousand dollars for that afternoon's work, but he did! Six months later, after I had entirely forgotten the incident, he called on me again and asked how much salary I was receiving. When I told him, he informed me that he was ready to pay me the thousand dollars that I had laughingly said I would charge him, and he *did* pay it—by giving me a position at a thousand dollars a year increase in salary.

Unconsciously, I had put the law of increasing returns to work on my behalf that afternoon by giving up the ball game and rendering a service that was obviously rendered out of a desire to be helpful and not for the sake of a monetary consideration.

It was not my duty to give up my Saturday afternoon, but it was my *privilege!* Furthermore, it had been a profitable privilege, because it yielded me a thousand dollars in cash and a much more responsible position than the one I had formerly.

I have been thinking for more than twenty-five years about this *privilege* of Doing More Than Paid For, and my thoughts have led me to the conclusion that a single hour devoted each day to rendering service for which we are not paid can be made to yield bigger returns than what we receive from all the rest of the day when we are merely performing our *duty*.

COMMENTARY

In A Lifetime of Riches, *author Michael Ritt tells the story of a letter Hill wrote, just prior to his graduation from business school, to Rufus Ayers, a prominent attorney and "big men" businessman with whom he aspired to work:*

"I have just completed a business college course and am well qualified to serve as your secretary, a position I am very anxious to have. Because I have no

previous experience, I know that at the beginning working for you will be of more value to me than it will be to you. Because of this I am willing to pay for the privilege of working with you.

"You may charge any sum you consider fair, provided at the end of three months that amount will become my salary. The sum I am to pay you can be deducted from what you pay me when I start to earn money."

Ayers quickly hired him, with pay, and Hill "was an instant success. He came to the office early, stayed late, and worked tirelessly in between. He was an excellent bookkeeper, fastidiously accurate and willing 'to go the extra mile to render more service than compensated for'—an axiom that would one day become one of his principles for success."

The law of increasing returns is no invention of mine, nor do I lay claim to the discovery of the principle of Doing More Than Paid For as a means of utilizing this law. I merely appropriated them, after many years of careful observation of those forces which enter into the attainment of success, just as *you* will appropriate them after you understand their significance.

You can begin this process now by trying an experiment that will open your eyes and give you powers that you did not know you possessed.

Let me caution you, however, not to attempt this experiment in the same spirit in which a certain woman experimented with the biblical passage that says something to the effect that if you have faith the size of a grain of mustard, and say to yonder mountain be removed to some other place, it will be removed.

This woman lived near a high mountain which she could see from her front door. As she retired one night she commanded the mountain to remove itself to some other place. Next morning she jumped out of bed, rushed to the door, and looked out, but the mountain was still there. Then she said, "Just as I had expected! I knew it would be there."

THERE ARE TEN WEAKNESSES

AGAINST WHICH MOST OF US

MUST GUARD OURSELVES.

ONE OF THESE IS THE HABIT OF TRYING

TO REAP BEFORE WE HAVE SOWN,

AND THE OTHER NINE ARE

ALL WRAPPED UP IN THE ONE PRACTICE

OF CREATING ALIBIS TO

COVER EVERY MISTAKE MADE.

—Napoleon Hill

I am going to ask you to approach this experiment with full faith that it will mark one of the most important turning points of your entire life. I am going to ask you to make the object of this experiment the removal of a mountain that is standing where your *success* should stand, but where it can never stand until you have removed the mountain.

You may never have noticed the mountain to which I refer, but it is standing there in your way just the same, unless you have already discovered and removed it. And what is this mountain? It is the feeling that you have been cheated unless you receive material pay for all the service you render. That feeling may be unconsciously expressing itself and destroying the very foundation of your success in scores of ways that you have not realized.

In its basic form, this feeling usually seeks outward expression in terms something like, "I am not paid to do this and I'll be damned if I'll do it." You know the attitude to which I refer. You have met with it many times, but have you ever found a single person of this type who was successful? I don't expect that you ever will.

Success must be attracted through understanding and application of laws that are as immutable as is the law of gravity. For this reason you are requested to enter into the following experiment with the object of further familiarizing yourself with the all-important law of increasing returns.

During the next six months make it your business to render useful service to at least one person every day, for which you neither expect nor accept monetary pay.

Do this experiment with faith that it will reveal one of the most powerful laws of achieving success, and you will not be disappointed.

The rendering of this service may take any form you choose. For example, it may be rendered personally to one or more specific persons. Or it may be rendered to your employer as work that you perform after hours. Or it may be rendered to entire strangers whom you never expect to see again. It doesn't matter to whom you render this service so long as you render it with willingness, and solely for the purpose of benefiting others.

If you carry out this experiment with the proper attitude, you will discover what all others who have become familiar with the law on which it is based have discovered—that you can no more render service without receiving compensation than you can withhold the rendering of it without suffering the loss of reward.

Ralph Waldo Emerson wrote in his essay Compensation:

> . . . If you serve an ungrateful master, serve him the more. Put God in your debt. Every stroke shall be repaid. The longer the payment is withholden, the better for you; for compound interest on compound interest is the rate and usage of this exchequer. . . .
>
> . . . The law of Nature is, Do the thing and you shall have the power; but they who do not the thing have not the power. . . .
>
> . . . Men suffer all their life long, under the foolish superstition that they can be cheated. But it is as impossible for a man to be cheated by anyone but himself, as for a thing to be, and not to be, at the same time. There is a third silent party to all our bargains. The nature and soul of things takes on itself the guaranty of fulfillment of every contract, so that honest service cannot come to loss. . . .

Before you begin the experiment, let me suggest that you read all of Emerson's Compensation, for it will go a very long way toward helping you to understand *why* you are doing the experiment.

Perhaps you have read Compensation before. Read it again! Every time you read it you will discover new truths that you did not notice during previous readings.

COMMENTARY

> *Anyone interested in reading Ralph Waldo Emerson's Compensation online can find it at http://www.rwe.org/works/Essays-1st_Series_03_Compensation.htm.*

A few years ago I was invited to deliver the graduation address before the students of a college. During my address I dwelt at length, and with all the emphasis at my command, on the importance of rendering more service and better service than that for which one is paid.

After the address was delivered, the president and the secretary of the college invited me to lunch. While we were eating, the secretary turned to the president and said, "I have just found out what this man is doing. He is putting himself ahead in the world by first helping others to get ahead."

In that brief statement he had epitomized the most important part of my philosophy on the subject of success: It is literally true that you can succeed best and quickest by helping others to succeed.

Some years ago, when I was in the advertising business, I built my entire clientele by applying the fundamentals upon which this lesson is founded. By having my name placed on the follow-up lists of various mail-order houses, I received their sales literature. When I received a sales letter or a booklet or a folder that I believed I could improve, I went right to work on it and made the improvement, then sent it back to the firm that had sent it to me, with a letter stating that this was but a trifling sample of what I could do—that there were plenty of other good ideas where that one came from—and that I would be glad to render regular service for a monthly fee.

Invariably this brought an order for my services. On one occasion a firm was dishonest enough to appropriate my idea and use it without paying me for it, but this later turned out to be an advantage to me. A member of the firm who was familiar with the situation started another business, and as a result of the work I had done for his former associates, for which I was not paid, he hired me at more than double the amount I would have realized from his original firm.

SELF-SACRIFICE IS NEVER

ENTIRELY UNSELFISH,

FOR THE GIVER

NEVER FAILS TO RECEIVE.

—Dolores E. McGuire

Thus the law of compensation gave back to me, and with compound interest added, that which I had lost by rendering service to those who were dishonest.

Several years ago I had been invited to deliver a lecture before the students of the Palmer School in Davenport, Iowa. My manager had completed arrangements for me to accept the invitation under the regular terms in effect at that time, which were $100 for the lecture plus my travel expenses.

When I arrived at Davenport I found a reception committee awaiting me at the depot, and that evening I was given one of the warmest welcomes I had ever received during my public career, up to that time. I met many delightful people from whom I gathered many valuable facts that were of benefit to me. Therefore, when I was asked to make out my expense account so the school could give me a check, I told them that I had received my pay, many times over, by what I had learned while I was there. I refused my fee and returned to my office in Chicago feeling well repaid for the trip.

The following morning Dr. Palmer went before the two thousand students of his school and announced what I had said about feeling repaid by what I had learned, and he added: "In the twenty years I have been conducting this school I have had scores of speakers address the student body, but this is the first time I ever knew a man to refuse his fee because he felt that he had been repaid for his services in other ways. This man is the editor of a national magazine and I advise every one of you to subscribe to that magazine, because such a man as this must have much that each of you will need when you go into the field and offer your services."

By the middle of that week I had received more than $6,000 for subscriptions. During the following two years these same two thousand students and their friends sent in more than $50,000 for subscriptions. Tell me how or where I could have invested $100 as profitably as this.

PEOPLE ARE ALWAYS BLAMING THEIR

CIRCUMSTANCES FOR WHAT THEY ARE.

I DON'T BELIEVE IN CIRCUMSTANCES.

THE PEOPLE WHO GET ON

IN THIS WORLD ARE THE PEOPLE

WHO GET UP AND LOOK FOR THE

CIRCUMSTANCES THEY WANT,

AND IF THEY CAN'T FIND THEM,

THEY MAKE THEM.

—George Bernard Shaw

COMMENTARY

The magazine to which Napoleon Hill refers was Hill's Golden Rule. *In 1918, on the day the First World War ended, he was again looking for his definite purpose in life through which he could also earn a living. As reproduced in Michael Ritt's book* A Lifetime of Riches, *this is from the essay Hill wrote as he contemplated his future:*

"Out of this war will come a new idealism—an idealism that will be based on the Golden Rule philosophy; an idealism that will guide us, not to see how much we can 'do our fellow man for' but how much we can do for him, that will ameliorate his hardships and make him happier as he tarries by the wayside of life. . . . To get this philosophy into the hearts of those who need it, I shall publish a magazine to be called Hill's Golden Rule.*"*

He took his essay to George Williams, a Chicago printer he had met while working at the White House, and by early January of 1919 the magazine was on the newsstands. Having no money to pay other writers, Hill wrote every word himself.

We go through two important periods in this life. One is that period during which we are gathering, classifying, and organizing knowledge, and the other is that period during which we are struggling for recognition. We must first learn something, which requires more effort than most of us are willing to put into the job, but even after we have learned much that can be of useful service to others, we are still confronted with the problem of convincing them that we can serve them.

One of the most important reasons why we should always be not only ready but also *willing* to render service is that every time we do so, we gain an opportunity to prove to someone that we have ability. We go just one more step toward gaining the necessary recognition that we must all have.

Instead of saying to the world, "Show me the color of your money and I will show you what I can do," reverse the rule and say, "Let me show you the color of my service so that I may take a look at the color of your money if you like my service."

In 1917 a woman, who was then nearing fifty, was working as a stenographer at fifteen dollars a week. Judging by the salary, she must have been none too competent in that work.

About ten years later, this same woman was clearing a little over $100,000 on the lecture circuit. What bridged that mighty chasm between her two earning capacities? The Habit of Doing More Than Paid For.

This woman became well known throughout the country as a prominent lecturer on the subject of applied psychology.

Let me show you how she harnessed the law of increasing returns. First she went into a city and delivered a series of fifteen free lectures. Anyone could attend, at no charge. As she was delivering these lectures she had the opportunity of "selling herself" to her audience, and at the end of the series she announced the formation of a class for which she charged twenty-five dollars per student.

That's all there was to her plan. While she was commanding a small fortune for a year's work, there were scores of much more proficient lecturers who were barely getting enough from their work to pay their expenses, simply because they had not yet familiarized themselves, as she had, with the fundamentals on which this lesson is based.

COMMENTARY

At a later time, Hill himself used the same principle but he combined it with the leading technology of his day. Napoleon Hill took his lecture series and turned it into radio programs and later television shows that were broadcast all over America. These were but a more sophisticated version of "free" lectures that enticed listeners and viewers to see him for themselves and perhaps buy his books.

The Silva Method, a success system developed by Jose Silva and based on concepts very similar to those espoused by Napoleon Hill, became popular using essentially that same principle. Beginning in the late 1960s, every weekend in newspapers in most major cities in North America, advertisements would appear offering a free introductory course provided by a local trainer certified in the Silva Method. These free introductions convinced enough participants to become paying customers that the Silva Method grew into one of the most successful self-help courses of all time.

In the 1980s the principle evolved again, only this time the free lecture was called an infomercial. But in essence it was the same concept: it was a way for audiences to sample ideas and speakers. Once again the principle worked, and in the case of Anthony Robbins, for example, it launched a true phenomenon into the world of motivational speaking.

If this woman, who had no extraordinary qualifications, could harness the law of increasing returns and make it raise her from the position of stenographer at fifteen dollars a week to that of lecturer at over $100,000 a year, why can you not apply this same law so that it will give you advantages that you do not have now?

You are struggling to make a place for yourself in the world. You may already be exerting enough effort to bring you success of the highest order, if only that effort were coupled with and supported by the law of increasing returns. For this reason, you owe it to yourself to find out how you can apply this law to best advantage.

After you have finished reading this lesson, if you will go back and review the previous lessons on Initiative and Leadership and on Enthusiasm, you will better understand them. Those lessons and this one clearly establish the necessity of taking the Initiative, following it with aggressive action, and doing more than you are paid to do. If you will burn the fundamentals of these three lessons into your consciousness, you will be a changed person, and I make this statement regardless of who you are or what your calling may be.

I hope you will profit by the counsel of one who has made many more mistakes than you ever made—and for that reason learned a few of the fundamental truths of life.

———————

THINK NOT THOSE FAITHFUL

WHO PRAISE ALL THY WORDS,

BUT THOSE WHO KINDLY

REPROVE THY FAULTS.

—Socrates

———————

THE PRIVILEGE OF RENDERING MORE SERVICE

Still another important feature of this habit of offering more and better service than you are paid to do is that this habit can be developed without having to ask permission to do so. Such service may be rendered through your own Initiative, without the consent of anyone else. You do not have to consult those to whom you render the service, for it is a privilege that you control.

There are many things you could do that would tend to promote your interests, but most of them require the Cooperation or the consent of others. And if you render *less* service than that for which you are paid, you must do this with the agreement of the purchaser of the service, or the market for your service will soon cease.

I want you to get the full significance of your prerogative to render more and better service than that for which you are paid, for this places squarely on your shoulders the responsibility of rendering such service. If you fail to do so, you haven't a plausible excuse to offer, or an alibi on which to fall back, if you fail in the achievement of your Definite Chief Aim in life.

One of the most essential yet most difficult truths that I have had to learn is that every person should be their own hardest taskmaster. We are all fine builders of alibis and creators of excuses in support of our shortcomings. When we do this we are not seeking facts and truths as they are, but as we wish them to be. We prefer words of flattery to those of cold, unbiased truth.

Furthermore, we usually become resentful toward those who dare to uncover the truth for our benefit. One of the most severe shocks I received in the early part of my public career was the knowledge that people are still being crucified for the high crime of telling the truth. I recall an experience I had some years ago with a man who had written a book advertising his business school. He submitted this book to me and paid me to review it and give him my candid opinion. I reviewed the book with painstaking care, then did my duty by showing him where I believed the book was weak.

Here I learned a great lesson, for that man became so angry that he has never forgiven me for allowing him to look at his book through my eyes. When he had asked me to tell him frankly what "criticism" I had to offer, what he really meant was that I should tell him what I saw in the book that I could "compliment."

That's human nature for you. We court flattery more than we do truth. I know, because I am human.

All of which is in preparation for the unkindest cut of all: to suggest that you have not done as well as you might have done to charge yourself with your own mistakes and shortcomings. To do this takes Self-Control and plenty of it.

If you paid someone, who had the ability and the courage to do it, a hundred dollars to strip you of your vanity and conceit and love for flattery, so that you might see the weakest part of your makeup, the price would be more than reasonable.

We go through life stumbling and falling and struggling to our knees, and struggling and falling some more, making asses of ourselves, and going down finally in defeat, largely because we either neglect or flatly refuse to learn the truth about ourselves.

I have come to discover some of my own weaknesses through my work of helping others discover theirs, and I blush with shame when I take a retrospective view and think how ridiculous I must have seemed in the eyes of those who could see me as I *wouldn't* see myself.

We parade before the enlarged shadows of our own vanity and imagine that those shadows are our real selves, while the few knowing souls with whom we meet stand in the background and look at us with pity or with scorn.

Not only have you been fooling yourself as to the real cause of your past failures, but you have also tried to blame those causes on someone else. When things did not go your way, instead of accepting full responsibility for the cause, you have said, "Oh, hang this job! I don't like the way *they* are treating me, so I'm going to quit."

Don't deny it!

Now let me whisper a secret in your ear—a secret that I have had to gather from grief and heartaches and unnecessary punishment of the hardest sort: Instead of "quitting" the job because there were obstacles to master and difficulties to be overcome, if you had faced the facts you would have better understood that life itself is just one long series of mastery of difficulties and obstacles.

The measure of a person may be taken very accurately by the extent to which they adapt themself to their environment and make it their business to accept responsibility for every adversity with which they meet, whether the adversity grows out of a cause within their control or not. If you feel that what I am saying is rather severe, know that I have had to punish myself even more before I learned the truth that I am passing on to you for your use and guidance.

I have a few enemies—and thank God for them!—for they have been vulgar and merciless enough to say some things about me that *forced* me to rid myself of some of my most serious shortcomings, mainly those I did not know I had. I have profited by the criticism of these enemies without having to pay them for their services in dollars, although I have paid in other ways.

However, it was not until some years ago that I caught sight of some of my most glaring faults which were brought to my attention as I studied Emerson's essay Compensation, particularly this part:

Our strength grows out of our weakness.

Not until we are pricked, and stung, and sorely shot at, awakens the indignation which arms itself with secret forces. A great man is always willing to be little. While he sits on the cushion of advantage he goes to sleep. When he is pushed, tormented, defeated, he has a chance to learn something; he has been put on his wits, on his manhood; he has gained facts; learned his ignorance; is cured of the insanity of conceit; has got moderation and real skill. The wise man always throws himself on the side of his assailants. It is more his

IN THE ARENA OF HUMAN LIFE

THE HONORS AND REWARDS FALL

TO THOSE WHO SHOW THEIR

GOOD QUALITIES IN ACTION.

—Aristotle

interest than it is theirs to find his weak point. Blame is safer than praise. I hate to be defended in a newspaper. As long as all that is said is said against me, I feel a certain assurance of success. But as soon as honeyed words of praise are spoken of me, I feel as one that lies unprotected before his enemies.

Study this, the philosophy of the immortal Emerson, for it may serve as a modifying force that will temper your metal and prepare you for the battles of life, as carbon tempers the steel. If you are very young, you need to study it all the more, for it often requires the stern realities of many years of experience to prepare one to assimilate and apply this philosophy.

It is better that you should understand these great truths as a result of my undiplomatic presentation of them than to be forced to gather them from the less sympathetic sources of cold experience—a teacher that knows no favorites. But when I permit you to profit by the truths I have gathered from the teachings of this unsympathetic teacher called experience, I am doing my best to show you favoritism, which reminds me somewhat of the times that my father used to "do his duty" by me, in the woodshed, always starting with this bit of encouraging philosophy: "Son, this hurts me worse than it does you."

There's a story that should leave in your mind the importance of this lesson. The story had its setting in the city of Antioch, in ancient Rome, two thousand years ago, when the great city of Jerusalem and all the land of Judea were under the oppressive heel of Rome.

The star figure of the story was a young Jewish man by the name of Ben Hur, who was falsely accused of crime and sentenced to hard labor at the galley's oar. Chained to a bench in the galley, and being forced to tug wearily at the oars, Ben Hur developed a powerful body. Little did his tormentors know that out of his punishment would grow the strength with which he would one day gain his freedom. Perhaps Ben Hur himself had no such hopes.

Then came the day of the chariot races. One span of horses was without a driver. In desperation the owner sought the aid of the young slave because of his mighty arms, and begged him to take the place of the missing driver.

As Ben Hur picked up the reins, a great cry went up from the onlookers. "Look! Look! Those arms! Where did you get them?" they howled, and Ben Hur answered, "At the galley's oar!"

The race was on. With those mighty arms Ben Hur calmly drove that charging span of horses on to victory—a victory that won for him his freedom.

Life itself is a great chariot race, and the victory goes only to those who have developed the strength of character and determination and willpower to win. It doesn't matter if we develop this strength through cruel confinement at the galley's oar, as long as we use it so that it brings us, finally, to victory and freedom.

It is an unvarying law that strength grows out of resistance. If we pity the poor blacksmith who swings a five-pound hammer all day, we must also admire the wonderful arm that he develops in doing it.

"... Because of the dual constitution of all things, in labor as in life, there can be no cheating," says Emerson. "The thief steals from himself. The swindler swindles himself. For the real price of labor is knowledge and virtue, whereof wealth and credit are signs. The signs, like paper money, may be counterfeited or stolen, but that which they represent, namely, knowledge and virtue, cannot be counterfeited or stolen."

Henry Ford receives fifteen thousand letters a week from people begging for a part of his wealth. Yet few of these poor ignorant souls understand that Ford's real wealth is not measured by the dollars he has in the bank, nor the factories he owns, but by the *reputation* he has gained through rendering useful service at a reasonable price.

And how did he gain that reputation? Certainly not by rendering as little service as possible and collecting all he could filch from the purchasers. The very essence of Ford's business philosophy was this: "Give the people the best product at the lowest price possible."

When other automobile manufacturers raised their prices, Ford lowered his. When other employers lowered wages, Ford increased them. What happened? This policy made the law of increasing returns work so effectively for Ford that he became the richest and most powerful man in the world.

Oh, you foolish and shortsighted seekers after wealth, who are returning from the daily chase empty-handed, why do you not take a lesson from men like Ford? Why do you not reverse your philosophy and *give* in order that you may get?

Life is but a short span of years at best. If we were placed here for the purpose of laying up treasures for use in a life that lies beyond the dark shadow of Death, may it not be possible that we can best collect these treasures by rendering all the service we can, to all the people we can, in a loving spirit of kindness and sympathy?

I hope you agree with this philosophy.

Here this lesson must end, but it is by no means completed. Where I lay down the chain of thought it is now your duty to take it up and develop it, in your own way and to your own benefit.

By the very nature of its subject, this lesson can never be finished. Its purpose is to inspire you to take the fundamentals on which it is based and use them as a stimulus that will open your mind, thereby releasing the latent forces within you.

This lesson was not written specifically for the purpose of teaching you, but was intended as a means of enabling you to teach yourself one of the great truths of life. It was intended as a source of education, in the true sense of *educing*, drawing out, developing from within, those forces of mind that are available for your use.

When you deliver the best service of which you are capable, striving each time to exceed all your previous efforts, you are making use of the highest form of education. Therefore, when you render more service and better service than that for which you are paid, you, more than anyone else, are profiting by the effort.

ANY MAN MAY BECOME GREAT

BY DOING THE COMMONPLACE

THINGS OF LIFE IN A GREAT SPIRIT,

WITH A GENUINE DESIRE TO BE

OF HELPFUL SERVICE TO OTHERS,

REGARDLESS OF HIS CALLING.

—Napoleon Hill

COMMENTARY

Andrew Carnegie had told Napoleon Hill that during the twenty years it would take to compile the research and information that would go into the development of "the world's first philosophy of individual achievement," he must be willing to starve rather than quit. There were many times when he was nearly doing the former, but he never gave in to the latter.

Hill believed so strongly in service to others and in doing more than what he was paid to do, that on at least two occasions—first in 1917 during the First World War, when he wrote material for President Woodrow Wilson to keep the industrial workers motivated, and again in 1933 during the depression, when he joined President Franklin Roosevelt's White House staff as an adviser, speechwriter, and p.r. man for the National Recovery Administration—Hill willingly worked for the government for just one dollar a year, when he had barely enough money to live on.

It is only through the delivery of such service that mastery in your chosen field can be attained. For this reason you should make it a part of your Definite Chief Aim to strive to surpass all previous records in all that you do. Make this a part of your daily habits, and follow it with the same regularity with which you eat your meals.

Make it your business to render more and better service than that for which you are paid, and before you realize what has happened, you will find that the world is willingly paying you for more than you do!

Compound interest upon compound interest is the rate that you will be paid for such service. Just how this pyramiding of gains takes place is left entirely to you to determine.

Now, what are you going to do with what you have learned from this lesson? and when? and how? and why? This lesson can be of no value to you unless it moves you to adopt and use the knowledge it has brought you. Knowledge becomes power only through organization and use. Do not forget this.

You can never become a leader without doing more than you are paid for, and you cannot become successful without developing Leadership in your chosen occupation.

Lesson Ten

Pleasing Personality

WHAT YOU WANT

TO BE EVENTUALLY,

THAT YOU MUST BE EVERY DAY;

AND BY AND BY

THE QUALITY OF YOUR DEEDS

WILL GET DOWN

INTO YOUR SOUL.

—Napoleon Hill

Lesson Ten

_____

PLEASING PERSONALITY

_____

"You Can Do It if You Believe You Can!"

WHAT IS A PLEASING PERSONALITY? IT IS a personality that attracts, and in this lesson we will look at what causes that attraction and how to create it.

Your personality is the sum total of your own characteristics and appearances that distinguish you from all others. The clothes you wear, the lines in your face, the tone of your voice, the thoughts you think, the character you have developed by those thoughts—all constitute parts of your personality. Whether your personality is attractive or not is another matter.

By far, the most important part of your personality is that which is represented by your character. Therefore it is also the part that is not visible.

The style of your clothes and their appropriateness undoubtedly constitutes a very important part of your personality, for it is true that people form first impressions of you from your outward appearance.

Even the way you shake hands forms an important part of your personality and goes a long way toward attracting or repelling those with whom you shake hands. But this art can be cultivated.

The expression in your eyes also forms an important part of your personality, for there are people, and they are more numerous than one might imagine, who can look through your eyes into your heart and see the nature of your most secret thoughts.

The vitality of your body—which is sometimes called personal magnetism—also constitutes an important part of your personality.

ELEMENTS OF
A PLEASING PERSONALITY

There is one way in which you can express the composite of your personality so that it will always attract, even though you may seem outwardly unattractive, and this is by taking an honest interest in other people.

Let me illustrate exactly what I mean, by relating an incident that happened some years ago from which I was taught a lesson in master salesmanship. You, too, may learn that lesson from this incident.

One day an elderly lady called at my office and sent in her card with a message saying that she must see *me* personally. No amount of coaxing by secretaries could induce her to disclose the nature of her visit, therefore I made up my mind that she was some poor old soul who wanted to sell me a book. Thinking of my own mother, I decided to go out to the reception room and buy her book, whatever it might be.

As I walked down the hallway from my private office, this lady, who was standing just outside the railing that led to the main reception room, began to smile. I had seen many people smile, but never before had I seen one who smiled so sweetly as did this lady. It was one of those contagious smiles, because I caught the spirit of it and began to smile too.

As I reached the railing, this lady extended her hand to shake hands with me. Now, as a rule, I do not become too friendly on first acquaintance when a person calls at my office, because it is very hard to say no if the caller should ask me to do something that I do not wish to do.

However, this dear lady looked so sweetly innocent and harmless that I extended my hand and she began to shake it, whereupon I discovered that she not only had an attractive smile but she also had a magnetic handshake. She took hold of my hand firmly, but not too firmly, and the very manner in which she went about it telegraphed the thought that it was *she* who was doing the honors. She made me feel that she was really and truly glad to shake my hand, and I believe that she was. I believe that her handshake came from her heart as well as from her hand.

I have shaken hands with many thousands of people during my public career, but I do not recall ever shaking hands with anyone who understood the art as well as this lady did. The moment she touched my hand I could feel myself "slipping" and I knew that whatever it was that she had come after, she would go away with it, and that I would aid and abet her all I could toward this end. That penetrating smile and that warm handshake had disarmed me and made me a willing victim.

At a single stroke, this lady had cut through that false shell into which I crawl when salespeople come around. This gentle visitor had "neutralized" my mind and made me want to listen.

Ah, but here is the point at which most salespeople stumble, for it is as useless to try to sell someone anything until you have first made them *want* to listen, as it would be to command the earth to stop rotating.

NOTHING IS EVER LOST BY COURTESY.

IT IS THE CHEAPEST OF PLEASURES,

COSTS NOTHING, AND CONVEYS MUCH.

IT PLEASES HIM WHO GIVES AND

HIM WHO RECEIVES, AND THUS,

LIKE MERCY, IS TWICE BLESSED.

—Erastus Wiman

Note well how this elderly lady used a smile and a handshake as the tools with which to pry open a doorway to my heart. Slowly and deliberately, as if she had all the time in the world (which she did have, as far as I was concerned at that moment) she began to crystallize the first step of her victory into reality by saying, "I just came here to tell you [what seemed to me to be a long pause] that I think you are doing the most wonderful work of any man in the world today."

Every word was emphasized by a gentle, though firm, squeeze of my hand, and she was looking through my eyes and into my heart as she spoke.

After I had regained consciousness (for it became a standing joke among my assistants at the office that I fainted dead away) I reached down and unlocked the little secret latch that fastened the gate, and said, "Come right in, dear lady—come right into my private office," and with a gallant bow that would have done credit to the cavaliers of olden times, I bade her come in and "sit awhile."

As she entered my private office, I motioned her to the big easy-chair behind my desk while I took the little hard-seated chair which, under ordinary circumstances, I would have used as a means of discouraging her from taking up too much of my time.

For three-quarters of an hour I listened to one of the most brilliant and charming conversations I have ever heard, and my visitor was doing *all* the conversing. From the very start she had assumed the initiative and taken the lead, and up to the end of that first three-quarters of an hour, she found no inclination on my part to challenge her right to it.

I repeat, lest you did not get the full importance of it, that I was a *willing* listener!

Now comes the part that could make me blush with embarrassment. As I have stated, my visitor entranced me with brilliant and captivating conversation for all of that time. And not once did she use the personal pronoun "I." Now, what do you suppose she had been talking about? Was she trying to sell me a book? No. However, she was not only trying, but actually selling me something, and that something was myself.

THE MOST IMPORTANT

SINGLE INGREDIENT IN THE

FORMULA OF SUCCESS IS

KNOWING HOW TO GET

ALONG WITH PEOPLE.

—Theodore Roosevelt

She had no sooner been seated in that big cushioned chair than she unrolled a package, and sure enough, there was a book in it. In fact several of them. But what she had was a complete year's file of the magazine of which I was then editor, *Hill's Golden Rule.* She turned the pages of those magazines and read places she had marked here and there, assuring me in the meanwhile that she had always believed the philosophy behind what she was reading.

Then, after I was in a state of complete mesmerism, and thoroughly receptive, my visitor tactfully switched the conversation to a subject which, I suspect, she had in mind to discuss with me long before she presented herself at my office. But—and this is another point at which most salespeople blunder—had she reversed the order and begun the conversation where she finished, chances are she never would have had the opportunity to sit in that big easy-chair.

During the last three minutes of her visit, she skillfully laid before me the merits of some securities she was selling. She did not ask me to purchase, but the way in which she told me about the securities had the psychological effect of making me want to purchase. And even though I made no purchase of securities from her, she made a sale—because I picked up the telephone and introduced her to a man to whom she later sold more than five times the amount that she had intended selling me.

If that same woman, or another woman, or a man, who had the tact and Pleasing Personality that she had, should call on me, I would again sit down and listen for three-quarters of an hour.

We are all human, and we are all more or less vain. And we are all alike in this respect: We will listen with intense interest to those who talk to us about that which lies closest to our hearts. Then, out of a sense of reciprocity, we will also listen with interest when the speaker finally switches the conversation to the subject closest to his or her heart, and in the end we will not only "sign on the dotted line" but we will also say, "What a wonderful personality!"

In the city of Chicago, some years ago, I was conducting a sales course for an investment house which employed more than fifteen hundred salespeople. To keep the ranks of that big organization filled, we had to train and employ six hundred new salespeople every week. Of the thousands of men and women who went through that school, there was but one man who grasped the significance of the principle I have just described.

This man had never tried to sell securities, and frankly admitted when he entered the class that he was not a salesman.

After he had finished his training, one of the "star" salesmen, a man by the name of Perkins, took a notion to play a practical joke on him. This star gave him an inside "tip" as to where he would be able to sell some securities without any great effort. Perkins would make the sale himself, he said, but the man to whom he referred as being a likely purchaser was an ordinary artist who would purchase with so little urging that he, being a star, did not wish to waste time on him.

The new salesman was delighted to receive this tip, and he went quickly on his way to make the sale. As soon as he was out of the office, the star gathered together the other "stars" and told of the joke he was playing, for in reality the artist was a very wealthy man and Perkins had spent nearly a month trying to sell to him, without success. It then came out that all the "stars" of that particular group had also called on this same artist but had failed to interest him.

The new salesman was gone about an hour and a half. When he returned he found the stars waiting for him with smiles on their faces. To their surprise, this new salesman also wore a broad smile on his face. They looked at each other inquiringly.

"Well, did you sell to your man?" asked the originator of the joke. "Certainly," replied the uninitiated one, "and I found that artist to be all you said he was—a perfect gentleman and a very interesting man."

Reaching into his pocket he pulled out an order and a check for two thousand dollars. The stars wanted to know how he did it.

"Oh, it wasn't difficult," replied the new salesman. "I just walked in and talked to him a few minutes, and he brought up the subject of the securities himself and said he wanted to purchase. Therefore, I really did not sell to him. He purchased of his own accord."

When I heard of the transaction, I called this new salesman in and asked him to describe, in detail, just how he made the sale.

He said that when he reached the artist's studio he found him at work on a picture. The artist had been so engaged in his work that he did not see the salesman enter. So the salesman walked over to where he could see the picture and stood there looking at it without saying a word. When the artist finally saw him, the salesman apologized for the intrusion and began to talk—about the picture the artist was painting.

He knew just enough about art to be able to discuss the merits of the picture with some intelligence, and he was really interested in the subject. He liked the picture and frankly told the artist so.

For nearly an hour those two men talked of nothing but art, particularly the picture that stood on the artist's easel. Finally, the artist asked the salesman his name and his business, and the salesman replied, "Oh, never mind my business or my name. I am more interested in you and your art."

The artist beamed. But not to be outdone by his polite visitor, he insisted on knowing what mission had brought him to his studio.

Then, with an air of genuine reluctance, this salesman—this *real* star—introduced himself and told his business. Briefly he described the securities he was selling, and the artist listened as if he enjoyed every word that was spoken.

After the salesman had finished, the artist said, "Well, well! Other salesmen from your firm have been here trying to sell me some of those securities, but they talked of nothing but business. In fact, they annoyed me so much that I had to ask one of them to leave; I believe his name was Perkins. But you present the matter so differently, and I want you to let me have two thousand dollars' worth of those securities."

Remember that: *"You present the matter so differently."*

And how did this new salesman present the matter so differently? What did this *master* salesman really sell that artist? Did he sell him securities?

No! He sold him his own picture that he was painting on his own canvas. The securities were almost incidental.

It happens that in a class attended by this new salesman early on, I had told the story of the elderly lady who entertained me for three-quarters of an hour by talking about that which was nearest my heart, and it had so impressed him that he made up his mind to study his prospective purchasers and find out what would interest them most, so he could talk about that.

This "green" salesman earned $7,900 in commissions the first month he was in the field, leading the next-highest man by more than double, and the tragedy of it was that not one person out of the entire organization of fifteen hundred salespeople took the time to find out how and why he became the real star of the organization.

COMMENTARY

As noted earlier, throughout this revised and updated edition of Law of Success *the editors have made it a practice to suggest relevant books and audiobooks by other authors that relate to the principles and concepts presented by Napoleon Hill in his original manuscript. That being the case, in this section you would expect to find one or two suggestions for books on salesmanship. But because salesmanship is a subject that has been written about so extensively, selecting a mere one or two examples would have proven almost impossible had it not been for a gentleman with the unusual name of Og Mandino, and Napoleon Hill himself.*

Mandino's personal story is far too powerful to do it justice in the few lines available here, but you should know something of his background in order to understand why we have singled out his book. In brief, when Og Mandino returned a decorated hero after his service in World War II, he struggled for a year trying to make a go of it as a writer in New York City. When his savings were exhausted he started on a fifteen-year merry-go-round of brief ups, followed by crashing downs that finally brought him so low he was literally a drunken bum on the streets of Cleveland, too poor to buy a gun to commit suicide. Then, in a public library, he came across a copy of Success Through a Positive Mental Attitude, *the classic motivational book co-written by Napoleon Hill and W. Clement Stone. It transformed his life.*

With a renewed sense of purpose, Og Mandino set out for Boston where he managed to convince the people at W. Clement Stone's Combined Insurance Company of America that they should hire him as an insurance salesman. Within three years he had elevated himself within the organization to the point where he was named to the position of executive editor of Success Unlimited, *a magazine published by Stone and Hill. A few years later, in 1968, a New York publisher took a chance on this first-time author and published Mandino's book* The Greatest Salesman in the World.

The details of Og Mandino's life, only hinted at here, and the equally extraordinary story of how his book earned its success, are intentionally being left for you to discover on your own. However, we will tell you this: The Greatest Salesman in the World *has sold well over four million copies, has gone through more than one hundred and thirty printings in seventeen languages, and is widely acknowledged as the bestselling book about sales in the entire world.*

The second source of additional material that the editors recommend is the audiobook Selling You! *It is a two-cassette program based on Napoleon Hill's bestseller* How to Sell Your Way through Life *(which is not currently available but there are plans to reprint it in the future). The audio program is narrated by Joe Slattery, features an introduction by W. Clement Stone, and is augmented with archival recordings of Napoleon Hill personally explaining some of his most compelling ideas. It also includes a 32-page booklet featuring additional sales techniques.*

VICTORY COMES ONLY AFTER

MANY STRUGGLES AND

COUNTLESS DEFEATS. . . .

EACH REBUFF IS AN

OPPORTUNITY TO MOVE FORWARD;

TURN AWAY FROM THEM,

AVOID THEM, AND YOU

THROW AWAY YOUR FUTURE.

—Og Mandino

A Carnegie or a Rockefeller or a James J. Hill or a Marshall Field accumulates a fortune through the application of the same principles available to all of us, but we envy them their wealth without ever thinking of studying their philosophy and applying it to ourselves.

We look at a successful person in the hour of their triumph and wonder how they did it, but we overlook the importance of analyzing their methods. And we forget the price they had to pay in the careful, well-organized preparation that had to be made before they could reap the fruits of their efforts.

Throughout this course you will not find a single new principle. Every one of them is as old as civilization itself, yet you will find few people who seem to understand how to apply them.

The salesman who sold the securities to that artist was not only a master salesman but he was also a man with a Pleasing Personality. He was not much to look at, and perhaps that was why the "star" conceived the idea of playing the joke on him, but even a homely person may have a very attractive personality in the eyes of those whose handiwork he or she has praised.

Of course, there are some who will get the wrong idea of the principle by drawing the conclusion that any sort of cheap flattery will take the place of genuine heart interest. I hope that you are not one of these. I hope that you are one who understands the real psychology on which this lesson is based, and that you will make it your business to study others closely enough to find something about them or their work that you *genuinely* admire. Only in this way can you develop a personality that will be irresistibly attractive.

Cheap flattery has just the opposite effect to that of constituting a Pleasing Personality. It repels instead of attracting. It is so shallow that even the ignorant easily detect it.

Perhaps you have noticed that this lesson emphasizes at length the importance of making it your business to take a keen interest in other people and in their work, business, or profession.

You will quickly observe that the principles upon which this lesson is based are very closely related to those that constitute the foundation of Lesson Six on Imagination, and also, later, many of the same general principles as those that form the most important part of Lesson Thirteen on Cooperation.

SELLING YOU AND YOUR IDEAS

I would like to introduce some very practical suggestions as to how the laws of Imagination, Cooperation, and Pleasing Personality can be coordinated to create usable ideas.

Every thinker knows that "ideas" are the beginning of all successful achievement. The question most often asked, however, is, "How can I learn to create ideas that will earn money?"

In part we will answer that question in this lesson by suggesting some novel ideas that might be developed and made very profitable, by almost anyone, in practically any locality.

COMMENTARY

A 1998 column in the Houston Business Journal *by syndicated columnist and business consultant Scott Clark of The HTC Group offers some interesting insight into the entrepreneurial process. He writes that while financiers perceive management, opportunity, and resources as the three driving forces behind any business venture, most entrepreneurs focus on just one driving force— opportunity. Although they define this as their product idea, an idea is just a brainstorm that seems to have great possibilities. If an entrepreneur learns of someone else with the same idea, they believe it was stolen from them.*

Clark says that when we are exposed to a sufficient number of life events and are able to filter them creatively, an idea may emerge. Others who have been exposed to the same events, but under different circumstances, are still capable of conceiving the same ideas. As a result, most of the great "ideas" in business/science history have been simultaneously developed by several people who had no direct contact with each other. Examples include the airplane, the integrated circuit, and the computer—each invented concurrently by two people at remote locations from each other.

What transforms an idea into an opportunity that will interest investors, says Clark, is determining a use that consumers really want, then being able to imple-ment it at an affordable price. Most entrepreneurs just devise an interesting concept, conduct market research by asking their friends what they think, then use that feedback to justify leaving their jobs and starting a business.

Clark explains that what they should do first is identify a specific market need, conduct extensive market research to verify the strength and price point of that need, then develop a marketing strategy to meet the demand—before approaching financiers. A failure to first prove the viability of a market for their product is one of the most common mistakes that many entrepreneurs make.

As for management and resources, Clark says that when financiers scrutin-ize a potential business deal, the first thing they look at is not the opportunity but the strength of the management team. According to George Doriot, one of the founders of modern venture capital, "Always consider investing in a grade A entrepreneur with a grade B idea, but never invest in a grade B entrepreneur with a grade A idea."

If you don't present the image of experience—the appropriate background as well as a detailed understanding of your market—investors will never provide you with the resources.

Idea Number One

If, for example, you wanted to manufacture toys, you would have to determine what sort of toys to manufacture and where to get the capital with which to operate the business.

First, go to your local toy store and find out what kinds of toys are currently selling best. If you do not feel competent yourself to make improvements on some of the toys now on the market, advertise for an inventor "with an idea for a marketable toy" and you will soon find a person who will supply this missing link.

———————————

THE ENTREPRENEUR IS ESSENTIALLY

A VISUALIZER AND AN ACTUALIZER . . .

HE CAN VISUALIZE SOMETHING,

AND WHEN HE VISUALIZES IT HE SEES

EXACTLY HOW TO MAKE IT HAPPEN.

—Robert L. Schwartz

———————————

Have that inventor make you a working model, then go to some small manufacturer and arrange to have your toy manufactured.

You now know just what your toy will cost, so you are ready to go to some big jobber, wholesaler, or distributor and arrange for the sale of your product.

If you are a good salesperson you can finance this whole project on the few dollars required to advertise for the inventor. When you find this person, you can probably arrange with them to create a model for you, with a promise that you will give them a better job when you are manufacturing your own toys, or they may do the work in return for an interest in the business.

You should be able to get the manufacturer of your toys to wait for their money until you are paid by the firm to which you sell them, and, if necessary, you can assign to the manufacturer the invoices for the toys sold and let the money come directly to them.

Of course if you have an unusually pleasing and convincing personality, and considerable ability to organize, you will be able to take the model of your toy to someone of means and, in return for an interest in the business, secure the capital with which to do your own manufacturing.

Common sense is all that is necessary. Simply find out what it is that the people want, and then produce it. Produce it well—better than anyone else is doing. Give it a touch of individuality. Make it distinctive.

We spend millions of dollars annually for toys to entertain our children. Make your new toy useful as well as interesting. Make it educational if possible. If it entertains and teaches at the same time it will sell readily and live forever. If your toy is a game, make it teach the child something, such as geography, arithmetic, English, science, and so on. Or, better still, produce a toy that will cause the child to exercise.

EVERYTHING THAT

CAN BE INVENTED

HAS BEEN INVENTED.

—Charles H. Duell*

*director of the U.S. Patent Office,
at the end of the nineteenth century;
referred to by *Time* magazine at the
end of the twentieth century as
"the boneheaded prediction . . ."

COMMENTARY

In reading Napoleon Hill's example of starting a toy company you may have thought to yourself, "How quaint, toy trucks and rag dolls, but that idea belongs to another era. You could never do that today."

Be assured, the basic principles Hill outlines are exactly the principles upon which companies making today's latest computer games are founded. And not only can you do it today but someone is doing it, right now.

Every January or February in New York City, in lower Manhattan where Broadway and Fifth Avenue intersect, as well as at the Javits Convention Center, Toy Fair happens. Everybody who is anybody in the toy business is there displaying their latest toys and games and trying to convince the buyers for the major retail stores that they've got the one that's going to be the big seller at Christmas. And every year, just like at any other trade show, the big guys have the big displays and the big announcements. And every year some little guy with nothing more than a ten-by-ten booth and an original idea will catch the fancy of the buyers.

Clearly, the editors acknowledge that it's the big toy companies that consistently turn out the bestselling toys. The well-known brands have the resources to develop many different lines each year for Toy Fair, and they have established relationships with the buyers. But it is surprising how often it's been a little guy who had the hit of the show that really did become the big seller the following Christmas.

Toy companies aside, the larger point that Hill was making was that new products are coming into the market all the time, and not all of them are created by established companies. It was true when Hill first wrote Law of Success *and it remains true. As this updated edition is being written, new products are still being created and someone with imagination and a pleasing personality is getting the cooperation of other people to help finance and manufacture those products.*

Idea Number Two

This idea will be of interest only to the man or woman who has the Self-Confidence and the ambition to "run the risk" of making a big income, which, I might add, many people do not have.

It is intended for the man or woman who is creative and has the talent to write advertising and sales materials. To make practical and profitable use of this suggestion you will need the Cooperation of a good advertising agency and from one to five firms or individuals who do enough advertising to warrant going through an agency.

This is where you will need Imagination, Cooperation, and a Pleasing Personality, as you will first need to go to an agency and sell them on the idea of paying you a percentage on gross expenditures of all accounts that you bring to it. This percentage is to compensate you for getting the account and for writing the copy and otherwise serving the client in the management of their advertising.

Then you go to a firm or individual whose advertising account you wish to handle and say in effect that you wish to go to work *without compensation.* Tell what you can do and what you intend to do for that particular firm that will help them to sell more goods. If this firm employs an advertising manager, you are to become virtually his or her assistant, *without pay,* on one condition—that the company's advertising is to be placed through the agency with which you have the connection.

Through this arrangement the firm or individual whose account you thus secure will get the benefit of your personal services, *without cost,* and will pay no more for placing its advertising through your agency than it would through any other. If you are convincing and you really take the time to prepare your case, you will get the account without much argument.

You will also give the advertising agency a reputation for effective service, and you will please your clients because they will see satisfactory returns from your efforts. As long as you keep the agency and the clients whom you serve satisfied, your job is safe and you will make money. You can repeat this transaction until you have as many accounts as you can handle.

You can see that the plan has possibilities. It supplies independent work and gives you 100 percent of your earning power. It is better than a position as advertising manager, even if the position paid the same money, because it practically places you in a business of your own—one in which your name is constantly developing a survival value.

Idea Number Three

This plan can be put into operation by almost any man or woman of average intelligence, and with little preparation. Go to any first-class printer and make arrangements with them to handle all the business you bring to them, allowing you a commission of, say, 10 percent on the gross amount. Then go to the largest users of printed matter and get samples of everything that they use in the way of printing.

Form a partnership or working arrangement with a commercial artist who will go over all this printed matter and, wherever suitable or appropriate, improve the illustrations. Then, if you are not a copy writer, form a working arrangement with someone who is, and get him or her to go over the copy of the printed materials and improve on it in every respect possible.

When the work is complete, go back to the firm from which you get the printed matter and show how much more effective you can make it.

If you perform your service properly you will soon have all the business your commercial artist, your copywriter, and you can handle.

Any profits that you earn from the work of others will be a legitimate profit in return for your ability to organize and bring together all the necessary talent and ability with which to perform satisfactory service.

IF YOU WANT TO GET ACROSS AN IDEA,

WRAP IT UP IN A PERSON.

—Ralph Bunche

COMMENTARY

Napoleon Hill's second and third suggestions are really variations on the same theme, and no doubt he chose these examples because he had personally succeeded in doing something very similar. Although Hill was always a writer, the difference between being a writer and being an author was years of research and hard work. During those years he often put his talents to work as a freelancer writing promotional and advertising materials.

Since Hill's time, advertising and marketing have overlapped into other areas and become a part of a larger whole that is vaguely referred to as "the media." This amorphous thing called the media now encompasses everything from the copywriters and illustrators that Hill was familiar with to computer-graphics designers, specialized artists, photographers, performers, interactive-games designers, digital animators, infomercial producers, product-placement specialists, creators of Web sites, and consultants of every stripe.

As new and different as all of these media types may seem, Napoleon Hill would have been right at home with them. Like Hill, they are either freelancers themselves or they rely on freelancers to run their business. Just as you don't have to be the one who creates a toy in order to create a successful toy-manufacturing company, in the service industry it's also not essential that you be the writer or the computer designer to launch a successful media company.

What you do need is the imagination to find out what kind of talent and services are in demand and who the people or businesses are who need those talents. Combine that imaginative idea with the kind of pleasing personality that can elicit the cooperation of freelancers who have the talents to fill that demand, and you have just taken Napoleon Hill's 1927 business model as a blueprint for creating a leading-edge media company.

You want to stop being an employee and become an employer. I do not blame you for that. Most people want to do the same. The best first step to take is to serve the firm or individual for whom you are working just as you would wish to be served if you were that individual or the head of that firm.

Who are the big employers today? They are the men and women who have come up from the ranks; people who have had no greater opportunity than you have. They are in the positions that they hold because their superior ability has enabled them to intelligently direct others. You can acquire that ability if you will try.

Right in the town or city where you live there are people who probably could benefit by knowing you, and who could undoubtedly benefit you in return. In one section of the city lives Mr. John Smith who wishes to sell his grocery store and then open a movie theater. In another section of the city is a man who has a movie theater that he would like to trade for a grocery store. Can you bring them together? If you can, you will serve both and earn a nice commission.

In your town or city are people who want the products raised on the farms in the surrounding community. On those farms there are farmers who raise farm products and who want to get them into the hands of those who live in the towns. If you can find a way of carrying the farm products direct from the farm to the city or town consumer, you will thereby enable the farmer to get more for his products and the consumer to get those products for less, and still there will be a margin to pay you for your ingenuity in shortening the route between producer and consumer.

If you can create such a plan—to shorten that route within any business—you are entitled to a fair percentage of what you *save* for the consumer and also a fair percentage of what you *make* for the producer.

And let me warn you that whatever plan you create as a means of making money, you had better see that it slices off a little of the cost to the consumer instead of adding a little to that cost. If you crave wealth and are really brave enough to shoulder the burdens that go with it, reverse the usual method of acquiring it by giving your goods and wares to the world at the lowest possible profit you can afford instead of exacting all that you can with safety.

The business of bringing together producer and consumer is a profitable business when it is conducted fairly to both, without a greedy desire to get all that you can. The American public is wonderfully patient with profiteers, but there is a point beyond which even the shrewdest dare not go.

There may be some perfectly good plans through which you could squeeze the consumer and still manage to keep out of jail, but you will enjoy much more peace of mind, and in all probability also more profits in the long run, if your plan is built along the lines of Henry Ford's, who found it profitable to pay his workers not as little as he could get them for but as much as his profits would permit. He also found it profitable to reduce the price of his automobile to the consumer while other manufacturers, many of whom have long since failed, continued to increase theirs.

John D. Rockefeller has been abused considerably, but most of this abuse has been prompted by sheer envy on the part of those who would like to have his money but haven't the inclination to earn it.

Regardless of your opinion of Rockefeller, do not forget that he began as a humble bookkeeper and that he gradually climbed to the top because of his ability to organize and direct others intelligently. I can remember when I had to pay twenty-five cents for a gallon of lamp oil and walk two miles through the hot sun, carrying it home in a tin can. Now Rockefeller's wagon will deliver it at the back door, in the city or on the farm, at a little over half that sum.

Who has a right to begrudge Rockefeller his millions when he has reduced the price of a needed commodity? He could just as easily have increased the price of lamp oil to half a dollar, but I seriously doubt that he would be a multimillionaire today if he had done so.

There are a lot of us who want money, but ninety-nine out of every hundred who start to create a plan through which to get money give all their thought to the scheme through which to get it and no thought to the service to be given in return for it.

———

A MAN WITHOUT A SMILING FACE

MUST NOT OPEN A SHOP.

—Chinese proverb

———

COMMENTARY

> In Time magazine's 100 Most Important People of the Twentieth Century, an article by Grace Mirabella, former Vogue editor-in-chief and the founder of Mirabella magazine, quotes Leonard Lauder, chief executive of the Estée Lauder cosmetics company, as saying his mother always thought she "was growing a nice little business."
>
> Lauder, while living above her father's hardware store in a section of Queens, NY, began selling creams created by her uncle who was a chemist. Long before getting her products into major stores, she was selling them in beauty shops, beach clubs, and resorts. In the beginning, the only person available to answer the phones "changed her voice to become the shipping or billing department as needed." Later Estée Lauder is said to have "stalked" the bosses at Saks Fifth Avenue until she got counter space, where her personal selling approach—including promotions and samples—was instrumental in her success.
>
> In addition to being extremely focused, and a quality fanatic, Estée Lauder "outworked everyone else in the cosmetics industry." Leonard Lauder attributes his mother's success to ambition. Former Neiman Marcus chief Stanley Marcus was obviously referring to Lauder's pleasing personality when he said, "She was determined and gracious and lovely through it all. It was easier to say yes to Estée than to say no."
>
> At the end of the century, that "nice little business" controlled 45 percent of the cosmetics market in U.S. department stores, had $3.6 billion in sales in 118 countries, and the Lauder family's shares were worth more than $6 billion.

A Pleasing Personality is one that makes use of Imagination and Cooperation. I have cited the foregoing illustrations, of how ideas may be created, to show you how to coordinate the laws of Imagination, Cooperation, and a Pleasing Personality.

Analyze any person who does not have a Pleasing Personality and you will also find lacking in that person the faculties of Imagination and Cooperation.

THE PERSUASIVE PERSONALITY

This brings us to a suitable place at which to introduce one of the greatest lessons on personality ever placed on paper. It is also one of the most effective lessons on salesmanship ever written, for the subjects of a Pleasing Personality and salesmanship must always go hand in hand; they are inseparable.

I am referring to Shakespeare's masterpiece, Marc Antony's speech at the funeral of Caesar. I present it here with my bracketed interpretations, which may help you to gather a new meaning from it.

The setting for that oration was something like this: Caesar is dead, and Brutus, his slayer, is called on to tell the Roman mob, which has gathered at the undertaker's, why he put Caesar out of the way. Imagine a howling mob that was none too friendly to Caesar, and which already believed that Brutus had done a noble deed by murdering him.

Brutus takes the platform and makes a short statement of his reasons for killing Caesar. Confident that he has won the day, he takes his seat. His whole demeanor is that of one who believes his word will be accepted without question; it is one of haughtiness.

Marc Antony now takes the platform, knowing that the mob is antagonistic to him because he was a friend of Caesar's. In a low, humble tone of voice Antony begins to speak:

Antony: For Brutus' sake, I am beholding to you.

Fourth Citizen: What does he say of Brutus?

Third Citizen: He says, for Brutus' sake, he finds himself beholding to us all.

Fourth Citizen: 'Twere best he speak no harm of Brutus here.

First Citizen: This Caesar was a tyrant.

Third Citizen: Nay, that's certain; we are blest that Rome is rid of him.

Second Citizen: Peace! Let us hear what Antony can say.

[Here you will observe, in Antony's opening sentence, his clever method of "neutralizing" the minds of his listeners.]

Antony: You gentle Romans—

All: Peace, ho! Let us hear him.

[Had Antony begun his speech by "knocking" Brutus, the history of Rome would have been different . . .]

Antony: Friends, Romans, Countrymen, lend me your ears; I come
to bury Caesar, not to praise him.

[Allying himself with what he knew to be his listeners' state of mind.]

The evil that men do lives after them;
The good is oft interred with their bones;
So let it be with Caesar. The noble Brutus
Hath told you Caesar was ambitious;
If it were so, it was a grievous fault;
And grievously hath Caesar answered it.
Here, under leave of Brutus and the rest—
For Brutus is an honorable man;
So are they all, all honorable men—
Come I to speak at Caesar's funeral.
He was my friend—faithful, and just to me;
But Brutus says he was ambitious;
And Brutus is an honorable man;
He hath brought many captives home to Rome,
Whose ransoms did the general coffers fill;
Did this in Caesar seem ambitious?
When the poor have cried, Caesar hath wept;
Ambition should be made of sterner stuff;
Yet Brutus says he was ambitious;
And Brutus is an honorable man.
You all did see that on the Lupercal

THE OBJECT OF ORATORY

IS NOT TRUTH,

BUT PERSUASION.

—Lord Macaulay

I thrice presented him a kingly crown,

Which he did thrice refuse. Was this ambition?

Yet Brutus says he was ambitious;

And, surely, he is an honorable man.

I speak not to disprove what Brutus spoke,

But here I am to speak what I do know.

You all did love him once, not without cause;

What cause withholds you then to mourn for him?

O judgment! thou art fled to brutish beasts,

And men have lost their reason. Bear with me,

My heart is in the coffin there with Caesar,

And I must pause till it come back to me.

[At this point Antony paused to give his audience a chance to discuss hurriedly, among themselves, his opening statements. His object in doing this was to observe what effect his words were having, just as a master salesperson always encourages their prospective purchaser to talk, so the salesperson may know what is in their mind.]

First Citizen: Methinks there is much in his saying.

Second Citizen: If thou consider rightly of the matter, Caesar has had great wrong.

Third Citizen: Has he, masters? I fear there will be worse come in his place.

Fourth Citizen: Mark'd ye his words? He would not take the crown? Therefore 'tis certain he was not ambitious.

First Citizen: If it be found so, someone will dear abide it.

Second Citizen: Poor soul! his eyes are red as fire with weeping.

Third Citizen: There's not a nobler man in Rome than Antony.

Fourth Citizen: Now mark him, he begins again to speak.

Antony: But yesterday the word of Caesar might

Have stood against the world; now lies he there,

THE PEOPLE ONLY UNDERSTAND

WHAT THEY CAN FEEL;

THE ONLY ORATORS THAT CAN

AFFECT THEM ARE

THOSE WHO MOVE THEM.

—Alphonse De Lamartine

And none so poor to do him reverence.
O masters [appealing to their vanity], if I were disposed to stir
Your hearts and minds to mutiny and rage,
I should do Brutus wrong and Cassius wrong,
Who, you all know, are honorable men.

[Observe how often Antony has repeated the term *honorable*. Observe also how cleverly he brings in the first suggestion that perhaps Brutus and Cassius may not be as honorable as the Roman mob believes them to be. This suggestion is carried in the words *mutiny* and *rage*, which he uses for the first time here, after his pause gave him time to observe that the mob was swinging over toward his side of the argument. Observe how carefully he is "feeling" his way and making his words fit what he knows to be the frame of mind of his listeners.]

Antony: I will not do them wrong; I rather choose
To wrong the dead, to wrong myself and you,
Than I will wrong such honorable men.

[Crystallizing his suggestion into hatred of Brutus and Cassius, he then appeals to their curiosity and begins to lay the foundation for his climax—a climax he knows will win the mob because he is reaching it so cleverly that the mob believes it to be its own conclusion.]

But here's a parchment, with the seal of Caesar;
I found it in his closet; 'tis his will;
Let but the commons hear this testament,
Which, pardon me, I do not mean to read—

[Tightening up on his appeal to their curiosity by making them believe he does not intend to read the will.]

And they would go and kiss dead Caesar's wounds
And dip their napkins in his sacred blood,
Yea, beg a hair of him for memory,
And, dying, mention it within their wills,
Bequeathing it as a rich legacy
Unto their issue.

[Human nature *always* wants that which is difficult to get, or that of which it is about to be deprived. Observe how craftily Antony has awakened the interest of the mob and made them want to hear the reading of the will, thereby preparing them to hear it with open minds. This marks his second step in the process of "neutralizing" their minds.]

All: The will, the will! We will hear Caesar's will.

Antony: Have patience, gentle friends, I must not read it;
    It is not meet you know how Caesar loved you.
    You are not wood, you are not stones, but men;
    And, being men, hearing the will of Caesar,
    It will inflame you;

[Exactly what he wishes to do.]

    It will make you mad;
    'Tis good you know not that you are his heirs,
    For if you should, O what will come of it!

Fourth Citizen: Read the will; we'll hear it, Antony;
    You shall read us the will; Caesar's will.

Antony: Will you be patient? Will you stay awhile?
    I have o'ershot myself to tell you of it;
    I fear I wrong the honorable men
    Whose daggers have stabb'd Caesar, I do fear it.

["Daggers" and "stabb'd" suggest cruel murder. Observe how cleverly Antony injects this suggestion into his speech, and observe, also, how quickly the mob catches its significance, because, unknown to the mob, Antony has carefully prepared their minds to receive this suggestion.]

Fourth Citizen: They were traitors, honorable men!

All: The will! The testament!

Second Citizen: They were villains, murderers; the will!

[Just what Antony would have said in the beginning, but he knew it would have a more desirable effect if he planted the thought in the minds of the mob and permitted them to say it themselves.]

Antony: You will compel me then to read the will?
Then make a ring about the corpse of Caesar,
And let me show you him that made the will.
Shall I descend, and will you give me leave?

[This was the point at which Brutus should have begun to look for a back door through which to make his escape.]

All: Come down.

Second Citizen: Descend.

Third Citizen: Room for Antony, most noble Antony.

Antony: Nay, press not so upon me, stand far off.

[He knew this command would make them want to draw nearer, which is what he wanted them to do.]

All: Stand back. Room.

Antony: If you have tears, prepare to shed them now.
You all do know this mantle; I remember
The first time ever Caesar put it on;
'Twas on a summer's evening, in his tent,
That day he overcame the Nervii;
Look, in this place ran Cassius' dagger through;
See what a rent the envious Casca made;
Through this the well-beloved Brutus stabb'd;
And as he plucked his cursed steel away,
Mark how the blood of Caesar followed it,
As rushing out of doors, to be resolved
If Brutus so unkindly knock'd or no;
For Brutus, as you know, was Caesar's angel;
Judge, O you gods, how dearly Caesar loved him!

IT USUALLY TAKES MORE THAN

THREE WEEKS TO PREPARE

A GOOD IMPROMPTU SPEECH.

—Mark Twain

This was the most unkindest cut of all;
For, when the noble Caesar saw him stab,
Ingratitude, more strong than traitor's arms,
Quite vanquish'd him; then burst his mighty heart;
And, in his mantle muffling up his face,
Even at the base of Pompey's statua,
Which all the while ran blood, great Caesar fell.
O, what a fall was there, my countrymen!
Then I, and you, and all of us fell down
While bloody treason flourish'd over us.
O, now you weep, and I perceive you feel
The dint of pity; these are gracious drops.
Kind soul, why weep you when you but behold
Our Caesar's vesture wounded? Look you here;
Here is himself, marr'd, as you see, with traitors.

[Observe how Marc Antony now uses the word *traitors* quite freely, because he knows that it is in harmony with what is in the minds of the Roman mob.]

First Citizen: O piteous spectacle!

Second Citizen: O woeful day!

Third Citizen: O woeful day!

First Citizen: O most bloody sight!

Second Citizen: We will be revenged.

[Had Brutus been a wise man instead of a braggart, he would have been many miles from the scene by this time.]

All: Revenge! About! Seek! Burn! Fire! Kill! Slay! Let not a traitor live!

[Here Antony takes the next step toward crystallizing the frenzy of the mob into action; but, clever salesman that he is, does not try to force this action.]

THERE ARE TWO LEVERS

FOR MOVING MEN:

INTEREST AND FEAR.

—Napoleon Bonaparte

Antony: Stay, countrymen.

First Citizen: Peace there! Hear the noble Antony.

Second Citizen: We'll hear him, we'll follow him, we'll die with him.

[From these words, Antony knows that he has the mob with him. Observe how he takes advantage of this psychological moment—the moment for which all master salespeople wait.]

Antony: Good friends, sweet friends, let me not stir you up to such a
    sudden flood of mutiny.
  They that have done this deed are honorable.
  What private griefs they have, alas, I know not,
  That made them do it; they were wise and honorable,
  And will, no doubt, with reasons answer you.
  I come not, friends, to steal away your hearts:
  I am no orator as Brutus is;
  But, as you know me all, a plain, blunt man,
  That love my friend; and that they know full well
  That gave me public leave to speak of him;
  For I have neither wit, nor words, nor worth,
  Action, nor utterance, nor the power of speech,
  To stir men's blood; I only speak right on;
  I tell you that which you yourselves do know;
  Show you sweet Caesar's wounds, poor, poor, dumb mouths.
  And bid them speak for me; but were I Brutus,
  And Brutus Antony, there an Antony
  Would ruffle up your spirits, and put a tongue
  In every wound of Caesar that should move
  The stones of Rome to rise and mutiny.

All: We'll mutiny.

First Citizen: We'll burn the house of Brutus.

Third Citizen: Away, then! Come, seek the conspirators.

Antony: Yet hear me, countrymen; yet hear me speak!

All: Peace, ho! Hear Antony. Most noble Antony!

Antony: Why, friends, you go to do you know not what;
    Wherein hath Caesar thus deserved your love?
    Alas, you know not; I must tell you, then;
    You have forgot the will I told you of.

[Antony is now ready to play his trump card; he is ready to reach his climax. Observe how well he has marshaled his suggestions, step by step, saving until the last his most important statement, the one on which he relied for action. In the field of salesmanship and in public speaking many try to reach this point too soon, try to "rush" the audience or the prospective purchaser, and thereby lose their appeal.]

All: Most true; the will! Let's stay and hear the will.

Antony: Here is the will, and under Caesar's seal.
    To every Roman citizen he gives,
    To every several man, seventy-five drachmas.

Second Citizen: Most noble Caesar! We'll revenge his death.

Third Citizen: O royal Caesar!

Antony: Hear me with patience.

All: Peace, ho!

Antony: Moreover, he hath left you all his walks,
    His private arbors and new planted orchards,
    On this side Tiber; he hath left them you,
    And to your heirs forever; common pleasures,
    To walk abroad and recreate yourself.
    Here was a Caesar! When comes such another?

First Citizen: Never, never. Come, away, away!
    We'll burn his body in the holy place,
    And with the brands fire the traitors' houses.
    Take up the body.

Second Citizen: Go fetch fire.
Third Citizen: Pluck down benches.
Fourth Citizen: Pluck down forms, windows, anything.

And that was Brutus's finish. He lost his case because he lacked the *personality* and the good judgment with which to present his argument from the viewpoint of the Roman mob, as Marc Antony did. His whole attitude clearly indicated that he thought pretty well of himself, that he was proud of his deed. We have all seen people who somewhat resemble Brutus in this respect, but if we observe closely, we notice that they do not accomplish very much.

Suppose that Marc Antony had mounted the platform in a strutting attitude, and had begun his speech in this way: "Now let *me* tell you Romans something about this man Brutus. He is a murderer at heart and—" he would have gone no further, for the mob would have howled him down.

Go back to Lesson Five, on Initiative and Leadership, and read it again, and as you read, compare the psychology of it with that of Marc Antony's speech. Observe how the "you" and not the "I" attitude toward others is emphasized. This same point is emphasized throughout this course, especially in Lesson Seven on Enthusiasm. Shakespeare was, by far, the most able psychologist and writer known to civilization; for that reason, all of his writings are based upon unerring knowledge of the human mind. Throughout this speech which he placed in the mouth of Marc Antony, notice how carefully he assumed the "you" attitude—so carefully that the Roman mob was sure that its decision was of its own making.

Notice, however, that Marc Antony's appeal to the self-interest of the Roman mob was of the crafty type, and was based on the stealth with which dishonest men often make use of this principle in appealing to the excessive desire and greed of their victims. While Marc Antony displayed evidence of great Self-Control in being able to assume, at the beginning of his speech, an attitude toward Brutus that was not real, at the same time it is obvious that Antony's entire appeal was based on his knowledge of how to influence the minds of the Roman mob, through flattery.

The two letters which are reproduced in Lesson Seven *[pages 457 and 459]* illustrate, in a very concrete way, the value of the "you" and the fatality of the "I" appeal. Go back and read these letters again, and observe how the more successful of the two follows closely the Marc Antony appeal, while the other is based on an appeal of just the opposite nature. Whether you are writing a sales letter or preaching a sermon or writing an advertisement or a book, you will do well to follow the same principles employed by Marc Antony in his famous speech.

CHARACTER COUNTS

To study the ways and means through which one may develop a Pleasing Personality, I will begin with the first essential, which is *character*, for no one can have a Pleasing Personality without also having the foundation of a sound, positive character. Through the principle of telepathy you "telegraph" the nature of your character to those with whom you come in contact, which is also why you may have had an "intuitive" feeling that the person you had just met, but about whom you did not know very much, was not trustworthy.

You may wear the best and latest clothes, and conduct yourself in a most pleasing manner outwardly, but if there is greed and envy and hatred and jealousy and selfishness in your heart, you will never attract anyone except those who are the same. Like attracts like, and you may be sure, therefore, that those who are attracted to you are those whose inward natures parallel your own.

You may present an artificial smile and you may practice handshaking so that you can imitate, perfectly, the handshake of a person who is adept at this art, but if these outward manifestations of a

Pleasing Personality lack that vital factor called *earnestness of purpose*, they will turn people away rather than attract them to you.

How, then, does one build character? The first step in character building is rigid self-discipline.

In both the second and eighth lessons of this course, you will find the formula through which you may shape your character after any pattern that you choose. But I repeat it here, as it is based on a principle that deserves much repetition.

First, think of those people whose characters are made up of the qualities you wish to build into your own character, and then proceed, in the manner described in Lesson Two, to take on these qualities, through the aid of *autosuggestion*. Create in your Imagination a council table, and gather your characters around it each night, first having written out a clear, concise statement of the particular qualities you wish to assume from each. Then proceed to affirm or suggest to yourself, aloud, that you are developing those desired qualities. As you do this, close your eyes and see, in your Imagination, the figures seated around your imaginary table, in that same manner described in Lesson Two.

Second, through the principles described in Lesson Eight, Self-Control, focus your thoughts and keep your mind energized with thoughts of a positive nature. Let the dominating thought of your mind be a picture of the person that you intend to be: the person that you are deliberately building, through this process. At least a dozen times a day, when you have a few minutes to yourself, shut your eyes and direct your thoughts to the figures you have selected to sit at your imaginary council table. Then feel—with a faith that knows no limitation—that you are actually growing to resemble in character those figures of your choice.

Third, find at least one person each day, and more if possible, in whom you see some good quality that is worthy of praise—and praise them for it. Remember, however, that this praise must not be

ASSUME A VIRTUE,

IF YOU HAVE IT NOT.

—William Shakespeare

in the nature of cheap, insincere flattery; it must be genuine. Speak your words of praise with such earnestness that they will impress those to whom you speak.

Then watch what happens. You will have rendered those whom you praise a decided benefit of great value to them, and you will have gone just one more step in the direction of developing the habit of looking for and finding the good qualities in others.

I cannot overemphasize the far-reaching effects of this habit of praising, openly and enthusiastically, the good qualities in others, for this habit will soon reward you with a feeling of self-respect and manifestation of gratitude from others that will modify your entire personality. Here, again, the law of attraction enters, and those whom you praise will see, in you, the qualities that you see in them. Your success in the application of this formula will be in exact proportion to your *faith* in its soundness.

I do not merely believe that it is sound—I *know* that it is—and the reason I know is that I have used it successfully and I have also taught others how to use it successfully. Therefore I have a right to promise you that you can use it with equal success.

Furthermore, you can, with the aid of this formula, develop a Pleasing Personality so quickly that you will surprise all who know you. The development of such a personality is entirely within your own control, which gives you a tremendous advantage and at the same time places the responsibility on *you* if you fail or neglect to exercise your privilege.

I would like to point out the reason for speaking, aloud, the affirmation that you are developing the qualities you have selected as the materials out of which to develop a Pleasing Personality. This procedure has two desirable effects.

First, speaking it aloud sets into motion the vibration through which the thought behind your words reaches and embeds itself in your

SPEECH IS POWER:

SPEECH IS TO PERSUADE,

TO CONVERT,

TO COMPEL.

—Ralph Waldo Emerson

subconscious mind. There it takes root and grows until it becomes a great moving force in your outward, physical activities, leading to the transformation of the thought into reality.

Second, it helps you develop the ability to speak with force and conviction, which can lead to great ability as a public speaker. No matter what your calling in life may be, you should be able to stand on your feet and speak convincingly.

Put feeling and emotion into your words as you speak, and develop a deep, rich tone of voice. If your voice is inclined to be high-pitched, tone it down until it is soft and pleasing. You can never express an attractive personality, to best advantage, through a harsh or shrill voice. You must cultivate your voice until it becomes rhythmical and pleasing to the ear.

Remember that speech is the chief method of expressing your personality, and for this reason it is to your advantage to cultivate a style that is both forceful and pleasing.

I do not recall a single outstanding Pleasing Personality that was not made up, in part, of an ability to speak with force and conviction. Study the outstanding figures of the past in politics and statesmanship and observe that the most successful ones were those who were noted for their ability to speak with force and conviction. Study the prominent men and women of today, wherever you find them, and observe the significant fact that the more prominent they are, the more efficient they are in speaking forcefully.

In the field of business, industry, and finance it seems significant also that the most prominent leaders are men and women who are able public speakers. In fact no one may hope to become a prominent leader in any noteworthy undertaking without developing the ability to speak with a forcefulness that carries conviction. While the salesperson may never deliver a public address, they will profit, nevertheless, if they develop the ability to do so, because this ability increases his or her power to speak convincingly in ordinary conversation.

COMMENTARY

To hear how your voice sounds to others, record yourself in conversation. You will likely be surprised by how different it sounds when you hear the recording played back. If you don't like what you hear, and if you can be objective, study the tape to see where you could make improvements. Note the tone, the pitch, and the rhythm of your speech patterns. If you continue to work with the tape recorder and are still not pleased with the changes you can effect on your own, you might consider buying one of the audio programs available, or perhaps consulting a voice coach.

As important as the sound of your voice, if not more important, are the words you use, and this is another way by which people will judge you. Unless you are certain of the exact meaning of a word, don't use it. Opt instead for one that is more familiar to you. There are many books that point out some of the common mistakes people make in an attempt to sound more knowledgeable, and these books can be invaluable. One of the best-known is The Elements of Style *by William Strunk Jr. and E. B. White, which offers information for both the spoken and written word.*

There are also audio courses that not only teach new vocabulary but also allow you to hear the words used in context while at the same time hearing the correct pronunciation. You will find many of these audio programs in the audio-book section of most large bookstores.

Let us now summarize the seven chief factors which enter into the development of a Pleasing Personality:

1. Form the habit of interesting yourself in other people, and make it your business to find their good qualities and speak of them in terms of praise.

2. Develop the ability to speak with force and conviction, both in your ordinary conversational tones and before public gatherings, where you must use more volume.

3. Dress in a style that is becoming to you and appropriate to the work in which you are engaged.

4. Develop a positive character, through the aid of the methods outlined in this lesson.

5. Learn how to shake hands so that you will express warmth
   and Enthusiasm through this form of greeting.

6. Attract other people to you by first "attracting yourself" to them.

7. Remember that your only limitation, within reason, is the one that
   you set up in your own mind.

These seven points cover the most important factors, although
such a personality will obviously not develop of its own accord. It
will develop, however, if you submit yourself to the discipline herein
described, with a firm determination to transform yourself into
the person that you would like to be.

I stress the second and the fourth as being the most important.
If you will cultivate those finer thoughts, feelings, and actions out of
which a positive character is built, and then learn to express yourself
with force and conviction, you will have developed a Pleasing Personality, for you will see that out of this will come the other qualities here
outlined.

There is a great power of attraction in the person who has a
positive character, and this power expresses itself in unseen as well
as visible ways. The moment you come within speaking distance of
such a person, even though not a word is spoken, the influence of the
"unseen power within" makes itself felt.

Every "shady" transaction in which you engage, every negative
thought that you think, and every destructive act destroys something
within your character.

Emerson wrote: "There is full confession in the glances of our
eyes; in our smiles; in salutations; in the grasp of the hands. His
sin bedaubs him, mars all his good impression. Men know not why
they do not trust him, but they do not trust him. His vice glasses
his eye, demeans his cheek, pinches the nose, sets the mark of beast

TO CULTIVATE KINDNESS

IS A VALUABLE PART OF

THE BUSINESS OF LIFE.

—Samuel Johnson

on the back of the head, and writes, 'O fool! fool!' on the forehead of a king."

Pay close attention to the first of the seven factors in developing a Pleasing Personality. All through this lesson I have gone into lengthy detail to show the material advantages of being agreeable to others. The biggest advantage of all, however, lies not in the possibility of monetary or material gain, but in the enhancing effect that it has on the character of all who practice it.

Acquire the habit of making yourself agreeable and you profit both materially and emotionally, for you will never be as happy in any other way as you will be when you know that you are making others happy.

Get the chip off your shoulder and stop challenging people to engage you in useless arguments. Remove the dark glasses through which you see what you believe to be the negative side of life, and behold the shining sunlight of friendliness instead. Throw away your hammer and quit knocking, for surely you must know that the big prizes of life go to the builders and not to the destroyers.

The man who builds a house is an artist; the man who tears it down is a junkman. If you are a person with a grievance, the world will listen to your caustic rantings only if it does not see you coming. But if you are a person with a message of friendliness and optimism, it will listen because it wishes to do so.

No person with a grievance can also be a person with an attractive personality. The art of being agreeable—just that one simple trait—is the very foundation of all successful salesmanship.

I drive my automobile five miles to the outskirts of the city to purchase gasoline, which I could get within two blocks of my own garage, because the man who runs the filling station is an artist; he makes it his business to be agreeable. I go there not because he has cheaper gasoline, but because I enjoy the vitalizing effect of his Pleasing Personality.

I purchase my shoes at the Regal Shoe Store at Fiftieth Street and Broadway in New York, not because I cannot find other good shoes at the same price, but because Mr. Cobb, the manager of that particular Regal store, has a Pleasing Personality. While he is fitting me with shoes, he makes it his business to talk with me about subjects that he knows to be close to my heart.

I do my banking at the Harriman National Bank at Forty-fourth Street and Fifth Avenue, not because there are not scores of other good banks much nearer my place of business, but because the tellers, the cashiers, the lobby detective, Mr. Harriman, and all the others with whom I come in contact make it their business to be agreeable. My account is small but they receive me as though it were large.

I greatly admire John D. Rockefeller Jr., not because he is the son of one of the world's richest men, but because he, too, has acquired the art of being agreeable.

In the little city of Lancaster, Pennsylvania, lives M. T. Garvin, a very successful merchant whom I would travel hundreds of miles to visit because he makes it his business to be agreeable. I have no doubt that his material success is closely related to this noble art that he has acquired.

I have in my vest pocket a Parker fountain pen, and my wife and children have pens of the same brand, not because there are not other good fountain pens, but because I admire George S. Parker for his habit of being agreeable.

My wife subscribes to the *Ladies' Home Journal* not because there are not other good magazines of a similar nature, but because we became attracted to the *Journal* several years ago while Edward Bok was its editor, and he, too, had acquired the art of being agreeable.

O ye struggling pilgrims who are searching for the rainbow's end, ye drawers of water and hewers of wood, tarry for a moment by the wayside—and learn a lesson from the successful men and women who have succeeded because they acquired the art of being agreeable!

You can win, for a time, through ruthlessness and stealth; you can acquire more worldly goods than you will need, by sheer force and shrewd strategy, without taking the time or going to the trouble of being agreeable. But sooner or later you will come to that point in life when you will feel the pangs of remorse and the emptiness of your well-filled purse.

I never think of power and position and wealth that was attained by force, without feeling, very deeply, the sentiment expressed by a man whose name I dare not mention, as he stood at the tomb of Napoleon Bonaparte:

COMMENTARY

The editors have learned that the following was by Robert Green Ingersoll, who in the late 1800s was America's best-known orator, particularly on behalf of Republican causes and candidates. Ingersoll was also friends with and admired by Napoleon Hill's mentor, Andrew Carnegie.

A little while ago I stood by the grave of the old Napoleon—a magnificent tomb of gilt and gold, fit almost for a deity dead—and gazed upon the sarcophagus of rare and nameless marble, where rest at last the ashes of that restless man. I leaned over the balustrade and thought about the career of the greatest soldier of the modern world.

I saw him at Toulon. I saw him walking upon the banks of the Seine contemplating suicide. I saw him putting down the mob in the streets of Paris. I saw him at the head of the army in Italy. I saw him crossing the bridge at Lodi with the tri-color in his hand. I saw him in Egypt, in the shadows of the pyramids. I saw him conquer the Alps and mingle the eagles of France with the eagles of the crags. I saw him at Marengo, at Ulm, and at Austerlitz. I saw him in Russia, when the infantry of the snow and the cavalry of the wild

TRY NOT TO BECOME

A MAN OF SUCCESS,

BUT RATHER TO BECOME

A MAN OF VALUE.

—Albert Einstein

blast scattered his legions like winter's withered leaves. I saw him at Leipsic in defeat and disaster—driven by a million bayonets back upon Paris—clutched like a wild beast—banished to Elba. I saw him escape and re-take an empire by the force of his genius. I saw him upon the frightful field of Waterloo, where chance and fate combined to wreck the fortunes of their former king. And I saw him at St. Helena, with his hands crossed behind him, gazing out upon the sad and solemn sea.

I thought of the widows and orphans he had made, of the tears that had been shed for his glory, and of the only woman who ever loved him, pushed from his heart by the cold hand of ambition. And I said I would rather have been a French peasant and worn wooden shoes; I would rather have lived in a hut with a vine growing over the door, and the grapes growing purple in the amorous kisses of the autumn sun; I would rather have been that poor peasant, with my wife by my side knitting as the day died out of the sky, with my children upon my knees and their arms about me; I would rather have been this man and gone down to the tongueless silence of the dreamless dust than to have been that imperial personation of force and murder, known as Napoleon the Great.

I leave with you, as a fitting climax for this lesson, the thought of this deathless dissertation on a man who lived by the sword of force and died an ignominious death, an outcast in the eyes of his fellow men; a sore to the memory of civilization; a failure because—he did not acquire the art of being agreeable! He could not or would not subordinate "self" for the good of his followers.

—— Lesson Eleven ——

Accurate Thinking

BE A COLUMBUS TO

WHOLE NEW CONTINENTS

AND WORLDS WITHIN YOU,

OPENING NEW CHANNELS,

NOT OF TRADE,

BUT OF THOUGHT.

—Henry David Thoreau

Lesson Eleven

ACCURATE THINKING

"You Can Do It if You Believe You Can!"

THIS IS THE MOST IMPORTANT, THE MOST interesting, and the most difficult-to-present lesson of this entire course on the Law of Success.

It is important because it deals with a principle that runs through the entire course. It is interesting for the same reason. It is difficult to present because it will carry the average student far beyond the boundary line of his or her common experiences and into a realm of thought in which they are unaccustomed to being.

Unless you study this lesson with an open mind, you will miss the very keystone to the arch of this course, and without this stone you can never complete your temple of success.

This lesson will bring you a concept of thought that may carry you far beyond the level you have reached through your previous evolutionary processes, and, for this reason, you should not be disappointed if, at first reading, you do not fully understand it. Most of us disbelieve that which we cannot understand, and it is with my knowledge of this human tendency that I caution you against closing your mind if you do not at first grasp everything that is in this lesson.

For thousands of years men made ships of wood, and of nothing else. They used wood because they believed it was the only substance that would float. But that was because they had not yet advanced far enough in their thinking process to understand the truth that steel will float and that it is far superior to wood for the building of ships. They did not know that anything could float that was lighter than the amount of water it displaced, and until they learned of this great truth they went on making ships of wood.

Until early in this century, most people thought only birds could fly. Now we know that humans can not only equal the flying of the birds but we can exceed it. We did not know, until quite recently, that the air is more alive and more sensitive than anything on the earth. We did not know that the spoken word would travel with the speed of lightning, without the aid of wires. How could we know this when our minds had not been sufficiently unfolded to enable them to grasp it?

The purpose of this lesson is to aid *you* in unfolding and expanding your mind so that you will be able to think with accuracy. This will open to you a door that leads to all the power you will need in completing your temple of success.

All through the preceding lessons we have dealt with principles that anyone could easily grasp and apply, and they have been presented so as to lead to success as measured by material wealth. I was aware the majority of students would be disappointed if I showed them a roadway to success that leads other than through the doorways of business, finance, and industry. To most people the word *success* and the word *money* are synonymous—they want success that is spelled *$ucce$$*.

Very well, let those who are satisfied with this standard of success have it. But there are some who will want to go higher up the ladder, in search of success that is measured other than in material standards, and it is for their benefit in particular that this and the subsequent lessons of this course are intended.

DEDUCTIVE REASONING

Accurate Thinking involves two fundamentals. First, in order for you to think accurately you must separate facts from mere information. There is much "information" available to you that is not based on facts. Second, you must separate facts into two classes: the important and the unimportant, or the relevant and the irrelevant.

All facts that you can use in the attainment of your Definite Chief Aim are important and relevant; all that you cannot use are unimportant and irrelevant. It is mainly the neglect of some to make this distinction that so widely separates those people who appear to have equal *ability* and those who have had equal *opportunity*. Within your own circle of acquaintances you can likely point to one or more who have had no greater opportunity than you, and who have no more ability than you, but who are achieving far greater success.

And you wonder why. The answer is that they have acquired the habit of combining and using the important facts that affect their line of work. Far from working harder than you, they are perhaps working less and with greater ease. By separating the important facts from the unimportant, they have provided themselves with a sort of fulcrum and lever with which they can move, with their little fingers, loads that you cannot budge with the entire weight of your body.

So that you may understand the importance of distinguishing between facts and mere information, study the type of person who is guided entirely by what they hear—the type who is influenced by gossip; who accepts, without analysis, all that they read or hear in

---

SCIENCE IS ORGANIZED KNOWLEDGE.

WISDOM IS ORGANIZED LIFE.

—Immanuel Kant

---

the news, and who judges others by what their enemies, competitors, and contemporaries say about them.

From among your circle of acquaintances, pick out one of this type as an example to keep in mind while we are on this subject. Observe that this person usually begins conversations with phrases such as "I see by the papers . . ." or "they say . . ." The accurate thinker knows that the newspapers are not always accurate in their reports, and that what "they say" usually carries more falsehood than truth.

In searching for facts it is often necessary to gather them through the knowledge and experience of others. It then becomes necessary to carefully examine both the evidence submitted and the person from whom the evidence comes. When the evidence is such that it affects the interest of the witness who is giving it, scrutinize it all the more carefully. Witnesses who have an interest in the evidence often yield to the temptation to color and misuse it to protect that interest.

If one person slanders another, those remarks should be accepted with some caution, for it is a common human tendency for people to find nothing but evil in those they do not like. Anyone who has reached the degree of Accurate Thinking that enables them to speak of their enemy without exaggerating that person's faults and minimizing their virtues is the exception and not the rule.

Before you can become an accurate thinker, you must understand and make allowance for the fact that the moment a man or a woman begins to assume Leadership in any walk of life, the slanderers begin to circulate rumors and innuendos reflecting on his or her character.

No matter how fine one's character, or what service that person may be rendering to the world, no one can escape the notice of those misguided people who delight in destroying instead of building.

The moment anyone begins to make themself felt in the field of industry or business, this chorus becomes active. If one makes a better mousetrap than their neighbor, the world will beat a path to their door, and in the gang that will trail along will be those who come not to commend but to condemn and to destroy that person's reputation.

As an accurate thinker, it is both your privilege and your duty to avail yourself of facts, even though you must go out of your way to get them. If you permit yourself to be swayed by all manner of information that comes to your attention, you will never become an accurate thinker. And if you do not think accurately, you cannot be sure of attaining your Definite Chief Aim in life.

Many have gone down to defeat because, due to their prejudice and hatred, they underestimated the virtues of their enemies or competitors. The eyes of the accurate thinker see *facts*—not the delusions of prejudice, hate, and envy.

As an accurate thinker you must be fair enough, with yourself at least, to look for virtues as well as faults in other people.

"I do not believe that I can afford to deceive others. I *know* that I cannot afford to deceive myself." This must be the motto of the accurate thinker.

COMMENTARY

To the modern reader it may seem that in the first pages of this section Napoleon Hill belabors unnecessarily his point about needing factual information upon which to base opinions and make decisions. Surely that is self-evident to anyone seeking advice on how to achieve success. Understanding the context in which Hill wrote the advice will explain why he felt it was necessary to place so much emphasis on the point. Following that are some "facts" that will make it clear why his point is still just as valid today.

In 1927 most Americans got their information from newspapers. Every city of any size had a half-dozen or more dailies publishing morning editions, home editions, late editions, and hawking Extras on the street corners when there was breaking news. These were the days of the great newspaper wars, scandal sheets, yellow journalism, and political cronyism. It was a time when newspapers were often blatantly biased and publishers thought nothing of slanting stories to fit their personal prejudices and political agendas.

Though science and medicine had made tremendous advances in the first part of the century, it would still be a generation or two before that knowledge would become a part of the general education of the average American. Newspapers were still the main source of information about such things, and the back pages were filled with advertisements for pseudoscientific contraptions that promised to cure diseases by harnessing the power of magnetism or the miraculous effects of radio waves. Quack doctors touted patent medicines and pills that were often mostly opium or cocaine that dulled the senses but did little to cure anything. When viewed in that context, it is little wonder that Napoleon Hill felt it was important to caution his readers about the source of their information.

But what significance does his advice have for the modern reader? America has advanced since then through the information age, the communication age, and the Internet age. News is delivered to us as it happens from anywhere on earth, and even children have instant access to information data banks that stagger the imagination.

The world has indeed changed, but as the editors of this edition have often pointed out, the times may be different but the basic principles Hill writes about remain just that: basic principles. Though journalistic standards have improved tremendously, and it is rare to find an executive of a reputable news organization who blatantly manipulates the news, it would be a mistake to believe that what you hear, see, or read is fact. It only means that today bias is less obvious and we must be even more astute when searching for the facts necessary for accurate thinking.

By the end of the twentieth century, the term "spin doctor" came into common usage. It was used to describe political or government officials, or p.r. professionals whose job was to take the news and "spin" it in the way that served a particular purpose and advanced his or her political agenda. Another commonly heard term was "the liberal media," used often in reference to television news and the perception that there was a left-leaning bias among the major networks.

However, in radio broadcasting at that same time, the majority of talk shows featured highly opinionated hosts whose popularity was based on their controversial right-wing views. The two most popular cable-television news networks were evenly divided, with CNN usually identified as liberal and the Fox News Channel usually regarded as conservative.

MOST OF THE PEOPLE SAY THEY . . .

GET THEIR NEWS FROM TELEVISION.

THAT MEANS THEY'RE

INADEQUATELY INFORMED,

TOO POORLY INFORMED TO EXERCISE

THEIR RIGHTS IN A DEMOCRACY.

YOU CANNOT GIVE PEOPLE

ENOUGH INFORMATION

ON THE NIGHTLY NEWS.

—Walter Cronkite

Clearly, what you believe to be fact or truth today would still depend greatly on how and where you get your information. As to the enormous amount of facts and information made easily accessible to anyone now, in researching material for this section (in an Internet search) the editors found many "facts" about the discovery of penicillin.

One version of the facts said that in 1928 Scottish researcher Alexander Fleming went on vacation leaving a lab dish growing bacteria. During his absence it became contaminated with a penicillium mold spore. On his return he noticed that the mold had stopped the growth of the germs. This version also says that Fleming did nothing further to develop penicillin, but others did.

Another version is that Fleming was such a hardworking bacteriologist that he wouldn't even go out for lunch. One day, at a time when he was suffering from boils, he ate a forgotten sandwich that had turned green with mold. When it seemed that his boils had been cured, he proceeded to research the mold.

Still another version is that amidst the disorderly mess in Fleming's lab were several petri dishes in which he had (intentionally) been growing bacteria. As he was cleaning up and about to throw these out, he noticed in one that all around the mold the staph bacteria had been killed. He researched it further and the following year published a report on the potential uses of penicillin. His work was eventually taken over by a team of chemists and mold specialists, several of whom moved or died. Then in 1935 a professor and researchers at Oxford became interested, took the study further, and in 1945 Alexander Fleming, Howard Florey (professor), and Ernst Chain (researcher) shared the Nobel Prize for the discovery of penicillin.

It is stunning that there can be such inconsistency in the "facts" about something as significant as the discovery of penicillin. For an even more revealing picture of how widespread the belief is in some "well-known facts" that may not be facts at all, the editors suggest that you check out the many Web sites and books available on the subject of urban legends, as well as the book Why People Believe Weird Things *by Michael Shermer, who is also publisher of* Skeptic *magazine and director of the Skeptics Society. In doing so you may find challenges to some of your own beliefs that you've based on what you assume to be well-known facts.*

In the realm of legal procedure there is a principle called the law of *evidence*, and the object of this law is to get at the facts. Any judge can proceed with justice to all concerned if they have the *facts* upon which to base their judgment, but they may play havoc with innocent people if they circumvent the law of evidence and reach a conclusion or judgment that is based on hearsay information.

The specific rules of evidence vary according to the subject and circumstances with which they are used, but you will not go far wrong if you follow this rule: If you do not have hard facts to work from, form your judgment on the part of the evidence before you that furthers your own interests—*without working any hardship on others*—and is based on facts.

The phrase "without working any hardship on others" is a crucial and important point in this lesson. Many people mistake, knowingly or otherwise, expediency for fact—doing something, or refraining from doing it, for the sole reason that their action furthers their own interests—without consideration as to whether it interferes with the rights of others.

It is amazing, to the more advanced student of Accurate Thinking, how many people there are who are "honest" when it is profitable to them, but find innumerable "facts" to justify themselves in following a dishonest course when that course seems to be more profitable or advantageous.

The accurate thinker deals with facts, regardless of how they affect his or her own interests, for they know that ultimately this policy will bring them out on top, in full possession of the object of their Definite Chief Aim in life. They understand the soundness of the philosophy that Croesus had in mind when he said, "There is a wheel on which the affairs of men revolve, and its mechanism is such that it prevents *any* man from being *always* fortunate."

The accurate thinker adopts a standard by which they guide themself, and they follow that standard at all times. The standard is observed as faithfully when it brings temporary disadvantage as it is when it brings outstanding advantage. Using Accurate Thinking, they know that by the law of averages they will more than regain, at some future time, that which is lost when the result of applying this standard is to their own temporary detriment.

You must understand that it requires the staunchest and most unshakable *character* to become an accurate thinker, for there can be a certain amount of temporary penalty attached to Accurate Thinking. But the compensating reward is so overwhelmingly greater that you will gladly pay this penalty.

COMMENTARY

Napoleon Hill was able to refine his philosophy of personal achievement and write Law of Success *because Andrew Carnegie introduced him to the leaders of business and industry in such a way that they were prepared to share with him the secrets of their success. But he also wrote from his personal experience. As the following story demonstrates, at an early age Napoleon Hill proved that he himself was a person of unshakable character.*

As told by author Michael Ritt in A Lifetime of Riches, *in 1902 after Hill had been promoted to chief clerk at one of Rufus Ayers' coal mines, the manager of the mine and his brother, who was cashier of a bank owned by Ayers, had gone on a drinking spree. At one of their later stops at a hotel, the brother dropped a loaded revolver he was carrying and it discharged, killing a bellboy.*

Hill heard the news almost immediately and went to the hotel. He learned that the brother had left the bank the previous day and hadn't returned. Rushing to the bank, Hill found the vaults open and money scattered everywhere. He then wired the news to Ayers, who told him to count the money and charge Ayers' own account for any shortage. He counted it, found that no money was missing, and informed Ayers. Impressed by Hill's honesty, Ayers instantly promoted him to replace the manager—making this nineteen-year-old the youngest manager of a mine, and in charge of three hundred and fifty men.

TO MANY A MAN,

AND SOMETIMES TO A YOUTH,

THERE COMES THE OPPORTUNITY

TO CHOOSE BETWEEN HONORABLE

COMPETENCE AND TAINTED WEALTH.

THE YOUNG MAN WHO STARTS OUT

TO BE POOR AND HONORABLE,

HOLDS IN HIS HAND ONE OF THE

STRONGEST ELEMENTS OF SUCCESS.

—Orison Swett Marden

Hill's honesty received widespread publicity, which also served him well in his next ventures, but it's believed that he never spoke publicly of the moral dilemma he'd found himself in. He wrote of it in his memoirs only to point out the virtues of honesty. And while he likely wouldn't have known the term in 1902, it was also an excellent example of accurate thinking.

Assuming that the foregoing was sufficient to impress upon your mind the importance of searching for *facts* until you are reasonably sure you have found them, we will now look at organizing, classifying, and using those facts.

Consider again your own circle of acquaintances and find someone who appears to accomplish more with less effort than do any of their associates. Study this person and you observe that he or she is a strategist, in that they have learned how to arrange facts so as to bring to their aid the law of increasing returns, which was described in Lesson Nine.

The person who *knows* they are working with facts goes about their task with a feeling of Self-Confidence that enables them to refrain from procrastinating, hesitating, or waiting to make sure of their ground. They know in advance what the outcome of their efforts will be. Therefore, they move more rapidly and accomplish more than does the person who must "feel their way" because they are not sure they are working with facts.

The person who has learned of the advantages of searching for facts as the foundation of their thinking has gone a very long way toward the development of Accurate Thinking. But the person who has learned how to separate facts into the *important* and the *unimportant* has gone still further.

Inasmuch as this is an age in which money is looked upon as being the most concrete proof of success, let us look again at a man who has accumulated almost as much of it as has any other man in the history of the world—John D. Rockefeller.

WISDOM DENOTES THE PURSUING

OF THE BEST ENDS

BY THE BEST MEANS.

—Francis Hutcheson

Mr. Rockefeller has one quality that stands out, like a shining star, above all of his other qualities. It is his habit of dealing only with the relevant facts pertaining to his lifework. As a very young man (and a very poor young man, at that) Mr. Rockefeller adopted, as his Definite Chief Aim, the accumulation of great wealth. It is not my purpose, nor is it of any particular advantage, to look into Mr. Rockefeller's method of accumulating his fortune, other than to observe that his most pronounced quality was that of insisting on facts as the basis of his business philosophy.

There are some who say that John D. Rockefeller was not always fair with his competitors. That may or may not be true (as accurate thinkers we will leave the point undisturbed), but no one, not even his competitors, ever accused Mr. Rockefeller of forming snap judgments or of underestimating the strength of his competitors. He not only recognized facts that affected his business, wherever and whenever he found them, but he also made it his business to search for them until he was *sure* he had found them.

Thomas A. Edison is another example of a man who has attained to greatness through the organization, classification, and use of relevant facts. Mr. Edison works with natural laws as his chief aids, so he *must* be sure of his facts before he can harness those laws. Every time you switch on an electric light, remember that it was Mr. Edison's capacity for organizing relevant facts that made this possible.

In the field of science, relevant facts are the tools with which men and women work. Mere information, or hearsay evidence, is of no value to Mr. Edison. Yet he might have wasted his life working with it, as millions of other people are doing.

Hearsay evidence could never have produced the incandescent electric light, the phonograph, or the moving picture, and if it had, the phenomenon would have been "an accident." In this lesson we are trying to prepare the student to avoid "accidents."

The question now arises as to what constitutes an important and relevant fact.

The answer depends entirely on what constitutes your Definite Chief Aim in life, for an important and relevant fact is any fact that you can use, without interfering with the rights of others, in the attainment of that purpose.

All other facts, as far as you are concerned, are superfluous and of minor importance at most. You can, however, work just as hard in organizing, classifying, and using unimportant and irrelevant facts as you can in dealing with their opposites—but you will not accomplish as much.

CREATIVE THOUGHT
AND INFINITE INTELLIGENCE

Up to this point we have been discussing only one factor of Accurate Thinking—that which is based on deductive reasoning. Some of you may now have to think along lines that are not familiar to you, for we have come to the discussion of thought that does much more than gather, organize, and combine facts.

Let us call this *creative thought*. So that you can understand why it is called creative thought, it is necessary to briefly study the process of evolution through which the *thinking man* has been created.

Thinking man has been a long time on the road of evolution and has traveled a very long way. In the words of Judge T. Troward in *Bible Mystery and Bible Meaning,* "Perfected man is the apex of the Evolutionary Pyramid, and this by a necessary sequence."

Let us trace the five evolutionary steps through which we believe life has evolved, beginning with the very lowest:

1. *Mineral Period.* Here we find life in its lowest form, lying motionless and inert, a mass of mineral substances with no power to move.

2. *Vegetable Period.* Here life is in a more active form, with intelligence sufficient to gather food, grow, and reproduce, but still unable to move from its fixed moorings.

3. *Animal Period.* Here we find life in a still higher and more intelligent form, and with the ability to move from place to place.

4. *Human or Thinking Man Period.* Here we find life in its highest known form—the highest because man can *think,* and because thought is the highest known form of organized energy. In the realm of thought, man knows no limitations. He can gather facts and assemble them in new and varying combinations. He can also create hypotheses and translate them into physical reality through thought. He can reason both inductively and deductively.

5. *Spiritual.* On this plane the lower forms of life described in the previous four periods converge and become infinitude in nature. At this point thinking man has unfolded, expanded, and grown until he has projected his thinking ability into *infinite intelligence.* As yet, thinking man is but an infant in this fifth period, for he has not learned how to make use of this infinite intelligence called *spirit.* Moreover, with a few rare exceptions, man has not yet recognized thought as the connecting link that gives him access to the power of infinite intelligence. These exceptions have been such men as Moses, Solomon, Christ, Plato, Aristotle, Socrates, Confucius, and a comparatively small number of others. Since their time we have had many who partly uncovered this great truth, yet the truth itself is as available now as it was then.

To make use of creative thought, one must work largely on faith, which is the chief reason why more of us do not indulge in this sort of thought. The most ignorant of us can think in terms of deductive reasoning, in connection with issues of a purely physical and material nature, but to go a step higher and think in terms of infinite intelligence is another matter.

The average person is totally lost the moment they get beyond that which they can comprehend with the aid of their five physical senses of seeing, hearing, feeling, smelling, and tasting. Infinite intel-

OUR MIND IS CAPABLE OF

PASSING BEYOND THE DIVIDING LINE

WE HAVE DRAWN FOR IT.

BEYOND THE PAIRS OF OPPOSITES

OF WHICH THE WORLD CONSISTS,

OTHER, NEW INSIGHTS BEGIN.

—Hermann Hesse

ligence works through none of these agencies and we cannot invoke its aid through any of them.

The only way to use the power of infinite intelligence is through creative thought.

To make clear the exact manner in which this is done I will refer to some of the preceding lessons of this course through which you have been prepared to understand the meaning of creative thought.

In the second lesson, and to some extent in practically every subsequent lesson up to this one, you have observed the use of the term *autosuggestion*—suggestion that you make to yourself. We now come back to that term, because autosuggestion is the way in which you may register in your subconscious mind a description or plan of what you wish to create or acquire in physical form. It is a process you can easily learn to use.

The subconscious mind is the intermediary between the conscious *thinking* mind and infinite intelligence, and you can invoke the aid of infinite intelligence only through the medium of the subconscious mind, by giving it clear instructions as to what you want. Here you become familiar with the psychological reason for a Definite Chief Aim.

If you have not already seen the importance of creating a Definite Chief Aim as the object of your life's work, you will undoubtedly do so before this lesson has been mastered.

Knowing from my own experience how little I understood about such terms as *subconscious mind, autosuggestion,* and *creative thought,* throughout this course I have described these terms through every conceivable simile and illustration, with the object of making their meaning and the method of their application so clear that no student of this course can possibly fail to understand. This accounts for the repetition of terms, and at the same time serves as an apology to those who have already advanced far enough to grasp the meaning of much that the beginner will not understand at first reading.

An outstanding characteristic of the subconscious mind is that it records the suggestions that you send it through autosuggestion and it invokes the aid of infinite intelligence in translating these suggestions into their natural physical form. It is important that you understand this last sentence, for if you fail to understand it, you are likely to also fail to understand the importance of the very foundation upon which this entire course is built—the principle of infinite intelligence, which may be reached and used at will through the aid of the law of the Master Mind described in Lesson One.

Study carefully, thoughtfully, and with meditation, the entire preceding paragraph.

An outstanding characteristic of the subconscious mind is that it accepts and acts upon all suggestions that reach it, whether they are constructive or destructive, and whether they come from the outside or from your own conscious mind.

You can see, therefore, how essential it is to observe the law of evidence, and to carefully follow the principles laid down at the beginning of this lesson, in your selection of what you will pass on to your subconscious mind through autosuggestion. You can see why you must search diligently for facts, and why you cannot afford to listen to the slanderer or the scandalmonger, for to do so would be poisonous to the subconscious mind and ruinous to creative thought.

The subconscious mind may be likened to the sensitive plate of a camera on which the picture of any object placed before the camera will be recorded. The plate does not choose the sort of picture to be recorded on it; it records anything that reaches it through the lens. The conscious mind may be likened to the shutter, which shuts off the light from the sensitized plate, permitting nothing to reach it for record except what the operator wishes to reach it. The lens of the camera may then be likened to autosuggestion, for it is the medium that carries to the sensitized plate of the camera the image of the object to be registered.

Infinite intelligence, by this example, may be likened to the one who develops the sensitized plate after a picture has been recorded on it, thus bringing the picture into physical reality.

COMMENTARY

The concept of what Hill refers to here as the "plate" is the same concept as roll film, which was invented in the late 1800s by George Eastman, founder of Kodak Eastman, and used then primarily by the amateur photographer. But perhaps Hill was more familiar with professional photography studios, where plates were used.

In the foreword by George M. C. Fisher, former chairman and CEO of the Eastman Kodak Company, to George Eastman: A Biography *by Elizabeth Brayer, the man whom Fisher describes is an excellent example of much that Hill espouses:*

"Like Alexander Graham Bell, Eastman tinkered his way to a universally welcome invention. Like Henry Ford, he put his name on his company. Like Thomas Edison, he shaped his products to world markets hungry for their startling benefits. . . . We see the young Eastman staying awake around the clock for five days straight—week after week—to get his fledgling dry photographic plate business off the ground. We see him personally mixing 450 batches of emulsion only to fail to fix a quality problem, then sailing off to Europe to find its source."

Like many of the successful men whom Hill cites as examples and who had little formal education, George Eastman dropped out of school when he was thirteen. But according to Fischer he had tenacity, "sticktoitiveness," and he used his wits. Eastman was obviously an accurate thinker. In fact, it seems that he employed all of Hill's principles, with the possible exception of a pleasing personality (depending on which reports you choose to believe).

The camera makes a perfect allegory for the process of creative thought. First comes the selection of the object to be exposed before the camera. This represents one's Definite Chief Aim in life. Then comes the actual operation of recording a clear outline of that purpose, through the lens of autosuggestion, on the sensitized plate of

THE ELEVATOR TO SUCCESS

IS OUT OF ORDER.

YOU'LL HAVE TO USE THE STAIRS . . .

ONE STEP AT A TIME.

—Joe Girard

the subconscious mind. Here infinite intelligence steps in and develops the outline of that purpose into a physical form appropriate to the nature of the purpose.

The part that *you* must play is clear. You select the picture to be recorded (your Definite Chief Aim), then you fix your conscious mind on this purpose with such intensity that it communicates with the subconscious mind, through autosuggestion, and registers that picture. You then begin to watch for and to expect manifestations of physical realization of the subject of that picture.

Bear in mind that you do not sit down and wait, nor do you go to bed and sleep, with the expectation of awaking to find that infinite intelligence has showered you with the object of your Definite Chief Aim. You must work to make it happen, in accordance with the instructions laid down in Lesson Nine—with full faith and confidence that natural ways and means for the attainment of the object of your *definite purpose* will open to you at the proper time and in a suitable manner.

The way may not open suddenly, from the first step to the last. Often it opens only one step at a time. Therefore, when you are conscious of an opportunity to take the first step, take it without hesitation. And do the same when the second, and the third, and all subsequent steps essential for the attainment of the object of your Definite Chief Aim are manifested to you.

Infinite intelligence will not build you a home and deliver that home to you, ready to enter, but infinite intelligence will open the way and provide the necessary means with which *you* may build your own house.

Infinite intelligence will not command your bank to place a definite sum of money in your account, just because you suggested this to your subconscious mind, but infinite intelligence will open to you the way in which you may earn or borrow that money and place it in your account yourself.

Infinite intelligence will not throw out the present incumbent of the White House and make you the president instead. But infinite intelligence would most likely, under the proper circumstances, influence you to prepare yourself to fill that position and then help you to attain it through regular methods of procedure.

Do not rely on miracles for the attainment of the object of your Definite Chief Aim; rely on the power of infinite intelligence to guide you, through natural channels and with the aid of natural laws, toward its attainment. Do not expect infinite intelligence to bring to you the object of your Definite Chief Aim; instead, expect infinite intelligence to direct you toward that object.

As a beginner, do not expect infinite intelligence to move quickly in your behalf. But as you become more adept in the use of the principle of autosuggestion, and as your faith and understanding grow, you will see the realization of your Definite Chief Aim and its translation into physical reality.

You did not walk the first time you tried, but as you matured you walked without effort. Keep this in mind and you will understand why you cannot reasonably expect infinite intelligence to circumvent natural laws and provide you with its full knowledge and power until you have prepared yourself to use this knowledge and power.

If you want a fair example of what may happen to a person who suddenly comes into control of power, study some newly rich or someone who has inherited a fortune. Money-power in the hands of John D. Rockefeller is not only in safe hands, but it is also in hands where it is serving mankind throughout the world, blotting out ignorance, destroying diseases, and serving in a thousand other ways. But place Rockefeller's fortune in the hands of a young person who has not yet finished high school, and you would have another story to tell. I will have more to say on this subject in Lesson Fourteen.

If you have ever done any farming, you understand that certain preparations are necessary before a crop can be produced from the ground.

You know, of course, that grain will not grow in the woods —that it requires sunshine and rain for its growth. Likewise, you understand that the farmer must plow the soil and properly plant the grain. After this has been done, he then waits for Nature to do her share of the work, and she does it in due time, without outside help.

This is a perfect simile to illustrate the method through which one may attain the object of one's Definite Chief Aim. First comes the preparing of the soil to receive the seed, which is represented by faith and infinite intelligence and understanding of the principle of autosuggestion through which the seed of a *definite purpose* may be planted. Then comes a period of waiting and working for the realization of the object of that purpose. During this period, there must be continuous, intensified faith, which serves as the sunshine and the rain, without which the seed would wither and die in the ground. Then comes realization—harvest time—and a wonderful harvest can be brought forth.

I am fully aware that much of what I am proposing will not be understood or believed by the beginner. I remember my own experiences at the start. However, as the evolutionary process carries on its work—and it will do so; make no mistake about this—all the principles described in this and all other lessons of this course will become as familiar to you as did the multiplication table after you had mastered it. And what is of greater importance still, these principles will work with the same unvarying certainty as does the principle of multiplication.

Each lesson has provided you with definite instructions to be followed. The instructions have been simplified as far as possible, so anyone can understand them. Nothing has been left to the student except to follow these instructions and supply the faith in their soundness—without which they would be useless.

I remind you to familiarize yourself with the four major factors in this lesson on Accurate Thinking: autosuggestion, the subconscious mind, creative thought, and infinite intelligence. They are the four

THE ACTION REQUIRED

TO SUSTAIN HUMAN LIFE

IS PRIMARILY INTELLECTUAL:

EVERYTHING MAN NEEDS

HAS TO BE DISCOVERED

BY HIS MIND AND PRODUCED

BY HIS EFFORT.

—Ayn Rand

roadways over which you must travel in your upward climb in quest of knowledge.

You are in control of the first three, and how you travel these three roadways will be up to you. Therefore it will also depend on you as to the time and place at which they will converge into the fourth: infinite intelligence.

You understand what is meant by the terms *autosuggestion* and *subconscious mind.* Let us again make sure that you also understand what is meant by the term *creative thought.* It means thought of a positive, nondestructive, creative nature. The object of Lesson Eight on Self-Control was to prepare you to understand and successfully apply the principle of creative thought. If you have not mastered that lesson you are not ready to make use of creative thought in the attainment of your Definite Chief Aim.

Remember, it is in your subconscious mind that the seed of your Definite Chief Aim is planted, and it is with creative thought that you awaken that seed into growth and maturity. Your subconscious mind will not germinate the seed of your Definite Chief Aim, nor will infinite intelligence translate that purpose into physical reality, if you fill your mind with hatred, envy, jealousy, selfishness, and greed. These negative or destructive thoughts will choke out the seed of your *definite purpose.*

Creative thought presupposes that you will keep your mind in a state of expectancy of attainment of the object of your Definite Chief Aim; that you will have full faith and confidence in its attainment in due course and in due order.

If this lesson does what it was intended to do, it will bring you a fuller and deeper realization of the third lesson, on Self-Confidence, and it will also become clear that it is not Self-Confidence, but, rather, infinite intelligence that is the real source from which you are drawing your power.

SUGGESTION AND
THE SUBCONSCIOUS MIND

Autosuggestion is a powerful weapon with which one may rise to heights of great achievement, when it is used constructively. Used in a negative manner, however, it may destroy all possibility of success, and if so used continuously it will actually destroy health.

Careful comparison of the experiences of leading physicians and psychiatrists disclosed the startling information that approximately 75 percent of those who are ill are suffering from hypochondria, which is a morbid state of mind causing useless anxiety about one's health.

Stated in plain language, the hypochondriac is a person who believes he or she is suffering with some sort of imaginary disease, and often believes they have every disease of which they ever heard.

The person who suffers with such a condition is not only unable to think with accuracy, but also suffers from all sorts of destructive, illusory thoughts. Dr. Henry R. Rose is an authority for the following typical example of the power of autosuggestion:

"'If my wife dies I will not believe there is a God.' His wife was ill with pneumonia, and this is the way he greeted me when I reached his home. She had sent for me because the doctor had told her she could not recover. [Most doctors know better than to make a statement such as this in the presence of a patient.] She had called her husband and two sons to her bedside and bidden them good-bye. Then she asked that I, her minister, be sent for. I found the husband in the front room sobbing and the sons doing their best to brace her up. When I went into her room she was breathing with difficulty, and the trained nurse told me she was very low.

"I soon found that Mrs. N—— had sent for me to look after her two sons after she was gone. I said to her: 'You mustn't give up. You are not going to die! You have always been a strong and healthy woman and I do not believe God wants you to die and leave your boys to me or anyone else.'

"I talked to her along this line, then read the 103d Psalm and made a prayer in which I prepared her to get well rather than to enter eternity. I told her to put her faith in God and to throw her mind and will against every thought of dying. Then I left, saying, 'I will come again after the church service, and I will then find you much better.'

"This was Sunday morning. I called that afternoon. Her husband met me with a smile. He said that the moment I had gone, his wife called him and the boys into the room and said: 'Dr. Rose says that I am not going to die, that I am going to get well. And I am.'

"She did get well. But what did it? Two things: autosuggestion, superinduced by the suggestion I had given her, and faith on her part. I came just in the nick of time, and so great was her faith in me that I was able to inspire faith in herself. It was that faith that tipped the scales and brought her through the pneumonia. There are cases of pneumonia, perhaps, that nothing can cure. We all sadly agree to that. But there are times, as in this case, when the mind, if worked with in just the right way, will turn the tide. While there is life there is hope, but hope must rule supreme and do the good that it was intended to do.

"Here is another remarkable case showing the power of the human mind when used constructively. A physician asked me to see Mrs. H———. He said there was nothing organically wrong with her, but having made up her mind that she could not retain anything in her stomach, she had quit eating and was slowly starving herself to death. I went to see her and found also that she had no religious belief. She had lost her faith in God.

"My first effort was to restore her faith in the Almighty and to get her to believe that He was with her and would give her power. Then I told her she could eat anything she wanted. Her confidence in me was great and my statement impressed her. She began to eat from that day! She was out of her bed in three days, for the first time in weeks. She is a normal, healthy, and happy woman today.

THE MIND THAT MADE YOU SICK

CAN ALSO MAKE YOU WELL.

—unknown

"What did it? The same forces as those described in the preceding case: outside suggestion—which she accepted in faith, and applied through self-suggestion—and inward confidence.

"There are times when the mind is sick and it makes the body sick. At such times it needs a stronger mind to heal it by giving it direction and especially by giving it confidence and faith in itself. This is called suggestion. It is transmitting your confidence and power to another, and with such force as to make the other believe as you wish and do as you will. It need not be hypnotism. You can get wonderful results with the patient wide awake and perfectly rational. But they must believe in you and you must understand the workings of the mind in order to meet the arguments and questions of the patient. Each of us can be a healer of this sort and thus help our fellow men.

"It is the duty of every person to read some of the best books on the forces of the human mind and learn what amazing things the mind can do to keep people well and happy. We see the terrible things that wrong thinking does to people, even going to such lengths as to make them positively insane. It is high time we found out the good things the mind can do, not only to cure mental disorders, but physical diseases as well."

COMMENTARY

As was also noted in earlier lessons, numerous medical professionals have incorporated the concept of autosuggestion under the term "the body-mind connection," and the belief that the mind can manifest physical changes in the body has become a part of mainstream medical practice.

In the previous volumes the editors listed the titles of several seminal books and audiobooks that explain in greater detail the medical applications of the power of suggestion. If you have yet to read any of the suggested books or listen to the tapes, we encourage you to do so, and we again offer the following list: Visualization by Adelaide Bry; Ageless Body, Timeless Mind by Deepak Chopra, M.D.; Creative Visualization by Shakti Gawain; Focusing by Eugene Gendlin, Ph.D.;

GOOD FOR THE BODY

IS THE WORK OF THE BODY,

GOOD FOR THE SOUL

IS THE WORK OF THE SOUL,

AND GOOD FOR EITHER

THE WORK OF THE OTHER.

—Henry David Thoreau

You Can Heal Your Life *by Louise Hay;* Healing with Body Energy *by W. Brugh Joy, M.D.;* Psycho-Cybernetics *by Maxwell Maltz, M.D.;* Superimmunity *by Paul Pearsall, Ph.D.;* Healing Back Pain *by John E. Sarno, M.D.;* Love, Medicine, and Miracles *by Bernie S. Siegel, M.D.;* Getting Well *by O. Carl Simonton, M.D.;* Eight Weeks to Optimum Health and Spontaneous Healing *by Andrew Weil, M.D.*

Napoleon Bonaparte, during his campaign in Egypt, went among his soldiers who were dying by the hundreds of the bubonic plague. He touched one of them and lifted a second, to inspire the others not to be afraid, for the awful disease seemed to spread as much by the aid of the Imagination as in any other way. The German philosopher Goethe tells us that he himself went where there was malignant fever and never contracted it because he put forth his will.

These giants among men knew something that we are slowly beginning to find out: the power of autosuggestion. We can influence ourselves by *believing* we cannot catch a disease or be sick.

Imagination can kill a person, or it can help you rise to heights of achievement of the most astounding nature, providing it is used as the basis of Self-Confidence. There are authentic cases on record of men having actually died because they imagined they were cut by a knife across the jugular vein, when in reality a piece of ice was used and water was allowed to drip so they could hear it and imagine their blood was running out. They had been blindfolded before the experiment was begun.

The imaginative faculty of the human mind is a marvelous piece of mental machinery, but it may, and usually does, play tricks on us unless we keep constantly on guard and control it.

If you allow your Imagination to "expect the worst" it will play havoc with you. Young medical students not infrequently become frightened and believe they have every disease in the medical books, as a result of the lectures and classroom discussions of the various diseases.

Dr. Schofield describes the case of a woman who had a tumor. They placed her on the operating table, gave her anesthetics, when suddenly the tumor disappeared and no operation was necessary. But when she came back to consciousness the tumor returned. The physician then learned that she had been living with a relative who had a real tumor, and the woman's Imagination was so vivid that she had imagined this one upon herself.

She was placed on the operating table again, given anesthetics, then bandaged around the middle so the tumor could not artificially return. When she awoke, she was told the operation had been a success but it would be necessary to wear the bandage for several days.

The woman believed the doctor, and when the bandage was finally removed, the tumor did not return. No operation whatsoever had been performed. She had simply relieved her subconscious mind of the thought that she had a tumor, leaving her Imagination nothing to work on but the idea of health. And as she had never really been sick, of course she remained normal.

The mind may be cured of imaginary ills in exactly the same manner that it became diseased with those ills—by autosuggestion. The best time to work on a faulty Imagination is at night, just as you are ready to go to sleep, for then the thoughts or suggestions you give your subconscious mind, just as your conscious mind is about to go off duty, will be taken up and worked on during the night.

This may seem impossible, but you can easily test the principle: You wish to get up at seven tomorrow morning, or some hour other than your regular time. Say to yourself, as you are ready to go to sleep, "I must arise at seven o'clock tomorrow without fail." Repeat this several times, impressing on your mind that you *must* arise at that precise moment. Turn this thought over to your subconscious mind with absolute confidence that you will awaken at seven o'clock, and when that hour arrives your subconscious mind will awaken you. But you must give the command in no uncertain or indefinite terms.

In this same way, the subconscious mind may be given any other sort of orders and it will carry them out as readily as it will awaken you at a given hour. For example, give the command, as you are about to go to sleep each night, for your subconscious mind to develop Self-Confidence, Initiative, courage, or any other desired quality, and it will do your bidding. If the Imagination can create imaginary ills and send one to bed with those ills, it can also, and just as easily, remove the cause of those ills.

The mind seems to be a complicated machine, but in reality it is the nearest thing to perpetual motion that is known. It works automatically when we are asleep; it works both automatically and in conjunction with the will when we are awake.

The mind is deserving of the minutest possible analysis in this lesson, because the mind is the energy with which all thinking is done. To learn how to use Accurate Thinking, one must thoroughly understand the following:

1. The mind can be controlled, guided, and directed to creative, constructive ends.

2. The mind can also be directed to destructive ends, and it may, voluntarily, tear down and destroy unless it is carefully controlled and directed constructively.

3. The mind has power over every cell of the body, and it can be made to cause every cell to do its intended work perfectly, or it may, through neglect or wrong direction, destroy the normal functionary purposes of any or all cells.

4. All achievement is the result of thought. The physical body is of secondary importance, and in many instances of no importance whatsoever except as a place to house the mind.

5. The greatest of all achievements, whether in literature, art, finance, industry, commerce, transportation, religion, politics, or scientific discoveries, are usually the results of ideas conceived in one person's brain—but actually transformed into reality by others, through the combined use of their minds and bodies. (Meaning that the conception of an idea is of greater importance than the transformation of that idea into more material form, because relatively few people can conceive useful ideas, while there are millions who can develop an idea and give it material form after it has been conceived.)

6. The majority of all thoughts that are conceived in people's minds are *not accurate*, being more in the nature of "opinions" or "snap judgments."

"Accurate thoughts" have conquered the air and the sea, explored practically every square mile of the little earth on which we live, and wrested from Nature thousands of "secrets" that, a few generations ago, would have been set down as "miracles" of the most astounding and imponderable sort.

All scientists who have made a study of the human mind readily agree that the surface has not yet been scratched in the study of the wonderful power that lies dormant, waiting, as the oak tree sleeps in the acorn, to be aroused and put to work. Those who have expressed an opinion on the subject believe that the next great cycle of discovery lies in the realm of the human mind.

The possible nature of these discoveries has been suggested, in many different ways, in practically every lesson of this course, particularly in this and the following lessons. If these suggestions appear to lead the student of this philosophy deeper than he or she is accustomed, that student has the privilege of stopping at any depth desired, until ready, through thought and study, to go further.

It is not expected that the beginner will immediately assimilate and put into use all that is included in this philosophy. But if the net result is nothing more than to sow the seed of constructive thought in the mind of the student, my work will have been done. Time, plus the student's own desire for knowledge, will do the rest.

Frankly, many of the suggestions passed on through this course would, if literally followed, lead you far beyond the bounds of what is ordinarily called business philosophy. The course goes more deeply into the functioning processes of the human mind than is necessary for the use of this philosophy as a means of achieving business or financial success. However, it is presumed that many students of this course will wish to do just that, and I have had these students in mind throughout the labor of organizing and writing this course.

SUMMARY OF THE
PRINCIPLES OF ACCURATE THINKING

We have discovered that the human body consists of billions of living, intelligent, individual cells that carry on a very definite, well-organized work of building, developing, and maintaining the body.

We have discovered that these cells are directed, in their respective duties, by the subconscious or automatic action of the mind; that the subconscious section of the mind can be, to a very large extent, controlled and directed by the conscious or voluntary section of the mind.

We have found that any idea or any thought that is held in the mind, through repetition, has a tendency to direct the physical body to transform such thought or idea into its material equivalent. We have found that any order that is *properly* given to the subconscious section of the mind, through the law of autosuggestion, will be carried out unless it is sidetracked or countermanded by another and stronger order. We have found that the subconscious mind does not question the source from which it receives orders, nor the soundness of those orders, but it will proceed to direct the body to carry out any order it receives.

WHAT IS A DEMANDING PLEASURE?

A PLEASURE THAT DEMANDS

THE USE OF ONE'S MIND;

NOT IN THE SENSE OF

PROBLEM SOLVING,

BUT IN THE SENSE OF

EXERCISING DISCRIMINATION,

JUDGMENT, AWARENESS.

—Nathaniel Branden

This explains the necessity for closely guarding how and from where we receive suggestions. It is a fact that we can be subtly and quietly influenced at times and in ways of which we are not consciously aware.

We have found that every movement of the human body is controlled by either the conscious or the subconscious section of the mind, and that not a muscle can be moved until an order to do so has been sent out by one or the other of these two sections of the mind.

When this principle is thoroughly understood, we also understand the powerful effect of any idea or thought that we create and hold in the conscious mind until the subconscious mind has time to take over that thought and begin the work of transforming it into its material counterpart. When we understand the principle through which any idea is first placed in the conscious mind, and held there until the subconscious picks it up and appropriates it, we have a practical working knowledge of the law of Concentration, which will be covered in the next lesson.

The Value of Adopting a Chief Aim

This lesson on Accurate Thinking not only describes the real purpose of a Definite Chief Aim, but it also explains in simple terms the principles through which such an aim or purpose may be realized.

First create the objective toward which you are striving, through the imaginative faculty of your mind, then transfer an outline of this objective to paper by writing out a definite statement of it in the nature of a Definite Chief Aim.

By daily reference to this written statement, the idea or thing aimed for is taken up by the conscious mind and handed over to the subconscious mind, which in turn directs the energies of the body to transform the desire into reality.

Desire

Strong, deeply rooted *desire* is the starting point and seed of all achievement. It is the starting place behind which there is nothing, or at least nothing of which we have any knowledge.

A Definite Chief Aim, which is only another name for desire, would be meaningless unless based on a strong desire for the object of that aim. Many people "wish" for many things, but a wish is not the equivalent of a strong desire, and therefore wishes are of little or no value unless crystallized into the more definite form of desire.

It is believed that all energy and all matter respond to and are controlled by a law of attraction that causes elements and forces of a similar nature to gather around certain centers of attraction. Likewise, constant, deeply seated desire attracts the physical equivalent or counterpart of the thing desired, or the means of securing it.

Suggestion and Autosuggestion

Through this and other lessons of the Law of Success course, you have learned that sense impressions arising out of one's environment, or from statements or actions of other people, are called suggestions, while sense impressions that we place in our own minds are placed there by self-suggestion, or autosuggestion.

All suggestions coming from others, or from our environment, influence us only after we have accepted them and passed them on to the subconscious mind through the principle of autosuggestion. Thus it is seen that suggestion must become autosuggestion before it influences the mind of the one receiving it.

Stated another way, no one may influence another without the consent of the one influenced, as the influencing is done through one's own power of autosuggestion.

The conscious mind stands, during the hours when one is awake, as a sentinel, guarding the subconscious mind and warding off all suggestions that try to reach it from the outside until those suggestions have been examined, and accepted, by the conscious mind. This is Nature's way of safeguarding the human being against intruders who would otherwise take control of any mind at will.

It is a wise arrangement.

The Value of Autosuggestion in Achieving Your Definite Chief Aim

One of the greatest uses to which you may direct the power of auto-suggestion is in having it help accomplish the object of your Definite Chief Aim in life.

The way to do this is very simple. While the exact formula has been stated in Lesson Two, and referred to in many other lessons of the course, I will describe again the principle on which it is based:

Write out a clear, concise statement of what you intend to accomplish as your Definite Chief Aim, covering a period of perhaps the next five years. Make at least two copies of your statement, one to be placed where you can read it several times a day while you are at work, and another to be placed where it can be read several times each evening before you go to sleep, and just after you arise in the morning.

The suggestive influence of this procedure, impractical though it may seem, will soon impress the object of your Definite Chief Aim on your subconscious mind. Within a very short time you will begin to observe events taking place that will lead you nearer and nearer the attainment of that object.

From the very day that you reach a definite decision in your own mind as to the precise thing, condition, or position in life that you deeply desire, you will observe, if you read books, newspapers, and magazines, that important news items and other data bearing on the object of your Definite Chief Aim will begin to come to your attention. You will also observe opportunities beginning to come to you that will, if embraced, lead you nearer and nearer the coveted goal of your desire.

THE SUBJECTIVE MIND IS

ENTIRELY UNDER THE CONTROL

OF THE OBJECTIVE MIND.

WITH THE UTMOST FIDELITY

IT REPRODUCES AND WORKS OUT

TO ITS FINAL CONSEQUENCES

WHATEVER THE OBJECTIVE MIND

IMPRESSES UPON IT.

—Thomas Troward

No one knows better than I how impossible and impractical this may seem to the person who is not a student of psychology. However, the best thing for anyone to do is to experiment with this principle until its practicality has been established.

The word *impossible* means less now than it ever did before in the history of the human race. There are some who have actually removed this word from their vocabularies, believing that we can do anything we can imagine and *believe* we can do!

We know now that the universe is made up of two substances: matter and energy. Through patient scientific research we have discovered that everything that is or ever has been in the way of matter, when analyzed to the finest point, is nothing but a form of energy.

On the other hand, every material thing that man has created began in the form of energy, through the seed of an idea that was released through the imaginative faculty of the human mind. In other words, the beginning of every material thing is energy and the ending of it is energy.

All matter obeys the command of one form or another of energy. The highest known form of energy is that which functions as the human mind. The human mind, therefore, is the sole directing force of everything man creates, and what he may create with this force in the future, as compared with what he has created with it in the past, will make his past achievements seem petty and small.

We do not have to wait for future discoveries for evidence that the mind is the greatest force known to mankind. We know now that any idea, aim, or purpose that is fixed in the mind and held there with a will to achieve or attain its physical or material equivalent, puts into motion powers that cannot be conquered.

English author Charles Buxton said: "The longer I live the more certain I am that the great difference between men, between the feeble and the powerful, the great and the insignificant, is energy— invincible determination—a purpose once fixed, and then death or victory. That quality will do anything that can be done in this world —and no talents, no circumstances, no opportunities will make a two-legged creature a man without it."

Author Donald G. Mitchell has well said: "Resolve is what makes a man manifest. Not puny resolve; not crude determinations; not errant purposes—but that strong and indefatigable will which treads down difficulties and danger, as a boy treads down the heaving frost-lands of winter, which kindles his eye and brain with proud pulse-beat toward the unattainable. Will makes men giants!"

The great Benjamin Disraeli said: "I have brought myself, by long meditation, to the conviction that a human being with a settled purpose must accomplish it, and that nothing can resist a will which will stake even existence upon its fulfillment."

Sir John Simpson said: "A passionate desire and an unwearied will can perform impossibilities, or what may seem to be such to the cold, timid and feeble."

And John Foster adds his testimony when he says: "It is wonderful how even the casualties of life seem to bow to a spirit that will not bow to them, and yield to subserve a design which they may, in their first apparent tendency, threaten to frustrate. When a firm, decisive spirit is recognized, it is curious to see how the space clears around a man and leaves him room and freedom."

Abraham Lincoln said of General Grant: "The great thing about Grant is his cool persistency of purpose. He is not easily excited, and he has got the grip of a bulldog. When he once gets his teeth in, nothing can shake him off."

It seems appropriate to state here that a strong desire, to be transformed into reality, must be backed with persistency until it is taken over by the subconscious mind. It is not enough to feel very deeply the desire for achievement of a Definite Chief Aim, for just a few hours or a few days. The desire must be placed in the mind and held there—with persistence that knows no defeat—until the automatic or subconscious mind takes it over. Up to this point you must stand behind the desire and push it; beyond this point the desire will stand behind you and push you on to achievement.

Persistence may be compared to the dropping of water that finally wears away the hardest stone. When the final chapter of your life has been completed, it will be found that your persistence, or lack of this sterling quality, played an important part in either your success or your failure.

I watched the Tunney-Dempsey fight in Chicago. I also studied the psychology leading up to and surrounding their previous bout. Two things helped Tunney defeat Dempsey, on both occasions, despite Dempsey being the stronger of the two men and, as many believe, the better fighter. And the two things that spelled Dempsey's doom were, first, his own lack of Self-Confidence—the fear that Tunney might defeat him—and second, Tunney's complete self-reliance and his belief that he could whip Dempsey.

Tunney stepped into the ring with his chin in the air, an atmosphere of self-assurance and certainty written in his every movement. Dempsey walked in with a sort of uncertain stride, eyeing Tunney in a manner that plainly queried, "I wonder what you'll do to me?"

Dempsey was whipped, in his own mind, before he entered the ring. Press agents and propagandists had done the trick, thanks to the superior thinking ability of his opponent, Tunney.

And so the story goes, from the lowest and the most brutal of occupations, prize-fighting, on up to the highest and most commendable professions. Success is won by the person who understands how to use their power of thought.

Throughout this course much stress has been put on the importance of environment and habit, out of which grow the stimuli that put the wheels of the human mind into operation. Fortunate is the person who has found how to stimulate his or her mind so that its powers will function constructively when placed behind any strong, deeply seated desire.

WE ARE WHAT WE THINK.

ALL THAT WE ARE

ARISES WITH OUR THOUGHTS.

WITH OUR THOUGHTS,

WE MAKE THE WORLD.

—Buddha

Accurate Thinking is thinking that makes intelligent use of all the powers of the human mind, and it does not stop with the mere examination, classification, and arranging of ideas. Accurate Thinking creates ideas and it may be made to transform these ideas into their most profitable, constructive form.

You will perhaps be better prepared to analyze, without a feeling of skepticism and doubt, the principles laid down in this lesson if you keep in mind that the conclusions and hypotheses are not solely mine. I have had the benefit of close Cooperation from some of the leading investigators in the field of mental phenomena.

COMMENTARY

To illustrate Hill's point that the principles he proposed were accepted by other experts, the editors offer the following list of books and audiobooks by a variety of experts, all of whom are leaders in their fields, and whose principles parallel Hill's. Many of these books have been recommended in other lessons, but they are equally applicable to this section on accurate thinking: Super Creativity *by Tony Buzan;* The Artist's Way *by Julia Cameron;* The 7 Habits of Highly Effective People *by Stephen Covey;* Lateral Thinking, Six Thinking Hats, *and* Super Thinking *by Edward De Bono;* Drawing on the Right Side of the Brain *by Betty Edwards;* The Zen of Seeing *by Frederick Franck;* Writing Down the Bones *by Natalie Goldberg;* Peak Learning *by Ronald Gross;* Feel the Fear and Do It Anyway *by Susan Jeffers;* Thinkertoys *by Michael Michalko;* Superlearning *by Sheilah Ostrander and Lynn Schroeder;* Writing the Natural Way *by Gabriele Rico;* Awaken the Giant Within *by Anthony Robbins, and the complete Anthony Robbins library of* PowerTalk! *audiobooks;* Wishcraft *by Barbara Sher;* Do What You Love, the Money Will Follow *by Marsha Sinetar;* A Kick in the Seat of the Pants *by R. von Oech;* Sell Your Way to the Top *by Zig Zigler.*

In the next lesson, Concentration, you will be further instructed in the method of using autosuggestion. In fact, throughout this course, the principle of gradual unfoldment has been followed, paralleling

WHAT A PECULIAR PRIVILEGE HAS

THIS LITTLE AGITATION OF THE BRAIN

WHICH WE CALL "THOUGHT."

—Hume

that of the principle of evolution as nearly as possible. The first lesson laid the foundation for the second, and the second prepared the way for the third, and so on. I have tried to build this course by a series of steps, each of which lifts the student just another level higher and nearer the apex of the pyramid that the course, as a whole, represents.

The purpose in building the course in this manner cannot be described in words, but that purpose will become clear when you have mastered it, for its mastery will open to you a source of knowledge that cannot be imparted by one to another. It is attainable only by drawing out and expanding from *within one's own mind.*

With this vague hint as to the reward that awaits all who earnestly and intelligently search for the hidden passageway to knowledge to which I refer, we will now discuss the phase of Accurate Thinking that will take you as high as you can go—except through the discovery and use of that secret passageway.

> *You never can tell what your thoughts will do*
> *In bringing you hate or love,*
> *For thoughts are things, and their airy wings*
> *Are swifter than a carrier dove.*
> *They follow the law of the universe,*
> *Each thing must create its kind,*
> *And they speed o'er the track to bring you back*
> *Whatever went out from your mind.*
>
> —ELLA WHEELER WILCOX

Thoughts are things. It is the belief of many that every completed thought starts an unending vibration with which the one who releases it will have to contend at a later time; that man is but the physical reflection of thought that was put into motion by infinite intelligence.

All thought is creative. However, not all thought is constructive or positive. If you think thoughts of misery and poverty and see no way to avoid them, then your thoughts will create those very conditions. But reverse the order, and think thoughts of a positive, expectant nature, and your thoughts will create *those* conditions.

Your thoughts affect your entire personality and attract to you the outward, physical things that harmonize with the nature of your thoughts. This has been made clear in almost every lesson and will be repeated many times more in the lessons that follow. The reason for this repetition is that nearly all beginners in the study of the mind overlook the importance of this fundamental and eternal truth.

When you suggest to your subconscious mind a Definite Chief Aim that embodies a definite desire, you must accompany it with such faith and belief in the ultimate realization of that purpose that you can actually see yourself in possession of it. Conduct yourself as you would if you were already in possession of the object of your *definite purpose*—from the moment that you suggest it to your subconscious mind. Enrich it with full belief that infinite intelligence will step in and mature that purpose into reality in exact accordance with its nature. Anything short of such belief will bring you disappointment.

Do not question whether the principles of autosuggestion will work. Do not doubt, but believe! The power to think as you wish to think is the only power over which you have absolute control.

Please read and study that last sentence until you grasp its meaning. If it is within your power to control your thoughts, the responsibility then rests with you as to whether your thoughts will be of the positive or negative type, which brings to mind one of the world's most famous poems:

> *Out of the night that covers me,*
> *   Black as the pit from pole to pole,*
> *I thank whatever gods may be*
> *   For my unconquerable soul.*

In the fell clutch of circumstance
　　I have not winced or cried aloud.
Under the bludgeonings of chance
　　My head is bloody, but unbowed.

Beyond this place of wrath and tears
　　Looms but the horror of the shade,
And yet the menace of the years
　　Finds, and shall find, me unafraid.

It matters not how strait the gate,
　　How charged with punishments the scroll,
I am the master of my fate,
　　I am the captain of my soul.

—WILLIAM ERNEST HENLEY

Henley did not write this poem until after he had discovered the door to that secret passageway to which I referred.

You are the "master of your fate" and the "captain of your soul" because *you control your own thoughts.* With the aid of your thoughts you may create whatever you desire.

As we approach the close of this lesson, let us pull aside the curtain that hangs over the gateway called Death and take a look into the Great Beyond. Look closely and observe that you look at a world of beings of your own creation; they correspond exactly to the nature of your own thoughts as you expressed them before death. There they are, the children of your own heart and mind, patterned after the image of your own thoughts.

Those that were born of your hatred, envy, jealousy, selfishness, and injustice toward others will not make very desirable neighbors, but you must live with them just the same, for they are your children and you cannot turn them out.

THE PROBLEM WITH MOST PEOPLE

IS THAT THEY THINK WITH THEIR

HOPES OR FEARS OR WISHES

RATHER THAN THEIR MINDS.

—Walter Duranty

You will be unfortunate indeed if you find there no children that were born of love, justice, truth, and kindness toward others.

In the light of this allegorical suggestion, the subject of Accurate Thinking takes on a new and much more important aspect, doesn't it? If there is a possibility that every thought you release during this life will step out to greet you after death, then you need no further reason for guarding all your thoughts carefully.

The term *accurate thought*, as used in this lesson, refers to thought that is of your own creation. Thought that comes to you from others, through either suggestion or direct statement, is not accurate thought within the meaning and purpose of this lesson, although it may be thought that is based on *facts.*

I can take you no further in this lesson on Accurate Thinking. However, you have not yet gone the entire distance; you have only just started. From here on you must be your own guide. But if you have understood the great truth upon which this lesson is founded, you will not have difficulty finding your own way.

Let me caution you *again,* however, not to become discouraged if the fundamental truth of this lesson has not become clear to you at first reading. This is the one lesson of the entire course that cannot be fully assimilated by the beginner through one reading. You will gain the knowledge only through thought, reflection, and meditation. For this reason you are instructed to read this lesson at least four times, at intervals of one week apart.

It may require weeks or even months of meditation for you to fully comprehend, but this truth is worth working for.

You are also instructed to again read Lesson One, so that you may better understand the law of the Master Mind and the relationship between that law and the subjects covered by this lesson on Accurate Thinking. The Master Mind is the principle through which you may become an accurate thinker.

Lesson Twelve

Concentration

CONCENTRATION IS MY MOTTO—

FIRST HONESTY, THEN INDUSTRY,

THEN CONCENTRATION.

—Andrew Carnegie

Lesson Twelve

CONCENTRATION

"You Can Do It if You Believe You Can!"

THIS LESSON HOLDS A KEYSTONE POSITION in this course, because the psychological law upon which it is based is of vital importance to every other lesson of the course.

Let me first define the word *concentration* as it is used in this lesson: "Concentration is the act of focusing the mind on a given desire until ways and means for its realization have been worked out and successfully put into operation."

Two important laws enter into the act of concentrating the mind on a given desire. One is the law of autosuggestion and the other is the law of *habit*. The former having been fully described in previous lessons, I will now briefly describe the law of habit.

Habit grows out of environment—the sum total of all sources by which you are influenced through the aid of the five senses of seeing, hearing, smelling, tasting, and feeling—and out of doing the same thing in the same way over and over again, out of repetition, out of thinking the same thoughts over and over.

Except on rare occasions when it rises above environment, the human mind draws from its surroundings the material out of which thought is created. Habit crystallizes this thought into a permanent fixture, storing it away in the subconscious mind where it becomes a vital part of our personality and silently influences our actions, forms our prejudices and our biases, and controls our opinions.

A great philosopher had in mind the power of habit when he said: "We first endure, then pity, and finally embrace," in speaking of the manner in which honest men come to indulge in crime.

We begin to see, therefore, the importance of selecting our environment with the greatest of care, because environment is the mental feeding ground out of which the food that goes into our minds is extracted.

THE FORCES OF HABIT

It has been said that all people are the creatures of habit, and that habit is a cable; we weave a thread of it each day and it becomes so strong that we cannot break it.

If it is true that habit can compel us against our will, desire, and inclination, and thereby dominate our actions and character, then it can also be mastered, harnessed, and directed for our good. Thousands of people have applied this knowledge and have turned the force of habit into new channels.

A habit is a "mental path" over which our actions have traveled for some time, each passing making the path a little deeper and a little wider. If you have had to walk over a field or through a forest, you know how natural it is to choose the clearest path. The line of mental action is precisely the same. It is movement along the lines of least resistance—passage over the well-worn path.

Habits are created by repetition and are formed in accordance to a natural law, observable in all animate things and some would say in inanimate things as well. For instance, a piece of paper once folded in a certain way will fold along the same lines the next time. Clothing forms into creases according to the person wearing it and these creases once formed will remain. All users of any kind of machinery know that as a machine is first "broken in," so it will tend to run thereafter. Rivers and streams cut their courses through the land along the lines of least resistance. The law is in operation everywhere.

These examples will give you the idea of the nature of habit and will aid you in forming new mental paths—new mental creases. The best, and one might say the only, way that old habits may be broken is to form new habits to counteract and replace the undesirable ones. Form new mental paths over which to travel, and soon the old ones will become less distinct. Every time you travel over the path of the desirable mental habit, you make that new path deeper and wider—and so much easier to travel thereafter.

This mental path-making is very important, and I cannot urge you too strongly to start making the desirable mental paths over which you wish to travel.

The following are the rules through which you may form the habits you desire:

I. At the beginning of the formation of a new habit, put force and Enthusiasm into your expression. Feel what you think. Remember that you are taking the first steps toward making your new mental paths, and it is much harder at first than it will be afterward. At the beginning make each path as clear and as deep as you can, so that you can readily see it the next time you wish to follow it.

EXCELLENCE IS AN ART WON

BY TRAINING AND HABITUATION.

WE DO NOT ACT RIGHTLY BECAUSE

WE HAVE VIRTUE OR EXCELLENCE,

BUT WE RATHER HAVE THOSE BECAUSE

WE HAVE ACTED RIGHTLY.

WE ARE WHAT WE REPEATEDLY DO.

EXCELLENCE, THEN, IS NOT AN ACT

BUT A HABIT.

—Aristotle

2. Keep your attention firmly concentrated on your new path-building, and forget all about the old paths. Concern yourself only with the new ones that you are building to order.

3. Travel over your newly made paths as often as possible. Create opportunities for doing so, without waiting for them to arise through luck or chance. The more often you go over the new paths, the sooner they will become well worn and easily traveled.

4. Resist the temptation to travel over the older, easier paths you have been using in the past. Every time you resist a temptation, the stronger you become and the easier it will be for you to do so the next time. But every time you yield to the temptation, the easier it becomes to yield again and the more difficult it becomes to resist the next time. This is the critical time. Prove your determination, persistency, and willpower now, at the very beginning.

5. Be sure you have mapped out the right path as your Definite Chief Aim, then go ahead without fear and without allowing yourself to doubt. Select your goal and make good, deep, wide mental paths leading straight to it.

As you will have observed, there is a close relationship between habit and autosuggestion. Through habit, an act repeatedly performed in the same manner has a tendency to become permanent, and eventually we come to perform the act automatically or unconsciously. In playing a piano, for example, the artist can play a familiar piece while his or her conscious mind is on some other subject.

Autosuggestion is the tool with which we dig a mental path, Concentration is the hand that holds that tool, and habit is the map or blueprint that the mental path follows. An idea or desire, to be transformed into terms of action or physical reality, must be held in the conscious mind faithfully and persistently until habit begins to give it permanent form.

YOU ARE A PRODUCT OF

YOUR ENVIRONMENT.

SO CHOOSE THE ENVIRONMENT

THAT WILL BEST DEVELOP YOU

TOWARD YOUR OBJECTIVE. . . .

ARE THE THINGS AROUND YOU

HELPING YOU TOWARD SUCCESS—

OR ARE THEY HOLDING YOU BACK?

—W. Clement Stone

We absorb the material for thought from our surrounding environment. The term *environment* covers a very broad field. It consists of the books we read, the people with whom we associate, the country and community in which we live, the nature of the work we do, the clothes we wear, the songs we sing, and, most important of all, the religious and intellectual training we receive prior to the age of fourteen years.

The purpose of analyzing the subject of environment is to show its direct relationship to the personality we are developing, and how its influence will give us the materials out of which we may attain our Definite Chief Aim in life.

The mind feeds upon that which we supply it, or that which is forced upon it, through our environment. Therefore, let us select our environment, as much as possible, with the object of supplying the mind with suitable material out of which to carry on its work. If your environment is not to your liking, change it!

The first step is to create in your own mind a clear, well-defined picture of the environment in which you believe you could best attain your Definite Chief Aim. Then *concentrate* your mind on this picture until you transform it into reality.

Just as you learned in Lesson Two, A Definite Chief Aim, the first step you must take in the accomplishment of *any* desire is to have in your mind an exact picture of what it is that you intend to accomplish. This is also the first principle to be observed in your plans for the achievement of success, and if you fail to observe it you cannot succeed except by chance.

Your daily associates constitute one of the most important and influential parts of your environment, and they may work for your progress or against it. As much as possible, you should select as your closest daily associates those who are in sympathy with your aims and ideals—especially those represented by your Definite Chief Aim.

You should make it a point to associate with people whose mental attitudes inspire you with Enthusiasm, Self-Confidence, determination, and ambition.

Remember that every word spoken within your hearing, every sight that reaches your eyes, and every sense impression that you receive through any of the five senses, will influence your thoughts. This being true, can you not see the importance of controlling, as far as possible, the environment in which you live and work? Can you not see the importance of reading books which deal with subjects that are directly related to your Definite Chief Aim? Can you not see the importance of talking with people who are in sympathy with your aims, and who will encourage you and spur you on toward their attainment?

An observant person could accurately analyze someone by seeing their work environment. A well-organized desk will usually indicate a well-organized mind. Show me the shelves in a store and I will tell you whether the manager of that store has an organized or disorganized mind. There is a close relationship between one's mental attitude and one's physical environment.

The effects of environment so vitally influence those who work in factories, stores, and offices, that most employers have become well aware of the importance of creating an environment that inspires and encourages their workers.

THE POWER OF CONCENTRATION

This would be an appropriate place at which to describe the method through which you may apply the principles directly and indirectly related to the subject of Concentration. I call this method the Magic Key to Success.

In presenting you with this magic key, let me first explain that it is no invention or discovery of mine. It is the same key that is used, in one form or another, by all groups that are founded on the philosophy of optimism.

The magic key offers an irresistible power that all may use. It will unlock the door to riches. It will unlock the door to fame. And, in many instances, it will unlock the door to physical health. It will unlock the door to education and let you into the storehouse of all your latent ability. It will act as a passkey to any position in life for which you are suited.

Through the aid of this magic key we have unlocked the secret doors to all of the world's great inventions. Through its magic powers all of our great geniuses of the past have been developed.

Suppose you are working in a menial position and desire a better place in life. The magic key will help you attain it. It will unlock prison doors and turn human derelicts into useful, trustworthy men and women. It will turn failure into success and misery into happiness.

This magic key is—Concentration.

Now let me once again define *concentration* as I use the term. It means the ability, through fixed habit and practice, to keep your mind on one subject until you have thoroughly familiarized yourself with that subject and mastered it. It means the ability to control your attention and focus it on a given problem until you have solved that problem. It means the ability to throw off the effects of those habits you wish to discard, and the power to build new habits. It means complete self-mastery.

Concentration is the ability to think as you wish to think, the ability to control your thoughts and direct them to a definite end, and the ability to organize your knowledge into a plan of action that is sound and workable.

You can readily see that in concentrating your mind on your Definite Chief Aim in life, you must also cover many closely related subjects that blend into each other and complete the main subject on which you are concentrating.

COMMENTARY

In the year 2000, Albert Einstein was chosen by Time *magazine as Person of the Century. He was described by managing editor Walter Isaacson as "both the greatest mind and paramount icon of our age" whose "extraordinary brilliance made his face a symbol and his name a synonym for genius."*

Had Einstein been born today, however, he might have been diagnosed in his early years as having attention deficit disorder. As a child he was slow to learn to talk. As a student he showed little promise and was even expelled from school. Isaacson refers to him as "the patron saint of distracted schoolkids."

But what Einstein could do *was the very thing Napoleon Hill refers to in this lesson, for once Einstein set himself a "definite chief aim," he had a phenomenal ability to focus his* concentration. *His famous theories were all the result of "thought experiments"—experiments that took place inside his mind! His breakthroughs came, just as Hill suggests, by mentally organizing his knowledge and "concentrating on many closely related subjects that blend into each other and complete the main subject."*

Ambition and desire are the major factors that enter into the act of successful Concentration. Without these factors the magic key is useless, and the main reason why so few people make use of this key is that most people lack ambition, and desire nothing in particular.

Desire whatever you may, and if your desire is within reason and if it is strong enough, the magic key of Concentration will help you attain it. There are many scientists and research psychologists who believe that the power of prayer operates through the principle of Concentration on the attainment of a deeply seated desire.

Nothing was ever created by a human being that was not first created in the Imagination, through desire, and then transformed into reality through Concentration.

Let us put the magic key to a test through the aid of a definite formula.

First you must get rid of skepticism and doubt. No unbeliever ever enjoyed the benefits of this magic key. You must *believe* in the test that you are about to make.

Perhaps you have thought something about becoming a successful writer, or perhaps a powerful public speaker, or a successful business executive, or an able financier. We will take public speaking as the subject of this test, but you can change that to your own objective. Just remember you must follow instructions to the letter.

On a plain sheet of letter-size paper write the following:

> I am going to become a powerful public speaker because this will enable me to render the world useful service that is needed—and because it will yield me a financial return that will provide me with the necessary material things of life.
>
> I will concentrate my mind on this desire for ten minutes daily, just before retiring at night and just after arising in the morning, for the purpose of determining just how I shall proceed to transform it into reality.
>
> I know I can become a powerful and magnetic speaker, therefore I will permit nothing to interfere with my doing so.
>
> Signed . . . .

After signing this pledge, proceed to do as you have given your word that you would do. Keep it up until the desired results have been realized.

When you come to do your concentrating, look ahead one, three, five, or even ten years, and see yourself as the most powerful speaker of your time. See, in your Imagination, an appropriate income. See yourself in your own home that you have purchased with the proceeds from your efforts as a speaker or lecturer. See yourself in possession of a nice bank account for your retirement. See yourself as a person of

SUCCESS IS

FOCUSING THE FULL POWER

OF ALL YOU ARE

ON WHAT YOU HAVE

A BURNING DESIRE

TO ACHIEVE.

—Wilferd A. Peterson

influence, due to your great ability as a public speaker. See yourself engaged in a life-calling in which you will not fear the loss of your position.

Paint this picture clearly, through the powers of your Imagination, and it will soon become transformed into a beautiful picture of deeply seated desire. Use this desire as the chief object of your Concentration and observe what happens.

You should now understand how the secret of the magic key is Concentration. Do not underestimate its power because it did not come to you clothed in mysticism, or because it is described in language that anyone can understand. All great truths are simple in final analysis, and easily understood. If they are not, they are not *great* truths.

Use the magic key with intelligence and only for the attainment of worthy ends, and it will bring you enduring happiness and success. Forget the mistakes you have made and the failures you have experienced. Quit living in the past, for your yesterdays never return. If your previous efforts have not turned out well, start all over again and make the future tell a story of success.

Make a name for yourself and render the world a great service, through ambition, desire, and *concentrated effort.*

You can do it if you believe you can!

COMMENTARY

It is impossible to read this or any of the other lessons of Law of Success *without recognizing that the principles Napoleon Hill wrote about are so interrelated, and they intersect with each other in so many ways and on so many levels, that a key concept or idea may be stated and restated numerous times with slightly different shadings. Hill comments on this himself, pointing out that the repetition is intentional in his structure of lessons that are designed to build one upon the other.*

Consequently, the editors of this edition have found that in suggesting supplemental materials, certain books and audiobooks also recur frequently. Such is the case with this subject of concentration and Hill's advice to "see yourself" as you will be when you have already achieved your objective. What Napoleon Hill is advising is not simply daydreaming. It is a very specific technique called "visualization," and many people have difficulty achieving the kind of vivid imagery that is required for it to have any real effect.

The following books are suggested here because they are particularly helpful in developing the technique of creating powerful mental imagery. Most are also available on audio: Visualization: Directing the Movies of Your Mind *by Adelaide Bry,* Creative Visualization *by Shakti Gawain,* Psycho-Cybernetics *by Dr. Maxwell Maltz,* Getting Well *by Dr. O. Carl Simonton, and* The Initiation *by Donald Schnell, which includes a description of the visualization technique in spiritual story form. Also suggested are all of the audiobooks featuring the Silva Method trainer Hans DeJong, whose tapes include an unusual method of quieting the mind using an audio tone that is designed to put the mind in the alpha state.*

When you become familiar with the powers of Concentration, it becomes clear why it is so important to choose a Definite Chief Aim as the first step in the attainment of enduring success.

The presence of any idea or thought in your consciousness tends to produce an "associated" feeling and urge you to an appropriate or corresponding action. Hold a deeply seated desire in your consciousness, through the principle of Concentration, and if you do it with full faith in its realization, this act will attract powers that the entire scientific world has failed to understand or explain.

Concentrate your mind on the attainment of the object of your deeply seated desire and soon you will attract, through those forces that no one can explain, the material counterparts of that desire.

This now brings us to the principle that constitutes the most important part of this lesson, if not the most important part of the entire course: When two or more people ally themselves, in a spirit of perfect harmony, for the purpose of attaining a definite end, if that alliance is faithfully observed by all of whom it is composed, the alliance brings, to each of them, power that is superhuman and seemingly irresistible in nature.

Science has yet to determine the name of the law behind this statement, but it is this law that I have had in mind, throughout this course, when I repeatedly refer to the power of *organized effort.*

COMMENTARY

> The organized effort of Steven Spielberg, Jeffrey Katzenberg, and David Geffen in the formation of DreamWorks SKG is an excellent contemporary example, since 1994, of an alliance for the purpose of attaining a definite end—theirs being to produce live-action motion pictures, animated feature films, television programming, home video entertainment, records, books, toys, and consumer products.
>
> To that end, they continue to further ally with other companies and individuals in the pursuit of each of those goals. In 1998 Paul Allen, already a board member, increased his investments in DreamWorks, demonstrating his faith in the company and its partners, said a spokesperson for Allen's Vulcan Ventures. Allen is the billionaire cofounder, with Bill Gates, of Microsoft.
>
> Early in 2002, DreamWorks and Hewlett-Packard Company announced, according to the HP press release, "a three-year, multimillion-dollar technology strategic alliance aimed at revolutionizing animation production. HP will provide computing infrastructure for DreamWorks' next-generation digital studio at its main facility in Glendale [California], which will make it possible to create the latest computer-generated animation more quickly, cost effectively, and with greater artistic quality than ever before."
>
> These are just two of the many alliances that have gone into the creation of this dynamic company, and they are also examples of the basis for growth of an endless number of other successful businesses.

THE EMPIRES OF THE FUTURE

ARE THE EMPIRES OF THE MIND.

—Winston Churchill

In chemistry we learn that two or more elements may be so compounded that the result is something entirely different in nature from any of the individual elements. For example, ordinary water, known by the formula H_2O, is a compound consisting of two atoms of hydrogen and one atom of oxygen, but water is neither hydrogen nor oxygen. This "marrying" of elements creates an entirely different substance from that of either of its component parts.

The same law through which this transformation of physical elements takes place may be responsible for the powers resulting from the alliance of two or more people—in a perfect state of harmony and understanding—for the attainment of a given end.

This world, and all matter, is made up of a form of energy. On the other hand, thought, and that which we call the "mind," is also a form of energy. Thought, in other words, is *organized energy.*

Now, if all matter, in final analysis, consists of energy, and if the mind is nothing but a form of highly organized energy, it is possible that the laws which affect matter may also govern the mind.

And if combining two or more elements of matter, in the proper proportion and under the right conditions, will produce something entirely different from those original elements, as in the case of H_2O, do you not see how it is possible to so combine the energy of two or more minds that the result will be a sort of composite mind that is totally different from the individual minds of which it consists?

You have undoubtedly noticed how you are influenced in the presence of other people. Some people inspire you with optimism and Enthusiasm. Their very presence seems to stimulate your own mind to greater action, and this not only *seems* to be true but it *is* true. You have also noticed that the presence of some others had a tendency to lower your vitality and depress you; a tendency which I can assure you was very real!

What, then, do you imagine could be the cause of these changes that come over us when we come within range of certain people, unless it is a change resulting from the blending or combining of their minds with our own and producing something entirely different from the original elements?

There is no known method for proving this to be true, but I have given it many years of serious thought and I always come to the conclusion that it is at least a sound hypothesis.

You need no proof, however, that the presence of some people inspires you, while the presence of others depresses you. So it stands to reason that the person who inspires you and arouses your mind to a state of greater activity gives you more power to achieve, while the person whose presence depresses you and lowers your vitality has just the opposite effect on you. You can understand this much without the aid of a hypothesis and without further proof than what you have experienced time after time.

Come back now to the original statement: "When two or more people ally themselves, *in a spirit of perfect harmony*, for the purpose of attaining a definite end, if that alliance is *faithfully observed by all of whom it is composed*, the alliance brings, to each of them, power that is superhuman and seemingly irresistible in nature."

Study closely the emphasized parts of the foregoing statement, for there you will find the "mental formula" which, if not faithfully observed, destroys the effect of the whole.

One atom of hydrogen combined with one atom of oxygen will not produce water, and nor will an alliance in name only—that is not accompanied by "a spirit of perfect harmony" between those forming the alliance—produce "power that is superhuman and seemingly irresistible in nature."

Plant a tiny apple seed in the right sort of soil, at the right time of the year, and gradually it will burst forth into a tiny sprig, then in time it will expand and grow into an apple tree. That tree does not come from the seed alone, or from the soil, or from the elements of the air, but from all of these sources working together.

When two or more people ally themselves, "in a spirit of perfect harmony, for the purpose of attaining a definite end," the end itself, or the desire for that end, may be likened to the apple seed, and the blending of the forces of energy of the two or more minds may be likened to the seed, the air, and the soil out of which come the elements that form the material objects of that desire.

I know of a family of mountain folk who, for more than six generations, have lived in the mountainous region of Kentucky. Generation after generation of this family came and went without any noticeable improvement of a mental nature, with each generation following in the footsteps of its ancestors. They made their living from the soil, and as far as they knew, or cared, the universe consisted of a little spot of territory known as Letcher County. They married strictly in their own set, and in their own community.

Finally, one of the members of this family strayed away from the flock, so to speak, and married a well-educated and highly cultured woman from the neighboring state of Virginia. This woman was an ambitious person who was well aware that the universe extended beyond the borders of Letcher County, and covered, at least, the whole of the southern states. She had heard of chemistry, botany, biology, pathology, psychology, and of many other subjects that were of importance in the field of education.

When her children reached an age of understanding, this woman would talk to them of these subjects, and they in turn began to show a keen interest in them. One of her children is now the president of a great educational institution, where most of these subjects are taught. Another of them is a prominent lawyer, while still another is a successful physician.

Her husband, thanks to the influence of her mind, is a well-known dental surgeon and the first of his family, for six generations, to break from the traditions by which the family had been bound.

The blending of her mind with his gave him the needed stimulus to spur him on and it inspired him with ambition such as he would never have known without her influence.

EXAMPLE IS NOT THE MAIN THING

IN INFLUENCING OTHERS.

IT IS THE ONLY THING.

—Albert Schweitzer

COMMENTARY

It is indeed possible that Hill knew of this family from his childhood, when he lived in Wise County, Virginia, deep in the Blue Ridge Mountains on the Kentucky border. It's also possible that he created the story by way of example, based it somewhat loosely on his own family, and combined it with details of others he knew.

As told in A Lifetime of Riches, *Napoleon's father, James Monroe Hill, immigrated to America from England and adapted well to mountain living. Having learned the printing trade from his father, after he was married he made his own printing press and published the county's first newspaper. But it provided little income, so in 1883 when "Nap" was born James gave up the paper to work as a blacksmith and farmer. Later he helped establish a local post office, where he became postmaster, and was also a trader and ran a general store.*

When Napoleon was nine his mother died. A year later his father married Martha Ramey Banner, a well-educated, cultured woman who, in addition to imparting knowledge and values to Napoleon and his brother, would later encourage James to become a dentist. But Martha's greatest contribution may have been to turn Napoleon from a wild kid, who terrorized the county, toted a six-shooter, and posed a serious disciplinary problem, into a young man with a direction and dreams of success.

When Napoleon was twelve Martha offered to replace his gun with a typewriter, saying, "If you become as good with a typewriter as you are with that gun, you may become rich and famous and known throughout the world." Whether he accepted her offer as quickly as he accepted Carnegie's is unlikely, but her early influences would certainly have prepared him for that day.

For many years I have been studying the biographies of many of those whom the world calls *great,* and it seems to me more than a mere coincidence that in every instance where the facts were available, the person who was really responsible for the greatness was in the background, behind the scenes, and seldom heard of by the hero-worshiping public.

DEPENDENT PEOPLE NEED OTHERS

TO GET WHAT THEY WANT.

INDEPENDENT PEOPLE CAN

GET WHAT THEY WANT

THROUGH THEIR OWN EFFORTS.

INTERDEPENDENT PEOPLE

COMBINE THEIR OWN EFFORTS

WITH THE EFFORTS OF OTHERS

TO ACHIEVE THEIR GREATEST SUCCESS.

—Stephen Covey

Henry Ford is one of the modern miracles of this age, and I doubt that this country, or any other, ever produced an industrial genius of his equal. If the facts were known they might trace the cause of Mr. Ford's phenomenal achievements to a woman about whom the public hears but little—his wife.

We read of Ford's achievements and of his enormous income and imagine him to be blessed with matchless ability, and he is—ability of which the world would never have heard had it not been for the modifying influence of his wife, who cooperated with him during all his years of struggle, "in a spirit of perfect harmony, for the purpose of attaining a definite end."

I have in mind another genius who is well known to the entire civilized world, Thomas Edison, who is married to one of the most remarkable women in America. Few outside of their family know to what extent her influence has made Edison's achievements possible. Mrs. Edison once told me that Mr. Edison's outstanding quality, his greatest asset above all others, was that of Concentration.

When Thomas Edison begins an experiment or research or an investigation, he never "lets go" until he either finds what he is looking for or exhausts every possible effort to do so. Night after night Mr. Edison works with such Enthusiasm that he requires but three or four hours of sleep.

Behind Mr. Edison stand two great powers: one is Concentration and the other is Mrs. Edison!

In Lesson Thirteen you will see the principle of allied effort carried to proportions that almost stagger the minds of all who have not trained themselves to think in terms of organized thought.

This course itself is a very concrete illustration of the principle underlying *organized effort*, but you will observe that it requires all the lessons of this entire course to complete the description of this principle. Omit even one of the lessons and the omission would affect the whole as the removal of one link would affect the whole of a chain.

As I have already stated in many different ways, there is a well-founded hypothesis that when one concentrates one's mind on a given subject, facts of a nature closely related to that subject will "pour" in from every conceivable source. The theory is that a deeply seated desire, when planted in the right sort of "mental soil," serves as a center of attraction for everything that harmonizes with the nature of the desire.

Dr. Elmer Gates of Washington, D.C., is perhaps one of the most competent psychologists in the world. He is recognized both in the field of psychology and in other directly and indirectly related fields of science, throughout the world, as being a man of the highest scientific standing.

After Dr. Gates has followed a line of investigation as far as is possible through the usual channels of research, and he has all the recorded facts at his command, he takes a pencil and a notepad and "sits" for further information, by *concentrating* on that subject until thoughts related to it begin to flow in upon him. He told me that many of his most important discoveries came through this method.

It was more than twenty years ago that I first talked with Dr. Gates on this subject. Since that time, through the discovery of radio, we have been provided with a reasonable hypothesis through which to explain the results of these "sittings." The ether, as we have discovered through the modern radio apparatus, is in a constant state of agitation. Soundwaves are floating through the ether at all times, but these waves cannot be detected, beyond a short distance from their source, except by the aid of properly attuned instruments.

COMMENTARY

In Napoleon Hill's reference here to the discovery of "the modern radio apparatus," we are reminded that when he was writing this the average person's knowledge of radio was less than twenty-five years old.

In the early 1890s a number of people had been experimenting with radio signals. Professor Oliver Lodge, a British physicist at Oxford, had already succeeded in transmitting Morse signals over a relatively short range, but for him it was just an academic exercise and he didn't pursue it further.

In 1895, after building the equipment and transmitting electrical signals over short distances at home, Italian inventor Guglielmo Marconi became obsessed with the idea of sending messages across the ocean. In 1901 he built a powerful transmitter at the southwest tip of England, then installed a receiving station at St. John's, Newfoundland, and on December 12, 1901, he received signals from across the Atlantic.

Following Marconi's success, one report said that his ideas were the products of Lodge's mind, not his own. Lodge, however, had failed to see the potential application of wireless, while Marconi understood it and set about applying it.

In light of the thinking of the time, it is not hard to see why Hill might have seen this new principle of sending and receiving radio-wave vibrations as being the answer to the phenomenon we've all experienced of picking up "vibes" from other people. Although Hill's theory was not proven to be right, it should also be pointed out that no one has yet come up with a better explanation.

Now, it seems reasonable to suppose that *thought*, being the most highly organized form of energy known, is constantly sending waves through the ether, but these waves, like those of sound, can only be detected and correctly interpreted by a properly attuned mind.

I have not a doubt that when Dr. Gates sat down in a room and put himself in a quiet, passive state of mind, the dominating thoughts in his mind served as a force that attracted the related or similar thought waves of others.

Taking the hypothesis just a step further, it has occurred to me many times that every thought that has ever been released in organized form, from the mind of any human being, is still in existence in the form of a wave and is constantly passing around and around in

WISDOM IS LIKE ELECTRICITY.

THERE IS NO PERMANENTLY WISE MAN,

BUT MEN CAPABLE OF WISDOM, WHO,

BEING PUT INTO CERTAIN COMPANY,

OR OTHER FAVORABLE CONDITIONS,

BECOME WISE FOR A WHILE,

AS GLASSES BEING RUBBED ACQUIRE

ELECTRIC POWER FOR A WHILE.

—Ralph Waldo Emerson

a great endless circle. It may be that by the act of concentrating your mind with intensity on a given subject you send out thought waves that reach and blend with those of a related or similar nature, thereby establishing a line of communication between the one doing the concentrating and the thoughts of a similar nature that have been previously set into motion.

Going still a step further, may it not be possible to so attune one's mind, and harmonize the rate of vibration of thought with the rate of vibration of the ether, that all knowledge that has been accumulated through the *organized thoughts* of the past is still available?

With these hypotheses in mind, go back to Lesson Two and study Andrew Carnegie's description of the Master Mind through which he accumulated his great fortune.

When Carnegie formed an alliance between more than a score of carefully selected minds, he created one of the strongest industrial forces that the world has ever witnessed. With a few notable (and very disastrous) exceptions, the men constituting the Master Mind that Carnegie created *thought* and *acted* as one!

And that Master Mind, composed of many individual minds, was concentrated on a single purpose, the nature of which is familiar to everyone who knew Mr. Carnegie, particularly those who were competing with him in the steel business.

You will understand from this lesson that the object of forming an alliance between two or more people, and thereby creating a Master Mind, is to apply the law of Concentration more effectively than it could be applied through the efforts of one person.

The principle referred to as the Master Mind is nothing more nor less than group Concentration of mind power on the attainment of a definite object or end. Greater power comes through group mind Concentration because of the "stepping up" process produced through the reaction of one mind on another or others.

If you have followed Henry Ford's record, even slightly, you will undoubtedly have observed that *concentrated effort* has been one of the outstanding features of his career. Nearly thirty years ago he adopted a policy of standardization as to the general type of automobile he would build, and he consistently maintained that policy until the change in public demand forced him, in 1927, to change it.

COMMENTARY

Henry Ford's consistency extended also to the color of the Model T, fifteen million of which, in nineteen years of production from 1908 to 1927, were made only in black and with little change in the design.

A few years after its introduction, Napoleon Hill met with Ford to talk about the principles of success. According to Hill, in Michael Ritt's A Lifetime of Riches, *Henry Ford was "cold, indifferent, unenthusiastic, and spoke only when forced to." Early on, few people other than Carnegie could foresee the success Ford would achieve, which Hill, as he says here, attributed in large part to Ford's concentrated effort. At Hill's first meeting with him in 1911, the only thing Ford was interested in talking about was his Model T. After Ford took him for a "spin around the factory," Hill bought one for $680.*

When I met the former chief engineer of the Ford plant a few years ago, he told me of an incident that happened during the early stages of Mr. Ford's automobile experience which very clearly points to *concentrated effort* as being one of his prominent fundamentals of economic philosophy.

On this occasion the engineers of the Ford plant had gathered in the engineering office to discuss a proposed change in the design of the rear axle construction of the Ford automobile. Mr. Ford stood around and listened to the discussion until each man had had his say, then he walked over to the table, tapped the drawing of the proposed axle with his finger, and said, "Now listen! The axle we are using does the work for which it was intended, and does it well, and there's going to be no more change in that axle!"

He turned and walked away, and from that day until this, the rear axle construction of the Ford automobile has remained substantially the same. It is not improbable that Mr. Ford's success in building and marketing automobiles has been due, very largely, to his policy of consistently concentrating his efforts behind one plan, with but one *definite purpose* in mind at a time.

A few years ago I read Edward Bok's book *Man from Maine,* which is the biography of his father-in-law, Mr. Cyrus H. K. Curtis, the owner of the *Saturday Evening Post,* the *Ladies' Home Journal,* and several other publications. All through the book I noticed that the outstanding feature of Mr. Curtis's philosophy was that of *concentrated effort* behind a *definite purpose.*

During the early days of his ownership of the *Saturday Evening Post,* as he was pouring money into a losing venture by the hundreds of thousands of dollars, it required *concentrated effort,* backed by courage such as but few men possess, to enable him to carry on.

Read *Man from Maine.* It is a splendid lesson on the subject of Concentration and it supports, to the smallest detail, the fundamentals upon which this lesson is based.

The *Saturday Evening Post* is now one of the most profitable magazines in the world, but its name would have been long since forgotten had Mr. Curtis not concentrated his attention and his fortune on the one *definite purpose* of making it a great magazine.

COMMENTARY

Man from Maine *was reprinted as recently as 1993 but at this writing it is not in current stock at either Barnes & Noble or Amazon. There are, however, used copies available through both, and no doubt used-book dealers would also be able to locate copies.*

I DO NOT THINK THERE IS

ANY OTHER QUALITY SO ESSENTIAL

TO SUCCESS OF ANY KIND AS THE

QUALITY OF PERSEVERANCE.

IT OVERCOMES ALMOST EVERYTHING,

EVEN NATURE.

—John D. Rockefeller

In the time since Hill wrote his ringing endorsement of Man from Maine *there have been numerous such biographies and autobiographies that speak to the importance of concentrated effort and to all of Hill's other principles as well.*

As of the 1980s, and continuing into the twenty-first century, the business biography bestseller has practically become its own publishing genre. So much so that there are literally too many bestsellers from which to select a "best-of" listing for inclusion here. Any such choice we would make would not necessarily be the best, but merely reflective of the interests of the person doing the choosing. There are bestselling books and audiobooks by and about the insiders who run every industry from airlines, automobiles, cosmetics, computers, department stores, hotels, Internet companies, movie studios, multinational conglomerates, real estate empires, television networks, toy companies, sports teams, and wineries, to whatever industries start with x, y, and z.

However, there are two books that the editors recommend which are not by or about a single individual or industry. These books are In Search of Excellence *by Tom Peters and* Breakthroughs! *by P. R. Nayak and John M. Ketteringham. Each of these books deals with a broad spectrum of industries, and within each industry they single out certain companies and individuals for analysis.*

Both were published at the beginning of the business-book trend in the 1980s, but there have been few books since then that better convey the importance of the person focused on a good idea. In Search of Excellence, *recently chosen by a panel of experts as the most influential book of the past twenty years, was a runaway bestseller and will likely be in print for years to come.* Breakthroughs! *may be harder to find but it will be well worth the effort.*

MEMORY TRAINING

We have seen what an important part environment and habit play in connection with Concentration. We shall now discuss a third subject related to Concentration, and that is *memory*.

The three principles through which an accurate and unfaltering memory may be trained are few and comparatively simple:

1. *Retention:* The receiving of a sense impression through one or more of the five senses, and the recording of this impression in the mind. As stated earlier, this process may be likened to the recording of a picture on the plate of a camera.

2. *Recall:* The reviving or recalling into the conscious mind of those sense impressions that have been recorded in the subconscious mind. This process could be compared to going through a card index and pulling out a card on which information had been previously recorded.

3. *Recognition:* The ability to recognize a sense impression when it is called into the conscious mind, to identify it as being a duplicate of the original impression, then to associate it with the source from which it came when it was first recorded. This process enables us to distinguish between memory and imagination.

Now let us make application of these principles and determine how to use them effectively.

First, when you wish to be sure of your ability to recall a sense impression, such as a name, a date, or a place, be sure to make the impression vivid by concentrating on it to the finest detail. An effective way to do this is to repeat the information several times. Just as a photographer must give an exposure proper time to record itself on the plate of the camera, so must we give the subconscious mind time to properly and clearly record any sense impression that we wish to be able to recall readily.

Next, associate whatever you wish to remember with some other object, name, place, or date that is familiar to you, such as the name of your hometown, a close friend, your birth date, and so on. Along with the sense impression you can easily recall, your mind will also store the one you may not recall as easily. Later, bringing the familiar impression into the conscious mind will also bring the other with it.

Repeat what you wish to remember, a number of times, while at the same time *concentrating* your mind on it. The common failing of not being able to remember the names of other people, which most of us have, is due entirely to the fact that we do not properly record the name in the first place. When you are introduced to a new person, repeat their name four or five times, first making sure you understood the name correctly. If the name is similar to that of someone else you know, associate the two names, thinking of both as you repeat the name of the new person.

The law of association is the most important feature of a well-trained memory and it is also a very simple law.

If someone gives you a letter to be mailed, look at the letter, then increase its size in your Imagination and see it hanging over a mailbox. Fix in your mind a letter approximately the size of a door, then associate it with a mailbox, and you will find that the first mailbox you pass on the street will cause you to recall that big, odd-looking letter that you have in your pocket.

Suppose you were introduced to a lady whose name was Elizabeth Shearer and you wished to be able to recall her name at will. As you repeat her name, associate with it a large pair of scissors, perhaps ten feet in length, and Queen Elizabeth, and you will observe that recalling either the large pair of scissors or the name of Queen Elizabeth will also help you recall the name of Elizabeth Shearer.

Nearly ten years ago a friend gave me his residence telephone number in Milwaukee, Wisconsin, and although I did not write it down, I remember it today as well as I did the day he gave it to me. The exchange and number were Lakeview 2651. At the time he gave it to me we were standing at the railroad station, in sight of Lake Michigan.

Therefore I used the lake as an associated object with which to file the name of the telephone exchange. It so happened that the telephone number was made up of the age of my brother, who was

WHAT YOU SEE (IN YOUR MIND'S EYE)

IS WHAT YOU GET.

PROOF: WHAT YOU SAW

IS PRETTY MUCH WHAT YOU GOT!

—Joe Klock

26, and my father, who was 51. So I associated their names and ages with the number. To recall the telephone exchange and number, I had only to think of Lake Michigan, my brother, and my father.

COMMENTARY

> *As Napoleon Hill notes, there are only a few basic memory techniques, and while his explanation covers the classic methods, he does so in rather simple terms. From the many books on the subject and the memory courses that are widely promoted in every media from magazines to infomercials, it would seem that there must be more to it.*
>
> *And there is. The "more to it" is the many variations on the basic techniques. Though it may all boil down to repetition, association, and recall of sense impressions, there are many inventive methods by which you can put them into practice, especially the techniques of association and sense impression. None of the available books or courses can offer magic, but they do give you interesting tools to work with.*

An acquaintance of mine found himself to be suffering from what is often called a "wandering mind." He was becoming absent-minded and unable to remember. In his own words, this is how he overcame that handicap:

"I am fifty years old. For a decade I have been a department manager in a large factory. At first my duties were easy, then the firm had a rapid expansion of business which gave me added responsibilities. Several of the young men in my department developed unusual energy and ability, and at least one of them had his eye on my job.

"I had reached the age in life when a man likes to be comfortable, and having been with the company a long time, I felt that I could safely settle back into an easy berth. The effect of this attitude was disastrous to my position.

"About two years ago I noticed that my power of concentration was weakening. I neglected my correspondence until I looked with dread upon the formidable pile of letters. Reports accumulated and subordinates were inconvenienced by the delay. I sat at my desk with my mind wandering elsewhere.

"Other circumstances also showed plainly that my mind was not on my work. I forgot to attend an important meeting of the officers of the company. Another time one of the clerks under me caught a bad mistake I had made in an estimate on a carload of goods, and, of course, saw to it that the manager learned of the incident.

"I was thoroughly alarmed at the situation and asked for a week's vacation to think things over. I was determined either to resign or to find the trouble and remedy it. A few days of earnest introspection at an out-of-the-way mountain resort convinced me that I was suffering from a plain case of mind-wandering. My physical and mental activities at my desk had become haphazard. I was careless, shiftless, and neglectful—all because my mind was not alertly on the job. I needed a complete new set of working habits, and I made a resolve to acquire them.

"With paper and pencil I outlined a schedule to cover the working day: first the morning mail, then the orders to be filled, dictation, conference with subordinates, and miscellaneous duties, ending with a clean desk before I left.

"I asked myself how habits are formed, and my answer was by repetition. I realized that I have been doing these things over and over thousands of times, but not in an orderly concentrated fashion.

"I returned to the office and put my new working schedule in force at once. I performed the same duties with the same zest and, as nearly as possible, at the same time every day. When my mind started to slip away I quickly brought it back. From a mental stimulus created by willpower, I progressed in habit-building. Day after day I practiced concentration of thought. When I found repetition becoming comfortable, then I knew that I had won."

Your ability to train your memory, or to develop any desired habit, is solely a matter of being able to fix your attention on a given subject until the outline of that subject has been thoroughly impressed upon your mind. Concentration itself is nothing but a matter of control of your attention.

You will observe that by reading a line of print with which you are not familiar and which you have never seen before, and then closing your eyes, you can see that line as plainly as though you were looking at it on the printed page. In reality, you are "looking at it" not on the page but on the sensitized plate of your own mind. If you try this experiment and it does not work the first time, it is because you did not concentrate your attention on the line closely enough. Repeat the process a few times and finally you will succeed.

If you wish to memorize poetry, for example, you can do so very quickly by training yourself to fix your attention on the lines so closely that, again, you can shut your eyes and see them in your mind as plainly as you see them on the printed page.

So significant is this subject of control of attention that I must emphasize it strongly. I consider it, by far, the most important part of the lesson.

Put this hypothesis to a test of your own. You can select no better subject than your Definite Chief Aim in life. Memorize your Definite Chief Aim so that you can repeat it without looking at the written page, then make a practice of fixing your attention on it at least twice a day.

Go to a quiet place where you will not be disturbed. Sit down and completely relax your mind and your body. Then close your eyes and place your fingers in your ears, thereby blocking all light and all ordinary sound waves.

"BUT CAN YOU PERSUADE US, IF WE

REFUSE TO LISTEN TO YOU?" HE SAID.

"CERTAINLY NOT," REPLIED GLAUCON.

"THEN WE ARE NOT GOING TO LISTEN;

OF THAT YOU CAN BE ASSURED."

—*The Republic* by Plato

Then repeat your Definite Chief Aim in life, and as you do so, in your Imagination see yourself in full possession of the object of that aim. If a part of your aim is the accumulation of money, as it undoubtedly is, then see yourself in possession of that money. If a part of the object of your Definite Chief Aim is to own a home, then see a picture of that home in your Imagination just as you expect to see it in reality. If a part of your Definite Chief Aim is to become a powerful and influential public speaker, then see yourself before an enormous audience, and *feel* yourself playing on the emotions of that audience as a great violinist would play on the strings of a violin.

Begin now to cultivate the ability to fix attention, at will, on a given subject, with a feeling that this ability when fully developed would bring you the object of your Definite Chief Aim in life.

PERSUASION VS. FORCE

Success, as has been stated in dozens of different ways throughout this course, is very largely a matter of tactful and harmonious negotiation with other people. Generally speaking, one who understands how to get people to do the things they want done may succeed in any calling.

I will now describe those principles through which people are influenced, through which Cooperation is gained, and through which antagonism is eliminated and friendliness developed.

Force sometimes gets what appear to be satisfactory results, but force alone never has built and never can build enduring success.

The human body can be imprisoned or controlled by physical force, but it is not so with the human mind. No one can control the mind of a normal, healthy person if that person chooses to exercise their God-given right to control their own mind.

The majority of the people do not exercise this right. They go through the world, thanks to our faulty educational system, without having discovered the strength that lies dormant in their own minds. Now and then something happens that awakens a person and causes them to discover where their real strength lies and how to use it in the development of industry or one of the professions. Result: a genius is born!

There is a given point at which the human mind stops rising or exploring unless something out of the daily routine happens to "push" it over this obstacle. The individual who discovers a way to stimulate his or her mind artificially, to cause it to go beyond this average stopping point frequently, is sure to be rewarded with fame and fortune if their efforts are of a constructive nature.

COMMENTARY

Hill's own mind never did reach its stopping point, although he found it taking an unexpected direction at the same time he reached what he'd intended would be semiretirement.

W. Clement Stone had been a devotee of Napoleon Hill's philosophies since he first read Think and Grow Rich *in 1938. The owner of an insurance company selling one-dollar travel policies, Stone had purchased many thousands of copies of the book, making it required reading for each of his thousands of salespeople.*

In 1952 Stone's friend and dentist, Dr. Herb Gustafson, had recommended Napoleon Hill as speaker for a dental convention in Chicago. It was to have been one of Hill's last public engagements, and Gustafson invited Stone to attend.

When they met, Stone told Hill of the numerous copies he had bought of Think and Grow Rich *and said that he attributed his success and great wealth to that book. In* A Lifetime of Riches, *author Michael Ritt says that to Hill it "was an endorsement of his life's work, and it came from a man who was more than accomplished—Stone was, in Hill's eyes, an empire builder cut from the same mold as the giants of early twentieth-century American industry whose philosophies had provided the basis for Hill's principles of success."*

W. Clement Stone's primary goals were to increase his business from a thirty-two-million-dollar enterprise to one hundred million and, personally, to

use his wealth and knowledge to "create a better world for this and future genera-
tions." He called this his "magnificent obsession."

They were philosophically in perfect harmony. Stone persuaded Hill to forget
about retirement, and by the end of the luncheon they had created the foundation
for what would become the strongest Master Mind alliance of Hill's career. To
further spread Hill's message, Stone would manage his activities and provide
financial backing. They formed Napoleon Hill Associates.

Stone's business goal was more than realized. With Hill motivating his staff,
the company's assets reached nine hundred million dollars. To reach what was
the personal goal of both, Napoleon Hill Associates produced books, courses,
lectures, inspirational films, radio programs, and eventually television shows.

The success of their business partnership and Master Mind alliance
continued until 1961—always with a handshake, never a contract. Their friend-
ship continued throughout the rest of Hill's life.

Napoleon Hill died November 8, 1970, at the age of eighty-seven. W. Clement
Stone died September 3, 2002, at the age of one hundred, having fulfilled his
magnificent obsession by donating more than $275 million to various charities
over his lifetime.

The educator who discovers a way to stimulate any mind and cause it to rise above its usual stopping point, without any bad reactionary effects, will confer a blessing on humanity second to none. I am not referring to physical stimulants. I am referring to a purely mental stimulant, such as that which comes through intense interest, desire, Enthusiasm, love, and so on—the factors out of which a Master Mind may be developed.

The person who makes this discovery will also do much toward solving the crime problem. You can do almost anything with a person when you learn how to influence their mind. The human mind may be likened to a great field. It is a very fertile field that always produces a crop of the kind of seed that is sown in it. The problem, then, is to learn how to select the right sort of seed and how to sow that seed so that it takes root and grows quickly.

———————————

I DO NOT FEEL OBLIGED TO BELIEVE

THAT THE SAME GOD WHO HAS

ENDOWED US WITH SENSE,

REASON, AND INTELLECT HAS

INTENDED US TO FORGO THEIR USE.

—Galileo Galilei

———————————

We are sowing seed in our minds every second, but we are doing it more or less unconsciously. We must learn to do it following a carefully prepared plan, according to a well laid-out design. Haphazardly sown seed in the human mind brings back a haphazard crop. There is no escape from this result.

History is full of notable cases of those who have been transformed from law-abiding, peaceful, constructive citizens to vicious criminals. We also have thousands of cases wherein criminals have been transformed into constructive, law-abiding citizens. In every one of these cases the transformation of the human being took place in the mind of the person. Each created in their own mind, for one reason or another, a picture of what they desired and then proceeded to transform that picture into reality.

If a picture of any environment, condition, or thing is envisioned in the human mind, and if the mind is focused or concentrated on that picture long enough and persistently enough and backed up with a strong desire for the thing pictured, it is but a short step from the picture to the realization of it in physical or mental form.

The world war brought out many startling tendencies of the human mind which corroborate the work that psychologists have been doing in their research into the workings of the mind. The following account of a rough, unschooled, undisciplined young mountain man is an excellent case in point.

COMMENTARY

By including the following story of World War I hero Alvin York, as written by George W. Dixon, Napoleon Hill's intent was not just to tell the story of a hero but also to illustrate his point that given a powerful enough stimulus, an individual can change his or her mind and thereby change his or her life.

In the case of Alvin York, he went through two profound changes: the first self-directed, and the second inspired by others whom he respected. Though the modern reader may find the storytelling style a little florid and melodramatic, the editors of this edition have chosen to reprint it exactly as it first appeared. Mr. Dixon's passionate literary style also says something about how powerfully affected the public of the day was by Alvin York's story of self-transformation.

In 1941 York's story was made into the motion picture Sergeant York, *starring Gary Cooper, a role for which Cooper won the Academy Award for Best Actor. Alvin York acted as a consultant on the film, so the events portrayed are not as overly dramatic or romanticized as many other Hollywood biographies.* Sergeant York *is available on video and it still holds up as a well-made, powerful, and affecting movie.*

FOUGHT FOR HIS RELIGION; NOW GREAT WAR HERO

ROTARIANS PLAN TO PRESENT FARM TO ALVIN YORK,
UNLETTERED TENNESSEE SQUIRREL HUNTER

by George W. Dixon

How Alvin Cullom York, an unlettered Tennessee squirrel hunter, became the foremost hero of the American Expeditionary Forces in France, forms a romantic chapter in the history of the world war.

York is a native of Fentress County. He was born and reared among the hardy mountaineers of the Tennessee woods. There is not even a railroad in Fentress County. During his earlier years he was reputed to be a desperate character. He was what was known as a gunman. He was a dead shot with a revolver, and his prowess with the rifle was known far and wide among the plain people of the Tennessee hills.

One day a religious organization pitched its tent in the community in which York and his parents lived. It was a strange sect that came to the mountains looking for converts, but the methods of the evangels of the new cult were full of fire and emotionalism. They denounced the sinner, the vile character and the man who took advantage of his neighbor. They pointed to the religion of the Master as an example that all should follow.

Alvin Gets Religion

Alvin Cullom York startled his neighbors one night by flinging himself down at the mourners' bench. Old men stirred in their seats and women craned their necks, as York wrestled with his sins in the shadows of the Tennessee mountains.

York became an ardent apostle of the new religion. He became an exhorter, a leader in the religious life of the community, and, although his marksmanship was as deadly as ever, no one feared him who walked in the path of righteousness.

When the news of the war reached that remote section of Tennessee, and the mountaineers were told that they were going to be "conscripted," York grew sullen and disagreeable. He didn't believe in killing human beings, even in war. His Bible taught him, "Thou shalt not kill." To his mind this was literal and final. He was branded as a "conscientious objector."

The draft officers anticipated trouble. They knew that his mind was made up, and they would have to reach him in some manner other than by threats of punishment.

War in a Holy Cause

They went to York with a Bible and showed him that the war was in a holy cause—the cause of liberty and human freedom. They pointed out that men like himself were called upon by the Higher Powers to make the world free; to protect innocent women and children from violation; to make life

IT IS EASY TO FLY INTO A PASSION—

ANYBODY CAN DO THAT—

BUT TO BE ANGRY WITH THE

RIGHT PERSON TO THE RIGHT EXTENT

AND AT THE RIGHT TIME

WITH THE RIGHT OBJECT

AND IN THE RIGHT WAY—

THAT IS NOT EASY, AND IT IS NOT

EVERYONE WHO CAN DO IT.

—Aristotle

worth living for the poor and oppressed; to overcome the "beast" pictured in the Scriptures; and to make the world free for the development of Christian ideals and Christian manhood and womanhood. It was a fight between the hosts of righteousness and the hordes of Satan. The devil was trying to conquer the world through his chosen agents, the Kaiser and his generals.

York's eyes blazed with a fierce light. His big hands closed like a vise. His strong jaws snapped. "The Kaiser," he hissed between his teeth. "The beast! The destroyer of women and children! I'll show him where he belongs if I ever get within gunshot of him!"

He caressed his rifle, kissed his mother good-by, and told her he would see her again when the Kaiser had been put out of business. He went to the training camp and drilled with scrupulous care and strict obedience to orders.

His skill at target practice attracted attention. His comrades were puzzled at his high scores. They had not reckoned that a backwoods squirrel hunter would make fine material for a sniper in the front-line trenches.

York's part in the war is now history. General Pershing has designated him as the foremost individual hero of the war. He won every decoration, including the Congressional Medal, the Croix de Guerre, the Legion of Honor. He faced the Germans without fear of death. He was fighting to vindicate his religion, for the sanctity of the home; the love of women and children; the preservation of the ideal of Christianity and the liberties of the poor and oppressed.

Fear was not in his code or his vocabulary. His cool daring electrified more than a million men and set the world to talking about this strange, unlettered hero from the hills of Tennessee.

Here we have a case of a young mountain man who, had he been approached from just a slightly different angle, undoubtedly would have resisted conscription and, likely as not, would have become so embittered toward his country that he would have become an outlaw, looking for an opportunity to strike back at the first chance.

Those who approached him knew something of the principles through which the human mind works. They knew how to connect with young York by first overcoming the resistance he had worked up in his own mind. This is the very point at which thousands of men, through improper understanding of these principles, are arbitrarily classed as criminals and treated as dangerous, vicious people. Through suggestion, these people could have been handled as effectively as young York was handled and they could have developed into useful, productive human beings.

In your search for ways and means of understanding and manipulating your own mind so that you can persuade it to create what you desire in life, let me remind you that, without a single exception, anything that irritates you and arouses you to anger, hatred, dislike, or cynicism, is destructive to you.

You can never get the maximum or even a fair average of constructive action out of your mind until you have learned to control it and keep it from becoming stimulated through anger or fear.

These two negatives—anger and fear—are, without question, destructive to your mind. As long as you allow them to remain, you can be sure of results that are unsatisfactory and far below what you are capable of producing.

In our discussion of environment and habit, we learned that the individual mind is amenable to the suggestions of environment and that the minds of the individuals of a crowd blend with one another, conforming to the suggestion of the leader or dominating figure.

Following are comments by leading authorities that will give you a better understanding of the law of Concentration as it is often used by those who wish to "blend" or "fuse" the minds of a crowd so they will function as a single mind.

COMMENTARY

In the original edition of Law of Success, *following the above introduction, Napoleon Hill had included an extremely lengthy digression on religious revival meetings.*

As readers of this book are well aware, Hill was intrigued by the workings of the mind, the study of psychology in general, and in particular the serious study of hypnosis. To his dismay, the scientific work done in these areas was being abused. Hypnosis was falling into disrepute because stage magicians, who were extremely popular at the time, often used it as a part of their act. At the same time the phenomenon of the religious revival meeting was sweeping America. Hill was very critical of the ways in which the leaders of these "tent meetings" manipulated the emotions of their followers by using the techniques of mass psychology and hypnosis to create the illusion of religious epiphany. Apparently Hill felt that his readers needed to be warned of these abuses and he extensively quoted numerous experts to support his position.

At the time of this writing, revival meetings are far from being a widespread phenomenon, the magicians of note are creating grand illusions in the casinos of Las Vegas, and hypnosis has regained its status as a serious psychological technique used in hypnotherapy. Knowing that the reader of this edition is not in danger of being bamboozled, the editors have limited the number of repetitive supporting quotations. There are, however, some interesting points made in this quoted material about the mass psychology of revival meetings, which the modern reader may even have experienced at a seminar or workshop given by one of today's powerful motivational speakers.

EVERY MAN HAS A MOB SELF

AND AN INDIVIDUAL SELF,

IN VARYING PROPORTIONS.

—D. H. Lawrence

Here Mr. J. A. Fisk gives an interesting account of the influence of mental suggestion in a revival meeting.

MENTAL SUGGESTION IN THE REVIVAL

Modern psychology has firmly established the fact that the greater part of the phenomena of the religious "revival" are *psychical* rather than spiritual in their nature. The leading authorities recognize the fact that the mental excitement of the emotional appeals of the "revivalist" must be classified with the phenomena of hypnotic suggestion rather than with that of true religious experience. In fact, by some careful observers, familiar with the respective phenomena, the religious "revival" meeting is classed with the public hypnotic "entertainment". . . .

In order to understand the principle of the operation of mental suggestion in the revival meeting, we must first understand something of what is known as the *psychology of the crowd.*

Psychologists are aware that the psychology of a crowd differs from that of the separate individuals composing that crowd. There is a crowd of separate individuals, and a composite crowd in which the emotional natures of the units seem to blend and fuse.

The change arises from the influence of earnest attention, or deep emotional appeals, or common interest. When this change occurs, the crowd becomes a composite individual whose intelligence and emotional control is little above that of its weakest member. . . . The predominant characteristics of this "composite-mindedness" of a crowd are the evidences of extreme suggestibility, response to appeals of emotion, vivid imagination, and action arising from imitation. . . .

Diall, in his *Psychology of the Aggregate Mind of an Audience*, holds that the mind of an assemblage listening to a powerful speaker undergoes a curious process called "fusion," by which the individuals in the audience, losing their personal traits for the time being . . . are reduced, as it were, to a single individual, whose characteristics are those of an impulsive youth, imbued in general with high ideals, but lacking in reasoning power and will. Tarde, the French psychologist, advances similar views.

Professor Joseph Jastrow, in his *Fact and Fable in Psychology*, says:

". . . The conjurer finds it easy to perform to a large audience, because, among other reasons, it is easier to arouse their admiration and sympathy, easier to make them forget themselves and enter into the uncritical spirit of wonderland. It would seem that in some respects the critical tone of an assembly, like the strength of a chain, is that of its weakest member."

Professor [Gustave] Le Bon, in his *The Crowd*, says:

"The sentiments and ideas of all the persons in the gathering take one and the same direction, and their conscious personality vanishes. . . . The most careful observations seem to prove that an individual immerged for some length of time in a crowd in action soon finds himself in a special state, which most resembles the state of fascination in which the hypnotized individual finds himself. . . . The conscious personality has entirely vanished, will and discernment are lost. All feelings and thoughts are bent in the direction determined by the hypnotizer. . . .

"Moreover, by the mere fact that he forms part of an organized crowd, a man descends several rungs in the ladder of civilization. Isolated, he may be a cultured individual; in a crowd, he is a barbarian—that is, a creature acting by instinct. . . . An individual in a crowd is a grain of sand amid other grains of sand, which the wind stirs up at will."

Professor [Frederick Morgan] Davenport, in his book *Primitive Traits in Religious Revivals*, says:

"The mind of the crowd is strangely like that of primitive man. Most of the people in it may be far from primitive in emotion, in thought, in character; nevertheless, the result tends always to be the same. Stimulation immediately begets action. Reason is in abeyance. The cool, rational speaker has little chance beside the skillful emotional orator. The crowd thinks in images, and speech must take this form to be accessible to it. . . . It follows from this, of course, that appeals to the imagination have paramount influence. . . . The crowd is united and governed by emotion rather than by reason. . . . The explanation of this is that the attention of the crowd is always directed either by the circumstances of the occasion or by the speaker to certain common ideas—as 'salvation' in religious gatherings . . . and every individual in the gathering is stirred with emotion, not only because the idea or the shibboleth stirs him, but also because he is conscious that every other individual in the gathering believes in the idea or the shibboleth, and is stirred by it, too...."

As [Emile] Durkheim observed in his psychological investigations, the average individual is "intimidated by the mass" of the crowd around him, or before him, and experiences that peculiar psychological influence exerted by the mere number of people as against his individual self. Not only does the suggestible person find it easy to respond to the authoritative suggestions of the preacher and the exhortations of his helpers, but he is also brought under the direct fire of the imitative suggestions of those on all sides who are experiencing emotional activities and who are manifesting them outwardly. . . . Human beings, in times

IT IS A CHARACTERISTIC OF

ALL MOVEMENTS AND CRUSADES

THAT THE PSYCHOPATHIC ELEMENT

RISES TO THE TOP.

—Robert Lindner

of panic, fright, or deep emotion of any kind, manifest the imitative tendency of sheep, and the tendency of cattle and horses to "stampede" under imitation.

. . . [In both hypnosis and revival meetings] the attention and interest is attracted by the unusual procedure; the element of mystery and awe is induced by words and actions calculated to inspire them; the senses are tired by monotonous talk in an impressive and authoritative tone; and finally the suggestions are projected in a commanding, *suggestive* manner familiar to all students of hypnotic suggestion. The subjects in both cases are prepared for the final suggestions and commands by previously given minor suggestions such as, in the case of the hypnotist, "stand up" or "look this way" and so on; in the case of the revivalist, by something like "all those who think so-and-so, stand up" or "all who are willing to become better, stand up." The impressionable subjects are thus accustomed to obedience to suggestion by easy stages. And, finally, the commanding suggestion: "Come right up . . . right up . . . this way—right up . . . come, I say, come, come, come!" . . . which takes the impressed ones right off their feet and rushes them to the front are almost precisely the same in the hypnotic experiment or séance, on the one hand, and the sensational revival, on the other. Every good revivalist would make a good hypnotic operator, and every good hypnotic operator would make a good revivalist, if his mind were turned in that direction.

In the revival, the person giving the suggestions has the advantage of breaking down the resistance of his audience by arousing their sentiments and emotions. Tales depicting the influence of mother, home, and heaven . . . tend to reduce one to the state of emotional response, and render them most suscep-tible to strong, repeated suggestions along the same line....

The element of fear is also invoked in the revival. . . . The fear of a sudden death in an unconverted condition is held

WE MUST RESPECT THE

OTHER FELLOW'S RELIGION,

BUT ONLY IN THE SENSE AND

TO THE EXTENT THAT WE

RESPECT HIS THEORY THAT

HIS WIFE IS BEAUTIFUL AND

HIS CHILDREN SMART.

—H. L. Mencken

over the audience, and, "Why not now—why not tonight?"...
is asked....

The persons who show signs of being influenced are then
"labored with" by either the revivalist or his co-workers. They
are urged to surrender their will, and "Leave it all to the Lord."
They are told to "Give yourself to God, now, right now, this
minute"; or to "only believe now, and you shall be saved";
or, "Won't you give yourself to Jesus?" etc. They are exhorted
and prayed with; arms are placed around their shoulders, and
every art of emotional persuasive suggestion is used to make
the sinner "give up."

[Edwin Diller] Starbuck in his *The Psychology of Religion*
relates a number of instances of the experiences of converted
persons at revivals. One person wrote as follows:

"My will seemed wholly at the mercy of others, particularly
of the revivalist M———. There was absolutely no intellectual
element. It was pure feeling. There followed a period of ecstasy.
I was bent on doing good and was eloquent in appealing to
others. The state of moral exaltation did not continue. It was
followed by a complete relapse from orthodox religion."

... While there have undoubtedly been many instances
of persons attracted originally by the emotional excitement
of the revival, and afterwards leading worthy religious lives in
accordance with the higher spiritual nature, still in too many
cases the revival has exerted but a temporary effect for good
upon the persons yielding to the excitement, and after the
stress has passed has resulted in creating an indifference and
even an aversion for true religious feeling.... In others there
is merely awakened a susceptibility to emotional excitement,
which causes the individual to undergo repeated stages of
"conversion" at each revival, and a subsequent "backsliding"
after the influence of the meeting [has passed].

APPLY CONCENTRATION TO
THE LAWS OF SUCCESS

By now you will have learned that the one thing over which you have complete control is your thoughts. You may not be able to determine every circumstance of your life, but with Concentration and Accurate Thinking you can determine your reaction to those circumstances.

The law of Concentration is one of the major principles that must be understood and applied intelligently by all who would successfully experiment with what I have described as the Master Mind.

I have striven throughout this course to give you practical means for putting to work everything you learn. You have no doubt noticed that with each lesson the ideas of the previous lessons have also been integrated. The Law of Success course is arranged in this manner so that your understanding of each new lesson also increases your comprehension of, and ability to apply, all the previous lessons.

THE MASTER MIND—AN AFTER-THE-LESSON
VISIT WITH THE AUTHOR

With the aid of the mind, man has discovered many interesting facts about the earth on which we live, the air and the endless space about us, and the millions of other planets and heavenly bodies that float through space. With the aid of a little mechanical contrivance (which man's mind conceived) called a "spectroscope," man has discovered, at a distance of 93,000,000 miles, the nature of the substances of which the sun is made.

We have lived through the Stone Age, the Iron Age, the Copper Age, the religious fanatic age, the Industrial Age, the scientific research age, and now we enter the age of thought.

Out of the spoils of the dark ages through which we have passed has come much material that is sound food for thought. While for more than ten thousand years the battle has raged between ignorance, superstition, and fear on the one side, and intelligence on the other, we have picked up some useful knowledge.

Among the fragments of useful knowledge gathered, we have discovered and classified the elements of which all physical matter consists. By study and analysis and comparison, we have discovered the "bigness" of the material things in the universe as they are represented by the suns and stars, some of them over ten million times as large as the earth.

We have also discovered the "littleness" of things by reducing matter to molecules, then to atoms, which are in turn made up of electrons that are themselves comprised of even smaller units, all constantly in rapid motion. And thus it is said that in every drop of water and every grain of sand the entire principle upon which the whole universe operates is duplicated.

How do we know these things to be true? Through the aid of the mind.

In the physical or material world, whether one is looking at the largest star that floats through the heavens or the smallest grain of sand to be found on earth, the object under observation is but an organized collection of molecules, atoms, and electrons.

Man knows much about the physical facts of the universe. The next great scientific discovery may well be proof of my belief that in some way every human brain may be both a broadcasting and a receiving station; that every thought vibration released by the brain may be picked up and interpreted by all other brains that are in harmony with the rate of vibration of the broadcasting brain.

I am of the opinion, and not without substantial evidence to support me, that it is possible for one to develop the ability of fixing their attention so highly that they may "tune in" and understand what is in the mind of any person. But this is not all, nor is it the most important part of a hypothesis at which I have arrived after many years of careful research, for I believe that one may just as easily go a step further and "tune in" on the universal mind in which all knowledge is stored.

To a highly orthodox mind, these statements may seem very irrational. But to the student who has studied this subject, these hypotheses seem not only possible but also absolutely probable.

COMMENTARY

As was noted in Lesson One, Introduction to the Master Mind, when Napoleon Hill was writing this book in 1927, the two founders of modern psychology, Sigmund Freud and Carl Jung, were still developing their theories of how the human mind worked.

In the time since, much of Freudian psychology has been supplanted by other theories and techniques. But this is not true of Jung. If anything, Jungian psychology has gained greater acceptance. It is interesting to note that one of the cornerstones of Jung's theory is what he called the collective unconscious, a concept that is not dissimilar to what Hill is proposing here as well as in his explanations of the Master Mind.

How did we acquire the knowledge that we possess concerning the physical laws of this earth? How did we learn what has taken place before our time, and during the uncivilized period? We gathered this knowledge by turning back the pages of Nature's bible and there viewing the unimpeachable evidence of millions of years of struggle among animals of a lower intelligence. By turning back the great stone pages, we have uncovered the bones, skeletons, footprints, and other unmistakable evidence that Mother Nature has held for our inspection throughout unbelievable periods of time.

Now we are turning our attention to another section of Nature's bible—a history of the great mental struggle that has taken place in the realm of *thought.* Thanks to education (meaning the unfolding and developing from within of the human mind) Nature's bible is now being interpreted. The story of humankind's long and perilous struggle upward has been written on the pages of this, the greatest of all bibles.

All who have at least partly conquered the six basic fears described in Lesson Three, and who have successfully conquered superstition and ignorance, may read the records that have been written in Nature's bible.

COMMENTARY

As explained in detail in Lesson Three and also in Napoleon Hill's Think and Grow Rich, *the six basic fears are the fear of poverty, the fear of old age, the fear of criticism, the fear of loss of love of someone, the fear of ill health, and the fear of death. In fact Hill reexamined these fears, in varying ways, in most of his works.*

Come for a short visit with a few of the powerful men who are making use of power created through the blending, in a spirit of harmony, of two or more minds.

Henry Ford, Thomas A. Edison, and Harvey Firestone are men of great achievement in their respective fields of endeavor. Of the three, Henry Ford is the most powerful, with reference to economic power. So great is his power that he may have anything of a physical nature that he desires, or its equivalent. Millions of dollars, to him, are but playthings, no harder to acquire than the grains of sand with which the child builds sand tunnels.

Mr. Edison has such a keen insight into Mother Nature's bible that he has harnessed and combined, for the good of man, more of Nature's laws than any other man who ever lived.

Mr. Firestone's industrial achievement has made dollars multiply themselves so rapidly that his name has become a byword wherever automobiles are operated.

All three men began their business and professional careers with no capital and but little schooling of the nature usually referred to as "education."

Perhaps Mr. Ford's beginning was, by far, the most humble of the three. Cursed with poverty and with lack of even the most elementary form of schooling, and handicapped by ignorance in many forms, he has mastered all of these in the inconceivably short period of twenty-five years.

Thus might we briefly describe the achievements of three well-known, successful men of power. But we have been dealing with effect only. The true philosopher wishes to know something of the cause that produced these desirable effects.

It is a matter of public knowledge that Mr. Ford, Mr. Edison, and Mr. Firestone are close personal friends, that they go away to the woods once a year for a period of recuperation and rest.

But it is not generally known—it is doubtful if these three men, themselves, even know it—that there exists between the three men a bond of harmony out of which has grown a Master Mind that is being used by each of the three; a mind that has the capacity to "tune in" on forces with which most men are to no extent familiar.

Let us repeat the statement that out of the blending and harmonizing of two or more minds (twelve or thirteen minds appear to be the most favorable number) may be produced a mind that has the capacity to "tune in" and pick up kindred thoughts on any subject.

Through the principle of harmony of minds, Ford, Edison, and Firestone have created a Master Mind which now supplements the efforts of each of the three, and whether consciously or unconsciously, this Master Mind is the cause of the success of each of the three.

There is no other answer to their attainment of great power and far-reaching success in their respective fields of endeavor, and this is true despite the fact that none of them may be conscious of the power they have created, or the manner in which they have done so.

COMMENTARY

Throughout Law of Success, *Napoleon Hill often names the same individuals and companies over and over when citing examples to illustrate how to apply the principles of success. These were the people Andrew Carnegie made available to Hill, and so when he spoke of how they used these principles he did so from close observation and personal knowledge.*

It's interesting to speculate whom Napoleon Hill might have written about had he been writing Law of Success *at the beginning of the twenty-first century. Which of the leaders of business and industry would he choose as examples of each principle of personal achievement? Had he known him, what would Hill have had to say about someone such as Sir Richard Branson, one of the more interesting and unusual of today's billionaires and renowned for his flamboyant, often outrageous, business and promotional style?*

Like Hill's examples above, Branson's school education was not extensive. But despite learning difficulties due to dyslexia, he was already coming up with business ideas while still in high school. In 1968 he and friend Jonny Gems created a newspaper called Student, *selling subscriptions not just to students at their own school but also to those at several other British schools. And like Hill's three examples, Branson also had no capital, other than four pounds from his mother for postage and telephone expenses. But with grand dreams, and articles written by such diverse contributors as government officials, musicians, and celebrities, they soon managed to sell corporate advertising.*

Soon afterward, when the British government lifted price controls on retail products, Branson noticed that none of the music stores were discounting records, so he ran ads in his newspaper offering discounted records by mail order. Finding that the record sales were more profitable than newspaper sales, he and Jonny acquired retail space above a shoe store by convincing the owner that their customer traffic would so greatly benefit his shoe business that it justified free rent. This was the first Virgin Records store, so named by these virgins at business.

Though Branson has retained that company name, the original reasoning was not applicable for long. Virgin has become such a well-recognized brand name that the majority of the companies in the Virgin empire are partnerships with other companies wanting to benefit from that brand association. Singapore Airlines, for example, in 1999 purchased 49 percent of Virgin Atlantic Airlines.

Despite his success and with more than three hundred business enterprises by 2002, Richard Branson has never had a corporate office or a corporate staff. His "office," usually in one of his residences, is his notebook and a telephone.

What is said to be Branson's most valuable asset is his ability to connect with people—in the true sense of the Master Mind—and to empower their ideas, to his own benefit as well as to theirs. He seems to create a new Master Mind group with each new venture, bringing into it the people or companies best able to provide the necessary links.

When Branson wanted to expand the Virgin brand into mobile phones, he did it as a co-venture with Britain's One2One. When he decided to expand into e-commerce, and being admittedly computer illiterate, who did he bring into this venture? None other than Microsoft cofounder Paul Allen.

There are aspects of this entrepreneur's story that are applicable to most all of Hill's principles, but we have chosen to mention Richard Branson in connection with this lesson because concentration and the Master Mind principle seem to best exemplify—or perhaps be the only feasible explanation for—his determination and success in implementing his ideas to the degree that he has.

These men, whether by accident or design, have blended their minds in such a way that the mind of each has been supplemented by the power of the Master Mind, and that mind has brought each of them more worldly gain than any person could possibly use.

The law upon which the principle of a Master Mind operates was discovered by Christ, when he surrounded himself with twelve disciples and created the first Thirteen Club of the world. Despite the fact that one of the thirteen (Judas) broke the chain of harmony, sufficient seed had been sown during the period of harmony that originally existed between these thirteen people to ensure the continuation of the greatest and most far-reaching philosophy known to the inhabitants of this earth.

Many millions of people believe themselves to possess wisdom. Many of these do possess wisdom, in certain elementary stages, but no one may possess real wisdom without the aid of the power of a Master Mind, and such a mind cannot be created except through the principle of blending, in harmony, of two or more minds.

Through many years of practical experimentation it has been found that thirteen minds, when blended in a spirit of perfect harmony, produce the most practical results. On this principle, whether consciously or unconsciously, is founded all of the great industrial and commercial successes that are so abundant in this age.

The successful business, industrial, and financial enterprises are those managed by leaders who either consciously or unconsciously apply the principle of coordinated effort described here. If you would be a great leader in any undertaking, surround yourself with other minds that can be blended in a spirit of Cooperation so that they act and function as one. If you can grasp this principle and apply it, you may have, for your efforts, whatever you want.

Lesson Thirteen

Cooperation

THE WORLD BASICALLY AND

FUNDAMENTALLY IS CONSTITUTED

ON THE BASIS OF HARMONY.

EVERYTHING WORKS IN COOPERATION

WITH SOMETHING ELSE.

—Preston Bradley

Lesson Thirteen

COOPERATION

"You Can Do It if You Believe You Can!"

COOPERATION IS THE BEGINNING OF ALL *organized effort.* As has already been stated, particularly in Lesson Two of this course, Andrew Carnegie accumulated a gigantic fortune through the *cooperative efforts* of a small group of men numbering not more than twenty. You, too, can learn how to use this principle.

There are two forms of Cooperation that will be discussed in this lesson.

The first form is the Cooperation between people who group themselves together or form alliances for the purpose of attaining a given end, under the principles described throughout this course as the law of the Master Mind.

The second is the Cooperation between the conscious and the subconscious minds, which is the basis upon which I have built my hypothesis that we can develop the ability to contact, communicate with, and draw upon *infinite intelligence.*

Although the foregoing hypothesis may seem unreasonable to you at this point, study the facts upon which the hypothesis is based, and then draw your own conclusions.

Let us begin with a brief review of the physical construction of the body.

COMMENTARY

In the material that follows, Napoleon Hill quotes from The Edinburgh Lectures on Mental Science *by Judge Thomas Troward. The book was first published in 1909 and most recently reprinted in 1989 in paperback. The reviews on Amazon.com are relatively current and generally favorable despite new theories having been developed since it was first written and despite some of the rather archaic writing.*

A review posted in 2002 says that it's very easy to understand and calls it "a classic by one of the pioneers of New Thought." That reviewer also recommends Troward's "masterpiece," The Creative Process in the Individual. *A 2000 review calls it "half philosophy, half science," saying "the premise, condensed down to three words, is 'faith changes reality.'" And a 1998 review also recommends* Your Invisible Power *by Genevieve Behrend, Troward's student, saying that her book outlining the same principles is more basic.*

We know that the whole body is traversed by a network of nerves that serve as the channels of communication between the indwelling spiritual ego, which we call mind, and the functions of the external organism.

This nervous system is dual. One system, known as the sympathetic, is the channel for all those activities which are not consciously directed by our volition, such as the operation of the digestive organs, the repair of the daily wear and tear of the tissues, and the like.

The other system, known as the voluntary or cerebro-spinal system, is the channel through which we receive conscious perception from the physical senses and exercise control over the movements of the body. This system has its center in the brain, while the other has its center in the ganglionic mass at the back of the stomach known as the solar plexus, and sometimes spoken of as the abdominal brain. The cerebro-spinal system is the channel of our volitional or conscious mental action, and the sympathetic system is the channel of that mental action which unconsciously supports the vital functions of the body.

Thus the cerebro-spinal system is the organ of the conscious mind and the sympathetic is that of the subconscious mind.

But the interaction of conscious and subconscious minds requires a similar interaction between the corresponding systems of nerves, and one conspicuous connection by which this is provided is the "vagus" nerve. This nerve passes out of the cerebral region as a portion of the voluntary system, and through it we control the vocal organs; then it passes onward to the thorax, sending out branches to the heart and lungs; and finally, passing through the diaphragm, it loses the outer coating which distinguishes the nerves of the voluntary system and becomes identified with those of the sympathetic system, *so forming a connecting link* between the two and making the man physically a single entity.

Similarly different areas of the brain indicate their connection with the objective and subjective activities of the mind

SOMETIMES THE SUBCONSCIOUS MIND

MANIFESTS A WISDOM

SEVERAL STEPS OR EVEN YEARS AHEAD

OF THE CONSCIOUS MIND,

AND HAS ITS OWN WAY OF

LEADING US TOWARD OUR DESTINY.

—Nathaniel Branden

respectively, and, speaking in a general way, we may assign
the frontal portion of the brain to the former, and the posterior portion to the latter, while the intermediate portion
partakes of the character of both.

The intuitional faculty has its correspondence in the
upper area of the brain, situated between the frontal and
the posterior portions, and, physiologically speaking, it is
here that intuitive ideas find entrance. These, at first, are
more or less unformed and generalized in character but are,
nevertheless, perceived by the conscious mind; otherwise,
we should not be aware of them at all. Then the effort of
Nature is to bring these ideas into more definite and usable
shape, so the conscious mind lays hold on them and induces
a corresponding vibratory current in the voluntary system
of nerves, and this in turn induces a similar current in the
involuntary system, *thus handing the idea over to the subjective
mind.* The vibratory current which had first descended from
the apex of the brain to the frontal brain and thus through
the voluntary system to the solar plexus is now reversed
and ascends from the solar plexus through the sympathetic
system to the posterior brain, this return current indicating
the action of the subjective mind.

If we were to remove the surface portion of the apex of
the brain we should find immediately below it the shining
belt of brain substance called the "corpus callosum." *This
is the point of union between the subjective and objective,* and, as
the current returns from the solar plexus to this point, it
is restored to the objective portion of the brain in a fresh
form *which it has acquired by the silent alchemy of the subjective
mind.* Thus the conception which was at first only vaguely
recognized is restored to the objective mind in a definite and
workable form, and then the objective mind, acting through

the frontal brain—the area of comparison and analysis—
proceeds to work upon a clearly perceived idea and to bring
out the potentialities that are latent in it.

The term "subjective mind" is the same as the term "subconscious
mind," and the term "objective mind" is the same as the term "conscious mind."

Please understand these different terms.

By studying this *dual system* through which the body transmits
energy, we discover the exact points at which the two systems are
connected, and the manner in which we may transmit a *thought* from
the conscious to the subconscious mind.

This cooperative dual nervous system is the most important
form of Cooperation known to man, for it is through the aid of
this system that the principle of evolution carries on its work of
developing Accurate Thinking, as described in Lesson Eleven.

When you impress any idea on your subconscious mind, through
the principle of autosuggestion, you do so with the aid of this dual
nervous system, and when your subconscious mind works out a definite plan of any desire with which you impress it, the plan is delivered
back to your conscious mind through this same dual nervous system.

This cooperative system of nerves literally constitutes a direct
line of communication between your ordinary conscious mind and
infinite intelligence.

COMMENTARY

*Napoleon Hill discusses infinite intelligence at length in Lesson Eleven, as
well as in* Think and Grow Rich. *While the term itself is used only twice in
this lesson, the concept is frequently applicable. Therefore, for the benefit
of readers who may be not be reading these lessons consecutively, we
provide a brief explanation based on Hill's other writings.*

As he says here, the subconscious mind is the connecting link, or intermediary, between the conscious mind and infinite intelligence. In Think and Grow Rich *Hill describes infinite intelligence as a power "which permeates every atom of matter, and embraces every unit of energy perceptible to man . . . converts acorns into oak trees, causes water to flow downhill in response to the law of gravity, follows night with day, and winter with summer, each maintaining its proper place and relationship to the other. This intelligence may, through the principles of this philosophy, be induced to aid in transmuting desires into concrete, or material, form." This concept will be better understood after reading the last lesson in this volume.*

Hill at times refers to infinite intelligence as "spirit," and also describes it as the "receiving set" through which thoughts, ideas, hunches, and inspirations flash into the mind. He says it is also through infinite intelligence that one may "tune in" or communicate with the subconscious minds of others.

However, he stresses that it is only through faith—by which Hill means conviction or belief, not necessarily religious faith—that the force of infinite intelligence can be accessed and applied.

In Think and Grow Rich *Hill writes: "If you pray for a thing, but have fear as you pray that you may not receive it, or that your prayer will not be acted upon by infinite intelligence, your prayer will have been in vain."*

Knowing, from my own previous experience as a beginner in the study of this subject, how difficult it is to accept this hypothesis, I will illustrate the soundness of the hypothesis in a simple way that you can both understand and demonstrate for yourself.

Before going to sleep at night impress upon your mind the desire to arise the next morning at a given hour, say 4:00 A.M., and if your impression is accompanied by *positive determination* to arise at that hour, your subconscious will register the impression and awaken you at precisely that time.

THERE IS NO SUCH THING

AS A SELF-MADE MAN.

YOU WILL REACH YOUR GOALS

ONLY WITH THE HELP OF OTHERS.

—George Shinn

Now, the question might well be asked: "If I can impress my subconscious mind with the desire to arise at a specified time and it will awaken me at that time, why do I not form the habit of impressing it with other and more important desires?"

If you will ask yourself this question, and insist on an answer, you will find yourself on the pathway that leads to the secret door to knowledge, as described in Lesson Eleven.

THE POWER OF
COOPERATIVE ORGANIZED EFFORT

We will now take up the subject of Cooperation between those who unite, or group themselves together, for the purpose of attaining a given end.

In Lesson Two I referred to this sort of Cooperation as *organized effort*. This course touches on some phase of Cooperation in practically every lesson. This was inevitable because one object of the course is to help the student develop *power*, and power is developed only through *organized effort*.

The three most important factors that enter into the process of organizing effort are Concentration, Cooperation, and coordination.

We are living in an age of *cooperative effort*. Nearly all successful businesses are conducted under some form of Cooperation. The same is true in the field of industry and finance, as well as in the professional field.

Doctors and lawyers have their alliances for mutual aid and protection in the form of bar associations and medical associations. Bankers have both local and national associations for their mutual aid and advancement. Retail merchants have their associations for the same purpose. Automobile owners have grouped themselves into clubs and associations. Printers have their associations and plumbers have theirs.

Cooperation is the object of all these associations. The laborers have unions, and those who supply the working capital and supervise the efforts of laborers have their alliances, under various names.

It is slowly becoming obvious that those who most efficiently apply the principle of *cooperative effort* survive longest, and that this principle applies from the lowest form of animal life to the highest form of human endeavor.

Mr. Carnegie and Mr. Rockefeller, and Mr. Ford have taught the businessman the value of *cooperative effort.* That is, they have taught all who cared to observe, the principle through which they themselves accumulated vast fortunes.

Cooperation is the very foundation of all successful Leadership. Henry Ford's most tangible asset is the well-organized network of car dealerships that he has established. This organization not only provides him with an outlet for all the automobiles he can manufacture, but, of greater importance still, it provides him with financial power sufficient to meet any emergency that may arise.

As a result of his understanding of the value of the cooperative principle, Ford has removed himself from the usual position of dependence upon financial institutions and at the same time provided himself with more commercial power than he can possibly use.

The chain-store systems constitute another form of commercial Cooperation that provides advantage through both the purchasing and the distributing end of the business.

The modern department store, which is the equivalent of a group of small stores operating under one roof, one management, and one overhead expense, is another illustration of the advantage of *cooperative effort* in the commercial field.

In Lesson Fifteen you will observe the possibilities of *cooperative effort* in its highest form and at the same time you will see the important part that it plays in the development of power.

Personal power is developed by organizing and coordinating the faculties of the mind. This may be accomplished by mastering and applying the seventeen major principles upon which this course is founded. The necessary procedure through which these principles may be mastered is thoroughly described in the sixteenth lesson.

The development of personal power is just the first step to be taken in the development of the potential power that is available to you through the medium of allied effort, or Cooperation, which may be called group power.

It is a well-known fact that all who have amassed large fortunes have been known as able "organizers." This means that they had the ability to enlist the *cooperative efforts* of others who supplied talent and ability which they themselves did not possess.

One of the chief objects of this course is to present the principles of *organized* and *cooperative* or allied effort so that you will comprehend their significance and make them the basis of your own philosophy.

Take, as an example, any business or profession that you choose and you will observe, by analysis, that it is limited only by a lack of application of *organized* and *cooperative effort.* As an illustration, consider the legal profession.

If a law firm consists of only one type of mind it will be greatly handicapped, even though it may be made up of a dozen able people of this particular type. The complicated legal system calls for a greater variety of talent than any one type of mind could possibly provide.

It is evident, therefore, that mere *organized effort* is not sufficient to ensure outstanding success. The organization must also consist of individuals who each supply some specialized talent that the other members of the organization do not have.

A well-organized law firm would include talent that was specialized in the preparation of cases; people of vision and Imagination who understood how to harmonize the law and the evidence of a case

THE MAN WHO GETS

THE MOST SATISFACTORY RESULTS

IS NOT ALWAYS THE MAN WITH

THE MOST BRILLIANT SINGLE MIND,

BUT RATHER THE MAN WHO

CAN BEST COORDINATE THE BRAINS

AND TALENTS OF HIS ASSOCIATES.

—W. Alton Jones

under a sound plan. But those who have such ability do not always have the ability to try a case in court. Therefore, people who are proficient in court procedure must also be available.

Carrying this analysis a step further, it will be seen that there are many different types of cases that call for people of various specialized abilities in both the preparation and trial of these cases. A lawyer who was a specialist in corporate law might be wholly unprepared to handle a case in criminal procedure.

In forming a law partnership, the person who understood the principles of *organized, cooperative effort* would surround themselves with talent that was specialized in every branch of law and legal procedure in which they intended to practice. The person who had no concept of the potential power of these principles would probably select their associates by the usual hit-or-miss method, basing their selections more on personality or acquaintanceship than on consideration of the particular type of legal talent that each possessed.

The subject of *organized effort* has been covered in the preceding lessons of this course, but it is again brought up in connection with this lesson for the purpose of indicating the necessity of forming alliances or organizations consisting of individuals who supply *all* of the necessary talent that may be needed for the attainment of the object in mind.

In nearly all commercial undertakings, there is a need for at least three kinds of talent: buyers, salespeople, and those who are familiar with finance. It will be readily seen that when these three organize and coordinate their efforts they avail themselves, through this form of Cooperation, of a power that no single individual of the group has.

Many a business fails because all of the people behind it are salespeople, or financial people, or buyers. By nature, the most able salespeople are optimistic, enthusiastic, and emotional, while able financial people, as a rule, are unemotional, deliberate, and conservative. Both types are essential to the success of a commercial enterprise, but either will prove too much of a burden for any business, without the modifying influence of the other.

It is generally conceded that James J. Hill was the most efficient railroad builder that America ever produced, but it is equally well known that he was not a civil engineer or a bridge builder or a locomotive engineer or a mechanical engineer or a chemist, although these highly specialized talents are all essential in the building of railroads. Mr. Hill understood the principles of *organized effort* and Cooperation. Therefore, he surrounded himself with men who possessed all the necessary ability which he lacked.

Analyze power, no matter where or in what form it may be found, and you will find organization and Cooperation as the chief factors behind it. You will find these two principles in evidence in the lowest form of vegetation no less than in the highest form of animal, which is man.

Off the coast of Norway is the most famous and irresistible maelstrom in the world. This great whirlpool of ceaseless motion has never been known to give up any victim who was caught in its circling embrace of foaming water.

No less sure of destruction are those unfortunate souls who are caught in the great maelstrom of life toward which all who do not understand the principle of *organized, cooperative effort* are traveling. We are living in a world in which the law of the survival of the fittest is everywhere in evidence. Those who are "fit" are those who have power, and power is *organized effort*.

Unfortunate is the person who, either through ignorance or because of egotism, imagines that they can sail this sea of life on independence. Such a person will discover that there are maelstroms more dangerous than any mere whirlpool of unfriendly waters. All natural laws and all of Nature's plans are based upon harmonious *cooperative effort,* as all who have attained high places in the world have discovered.

Wherever people are engaged in unfriendly combat, no matter what may be its nature or its cause, one may observe the nearness of one of these maelstroms that awaits the combatants.

Success in life cannot be attained except through peaceful, harmonious *cooperative effort.* Nor can success be attained single-handedly or independently. Even a person who lives as a hermit in the wilderness, far from all signs of civilization, is nevertheless dependent on forces outside of themselves for an existence. The more one becomes a part of civilization, the more dependent on *cooperative effort* they become. Whether they earn their living by working, or from the interest on the fortune they have amassed, they will earn it with less opposition through friendly Cooperation with others. Moreover, the person whose philosophy is based on Cooperation instead of competition will not only acquire the necessities and the luxuries of life with less effort, but they will also enjoy an extra reward in happiness such as others will never feel.

Fortunes that are acquired through *cooperative effort* inflict no scars on the hearts of their owners, which is more than can be said of fortunes that are acquired through conflict and competitive methods that border on extortion.

The accumulation of material wealth, whether the object is that of bare existence or of luxury, consumes most of the time that we put into this earthly struggle. If we cannot change this materialistic tendency of human nature, we can, at least, change the method of pursuing it by adopting Cooperation as the basis of the pursuit.

Cooperation offers the twofold reward of providing one with both the necessities and the luxuries of life and the peace of mind that the greedy never know. The avaricious and covetous person may amass a great fortune in material wealth, there is no denying this, but they will have sold their soul in the bargain.

I DO NOT BELIEVE IN

A FATE THAT FALLS ON MEN

HOWEVER THEY ACT;

BUT I DO BELIEVE IN

A FATE THAT FALLS ON THEM

UNLESS THEY ACT.

—Gilbert K. Chesterton

SUCCESS DEMANDS ACTION

All success is based on power, and power grows out of knowledge that has been organized and expressed in terms of *action.* The world pays for but one kind of knowledge—the kind that is expressed in constructive service.

In addressing the graduating class of a business college, one of the best-known bankers in America said:

"You ought to feel proud of your diplomas, because they are evidence that you have been preparing yourselves for action in the great field of business.

"One of the advantages of a business-college training is that it prepares you for action! Not to belittle other methods of education, but to exalt the modern business-college method, I am reminded to say that there are some colleges in which the majority of the students are preparing for practically everything else *except* action.

"You came to this college with but one object in view, and that object is to learn to render service and earn a living. The latest style of clothing has been of little interest to you because you have been preparing yourself for work in which clothes of the latest style will play no important part. You did not come here to learn how to pour tea at an afternoon party nor to become masters at affecting friendliness while inwardly feeling envy for those who wear finer gowns and drive costly motor cars. You came here to learn how to work!"

In the graduating class before which this man spoke were thirteen boys, all of whom were so poor that they had barely enough money with which to pay their way, and some were having to work before and after school hours.

That was twenty-five years ago. Last summer I met the president of the business college that these boys attended and he gave me the history of each one of them, from the time they graduated until the time I talked with him. One of them is president of one of the big wholesale drug companies, and a wealthy man; one is a successful lawyer; two men own large business colleges of their own; one man is a professor in the department of economics at one of the largest universities in America; one is president of one of the large automobile manufacturing companies; two are presidents of banks, and wealthy men; one man is the owner of a large department store; one is vice president of one of the great railway systems of this country; one is a well-established certified public accountant; one is dead; and the thirteenth is myself.

Eleven successes out of a class of thirteen boys is not a bad record, thanks to the spirit of action developed through the training from that business college.

It is not the schooling you have had that counts; it is the extent to which you express that which you learned from your schooling, through well-organized and intelligently directed action.

By no means would I belittle higher education, but I would offer hope and encouragement to those who have had no such education, provided that they express what they do know, no matter how little, in intensive action along constructive lines.

Abraham Lincoln, one of the greatest presidents who ever occupied the White House, had little schooling. But he did such a good job of expressing what knowledge he acquired by that little schooling, through properly directed action, that his name has been inseparably woven into the history of the United States.

Every city, town, and hamlet has its population of ne'er-do-wells, and if you will analyze these unfortunate people, you will observe that one of their most notable characteristics is *procrastination.*

Lack of action has caused them to slip backward into a rut, where they will remain unless they are unexpectedly forced out and unusual action becomes necessary. Don't let yourself get into that situation.

Every office and every shop and every bank and every store and every other place of employment has its outstanding victims of procrastination who are marching down the dusty road of failure because they have not developed the habit of expressing themselves through action.

You can pick out these unfortunates if you will begin to analyze those with whom you come in contact each day. If you will talk with them you will observe that they have built up a false philosophy, such as, "I am doing all I am paid to do, and I am getting by."

Yes, they are "getting by," but that is all they are getting.

Some years ago, at a time when labor was scarce and wages were unusually high, I observed scores of able-bodied men lying about in the parks of Chicago, doing nothing. I became curious to know what sort of an explanation they would offer for their conduct, so I went out one afternoon and interviewed seven of them.

With the aid of a generous supply of cigars and cigarettes and a little loose change, I bought myself into the confidence of those whom I interviewed and thereby gained a rather intimate view of their philosophy. All gave exactly the same reason for being there, unemployed, saying, "The world will not give me a chance."

Think of it—the world would not "give them a chance."

Of course the world wouldn't *give* them a chance. It never *gives* anyone a chance. Anyone who wants a chance may create it through action, but if they wait for someone to hand it to them on a silver platter, they will meet with disappointment.

I fear the excuse that the world does not *give* someone a chance is quite prevalent, and I strongly suspect that it is one of the commonest causes of poverty and failure.

The seventh man that I interviewed on that well-spent afternoon was an unusually fine-looking specimen, physically. He was lying on the ground asleep, with a newspaper over his face. When I lifted the paper, he reached up, took it out of my hands, put it back over his face, and went right on sleeping.

Then I used a little strategy by removing the paper from his face and placing it behind me, where he could not get it. He then sat up

AS I GROW OLDER

I PAY LESS ATTENTION TO

WHAT MEN SAY.

I JUST WATCH WHAT THEY DO.

—Andrew Carnegie

on the ground and I interviewed him. That fellow was a graduate from two of the great universities in the East, with a master's degree from one and a Ph.D. from the other.

His story was pathetic.

He had held job after job, but always his employer or his fellow employee "had it in for him." He hadn't been able to make them see the value of his college training. They wouldn't "give him a chance."

Here was a man who might have been at the head of some great business or an outstanding figure in one of the professions, had he not chosen to *procrastinate* and hold on to the false belief that the world should pay him for *what he knew.*

Fortunately, most college graduates do not opt for such choices, because no college can bring success to one who tries to collect for what they *know* instead of what they can *do* with what they know.

The man to whom I referred was from one of the best-known families of Virginia. He traced his ancestry back to the landing of the Mayflower. He threw back his shoulders, pounded himself on the chest with his fist, and said, "Just think of it, sir! I am a son of one of the first families of old Virginia!"

My observations led me to believe that being the son of a "first family" is not always fortunate for either the son or the family. Too often these sons of first families try to slide home from third base on their family names. This may be only a peculiar notion of mine, but I have observed that the men and women who are doing the world's work have but little time, and less inclination, to brag about their ancestry.

Not long ago I took a trip back to southwest Virginia, where I was born. It was the first time I had been there in over twenty years. It was a sad sight to compare the sons of some of those who were known as "first families" twenty years ago, with the sons of those who were but plain folk who made it their business to express themselves in action of the most intensive nature.

The comparison reflected no credit on the "first family" boys. It is with no feeling of exaltation that I express my gratitude for not having been brought into the world by parents from a "first family." That, of course, had not been a matter of choice, and if it had been perhaps I, too, would have selected parents of the "first family" type.

Not long ago I had been invited to deliver an address in Boston, Massachusetts. After my work was finished, a reception committee volunteered to show me the sights, including a trip to Cambridge, where we visited Harvard University. While there, I observed many sons of "first families," some of whom had Packard cars. Twenty years ago I would have felt proud to be a student at Harvard, with a Packard, but the illuminating effect of my more mature years has led me to conclude that had I had the privilege of going to Harvard I might have done just as well without the aid of a Packard.

COMMENTARY

For any readers unfamiliar with the Packard, they were expensive grand luxury cars known for their quality construction, extreme durability, and classic styling, the latter no doubt being why they showed up at Harvard.

The first Packard automobile was produced in 1899 in Warren, Ohio, at the Packard Electric Company's subsidiary plant, the New York and Ohio Company. The Packard division began as the Ohio Automobile Company and became the Packard Motor Car Company in 1902. Production ceased in 1958, but today there are still Packard car clubs, a museum, and The Packard Motor Car Foundation, a nonprofit educational organization dedicated to the preservation of the products and history of The Packard Motor Car Company.

I noticed some Harvard boys who had no Packards. They were working as waiters in a restaurant where I ate, and as far as I could see they were missing nothing of value by not owning a Packard; nor did they seem to be suffering by comparison with those who could boast of "first family" parents.

All of which is no reflection upon Harvard University—one of the great universities of the world—nor upon the "first families" who send boys to Harvard. To the contrary, it is intended as a bit of encouragement to those unfortunates who, like myself, have but little and know but little, but express what little they know in terms of constructive, useful action.

The psychology of *in*action is one of the chief reasons why some towns and cities are dying. In one city in Maine, for example, laws have closed up all the restaurants on Sunday. Railroad trains must slow down to twelve miles an hour while passing through the city. There are "keep off the grass" signs prominently displayed in the parks. Unfavorable city ordinances of one sort or another have driven the best industries to other cities. Evidence of restraint can be seen everywhere. The people on the streets show signs of restraint in their faces and in their manner and in their walk.

The mass psychology of the city is negative. The moment one gets off the train at the depot, this negative atmosphere becomes depressingly obvious and makes one want to take the next train out again. The place reminds one of a graveyard and the people resemble walking ghosts. They register no signs of action!

The financial statements of the banking institutions reflect this negative, inactive state of mind. The stores reflect it in their show windows and in the faces of their salespeople. I went into one of the stores to buy a pair of socks. A young woman with bobbed hair, who would have been a "flapper" if she hadn't been too lazy, threw a box of socks on the counter. When I picked up the box, looked at the socks, and registered a look of disapproval on my face, she languidly yawned, "They're the best you can get in this dump."

She must have been a mind reader, for *dump* was the word in my mind before she spoke. The store reminded me of a rubbish dump;

THE MOST OMINOUS OF FALLACIES:

THE BELIEF THAT THINGS CAN BE

KEPT STATIC BY INACTION.

—Freyda Stark

the city reminded me of the same. I felt the stuff getting into my blood. The negative psychology of the people was actually reaching out and gathering me in.

Maine is not the only state that is afflicted with a city such as the one I have described. I could name others, but I might wish to go into politics someday; therefore, I will leave it to you to do your own analyzing and comparing of cities that are alive with action and those that are slowly dying from inaction.

I know of some business concerns that are in this same state of inaction, but I will omit their names. You probably know some too.

Many years ago Frank A. Vanderlip, who is one of the best-known and most capable bankers in America, went to work for the National City Bank of New York City. His salary was above average from the start, because he was capable and had a record of successful achievement that made him a valuable man.

He was assigned to a private office that was equipped with a fine mahogany desk. On the desk was an electric push button connected to a secretary's desk outside.

The first day went by without any work coming to his desk. The second and third and fourth days went by without any work. No one came in or said anything to him. He was feeling very uneasy. Men of action always feel uneasy when there is no work in sight.

So Mr. Vanderlip went into the president's office and said, "Look here, you are paying me a big salary and giving me nothing to do and it is grating on my nerves."

The president looked up with a lively twinkle in his keen eyes.

"I have been thinking," Mr. Vanderlip continued, "while sitting in there with nothing to do, of a plan for increasing the business of this bank."

The president assured him that both "thinking" and "plans" were valuable and asked him to continue. "I have thought of a plan," Mr.

Vanderlip went on, "that will give the bank the benefit of my experience in the bond business. I propose to create a bond department for this bank and advertise it as a feature of our business."

"What! This bank advertise?" queried the president. "Why, we have never advertised since we began business, and we have managed to get along without it."

"Well, this is where you are going to begin advertising," said Mr. Vanderlip, "and the first thing you are going to advertise is this new bond department that I have planned."

Mr. Vanderlip won. Men of action usually win—that is one of their distinctive characteristics. The National City Bank also won, because that conversation was the beginning of one of the most progressive and profitable advertising campaigns ever carried on by any bank, with the result that the National City Bank became one of the most powerful financial institutions of America.

There were other results too. Mr. Vanderlip grew with the bank, as men of action usually grow in whatever they help to build, until finally he became the president of that great banking house.

COOPERATION OF MIND AND BODY

In the lesson on Imagination you learned how to recombine old ideas into new plans. But no matter how practical your plans may be, they will be useless if they are not expressed in action. To dream dreams and see visions of the person you would like to be or the station in life you would like to attain are admirable, provided you transform your dreams and visions into reality through intensive action.

There are some people who dream but do nothing more. There are others who take the visions of the dreamers and translate them into stone, and marble, and music, and good books, and railroads, and steamships. There are still others who both dream and transform their dreams into reality. They are the dreamer-doer types.

There is a psychological as well as an economic reason why you should form the habit of intensive action. Your body is made up of billions of tiny cells that are highly sensitive and amenable to the influence of your mind. If your mind is lethargic and inactive, the cells of your body become lazy and inactive also. If you doubt this, the next time you feel lazy think about an activity of which you are fond and notice how quickly the cells of your body will respond to your Enthusiasm and your lazy feeling will disappear.

The cells of the human body respond to a person's state of mind in exactly the same manner that the people of a city respond to the mass psychology that dominates the city. If a group of leaders engages in sufficient action to give a city the reputation of being an "alive" city, this action influences all who live there. The same principle applies to the relationship between the mind and the body. An active, dynamic mind keeps the cells of the body in a constant state of activity.

The amount of work that I perform every day and still keep in good physical condition is a source of wonderment and mystery to those who know me well, yet there is no mystery to it, and the system I follow does not cost anything.

First, I drink a cup of hot water when I get up in the morning, before I have breakfast. My breakfast consists of rolls made of whole wheat and bran, breakfast cereal, fruit, soft-boiled eggs once in a while, and a cup of coffee. For lunch I eat vegetables (most any kind), whole-wheat bread, and drink a glass of buttermilk. And for supper, a well-cooked steak once or twice a week, vegetables (especially lettuce), and coffee.

I walk an average of ten miles a day, five miles into the country and five miles back, using this period for meditation and thought. Perhaps the thinking is as valuable to my health as the walk.

You cannot be a person of action if you overeat and underexercise. Neither can you be a person of action if you run to the pill bottle

THE OLDER I GET,

THE MORE I REALIZE THE

IMPORTANCE OF EXERCISING

THE VARIOUS DIMENSIONS OF MY

BODY, SOUL, MIND, AND HEART. . . .

INTELLECTUAL, EMOTIONAL, AND

PHYSICAL ACTIVITY ARE NOT

SEPARATE ENTITIES. RATHER,

THEY ARE DIMENSIONS OF

THE SAME HUMAN BEING.

—Robert Fulghum

every time you have, or imagine you have, an ache or a pain. I have not touched a drug in more than five years, and I have not been either sick or ailing during that time, in spite of the fact that I perform more work each day than most men of my profession. I have Enthusiasm, endurance, and action because I eat the simple foods that contain the body-building elements that I require.

There is another enemy you must conquer before you can become a person of action, and that is the *worry* habit.

Worry, envy, jealousy, hatred, doubt, and fear are all states of mind that are fatal to action. These negative states of mind destroy the most essential factor in the achievement of success—the *desire* to achieve.

In A Definite Chief Aim, the second lesson of this course, you learned that your chief aim in life should be supported by a burning desire for its realization. You can have no burning desire for achievement when you are in a negative state of mind, no matter what the cause may be.

I have discovered a very effective way to keep myself in a positive frame of mind. When I feel out of sorts or inclined to argue with somebody over something that is not worthy of discussion, I get away to where I will disturb no one and I have a good hearty laugh. If I can find nothing really funny to laugh about, I simply have a forced laugh. The effect is the same in both cases. Five minutes of this sort of mental and physical exercise—for it is both—will stimulate action that is free from negativity. Do not just take my word for this. Try it!

Not long ago I heard a record entitled, as I recall, "The Laughing Fool." It was all that its name implies. The record was made by a man and a woman; the man was trying to play a cornet and the woman was laughing at him. She laughed so effectively that she finally made the man laugh, and the suggestion was so pronounced that all who heard it usually joined in, whether they felt like it or not.

COMMENTARY

> Many of Napoleon Hill's beliefs about the power of the mind that were considered unconventional in his time became part of mainstream medical and psychological practice by the latter years of the twentieth century.
>
> A number of seminal books on what is now commonly referred to as "the body-mind connection" were published in the 1970s and 1980s. One such book is Anatomy of an Illness, in which author Norman Cousins documents his use of laughter to help heal a painful and near-fatal illness. Other books that speak to the power of laughter are The Laughter Prescription by Dr. Laurence J. Peter, The Healing Power of Humor by Allen Klein, and Laughter: The Best Medicine by Robert Holden.

"As a man thinketh in his heart, so is he."

You cannot think fear and act courageously. You cannot think hatred and act in a kindly manner toward others. And the dominating thoughts of your mind—meaning the strongest, deepest, and most frequent of your thoughts—influence the physical action of your body.

Every thought put into action by your brain reaches and influences every cell in your body. When you think fear, your mind will telegraph this thought to the cells that form the muscles of your legs and tell those muscles to get into action and carry you away as rapidly as they can. A person who is afraid runs away because their legs carry them, and they carry them because the fear thought in the person's mind instructed them to do so, even though the instructions were given unconsciously.

In Lesson One of this course you learned how thought travels from one mind to another, through the principle of telepathy. In this lesson you should go a step further and learn that your thoughts not only register themselves in the minds of other people through the principle of telepathy, but what is a million times more important for you to understand is that they register themselves on the cells of your own body and affect those cells in a manner that harmonizes with the nature of the thoughts.

Action, in the sense the term is used in this lesson, is of two forms. One is physical and the other is mental. You can be very active with your mind while your body is entirely inactive. Or you can be very active with both body and mind.

INSPIRE COOPERATIVE AND PERSONAL ACTION

There are essentially two kinds of people of action. One might be called the caretaker type and the other the promoter or salesperson type. Both types are essential in business, industry, and finance. One of them is known as a dynamo while the other is often referred to as a balance wheel.

Once in a great while you find someone who is both a dynamo and a balance wheel, but such a personality combination is rare. Most successful business organizations are made up of both types.

The balance-wheel type who does nothing but compile facts and figures and statistics is just as much a person of action as the one who gets on a stage and sells an idea to a thousand people by the sheer power of their *active* personality. To determine whether or not someone is a person of action, it is necessary to analyze both their mental and their physical habits.

Earlier in this lesson I said that the world pays you for what you do and not for what you know. That statement might easily be misconstrued. What the world really pays you for is what *you* do or what you can get *others* to do.

A person who can induce others to cooperate and do effective teamwork, or inspire others so that they become more active, is no less a person of action than the one who renders effective service in a more direct manner.

In the field of industry and business there are people who have the ability to so inspire and direct the efforts of others that all under

LEADERSHIP:

THE ART OF GETTING

SOMEONE ELSE TO DO

SOMETHING YOU WANT DONE

BECAUSE HE WANTS TO DO IT.

—Dwight D. Eisenhower

their direction accomplish more than they could without this directing influence. Andrew Carnegie so ably directed the efforts of those who constituted his personal staff that he made many wealthy men of those who would never have become wealthy without the directing genius of his mind. The same may be said of practically all the great leaders in the field of industry and business—the gain is not all on the side of the leaders. Those under their direction often profit most by their Leadership.

In the first lesson of this course the value of allied effort was particularly emphasized for the reason that some people have the vision to plan, while others, although they do not have the Imagination or the vision to create the plans, have the ability to carry those plans into action.

It was his understanding of this principle of allied effort that enabled Andrew Carnegie to surround himself with a group of men which was made up of those who could plan and those who could execute. Carnegie had in his group of assistants some of the most efficient salesmen in the world, but if his entire staff had been made up of men who could do nothing but sell, he could never have accumulated the fortune that he did. Action, in the sense that it is used in this lesson, must be intelligently guided.

One of the best-known law firms in America is made up of two lawyers, one of whom never appears in court. He prepares the firm's cases for trial and the other member of the firm goes to court and tries them. Both are men of intense action, but they express it in different ways.

In most undertakings, there can be as much action in the preparation as in the execution.

In finding your own place in the world, you should analyze yourself to find out whether you are a dynamo or a balance wheel, then select a Definite Chief Aim that harmonizes with your native ability. If you are in business with others, you should analyze them as well as yourself, and endeavor to see that each person takes the part for which their temperament and native ability best fit.

The dynamo, or promoter type, makes an able salesperson and organizer. The balance wheel, or caretaker type, makes an excellent conserver of assets after they have been accumulated.

Place the caretaker type in charge of a set of books and they are happy, but place them on the outside selling and they are unhappy and will be a failure at their job. Place the promoter type in charge of a set of books and they will be miserable. Their nature demands more intense action. Action of the passive type will not satisfy their ambitions, and if they are kept at work that does not give them the action that their nature demands, they will be a failure. It very frequently turns out that people who embezzle funds in their charge are of the promoter type and they would not have yielded to that temptation had their efforts been confined to the work for which they are best suited.

Give a person the sort of work that harmonizes with their nature, and the best there is in them will exert itself. One of the tragedies of the world is that most people never find the work for which they are best suited by nature.

Too often the mistake is made, in the selection of a life's work, of engaging only in the work that seems to be the most monetarily profitable. If money alone brought success, this procedure would be all right, but success in its highest and noblest form calls for peace of mind and enjoyment and happiness which come only to the person who has found the work that they like best.

An important purpose of this Law of Success course is to help you analyze yourself to determine what your native ability best fits you to do. You should make this analysis by carefully studying the comparison chart at the beginning of this book before selecting your Definite Chief Aim.

We come now to the discussion of the principle through which action may be developed. Understanding how to become active requires understanding how not to procrastinate. I offer these suggestions:

1. Form the habit of each day doing the most distasteful tasks first. This procedure will be difficult in the beginning, but after you have formed the habit you will take pride in first dealing with the hardest and most undesirable part of your work.

2. Place this sign in front of you where you can see it daily while you work, and put a copy where you can see it before you go to sleep and when you arise: "Do not tell them what you can do—show them!"

3. Repeat the following words, aloud, twelve times each night just before you go to sleep: "Tomorrow I will do everything that should be done, when it should be done, and as it should be done. I will perform the most difficult tasks first because this will destroy the habit of procrastination and develop the habit of action in its place."

4. Carry out these instructions with faith in their soundness and with belief that they will develop action, in body and in mind, sufficient to enable you to realize your Definite Chief Aim.

I would like to refer back to what I said about the value of a hearty laugh as a healthful stimulant to action, and add that singing produces the same effect and in some cases is far preferable to laughing.

Billy Sunday is one of the most dynamic and active preachers in the world, yet it has been said that his sermons would lose much of their effectiveness if it were not for the psychological effect of his song services.

I LOVE TO HEAR A CHOIR.

I LOVE THE HUMANITY, TO SEE THE

FACES OF REAL PEOPLE DEVOTING

THEMSELVES TO A PIECE OF MUSIC.

I LIKE THE TEAMWORK.

IT MAKES ME FEEL OPTIMISTIC

ABOUT THE HUMAN RACE WHEN I

SEE THEM COOPERATING LIKE THAT.

—Paul McCartney

COMMENTARY

> *William Ashley (Billy) Sunday, born in 1868 in Ames, Iowa, grew up in an orphanage, worked as a janitor while in high school, and in 1883 became a professional baseball player with the Chicago White Sox.*
>
> *In 1886 it was through "the psychological effect of the song service" at the Pacific Garden Mission in Chicago that Sunday became a born-again Christian. He later declined a $400 monthly baseball contract in favor of becoming a YMCA secretary, eventually accepted an assistant ministry position paying $84 a month, and in 1896 became an evangelical preacher himself.*
>
> *In his twenty years of preaching throughout America, Sunday's following was in the millions, with hundreds of thousands of converts, and at his Detroit revival there were five thousand singers in the choir.*
>
> *Billy Sunday was not only active but virtually acrobatic in his fire-and-brimstone preachings. His moralistic revival meetings condemned, among other "sins," birth control and liquor, and Sunday campaigned passionately for the passage of prohibition laws. Henry Ford is said to have told him that if the law were enacted in Michigan, the breweries could be converted to produce denatured alcohol as fuel for Ford's automobiles.*
>
> *By the time prohibition ended in 1934, Sunday's following had declined dramatically. Billy Sunday died in 1936.*

If church attendance had nothing else to recommend it except the psychological effect of the song service, that would be sufficient, for no one can join in the singing of a beautiful hymn without feeling better for it.

For many years I have observed that I could write more effectively after having participated in a song service. Prove my statement to your own satisfaction by going to church and participating in the song service with all the Enthusiasm at your command.

During the war I helped to devise ways and means of speeding production in industrial plants that were engaged in manufacturing war supplies. By actual test, in a plant employing three thousand men and women, the production was increased 45 percent in less than thirty days after we had organized the workers into singing groups and installed orchestras and bands that played at ten-minute intervals such stirring songs as "Over There" and "Dixie" and "There'll Be a Hot Time in the Old Town Tonight." The workers caught the rhythm of the music and speeded up their work accordingly.

Properly selected music would stimulate any group of workers to greater action, a fact which does not seem to be understood by all who direct the efforts of large numbers of people.

In all of my travels I have found only one business firm whose managers made use of music as a stimulant for their workers. This was the Filene Department Store in Boston, Massachusetts. During the summer months this store provides an orchestra that plays the latest dance music for half an hour in the morning before opening time. The salespeople use the aisles of the store for dancing and by the time the store opens they are in an active state of mind and body that carries them through the entire day.

Incidentally, I have also never seen more courteous or efficient salespeople than those employed by the Filene store. One of the department managers told me that every person in his department performed more service, and with less real effort, as a result of the morning music program.

There is a book entitled *Singing Through Life with God* by George Wharton James, which I recommend to all who are interested in the psychology of song.

COMMENTARY

It is interesting that the majority of books Napoleon Hill recommended in 1927 are still available today, although this one is among the harder to come by. It is out of print but available through used-book dealers.

The three copies listed in Barnes & Noble's out-of-print books ranged in price from $47 to $101.

Needless to say, in the time since Hill reported that he could find only one business that used music to stimulate workers, it is now hard to find a retail store that doesn't have music playing from the time they open 'til they close at the end of the day. The major departure from Hill's theory is that today music is used to influence the customers as much as to stimulate employees. The companies that specialize in providing piped-in music conduct research into everything from musical theory to traffic-flow patterns and changing blood-sugar levels in order to program the right kind of music for the right customer demographics and the right time of day.

Although the contemporary use of music in American retail stores became a modification of Napoleon Hill's idea, others took the suggestion literally. One of the most talked-about examples of the effectiveness of music to stimulate employees comes from modern industrial Japan. During the 1970s, as the large Japanese automobile and electronics manufacturers were rising to world prominence, much attention was focused on the way the Japanese managers motivated their workers. The stories and pictures that appeared in business magazines startled their American counterparts. What the pictures showed was exactly what Hill had in mind—whole Japanese workforces gathering, before the workday began, to exercise together and sing what amounted to corporate team songs or cheers.

Any form of group effort, where two or more people form a cooperative alliance for the purpose of accomplishing a *definite purpose*, becomes more powerful than mere individual effort.

A football team may win consistently, by well-coordinated teamwork, even though the members of the team may be unfriendly and out of harmony in many ways outside of their work on the field.

THE GREATEST LEADER

IS NOT NECESSARILY THE ONE

WHO DOES THE GREATEST THINGS,

BUT THE ONE WHO GETS THE PEOPLE

TO DO THE GREATEST THINGS.

—Ronald Reagan

A group composing a board of directors may disagree with one another, they may be unfriendly and in no way in sympathy with one another, and still carry on a business that appears to be very successful.

A husband and wife may live together, raise a family, and accumulate a fair-sized or even a great fortune, without having the bond of harmony that is essential for the development of a Master Mind.

But all these alliances might be made more powerful and effective if based upon a foundation of perfect harmony, thus permitting the development of the supplemental power of the Master Mind.

All *cooperative effort* produces power, there can be no doubt about this, but *cooperative effort* that is based upon complete harmony of purpose develops superpower.

Let every member of any cooperative group set their hearts on the achievement of the same definite end, in a spirit of perfect harmony, and the way has been paved for the development of a Master Mind—providing all members of the group willingly subordinate their own personal interests for the attainment of the objective for which the group is aiming.

These United States were born as the result of one of the most powerful Master Minds ever created. The members of this Master Mind were the signers of the Declaration of Independence. The men who signed that document either consciously or unconsciously put into operation the power known as the Master Mind, and that power was sufficient to enable them to defeat all soldiers who were sent into the field against them. The men who fought to make the Declaration of Independence endure did not fight for money alone; they fought for a principle—the principle of freedom, which is the highest-known motivating force.

A great leader, whether in business, finance, industry, or statesmanship, is one who understands how to create a motivating objective that will be accepted with Enthusiasm by every member of their group of followers.

THE IMPORTANT THING TO RECOGNIZE

IS THAT IT TAKES A TEAM, AND

THE TEAM OUGHT TO GET CREDIT

FOR THE WINS AND THE LOSSES.

SUCCESSES HAVE MANY FATHERS,

FAILURES HAVE NONE.

—Philip Caldwell

In politics a "live issue" is everything. A live issue is some popular objective which the majority of the voters can be rallied toward the attainment of. These "issues" are generally broadcast in the form of snappy slogans, such as "Keep Cool with Coolidge," which suggested to the minds of the voters that to keep Coolidge was the equivalent of keeping prosperity. And it worked.

During Lincoln's election campaign the cry was "Stand back of Lincoln and preserve the Union." It worked.

Woodrow Wilson's campaign managers, during his second campaign, coined the slogan "He kept us out of war." It worked too.

The degree of power created by the *cooperative effort* of any group of people is measured, always, by the nature of the motive that the group is laboring to attain. This may be profitably kept in mind by all who organize group efforts for any purpose whatsoever. Find a motive around which people may be induced to rally in a highly emotionalized, enthusiastic spirit of perfect harmony and you have found the starting point for the creation of a Master Mind.

Most people will work harder for the attainment of an ideal than they will for mere money. In searching for a "motive" as the basis for developing cooperative group effort, it will be profitable to bear this in mind. Give someone a sufficiently vitalized motive and even the person of average ability, under ordinary circumstances, will suddenly develop superpower.

What a man can and will accomplish to please the woman of his choice has ever been a source of wonderment to students of the human mind.

There are three major motivating forces to which man responds in practically all of his efforts:

1. The motive of self-preservation

2. The motive of sexual contact

3. The motive of financial and social power

WE CANNOT BE

SEPARATED IN INTEREST OR

DIVIDED IN PURPOSE.

WE STAND TOGETHER

UNTIL THE END.

—Woodrow Wilson

Leaders who are seeking a motivating force out of which to secure action may find it under one or more of those three classifications.

The three major motivating forces have been noted here for the guidance of the leader who wishes the Cooperation of followers who will throw themselves into carrying out his or her plans in a spirit of unselfishness and perfect harmony. We do well that which we love to do, and fortunate is the leader who has the good judgment to assign all of their followers the roles that harmonize with this law.

Regardless of who you are, or what your Definite Chief Aim may be, if you plan to attain the object of your chief aim through the *cooperative efforts* of others, you must set up in the minds of those whose Cooperation you seek a motive strong enough to ensure their full, undivided, unselfish Cooperation. When you do, you will be empowering your plans with the law of the Master Mind.

As you will have observed, this lesson is very closely related to Lesson One and Lesson Two which cover the law of the Master Mind. It is possible for groups to function cooperatively without creating a Master Mind, such as when people cooperate merely out of necessity and without the spirit of harmony as the basis of their efforts. This sort of Cooperation may produce considerable power, but it doesn't compare with what is possible when every person in an alliance subordinates their own individual interests.

The extent to which people may be induced to cooperate, in harmony, depends on the motivating force that impels them to action. The perfect harmony essential for creating a Master Mind develops only when the motivating force of a group is sufficient to cause each member of the group to completely forget his or her own personal interests and work for the good of the group, or for the sake of attaining some idealistic, charitable, or philanthropic objective.

You are now ready for Lesson Fourteen, which will teach you how to make working capital out of all mistakes, errors, and failures that you have experienced, and also how to profit by the mistakes and failures of others.

The president of one of the great railway systems of the United States said, after reading the next lesson, that "this lesson carries a suggestion which, if heeded and understood, will enable any person to become a master in their chosen life's work."

For reasons that will be clear after you have read it, Profiting by Failure is my favorite lesson of this course.

INDECISION—
AN AFTER-THE-LESSON VISIT WITH THE AUTHOR

Procrastination robs you of opportunity. It is a significant fact that no great leader was ever known to procrastinate. You are fortunate if ambition drives you into action, never permitting you to falter or turn back once you have rendered a decision to go forward.

You may be shocked if you kept accurate account of the time you waste in a single day. Second by second, as the clock ticks off the distance, time is running a race with *you*. Delay means defeat, because no one may ever make up a second of lost time. Wasted time is one of the chief causes of failure.

Time is also, however, a master worker that heals the wounds of failure and disappointment, and rights all wrongs and turns all mistakes into capital. But it favors only those who kill off procrastination and remain in *action* when there are decisions to be made.

Life is a great checkerboard. The player opposite you is Time. If you hesitate you will be wiped off the board. If you keep moving you may win. The only real capital is time, but it is capital only when used.

The other player is Mr. Average Man; let us call him you. Move by move, Time has wiped off Mr. Average Man's men until he is finally cornered where Time will get him no matter which way he moves. Indecision has driven him into that corner.

Ask any well-informed salesperson and they will tell you that indecision is the outstanding weakness of the majority of people. Every salesperson is familiar with that old excuse "I will think it over," which is the last line of defense of those who do not have the courage to say either yes or no. While they can't decide which way to move, Time forces them into a corner where they can't move.

The great leaders of the world were people of quick decision.

General Grant had but little to commend him as an able general except the quality of firm decision, but this was sufficient to offset all of his weaknesses. The whole story of his military success may be gathered from his reply to his critics when he said, "We will fight it out along these lines if it takes all summer."

When Napoleon Bonaparte reached a decision to move his armies in a given direction, he permitted nothing to cause him to change that decision. If his line of march brought his soldiers to a ditch dug by his opponents to stop him, he would give the order to charge the ditch until it had been filled with dead men and horses sufficient to bridge it.

The suspense of indecision drives millions of people to failure. A condemned man once said that the thought of his approaching execution was not so terrifying once he had reached the decision in his own mind to accept the inevitable.

The lack of decision is the chief stumbling block of all revival-meeting workers. Their entire work is to get men and women to reach a decision in their own minds to accept a given religious tenet. Billy Sunday once said, "Indecision is the devil's favorite tool."

Andrew Carnegie visualized a great steel industry, but that industry would not be what it is today had he not reached a *decision* in his own mind to transform his vision into reality.

James J. Hill saw, in his mind's eye, a great transcontinental railway system, but that railroad never would have become a reality had he not reached a *decision* to start the project.

IN ANY MOMENT OF DECISION

THE BEST THING YOU CAN DO

IS THE RIGHT THING,

THE NEXT BEST THING

IS THE WRONG THING, AND

THE WORST THING YOU CAN DO

IS NOTHING.

—Theodore Roosevelt

Imagination alone is not enough to ensure success. Millions of people have Imagination and build plans that would easily bring them both fame and fortune, but those plans never reach the *decision* stage.

Demosthenes was a poor Greek lad who had a strong desire to be a great public speaker. Nothing unusual about that; others have "desired" this and similar ability without living to see their desires realized. But Demosthenes added *decision* to desire, and, despite the fact that he was a stammerer, he mastered this handicap and made himself one of the great orators of the world.

Samuel Insul was an ordinary stenographer, in the employ of Thomas A. Edison. Through the aid of his Imagination he saw the great commercial possibilities of electricity. But he did more than see the possibilities—he reached a decision to transform the mere possibilities into realities, and today he is a multimillionaire electric-light-plant operator.

Edwin C. Barnes reached a *decision* in his own mind to become the partner of Thomas Edison. Handicapped by lack of schooling, without money to pay his railroad fare, and with no influential friends to introduce him to Mr. Edison, young Barnes made his way to West Orange on a freight car and so thoroughly sold himself to Mr. Edison that he got his opportunity which led to a partnership. Today, just twenty years since that decision was reached, Edwin Barnes lives at Bradenton, Florida, retired, with all the money he needs.

William Wrigley Jr. reached a *decision* to devote his entire business career to the manufacture and sale of a five-cent package of chewing gum. He has made that decision bring him financial returns running into millions of dollars a year.

Henry Ford reached a *decision* to manufacture and sell a popular-priced automobile that would be within the means of all who wished to own it. That decision has brought enormous power to Ford, and has brought travel opportunity to millions of people.

OCCASIONS ARE RARE;

AND THOSE WHO KNOW

HOW TO SEIZE UPON THEM

ARE RARER.

—Josh Billings

All these men had two outstanding qualities: a *definite purpose* and a firm decision to transform that purpose into reality.

———————

The person of decision gets what he or she goes after, no matter how long it takes or how difficult the task.

An able salesman had wanted to meet a Cleveland banker but the banker would not see him. One morning this salesman waited near the banker's house until he saw him get into his car and head downtown. Watching his opportunity, the salesman drove his own car into the banker's, causing slight damage to the car. The salesman got out of his car, handed his card to the banker, expressed regret about the damage done, and promised the banker a new car exactly like the one he had damaged. That afternoon a new car was delivered to the banker and out of that transaction grew a friendship that developed into a business partnership that still exists.

The person of decision cannot be stopped. The person of indecision cannot be started. Make your own choice.

———————

> *Behind him lay the gray Azores,*
> *Behind the Gates of Hercules;*
> *Before him not the ghosts of shores;*
> *Before him only shoreless seas.*
> *The good mate said: "Now must we pray,*
> *For lo! the very stars are gone.*
> *Brave Adm'r'l, speak; what shall I say?"*
> *"Why, say: 'Sail on and on!'"*
>
> —JOAQUIN MILLER

When Columbus began his famous voyage he made one of the most far-reaching decisions in the history of mankind. Had he not

PROCRASTINATION IS SUICIDE

ON THE INSTALLMENT PLAN.

—Anon.

remained firm on that decision, the freedom of America as we know it today would never have been realized.

Take notice of those about you and observe this significant fact: The successful men and women are those who reach decisions quickly and then stand firmly by those decisions after they are made.

If you are one of those who make up their minds today then and change them again tomorrow, you are doomed to failure. If you are not sure which way to move, it is better to shut your eyes and move in the dark than to remain still and make no move at all.

The world will forgive you if you make mistakes, but it will never forgive you if you make no decisions, because it will never hear of you outside the community in which you live.

No matter who you are or what may be your life's work, you are playing checkers with Time! It is always your next move. Move with quick decision, and Time will favor you. Stand still and Time will wipe you off the board.

You cannot always make the right move, but if you make enough moves you may take advantage of the law of averages and pile up a creditable score before the great game of life is ended.

— Lesson Fourteen —

Profiting by Failure

DEFEAT, LIKE A HEADACHE,

WARNS US THAT SOMETHING

HAS GONE WRONG.

IF WE ARE INTELLIGENT

WE LOOK FOR THE CAUSE

AND PROFIT BY THE EXPERIENCE.

—Napoleon Hill

PROFITING BY FAILURE

"You Can Do It if You Believe You Can!"

ORDINARILY *FAILURE* IS A NEGATIVE TERM. But in this lesson the word will be given a new meaning, because it has been a very much misused word and for that reason has brought unnecessary grief and hardship to millions of people.

I will distinguish here between *failure* and *defeat,* and you will see if what is so often looked upon as failure is not, in reality, just temporary defeat. Moreover, you will see if this temporary defeat is not usually a blessing in disguise. You will also learn that sound character is often the product of reversals and setbacks.

Neither temporary defeat nor adversity amounts to failure in the mind of the person who looks upon it as a teacher of some needed lesson. There is a great and lasting lesson in every reversal and in every defeat, and usually it is a lesson that could be learned in no other way.

Defeat often talks to us in a language that we do not understand. If this were not true, we would not make the same mistakes over and over again without profiting by the lessons that they might teach us. If it were not true, we would observe more closely the mistakes that other people make and we would profit by them also.

SEVEN TURNING POINTS

Perhaps I can best help you to interpret the meaning of defeat by taking you back over some of my own experiences covering a period of approximately thirty years. Seven different times within this period I have come to the turning point that the uninformed call failure. At each one of these seven turning points I thought I had been a dismal failure, but now I know that what looked to be a failure was nothing more than a kindly, unseen hand that halted me in my chosen course and with great wisdom forced me to redirect my efforts along more advantageous pathways.

I realized this, however, only after I had taken a retrospective view of my experiences and had analyzed them in the light of many years of meditative thought.

First Turning Point

After finishing a course at a business college, I took a job as a stenographer and bookkeeper, a position that I held for the next five years. As a result of having practiced the habit of performing more work and better work than that for which I was paid, as described in Lesson Nine, I advanced rapidly until I was assuming responsibilities and receiving a salary far out of proportion to my age. I saved my money, and my bank account amounted to several thousand dollars. My reputation spread rapidly and found competitive bidders for my services. To meet these offers from competitors, my employer advanced me to the position of general manager of the mines where I was employed. I was quickly getting on top of the world, and I knew it.

Ah, but that was the sad part—*I knew it!*

Then Fate reached out and gave me a gentle nudge. My employer lost his fortune and I lost my position. This was my first real defeat, and even though it came about as a result of causes beyond my control, I didn't learn a lesson from it until many years later.

Second Turning Point

My next position was that of sales manager for a large lumber manufacturer in the South. I knew nothing about lumber, and little about sales management, but I had learned that it was beneficial to render more service than that for which I was paid. I had also learned that it paid to take the Initiative and find out what needed to be done without someone telling me to do it. A good-sized bank account, as well as a record of steady advancement in my previous position, gave me all the Self-Confidence I needed, with perhaps some to spare.

My advancement was rapid, my salary having been increased twice during the first year. I did so well in the management of sales that my employer took me into partnership with him. We began to make money and I began to see myself on top of the world again.

To stand "on top of the world" is a wonderful feeling, but it is a very dangerous place to stand unless one stands very firmly, because the fall is so long and hard if one should stumble.

But I was succeeding by leaps and bounds!

Up to that time it had never occurred to me that success could be measured in terms other than money and authority. Perhaps this was due to the fact that I had more money than I needed and more authority than I could manage safely at that age.

DO NOT LOOK WHERE YOU FELL,

BUT WHERE YOU SLIPPED.

—African proverb

Not only was I "succeeding"—from my viewpoint of success—but I knew I was working in the one and only business suited to my temperament. Nothing could have induced me to change into another line of endeavor. Nothing, that is, except what happened which forced me to change.

I strutted around under the influence of my own vanity until I began to feel my importance. In the light of my more mature years, I now wonder if that Unseen Hand does not purposely permit us foolish human beings to parade ourselves before our own mirrors of vanity until we come to see how vulgarly we are acting and we become ashamed of ourselves. At any rate, I seemed to have a clear track ahead of me. There was plenty of coal in the bunker, there was water in the tank, and my hand was on the throttle. I opened it wide and sped along at a rapid pace.

Alas, Fate awaited me just around the corner, with a stuffed club that was not stuffed with cotton. Of course, I did not see the impending crash until it came. Mine was a sad story—but not unlike that which many others might tell if they would be frank with themselves.

Like a stroke of lightning out of a clear sky, the 1907 panic swept down, and overnight it rendered me an enduring service by destroying our business and relieving me of every dollar that I had.

This was my first serious *defeat*. I mistook it, then, for failure. But it was not, and before I complete this lesson I will tell you why it was not.

COMMENTARY

The panic referred to by Napoleon Hill began in the summer of 1907 when a number of banks and stock brokerages declared bankruptcy. Nervous investors began selling shares, which caused stock prices to drop even further. Investors withdrew money from their banks to cover their losses, but only the largest banks had enough cash reserves to cover the demand. Smaller banks that didn't have enough cash in their vaults had to turn away customers.

As word spread to the general public it created a "run" on the banks as depositors lined up to demand they be given the money they had on deposit. Banks called in loans to meet the demand for cash. When the borrowers couldn't pay, the banks foreclosed on the businesses, homes, or whatever else had been put up as collateral.

America was caught in a downward spiral that was reversed only when the major Wall Street bankers and financial executives, who were themselves in danger of losing their businesses, stepped in to shore up troubled banks. In addition to arranging foreign loans, they themselves bought stocks as a show of faith in the market.

It was in large part because of the bank panic of 1907 that legislation was enacted in 1913 to create the Federal Reserve System.

Third Turning Point

It required the 1907 panic, and the defeat that it brought me, to divert and redirect my efforts from the lumber business to the study of law. Nothing on earth, except defeat, could have brought about this result. Thus, the third turning point of my life began in what most people would call failure, which reminds me to state again that every defeat teaches a needed lesson to those who are ready and willing to be taught.

When I entered law school it was with the firm belief that I would emerge doubly prepared to catch up with the end of the rainbow and claim my pot of gold, for I still had no other concept of success except that of money and power.

I attended law school at night and worked as an automobile salesman during the day. My sales experience in the lumber business was turned to good advantage. I prospered rapidly, doing so well— still performing more service and better service than that for which I

was paid—that the opportunity came to enter the automobile manufacturing business. I saw the need for trained automobile mechanics,
therefore I opened an educational department in the manufacturing
plant and began to train ordinary machinists in automobile assembly
and repair work. The school prospered, paying me over a thousand
dollars a month in net profits.

Again I was beginning to near the rainbow's end. Again I knew I
had at last found my niche and that nothing could swerve me from my
course or divert my attention, this time from the automobile business.

My banker knew that I was prospering, therefore he loaned me
money with which to expand. A peculiar trait of bankers, a trait which
may be more or less developed in the rest of us too, is that they will
loan us money without any hesitation when we are prosperous.

My banker loaned me money until I was hopelessly in his debt,
then he took over my business as calmly as if it had belonged to him.
Which it did.

From the station of a man of affairs who enjoyed an income of
more than a thousand dollars a month, I was suddenly reduced to
poverty.

COMMENTARY

*As was noted previously, according to one calculation source the value of
one dollar at the beginning of the twentieth century was the equivalent of
almost twenty dollars at the beginning of the twenty-first century. Using
that comparison, the thousand dollars Hill's business was earning then
would be worth close to twenty thousand dollars a month today. But,
as was also noted previously, there are many factors and variables in
making direct dollar comparisons when it comes to salaries, and the
conversion figures also vary among sources.*

*According to the Bureau of Labor Statistics it took $17.89 in 2002 to
buy what $1.00 bought in 1913. If the $17.89 figure were used relative*

AN OPTIMIST SEES AN OPPORTUNITY

IN EVERY CALAMITY;

A PESSIMIST SEES A CALAMITY

IN EVERY OPPORTUNITY.

—Winston Churchill

to salaries, that would translate to Hill's annual income being the equi-valent of $214,680.

That calculation, however, is based on all goods and services purch-ased by urban households, and as we've seen during recessions, the fact that consumers spend less freely doesn't mean salaries are suddenly decreased accordingly. And nor do salaries increase to match the freer spending in a particularly good economic climate.

Now, twenty years later, I thank the hand of Fate for this forced change. But at that time I looked upon the change as nothing but failure.

The rainbow's end had disappeared, and with it that proverbial pot of gold. It was many years later that I learned the truth—that this temporary defeat was probably the greatest single blessing that ever came my way, because it forced me out of a business that in no way helped me to develop knowledge of self or of others, and it steered my efforts in a direction that brought me the rich experience I needed.

For the first time, I began to ask myself if it were not possible for one to find something of value other than money and power at the rainbow's end. This temporary questioning did not amount to open rebellion, mind you, nor did I follow it far enough to get the answer. It came merely as a fleeting thought, as do so many other thoughts to which we pay no attention, and then passed out of my mind.

Had I known as much then as I know now about the law of compensation, and had I been able to interpret experiences as I can now interpret them, I would have recognized that event as a gentle nudge from the hand of Fate. But after putting up the hardest fight of my life, up to that time, I accepted my temporary defeat as failure and thus was ushered into my next and fourth turning point. It gave me an opportunity to put into use the knowledge of law that I had acquired.

Fourth Turning Point

Because my wife's family had influence, I secured the appointment as assistant to the chief counsel for one of the largest coal companies in the world. My salary was greatly out of proportion to what was usually paid to beginners, and still further out of proportion to what I was worth, but pull was pull and I was there just the same. It happened that what I lacked in legal skill I more than made up by performing more service than that for which I was paid, and by taking the Initiative and doing what needed to be done without being told to do it.

I was holding my position without difficulty. I practically had a soft berth for life had I cared to keep it. Then without consultation with my friends, and without warning, I resigned.

This was the first turning point that was of my own selection. It was not forced upon me. I saw the old man Fate coming and beat him to the door. When pressed for a reason for resigning, I gave what seemed to me to be a very sound one, but I had trouble convincing the family circle that I had acted wisely.

I quit that position because the work was too easy and I was performing it with too little effort. I saw myself drifting into the habit of inertia. I felt myself becoming accustomed to taking life easy and I knew the next step would be retrogression. I had so many friends at court that there was no particular motivation for me to keep moving. I was among friends and relatives, and I had a position I could keep for as long as I wished, without exerting myself. I received an income that provided me with all the necessities and some of the luxuries, including a car and enough gasoline to keep it running.

What more did I need? Nothing, I was beginning to say to myself.

This was the attitude toward which I felt myself slipping. It was an attitude that, for some reason still unknown to me, startled me so sharply that I made what many believed to be an irrational move by resigning. However ignorant I might have been in other matters at the time, I have felt thankful ever since for having had sense enough to realize that strength and growth come only through continuous effort and struggle; that disuse brings atrophy and decay.

This move proved to be the next most important turning point of my life, although it was followed by ten years of effort that brought almost every conceivable grief the human heart can experience. I quit my job in the legal field, where I was getting along well, living among friends and relatives, and where I had what they believed to be an unusually bright and promising future ahead of me. I am frank to admit that it has been an ever-increasing source of wonderment to me as to why and how I gathered the courage to make the move that I did. As far as I am able to interpret it, I arrived at my decision to resign more because of a "hunch"—or a sort of "prompting," which I did not understand at the time—than by logical reasoning.

I selected Chicago as my new field of endeavor. I did this because I believed Chicago to be a place where one might find out if they had those sterner qualities that are so essential for survival in a world of keen competition. I made up my mind that if I could gain recognition in Chicago, in any honorable sort of work, it would prove that I had something that might be developed into real ability.

That was an odd process of reasoning. At least it was an unusual process for me to indulge in at that time, which reminds me to say that we human beings often give ourselves credit to which we are not entitled. I fear we too often assume credit for wisdom and for results that accrue from causes over which we have absolutely no control.

I do not mean to convey the impression that I believe all of our acts to be controlled by causes beyond our power to direct, but I strongly urge you to study and correctly interpret those causes that mark the most vital turning points of your life—the points at which your efforts are diverted, from the old into new channels, in spite of what you might do. At least refrain from accepting any defeat as failure until you have had time to analyze the final result.

ONLY THOSE WHO

DARE TO FAIL GREATLY

CAN EVER ACHIEVE GREATLY.

—Robert Francis Kennedy

My first position in Chicago was that of advertising manager for a large correspondence school. I knew little about advertising, but my previous experience as a salesman, plus the advantage gained by rendering more service than that for which I was paid, enabled me to do particularly well.

The first year I earned $5,200. I was coming back by leaps and bounds, and gradually I again began to see the shining pot of gold almost within my reach. History is full of evidence that a feast usually precedes a famine. I was enjoying a feast but did not anticipate the famine that was to follow. I was getting along so well that I thoroughly approved of myself.

Self-approval is a dangerous state of mind.

This is a great truth that many people do not learn for the better part of a lifetime. Some never do learn it. But those who do are those who finally begin to understand the strange language of defeat.

I am convinced that we have few, if any, more dangerous enemies to combat than that of self-approval. Personally I fear it more than I fear defeat.

This brings me to my fifth turning point, which was also of my own choice.

Fifth Turning Point

I had done so well as advertising manager of the correspondence school that the president of the school induced me to resign and go into the candy manufacturing business with him. We organized the Betsy Ross Candy Company and I became its first president.

The business grew rapidly, and soon we had a chain of stores in eighteen different cities. Again I saw my rainbow's end almost within reach, and again I believed I had at last found the business in which I wished to remain for life. The candy business was profitable, and because I looked upon money as being the only evidence of success, I naturally believed I was about to corner that success.

THE PROBLEMS OF VICTORY ARE MORE

AGREEABLE THAN THOSE OF DEFEAT,

BUT THEY ARE NO LESS DIFFICULT.

—Winston Churchill

Everything went smoothly until my business associate and a third man, whom we had taken into the business, took a notion to gain control of my interest in the business without paying for it.

Their plan was successful, in a way, although I resisted more than they had anticipated I would. Therefore, for the purpose of "gentle persuasion," they proceeded to have me arrested on a false charge and then offered to withdraw the charge on condition that I turn over to them my interest in the business.

I began to learn, for the first time, that there was much cruelty and injustice and dishonesty in the hearts of men.

When the time for a preliminary hearing came, the complaining witnesses were nowhere to be found. But I had them brought to the courtroom and forced them to go on the witness stand to tell their stories. This resulted in my vindication, and a damage suit against the perpetrators of the injustice.

The incident brought about an irreparable breach between my business associates and myself, which finally cost me my interest in the business. But that was slight when compared with what it cost my associates, for they are still paying, and no doubt will continue to pay as long as they live.

My damage suit was brought under what is known as a tort action, through which damages were claimed for malicious damage to character. In Illinois, where the case was filed, judgment under a tort action gives the one in favor of whom the judgment is rendered the right to have the person against whom it is obtained placed in jail until the amount of the judgment has been paid.

In due time I got a heavy judgment against my former business associates, and could then have had both of them placed behind bars.

For the first time in my life I was brought face to face with the opportunity to strike back at my enemies in a manner that would hurt. I had in my possession a weapon with "teeth" in it—a weapon placed there by the enemies themselves.

A strange feeling swept over me. Would I have my enemies jailed, or would I take advantage of this opportunity to extend them mercy, thereby proving myself to be made of different material?

Then and there was laid, in my heart, the foundation upon which the sixteenth lesson of this course is built, for I made up my mind to permit my enemies to go free—as free as they could be made by my having extended them mercy and forgiveness.

But long before my decision had been reached, the hand of Fate had begun to deal roughly with these misguided men who had tried, in vain, to destroy me. Time, the master worker to which we must all submit sooner or later, had already been at work on my former associates and it had dealt with them less mercifully than I had done. One of them was later sentenced to a long term in the penitentiary, for another crime that he had committed against some other person, and the other one had meanwhile been reduced to poverty.

We can circumvent the laws in the statute books, but we can never circumvent the law of compensation.

The judgment that I obtained against these men stands on the records of the Superior Court of Chicago as silent evidence of vindication of my character. But it serves me in a more important way than that—it serves as a reminder that I could forgive enemies who had tried to destroy me, and for this reason, instead of destroying my character, I suspect that the incident served to strengthen it.

Being arrested seemed, at the time, a terrible disgrace, even though the charge was false. It was not a pleasant experience, and I would not wish to go through a similar experience again, but I must admit that it was worth all the grief it cost me, because it gave me the opportunity to find out that revenge was not a part of my makeup.

If you carefully analyze the events described in this lesson, you can see how this entire course has been evolved from these experiences. Each temporary defeat left its mark on my heart and provided some part of the material of which this course has been built.

We would not fear or run from trying experiences if we observed, from the biographies of the men of destiny, that nearly every one of them was sorely put through the mill of merciless experience before he "arrived." This leads me to wonder if the hand of Fate does not test our fortitude in various and sundry ways before placing great responsibilities on our shoulders.

It is significant to note that each turning point carried me nearer and nearer my rainbow's end and brought me some useful knowledge that would later become a permanent part of my philosophy of life.

Sixth Turning Point

This one is the turning point that probably brought me nearer that rainbow's end than any of the others had, because it brought me to where I found it necessary to use all the knowledge I had acquired to that time, about practically every subject with which I was acquainted, and it gave me an opportunity for self-expression and development that rarely comes to a person so early in life.

This turning point came shortly after my dreams of success in the candy business had been shattered, when I turned my efforts to teaching advertising and salesmanship as a department of one of the colleges in the Midwest.

Some wise philosopher has said that we never learn very much about a given subject until we begin teaching it to others. My first experience as a teacher proved this to be true. My school prospered from the very beginning. I had a resident class and also a correspondence school through which I was teaching students in nearly every English-speaking country. Despite the ravages of war, this school was growing rapidly and I once again saw the end of the rainbow within sight.

Then came the second military draft and it practically destroyed my school, as it caught most of those who were enrolled as students.

THERE IS SOMETHING GOOD

IN ALL SEEMING FAILURES.

YOU ARE NOT TO SEE THAT NOW.

TIME WILL REVEAL IT.

BE PATIENT.

—Sri Swami Sivananda

At one stroke I charged off more than $75,000 in tuition fees and at the same time contributed my own service to my country.

Once more I was penniless! Unfortunate is the person who has never had the thrill of being penniless at one time or another, for as Edward Bok has truthfully stated, poverty is the richest experience that can come to a person—an experience which, however, he advises one to get away from as quickly as possible.

COMMENTARY

Napoleon Hill knew something of the "value" of poverty from his own modest upbringing in the backwoods of Virginia. Edward Bok, whose writing on the subject is excerpted in Lesson Eight, Self-Control, *also wrote from personal experience. And this same sentiment was expressed to Hill by Andrew Carnegie at their first meeting in 1908.*

In telling Hill that his own humble beginnings had been his inspiration to reach seemingly impossible goals, Carnegie had also said, "The richest heritage a young man can have is to be born into poverty."

This story is told in greater detail in the book A Lifetime of Riches: The Biography of Napoleon Hill *by Michael J. Ritt Jr. and Kirk Landers. Ritt worked as Hill's assistant for ten years and was the first employee of the Napoleon Hill Foundation, where he served as executive director, secretary, and treasurer. The material in Ritt's book comes from his own personal knowledge of Hill as well as from Hill's unpublished autobiography.*

Again I was forced to redirect my efforts. But before I proceed to describe the next and last important turning point, I should mention that no single event described up to this point is, in itself, of any practical significance. The six turning points I have briefly described meant nothing to me taken singly, and they will mean nothing to you if analyzed singly. But take these events collectively and they form a very significant foundation for the next turning point. They constitute reliable evidence that we human beings are constantly under-going evolutionary changes as a result of the experiences of our lives, even though no single experience seems to necessarily convey a definite, usable lesson.

I must make this clear here, because my story has now reached the point at which people either go down in permanent defeat or they rise, with renewed energies, to heights of attainment of stupendous proportions—according to the way in which they interpret their past experiences and use those experiences as the basis of future plans. If my story stopped here it would be of no value to you, but there is another and more significant passage yet to be written.

It must have been obvious to you, all through my description of the six turning points already outlined, that I had not really found my place in the world. It must have been obvious too that most, if not all, of my temporary defeats were due mainly to the fact that I had not yet truly discovered the work into which I could throw my heart and soul. Finding the work that one likes best and for which one is best suited is also very much like finding the person whom one loves best.

There is no rule by which to make this search, but when the right niche is found, one immediately recognizes it.

Seventh Turning Point

To describe the seventh turning point of my life, I must go back to November 11, 1918—Armistice Day, the end of the world war. The war had left me without a penny, as I have already said, but I was happy to know that the slaughter had ceased and reason was about to reclaim civilization.

As I stood in front of my office window and looked out at the howling mob that was celebrating the end of the war, my mind went back to my yesterdays, especially to the day when that kindly gentleman had laid his hand on my shoulder and told me that if I would acquire an education I could make my mark in the world. I had been acquiring that education without knowing it.

Over a period of more than twenty years I had been going to school at the University of Hard Knocks, as you must have observed from my description of my various turning points. As I stood in front of that window my entire past, with its bitter and its sweet, its ups and its downs, passed before me in review.

The time had come for another turning point!

I sat down at my typewriter and, to my astonishment, my hands began to play a tune on the keyboard. I had never written so rapidly or so easily before. I did not plan or think about what I was writing —I just wrote whatever came into my mind.

Unconsciously, I was laying the foundation for the most important turning point of my life, for when I finished I had prepared a document through which I would finance a national magazine that would give me contact with people throughout the English-speaking world.

So greatly did that document influence my own career, and the lives of tens of thousands of other people, that I believe it will be of interest to the students of this course. Therefore, I am reproducing it just as it appeared in *Hill's Golden Rule* magazine, where it was first published:

A PERSONAL VISIT WITH YOUR EDITOR

I am writing on Monday, November eleventh, 1918. Today will go down in history as the greatest holiday.

On the street, just outside my office window, the surging crowds of people are celebrating the downfall of an influence that has menaced civilization for the past four years.

The war is over. Soon our boys will be coming back home from the battlefields of France. The lord and master of brute force is nothing but a shadowy ghost of the past!

TELL EVERYONE

WHAT YOU WANT TO DO

AND SOMEONE WILL

WANT TO HELP YOU DO IT.

—W. Clement Stone

Two thousand years ago the son of man was an outcast, with no place of abode. Now the situation has been reversed and the devil has no place to lay his head.

Let each of us take unto himself the great lesson that this world war has taught: namely, only that which is based upon justice and mercy toward all—the weak and the strong, the rich and the poor, alike—can survive. All else must pass on.

Out of this war will come a new idealism—an idealism that will be based on the Golden Rule philosophy; an idealism that will guide us, not to see how much we can "do our fellow man for," but how much we can do *for* him that will ameliorate his hardships and make him happier as he tarries by the wayside of life.

Emerson embodied this idealism in his great essay, Compensation. Another great philosopher embodied it in these words, "Whatsoever a man soweth, that shall he also reap."

The time for practicing the Golden Rule philosophy is upon us. In business as well as in social relationships, he who neglects or refuses to use this philosophy as the basis of his dealings will but hasten the time of his failure.

And while I am intoxicated with the glorious news of the war's ending, is it not fitting that I should attempt to do something to help preserve for the generations yet to come, one of the great lessons to be learned from William Hohenzollern's effort to rule the earth by force?

I can best do this by going back twenty-two years for my beginning. Come with me, won't you?

It was a bleak November morning, probably not far from the eleventh of the month, that I got my first job as a laborer in the coal mine regions of Virginia, at wages of a dollar a day. A dollar a day was a big sum in those days; especially to a boy of my age. Of this, I paid fifty cents a day for my room and board.

Shortly after I began work, the miners became dissatisfied and commenced talking about striking. I listened eagerly to all that was said. I was especially interested in the organizer who had organized the union. He was one of the smoothest speakers I had ever heard, and his words fascinated me. He said one thing, in particular, that I have never forgotten; and, if I knew where to find him, I would look him up today and thank him warmly for saying it. The philosophy which I gathered from his words has had a most profound and enduring influence upon me.

Perhaps you will say that most labor agitators are not very sound philosophers; and I would agree with you if you said so. Maybe this one was not a sound philosopher, but surely the philosophy he expounded on this occasion was sound.

Standing on a dry goods box, in the corner of an old shop where he was holding a meeting, he said:

"Men, we are talking about striking. Before you vote, I wish to call your attention to something that will benefit you if you will heed what I say.

"You want more money for your work, and I wish to see you get it, because I believe you deserve it. May I not tell you how to get more money and still retain the goodwill of the owner of this mine?

"We can call a strike and probably force them to pay more money, but we cannot force them to do this and like it. Before we call a strike, let us be fair with the owner of the mine and with ourselves; let us go to the owner and ask him if he will divide the profits of his mine with us fairly.

"If he says yes, as he probably will, then let us ask him how much he made last month and if he will divide among us a fair proportion of any additional profits he may make if we all jump in and help him earn more next month.

"He, being human like each of us, will no doubt say, 'Why, certainly boys, go to it and I'll divide with you.' It is but natural that he would say that.

"After he agrees to the plan, as I believe he will if we make him see that we are in earnest, I want every one of you to come to work with a smile on your face for the next thirty days. I want to hear you whistling a tune as you go into the mines. I want you to go at your work with the feeling that you are one of the partners in this business.

"Without hurting yourself you can do almost twice as much work as you are doing, and if you do more work, you are sure to help the owner of this mine make more money. And if he makes more money he will be glad to divide a part of it with you. He will do this for sound business reasons if not out of a spirit of fair play.

"If he doesn't, I'll be personally responsible to you, and if you say so I'll help blow this mine into smithereens! That's how much I think of the plan, boys! Are you with me?"

They were, to the man!

The following month every man in the mines received a bonus of twenty percent of his month's earnings. Every month thereafter each man received a bright red envelope with his part of the extra earnings in it. On the outside of the envelope were these printed words: *Your part of the profits from the work which you did that you were not paid to do.*

I have gone through some pretty tough experiences since those days of twenty-odd years ago, but I have always come out on top—a little wiser, a little happier, and a little better prepared to be of service to my fellow men, owing to my having applied the principle of performing more work than I was actually paid to perform.

THERE ARE TWELVE

GOOD REASONS FOR FAILURE.

THE FIRST ONE IS THE AVOWED

INTENTION OF DOING NO MORE

THAN ONE IS PAID TO DO, AND

THE PERSON WHO MAKES THIS AVOWAL

MAY SEE THE OTHER ELEVEN BY

STEPPING BEFORE A LOOKING-GLASS.

—Napoleon Hill

It may be of interest to you to know that the last position I held in the coal business was that of assistant to the chief counsel for one of the largest companies in the world. It is a considerable jump from the position of common laborer in the coal mines to that of assistant to the chief counsel—a jump that I never could have made without the aid of this principle of performing more work than I was paid to perform.

I wish I had the space in which to tell you of the scores of times that this idea of performing more work than I was paid to perform has helped me over rough spots.

Many have been the times that I have placed an employer so deeply in my debt, through the aid of this principle, that I got whatever I asked for, without hesitation or quibbling, without complaint or hard feelings, and what is more important, without the feeling that I was taking unfair advantage of my employer.

I believe most earnestly that anything a man acquires from his fellow man, without the full consent of the person from whom it is acquired, will eventually burn a hole in his pocket, or blister the palms of his hands, to say nothing of gnawing at his conscience until his heart aches with regret.

As I said in the beginning, I am writing on the morning of the eleventh of November, while the crowds are celebrating the great victory. Therefore, it is but natural that I should turn to the silence of my heart for some thought to pass on to the world today—some thought that will help keep alive in the minds of Americans the spirit of idealism for which they have fought and in which they entered the world war.

I find nothing more appropriate than the philosophy which I have related. To get this philosophy into the hearts of those who need it, I shall publish a magazine to be called *Hill's Golden Rule.*

It takes money to publish a national magazine, and I haven't very much of it at this writing. But before another month shall have passed, through the aid of the philosophy that I have tried to emphasize here, I shall find someone who will supply the necessary money and make it possible for me to pass on to the world the simple philosophy that lifted me out of the dirty coal mines and gave me a place where I can be of service to humanity. The philosophy which will raise you, my dear reader, whoever you may be and whatever you may be doing, into whatever position in life you may make up your mind to attain.

Every person has, or ought to have, the inherent desire to own something of monetary value. In at least a vague sort of way, every person who works for others (and this includes practically all of us) looks forward to the time when he will have some sort of a business or a profession of his own.

The best way to realize that ambition is to perform more work than you are paid to perform. You can get along with but little schooling; you can get along with but little capital; you can overcome almost any obstacle with which you are confronted, if you are honestly and earnestly willing to do the best work of which you are capable, regardless of the amount of money you receive for it.

It was in this somewhat dramatic manner that a desire which had lain dormant in my mind for nearly twenty years became translated into reality. During all that time I had wanted to become editor of a newspaper. Back more than thirty years ago, when I was a very small boy, I used to "kick" the press for my father when he was publishing a small weekly newspaper, and I grew to love the smell of printer's ink.

Perhaps this desire was subconsciously gaining momentum during all those years that I was going through the experiences outlined in these turning points of my life, until it finally burst forth in terms of action. Or it may be that there was another plan, over which I had no control, that urged me on and on, never giving me any rest in any other line of work, until I began the publication of my first magazine. But the important thing is that I found my proper niche.

COMMENTARY

Referring once again to Michael Ritt's A Lifetime of Riches: The Biography of Napoleon Hill, *and as we also noted in Lesson Nine, Hill took the fore-going postwar essay to George B. Williams, a Chicago printer he had met while working at the White House, and by early January of 1919 Hill's* Golden Rule *magazine was on the newsstands.*

The first issue was forty-eight pages. In the beginning, with no money to pay anyone else, Hill wrote and edited every word himself, changing his writing style for each article as well as using a variety of pen names. Additional staff was hired later, which soon led to problems on the inside and on the outside, and Williams attempted to buy out Hill's share of the business. But when Hill realized that one stipulation of the buyout prevented him from any involvement in a competing publication, in October of 1920 he simply left.

By April of 1921 Hill had raised the money for a new publication, Napoleon Hill's Magazine, *the foundation of which was again the Golden Rule, but it also expanded into presenting many of the principles of success that would become the basis of his later books. The magazine's acceptance and success also led to Hill's success as a speaker and motivator, which led to even greater success for the magazine.*

At the same time, Napoleon Hill was working with one of the inmates of a penitentiary to develop a correspondence course which he took to the prisons to encourage prisoner rehabilitation. Most everything Hill did during this time was successful, and the success of the prison program was significant. But the greed of two members of the board of directors,

PROSPERITY IS ONLY

AN INSTRUMENT TO BE USED,

NOT A DEITY TO BE WORSHIPPED.

—Calvin Coolidge

one of whom was the prison chaplain, eventually led in 1923 to the
demise of not only the educational rehabilitation programs but also the
magazine and numerous other successful offshoot ventures.

"The bleak irony," as Michael Ritt notes, was that "few enterprises in
the 1920s could have been more idealistic or humanitarian in concept . . .
yet in seeking to stir goodness in men's souls these enterprises had stirred
mean-spirited men to a blood lust that destroyed everything."

As devastated as he was, Hill blamed himself and his own poor
judgment of the character of others.

Strangely enough, I entered into this work with never a thought of looking for either the end of the rainbow or the proverbial pot of gold. For the first time in my life I seemed to realize, without a doubt, that there was something else to be sought in life that was worth more than gold. I went at my editorial work with but one main thought in mind—to render the world the best service of which I was capable, whether my efforts brought me a penny in return or not.

The publication of *Hill's Golden Rule* magazine brought me in contact with thinking people all over the country. It was my big chance to be heard. My message of optimism and goodwill toward others became so popular that I was invited to go on a countrywide speaking tour during the early part of 1920, during which I had the privilege of meeting and talking with some of the most progressive thinkers of this generation. Contact with these people went a very long way toward giving me the courage to keep on doing the good work that I had started. This tour was a liberal education in itself, because it brought me in exceedingly close contact with people in practically all walks of life.

One day during my speaking tour I was sitting in a restaurant in Dallas, Texas, watching the hardest downpour of rain that I have ever seen. The water was pouring down over the plate-glass window in two great streams, and playing backward and forward from one of the streams to the other were little streams, creating what resembled a great ladder of water.

As I looked at this unusual scene, the thought flashed into my mind that I would have a splendid lecture if I organized all that I had learned from the seven turning points of my life, and all I had learned from studying the lives of successful men, and offered it under the title "The Magic Ladder to Success."

COMMENTARY

For anyone who may be reading this lesson before reading all of the previous lessons, or who may not have read the Editors' Note at the beginning of this book, we will repeat an explanatory portion of a commentary from Lesson Nine so that you will better understand what Napoleon Hill means by "studying the lives of successful men." The source of this information is again A Lifetime of Riches.

In 1908, during a particularly down time in the U.S. economy and with no money and no work, Hill took a job with Bob Taylor's Magazine. *Although it would not provide much in the way of income, it would provide the opportunity to meet and profile the giants of industry and business— the first of whom was the creator of America's steel industry, multimillionaire Andrew Carnegie, who was to become Hill's mentor.*

Carnegie was so impressed by Hill's perceptive mind that following their three-hour interview he invited Hill to spend the weekend at his estate. After two more days of conversation, Carnegie told Hill that he believed any person could achieve greatness if they understood the philosophy of success and the steps required to achieve it, and that this knowledge could be gained by interviewing those who had achieved greatness and then compiling the information and research into a comprehensive set of principles. He believed it would take at least twenty years, and offered Hill the challenge—for no more compensation than that Carnegie would make the necessary introductions and cover travel expenses.

> *It took Hill twenty-nine seconds to accept Carnegie's proposal. Carnegie told him afterward that had it taken him more than sixty seconds to make the decision he would have withdrawn the offer, for "a man who cannot reach a decision promptly, once he has all the necessary facts, cannot be depended upon to carry through any decision he may make."*
>
> *It was through Napoleon Hill's unwavering dedication that this book and his others were eventually written. Hill's conversations with Andrew Carnegie during their first meeting would later also become the basis for* Think and Grow Rich.

On the back of an envelope I outlined the fifteen points out of which this lecture would be built, and I later worked these points into a lecture that was literally built from the temporary defeats described in the seven turning points of my life. The material out of which my knowledge was gathered is nothing more nor less than the knowledge that was forced upon me through experiences that have undoubtedly been considered by some to be failures.

This course is but the sum total of what I have gathered through these "failures." If the information in the course proves to be of value to you, as I hope it will, you may give credit to the "failures" described in this lesson.

Perhaps you will want to know what material, monetary benefits I have gained from these turning points. All right, I'll tell you. To begin with, the estimated income from the sale of this course is all that I need, despite the fact that I have insisted my publishers apply the Ford philosophy and sell the course at a price that is within the reach of all who want it.

In addition to the income from the sale of the course, I am at this time engaged in writing a series of illustrated editorials that is to be syndicated and published in newspapers across the country. These editorials are based on the same fifteen principles of achievement as outlined in this course.

SUCCESS IS GOING FROM

FAILURE TO FAILURE

WITHOUT LOSING

YOUR ENTHUSIASM.

—Winston Churchill

COMMENTARY

Again for readers who may have missed the note at the beginning of this book, originally the Law of Success was indeed based on fifteen laws. The Master Mind was initially considered to be just an introductory lesson, then later became the first law and all the others moved down one. Later still, the Universal Law of Cosmic Habitforce was added, for a total of seventeen laws or principles.

The estimated net income from the sale of the editorials is more than enough to care for my needs.

I am now also working in collaboration with a group of scientists, psychologists, and businessmen in writing a postgraduate course that will soon be available to all students who have mastered this more elementary Law of Success course, covering not only the fifteen laws here outlined from a more advanced viewpoint, but also including still other laws which have but recently been discovered.

COMMENTARY

In the latter part of 1929, as a result of the October 29 stock market crash, book sales of Law of Success *declined dramatically.*

Napoleon Hill, ever the optimist, did not take the crash as seriously as others did. He thought that the economy would recover quickly, and he went to work turning his Magic Ladder to Success lecture series into another book. He also organized the lectures to become a class.

But in 1930 when The Magic Ladder to Success *was published, books were not a "luxury" that many people could afford, and few had any immediate hope for the opportunities the book proposed. With the book failing to sell, Hill realized that reports of the severe economic conditions had not been greatly exaggerated at all. At this same time, many of the newspapers that had been expected to become part of Hill's syndication deal were having their own financial difficulties and there was little to be made from this once-promising venture either.*

I include this information only because I know how common it is for all of us to measure success in terms of dollars and to refuse as unsound all philosophy that does not effect a good bank balance.

For most of my life I have been poor—exceedingly poor—as far as bank balances were concerned. This has been very largely a matter of choice, because I have been putting the best of my time into the toilsome job of gathering some much needed knowledge of life.

From the experiences described in my seven turning points, I have gathered a few golden threads of knowledge that I could have gained in no other way than through defeat. My own experiences have led me to believe that the language of defeat is the plainest and most effective language in the world, once one begins to understand it. I am almost tempted to say that I believe it to be the language in which Nature cries out to us when we will listen to no other language.

I am glad that I have experienced much defeat. It has had the effect of tempering me with the courage to undertake tasks that I would never have begun had I been surrounded by protecting influences. Defeat is a destructive force only when it is accepted as failure. When accepted as teaching some needed lesson it is always a blessing.

COMMENTARY

A defeat to which Napoleon Hill does not refer in this book, but which Michael Ritt mentions in A Lifetime of Riches, *was another shocking loss that he suffered in 1923.*

Returning to Chicago after the significant loss of his first magazine and subsequent businesses, Hill found that the building in which he kept some of his most treasured documents had been completely destroyed by a fire. Among the losses were numerous letters from Woodrow Wilson as well as an endorsement of Hill's proposal that Wilson had used to sell war bonds, and a letter from President Taft endorsing Hill to potential employers.

But most stunning was the loss of Napoleon Hill's entire collection of confidential questionnaires that had been completed by the most successful people of the day—the people he met through the introductions made by Andrew Carnegie. Those questionnaires had represented Hill's fifteen years of research, to that time, on the philosophy of success.

As with all of his adversities and defeats, Napoleon recovered and carried on, proving once again and without question that his lessons to readers are truly based on experience.

BLESSINGS IN DISGUISE

I used to hate my enemies. But that was before I learned how well they were serving me by keeping me everlastingly on the alert lest some weak spot in my character provide an opening through which they might damage me.

In view of what I have learned of the value of enemies, if I had none I would feel it my duty to create a few. They would discover my defects and point them out to me, whereas my friends, if they saw my weaknesses at all, would say nothing about them.

Of all Joaquin Miller's poems, none expressed a nobler thought than did this one:

> *"All honor to him who shall win a prize,"*
> *The world has cried for a thousand years;*
> *But to him who tries, and who fails, and dies,*
> *I give great honor, and glory, and tears.*
>
> *Give glory and honor and pitiful tears*
> *To all who fail in their deeds sublime;*
> *Their ghosts are many in the van of years,*
> *They were born with Time, in advance of Time.*
>
> *Oh, great is the hero who wins a name;*
> *But greater many, and many a time,*
> *Some pale-faced fellow who dies in shame*
> *And lets God finish the thought sublime.*

ACCEPT FAILURE AS A

NORMAL PART OF LIVING.

VIEW IT AS PART OF THE PROCESS

OF EXPLORING YOUR WORLD;

MAKE A NOTE OF ITS LESSONS

AND MOVE ON.

—Tom Hobson

And great is the man with a sword undrawn,
  And good is the man who refrains from wine;
But the man who fails and yet still fights on,
  Lo, he is the twin-brother of mine.

There can be no failure for the person who "still fights on." No one has ever failed until they accept temporary defeat as failure. And there is a wide difference between the two—a difference I have tried to emphasize throughout this lesson.

I am convinced that failure is Nature's plan through which she hurdlejumps those of destiny and prepares them to do their work. Failure is Nature's great crucible in which she burns the dross from the human heart and so purifies the mettle of the person that it can stand the test of hard usage.

I have found evidence to support this theory in the study of the records of scores of great men, from Socrates and Christ on down the centuries to the well-known men of achievement of our times. The success of each seemed to be in almost exact ratio to the extent of the obstacles and difficulties he had to surmount.

No one ever arose from the knockout blow of defeat without being stronger and wiser for the experience. Of course one must have considerable courage to look upon defeat as a blessing in disguise, but the attainment of any position in life that is worth having requires a lot of "sand." This brings to mind a poem that harmonizes with the philosophy of this lesson:

I observed a locomotive in the railroad yards
  one day,
It was waiting in the roundhouse where the
  locomotives stay;
It was panting for the journey, it was coaled
  and fully manned,
And it had a box the fireman was filling full
  of sand.

*It appears that locomotives cannot always
    get a grip
On their slender iron pavement, 'cause the wheels
    are apt to slip;
And when they reach a slippery spot, their tactics
    they command,
And to get a grip upon the rail, they sprinkle it
    with sand.
It's about the way with travel along life's
    slippery track—
If your load is rather heavy, you're always
    slipping back;
So, if a common locomotive you
    completely understand,
You'll provide yourself in starting with a good
    supply of sand.*

*If your track is steep and hilly and you have a
    heavy grade,
If those who've gone before you have the rails
    quite slippery made,
If you ever reach the summit of the
    upper tableland,
You'll find you'll have to do it with a liberal
    use of sand.
If you strike some frigid weather and discover
    to your cost,
That you're liable to slip upon a heavy coat
    of frost,
Then some prompt decided action will be called
    into demand,
And you'll slip 'way to the bottom if you haven't
    any sand.*

You can get to any station that is on life's
schedule seen,
If there's fire beneath the boiler of ambition's
strong machine,
And you'll reach a place called Flushtown at a
rate of speed that's grand,
If for all the slippery places you've a good supply
of sand.

It can do you no harm to memorize the poems quoted in this lesson and make the philosophy upon which they are based a part of your own.

There is a bit of philosophy taken from the works of the great Shakespeare that I wish to challenge as I believe it to be unsound. It is stated in the following quotation:

There is a tide in the affairs of men
Which, taken at the flood, leads on to fortune;
Omitted, all the voyage of their life
Is bound in shallows, and in miseries.
On such a full sea are we now afloat;
And we must take the current when it serves,
Or lose our ventures.

Fear and admission of failure are the ties that cause us to be "bound in shallows, and in miseries." We can break these ties, turn them to advantage, and make them serve as a towline with which to pull ourselves ashore if we observe and profit by the lessons they teach.

Who ne'er has suffered, he has lived but half,
Who never failed, he never strove or sought,
Who never wept is stranger to a laugh,
And he who never doubted never thought.

SOMETIMES A NOBLE FAILURE

SERVES THE WORLD AS FAITHFULLY

AS A DISTINGUISHED SUCCESS.

—Edward Dowden

GREAT FAILURES

As I near the end of this, my favorite lesson of this course, I close my eyes for a moment and see before me a great army of men and women whose faces show the lines of care and despair. Some are in rags, having reached the last stage of that long, long trail which some call failure.

Others are in better circumstances, but the fear of starvation shows plainly on their faces. The smile of courage has left their lips and they, too, seem to have given up the battle.

The scene shifts. I look again and I am carried backward into the history of man's struggle for a place in the sun. There I also see the "failures" of the past—failures that have meant more to the human race than all the so-called successes recorded in the history of the world.

I see the homely face of Socrates as he stood at the very end of that trail called failure, waiting, with upturned eyes, through those moments that must have seemed like an eternity, just before he drank the cup of hemlock that was forced upon him by his tormentors.

I see Christopher Columbus, a prisoner in chains, which was the tribute paid him for his sacrifice in having set sail on an unknown and uncharted sea to discover an unknown continent.

I see the face of Thomas Paine, the man whom the English sought to capture and put to death as the real instigator of the American Revolution. I see him lying in a filthy prison in France as he waited calmly, under the shadow of the guillotine, for the death he expected would be meted out to him for his part on behalf of humanity.

And I see the face of the Man of Galilee, as he suffered on the cross of Calvary—the reward he received for his efforts on behalf of suffering humanity.

"Failures" all.

Oh, to be such a failure. Oh, to go down in history, as these men did, as one who was brave enough to place humanity above the individual and principle above pecuniary gain. On such "failures" rest the hopes of the world.

Oh, men, who are labeled "failures"—
*   up, rise up! again and do!*
Somewhere in the world of action is room;
*   there is room for you.*
No failure was e'er recorded,
*   in the annals of truthful men,*
Except of the craven-hearted who fails,
*   nor attempts again.*
The glory is in the doing,
*   and not in the trophy won;*
The walls that are laid in darkness
*   may laugh to the kiss of the sun.*
Oh, weary and worn and stricken,
*   oh, child of fate's cruel gales!*
I sing—that it haply may cheer him—
*   I sing to the man who fails.*

Be thankful for the defeat that many call failure, because if you can survive it and keep on trying, it gives you a chance to prove your ability to rise to the heights of achievement in your chosen field of endeavor.

No one has the right to brand you as a failure except yourself.

If, in a moment of despair, you should feel inclined to brand yourself as a failure, just remember those words of the wealthy philosopher Croesus, adviser to Cyrus, king of the Persians:

"I am reminded, O king, and take this lesson to heart, that there is a wheel on which the affairs of men revolve and its mechanism is such that it prevents any man from being *always* fortunate."

What a wonderful lesson is wrapped up in those words—a lesson of hope and courage and promise.

Who of us has not seen "off" days, when everything seemed to go wrong? These are the days when we see only the flat side of the great wheel of life.

Let us remember that the wheel is always turning. If it brings us sorrow today, it will bring us joy tomorrow. Life is a cycle of varying events—fortunes and misfortunes.

We cannot stop this wheel of fate from turning, but we can modify the misfortune it brings by remembering that good fortune will follow, just as surely as night follows day, if we maintain faith in ourselves and earnestly and honestly do our best.

In his greatest hours of trial the immortal Lincoln was often heard to say, "And this, too, will soon pass."

If you are hurting from the effects of some temporary defeat that you find hard to forget, let me recommend the poem "Opportunity" by Walter Malone:

> *They do me wrong who say I come no more*
> *When once I knock and fail to find you in;*
> *For every day I stand outside your door,*
> *And bid you wake, and rise to fight and win.*
>
> *Wail not for precious chances passed away;*
> *Weep not for golden ages on the wane;*
> *Each night I burn the records of the day;*
> *At sunrise every soul is born again.*
>
> *Laugh like a boy at splendors that have sped,*
> *To vanished joys be blind and deaf and dumb;*
> *My judgments seal the dead past with its dead,*
> *But never bind a moment yet to come.*
>
> *Though deep in mire wring not your hands and weep,*
> *I lend my arm to all who say "I can!"*
> *No shamefaced outcast ever sank so deep*
> *But yet might rise and be again a man!*

THE MAJORITY OF PEOPLE

MEET WITH FAILURE BECAUSE OF

THEIR LACK OF PERSISTENCE IN

CREATING NEW PLANS TO TAKE

THE PLACE OF THOSE WHICH FAIL.

—Napoleon Hill

Dost thou behold thy lost youth all aghast?
Dost reel from righteous retribution's blow?
Then turn from blotted archives of the past
And find the future's pages white as snow.

Art thou a mourner? Rouse thee from thy spell;
Art thou a sinner? Sin may be forgiven;
Each morning gives thee wings to flee from hell,
Each night a star to guide thy feet to heaven.

FAILURE—
AN AFTER-THE-LESSON VISIT WITH THE AUTHOR

An all-wise Providence has arranged the affairs of mankind so that every person who comes into the age of reason must bear the cross of failure in one form or another.

The heaviest and most cruel of all the crosses is poverty.

Hundreds of millions of people living on this earth today find it necessary to struggle under the burden of this cross in order to enjoy the three bare necessities of life: a place to sleep, something to eat, and clothes to wear.

Carrying the cross of poverty is no joke, but it seems significant that some of the greatest and most successful men and women who ever lived found it necessary to carry this cross before they "arrived."

Failure is generally accepted as a curse. But few people ever understand that failure is a curse only when it is accepted as such, and few ever learn the truth that failure is seldom permanent.

Go back over your own experiences for a few years and you will see that your failures generally turned out to be blessings in disguise. Failure teaches people lessons that they would never learn without it. Among the great lessons taught by failure is that of humility.

No one may become great without feeling themself humble and insignificant when compared with the world around them, the stars above them, and the harmony with which Nature does her work.

For every rich man's child who becomes a useful, constructive worker on behalf of humanity, there are ninety-nine others rendering useful service who come up through poverty and misery. This seems more than a coincidence.

Most people who believe themselves to be failures are not failures at all. Most conditions that people look upon as failure are nothing more than temporary defeat.

Careful analysis of one hundred men and women whom the world accepts as being "great" shows that they were compelled to undergo hardship and temporary defeat and failure such as you probably have never known and never will know.

Lincoln died without ever knowing that his "failure" gave sound foundation to the greatest nation on this earth.

Columbus died without knowing that his "failure" meant the discovery of the great nation that Lincoln helped to preserve with his "failure."

Do not use the word *failure* carelessly.

Remember, carrying a burdensome cross temporarily is not failure. If you have the real seed of success within you, a little adversity and temporary defeat will only serve to nurture that seed and cause it to burst forth into maturity.

When Divine Intelligence wants a great man or woman to render some needed service in the world, the fortunate one is tested through some form of failure. If you are undergoing what you believe to be failure, have patience; you may be passing through your testing time.

No capable executive would ever select as their lieutenants those whom they had not tested for reliability, loyalty, perseverance, and other essential qualities. Responsibility, and all that goes with it in the way of remuneration, always gravitates to the person who will not accept temporary defeat as permanent failure.

> *The test of a man is the fight he makes,*
>   *The grit that he daily shows;*
> *The way he stands on his feet and takes*
>   *Fate's numerous bumps and blows.*
> *A coward can smile when there's naught to fear,*
>   *When nothing his progress bars;*
> *But it takes a man to stand up and cheer*
>   *While some other fellow stars.*
>
> *It isn't the victory, after all,*
>   *But the fight that a brother makes;*
> *The man who, driven against the wall,*
>   *Still stands up erect and takes*
> *The blows of fate with his head held high:*
>   *Bleeding, and bruised, and pale,*
> *Is the man who'll win in the by and by,*
>   *For he isn't afraid to fail.*
>
> *It's the bumps you get, and the jolts you get,*
>   *And the shocks that your courage stands,*
> *The hours of sorrow and vain regret,*
>   *The prize that escapes your hands,*
> *That test your mettle and prove your worth;*
>   *It isn't the blows you deal,*
> *But the blows you take on the good old earth,*
>   *That show if your stuff is real.*

Failure often places one in a position where unusual effort must be forthcoming. Many have wrung victory from defeat, fighting with their back to the wall, where they could not retreat.

I DON'T MEASURE A MAN'S SUCCESS

BY HOW HIGH HE CLIMBS

BUT HOW HIGH HE BOUNCES

WHEN HE HITS BOTTOM.

—George S. Patton

Caesar had long wished to conquer the British. He quietly sailed his soldier-laden ships to the British island, unloaded his troops and supplies, then gave the order to burn all the ships. Calling his soldiers about him, he said, "Now it is win or perish. We have no choice."

And they won. People will usually win when they make up their minds to do so.

Burn your bridges behind you and observe how well you work when you know that you have no retreat.

A streetcar conductor got a leave of absence while he tried out a position in a great commercial business. "If I do not succeed in holding my new position," he remarked to a friend, "I can always come back to the old job." At the end of the month he was back, completely cured of all ambition to do anything except work on a streetcar. Had he resigned instead of asking for a leave of absence he might have made good in the new job.

Observe that everyone who travels the road of life carries a cross. Remember, as you take inventory of your own burdens, that Nature's richest gifts will go to those who meet failure without flinching or whining.

Nature's ways are not easily understood. If they were, no one could be tested for great responsibility—through failure.

In her poem entitled "When Nature Wants a Man," Angela Morgan expressed a great truth in support of the theory set out in this lesson on Profiting by Failure: that adversity and defeat are generally blessings in disguise.

COMMENTARY

American journalist, author, poet, and lecturer Angela Morgan was born in Yazoo County, Mississippi, in what she claimed was 1883 but biographers think was likely closer to 1875.

I HAVE NOT FAILED.

I'VE JUST FOUND 10,000 WAYS

THAT WON'T WORK.

—Thomas Edison

Prior to the First World War, Morgan worked as a reporter and feature writer for the Chicago Daily American, the New York American, and the Boston American. In 1915 she was assigned to interview a prominent New York preacher. After he read her poem "God's Man" to his congregation, it was published in Collier's Weekly.

Mrs. John Henry Hammond soon became aware of her work, and Morgan became a full-time poet under the patronage of Mrs. Hammond and later Mrs. Andrew Carnegie (which may explain why Napoleon Hill has given her so many pages in this book). It was Mrs. Carnegie who had Morgan's poem "Battle Cry of the Mothers" printed in booklet form. In April of 1915, as a delegate to the International Congress of Women at The Hague, Holland, Morgan recited the poem and it became a feminist anthem for pacifism.

She later wrote under contract with the International Feature's Syndicate, as well as for most major magazines of the time, and in 1936 was named poet laureate of the National Federation of Women's Clubs. Morgan wrote more than fourteen books of poems, one novel, and a book of short stories. Angela Morgan died in 1957.

The following poem was published in 1918 in her book Forward March!

When Nature wants to drill a man,
And thrill a man,
And skill a man;
When Nature wants to mold a man
To play the noblest part;
When she yearns with all her heart
To create so great and bold a man
That all the world shall praise—
Watch her method, watch her ways!
How she ruthlessly perfects
Whom she royally elects;
How she hammers him and hurts him,

And with mighty blows converts him
Into trial shapes of clay which only
　　Nature understands—
While his tortured heart is crying and he lifts
　　beseeching hands!—
How she bends, but never breaks,
When his good she undertakes . . .
How she uses whom she chooses
And with every purpose fuses him,
By every art induces him
To try his splendor out—
Nature knows what she's about.

When Nature wants to take a man,
And shake a man,
And wake a man;
When Nature wants to make a man
To do the Future's will;
When she tries with all her skill
And she yearns with all her soul
To create him large and whole . . .
With what cunning she prepares him!
How she goads and never spares him,
How she whets him, and she frets him,
And in poverty begets him . . .
How she often disappoints
Whom she sacredly anoints,
With what wisdom she will hide him,
Never minding what betide him
Though his genius sob with slighting and his
　　pride may not forget!
Bids him struggle harder yet.

Makes him lonely
So that only
God's high messages shall reach him,
So that she may surely teach him
What the Hierarchy planned.
Though he may not understand,
Gives him passions to command.
How remorselessly she spurs him
With terrific ardor stirs him
When she poignantly prefers him!

When Nature wants to name a man
And fame a man
And tame a man;
When Nature wants to shame a man
To do his heavenly best . . .
When she tries the highest test
That she reckoning may bring—
When she wants a god or king!
How she reins him and restrains him
So his body scarce contains him
While she fires him
And inspires him!
Keeps him yearning, ever burning for a
    tantalizing goal—
Lures and lacerates his soul.
Sets a challenge for his spirit,
Draws it higher when he's near it—
Makes a jungle, that he clear it;
Makes a desert that he fear it
And subdue it if he can—
So doth Nature make a man.

ULTIMATELY, NOTHING MUCH

MATTERS VERY MUCH.

THE DEFEAT THAT SEEMS TO BREAK

YOUR HEART TODAY WILL BE BUT

A RIPPLE AMONG THE WAVES OF OTHER

EXPERIENCES IN THE OCEAN

OF YOUR LIFE FURTHER AHEAD.

—Napoleon Hill

Then, to test his spirit's wrath
Hurls a mountain in his path—
Puts a bitter choice before him
And relentlessly stands o'er him.
"Climb, or perish!" so she says . . .
Watch her purpose, watch her ways!

Nature's plan is wondrous kind
Could we understand her mind . . .
Fools are they who call her blind.
When his feet are torn and bleeding
Yet his spirit mounts unheeding,
All his higher powers speeding,
Blazing newer paths and fine;
When the force that is divine
Leaps to challenge every failure and his ardor
*   still is sweet*
And love and hope are burning in the presence
*   of defeat . . .*
Lo, the crisis! Lo, the shout
That must call the leader out.
When the people need salvation
Doth he come to lead the nation . . .
Then doth Nature show her plan
When the world has found—a man!

There is no failure. What appears to be failure is usually nothing but temporary defeat. Make sure that you do not accept it as permanent!

—— Lesson Fifteen ——

Tolerance

WE ALL NEED TO LEARN A LESSON

FROM CRAYONS. SOME ARE SHARP,

SOME HAVE WEIRD NAMES, AND

THEY ARE ALL KINDS OF COLORS.

BUT IN THE END, THEY ALL HAVE TO

LEARN TO LIVE IN THE SAME BOX.

—Nick Meno

Lesson Fifteen

TOLERANCE

"You Can Do It if You Believe You Can!"

I WILL BEGIN THIS LESSON ABOUT TOLERANCE by pointing out the two significant features of *in*tolerance.

The first is that intolerance is a form of ignorance which must be mastered before any form of enduring success can be attained. It makes enemies in business and in the professions. It disintegrates the organized forces of society in a thousand forms. It is the chief cause of all wars and a barrier to the abolition of war. It dethrones reason and substitutes mob psychology in its place.

The second is that intolerance is the chief disintegrating force in the organized religions of the world, where it plays havoc with the greatest power for good by breaking up that power into small sects and denominations that spend as much effort opposing each other as they do in destroying the evils of the world.

But this indictment against intolerance is general. Let us look at how it affects you, the individual. It is, of course, obvious that anything which impedes the progress of civilization also stands as a barrier to each individual. Stating it conversely, anything that clouds the mind of the individual and retards mental, moral, and spiritual development, also retards the progress of civilization.

All of this is an abstract statement of a great truth. And inasmuch as abstract statements are neither interesting nor informative, let me more concretely illustrate the damaging effects of intolerance.

INTOLERANCE

I will start by describing an incident that I have mentioned quite freely in practically every public address I have delivered within the past five years. But because the cold printed page has a modifying effect that makes it possible to misinterpret the incident described, I caution you not to read into it a meaning that I had not intended. You will do yourself an injustice if you neglect to study this illustration in the exact words and with the exact meaning that I have intended those words to convey.

As you read, place yourself in my position and see if you have not had a parallel experience. And if so, what lesson did it teach you?

One day I was introduced to a young man of unusually fine appearance. His clear eyes, his warm hand-clasp, the tone of his voice, and the splendid taste with which he was groomed marked him as a young man of high intellect, the typical young American college student type. As I looked him over, hurriedly studying his personality, as one will naturally do under such circumstances, I observed a Knights of Columbus pin on his vest.

Instantly, I released his hand as if it were a piece of ice!

This was done so quickly that it surprised both him and me. As I excused myself and started to walk away, I glanced down at the Masonic pin that I wore on my own vest, then took another look at his Knights of Columbus pin, and wondered why a couple of trinkets such as these could dig such a deep chasm between men who knew nothing of each other.

COMMENTARY

Although most readers today will have some familiarity with Masonic Lodges and the Knights of Columbus, their role in American society has changed considerably in the time since Napoleon Hill wrote this anecdote. A brief overview of the two organizations will help to put his story into perspective.

The Masons are a fraternal organization (some say a secret society) that began in Europe and adopted the name and tools of ancient architects and builders as symbolic of their beliefs. Although the exact date of origin of Freemasonry is unknown, the significant time as it pertains to Hill's story dates to the eighteenth-century Age of Enlightenment. While its membership was Catholic in the beginning, by the late 1600s Masonry required of its members only that they believe in a Supreme Being, to be worshiped as the individual saw fit. They also embraced public education; the separation of church and state; equality of all men, including the clergy, under the law; and other goals of the Enlightenment. These ideas were in direct opposition to the beliefs of the Roman Catholic Church of the day. Further, the Craft, as Freemasonry is also called, had secret vows and rituals, a practice that was forbidden by the Church because of the belief that nothing could be held secret from the confessional. Between 1738 and 1902 there were twenty-one papal bulls condemning Freemasonry.

By the time Hill was writing his story, Masonic Lodges in America were largely perceived as strongholds of pro-American Protestantism. In many cases this equated with anti-Catholicism, and it was believed by

MINDS ARE LIKE PARACHUTES;

THEY WORK BEST WHEN OPEN.

—Lord Thomas Dewar

some that Catholicism was irreconcilable with American citizenship. They pointed to the fact that the Vatican had issued encyclicals against freedom of speech, the press, and religion, and that the pope had proclaimed against the separation of church and state. They claimed that true Catholics subject to papal decree were not free, but were in fact under the control of a foreign power.

The Knights of Columbus is a fraternal organization (again, some say a secret society) that was originated by an Irish Catholic priest, Father Michael J. McGivney, in 1881 in New Haven, Connecticut. It was founded as a temperance society that also embraced the goal of providing insurance for widows and orphans. At the time, American insurance societies required secrecy from their members, so the organization devised secret rituals and rites that blended Catholic symbolism with American patriotism, and named itself in honor of Christopher Columbus. The Knights of Columbus were in the forefront of those Catholics referred to as Americanists, who proclaimed that in their view there was no conflict between Catholic faith and American freedom. The organization flourished and by the early twentieth century there were more than 300,000 members.

During the election year of 1912 there was a resurgence of anti-Catholicism in America and much of it was directed at the Knights of Columbus. It was claimed by some, and believed by many Freemasons, that the Knights of Columbus was a sham organization whose real goal was to undermine American institutions and that they were secretly acting on the orders of the pope.

Such was the political and religious climate of the America in which Napoleon Hill was raised.

All the remainder of that day I kept thinking of the incident, because it bothered me. I had always taken considerable pride in the thought that I was tolerant with everyone, but here was a spontaneous outburst of intolerance that proved there was something in my subconscious mind that was creating narrow-mindedness.

This discovery so shocked me that I began a systematic process of self-analysis through which I searched into the very depths of my soul for the cause of my rudeness. I asked myself over and over again why I had so abruptly released that young man's hand and turned away from him, when I knew nothing about him.

Of course the answer always led me back to that Knights of Columbus pin he wore, but that was not a real answer and therefore it did not satisfy me.

Then I began to do some research work in the field of religion. I began to study both Catholicism and Protestantism until I had traced both back to their beginnings, a process that I must confess brought me more understanding of the problems of life than I had gathered from all other sources. For one thing, it disclosed that Catholicism and Protestantism differ more in *form* than they do in *effect*; that both are founded on exactly the same *cause*, which is Christianity.

But this was by no means all, nor was it the most important of my discoveries, for my research led, of necessity, in many directions and forced me into the field of biology where I learned much that I needed to know about life in general and the human being in particular. My research also led to the study of Darwin's hypothesis of evolution, as outlined in his *The Origin of Species*, and this, in turn, led to a much wider analysis of the subject of psychology than any I had previously made.

As I reached out for knowledge, my mind began to unfold and broaden with such alarming rapidity that I almost found it necessary to wipe the slate of what I believed to have been my previously gathered knowledge, and to unlearn much of what I had until then believed to be truth.

Comprehend the meaning of what I have just said. Imagine yourself suddenly discovering that most of your philosophy of life had been built of bias and prejudice, making it necessary for you to acknowledge that, far from being a finished scholar, you were barely qualified to become an intelligent student!

That was exactly the position in which I had found myself, with respect to many of what I believed to be sound fundamentals of life. But of all the discoveries to which this research led, none was more important than that of the relative importance of physical and social heredity, for it was through this discovery that I came to understand the cause for my action when I turned away from a man I did not know.

It was this discovery that disclosed to me how and where I had acquired my views of religion, politics, economics, and of many other equally important subjects. I both regret and rejoice to say that I found most of my views on these subjects without support by even a reasonable hypothesis, much less sound facts or reason.

I then recalled a conversation between the late Senator Robert L. Taylor and myself, in which we were discussing the subject of politics. It was a friendly discussion, as we were of the same political faith, but the senator had asked me a question for which I never forgave him until I began this research.

"I see that you are a very staunch Democrat," he said, "and I wonder if you know why you are?"

I thought about the question for a few seconds, then blurted out this reply:

"I am a Democrat because my father was one, of course!"

With a broad grin on his face the senator then nailed me with this response:

"Just as I thought! Now wouldn't you be in a bad fix if your father had been a horse thief?"

It was many years later, after I began the research work I have mentioned, that I understood the real meaning of Senator Taylor's response. Too often we hold opinions that are based on no sounder a foundation than it being what someone else believes.

To better illustrate the far-reaching effects of one of the important principles uncovered by the incident to which I have referred—and that you may learn how and where you acquired your philosophy of

NEVER EXPRESS YOURSELF

MORE CLEARLY

THAN YOU THINK.

—Niels Bohr

life in general; that you may trace your prejudices and your biases to their original source; and that you may discover, as I discovered, how largely you are the result of the training you received before you reached the age of fifteen years—I will now quote from a plan that I submitted to Mr. Edward Bok's committee, The American Peace Award, for the abolition of war.

This plan covers not only the most important of the principles, but it also shows how the principle of *organized effort* may be applied to one of the most important of the world's problems. At the same time, it gives you a more comprehensive idea of how to apply this principle in the attainment of your Definite Chief Aim.

HOW TO ABOLISH WAR:
THE BACKGROUND

There are two important factors that constitute the chief controlling forces of civilization. One is *physical heredity* and the other is *social heredity.*

The size and form of the body, the texture of the skin, the color of the eyes, and the functioning power of the vital organs are all the result of physical heredity; they are static and fixed and cannot be changed, for they are the result of a million years of evolution. But by far the most important part of what we are is the result of social heredity, which is effected through our environment and our early training.

Our conception of religion, politics, economics, philosophy, and other subjects of a similar nature, including war, is entirely the result of those dominating forces of our environment and training.

The Catholic is a Catholic because of their early training, and the Protestant is a Protestant for the same reason. But this is hardly stating the truth with sufficient emphasis, for it might be properly said that the Catholic is a Catholic and the Protestant is a Protestant because they cannot help it! With few exceptions, the religion of the adult is the result of their religious training during the years between four and fourteen, when their religion was forced on them by their parents or those who had control of their schooling.

A prominent clergyman once indicated how well he understood the principle of social heredity when he said, "Give me the control of the child until it is twelve years old and after that time you can teach it any religion you may please. But I will have planted my own religion so deeply in its mind that no power on earth could undo my work."

The outstanding and most prominent of a person's beliefs are those that were forced upon them or that they absorbed of their own volition, under highly emotionalized conditions, when his or her mind was receptive. Under such conditions the evangelist can plant the idea of religion more deeply and permanently during an hour's revival service than he could through years of training under ordinary conditions when the mind was not in an emotionalized state.

The people of the United States have immortalized Washington and Lincoln because they were the leaders of the nation during times when the minds of the people were highly emotionalized, as the result of calamities that shook the very foundation of our country and vitally affected the interests of all the people. Through the principle of social heredity, operating through the schools as in the teaching of American history and through other forms of impressive teaching, the immortality of Washington and Lincoln is planted in the minds of the young and in that way kept alive.

The three great organized forces through which social heredity operates are the schools, the churches, and the press. Any ideal that has the active Cooperation of these three forces may, during the brief period of one generation, be forced upon the minds of the young so effectively that they cannot resist it.

COMMENTARY

The Great War that had ended just ten years previously had a profound effect on Napoleon Hill. At the time many people, Hill included, felt that after such widespread devastation the world had finally realized the futility of war. It was with that spirit of idealism that Hill included in this lesson an extensive dissertation in which he proposed a plan that he believed would ensure world peace. In retrospect it is apparent that Hill was too idealistic and naïve in his worldview. Events were already under way that within a dozen years would find the world torn apart by a second world war.

As it appeared in the original edition, Hill's peace plan made numerous references to people and events whose relevance has long since faded into history and would mean little to the modern reader. The edited version that follows presents the basic principles behind Hill's vision which pertain directly to the subject of this lesson.

However, before you read on, the editors would like to point out that although Napoleon Hill was overly optimistic about the world's desire for peace, he was not unaware that the key to his solution was actually a double-edged sword. As you read his observations about Germany, Japan, and Russia, Hill is once again proved prescient.

In 1914 the world awoke one morning to find itself aflame with warfare on a scale previously unheard of, and the outstanding feature of importance of that worldwide calamity was the highly organized German armies. For more than three years, these armies gained ground so rapidly that world domination by Germany seemed certain. The German military machine operated with efficiency such as had never before been demonstrated in warfare. With *"Kultur"* as her avowed ideal, Germany swept the opposing armies before her as though they were leaderless, despite the fact that the allied forces outnumbered her own on every front.

The capacity for sacrifice in the German soldiers, in support of *Kultur,* was the outstanding surprise of the war, and that capacity

POWER LASTS TEN YEARS;

INFLUENCE NOT MORE

THAN A HUNDRED.

—Korean proverb

was largely the result of the work of two men. Through the German educational system, which they controlled, the psychology that carried the world into war in 1914 was created in the definite form of *Kultur.* These men were Adalbert Falk, Prussian minister of education until 1879, and the German Emperor William II.

COMMENTARY

Kultur *as it is spelled and used here by Napoleon Hill was in common usage at the time to refer to those characteristics that distinguished the German nation in the late nineteenth and early twentieth century: a sense of national pride and a belief in Germany's natural superiority over other nations and peoples, a policy of militant expansionism, a highly system-ized social order, and the belief in the subordination of the individual to the good of the state.*

The agency through which these men produced this result was social heredity—the imposing of an ideal on the minds of the young, under highly emotionalized conditions.

The teachers and professors were forced to implant the national ideal of *Kultur* in the minds of the young of Germany, beginning first in the elementary schools and extending on up through the high schools and universities, and out of this teaching, in a single generation, grew a capacity for sacrifice of the individual for the interest of the nation that surprised the modern world.

As author Benjamin Kidd so well stated it: "The aim of the state of Germany was everywhere to orientate public opinion through the heads of both its spiritual and temporal departments, through the bureaucracy, through the officers of the army, through the State direction of the press; and, last of all, through the State direction of the entire trade and industry of the nation, so as to bring the idealism of the whole people to a conception of and to a support of the national policy of modern Germany."

Germany controlled the press, the clergy, and the schools. There-fore, is it any wonder that she grew an army of soldiers, during one generation, that represented to a man her ideal of *Kultur?* Is it any wonder that the German soldiers faced certain death with fearless impunity, when one stops to consider that they had been taught, from early childhood, that this sacrifice was a rare privilege?

Turn now from this brief description of the modus operandi through which Germany prepared her people for war, to Japan. No western nation, with the one exception of Germany, has so clearly manifested its understanding of the far-reaching influence of social heredity, as has Japan. Within a single generation Japan has advanced to the ranks of nations that are the recognized powers of the civilized world. Study Japan and you will find that she forces upon the minds of her young, through exactly the same agencies employed by Ger-many, the ideal of subordination of individual rights for the sake of accumulation of power by the nation.

In all of her controversies with China, competent observers have seen that behind the apparent causes of the controversies was Japan's stealthy attempt to control the minds of the young by controlling the schools. If Japan could control the minds of the young of China, she could dominate that gigantic nation within one generation.

To study the effect of social heredity as it is being used for the development of a national ideal by still another nation, observe what has been going on in Russia since the ascendency to power of the soviet government, which is now patterning the minds of the young to conform with a national ideal. That ideal, when fully developed during the maturity of the present generation, will represent exactly what the soviet government wishes it to represent.

Of all the flood of propaganda concerning the soviet govern-ment of Russia that has been poured into this country through the tens of thousands of columns of newspaper space devoted to it since the close of the war, the following brief dispatch is by far the most significant:

RUSS REDS ORDER BOOKS

Contracts being let in Germany for 20,000,000 volumes.
Educational propaganda is aimed chiefly at children.

BY GEORGE WITTS

*Special Cable to the Chicago Daily News Foreign Service.
Berlin, Germany, November 9th, 1920*

Contracts for printing 20,000,000 books *in the Russian language*, chiefly for children, are being placed in Germany on behalf of the soviet government by Grschebin, a well-known Petrograd publisher and a friend of Maxim Gorky.

Far from being shocked by this significant press dispatch, the majority of the newspapers in America did not publish it, and those that did give it space placed it in an obscure part of the paper, in small type. Its real significance will become more apparent some twenty-odd years from now, when the soviet government of Russia will have grown an army of soldiers who will support, to the man, whatever national ideal the soviet government sets up.

COMMENTARY

At the time, the Russian Revolution of 1917 in which the Czarist monarchy was overthrown was still much in the news. The future implications of such a massive Communist regime were not yet clear, but obviously Hill was concerned by the potential. As the world was to learn over the next seventy years, some of Hill's worst fears were realized.

The possibility of war exists as a stern reality today solely because the principle of social heredity has not only been used as a sanctioning force in support of war, but it has actually been used as a chief agency through which the minds of men have been deliberately prepared for war. For evidence with which to support this statement, examine any

WE ARE A NATION OF

MANY NATIONALITIES, MANY RACES,

MANY RELIGIONS—BOUND TOGETHER

BY A SINGLE UNITY, THE UNITY OF

FREEDOM AND EQUALITY.

WHOEVER SEEKS TO SET

ONE NATIONALITY AGAINST ANOTHER,

SEEKS TO DEGRADE ALL NATIONALITIES.

—Franklin Delano Roosevelt

national or world history and observe how tactfully and effectively war has been glorified and so described that it not only did not shock the mind of the student, but it actually established a plausible justification of war.

HOW TO ABOLISH WAR:
THE PLAN

War grows out of the desire of the individual to gain advantage at the expense of his fellow men, and the smoldering embers of this desire are fanned into a flame through the grouping of these individuals who place the interests of the group above those of other groups.

War cannot be stopped suddenly. It can be eliminated only by education, through the aid of the principle of subordination of individual interests to the broader interests of the human race as a whole.

Man's tendencies and activities, as I have already stated, grow out of the two great forces of physical heredity and social heredity. It is through physical heredity that man inherits these early tendencies to destroy his fellow men out of self-protection. This practice is a holdover from the age when the struggle for existence was so great that only the physically strong could survive.

Gradually man began to learn that the individual could survive under more favorable circumstances by allying himself with others, and out of that discovery grew our modern society through which groups of people have formed states, and these groups in turn have formed nations. There is but little tendency toward warfare between the individuals of a particular group or nation, for they have learned, through the principle of social heredity, that they can best survive by subordinating the interest of the individual to that of the group.

Now the problem is to extend this principle of grouping so that the nations of the world will subordinate their individual interests to those of the human race as a whole.

PEACE CANNOT BE

ACHIEVED THROUGH VIOLENCE,

IT CAN ONLY BE ATTAINED

THROUGH UNDERSTANDING.

—Ralph Waldo Emerson

This can be brought about only through the principle of social heredity, by forcing upon the minds of the young of all races the fact that war is horrible and does not serve either the interest of the individual engaging in it or the group to which the individual belongs.

The question then arises, how can this be done? Before I answer this question, let me again define the term *social heredity* and find out what its possibilities are.

Social heredity is the principle through which the young of the race absorb from their environment, and particularly from their earlier training by parents, teachers, and religious leaders, the beliefs and tendencies of the adults who dominate them.

Any plan to abolish war, to be successful, depends on the successful coordination of effort between all the churches and schools of the world for the avowed purpose of so implanting the minds of the young with the idea of abolishing war that the very word "war" will strike terror in their hearts.

There is no other way of abolishing war!

The next question that arises is how can the churches and schools of the world be organized with this high ideal as an objective? The answer is that not all of them can be induced to enter into such an alliance, at one time. But a sufficient number of the more influential ones can be induced and this, in time, will lead or *force* the remainder into the alliance—as rapidly as public opinion begins to demand it.

One other question remains. Who will start the machinery of the United States government into action to call this conference? And the answer is public opinion.

Universal peace between nations will grow out of a movement that will be begun and carried on, at first, by a comparatively small number of thinkers. Gradually this number will grow until it will be composed of the leading educators, clergymen, and publicists of the world, and these in turn will so deeply and permanently establish peace as a world ideal that it will become a reality.

This desirable end may be attained in a single generation under the right sort of Leadership. But, more likely, it will not be attained for many generations to come, because those who have the ability to assume this Leadership are too busy in their pursuit of worldly wealth to make the necessary sacrifice for the good of generations yet unborn.

War can be eliminated not by appeal to reason but by appeal to the emotional side of humanity. This appeal must be made by organizing and highly emotionalizing the people of the different nations of the world in support of a universal plan for peace, and this plan must be forced upon the minds of the oncoming generations with the same diligent care that we now force upon the minds of our young the ideal of our respective religions.

It is not stating the possibilities too strongly to say that the churches of the world could establish universal peace as an international ideal within one generation if they would apply just one-half of the effort that they now apply in opposing one another.

In brief, if the present organized forces of the world will not lend their support to establishing universal peace as an international ideal, then new organizations must be created that will do so.

It staggers the imagination what all the leading churches of all religions, and the leading schools, and the press of the world could accomplish, within a single generation, in forcing the ideal of universal peace upon both the adult and the child minds of the world.

The majority of the people of the world want peace, wherein lies the possibility of its attainment!

Those who do not want peace are the ones who profit by war. In numbers, this group constitutes but a fragment of the power of the world and could be swept aside as though it did not exist, if the multitude who do not want war were organized in their objective.

In closing, it seems appropriate to apologize for the unfinished state of this essay, but it may be pardonable to suggest that the bricks and the mortar, and the foundation stones, and all the other necessary materials for the construction of the temple of universal peace have been here assembled, where they might be rearranged and transformed into this high ideal as a world reality.

ECONOMICS AND SOCIAL HEREDITY

Let us now apply the principle of social heredity to the subject of business economy, and ascertain whether or not it can be made of practical benefit in the attainment of material wealth.

If I were a banker I would obtain a list of all the births in the families within a given distance of my place of business, and every child would receive an appropriate letter, congratulating it on its arrival in the world at such an opportune time, in such a favorable community, and from that time on it would receive from my bank a birthday reminder of an appropriate nature. When the child was old enough to read, it would receive from my bank an interesting storybook in which the advantages of saving would be told in story form. If the child were a girl, she would receive, as a birthday gift, doll-cutout books, with the name of my bank on the back of each doll. If it were a boy, he would receive baseball bats. One of the most important floors (or even a whole nearby building) of my bank would be set aside as a children's playroom, and it would be equipped with merry-go-rounds, slides, seesaws, scooters, games, and sandboxes, with a competent supervisor in charge. I would let that playroom become the popular habitat of the children of the community, where mothers might leave their youngsters in safety while shopping or visiting.

I would entertain those youngsters so royally that when they grew up and became bank depositors whose accounts were worthwhile, they would be inseparably bound to my bank. And meanwhile, I would in no way be lessening my chances of making depositors of the fathers and mothers of those children.

CHILDREN ARE

POOR MEN'S RICHES.

—English proverb

If I were the owner of a business school, I would begin cultivating the boys and girls of my community from the time they reached the fifth grade, on up through high school, so that by the time they were through high school and ready to choose a vocation, I would have the name of my business school well fixed in their minds.

If I were a grocer, or a department-store owner, or a druggist, I would cultivate the children, thereby attracting both them and their parents to my place of business. If I were a department-store owner and took whole pages of newspaper ads, as most of them do, I would run a comic strip at the bottom of each page, illustrating it with scenes from my playroom, and in this way induce the children to read my advertisements.

If I were a national advertiser, or the owner of a mail-order house, I would find appropriate ways and means of establishing a point of contact with the children of the country, for, let me repeat, there is no better way of influencing the parent than through the child.

If I were a barber, I would have a room equipped exclusively for children, for this would also bring me the patronage of both the children and their parents.

In every city there is an opportunity for a flourishing business for someone who will operate a restaurant and serve quality home-cooked meals and cater to families who wish to bring the children. If I were operating it, I would have the place equipped with well-stocked fishing ponds, ponies, and all sorts of animals and birds, in order to induce the children to come out regularly and spend the entire day. Why speak of gold mines when opportunities such as this are abundant?

These are but a few of the ways in which the principle of social heredity might be used to advantage in business—attract the children and you attract the parents!

If the nations can build soldiers of war to order, by bending the minds of their young in the direction of war, businessmen can build customers to order through the same principle.

WE DO NOT EXIST FOR OURSELVES . . .

—Thomas Merton

ALLIANCES

We come now to another important feature of this lesson through which we may see, from another angle, how power may be accumulated by cooperative *organized effort*.

In the plan for the abolition of war, you observed how coordination of effort between three of the great organized powers of the world—the schools, the churches, and the press—might serve to force universal peace.

We learned many lessons of value from the world war, outrageous and destructive as it was, but none of greater importance than that of the effect of *organized effort*. The tide of war began to break in favor of the allied armies just after all armed forces were placed under the direction of General Foch, which brought about complete coordination of effort in the allied ranks.

Never before in the history of the world had so much power been concentrated in one group of men as that which was created through the *organized effort* of the allied armies. One of the most outstanding and significant facts to be found in the analysis of these armies is that they were made up of the most cosmopolitan group of soldiers ever assembled. Every race and religion was represented.

If they had any differences on account of race or creed, they laid them aside and subordinated them to the *cause* for which they were fighting. Under the stress of war, that great mass of humanity was reduced to a common level where they fought shoulder to shoulder, side by side, without asking any questions as to one another's racial or religious beliefs.

If they could lay aside intolerance long enough to fight for their lives over there, why can we not do the same while we fight for a higher standard of ethics in business and finance and industry over here? Is it only when civilized people are fighting for their lives that they have the foresight to put aside intolerance and cooperate in the furtherance of a common end?

If it were advantageous to the allied armies to think and act as one thoroughly coordinated body, would it be less advantageous for the people of a city or a community or an industry to do so?

If all the churches, schools, newspapers, clubs, and civic organizations of your city allied themselves for the furtherance of a common cause, do you not see how such an alliance would create sufficient power to ensure the success of that cause?

Bring the idea still nearer your own interests by imagining in your own city an alliance between all the employers and all the employees for the purpose of reducing friction and misunderstandings, thereby enabling them to render better service at a lower cost to the public and greater profit to themselves.

We learned from the world war that we cannot destroy a part without weakening the whole; that when one nation or group of people is reduced to poverty and want, the rest of the world suffers as well. As we also learned, Cooperation and Tolerance are the very foundation of enduring success.

Surely the more thoughtful and observant among us will not fail to profit, as individuals, by these great lessons.

I realize that you are probably studying this course for the purpose of profiting in every way possible, from a purely personal point of view, by the principles upon which it is founded. For this very reason, I have endeavored to apply these principles to as wide a range of subjects as possible.

In this lesson you have had an opportunity to consider the application of the principles of Tolerance, *organized effort*, and social heredity in ways that should have given you much to think about. I have endeavored to show you how these principles may be applied both in the furtherance of your own individual interests, in whatever you may be involved, and for the benefit of civilization as a whole.

Whether your calling is that of preaching sermons, selling goods or personal services, practicing law, directing the efforts of others, or working as a day laborer, it seems not too much to hope that you will find in this lesson a stimulus to thought which may lead you to higher achievements. If you happen to be a writer of advertising copy, you will surely find in this lesson sufficient food for thought. If you offer personal services, it is not unreasonable to expect that this lesson will suggest ways and means of marketing those services to greater advantage.

In pointing out some of the sources from which intolerance can develop, this lesson should also lead you to the study of other thought-provoking subjects, which might easily mark a most profitable turning point in your life. Books and lessons in themselves are of but little value; their real value, if any, lies not in their printed pages but in the possible action they may arouse in the reader.

For example, when my proofreader had finished reading the manuscript of this lesson, she informed me that it had so impressed her and her husband that they intended to go into the advertising business and supply banks with an advertising service that would reach the parents through the children. She believes the plan is worth $10,000 a year to her.

Frankly, her plan so appealed to me that I would estimate its value at a minimum of more than three times that amount, and I do not doubt that it would yield five times that amount if it were properly organized and marketed by a good salesperson.

That is not all this lesson has accomplished before passing from the manuscript stage. A prominent business-college owner to whom I showed the manuscript has already begun to put into effect the suggestion of applying the principle of social heredity as a means of "cultivating" students. He also believes that a plan similar to the one he intends using could be sold to the majority of the 1500 business colleges in the United States and Canada, and that it would yield the promoter of the plan a yearly income greater than the salary of the president of the United States.

I HAVE SEEN

GROSS INTOLERANCE

SHOWN IN SUPPORT

OF TOLERANCE.

—Samuel Taylor Coleridge

An important objective of this course, and particularly of this lesson, is to *educate* more than it is to inform. It should awaken the power within you that awaits some appropriate stimulus to arouse you to action.

In conclusion, I leave with you my personal sentiments on Tolerance, in the following essay which I wrote in the hour of my most trying experience, when an enemy was trying to ruin my reputation and destroy the results of a lifetime of honest effort to do some good in the world.

COMMENTARY

The Tolerance essay on the following page also appears in the After-the-Lesson Visit with the Author at the end of Lesson Five. The slight variations in each of the two versions in this revised edition are the same as they were in the original edition of this book.

With the 1928 edition of the book, and with the course on which it was based, a wallhanger of this essay was sent to each person who returned the Personal Analysis Questionnaire referred to at the end of Lesson Seventeen. In the version on the following page we present the essay in a similar format.

IF WE COULD READ THE

SECRET HISTORY OF OUR ENEMIES,

WE SHOULD FIND IN EACH MAN'S LIFE

SORROW AND SUFFERING ENOUGH

TO DISARM ALL HOSTILITY.

—Henry Wadsworth Longfellow

Tolerance

When the dawn of Intelligence shall have spread its wings over the eastern horizon of progress, and ignorance and superstition shall have left their last footprints on the sands of time, it will be recorded in the book of man's crimes and mistakes that his most grievous sin was that of intolerance!

The bitterest intolerance grows out of racial and religious differences of opinion, as the result of early childhood training. How long, O Master of Human Destinies, until we poor mortals will understand the folly of trying to destroy one another because of dogmas and creeds and other superficial matters over which we do not agree?

Our allotted time on this earth is but a fleeting moment, at most! Like a candle, we are lighted, shine for a moment and flicker out! Why can we not so live during this short earthly sojourn that when the great caravan called Death draws up and announces this visit about finished we will be ready to fold our tents, and, like the Arabs of the desert, silently follow the caravan out into the darkness of the unknown without fear and trembling?

I am hoping that I will find no Jews or Gentiles, Catholics or Protestants, Germans or Englishmen, Frenchmen or Russians, Blacks or Whites, Reds or Yellows, when I shall have crossed the bar to the other side. I am hoping I will find there only human souls, brothers and sisters all, unmarked by race, creed, or color, for I shall want to be done with intolerance so I may lie down and rest an aeon or two, undisturbed by the strife, ignorance, superstition, and petty misunderstandings which mark with chaos and grief this earthly existence.

Lesson Sixteen

The Golden Rule

—————

THERE IS A DESTINY THAT

MAKES US BROTHERS:

NONE GOES HIS WAY ALONE;

ALL THAT WE SEND

INTO THE LIVES OF OTHERS

COMES BACK ONTO OUR OWN.

—Edwin Markham

—————

Lesson Sixteen

THE GOLDEN RULE

"You Can Do It if You Believe You Can!"

T HIS LESSON IS THE GUIDING STAR THAT will enable you to profitably and *constructively* use the knowledge assembled in the preceding lessons.

For more than twenty-five years I have been observing the manner in which people with power behave, and I have come to the conclusion that the person who attains it in any way other than by the slow, step-by-step process is constantly in danger of destroying themselves and all whom they influence.

This entire course can lead you to the attainment of power of proportions that may be made to perform the seemingly impossible. It becomes apparent, however, that this power can be attained only by the observance of many fundamental principles—all of which converge in this lesson which is based on a law that both equals and transcends in importance every other law outlined in the preceding lessons.

That power can endure only by faithful observance of this law, wherein lies the "safety valve" that protects the careless student from the dangers of their own follies. It also protects those whom they might endanger by trying to circumvent the injunction laid down in this lesson.

To frivolously use the power that may be attained through the knowledge from the preceding lessons, without a full understanding and strict observance of the law presented in this lesson, is the equivalent of being reckless with a power that may destroy as well as create.

I am speaking now not of what I suspect to be true, but of what I *know* to be true. I have observed the unvarying application of this truth in everyday life over all these years and I have appropriated as much of it as, in the light of my own human frailties and weaknesses, I could make use of.

If you want positive proof of the soundness of the laws upon which this course in general—and this lesson in particular—is founded, I can offer it only through one witness, and that is *you*. You may have positive proof only by testing and applying these laws for yourself.

For more substantial and authoritative evidence than my own, I refer you to the teachings and philosophies of Christ, Plato, Socrates, Epictetus, Confucius, Emerson, and two of the more modern philosophers, James and Münsterberg, from whose works I have appropriated the more important fundamentals of this lesson, with the exception of what I have gathered from my own limited experience.

COMMENTARY

William James, psychologist and philosopher as well as physician, Harvard professor, artist, religious thinker, psychic researcher, drug experimenter, writer, and lecturer, was born in New York City in 1842 and is considered to be the father of modern American psychology. His first book, The Principles of Psychology, *advanced the functionalism movement and launched psychology as a separate field. It was perhaps the focus in James' work on the mind and on thought, habit, memory, imagination, hypnotism, and free will that most appealed to Napoleon Hill. First published in 1890, this book is still available in paperback. (William James is the older brother of novelist Henry James.)*

It was at the urging of William James that idealist German psychologist and philosopher Hugo Münsterberg came to the U.S. as a professor of psychology at Harvard. Combining his career and outside interests, Münsterberg wrote several books on such varied subjects as social issues, film, the criminal justice system, and Asian art, and many of these books are also still available.

DO UNTO OTHERS . . .

For more than four thousand years, people have been preaching the Golden Rule as a suitable rule of conduct toward others. But while we have accepted the philosophy of it as a sound rule of ethical conduct, we have failed to understand the spirit of it or the law upon which it is based.

The Golden Rule essentially means to do unto others as you would wish them to do unto you if your positions were reversed.

There is an eternal law through the operation of which we reap what we sow. When you select the rule of conduct by which you guide yourself in your transactions with others, you will very likely be fair and just if you know that by your selection you are setting into motion a power that will run its course in the lives of others, returning finally to help or to hinder you, according to its nature.

If you fully understood the principles described in Lesson Eleven on Accurate Thinking—that one's thoughts are transformed into reality corresponding exactly to the *nature* of the thoughts—it will be quite easy for you to understand the law upon which the Golden Rule is based. You cannot divert or change the course of this law,

IT IS WELL TO THINK WELL;

IT IS DIVINE TO ACT WELL.

—Horace Mann

but you can adapt yourself to its nature and thereby use it as an irresistible power that will carry you to heights of achievement which could not be attained without its aid.

It is your privilege to deal unjustly with others, but if you understand this law, you must know that your unjust dealings will come home to roost. The law does not stop by merely flinging back upon you your *acts* of injustice and unkindness toward others; it goes further than this—much further—and returns to you the results of every *thought* that you release.

Therefore, it is not enough to "do unto others as you wish them to do unto you," but you must also "think of others as you wish them to think of you."

The law upon which the Golden Rule is based begins affecting you the moment you release a thought. It has amounted almost to a worldwide tragedy that people have not generally understood this. Despite the simplicity of this law, it is practically all there is to be learned that is of enduring value to man, for it is the medium through which we become the masters of our own destiny.

Understand this law and you understand *all* that the Bible has to unfold to you, for the Bible presents an unbroken chain of evidence in support of man being the maker of his own destiny, and his thoughts and acts being the tools with which he does the making.

During ages of less enlightenment and Tolerance than that of the present, some of the greatest thinkers the world has ever produced have paid with their lives for daring to uncover this law so that it might be understood by all. In light of the past history of the world, people are gradually throwing off the veil of ignorance and intolerance, and today I stand in no danger of bodily harm for writing what would have cost me my life a few centuries ago.

While this course deals with the highest laws of the universe that man is capable of interpreting, the aim nevertheless has been to show

how these laws may be used in the practical affairs of life. With this object of practical application in mind, let us now proceed to analyze the effect of the Golden Rule through the following illustration of the power of prayer:

"No," said the lawyer, "I won't press your claim against that man. You can get someone else to take the case."

"Think there isn't any money in it?"

"There probably would be a little money in it, but it would come from the sale of the little house that the man calls his home! But I don't want to meddle with the matter, anyhow."

"Got frightened out of it, eh?"

"Not at all."

"I suppose the fellow begged hard to be let off?"

"Well, yes, he did."

"And you caved in?"

"Yes."

"What did you do?"

"I shed a few tears."

"And the old fellow begged you hard, you say?"

"No, he didn't speak a word to me."

"Well, then, whom did he address in your hearing?"

"God Almighty."

"He prayed to be let off?"

"Not for my benefit, in the least. You see, when I went to the house the front door was open. I knocked but nobody heard me, so I stepped into the little hall and saw through the crack of a door a cozy sitting room. There on the bed, with her silver head high on the pillows, was an old lady who looked for all the world just like my mother did the last time I ever saw her on earth. Down on his knees by her side was an old, white-haired man, and I couldn't have knocked then, for the life of me.

"Then he began. First, he reminded God they were still His submissive children, and no matter what He saw fit to bring upon them they shouldn't rebel at His will. Of course it was going to be very hard for them to go out homeless in their old age, especially with poor mother so sick and helpless, and oh how different it all might have been if only one of the boys had been spared. Then his voice kind of broke, and a white hand stole from under the covers and moved softly over his snowy hair. Then he went on to repeat that nothing could be so painful again as the parting with those three sons—unless mother and he should be separated.

"But, at last, he comforted himself with the fact that the dear Lord knew that it was through no fault of his own that mother and he were threatened with the loss of their dear little home. And then he quoted a multitude of promises concerning the safety of those who put their trust in the Lord. In fact, it was the most moving plea to which I ever listened. And last, he prayed for God's blessing on those who were about to demand justice."

The lawyer continued, more lowly than ever: "And, I believe, I'd rather go to the poorhouse myself tonight than to stain my heart and hands with such a prosecution as that."

"Afraid to negate the old man's prayer?"

"You couldn't negate it!" said the lawyer. "He left it all to the will of God. He claimed that we were told to make known our desires unto God, and of all the pleadings I ever heard, that beat all. You see, I was taught that kind of thing myself in my childhood. Was I sent to hear that prayer? I am sure I don't know, but I hand the case over."

"I wish," said the client, twisting uneasily, "you hadn't told me about the old man's prayer."

"Why so?"

"Well, because I want the money the place would bring, and generally people's personal prayers don't enter into my business dealings, but I was taught the Bible when I was a youngster too."

I FEEL THE CAPACITY TO CARE

IS THE THING WHICH GIVES LIFE

ITS DEEPEST SIGNIFICANCE.

—Pablo Casals

The lawyer smiled.

"Maybe that's why I overheard it. Maybe it was meant for both of us to hear. My mother used to sing about God's moving in a mysterious way, as I remember it."

"Well, my mother used to say it too," said the claimant, as he twisted the claim papers in his fingers. "You can call in the morning, if you like, and tell them the claim has been met."

"In a mysterious way," added the lawyer.

Neither this lesson nor any other part of this course is intended as an appeal to maudlin sentiment. But there can be no escape from the truth that success—in its highest and noblest form—brings one finally to view all human relationships with a feeling of deep emotion such as this lawyer felt when he overheard the old man's prayer.

It may be an old-fashioned idea, but somehow I also can't get away from the belief that no one can attain success in its highest form without the aid of earnest prayer. In this age of mundane affairs—when the uppermost thought of the majority of people is centered on either the accumulation of wealth or the struggle for a mere existence—it is both easy and natural for us to overlook the power of prayer.

I am not saying that you should resort to prayer as a means of solving the daily problems that require your immediate attention. No, I am not going that far in a course that will be studied largely by those who are seeking the road to success that is measured in dollars. But may I not modestly suggest that you at least give prayer a trial after everything else fails to bring you a satisfying success?

I have another, although very different, illustration of the effect of the Golden Rule and the power of prayer:

Thirty men, red-eyed and disheveled, lined up before a judge at the San Francisco police court. It was the regular morning company of drunks and disorderlies. Some were old and hardened; others hung their heads in shame. Just as the momentary disorder of the bringing in of the prisoners quieted down, a strange thing happened. A strong, clear voice from below began singing:

> *Last night I lay asleeping,*
> *There came a dream so fair.*
> *I stood in old Jerusalem,*
> *Beside the Temple there . . .*

"Last night"! It had been for all of them a nightmare or a drunken stupor! The words of the song were such a contrast to the facts that it came as a shock.

The judge paused. He made a quiet inquiry. A former member of a famous opera company known all over the country was awaiting trial for forgery. It was he who was singing in his cell.

In the meantime the song went on, and every man in the line showed emotion. One boy at the end of the line, after a desperate effort at self-control, leaned against the wall, buried his face against his folded arms, and sobbed, "Oh, mother, mother."

The sobs, cutting to the very heart the men who heard, and the song, still welling its way through the courtroom, blended in the hush. At length one man protested. "Judge," he said, "have we got to submit to this? We're here to take our punishment, but this—" Then he, too, began to sob.

It was impossible to proceed with the business of the court, yet the court gave no order to stop the song. The police sergeant, after an effort to keep the men in line, stepped back and waited with the rest. The song moved on to its climax:

> *Jerusalem, Jerusalem!*
> *Sing, for the night is o'er!*
> *Hosanna, in the highest!*
> *Hosanna, for evermore!*

In an ecstasy of melody the last words rang out, then there was silence. The judge looked into the faces of the men before him. There was not one who was not touched by the song, not one in whom some better impulse was not stirred. He did not call the cases singly, but with a kind word of advice he dismissed them all. No man was fined or sentenced to the workhouse that morning. The song had done more good than punishment could possibly have accomplished.

You have read the stories of a Golden Rule lawyer and a Golden Rule judge. In these two commonplace incidents of everyday life you have observed how the Golden Rule works when applied.

A passive attitude toward the Golden Rule will bring no results. It is not enough merely to believe in the philosophy while at the same time failing to apply it in your relationships with others. If you want results you must *actively apply* the Golden Rule.

It will not avail you anything to proclaim to the world your belief in the Golden Rule while your actions are not in harmony with your proclamation and you use it to cover a greedy or selfish nature. Even the most ignorant person will see you for what you are.

COMMENTARY

In their book Be Loved for Who You Really Are, *husband-and-wife psychology team Judith Sherven, Ph.D. and Jim Sniechowski, Ph.D. offer an interesting variation on the traditional Golden Rule. They point out that in some circumstances doing for someone what you would like them to do for you can have exactly the opposite effect to what is intended.*

The example they give in their own book is of a couple, each of whom has very different expectations of how they would like to be treated when they're ill. She expects to be cared for and catered to; he prefers to be left alone. So when she fussed over him and he ignored her, she was hurt and he was irritated. Yet each felt they were following the Golden Rule

HE WHO WISHES TO

SECURE THE GOOD OF OTHERS

HAS ALREADY SECURED HIS OWN.

—Confucius

because each was doing for the other what they would prefer be done in that situation. Until they recognized this difference and discussed it, each had felt resentful of and disrespected by the other. Once they understood what the other would like, the issues were quickly resolved.

It is true that in most of our day-to-day relationships we cannot know what others would prefer. But with those we are close to, Judith and Jim suggest that a more golden Golden Rule is to "do unto others as they would like you to do unto them." And if you don't think you know what they would like, you can always ask.

Ralph Waldo Emerson was referring to the Golden Rule philosophy when he wrote the following:

Human character does evermore publish itself. It will not be concealed. It hates darkness—it rushes into light.... I heard an experienced counselor say that he never feared the effect upon a jury of a lawyer who does not believe in his heart that his client ought to have a verdict. If he does not believe it, his unbelief will appear to the jury, despite all his protestations, and will become their unbelief. This is that law whereby a work of art, of whatever kind, sets us in the same state of mind wherein the artist was when he made it. That which we do not believe we cannot *adequately say*, though we may repeat the words ever so often. It was this conviction which Swedenborg expressed when he described a group of persons in the spiritual world endeavoring in vain to articulate a proposition which they did not believe; but they could not, though they twisted and folded their lips even to indignation.

A man passes for what he is worth. What he is engraves itself on his face, on his form, on his fortunes, in letters of light which all men may read but himself. . . . If you would not be known to do anything, never do it. A man may play the fool in the drifts of a desert, but every grain of sand shall seem to see.

THE SHORTEST AND SUREST WAY TO

LIVE WITH HONOR IN THE WORLD,

IS TO BE IN REALITY WHAT

WE WOULD APPEAR TO BE;

ALL HUMAN VIRTUES INCREASE AND

STRENGTHEN THEMSELVES BY THE

PRACTICE AND EXPERIENCE OF THEM.

—Socrates

And it was this same law that Emerson had in mind when he wrote this:

> Every violation of truth is not only a sort of suicide in the liar, but is a stab at the health of human society. On the most profitable lie the course of events presently lays a destructive tax; whilst frankness proves to be the best tactics, for it invites frankness, puts the parties on a convenient footing and makes their business a friendship. Trust men and they will be true to you; treat them greatly and they will show themselves great, though they make an exception in your favor to all their rules of trade.

The following is from *Bible Mystery and Bible Meaning* by the late Judge Thomas Troward, who was the author of several interesting volumes including the previously mentioned and recommended *The Edinburgh Lectures.*

> Once grant the creative power of our thought and there is an end of struggling for our own way, and an end of gaining it *at someone else's expense;* for, since by the terms of the hypothesis we can create what we like, the simplest way of getting what we want is, not to snatch it from somebody else, but to make it for ourselves; and, since there is no limit to thought there can be no need for straining, and for everyone to have his own way in *this manner,* would be to banish all strife, want, sickness, and sorrow from the earth.
>
> Now, it is precisely on this assumption of the creative power of our thought that the whole Bible rests. If not, what is the meaning of being saved by Faith? Faith is essentially thought; and, therefore, every call to have faith in God is a call to trust in the power of our own thought about God. "According to your faith be it unto you," says the Old

Testament. The entire book is nothing but one continuous statement of the creative power of Thought.

The Law of Man's Individuality is, therefore, the Law of Liberty, and equally it is the Gospel of peace; for when we truly understand the law of our own individuality, we see that the same law finds its expression in everyone else; and, consequently, we shall reverence *the law in others* exactly in proportion as we value it in ourselves. To do this is to follow the Golden Rule of doing to others what we would they should do unto us; and because we know that the Law of Liberty in ourselves must include the free use of our creative power, there is no longer any inducement to infringe the rights of others, for we can satisfy all our desires by the exercise of our knowledge of the law.

As this comes to be understood, cooperation will take the place of competition, with the result of removing all ground for enmity, whether between individuals, classes, or nations. . . .

If you wish to know what happens to someone when they totally disregard the law upon which the Golden Rule philosophy is based, pick out anyone in your community whom you know to live for the single dominating purpose of accumulating wealth, and who has no conscientious scruples as to how they accumulate that wealth. Study this person and you will observe that there is no warmth to their soul, no kindness to their words, and no welcome to their face. They have become a slave to the desire for wealth; they are too busy to enjoy life and too selfish to wish to help others enjoy it. They walk and talk and breathe, but are nothing more than a human robot. Yet there are many who envy such a person and wish that they might be in their position, foolishly believing them to be a success.

There can never be success without happiness, and no one can be happy without bringing happiness to others. Moreover, it must be voluntary and with no other objective than that of spreading sunshine into the hearts of those who are burdened.

George D. Herron had in mind the law upon which the Golden Rule philosophy is based when he wrote:

> We have talked much of the brotherhood to come; but brotherhood has always been the fact of our life, long before it became a modern and inspired sentiment. Only we have been brothers in slavery and torment, brothers in ignorance and its perdition, brothers in disease, and war, and want, brothers in prostitution and hypocrisy. What happens to one of us sooner or later happens to all; we have always been unescapably involved in common destiny. The world constantly tends to the level of the downmost man in it; and that downmost man is the world's real ruler, hugging it close to his bosom, dragging it down to his death.
>
> You do not think so, but it is true, and it ought to be true. For if there were some way by which some of us could get free, apart from others, if there were some way by which some of us could have heaven while others had hell, if there were some way by which part of the world could escape some form of the blight and peril and misery of disinherited labor, then indeed would our world be lost and damned; but since men have never been able to separate themselves from one another's woes and wrongs, since history is fairly stricken with the lesson that we cannot escape brotherhood of some kind, since the whole of life is teaching us that we are hourly choosing between brotherhood in suffering and brotherhood in good, it remains for us to choose the brotherhood of a cooperative world, with all its fruits thereof—the fruits of *love* and *liberty*.

The world war ushered us into an age of *cooperative effort* in which the law of "live and let live" is meant to guide us in our relationships

IT IS ONE OF THE BEAUTIFUL

COMPENSATIONS OF THIS LIFE

THAT NO ONE CAN SINCERELY

TRY TO HELP ANOTHER

WITHOUT HELPING HIMSELF.

—Ralph Waldo Emerson

with one another. This call for *cooperative effort* is taking on many forms, not the least important of which are the Rotary clubs, the Kiwanis clubs, the Lions clubs, and the many other organizations that bring men together in a spirit of friendly communication, for these clubs mark the beginning of an age of friendly competition in business. The next step will be a closer alliance of all such clubs in an out-and-out spirit of friendly Cooperation.

The attempt by Woodrow Wilson and his contemporaries to establish the League of Nations, followed by the efforts of Warren G. Harding to give footing to the same cause under the name of the World Court, marked the first attempt in the history of the world to make the Golden Rule effective as a common meeting ground for the nations of the world.

There is no escape from the fact that the world has awakened to the truth in George D. Herron's statement that "we are hourly choosing between brotherhood in suffering and brotherhood in good." The world war has taught us—no, has forced upon us—the truth that a part of the world cannot suffer without injury to the whole world. I mention this not to preach morality, but to point out that the underlying law through which these changes are being brought about is the Golden Rule philosophy. The world has been thinking about this rule for more than four thousand years, and the benefits that come to those who apply it are now being realized.

If you can grasp the significance of the tremendous change that has come over the world since the close of the world war, and if you can interpret the meaning of all the luncheon clubs and other similar gatherings which bring men and women together in a spirit of friendly Cooperation, surely you will see that there is opportunity to profit by adopting this spirit of friendly Cooperation as the basis of your own business or professional philosophy.

And stated conversely, it must also be obvious to all who make any pretense of thinking accurately, that failure to adopt the Golden Rule as the foundation of one's business or professional philosophy is the equivalent of economic suicide.

COMMENTARY

As noted in the previous lesson, many people at the time thought the First World War was not only the defining moment of their generation but a turning point for the entire world. Just ten years before they had experienced the first large-scale, impersonal, mechanized war in which there was little chivalry or honor, and tanks, aircraft, submarines, bombs, poison gases, and scientifically engineered devices killed indiscriminately. The president of the United States, Woodrow Wilson, believed the war had been so horrifying that leaders throughout the world could not help but see that negotiation and conciliation were preferable to another such devastating conflict. He proposed the creation of a League of Nations, an organization through which the countries of the world could come together and world leaders could reason together in a way that would make future wars avoidable. Napoleon Hill was a staunch supporter of Wilson's dream, but it was not to be.

Even among the European allies there was widespread disagreement about the Treaty of Versailles that had redrawn the borders at the end of the war. At home, President Wilson was unable to effectively convince the public at large that the United States should be responsible for defending the borders of foreign countries. Further, the Congress and Senate were not persuaded that America should be subject to the decisions of a world body and forego its right to act unilaterally. In 1920 the Senate refused to ratify the Treaty of Versailles. The League of Nations foundered. By 1932 Adolph Hitler's rise to power was assured and a second, even more devastating, worldwide war was all but inevitable.

At the end of the Second World War the hope flourished once again that the nations of the world could come together and future wars could be prevented. On June 26, 1945, fifty nations including the United States

*signed the charter that established the United Nations as a body dedi-
cated to promoting peace, international cooperation, and economic and
social development.*

Perhaps you have wondered why the subject of *honesty* has not been
mentioned in this course as a prerequisite to success. If so, the answer
will be found in this lesson. The Golden Rule philosophy, when rightly
understood and applied, makes dishonesty impossible. It also makes
all the other destructive qualities—such as selfishness, greed, envy,
bigotry, hatred, and malice—impossible.

When you apply the Golden Rule, you become at the same time
both the judge and the judged, the accuser and the accused. Honesty,
then, begins in one's own heart, toward one's self, and extends to all
others with equal effect. Honesty based on the Golden Rule recognizes
more than just expediency.

It is no credit to be honest only when honesty is obviously the
most profitable policy so as not to lose a valuable client or be sent
to jail for deception. But when honesty means either a temporary or
permanent material loss personally, then it becomes an *honor* of the
highest degree to all who practice it. Such honesty has its appropriate
reward in the accumulated power of character and reputation enjoyed
by those who deserve it.

Those who understand and apply the Golden Rule philosophy are
always scrupulously honest, not only out of their desire to be just with
others but also because of their desire to be just with themselves. They
understand the eternal law upon which the Golden Rule is based and
they know that through the operation of this law every thought they
release and every act in which they indulge has its counterpart in some
fact or circumstance with which they will later be confronted.

Those who understand this law would poison their own drinking
water as quickly as they would indulge in acts of injustice to others,
for they know that such injustice starts a chain reaction that will not

THE EFFECTS OF OUR ACTIONS

MAY BE POSTPONED

BUT THEY ARE NEVER LOST.

THERE IS AN INEVITABLE REWARD

FOR GOOD DEEDS AND AN

INESCAPABLE PUNISHMENT FOR BAD.

MEDITATE UPON THIS TRUTH,

AND SEEK ALWAYS TO EARN

GOOD WAGES FROM DESTINY.

—Wu Ming Fu

only bring them physical suffering but will also destroy their characters, stain their reputations, and make it impossible for them to attain enduring success.

The law through which the Golden Rule philosophy operates is none other than the law through which the principle of autosuggestion operates.

If all your acts toward others, and even your thoughts of others, are registered in your subconscious mind through the principle of autosuggestion, thereby building your own character in exact duplicate of your *thoughts* and *acts,* can you not see how important it is to guard those thoughts and acts?

We are now at the very heart of the real reason for doing unto others as we would have them do unto us, for it is obvious that whatever we do unto others we also do unto ourselves.

You cannot indulge in an act toward another person without having first created the nature of that act in your own thought, and you cannot release a thought without planting the sum and substance and nature of it in your own subconscious mind, where it becomes an integral part of your own character, modifying it in exact conformity with the nature of the act or thought.

Grasp this simple principle and you will understand why you cannot afford to hate or envy another person. You will also understand why you cannot afford to strike back, in kind, at those who do you an injustice. Likewise you will understand the injunction "return good for evil."

Understand the law upon which the Golden Rule is based and you will also understand the law that eternally binds all mankind in a single bond of fellowship and renders it impossible for you to injure another person, by thought or deed, without injuring yourself. Similarly, the results of every *kind* thought and deed in which you indulge adds favorably to your own character.

Understand this law and you will then know, beyond room for the slightest doubt, that you are constantly punishing yourself for every wrong you commit and rewarding yourself for every act of constructive conduct.

. . . AS YOU WOULD HAVE THEM DO UNTO YOU

There are people who believe that the Golden Rule philosophy is nothing more than a theory and that it is in no way connected with an immutable law. They have arrived at this conclusion because of personal experience wherein they rendered service to others without enjoying the benefits of direct reciprocation.

How many have not rendered service to others that was neither reciprocated nor appreciated? I am sure that I have had such an experience, not once but many times, and I am equally sure that I will have similar experiences in the future. But I will not discontinue rendering service to others merely because *they* neither reciprocate nor appreciate my efforts. And here is the reason:

When I render service to another, or indulge in an act of kindness, I store away in my subconscious mind the effect of my efforts, which may be likened to the charging of a battery. By and by, if I indulge in a sufficient number of such acts I will have developed a positive, dynamic character that will attract people who harmonize with or resemble my own character. Those whom I attract to me will reciprocate the acts of kindness and the service that I have rendered others, thus the law of compensation will have balanced the scales of justice for me, bringing back from one source the results of service that I rendered through an entirely different source.

You have often heard it said that a salesperson's first sale should be to themselves, which means that unless they first convince themself of the merits of their wares they will not be able to convince others. Here again is this same law of attraction. Enthusiasm is contagious, and when a salesperson shows great Enthusiasm over their wares, they will arouse in the minds of others a corresponding interest.

You can comprehend this law quite easily by regarding yourself as a sort of human magnet that attracts those whose characters harmonize with your own dominating characteristics and repels all who do not so harmonize. Also keep in mind that you are the builder of that magnet, and that you may change its nature so that it will correspond to any ideal that you may wish to conform to.

Again, and most important of all, remember that this entire process of change takes place through *thought*—your character is but the sum total of your *thoughts* and *deeds.* This truth has been stated in many different ways throughout this course.

Because of this great truth it is impossible for you to render any useful service or indulge in any act of kindness toward others without benefiting thereby. Moreover, it is just as impossible for you to indulge in any destructive act or thought without paying the penalty in the loss of a corresponding degree of your own power.

Positive thought develops a dynamic personality. *Negative* thought develops a personality of an opposite nature. In many of the preceding lessons of this course, as in this one, instructions are given as to the exact method of developing your personality through positive thought. These instructions are particularly detailed in Lesson Three on Self-Confidence. In that lesson you have a very definite formula to follow. All of the formulas provided in this course are for the purpose of helping you to *consciously* direct the power of thought in the development of a personality that will attract to you those who will be of help in the attainment of your Definite Chief Aim.

You need no proof that your hostile or unkind acts toward others bring the effects of retaliation. Moreover, this retaliation is usually definite and immediate. Likewise, you need no proof that you can accomplish more by dealing with others in such a way that they

HE THAT DOES GOOD

FOR GOOD'S SAKE

SEEKS NEITHER PARADISE

NOR REWARD, BUT HE IS

SURE OF BOTH IN THE END.

—William Penn

will want to cooperate with you. If you have mastered the eighth lesson, on Self-Control, you now understand how to induce others—through your own attitude toward them—to act toward you as you wish them to act.

The law of "an eye for an eye and a tooth for a tooth" is based on the same law as that on which the Golden Rule operates. This is nothing more than the law of retaliation. Even the most selfish person will respond to this law. They cannot help it. If I speak ill of you, even though I tell the truth, you will not think kindly of me. Furthermore, you will most likely retaliate in kind. But if I speak of your virtues you will think kindly of me and, in the majority of instances, when there is an opportunity you will reciprocate in kind.

Through the operation of this law of attraction, the uninformed are constantly attracting trouble and grief and hatred and opposition from others by their unguarded words and destructive acts.

Do unto others as you would have them do unto you—bearing in mind that human nature has a tendency to retaliate in kind.

Confucius must have been thinking of the law of retaliation when he stated the Golden Rule philosophy in somewhat this way: Do *not* unto others that which you would *not* have them do unto you.

And he might well have added an explanation to the effect that the reason for his injunction was based on that very tendency of man to retaliate in kind.

Those who do not understand the law upon which the Golden Rule is based will argue that it will not work when people are inclined toward the law of retaliation. If they would go a step further in their reasoning they would understand that they are looking at the *negative* effects of this law, and that the selfsame law is capable of producing *positive* effects as well.

In other words, if you would not have your own eye plucked out, then ensure against this misfortune by refraining from plucking out the other fellow's eye. Furthermore, render the other fellow an act of kindly helpful service, and through the operation of this same law of retaliation he will render you a similar service.

And if he should fail to reciprocate your kindness, what then?

You will have profited nevertheless—because of the effect of your act on your own subconscious mind.

Thus, by indulging in acts of kindness and always applying the Golden Rule philosophy, you are sure of benefit from one source and at the same time you have a pretty fair chance of profiting from another source.

It might happen that you would base all your acts toward others on the Golden Rule without enjoying any direct reciprocation for a long period of time. It might also happen that those to whom you rendered those acts of kindness would never reciprocate. In the meantime, however, you have been strengthening your own character and sooner or later this positive character you have been building will begin to assert itself and you will discover that you have been receiving compound interest upon compound interest in return for those acts of kindness that appeared to have been wasted on those who neither appreciated nor reciprocated them.

Remember that your reputation is made by others, but your *character* is made by you.

You want your reputation to be a favorable one but you cannot be sure that it will be, because that is outside of your own control, in the minds of others. It is what others believe you to be. With your character it is different. Your character is what you *are*, as the result of your thoughts and deeds. You control it. You can make it weak, good, or bad. When you are satisfied and know in your mind that your character is above reproach, you need not worry about your reputation, for it is as impossible for your character to be destroyed or damaged by anyone except yourself as it is to destroy matter or energy.

It was this truth that Emerson had in mind when he wrote: "A political victory, a rise of rents, the recovery of your sick or the return of your absent friend, or some other quite external event raises your spirits, and you think your days are prepared for you. *Do not believe it.* It can never be so. *Nothing can bring you peace but yourself. Nothing can bring you peace but the triumph of principles.*"

One reason for being just toward others is that such action may cause them to reciprocate in kind, but as I have said, a better reason is that kindness and justice toward others develops positive character in all who do so.

You may withhold from me the reward to which I am entitled for rendering you helpful service, but no one can deprive me of the benefit I will derive from the rendering of that service insofar as it adds to my own *character.*

THE GOLDEN RULE
APPLIED TO CAPITAL AND LABOR

We are living in a great industrial age. We see the evolutionary forces working great changes in the method and manner of living, and rearranging the relationships between people in the ordinary pursuit of life, liberty, and earning a living.

Everywhere we see evidence that *organized effort* is the basis of all financial success, and while other factors enter into the attainment of success, organization is still of major importance.

This industrial age has created two comparatively new terms. One is called *capital* and the other *labor.* Capital and labor constitute the main wheels in the machinery of *organized effort.* These two great forces enjoy success in exact ratio to the extent that the Golden Rule philosophy is understood and applied. Harmony between these two forces does not always prevail.

During the past fifteen years I have devoted considerable time to studying those causes of disagreement between employers and employees, and I have also gathered much information on the subject

I BELIEVE IN THE DIGNITY OF LABOR,

WHETHER WITH HEAD OR HAND;

THAT THE WORLD OWES

NO MAN A LIVING BUT THAT IT OWES

EVERY MAN AN OPPORTUNITY

TO MAKE A LIVING.

—John D. Rockefeller

from others who have been studying this problem. There is but one solution that will, if understood by all concerned, bring harmony out of chaos and establish a perfect working relationship between capital and labor.

The remedy is based on a great law of Nature and has been well stated by one of the great men of this generation, in the following words:

COMMENTARY

We include this quoted material for your information, with due apology for there having been neither a reference to its source nor any indication as to who this great man may have been.

The question we propose to consider is exciting deep interest at the present time, but no more than its importance demands. It is one of the hopeful signs of the times that these subjects of vital interest to human happiness are constantly coming up for a hearing, are engaging the attention of the wisest men, and stirring the minds of all classes of people. The wide prevalence of this movement shows that a new life is beating in the heart of humanity, operating upon their faculties like the warm breath of spring upon the frozen ground and the dormant germs of the plant. It will make a great stir, it will break up many frozen and dead forms, it will produce great and, in some cases, it may be, destructive changes, but it announces the blossoming of new hopes, and the coming of new harvests for the supply of human wants and the means of greater happiness. There is great need of wisdom to guide the new force coming into action. Every man is under the most solemn obligation to do his part in forming a correct public opinion and giving wise direction to popular will.

The solution for the problems of labor, of want, of abundance, of suffering and sorrow can only be found by regarding them from a moral and spiritual point of view. They must be seen and examined in a light that is not of themselves. *The true relations of labor and capital can never be discovered by human selfishness.* They must be viewed from a higher purpose than wages or the accumulation of wealth. They must be regarded from their bearing upon the purposes for which man was created. It is from this point of view I propose to consider the subject before us.

Capital and labor are essential to each other. Their interests are so bound together that they cannot be separated. In civilized and enlightened communities they are mutually dependent. If there is any difference, capital is more dependent upon labor than labor upon capital. Life can be sustained without capital. Animals, with a few exceptions, have no property, and take no anxious thought for the morrow, and our Lord commends them to our notice as examples worthy of imitation. "Behold the fowls of the air," He says, "for they sow not, neither do they reap nor gather into barns, yet your heavenly Father feedeth them." The savages live without capital. Indeed, the great mass of human beings live by their labor from day to day, from hand to mouth. But no man can live upon his wealth. He cannot eat his gold and silver; he cannot clothe himself with deeds and certificates of stock.

Capital can do nothing without labor, and its only value consists in its power to purchase labor or its results. It is itself the product of labor. It has no occasion, therefore, to assume an importance that does not belong to it. Absolutely dependent, however, as it is upon labor for its value, it is an essential factor in human progress.

The moment man begins to rise from a savage and comparatively independent state to a civilized and dependent one, capital becomes necessary. Men come into more intimate relations with one another. Instead of each one doing everything, men generally begin to devote themselves to special employments, and to depend upon others to provide many things for them while they engage in some special occupation. In this way labor becomes diversified. One person works in iron, another in wood; one manufactures cloth, another makes it into garments; some raise food to feed those who build houses and manufacture implements of husbandry. This necessitates a system of exchanges, and to facilitate exchanges roads must be made, and men must be employed to make them. As population increases and necessities multiply, the business of exchange becomes enlarged, until we have immense manufactories, railroads girding the earth with iron bands, steamships plowing every sea, and a multitude of men who cannot raise bread or make a garment, or do anything directly for the supply of their own wants.

Now, we can see how we become more dependent upon others as our wants are multiplied and civilization advances. Each one works in his special employment, does better work, because he can devote his whole thought and time to a form of use for which he is specially fitted, and contributes more largely to the public good. While he is working for others, all others are working for him. Every member of the community is working for the whole body, and the whole body for every member. This is the law of perfect life, a law which rules everywhere in the material body. Every man who is engaged in any employment useful to body or mind is a philanthropist, a public benefactor, whether he raises corn on the prairie, cotton in Texas or India, mines coal in the chambers of the earth, or feeds it to engines in the hold of a steamship. If selfishness did not pervert and blast human motives, all men and women would be fulfilling the law of charity while engaged in their daily employment.

I PITY THE MAN WHO

WANTS A COAT SO CHEAP THAT

THE MAN OR WOMAN WHO

PRODUCES THE CLOTH WILL

STARVE IN THE PROCESS.

—Benjamin Harrison

To carry on this vast system of exchanges, to place the forest and the farm, the factory and the mine side by side, and deliver the products of all climes at every door, requires immense capital. One man cannot work his farm or factory, and build a railroad or a line of steamships. As raindrops acting singly cannot drive a mill or supply steam for an engine, but, collected in a vast reservoir, become the resistless power of Niagara, or the force which drives the engine and steamship like mighty shuttles from mountain to seacoast and from shore to shore, so a few dollars in a multitude of pockets are powerless to provide the means for these vast operations, but combined they move the world.

Capital is a friend of labor and essential to its economical exercise and just reward. It can be, and often is, a terrible enemy, when employed for selfish purposes alone; but the great mass of it is more friendly to human happiness than is generally supposed. It cannot be employed without in some way, either directly or indirectly, helping the laborer. We think of the evils we suffer, but allow the good we enjoy to pass unnoticed. We think of the evils that larger means would relieve and the comforts they would provide, but overlook the blessings we enjoy that would have been impossible without large accumulations of capital. It is the part of wisdom to form a just estimate of the good we receive as well as the evils we suffer.

It is a common saying at the present time, that the rich are growing richer and the poor poorer; but when all man's possessions are taken into the account there are good reasons for doubting this assertion. It is true that the rich are growing richer. It is also true that the condition of the laborer is constantly improving. The common laborer has conveniences and comforts which princes could not command a century

HUMAN HISTORY IS WORK HISTORY.

THE HEROES OF THE PEOPLE

ARE WORK HEROES.

—Meridel le Sueur

ago. He is better clothed, has a greater variety and abundance of food, lives in a more comfortable dwelling, and has many more conveniences for the conduct of domestic affairs and the prosecution of labor than money could purchase but a few years ago.

An emperor could not travel with the ease, the comfort, and the swiftness that the common laborer can today. He may think that he stands alone, with no one to help. But, in truth, he has an immense retinue of servants constantly waiting upon him, ready and anxious to do his bidding. It requires a vast army of men and an immense outlay of capital to provide a common dinner, such as every man and woman, with few exceptions, has enjoyed today.

Think of the vast combination of means and men and forces necessary to provide even a frugal meal. The Chinese man raises your tea, the Brazilian your coffee, the East Indian your spices, the Cuban your sugar, the farmer upon the western prairies your bread and possibly your beef, the gardener your vegetables, the dairyman your butter and milk; the miner has dug from the hills the coal with which your food was cooked and your house was warmed, the cabinetmaker has provided you with chairs and tables, the cutler with knives and forks, the potter with dishes, the Irishman has made your tablecloth, the butcher has dressed your meat, the miller your flour.

But these various articles of food, and the means of preparing and serving them, were produced at immense distances from you and from one another. Oceans had to be traversed, hills leveled, valleys filled, and mountains tunneled, ships must be built, railways constructed, and a vast army of men instructed and employed in every mechanical art before the materials for your dinner could be prepared and served. There must also be men to collect these materials, to buy and sell and distribute them. Everyone stands in his own place and does his own work, and receives his wages. But he is none the less working for you, and serving you as truly and effectively as he would be if he were in your special employment and received his wages from your hand.

In the light of these facts, which everyone must acknowledge, we may be able to see more clearly the truth, that every man and woman who does useful work is a public benefactor, and the thought of it and the purpose of it will ennoble the labor and the laborer. We are all bound together by common ties. The rich and the poor, the learned and the ignorant, the strong and the weak, are woven together in one social and civic web. Harm to one is harm to all; help to one is help to all.

You see what a vast army of servants it requires to provide your dinner. Do you not see that it demands a corresponding amount of capital to provide and keep this complicated machinery in motion? And do you not see that every man, woman and child is enjoying the benefit of it? How could we get our coal, our meat, our flour, our tea and coffee, sugar and rice? The laborer cannot build ships and sail them and support himself while doing it. The farmer cannot leave his farm and take his produce to the market. The miner cannot mine and transport his coal. The farmer in Kansas may be burning corn today to cook his food and warm his dwelling, and the miner may be hungry for the bread which the corn would supply, because they cannot exchange the fruits of their labor. Every acre of land, every forest and mine has been increased in value by railways and steamboats, and the comforts of life and the means of social and intellectual culture have been carried to the most inaccessible places.

But the benefits of capital are not limited to supplying present wants and comforts. It opens new avenues for labor. It diversifies it and gives a wider field to everyone to do the kind of work for which he is best fitted by natural taste and genius. The number of employments created by railways, steamships, telegraph, and manufactories by machinery can hardly be estimated. Capital is also largely invested in supplying the means of intellectual and spiritual culture. Books are multiplied at constantly diminishing prices, and the best thought of the world, by the means of our great publishing houses, is made accessible to the humblest workman.

There is no better example of the benefits the common laborer derives from capital than the daily newspaper. For two or three cents the history of the world for twenty-four hours is brought to every door. The laborer, while riding to or from his work in a comfortable car, can visit all parts of the known world and get a truer idea of the events of the day than he could if he were bodily present. A battle in China or Africa, an earthquake in Spain, a dynamite explosion in London, a debate in Congress, the movements of men in public and private life for the suppression of vice, for enlightening the ignorant, helping the needy, and improving the people generally, are spread before him in a small compass, and bring him into contact and on equality, in regard to the world's history, with kings and queens, with saints and sages, and people in every condition in life. *Do you ever think*, while reading the morning paper, how many men have been running on your errands, collecting intelligence for you from all parts of the earth, and putting it into a form convenient for your use? It required the investment of millions of dollars and the employment of thousands of men to produce that paper and leave it at your door. And what did all this service cost you? A few cents.

LABOR IS PRIOR TO,

AND INDEPENDENT OF, CAPITAL.

CAPITAL IS ONLY THE FRUIT OF LABOR,

AND COULD NEVER HAVE EXISTED

IF LABOR HAD NOT FIRST EXISTED.

LABOR IS THE SUPERIOR OF CAPITAL,

AND DESERVES MUCH THE

HIGHER CONSIDERATION.

CAPITAL HAS ITS RIGHTS,

WHICH ARE AS WORTHY OF PROTECTION

AS ANY OTHER RIGHTS.

—Abraham Lincoln

These are examples of the benefits which everyone derives from capital, benefits which could not be obtained without vast expenditures of money; benefits which come to us without our care and lay their blessings at our feet. Capital cannot be invested in any useful production without blessing a multitude of people. It sets the machinery of life in motion, it multiplies employment; it places the product of all climes at every door, it draws the people of all nations together; brings mind in contact with mind, and gives to every man and woman a large and valuable share of the product. These are facts which it would be well for everyone, however poor he may be, to consider.

If capital is such a blessing to labor; if it can only be brought into use by labor and derives all its value from it, how can there be any conflict between them? There could be none if both the capitalist and laborer acted from humane and Christian principles. But they do not. They are governed by inhuman and unchristian principles. Each party seeks to get the largest returns for the least service. Capital desires larger profits, labor higher wages. The interests of the capitalist and the laborer come into direct collision. In this warfare capital has great advantages, and has been prompt to take them. It has demanded and taken the lion's share of the profits. It has despised the servant that enriched it. It has regarded the laborer as menial, a slave, whose rights and happiness it was not bound to respect. It influences legislators to enact laws in its favor, subsidizes governments and wields its power for its own advantage. Capital has been a lord and labor a servant. While the servant remained docile and obedient, content with such compensation as its lord chose to give, there was no conflict. But labor is rising from a servile, submissive, and hopeless condition. It has acquired strength and intelligence; has gained the idea that it has rights that ought to be respected, and begins to assert and combine to support them.

Each party in this warfare regards the subject from its own selfish interests. The capitalist supposes that gain to labor is loss to him, and that he must look to his own interests first; that the cheaper the labor the larger his gains. Consequently it is for his interest to keep the price as low as possible. On the contrary, the laborer thinks that he loses what the capitalist gains, and, consequently, that it is for his interest to get as large wages as possible. From these opposite points of view their interests appear to be directly hostile. What one party gains the other loses; hence the conflict. Both are acting from selfish motives, and, consequently, must be wrong. Both parties see only half of the truth, and, mistaking that for the whole of it, fall into a mistake ruinous to both. Each one stands on his own ground, and regards the subject wholly from his point of view and in the misleading light of his own selfishness.

Passion inflames the mind and blinds the understanding; and when passion is aroused men will sacrifice their own interests to injure others, and both will suffer loss. They will wage continual warfare against each other; they will resort to all devices, and take advantage of every necessity to win a victory. Capital tries to starve the laborer into submission like a beleaguered city; and hunger and want are most powerful weapons. Labor sullenly resists, and tries to destroy the value of capital by rendering it unproductive. If necessity or interest compels a truce, it is a sullen one, and maintained with the purpose of renewing hostilities as soon as there is any prospect of success. Thus laborers and capitalists confront each other like two armed hosts, ready at any time to renew the conflict. It will be renewed, without doubt, and continued with varying success until both parties discover that they are mistaken, that their interests are mutual, and can only be secured to the fullest extent by cooperation and giving to each the reward it deserves. The capitalist and the laborer must clasp hands across the bottomless pit into which so much wealth and work has been cast.

How this reconciliation is to be effected is a question that is occupying the minds of many wise and good men on both sides at the present time. Wise and impartial legislation will, no doubt, be an important agent in restraining blind passion and protecting all classes from insatiable greed; and it is the duty of every man to use his best endeavors to secure such legislation both in state and national governments. Organizations of laborers for protecting their own rights and securing a better reward for their labor, will have a great influence. That influence will continue to increase as their temper becomes normal and firm, and their demands are based on justice and humanity.

Violence and threats will effect no good. Dynamite, whether in the form of explosives or the more destructive force of fierce and reckless passion, will heal no wounds nor subdue any hostile feeling. Arbitration is, doubtless, the wisest and most practicable means now available to bring about amicable relations between these hostile parties and secure justice to both. Giving the laborer a share in the profits of the business has worked well in some cases, but it is attended with great practical difficulties which require more wisdom, self-control, and genuine regard for the common interests of both parties than often can be found. Many devices may have a partial and temporary effect. But no permanent progress can be made in settling this conflict without restraining and finally removing its cause.

Its real central cause is an inordinate love of self and the world, and that cause will continue to operate as long as it

IN GIVING RIGHTS TO OTHERS

WHICH BELONG TO THEM,

WE GIVE RIGHTS TO OURSELVES

AND TO OUR COUNTRY.

—John Fitzgerald Kennedy

exists. It may be restrained and moderated, but it will assert itself when occasion offers. Every wise man must, therefore, seek to remove the cause, and as far as he can do it he will control effects. Purify the fountain, and you make the whole stream pure and wholesome.

There is a principle of universal influence that must underlie and guide every successful effort to bring these two great factors of human good which now confront each other with hostile purpose, into harmony. It is no invention or discovery of mine. It embodies a higher than human wisdom. It is not difficult to understand or apply. The child can comprehend it and act according to it. It is universal in its application, and wholly useful in its effects. It will lighten the burdens of labor and increase its rewards. It will give security to capital and make it more productive. It is simply the Golden Rule, embodied in these words: *"Therefore all things whatsoever ye would that men should do to you, do ye even so to them: for this is the law and the prophets."*

Before proceeding to apply this principle to the case in hand, let me call your special attention to it. It is a very remarkable law of human life which seems to have been generally overlooked by statesmen, philosophers, and religious teachers. This rule embodies the whole of religion; it comprises all the precepts, commandments, and means of the future triumphs of good over evil, of truth over error, and the peace and happiness of men, foretold in the glorious visions of the prophets.

Mark the words. It does not merely say that it is a wise rule; that it accords with the principles of the Divine order revealed in the law and the prophets. *It embodies them all; it "IS the law and the prophets."* It comprises love to God. It says we should regard Him as we desire to have Him regard us; that we should do to Him as we wish to have Him do to us. If we desire to have Him love us with all His heart, with all His soul, with all His mind, and with all His strength, we must love Him in the same manner. If we desire to have our neighbor love us as he loves himself, we must love him as we love ourself. Here, then, is the universal and Divine law of human service and fellowship. It is not a precept of human wisdom; it has its origin in the Divine nature, and its embodiment in human nature. Now, let us apply it to the conflict between labor and capital.

You are a capitalist. Your money is invested in manufactures, in land, in mines, in merchandise, railways, and ships, or you loan it to others on interest. You employ, directly or indirectly, men to use your capital. You cannot come to a just conclusion concerning your rights and duties and privileges by looking wholly at your own gains. The glitter of the silver and gold will exercise so potent a spell over your mind that it will blind you to everything else. You can see no interest but your own. The laborer is not known or regarded as a man who has any interests you are bound to regard. You see him only as your slave, your tool, your means of adding to your wealth. In this light he is a friend so far as he serves you, an enemy so far as he does not.

But change your point of view. Put yourself in his place; put him in your place. How would you like to have him treat you if you were in his place? Perhaps you have been there. In all probability you have, for the capitalist today was the laborer yesterday, and the laborer today will be the employer tomorrow. You know from lively and painful experience how you would like to be treated. Would you like to be regarded as a mere tool? As a means of enriching another? Would you like to have your wages kept down to the bare necessities of life? Would you like to be regarded with indifference and treated with brutality? Would you like to have your blood, your strength, your soul coined into dollars for the benefit of another?

These questions are easy to answer. Everyone knows that he would rejoice to be treated kindly, to have his interests regarded, his rights recognized and protected. Everyone knows that such regard awakens a response in his own heart. Kindness begets kindness; respect awakens respect. Put yourself in his place. Imagine that you are dealing with yourself, and you will have no difficulty in deciding whether you should give the screw another turn, that you may wring a penny more from the muscles of the worker, or relax its pressure, and, if possible, add something to his wages, and give him respect for his service. Do to him as you would have him do to you in changed conditions.

You are a laborer. You receive a certain sum for a day's work. Put yourself in the place of your employer. How would you like to have the men whom you employed work for you? Would you think it right that they should regard you as their enemy? Would you think it honest in them to slight their work, *to do as little and to get as much as possible?* If you had a large contract which must be completed at a fixed time or you would suffer great loss, would you like to have your workmen take advantage of your necessity to compel an increase of their wages? Would you think it right and wise in them to interfere with you in the management of your business? To dictate whom you should employ, and on what terms you should employ them?

Would you not rather have them do honest work in a kind and good spirit? Would you not be much more disposed to look to their interests, to lighten their labor, to increase their wages when you could afford to do so, and look after the welfare of their families, when you found that they also regarded yours? I know that it would be so.

It is true that men are selfish, and that some men are so mean and contracted in spirit that they cannot see any interest but their own; whose hearts, not made of flesh but of silver

HE WHO LIVES ONLY

TO BENEFIT HIMSELF

CONFERS ON THE WORLD

A BENEFIT WHEN HE DIES.

—Tertullian

and gold, are so hard that they are not touched by any human feeling, and care not how much others suffer if they can make a cent by it. But they are the exception, not the rule. We are influenced by the regard and devotion of others to our interests. The laborer who knows that his employer feels kindly toward him, desires to treat him justly and to regard his good, will do better work and more of it, and will be disposed to look to his employer's interests as well as his own.

I am well aware that many will think this Divine and humane law of doing to others as we would have them do to us, is impracticable in this selfish and worldly age. If both parties would be governed by it, everyone can see how happy would be the results. But, it will be said, they will not. The laborer will not work unless compelled by want. He will take advantage of every necessity. As soon as he gains a little independence of his employer he becomes proud, arrogant and hostile. The employer will seize upon every means to keep the workmen dependent upon him, and to make as much out of them as possible. Every inch of ground which labor yields capital will occupy and intrench itself in it, and from its vantage bring the laborer into greater dependence and more abject submission. But this is a mistake.

The history of the world testifies that when the minds of men are not embittered by intense hostility and their feelings outraged by cruel wrongs, they are ready to listen to calm, disinterested and judicious counsel. A man who employed a large number of laborers in mining coal told me that he had never known an instance to fail of a calm and candid response when he had appealed to honorable motives, as a man to man, both of whom acknowledged a common humanity. There is a recent and most notable instance in this city of the happy effect of calm, disinterested and judicious counsel in settling difficulties between employers and workmen that were disastrous to both.

TAKE THE TROUBLE TO

STOP AND THINK OF THE

OTHER PERSON'S FEELINGS,

HIS VIEWPOINTS, HIS DESIRES

AND NEEDS. THINK MORE OF

WHAT THE OTHER FELLOW WANTS,

AND HOW HE MUST FEEL.

—Maxwell Maltz

When the mind is inflamed by passion, men will not listen to reason. They become blind to their own interests and regardless of the interests of others. Difficulties are never settled while passion rages. They are never settled by conflict. One party may be subdued by power; but the sense of wrong will remain; the fire of passion will slumber, ready to break out again on the first occasion. But let the laborer or the capitalist feel assured that the other party has no wish to take any advantage, that there is a sincere desire and determination on both sides to be just and pay due regard to their common interests, and all the conflict between them would cease, as the wild waves of the ocean sink to calm when the winds are at rest.

The laborer and the capitalist have a mutual and common interest. Neither can permanently prosper without the prosperity of the other. They are parts of one body. If labor is the arm, capital is the blood. Devitalize or waste the blood, and the arm loses its power. Destroy the arm, and the blood is useless. Let each care for the other, and both are benefited.

Let each take the Golden Rule as a guide, and all cause of hostility will be removed, all conflict will cease, and they will go hand in hand to do their work and reap their just reward.

MY CODE OF ETHICS

It seems almost an act of Providence that the greatest wrong and the most severe injustice ever done me by one of my fellow men was done just as I began this lesson.

This injustice has worked a temporary hardship on me, but that is of little consequence compared with the advantage it has given me by providing a timely opportunity for me to test the soundness of the entire premise of this lesson.

THERE IS ONLY ONE CORNER

OF THE UNIVERSE YOU CAN

BE CERTAIN OF IMPROVING . . .

AND THAT'S YOUR OWN SELF.

—Aldous Huxley

The injustice to which I refer left two courses of action open to me. I could have struck back at my antagonist through both civil court action and criminal libel proceedings, or I could have exercised my right to forgive him. One course of action would have brought me a substantial sum of money and whatever joy and satisfaction there may be in defeating and punishing an enemy. The other course of action would have brought me the self-respect that is enjoyed by those who have successfully met the test and discovered that they have evolved to the point where they can repeat the Lord's Prayer and *mean it!*

I chose the latter course. I did so despite the recommendations of close personal friends to strike back and despite the offer of a prominent lawyer to do my "striking" for me without cost.

But the lawyer had offered to do the impossible, because no one can strike back at another *without* cost. Not always is the cost of a monetary nature, for there are other things with which one may pay that are dearer than money.

It would be as hopeless to try to make someone who was not familiar with the law of the Golden Rule understand why I refused to strike back at this enemy as it would be to try to describe the law of gravitation to an ape. If you understand this law you also understand why I chose to *forgive* my enemy.

In the Lord's Prayer we are admonished to forgive our enemies, but that admonition will fall on deaf ears unless the listener understands the law upon which it is based. And that law is none other than the law upon which the Golden Rule is based. It is the law through which we must inevitably reap that which we sow. There is no escape from the operation of this law, nor is there any cause to try to avoid its consequences if we refrain from putting into motion thoughts and acts that are destructive.

I have incorporated this law into a code of ethics that anyone who wishes to literally follow the injunction of the Golden Rule might appropriately adopt.

My Code of Ethics

I.   I believe in the Golden Rule as the basis of all human conduct. Therefore I will never do to another person that which I would not be willing for that person to do to me if our positions were reversed.

II.   I will be honest, even to the slightest detail, in all my transactions with others, not only because of my desire to be fair with them but also because of my desire to impress the idea of honesty on my own subconscious mind, thereby weaving this essential quality into my own character.

III.   I will forgive those who are unjust toward me, with no thought as to whether they deserve it or not, because I understand the law through which forgiveness of others strengthens my own character and wipes out the effects of my own transgressions, in my subconscious mind.

IV.   I will be just, generous, and fair with others always, even though I know these acts will go unnoticed and unrewarded, in the ordinary terms of reward, because I understand and intend to apply the law through the aid of which one's own character is but the sum total of one's own acts and deeds.

V.   Whatever time I may have to devote to the discovery and exposure of the weaknesses and faults of others I will devote, more profitably, to the discovery and *correction* of my own.

VI.   I will slander no person, no matter how much I may believe another person may deserve it, because I wish to plant no destructive suggestions in my own subconscious mind.

VII.   I recognize the power of thought as being an inlet leading into my brain from the universal ocean of life, therefore I will set no destructive thoughts afloat upon that ocean lest they pollute the minds of others.

VIII.   I will conquer the common human tendency toward hatred, and envy, and selfishness, and jealousy, and malice, and pessimism, and doubt, and fear, for I believe these to be the seed from which the world harvests most of its troubles.

IX.   When my mind is not occupied with thoughts that tend toward the attainment of my Definite Chief Aim in life, I will voluntarily keep it filled with thoughts of courage, and Self-Confidence, and goodwill toward others, and faith, and kindness, and loyalty, and love for truth and justice, for I believe these to be the seed from which the world reaps its harvest of progressive growth.

X.   I understand that a mere passive belief in the soundness of the Golden Rule philosophy is of no value whatsoever, either to myself or to others. Therefore, I will *actively* put into operation this universal rule for good in all my transactions with others.

XI.   I understand the law through the operation of which my own character is developed from my own acts and thoughts. Therefore, I will guard with care all that goes into its development.

XII.   Realizing that enduring happiness comes only through helping others find it, that no act of kindness is without its reward, even though it may never be directly repaid, I will do my best to assist others when and where the opportunity appears.

— Lesson Seventeen —

The Universal Law of
Cosmic Habitforce

HABIT IS A CABLE;

WE WEAVE A THREAD OF IT

EVERY DAY, AND AT LAST

WE CANNOT BREAK IT.

—Horace Mann

Lesson Seventeen

The Universal Law of Cosmic Habitforce

"You Can Do It if You Believe You Can!"

WE COME NOW TO THE LAW OF COSMIC Habitforce—the universal law through which Nature affixes all habits so that they may carry on automatically once they have been put into motion. This law applies to the habits of mankind in the same way that it applies to the habits of the universe.

COMMENTARY

As has been mentioned previously, Napoleon Hill's codification of the attributes necessary for personal success was an evolving philosophy. What started as an indefinite number of general theories eventually *developed into fifteen specific principles, which later grew to sixteen, and finally to seventeen principles comprising the laws of success.*

This lesson, The Universal Law of Cosmic Habitforce, defines the seventeenth principle in the evolution of Hill's philosophy. Although this law would become a part of many of his subsequent works, it had not evolved early enough to have been a part of the original editions of Law of Success.

Napoleon Hill's philosophy had its formal beginning when, in 1908, Andrew Carnegie offered him the opportunity to interview the most powerful men of his day in order to learn the secrets of their success. From the interviews, Hill came to realize that all these successful men had certain principles in common. Over the next twenty years, as he analyzed and organized the points he wanted to stress in his lectures, in magazine and newspaper articles, and in a home-study course, the principles became refined into specific laws.

Those principles became even more refined on that day in 1920 when Napoleon Hill observed that the rivulets of water running down a windowpane resembled the rungs of a ladder. In his mind it became transformed into not just any ladder but a ladder that could lead to success. In a flash of inspiration Hill resolved to create a series of lectures based on each of his fifteen principles representing another rung in this ladder. By mastering these principles the student would climb the Magic Ladder to Success.

It was these fifteen principles that became the fifteen main lessons of the first edition of Law of Success. *In later editions the number of principles and lessons was expanded to sixteen as Hill realized that the Master Mind, which had been the introduction to the first edition, was actually a separate principle.*

After the successful publication of Law of Success, *Napoleon Hill lectured widely and wrote numerous books on the subject of success including his classic bestseller,* Think and Grow Rich, *and, with W. Clement Stone,* The Success System That Never Fails. *As he continued to lecture and write, Hill further realized that there was another key principle that, in effect, unified the others. He termed this newly recognized principle Cosmic Habitforce, which, when he began working with W. Clement Stone, was also referred to as the Universal Law.*

In consultation with the Napoleon Hill Foundation, the editors of this revised and updated edition have drawn upon Napoleon Hill's later writings, including The Master Key to Riches *and* How to Raise Your Own Salary, *in order to incorporate the final evolution of Hill's philosophy. The inclusion of this seventeenth law makes this the most complete edition of* Law of Success.

Cosmic Habitforce is the greatest of all natural laws. It is Nature's comptroller through which all other natural laws are coordinated, organized, and operated through orderliness and system. It is the particular application of energy with which Nature maintains the relationship between the atoms of matter, the stars and the planets in their ceaseless motion, the seasons of the year, night and day, sickness and health, life and death.

We see the stars and the planets move with such precision that the astronomers can predetermine their exact location and their relationship to one another scores of years hence. We see the seasons of the year come and go with clocklike regularity. We know that an oak tree grows from an acorn, and a pine tree grows from the seed of its ancestor; that an acorn never makes a mistake and produces a pine tree, nor does a pine seed produce an oak tree. We know that nothing is ever produced that does not have its antecedents in something similar which preceded it.

Cosmic Habitforce is also the medium through which all habits and all human relationships are maintained in varying degrees of permanence. And it is the medium through which thought is translated into its physical equivalent in response to the desires and the purposes of individuals.

MEN OCCASIONALLY

STUMBLE OVER THE TRUTH,

BUT MOST OF THEM

PICK THEMSELVES UP AND

HURRY OFF AS IF

NOTHING HAPPENED.

—Winston Churchill

Mankind is only an instrument through which higher powers than his own are projecting themselves. This entire philosophy is designed to lead you to this important discovery and to enable you to make use of the knowledge it reveals—by placing yourself in harmony with the unseen forces of the universe so that they may aid you in the formation of the kind of habits that will carry you from where you are to where you wish to be in life.

Cosmic Habitforce is the medium by which every living thing is forced to take on and become a part of the environmental influences in which it lives and moves. Thus it is clearly evident that success attracts more success, and failure attracts more failure—a truth that has long been known, but few have understood the reason for this strange phenomenon.

It is known that a person who has seemed a failure may become a most outstanding success by close association with those who think and act in terms of success, but not everyone knows the reason this is true is that the law of Cosmic Habitforce transmits the "success consciousness" from the mind of the successful person to the mind of the unsuccessful one when they are closely associated in daily life.

Whenever any two minds make contact a third mind is created, patterned after the stronger of the two. Most successful people recognize this truth and frankly admit that their success began with their close association with someone whose positive mental attitude they either consciously or unconsciously appropriated.

Cosmic Habitforce is silent, unseen, and unperceived through any of the five physical senses. That is why it has not been more widely recognized, for most people do not attempt to understand the intangible forces of Nature, nor are they interested in abstract principles. However, these intangibles and abstractions represent the real powers of the universe. They are the *basis* of everything that is tangible and concrete.

UNIVERSAL LAW

Understand the working principle of Cosmic Habitforce and you will have no difficulty interpreting Emerson's essay Compensation, for he was rubbing elbows with the law of Cosmic Habitforce when he wrote this famous essay.

Sir Isaac Newton likewise came near to the complete recognition of this law when he made his discovery of the law of gravitation. Had he gone but a brief distance beyond where he stopped, he might have discovered that the same law that holds the earth in space and relates it systematically to all other planets in both time and space is the same law that relates human beings to one another in exact conformity with the nature of their own thoughts.

The term *habitforce* is self-explanatory. It is a force that works through established habits. Every living thing below the intelligence of man lives, reproduces itself, and fulfills its earthly mission in direct response to the power of Cosmic Habitforce through what we call *instinct.*

Man alone has been given the privilege of choice in connection with his living habits, and these he may fix by the patterns of his thoughts—the one and only privilege, as I have said previously, over which any individual has been given complete right of control.

One may think in terms of self-imposed limitations of fear, doubt, envy, greed, and poverty, and Cosmic Habitforce will translate these thoughts into their material equivalent. Or one may think in terms of wealth and plenty, and this same law will translate these thoughts into their physical counterpart.

In this manner, one may control their destiny to an astounding degree—simply by exercising the privilege of shaping one's own thoughts. Once these thoughts have been shaped into definite patterns they are taken over by the law of Cosmic Habitforce and are made into permanent habits, and they remain as such unless and until they have been supplanted by different and stronger thought patterns.

Now we come to the consideration of one of the most profound of all truths—that most who attain the higher brackets of success seldom do so until they have gone through some event that reached deeply into their souls and reduced them to that circumstance of life which most call failure.

The reason for this strange phenomenon is readily recognized by those who understand the law of Cosmic Habitforce, for it exists in the fact that these disasters and tragedies of life serve to break the established habits that have led the person to failure—and thus break the grip of Cosmic Habitforce, allowing the person to formulate new and better habits.

Wars grow out of maladjustments in the relationships between people, as the result of the negative thoughts that have grown until they assume mass proportions. The spirit of any nation is but the sum total of the dominating thought habits of its people.

The same is true of individuals, for the spirit of the individual is also determined by their dominating thought habits. Most individuals are at war, in one way or another, throughout their lives. They are at war with their own conflicting thoughts and emotions. They are at war in their family relationships and in their occupational and social relationships.

Recognize this truth and you will understand the real power and the benefits that are available to those who live by the Golden Rule, for this great rule will save you from the conflicts of personal warfare.

Recognize it and you will also understand the real purpose and benefits of a Definite Chief Aim, for once that purpose has been fixed in your consciousness by your habits, it will be taken over by Cosmic Habitforce and carried to its logical conclusion by whatever practical means there may be available.

Cosmic Habitforce does not suggest what you should desire, or whether your thought habits will be positive or negative, but it acts

YOU ARE TODAY WHERE

YOUR THOUGHTS HAVE BROUGHT YOU;

YOU WILL BE TOMORROW WHERE

YOUR THOUGHTS TAKE YOU.

—James Allen

upon *all* your thought habits by crystallizing them into varying degrees of permanency and translating them into their physical equivalent, through inspired motivation to action.

It not only fixes the thought habits of individuals but it also fixes the thought habits of groups and masses of people, according to the pattern established by the preponderance of their individual dominating thoughts.

The same rule applies to the individual who thinks and talks of disease. At first that person is regarded as a hypochondriac, one who suffers with imaginary illness. But when the habit is maintained, the disease thus manifested or one very closely akin to it generally makes its appearance. Cosmic Habitforce attends to this, for it is true that any thought held in the mind through repetition begins immediately to translate itself into its physical equivalent.

It is a sad commentary on the intelligence of people to observe how many go through life in poverty and want, although the reason for this is not difficult to understand if one recognizes the working principle of Cosmic Habitforce.

Poverty is the direct result of a "poverty consciousness," which results from thinking in terms of poverty, fearing poverty, and talking of poverty. But if you desire wealth, give orders to your subconscious mind to produce wealth, thus developing a "prosperity consciousness," and see how quickly your economic condition will improve.

First comes the "consciousness" of that which you desire. Then follows the physical or mental manifestation of your desires. The consciousness is your responsibility. It is something you must create by your daily thoughts, or by meditation if you prefer. In this manner one may ally themself with no less a power than that of the Creator of all things.

"I have come to the conclusion," said a great philosopher, "that the acceptance of poverty, or the acceptance of ill health, is an open confession of the lack of faith." We do a lot of proclaiming of faith, but our actions belie our words. *Faith* is a state of mind that may become permanent only by actions. Belief alone is not sufficient.

The law of Cosmic Habitforce, or the Universal Law, is a power equally available to the weak and the strong, the rich and the poor, the sick and the well. It provides the solution to all human problems.

Now let us examine the word *habit*. Webster's dictionary gives the word many definitions, among them: "Habit implies a settled disposition or tendency *due to repetition;* custom suggests the fact of repetition rather than the tendency to repeat; usage (applying only to a considerable body of people) adds the implication of long acceptance or standing; both custom and usage often suggest authority; as, we do many things mechanically from force of habit."

Webster's definition runs on into considerable additional detail, but no part of it comes within sight of describing the law that fixes all habits, this omission being due no doubt to the fact that the law of Cosmic Habitforce had not been revealed to the editors of this dictionary. But we observe one significant and important word in the Webster's definition—the word *repetition.* It is important because it describes the means by which any habit is begun.

The habit of a *definite purpose,* for example, becomes a habit only by repetition of the thought of that purpose, by bringing it into the mind repeatedly, and by repeatedly submitting that thought to the Imagination with a burning desire for its fulfillment, until the Imagination creates a practical plan for attaining this desire. By applying the habit of faith in connection with the desire, and by doing it intensely and repeatedly, one may see themself already in possession of the object of desire even before he or she begins to attain it.

The building of voluntary positive habits calls for the application of self-discipline, persistence, willpower, and faith—all of which are available to the person who has assimilated the sixteen preceding principles of this philosophy.

Voluntary habit-building is self-discipline in its highest and noblest form of application, and all voluntary positive habits are the products of willpower directed toward the attainment of definite ends. They originate with the individual, not with Cosmic Habitforce. And they must be grounded in the mind through the repetition of thoughts and deeds until they are taken over by Cosmic Habitforce and fixed in place, after which they will operate automatically.

The word *habit* is an important word in connection with this philosophy of individual achievement, for it represents the real cause of everyone's economic, social, professional, occupational, and spiritual condition in life. As has already been stated, we are where we are and what we are because of our fixed habits. And we may be where we wish to be and what we wish to be only by the development and the maintenance of our *voluntary* habits.

Thus we see that this entire philosophy leads inevitably to an understanding and application of the law of Cosmic Habitforce— the power of fixation of all habits.

Each of the sixteen preceding lessons is intended to aid you in the development of a particular specialized form of habit that is necessary as a means of enabling you to take full possession of your own mind. This too must become a habit. And the purpose of this philosophy is to enable you to develop and maintain habits of thought and of deed that keep your mind concentrated on success.

Mastery and assimilation of the philosophy, like anything desirable, has a definite price that must be paid before its benefits may be enjoyed. That price, among other things, is eternal vigilance, determination, persistence, and the will to make life pay off on your own terms instead of accepting substitutes of poverty and misery and disillusionment.

There are two ways of relating to Life. One is that of playing horse while Life rides. The other is that of becoming the rider while Life plays horse. The choice as to whether one becomes the horse or the rider is the privilege of every person, but this much is certain: If you

MAN BECOMES A SLAVE TO

HIS CONSTANTLY REPEATED ACTS.

WHAT HE AT FIRST CHOOSES,

AT LAST COMPELS.

—Orison Swett Marden

do not choose to become the rider of Life, you are sure to be forced to become the horse. Life either rides or is ridden. It never stands still.

THE EGO, THE MASTER MIND, AND COSMIC HABITFORCE

Everyone knows that practically everything we do, from the time we begin to walk, is the result of habit. Walking and talking are habits. Our manner of eating and drinking is a habit. Our relationships with others, whether they are positive or negative, are the results of habits. But few people understand why or how we form habits.

Habits are inseparably related to the human ego, which is a greatly misunderstood subject. The word *ego* is of Latin origin and it means *I*, but it is a common error to believe the ego to be only a medium for expression of vanity.

The ego is the driving force behind all forms of human action, and it is the medium for translating desire into faith. Therefore we must know something of its nature and possibilities in order that we may guide it to the attainment of definite ends.

The power of the ego is fixed entirely by the application of auto-suggestion, or self-suggestion, and the starting point of all individual achievements is to inspire one's ego with a "success consciousness." The person who succeeds must do so by impressing on their ego the object of their desires, and removing from it all forms of limitation, fear, and doubt which lead to the dissipation of the power of the ego.

A person's ego is the sum total of their thought habits that have been affixed through the automatic operation of the law of Cosmic Habitforce. It determines the manner in which they relate to all other people. It is one's greatest asset or greatest liability, according to the way they relate themself to it.

The egoist who makes themself offensive through the expression of their ego is one who has not discovered how to relate themself to their ego in a constructive manner. Constructive application of the ego is made through the expressions of one's hopes, desires, aims, ambitions, and plans, and not by boastfulness or self-love. The motto of the person who has their ego under control is "Deeds, not words." One of the major differences between those who make valuable contributions to mankind and those who merely take up space in the world is mainly a difference in egos.

The desire to be great, to be recognized, and to have personal power, is a healthy desire. But an open expression of one's belief in their own greatness is an indication that he or she has not taken possession of their ego, that they have allowed it to take possession of them. You can be sure that their proclamations of greatness are only to shield some fear or inferiority complex.

Understand the real nature of your ego and you will understand the real significance of the Master Mind principle. Moreover, you will recognize that to be of the greatest service to you, the members of your Master Mind alliance must be in complete sympathy with your hopes, aims, and purposes. They must not be in competition with you in any manner whatsoever.

They must have confidence in you and your integrity, and they must respect you. They must be willing to accentuate your virtues and make allowances for your faults. They must be willing to permit you to be yourself and live your own life in your own way at all times. Lastly, they must receive from you some form of benefit that will make you as beneficial to them as they are to you.

Failure to observe this last requirement will bring an end to the power of your Master Mind alliance.

People relate themselves to one another in whatever capacities they may be associated because of a motive or motives. There can be no permanent human relationship based upon an indefinite or vague motive, or upon no motive at all. Failure to recognize this truth has cost many the difference between poverty and wealth.

The law of Cosmic Habitforce is the power that takes over the ego and provides it with the material counterparts of the thoughts that shape it. This law does not give quality or quantity to the ego; it merely takes what it finds and translates it into its physical equivalent.

The people of great achievement are, and have always been, those who deliberately feed and shape their own ego, leaving nothing to luck or chance, or to the fluctuations of life.

Every person may control the shaping of their own ego, but from that point on he or she has no more to do with what happens than does the farmer have anything to do with what happens to the seed he sows in the soil of the earth. The inexorable law of Cosmic Habitforce causes every living thing to perpetuate itself after its kind, and it translates the picture that a person paints of their ego into its physical equivalent as definitely as it develops an acorn into an oak tree. And no outside aid whatsoever is required, except time.

From these statements it is obvious that I am not only advocating the deliberate development and control of the ego but I am also warning that no one can hope to succeed in any calling without such control over their ego.

A properly developed ego is the product of several factors, which I will outline for you here.

First you must ally yourself with one or more persons who will coordinate their minds with yours in a spirit of perfect harmony for the attainment of a *definite purpose*, and that alliance must be continuous and active. Moreover, the alliance must consist of people whose spiritual and mental qualities, education, and age are suited for aiding in the attainment of the purpose of the alliance.

For example, Andrew Carnegie's Master Mind alliance was made up of more than twenty men, each of whom brought to the alliance some quality of mind, experience, education, or knowledge that was directly related to the object of the alliance and not available through any of the other members of the alliance.

―――――――

KEEP AWAY FROM PEOPLE WHO

TRY TO BELITTLE YOUR AMBITIONS.

SMALL PEOPLE ALWAYS DO THAT,

BUT THE REALLY GREAT

MAKE YOU FEEL THAT YOU, TOO,

CAN BECOME GREAT.

—Mark Twain

―――――――

Once you have placed yourself under the influence of the proper associates, you must adopt some definite plan by which to attain the object of the alliance and proceed to put that plan into action. The plan may be a composite plan created by the joint efforts of all the members of the Master Mind group.

If one plan proves to be unsound or inadequate, it must be revised or replaced by others until a plan is found that will work. But there must be no change in the purpose of the alliance.

Then you must remove yourself from the range of influence of every person and every circumstance that has even a slight tendency to cause you to feel inferior or incapable of attaining the object of your purpose. Positive egos do not grow in negative environments. On this point there can be no excuse for a compromise, and failure to observe it will prove fatal to your chances of success.

The line must be so clearly drawn between you and those who exercise any form of negative influence over you that you close the door tightly against every such person, no matter what previous ties of friendship, obligation, or relationship may have existed between you.

You must close the door tightly against every thought of any past experience or circumstance that tends to make you feel inferior or unhappy. A strong, vital ego cannot be developed by dwelling on thoughts of past unpleasant experiences. Vital egos thrive on the hopes and desires of yet unattained objectives.

Thoughts are the building blocks from which the human ego is constructed, and Cosmic Habitforce is the cement that binds these blocks together in permanency, through fixed habits. When the job is finished it represents, right down to the smallest detail, the nature of the thoughts that went into the building.

You must surround yourself with every possible physical means of impressing your mind with the nature and the purpose of the ego you are developing. For example, if you are or aspire to be an author, you should decorate your work environment with pictures and the works of other authors whom you most admire. You should fill your bookshelves with books related to your own field of work. You should surround yourself with every possible means of conveying to your ego the exact picture of yourself that you expect to express, because that picture is the pattern that the law of Cosmic Habitforce will pick up—the picture that it translates into its physical equivalent.

The properly developed ego is at all times under the control of the individual. There must be no overinflation of the ego tending toward "egomania," by which some people destroy themselves. Egomania reveals itself by a mad desire to control others by force.

In the development of the ego, one's motto might well be "Not too much, not too little, of anything." When people begin to thirst for control over others, or begin to accumulate large sums of money that they cannot or do not use constructively, they are treading on dangerous ground. Power of this nature grows of its own accord and it soon gets out of control. Nature has provided us all with a safety valve through which she deflates the ego and relieves the pressure of its influence when an individual goes beyond certain limits in the development of the ego.

Napoleon Bonaparte began to die, because of his crushed ego, the day he landed on St. Helena Island.

People who quit work and retire from all forms of activity, after having led active lives, generally atrophy and die soon thereafter. If they live they are usually miserable and unhappy. A healthy ego is one that is always in use and under complete control.

The ego is constantly undergoing changes, for better or for worse, because of the nature of one's thought habits. The two factors that force these changes upon one are time—and the law of Cosmic Habitforce.

Just as seeds planted in the soil require definite periods of time to germinate, develop, and grow, so do the ideas, thought impulses, and desires that are planted in the mind require definite periods of time for the law of Cosmic Habitforce to give them life and action.

There is no adequate means of describing or predetermining the exact period of time that is required for the transformation of a desire into its physical equivalent. The nature of the desire, the circumstances related to it, and the intensity of the desire, are all determining factors in the time required for transformation from the thought stage to the physical stage.

The state of mind known as faith is so favorable for the quick change of desire into its physical equivalent that it has been known to make the change almost instantaneously.

Human beings tend to mature physically in about twenty years, but mentally—which means the ego—we require from thirty-five to sixty years for maturity. This explains why people seldom begin to accumulate material riches in great abundance, or to attain outstanding records of achievement in other areas, until they are about fifty years of age.

It is a necessity that the ego undergo self-discipline—through which one acquires Self-Confidence, definiteness of purpose, personal Initiative, Imagination, accuracy of judgment, and other qualities— before it has the power to acquire and hold wealth in abundance.

These qualities come through the proper *use* of time. Observe that I did not say they come through the *lapse* of time. Through the operation of Cosmic Habitforce, every individual's thought habits, whether negative or positive, whether of wealth or of poverty, are woven into the pattern of their ego, and there they are given permanent form which determines the nature and the extent of that person's spiritual and physical status.

I have shown you how Cosmic Habitforce is the determining factor that leads one to success and plenty or to poverty and misery, and how it can bring harmony and understanding or disappointment and

---

UNTIL YOU VALUE YOURSELF,

YOU WON'T VALUE YOUR TIME.

UNTIL YOU VALUE YOUR TIME,

YOU WILL NOT DO

ANYTHING WITH IT.

—M. Scott Peck

---

failure. To have merely said that it is the force with which nature keeps the stars and planets in their place would not have been enough to be of benefit to the average person who is more concerned with the solution of their daily problems.

I will leave you with an overview of the relationship between Cosmic Habitforce and three other important principles through which it becomes the most important factor in guiding people's lives. Two of these principles are associated with the method by which the force operates, and the third is the major principle through which the power of this force can be redirected and converted from positive to negative use by the individual.

These four important associated principles are:

1. *Cosmic Habitforce:* The principle through which Nature forces everyone to take on and become a part of the environmental influences that control their thinking.

2. *Drifting:* The habit of mental indifference, through which an individual allows chance and circumstance to fasten their environmental influences on them.

3. *Time:* The factor with which Cosmic Habitforce weaves together an individual's dominating thoughts and the influences of their environment, and transforms them into stumbling blocks or steppingstones according to their nature.

4. *Definiteness of Purpose:* The only medium, under the control of an individual, with which Cosmic Habitforce may be controlled.

The Universal Law of Cosmic Habitforce is the culmination of this entire philosophy of individual achievement. It is the key to all of the principles described in *Law of Success*, but its benefits are available only to those who also master and apply the instructions in the previous lessons.

LIVES OF GREAT MEN ALL REMIND US

WE CAN MAKE OUR LIVES SUBLIME,

AND, DEPARTING, LEAVE BEHIND US

FOOTPRINTS IN THE SANDS OF TIME.

—Henry Wadsworth Longfellow

Cosmic Habitforce guided me through an awe-inspiring maze of experiences before revealing itself to me. All through those years of struggle there was one *definite purpose* uppermost in my mind— the burning desire to organize a philosophy with which the average person can become self-determining. Nature had no alternative but that of yielding to me the working principle of Cosmic Habitforce, because I unwittingly complied with the law by persistently seeking the way to its discovery.

If I had known of the existence of the law and of its working principle at the beginning of my research, I could have organized this philosophy in a much shorter period of time.

YOUR STANDING ARMY—
AN AFTER-THE-LESSON VISIT WITH THE AUTHOR

The seventeen officers in your standing army are the Master Mind, Definite Chief Aim, Self-Confidence, Habit of Saving, Initiative and Leadership, Imagination, Enthusiasm, Self-Control, Habit of Doing More Than Paid For, Pleasing Personality, Accurate Thinking, Concentration, Cooperation, Profiting by Failure, Tolerance, the Golden Rule, and the Universal Law of Cosmic Habitforce.

These soldiers are the forces that enter into all *organized effort*— from which comes power. Master these seventeen forces and you may have whatever you want in life. Others will be helpless to defeat your plans.

This army is standing at attention, ready to do the bidding of any person who will command it. It is *your* army if you will take charge of it. It will give you the power sufficient to mow down all opposition with which you meet.

If you are a normal person you long for material success. Success and power are always found together. You cannot be sure of success unless you have power, and you cannot have power unless you develop it through the seventeen essential qualities.

Each of these qualities may be likened to the commanding officer of a regiment of soldiers. The most important of the commanding officers in this army is a Definite Chief Aim.

Without the aid of a *definite purpose,* the remainder of the army would be useless to you. Find out, as early as possible, what your major purpose in life shall be. Until you do this you are nothing but a drifter, subject to control by every stray wind of circumstance that blows in your direction.

Millions of people go through life without knowing what it is they want. All have a purpose, but only two out of every hundred have a *definite* purpose.

Nothing is impossible to the person who knows what it is that they want and makes up their mind to acquire it!

Columbus had a *definite purpose* and it became a reality. Lincoln had a *definite purpose* to free the slaves of the South and he turned that purpose into reality. Roosevelt's *definite purpose,* during his first term of office, was to build the Panama Canal. He lived to see that purpose realized. Henry Ford's *definite purpose* was to build the best popular-priced automobile, a purpose which has made him the powerful man that he is. Burbank's *definite purpose* was to improve plant life.

COMMENTARY

Horticulturist Luther Burbank, perhaps not as well known to some readers today as are the others mentioned, at the time was equally famous as the father of modern plant breeding. In 1871 he developed the Burbank potato, which was brought to Ireland to help combat the blight epidemic. He then sold the rights to the potato for $150 and used the money to *travel from Lancaster, Massachusetts, to Santa Rosa, California, where he established a nursery and experimental farms.*

His objective to improve the quality of plants in order to increase the world's food supply inspired such worldwide interest that he was recognized by an Act of Congress.

Burbank was also a freethinker, which he kept private until motivated by two events to go public. The first was the Scopes "monkey trial" of 1925. A strong believer in Darwinism, he felt he had to speak out. The second was when Henry Ford went public with his views in favor of reincarnation. Ford was a friend of his, but when interviewed by a reporter for the San Francisco Bulletin *about his reaction to Ford's theories, Burbank expressed his doubts about God and about an afterlife:*

". . . I must believe that rather than the survival of all, we must look for survival only in the spirit of the good we have done in passing through. This is as feasible and credible as Henry Ford's own practice of discarding the old models of his automobile. Once obsolete, an automobile is thrown to the scrap heap. Once here and gone, the human life has likewise served its purpose. If it has been a good life, it has been sufficient. There is no need for another."

On January 22, 1926, the front-page story appeared in the San Francisco Bulletin *under the headline "I'm an Infidel, Declares Burbank, Casting Doubt on Soul Immortality Theory."*

The article was reprinted around the world, creating shock waves, and Burbank was inundated with hate mail. In a desperate effort to make people understand, he attempted to reply to all the letters. But the physical task of doing so, especially amid all the harassment, was so overwhelming for the seventy-seven-year-old that Burbank took ill and died.

Twenty years ago Edwin C. Barnes formed a *definite purpose* in his mind. That purpose was to become the business partner of Thomas A. Edison. At the time his purpose was chosen, Mr. Barnes had no qualification entitling him to a partnership with the world's greatest inventor. Despite this handicap he became the partner of the great Thomas Edison. Five years ago he retired from active business, with more money than he needs or can use, wealth that he accumulated in partnership with Edison.

Opportunity, capital, Cooperation from others, and all other essentials for success gravitate to the person who knows what they want.

Vitalize your mind with a *definite purpose* and immediately your mind becomes a magnet which attracts everything that harmonizes with that purpose.

James J. Hill, the great railroad builder, had been a poorly paid telegraph operator. Moreover, he had reached the age of forty and was still ticking away at the telegraph key without any outward appearances of success.

Then something of importance happened—of importance to Hill and to the people of the United States. He formed the *definite purpose* of building a railroad across the great waste desert of the West. Without reputation, without capital, without encouragement from others, James J. Hill got the capital and built the Great Northern Railway Company, the greatest of all the railroad systems of the United States.

F. W. Woolworth had been a poorly paid clerk in a general store. In his mind's eye he saw a chain of novelty stores specializing in five-and-ten-cent sales. That chain of stores became his *definite purpose.* He made that purpose come true, and with it more millions than he could use.

Cyrus H. K. Curtis selected as his *definite purpose* the publishing of the world's greatest magazine. Starting with nothing but the name "Saturday Evening Post," and opposed by friends and advisers who said it couldn't be done, he transformed that purpose into reality.

Martin W. Littleton is the most highly paid lawyer in the world. He will accept no retainer under $50,000, and it is said that he is kept busy all the time. When he was twelve years old he had never even been inside a schoolhouse. But when he went with his father to hear a lawyer defend a murderer, the speech so impressed him that he grabbed hold of his father's hand and said, "Someday I am going to be the best lawyer in the United States and make speeches like that man."

"Fine chance for an ignorant mountain youth to become a great lawyer," one might say, but remember—nothing is impossible to the person who knows what they want and makes up their mind to get it.

Not one of the soldiers in your standing army is powerful enough alone to ensure success. Remove a single one of them and the entire army would be weakened.

The powerful person is the one who has developed, in their own mind, the entire seventeen qualities represented by the seventeen commanding officers of this standing army.

You must watch for every opportunity to apply and empower the law of the Master Mind.

Before you can have power you must have a Definite Chief Aim —*a definite purpose.*

You must have Self-Confidence with which to back up your purpose.

You must have Initiative and Leadership with which to exercise your Self-Confidence.

You must have Imagination in creating your *definite purpose* and in building the plans with which to transform that purpose into reality and put your plans into action.

You must mix Enthusiasm with your action or it will be bland and weak.

You must exercise Self-Control.

You must form the Habit of Doing More Than Paid For.

You must cultivate a Pleasing Personality.

HERE LIES A MAN

WHO KNEW HOW TO

ENLIST THE SERVICE OF

BETTER MEN THAN HIMSELF.

—tombstone of Andrew Carnegie

You must acquire the Habit of Saving.

You must use Accurate Thinking, remembering, as you develop this quality, that accurate thought is based upon facts and not upon hearsay evidence or mere information.

You must form the habit of Concentration by giving your undivided attention to but one task at a time.

You must acquire the habit of Cooperation and practice it in all your plans.

You must Profit by Failure, your own and that of others.

You must cultivate the habit of Tolerance.

You must make the Golden Rule the foundation of all you do that affects other people.

You must make use of the Universal Law of Cosmic Habitforce, through which all of these principles can be applied to transform not only your thoughts but also your habits.

Each day, one by one, call your seventeen soldiers out of the line and study them. Make sure that the counterpart of each is developed in your own mind.

All efficient armies are well-disciplined. The army that you are building in your own mind must also be disciplined. It must obey your command at every step.

When you call out of the line the fourteenth soldier, Failure, remember that nothing will go as far toward developing discipline as will failure and temporary defeat. While you are comparing yourself with this soldier, determine whether or not you have been profiting by your own failures and temporary defeats.

Failure comes to all at one time or another. Make sure, when it comes your way, that you will learn something of value from its visit. It would not visit you if there was not room for it in your makeup.

To make progress in this world you must rely solely upon the forces within your own mind for your start. After this start has been made you may turn to others for aid, but the first step must be taken without outside aid. It will then surprise you to observe how many willing people you will encounter who will volunteer to assist you.

Success is made up of many facts and factors, chiefly of the seventeen qualities represented by these seventeen soldiers. To enjoy a well-rounded success, one must appropriate as many of these seventeen qualities as may be missing in one's own inherited ability.

When you came into this world you were endowed with certain inborn traits, the result of millions of years of evolutionary changes, through thousands of generations of ancestors. You then acquired many other qualities, according to the nature of your environment and the teaching you received during early childhood. You are the sum total of what was inborn, what you have picked up from your experiences, what you have thought, and what you have been taught.

By the law of chance, one in a million people will have, through inborn heredity and from knowledge acquired after birth, all of the seventeen qualities. If you were not fortunate enough to have acquired all the essentials for success in this way, you must strongly plant the *desire* to develop yourself where you are now deficient.

A *definite purpose* may be transformed into reality only when one believes it can be done, and that belief must be backed with unqualified faith. Perhaps the inexplicable law that turns prayer based upon faith into reality, also transforms into reality a *definite purpose* that is founded upon belief. It can do no harm if you make your *definite purpose* in life the object of your daily prayer.

Develop in your own mind all of the seventeen qualities and you will find that the application of faith is not difficult. Master these seventeen qualities and you will have the power to get whatever you want in life—without violating the rights of others.

PERSONAL ANALYSIS

Seventeen major factors entered into the building of this course. Analyze yourself carefully, with the assistance of one or more other persons if necessary, for the purpose of ascertaining in which of the seventeen factors you are the weakest. Then concentrate your efforts on those particular lessons until you have fully developed the factors they represent.

COMMENTARY

> Readers will of course understand that many of the specifics of the following offer are no longer applicable. We include it, however, as a matter of interest—and as a further indication that Napoleon Hill did indeed dedicate himself to helping people and to fulfilling his commitment to Andrew Carnegie that he would teach this success philosophy to others.

As a student of this course you are entitled to a continuation of my services for the purpose of making a complete personal analysis that will indicate your general efficiency and your understanding of the laws of success.

To avail yourself of this service you must fill out the Personal Analysis Questionnaire which accompanies the course, and mail it to me at the address shown on the questionnaire.

You will, in due time, receive a graphic-chart diagram which will show you, at a glance, the percentage to which you are entitled in connection with each of the laws. It will be both interesting and instructive to compare this analysis with the one that you, yourself, have made through the aid of the chart shown at the beginning of this book.

The questionnaire should not be filled out until after you have read all the lessons of this course at least once. Answer the questions correctly, and frankly, as best you can. The data contained in

REMEMBER THAT YOUR REAL WEALTH

CAN BE MEASURED NOT BY

WHAT YOU HAVE,

BUT BY WHAT YOU ARE.

—Napoleon Hill

your answers will be strictly confidential, and will be seen by no one except myself.

Your analysis will be in the nature of a signed report, which may be used to great advantage in the marketing of your personal services, if you wish to so use it. This analysis will be the same, in every respect, as those for which I charged twenty-five dollars during the years I was engaged in research for the organization of this course, and it may, under some circumstances, be worth many times this amount to you, as similar analyses have been to the many people I have served.

COMMENTARY

> Although Napoleon Hill's services are no longer available, as he suggests here, as well as in his Personal Statement, you can also prepare your own success analysis. If you would prefer not to mark the comparison chart at the front of this book, the Napoleon Hill Foundation has developed a self-scoring Success Profile Questionnaire for this same purpose. You will find it online at www.naphill.org.
>
> Or to receive this questionnaire by mail, as well as a bookplate with Napoleon Hill's signature and a copy of one of Hill's famous success essays (suitable for framing), please send your request along with a stamped, self-addressed, nine-by-twelve envelope to: The Napoleon Hill Foundation, P.O. Box 1277, Wise, Virginia 24293.

Highroads Media, Inc. is the publisher of more books and audiobooks by Napoleon Hill than any other publisher in the world. Other titles available:

ALSO REVISED & UPDATED (HARDCOVER)
Think and Grow Rich: The 21st-Century Edition

LEATHER-BOUND, GILT-EDGED COLLECTOR'S EDITIONS
Think and Grow Rich (single volume)
Law of Success (available in four volumes)

AUDIOBOOKS AVAILABLE ON CD
Think and Grow Rich (unabridged and abridged audiobook editions)
Think and Grow Rich: Instant Motivator (original audiobook)
Law of Success (four-volume unabridged audiobook set)
Your Right to Be Rich (unabridged audiobook)
Napoleon Hill's Keys to Success (unabridged and abridged audiobooks)
Selling You! (original audiobook)
Believe and Achieve (abridged audiobook)
The Richest Man in Babylon & The Magic Story (original audiobook)
A Lifetime of Riches: The Biography of Napoleon Hill (abridged audiobook)

For more information about Napoleon Hill books and audiobooks, contact Highroads Media, Inc., 6 Commerce Way, Arden, NC 28704
telephone: (323) 822-2676
fax: (323) 822-2686
email: highroadsmedia@sbcglobal.net
visit us at our website: www.highroadsmedia.com